BASIC ETHICS IN ACTION

Medical Ethics

MICHAEL BOYLAN

Prentice Hall, Upper Saddle River, New Jersey 07458

Library of Congress Cataloging-in-Publication Data

Boylan, Michael, (date)
   Medical ethics / Michael Boylan.
     p. cm. — (Basic ethics in action)
   Includes bibliographical references.
   ISBN 0–13–773847–1
   1. Medical ethics. I. Title. II. Series.
  B724.B65 2000
  174'.2—dc21   99–046581

Editor-in-Chief: Charlyce Jones Owen
Assistant Editor: Emsal Hasan
Editorial Assistant: Jennifer Ackerman
AVP, Director of Manufacturing
   and Production: Barbara Kittle
Senior Managing Editor: Jan Stephan
Production Liaison: Fran Russello
Project Manager: Linda B. Pawelchak
Manufacturing Manager: Nick Sklitsis
Prepress and Manufacturing Buyer: Tricia Kenny
Cover Director: Jayne Conte
Cover Design: Bruce Kenselaar
Marketing Manager: Ilse Wolf
Copy Editing: JaNoel Lowe
Proofreading: Maria McColligan

This book was set in 10/12 Palatino by Pub-Set
and was printed and bound by R.R. Donnelley and Sons, Inc.
The cover was printed by Phoenix Color Corp.

© 2000 by Michael Boylan
Upper Saddle River, New Jersey 07458

Printed in the United States of America
10 9 8 7 6 5 4 3 2 1

ISBN 0-13-773847-1

Prentice-Hall International (UK) Limited, *London*
Prentice-Hall of Australia Pty. Limited, *Sydney*
Prentice-Hall Canada Inc., *Toronto*
Prentice-Hall Hispanoamericana, S.A., *Mexico*
Prentice-Hall of India Private Limited, *New Delhi*
Prentice-Hall of Japan, Inc., *Tokyo*
Pearson Education Asia Pte. Ltd., *Singapore*
Editora Prentice-Hall do Brasil, Ltda., *Rio de Janeiro*

For Arianne

Contents

Preface

The purpose of this book is to introduce the student to important ethical issues pertaining to the health care professions. As such, it fits into the Applied Professional Ethics branch of ethics. *Medical Ethics* is the second book in the series *Basic Ethics in Action*. This series also includes two other books on Applied Professional Ethics, *Environmental Ethics* and *Business Ethics*. The series is anchored by *Basic Ethics*, which discusses Normative Ethics and Metaethics. Instructors and students of ethics can use (1) *Basic Ethics* alone or with other primary texts in an ethics course; (2) *Basic Ethics* along with one of the applied texts in the series in an ethics course that emphasizes an integration of theory and practice; or (3) one or more of the applied texts in courses concentrating on practice.

DISTINCTIVE FEATURES OF THIS BOOK

This book includes original interviews with two prominent practitioners in biomedicine, articles on issues addressed in the chapters by noted authors in the field, a methodology for linking theory to action, an awareness of gender issues as they relate to biomedicine, and a method for students to follow to write an essay using the information presented.

The book begins by introducing the student to my theory of worldview, or *Weltanschauung*. This concept is one of the unifying themes of *Basic Ethics*. I believe that acknowledging one's worldview and its relation to the common worldview (the worldview created by a particular community) is a crucial element in explaining and justifying what we value.

Chapter Two presents an interview with one of the most prominent figures in biomedical ethics, Edward Pellegrino, M.D. Dr. Pellegrino presents some of his reactions to the major issues discussed in this volume along with major perspectives he has developed over the years.

Chapter Three presents an original essay by Deryck Beyleveld and Shaun Pattinson on an important linking principle in bioethical discourse. This linking principle connects normative theory to action. In this case, the linking principle is precautionary reasoning, which takes the place of tenets that seek to grant proportional status and rights to prospective agents. I believe this linking principle has wide application in biomedicine.

Chapters Four through Seven constitute the core chapters of the book. These chapters present readings to support several general themes. I begin with a look at the Hippocratic Oath and proceed to the subjects of paternalism and autonomy, privacy and confidentiality, informed consent, and gender issues.

In Chapter Five, euthanasia and abortion are the central topics. In addition to the usual distinction between killing and letting die, this section considers the persistent vegetative state and the subject of defective infants.

Chapter Six begins with my interview of Kevin Brown, M.D., Ph.D., a visiting scientist at the National Institutes of Health working in gene therapy research. Dr. Brown reviews key issues discussed in the readings and offers insights from his work in the field.

Finally, Chapter Seven examines health care policy in the United States, focusing on the right to health care and the allocation of human organs for transplant.

Beginning with Chapter Three, each chapter ends with a section on how to respond to case studies that contain ethical issues. Each section presents one step in this process so that by the end of Chapter Seven, the student should have developed the ability to write an essay responding to case studies involving ethical issues.

Part of these sections in the core chapters of the book are case studies depicting situations related to topics presented in the chapter's readings. These case studies are separated into two groups, macro cases and micro cases. The macro cases take the point of view of someone in a managerial or supervisory role who considers medical ethics from a systemic perspective. The point of view in the micro cases is of physicians, nurses, and other health care professionals who deal directly with patients and must make decisions that have ethical implications. Through these case studies, the student has an opportunity to react to the readings and test his or her own attitudes by writing an essay.

Basic Ethics in Action has an argument-based style and tone and intends to challenge the reader to think about some of the various ethical implications involved in specific situations. In a classroom setting, I have found that discussion of the more controversial premises focuses debate in a way that is satisfactory for both instructor and student.

Many may wish to read *Medical Ethics* along with an ethical theory text (such as *Basic Ethics*). Others will want to delve more deeply into issues of practice by finding topics that interest them and then doing their own interviews of people in the field. I believe that getting a sense of what real life is like is very important. It puts these cases and principles into a context that can be more easily integrated into the students' worldview. This is, after all, the purpose of a course on Medical Ethics. It helps students refine their practical decision-making skills so that they might be better able to live following a worldview that is, above all else, good.

As in all projects of this sort, there are many to thank. First, I would like to thank the participants of the Marymount University Faculty Ethics Seminar (1996–1998), who were subjected to versions of my developing ideas on professional ethics. I would also like to thank James A. Donahue, who worked with me on that seminar, for his criticisms and insights. My students were also guinea pigs as I class tested various approaches between 1994 and 1998.

Next, I would like to thank the following reviewers: John Dilworth, Western Michigan University; Ronald Glass, University of Wisconsin–La Crosse; Joan Whitman Hoff, Lock Haven University of Pennsylvania; Charles F. Kielkopf, Ohio State University; Steven Luper, Trinity University; and Richard L. Wilson, Towson University.

Third, I would like to thank Karita France, my former editor, for her persistent and thoughtful suggestions. My manuscript has profited from her guidance. I am also grateful to Jennifer Ackerman, her assistant, and my production editor, Linda B. Pawelchak.

Then, I must also acknowledge the help of Pat Milmoe McCarrick and the staff at the National Reference Center for Bioethics Literature. I also received important help from the reference librarians at Marymount University, especially Margaret Norden and Marge Runge.

Finally, I would like to mention my family: Arianne, Seán, Éamon, and Rebecca. Their lives and the values they teach me are a constant source of strength and sustenance.

Michael Boylan

Contributors

CHAPTER ONE: INTRODUCTION

Michael Boylan is professor of philosophy at Marymount University.

CHAPTER TWO: INTERVIEW WITH EDMUND D. PELLEGRINO, M.D.

Edmund D. Pellegrino is University Professor of Medicine and Medical Ethics at Georgetown University.

CHAPTER THREE: FROM THEORY TO PRACTICE

Deryck Beyleveld is professor of jurisprudence, Faculty of Law at the University of Sheffield.

Shaun Pattinson is a research student, Faculty of Law at the University of Sheffield.

Chapter Four: Physician, Nurse, and Patient—
The Practice of Medicine

Paternalism and Autonomy

Hilary Jones is a registered mental health nurse at the Meadowbrook Unit, Mental Health Services of Salford Trust, Salford.

Julian Savulescu is on the faculty of philosophy at Green College, Oxford.

Nancy S. Jecker is associate professor at the University of Washington School of Medicine and adjunct associate professor of philosophy and law at the University of Washington.

Robert D. Orr is a physician practicing in Loma Linda, California.

Privacy and Confidentiality

Paul Cain is a lecturer in the Department for Community Studies at the University of Reading.

Katharine V. Smith and Jan Russell are assistant professors in the School of Nursing at the University of Missouri–Kansas City, Missouri.

Carol A. Ford is with the Division of Community Pediatrics, Adolescent Medicine Section, Department of Pediatrics at the University of North Carolina at Chapel Hill.

Grant Kelly is the chair of the Joint Computing Group of the General Medical Services Committee and Royal College of General Practitioners, Keynor House, Sidlesham, Chichester, West Sussex.

Informed Consent

Julian Savulescu is on the philosophy faculty at Green College, Oxford.

Richard W. Momeyer is on the philosophy faculty at Miami University, Oxford, Ohio.

Ellen Agard is a Greenwall Fellow in Bioethics at Johns Hopkins University and at Georgetown University.

Daniel Finkelstein is a professor of ophthalmology at the Wilmer Ophthalmological Institute and on the core faculty at the Bioethics Institute at Johns Hopkins University School of Medicine.

Edward Wallach is J. Donald Woodruff Professor of Gynecology in the Department of Gynecology and Obstetrics at Johns Hopkins University School of Medicine.

Ronald Beyer is a professor in the Division of Sociomedical Sciences at Columbia University's School of Public Health.

Gender Issues

Mary B. Mahowald is a professor of philosophy at the University of Chicago.

Marcia Angell is editor-in-chief of the *New England Journal of Medicine.*

Debra Leners is an associate professor in the School of Nursing at the University of Northern Colorado.

Nancy Q. Beardslee is a professor in the School of Nursing at the University of Colorado.

CHAPTER FIVE: ISSUES OF LIFE AND DEATH

Euthanasia

Daniel Callahan is director of international programs at the Hastings Center.

Pieter V. Admiraal is an anesthesiologist at Delft, The Netherlands.

Leon R. Kass is Addie Clark Harding Professor for the College and the Committee on Social Thought at the University of Chicago.

John M. Dolan is co-chair of the Program in Human Rights and Medicine at the Human Rights Center, School of Law and associate professor of philosophy and American Studies at the University of Minnesota.

John Jefferson Davis is professor of theology and Christian ethics at Gordon-Conwell Theological Seminary.

Arthur Caplan is a professor at the Center for Bioethics at the University of Pennsylvania.

Cynthia B. Cohen is a professor of philosophy at Villanova University.

Winifred J. Pinch is an associate professor in the School of Nursing and the Center for Health Policy and Ethics at Creighton University.

Margaret L. Spielman is an assistant professor (retired) in the School of Nursing at Creighton University.

Abortion

John T. Noonan was professor of law at the University of California at Berkeley from 1967 to 1986. He now sits as a judge on the U.S. Court of Appeals, 9th Circuit.

Judith Jarvis Thomson is professor of philosophy at M.I.T.

Michael Boylan is professor of philosophy at Marymount University.

CHAPTER SIX: GENETIC ENGINEERING

Kevin Brown is a visiting scientist at the National Heart, Lung and Blood Institute, N.I.H.

Nils Hiltug is assistant professor of philosophy at the University of Copenhagen.

Edward M. Berger is professor of biology at Dartmouth College.

Bernard M. Gert is professor of philosophy at Dartmouth College.

Kathleen Nolan is associate for medicine at the Hastings Center.

Dorothy Nelkin is professor of sociology at New York University.

Søren Holm is reader in bioethics at the Centre for Social Ethics and Policy at the University of Manchester.

John Harris is Sir David Alliance Professor of Bioethics at the University of Manchester.

CHAPTER SEVEN: HEALTH CARE POLICY

The Right to Health Care

Michael Boylan is professor of philosophy at Marymount University.

Charles Fried is professor of law at Harvard University.

The Organ Allocation Problem

Rosamond Rhodes is director of bioethics education and associate professor of medical education at the Mount Sinai School of Medicine. She is also on the doctoral faculty in philosophy at the City University of New York Graduate Center.

Brian Smart is on the faculty of Keele University.

chapter one

Introduction

I. THE STRATEGY OF APPLIED ETHICS.

Applied Ethics assumes a theory of normative ethics and a linking principle or principles by which the ethical principles or maxims can be applied in real-life situations. It is a difficult branch of ethics because it assumes a certain facility with the subject matter of ethics and with the general practical imperatives involved. The series of books *Basic Ethics in Action* addresses practical imperatives of the professions. This book examines issues facing medicine and medical-related professions. Other books in the series address other professional issues such as business ethics.

I believe that the logical order of presentation begins with an ethical theory that we have chosen, moves to "linking principles," and finishes with a practical directive to action. However, as neat and logical as this order of presentation is, we live in the genetic order of existence that is constantly changing and developing. We also find ourselves changing to keep up with these alterations and developments. This means that we must regularly take time to engage in an assessment of our personal understanding of professional practice and ethical theory. Both work together in Medical Ethics to create an interdisciplinary attitude. Like all interdisciplinary perspectives, one side is often developed to the exclusion of the other.

1

For your study of this book, a certain amount of ethical material is prerequisite. This material concerns normative ethical theory. Although some of those issues are briefly addressed here, the discussion is not meant to be comprehensive. *Basic Ethics,* the anchor volume of this series, addresses in more detail the material that will help you better consider the problems inherent in Applied Ethics. Other books on ethical theory also address these issues. It would be very useful for the student to avail herself of one of these books to prepare herself for studying Applied Ethics. (The section "Evaluating a Case Study," a series of essays that follow the core chapters in this volume, gives some help to the student in this regard.)

After studying the various ethical theories, you must choose which one to adopt. I believe this choice is very important and depends on some self-conscious understanding of your personal worldview. The next section of this chapter briefly discusses some important features of the personal worldview along with the Personal Worldview Imperative, which gives direction to the nature of the worldview a person should adopt.

Finally, after presenting the worldview, the Personal Worldview Imperative, and some key ethical terms, I provide a broad overview of how these might be integrated with action. Chapters Two and Three will give more specific aspects of professional medical practice through the interview with Dr. Edward Pellegrino and one example of a very useful linking principle, precautionary reasoning.

II. Personal Worldview Imperative.

A.

The World was all before them, where to choose
Thir place of rest, and Providence thir guide:
They hand in hand with wand'ring steps and slow,
Through Eden took thir solitary way.
                              —Milton, *Paradise Lost*

This is the way the world ends
This is the way the world ends
This is the way the world ends
Not with a bang but with a whimper.
          —T.S. Eliot, "The Hollow Men"

B.

Little Lamb, who made thee?
Dost thou know who made thee?
    —William Blake, "The Lamb"

That bit of filth in dirty walls,
And all around barbed wire,
And 30,000 souls who sleep
Who once will wake
And once will see
Their own blood spilled.
>—Hanus Hachenburg, "Terezin" (1944, just before his death
>in a Nazi concentration camp at the age of 14)

In these two groups of paired poems, each has a definite *point of view*. Group A begins with an optimistic view of a tragedy (the human fall in the Garden of Eden at the beginning of the world) followed by an angst-ridden view of the end of the world.

Group B presents an innocent view of gentle questioning about the causes of life from the mind of a carefree rural child followed by the queries of a soon-to-be Holocaust victim about the nature of life in death and death in life.

Each passage reflects a different set of assumptions held by the poet. In literature, we call this *voice*. As a writer of poetry and fiction (and occasional reviewer of literary novels), I can attest to the fact that the ultimate judgment that we make when reading a piece of fictive literature revolves around the author's voice.

Charles Dickens did not achieve fame for his stylistic writing. In fact, his sentences are often clumsy, and he uses many words improperly. His characters are often wooden and his plots predictable. What sets Dickens apart from others in his century (who were his superior in these departments) is his voice. Dickens's voice is that of a champion for the rights of children and for the rights of the oppressed and against those who through their machinations seek to overreach themselves and grasp goods meant for others. A reader of a Dickens novel is impressed with the clarity of moral vision that suffuses the pages. This sense of literary voice is what I will call the worldview, or *Weltanschauung*.

Voice demarcates the world we enter when we open the covers of a fiction book. The world it presents is an escape, and we assent to it or not according to a myriad of factors. The act of reading is a knowing *suspension of disbelief*. We willingly enter into the author's worldview and test what it is like to be there. This is more than merely becoming a murderer (in a mystery story), a member of the opposite sex, or a person of a different race, religion, or culture; it is accepting a network of beliefs that together express values concerning the critical concerns of life: ethics, politics, religion, aesthetics, and so forth. When the world we enter is welcoming (meaning that it *accords* with some deeply held tenets within our own worldview), we feel comfortable and react to that world positively. When that world is foreign and hostile (meaning that it does not accord with our deeply held tenets within our own worldview), we are uncomfortable and react to the world negatively.

The composition of this worldview web of beliefs is not the same in everyone. Some (probably very few) may have a tree-structured logical pyramid of axiomatic primitives at the top and derivative theorems that follow from them. Others (many more) have an edifice that is *aporitic* in nature (meaning that a number of separate constructs owe their existence to specific problems that have arisen in each person's life). These aporitic constructs often exist in isolation from one another. I am reminded of Wemmick in *Great Expectations,* who had a life in Jaggers's office and another life with the aged-one in the "castle." Wemmick often advised Pip to bring up certain topics with him at one arena or the other, depending on the answer Pip wanted to receive because in each place, Wemmick took on a different worldview. There was (almost) no integration between the two.

I am also reminded of the metaphorical descriptions used by John Ruskin in *The Seven Lamps of Architecture* in which he declares that the composition of a building should reflect all of the architect's values. Under this view, if the architect's worldview is not well integrated, during the process of design the architect must create a single vision that is true to his materials, function, and execution (or else the project will ultimately be a failure). The construction of a building is a metaphor for how we are to construct ourselves. It speaks to personal values and their relationships within our lives. In this way, we can be viewed as the architects of ourselves. Some might believe that this is rather ephemeral for hard-nosed philosophy, but I believe that the ideas of the worldview rests at the edge of traditional philosophical discourse.

It is important for the position I am defending that it be possible for an individual to evaluate her worldview and life plan in a holistic fashion with reason as one of several key components. This holistic approach means that a person cannot separate worldview from philosophy. Some analytic philosophers have suggested that somehow it is possible for philosophy to work independently of any worldviews.[1]

These various views of analytic philosophy depict it as an objective tool that anyone can employ without assuming any of the characteristics, values, or worldview of the practitioner. This position seems wrong to me. I believe that the philosopher always brings his worldview along with him. This is not a position of epistemological relativism but merely an admission that the subjective and objective do not neatly segregate.[2]

Although they are subjective in nature, these worldviews are themselves subject to evaluative criteria. They are formal and logical principles that are virtually devoid of empirical content. Together, these criteria can be put together to form the Personal Worldview Imperative: *All people must develop a single, comprehensive and internally coherent worldview that is good and that we strive*

---

[1]Kai Nielsen discussed this briefly in his article "Philosophy and *Weltanschauung*," *The Journal of Value Inquiry* 27 (1993): 179–86.

[2]This is similar to Quine's insistence that analytic and synthetic truths do not easily segregate. See Willard Quine, "Two Dogmas of Empiricism," *From a Logical Point of View* (Cambridge, MA: Harvard University Press, 1953).

to act out in our daily lives.[3] In my opinion, every agent acting or potentially acting in the world falls under the normative force of the Personal Worldview Imperative. This principle could probably be analyzed to cover a wide range of axiological issues and may be the topic of some future work, but here I simply highlight three separate criteria that I believe are imbedded within the Personal Worldview Imperative and that bear closer examination.

The first criterion is this: *We have a duty to develop and to act out our worldview.* This means that we are expected to *choose* and *fashion* a point of view that will do much to condition our day-to-day consciousness. It is not enough merely to accept another's general beliefs and attitudes about ethics, politics, aesthetics, and religion. Doing so would be tantamount to becoming the slave of another. If some modicum of freedom and autonomy is a part of our human nature and if ultimately we are content only if we act out our human nature (assuming that all wish to be ultimately content), then we should all seek to exercise our freedom in the most practically fundamental way by choosing and fashioning a worldview.

Our power of choice in adopting a worldview may not be absolute, but that does not prevent us from exercising our freedom within a limited domain. Let us use another metaphor. Having a limited choice in adopting a worldview would be akin to moving into someone else's house. Suppose that the house had many features that we decided we did not like. We have some money, so we might remodel the house a room at a time, taking care that the remodeling concept is in accord with some larger plan or aesthetic point of view. The word *fashion* used earlier is meant to embody some of this sense of re-creation or remodeling.

Depending on our circumstances, this process of fashioning a worldview, like remodeling the house, could take a considerable length of time, especially given difficult exterior or interior factors. No two people's tasks are identical.

The second criterion is this: *We have a duty to develop a single worldview that is both comprehensive and internally consistent.* This second duty involves rather prudential concerns of what would count as a serviceable worldview. A worldview that is not unitary and comprehensive might not give us direction at some future time when such direction is sorely needed. We cannot depend on a worldview that is not comprehensive to help us grow and develop in life.

Likewise, a worldview that is not internally consistent might offer us contradictory directions of action in the future because each area of inconsistency (call them A and non-A) might develop a line of reasoning that maintains its original character (logical heritability). The resulting "offspring" of A

---

[3]Some might contend that my depiction of this imperative places an overreliance on form over content. It is a procedure and thus cannot have normative content. Against this attack, I reply that although the prescription, by itself, is procedural, it will result in some content. And, if taken in the Socratic spirit of living an examined life, the force of the normativity is toward participation in a process that must be sincere because it represents each of our very best versions of the "good, true, and beautiful."

and non-A would also be opposed. If these offspring are imperatives of action, then we are in a dilemma.[4] Such a worldview is inadequate because it may not be able to offer clear direction for action at some time in the future.

The third criterion is this: *We have a duty to create a worldview that is good.* This final criterion is the most difficult to justify in moral terms. Clearly, the word *good* in this instance may mean merely good for the agent's prudential interests. Certainly, we would not want to create a worldview that is self-destructive. Few would argue against the premise that our worldview ought to support a plan of life and development, which will be personally advantageous to us. But I assert that the type of worldview I am talking about should be morally good as well. Such a moral interpretation of the Personal Worldview Imperative is essential if this principle is to be of use in moral analysis.

III. AN OVERVIEW OF SOME KEY ETHICAL TERMS.

A. Metaethics.

Metaethics refers to the most general investigation about how to go about creating and applying a theory that prescribes how we should act. Many issues are pertinent to this area of ethical study—more than we can investigate in a brief treatment such as this; however, for a discussion of numerous ethical theories, I direct the reader to the core chapters of *Basic Ethics.*

One central issue concerns the *origins* of the theories. This, in turn, engenders several related questions: How do we know these theories are correct? How are these theories justified? What do these theories tell us about the world? These (and other) questions are important because they set the stage for us to be able to construct a normative theory of ethics. In this way, metaethics serves normative ethics just as philosophy of science serves those who create theories of science; there is a sense of creating the boundaries of acceptable discourse.

One of the principal questions in metaethics in the twentieth century has been whether an "ought" statement could be derived from an "is" statement. If not, then oughts occur from nonfactual (i.e., nonrational) sources. Let's examine the relationship between *is* and *ought* through an example.

> Premise—John says to Mary, "There is a poisonous cobra under your chair."
>
> Conclusion—John then says, "You ought to get out of your chair and run" or, more simply, "Run!"

---

[4]A moral dilemma occurs when a person, through no fault of her own, finds herself in a situation in which the only available choices of action are both evil.

What is the relationship between the premise and the conclusion? On first glance, it might seem that the factual premise 1 implies the normative action-guiding conclusion. In this case, an "is" (or factual statement) implies an "ought" (or prescriptive statement). However, others might demur. They would say that this paradigm has suppressed premises, which might include the following:

1'.   A poisonous cobra will kill Mary.
1".   Mary does not wish to be killed.
1"'. The only way to avoid being killed is for Mary to get out of her chair and run.

Premise 1' and 1"' are both factual statements, but 1" is a suppressed premise that is also normative. The entire argument would be different if we were to assert that Mary were indifferent to being killed. This means that 1" is really equivalent to saying that Mary *ought* not to wish to be killed. By understanding 1" in this way the detractor would contend that a hidden ought has been smuggled into the premises. If it has, then an ought has not been derived from an is; instead, an ought has been derived from an ought.

Thus, the detractor of an ought being derived from an is would assert that every supposed example of such a purported derivation is a suppressed premise that contains a "hidden 'ought.' "

An example of another important question in metaethics concerns whether the basis of ethical value can be determined rationally. Those who would assert that it cannot fall into two camps: (a) the cognitivists, who emphasize the role of rationally informed emotion such as "sympathy" and "care" (as in Ethical Feminism) and (b) the noncognitivists.

The noncognitivists believe that the basis of ethical theory is not legitimately in knowledge but in a deep sense is a matter of "taste." For example, few of us would contend that an intellectual basis exists for liking Fortnum and Mason's Irish Breakfast Tea over Bewley's variety. Some prefer the softer taste of the former but others choose the sharper, tannic aspect of the latter.

The noncognitivists contend that no matter how much one tries, matters of value cannot be traced back to matters of fact. For example, in the example concerning tea, we could say that good tea has a sharper, tannic taste; therefore, Bewley's, which has these qualities, is better. However, the critic might contend, how do we know that sharper and tannic are better and how do we measure them? This can be a problem, the noncognitivists contend. There is no pure standard for good tea to which everyone would agree; for this reason, we have many types of tea!

I will not elaborate on other noncognitivist strategies—such as linguistic analysis and emotivism—here. For a more detailed treatment, I refer the reader to *Basic Ethics* or to other general books that consider issues of metaethics.

B. Normative Ethics.

Normative Ethics involves creating[5] norms or standards of human conduct. Each theory in normative ethics comes complete with its own internal justification and metaethical assumptions. Of the many important normative theories, I will sketch out only four in this abbreviated presentation: Ethical Intuitionism, Virtue Ethics, Utilitarianism, and Deontology. In addition to these traditional theories, various modifications of them—Feminist Ethics, Religion and Ethics, and Professional Ethics—have been made.[6] Each presents a prescriptive set of directives designed to offer judgments about our actions.

Ethical Intuitionism.

One can generally describe Ethical Intuitionism as a theory of justification of the immediate grasping of self-evident ethical truths. Ethical Intuitionism can operate on the level of general principles or on the level of daily decision making. In the latter mode, many of us have experienced a form of Ethical Intuitionism through the teaching of timeless adages such as "Look before you leap" and "Faint heart never won fair maiden." The truth of these sayings is justified through intuition. Many adages or maxims contradict each other (as these two do), so that the ability to apply these maxims properly is also understood through intuition.

In practice, Ethical Intuitionism works from an established list of moral maxims that have no justification other than the fact that they are immediately perceived to be true. To understand better how this ethical theory works, try the following exercise:

Step One: Make a list of general moral maxims that you believe will cover most moral situations (e.g., don't lie). Choose at least three but no more than ten.

Step Two: Establish a hierarchy among your maxims that will apply for the most part.

Step Three: Create a moral situation that involves at least two moral maxims from your list. Determine which moral maxim best applies in the situation and state the reasons for your choice. How would you respond to someone who disagrees with your choice?

---

[5]I use the word *creating* here because I believe that we legislate moral maxims over a universal sample space. Those who advocate Virtue Ethics or Utilitarianism would demur because for them the process is not one of creating but of scientific discovery. Emotivists would also concur.

[6]Many advocates of Feminist Ethics, Religion and Ethics, and Professional Ethics would criticize me here by saying that their theories are not "overlays" to some other theory but should stand by themselves. I would concur that this is one way to view these theories. However, I would add that in my treatment, their status would be as an overlay to enrich other theories.

Virtue Ethics.

Virtue Ethics is sometimes called *Agent-Based Ethics.* It takes the viewpoint that in living, we should try to cultivate excellence in all that we do. These excellences or virtues are both moral and nonmoral. Through conscious training, for example, an athlete can achieve excellence in a sport (a nonmoral example). A person can achieve moral excellence in the same way. The development of these habits and the type of community that nurtures them come under the umbrella of Virtue Ethics.

Virtue Ethics works from an established list of accepted character traits called *virtues.* These virtues are acquired by habit and guide the practitioner in making moral decisions. Aristotle described these character traits as being a mean between extremes: The good man so habituates his behavior to these virtues that he will carry out the good actions over and over again throughout his life.

To better understand Virtue Ethics, try the following exercise:

Step One: Make a list of traits you believe to be virtues. Make sure you have at least three virtues but no more than ten.

Step Two: Establish the mean by outlining how the virtues in step one are really somewhere in the middle of two extremes.

Step Three: Describe how you might ingrain this virtue into your character. What consequences would this virtue have on you?

Step Four: Create a moral situation and show how being guided by Virtue Ethics would help you to resolve it. How does Virtue Ethics make a difference in this situation?

Utilitarianism.

Utilitarianism suggests that an action is morally right when that action produces a consequence with more total utility for the group than any other alternative would. Sometimes this explanation has been shortened to the slogan "The greatest good for the greatest number." The emphasis on quantitatively calculating the general population's projected consequential utility among competing alternatives appeals to many of the same principles that underlie democracy and capitalism (the reason that this theory has always been very popular in the United States and other Western capitalistic democracies).

Since Utilitarianism commends the moral choice that produces the greatest happiness for the greatest number of people, under this system, we must have a mechanism for determining (a) the alternatives involved, (b) the possible outcome of each alternative, (c) a clear definition of the population sample to be affected by the alternatives, and (d) a way to measure the possible impact that each alternative would have on the population sample so that it will be clear which alternative will yield the most pleasure/utility. The test chosen must be one that can be carried out and have relatively uncontroversial units by which the happiness impact can be measured and examined. To better understand what is involved in choosing Utilitarianism as a moral theory, try the following exercise:

> *Step One:* Create a moral situation that involves a difficult choice of alternative actions. (Cases, which pit the majority interests against rights of the minority, are often good for this exercise.)
>
> *Step Two:* List the possible alternatives and their projected outcomes.
>
> *Step Three:* Define the population that is affected by your case.
>
> *Step Four:* Propose a way to measure the happiness of the parties involved. Be sure that your measuring system can be quantified. What criticisms of your test could people make? How would you respond to their criticisms?
>
> *Step Five:* Run your test on your sample population and give the actual numbers of the happiness coefficients that each group will possess according to each alternative.
>
> *Step Six:* Defend your choice in step five against possible attacks.

Deontology.

Deontology is a moral theory that emphasizes a person's duty to a particular action because the action itself is inherently right, not for any other calculation, such as the consequences of the action. Because of this nonconsequentialist bent, Deontology is often contrasted with Utilitarianism, which defines the right action in terms of its ability to bring about the greatest aggregate utility. In contradistinction to Utilitarianism, Deontology recommends an action based on "principle," which is justified through an understanding of the structure of action, the nature of reason, and the operation of the will. The result is a moral command to act that does not justify itself by calculating consequences.

The moral principle is derived from and justified by the nature of reason and the structure of human action. Both its justification and its scope are general. The principle defines duty concerning moral situations in general. One way to understand this level of generality is to compare it to a scientific law, which is universal and absolute, covering all societies in all historical epochs.

One difficulty people often face with such a general principle is that moral cases are presented to us as particulars. In logic, general or universal propositions are contrasted to particular or individual propositions. They are different logical types and cannot be directly compared. The moral problem must be "translated" into general language at the same level as the moral principle, which permits a definitive outcome to be determined. However, this translation is not so easy. For example, consider Sarah, who is contemplating an abortion. All particulars of her individual situation must be translated into the form of a general moral principle or general moral law.

For this example, let us assume Kant's Categorical Imperative as our general principle. This principle states that we should act only on that maxim through which we can at the same time will that it become a universal law. This principle prohibits murder[7] because a universal law allowing murder in some society is logically contradictory. (If everyone murdered everyone else, there would be no society.) Logically contradictory universal laws are immoral; therefore, murder is immoral.

Autonomy, however, is also dictated by the Categorical Imperative and becomes the cornerstone of a formulation of the Categorical Imperative that addresses people as ends, not means only.

An example of the problem of moving from the particular to the general level (necessary for applying the moral laws/principles of Deontology) is in the translation of abortion. Is abortion an instance of *killing* or of *autonomy?* If it is the former, it is prohibitted. If it is the latter, it is permitted.

The real debate rests in the translation. Once a moral situation is translated, the application to the moral law is easy. The moral law determines our duty in the situation, and we must do our duty or else we repudiate our human nature; we are rational beings.

To better understand how Deontology works, try the following exercise:

Step One: Choose a universal moral principle (it can be Kant's or any other principle stated in general "lawlike" terminology).

Step Two: Create a particular moral situation that seems to involve a difficult choice of alternative actions. (Cases, which pit two moral duties against each other, are often good for this exercise.)

Step Three: Determine the possible alternative ways to translate the particular case into more general language (i.e., as an instance of truth telling, murder, autonomy).

Step Four: Justify your translation and point out the flaws in alternative translations.

Step Five: Show how your translation fits a general corollary of the universal moral principle. Explain how you arrived at the corollary and the outcome of translation to the corollary. What criticism of your translation, corollary derivation, or outcomes application could people make? How would you defend yourself against these criticisms?

---

[7]The mode of this prohibition is that all moral maxims generated from the notion of a universal society of murderers are shown to be incoherent. This means that a moral maxim such as "It is permissable to murder" is found to contain a logical contradiction. Like Plato, Kant believes that logical contradictions indicate immorality because morality means the right and wrong in human action. *Right* and *wrong* are determined by reference to logic. Illogic, therefore, is wrong. This is the driving force behind the universality of the Categorical Imperative in its various forms.

The criteria for deciding between ethical theories are elaborated by metaethics. Once you endorse a theory, you must determine how to apply it. One commonly held principle of application states that similar cases are to be treated similarly. Let this principle be termed the *just implementation of rules.* This principle is a purely formal principle of distributive justice.[8] (Distributive justice is that subbranch of morality that provides criteria by which goods and services may be parsed to recipients.) As a formal principle, this tells us that no matter what the content of the rule, all things being equal it is just to treat like cases in the same way.

The just implementation of rules is a necessary but not a sufficient principle. For example, if the Nazis held that the right to live is to be distributed only to non-Jews, then the application of the just implementation of rules would suggest that all Jews be killed!

What is needed are specifications on the *content* of the rule. When the content of the rule is included (as per the Personal Worldview Imperative), it is obvious that the imperative is inconsistent because no morally relevant difference exists between Jews and non-Jews. Since the Nazis contended that such a difference existed, they can be accused of being logically inconsistent.

Some might contend that makes no difference. These bestial creatures could care less. The answer would be that they diminish themselves—whether they know it or not—by violating the Personal Worldview Imperative.

Specifications on the content of the rule also address issues of what is the best system of distributive justice. Traditional candidates of distributive justice have included *capitalism* (to each according to her production), *socialism* (to each according to his need), *egalitarianism* (to each equally), *aristocracy* (to each according to her inherited station), and *kraterism* (to each according to his ability to snatch it for himself). There are other candidates, but this list provides the flavor of various formulae, which are often referred to in answering the question of how goods and services are to be distributed.

Once we have argued for and accepted a theory, according to the just implementation of rules, we must apply it consistently to all similar cases.

In the preceding example concerning the Nazis, the theory of justice we adopt constitutes the material element in the theory and the just implementation of rules represents merely a formal implementation tool.

This example of the Nazis is meant to illustrate the types of issues with which normative ethics concerns itself. In this domain, we are interested in creating norms for conduct, including justifying and defending all issues involved with the creation, understanding, or general application of such ethical norms. Such is the purview of normative ethics.

---

[8]Distributive justice is only one form of justice. The other most prominent form is retributive justice, which outlines how we are to punish others and the conditions on which these decisions are made and justified.

C. Applied Ethics.

Applied Ethics involves solving particular moral problems. Obviously, this process relates to the theories we adopt (normative ethics). Applied Ethics thus involves making actual ethical decisions. It is aligned to decision theory in which a normative ethical theory is included in the decision-making rubric.

This volume is principally concerned with Applied Ethics. The student who desires more information on metaethics and normative ethics may refer to *Basic Ethics* or another general treatment.

IV. WORLDVIEW INTEGRATION.

The basic approach to worldview integration was suggested in *Basic Ethics*. In that book, I argue that in constructing our worldview, we might combine personal inclinations toward other essential values such as the principles of aesthetics, feminism, religion, and professional practices into a general system of ethics.

Many people actually reside in several self-contained worlds that dictate how they should act in this or that situation. These specifications can often be contradictory. For example, I have been a volunteer baseball coach for youth sports for a number of years. One day I had a baseball game scheduled on a field that was occupied by another team holding a practice. I approached the man running the practice and showed him my permit for the field. He refused to leave and continued with his practice. When the umpires arrived for our game, they confirmed our reservation for the field. But the man holding the practice told us that we would have to call the police to have him evicted from the field.

I was not eager to call the police[9] and began to exhort the usurper in rational terms. First, I mentioned that he was not setting a good example of reasonableness and good will in front of the children of both teams. Both teams that rightfully had the field were being bullied by someone without a permit whose only claim to the field was that he was using it. I asked the man if he believed in societies without the rule of law—for that was what a *krateristic* (might makes right) position amounts to. Then I started naming various *krateristic* regimes in the twentieth century, starting with Joseph Stalin and Adolf Hitler. At the mention of those two names, the man yielded the field.

I found out later that the man was the coach of a church-sponsored team and was a prominent lay leader in that church. He was a respected corporate tax lawyer. I believe that when he was doggedly holding a field for which he had no permit, he was in the worldview of the aggressive corporate tax lawyer.

---

[9]I thought that calling the police to force the man from the field was merely to fight force with force and would represent a defeat for reason. Instead, I presented an argument in a controlled and level tone.

However, when I began speaking about lawlessness and historical instances of how *kraterism* has resulted in tyranny, the worldview of the church leader took over and he yielded the field.

This man lived in at least two different worlds. Each world contained its own practices and endorsed different approaches to solving problems. It was also probable that each of these worlds had little interaction with the other. The Personal Worldview Imperative calls for us to create a single worldview. This means that people who hold multiple worldviews that refer, in turn, to multiple and contradictory practices must work to create unity and coherence among these worldviews. By integrating these various beliefs, general attitudes, and life values, these people confront the world more authentically than they did when their worldviews were fragmented. Such a process of integration obviously requires introspection and self-knowledge.

A similar example is someone who has a serviceable single worldview but makes certain exceptions now and again for activities that the worldview explicitly forbids. This is not an instance of weakness of the will (in which the person maintains her worldview but fails to follow its prescriptions because she is overwhelmed by contrary desires) but is a set of ad hoc amendments to the worldview that are patently inconsistent with its other tenets. Consider a person who has a general rule against belittling people because of their national origin or religion. But this person harasses an employee in a manner that directly contradicts his general rule. He forms a new amendment to his worldview that allows him to act in this way. Obviously, this is an instance of incoherence and is thus disallowed by the Personal Worldview Imperative.

In the process of integration, we relate the empirical world (in which we live and make sense of by continually wrestling and striving with these issues) to various more abstract principles in such a way that life becomes rationally comprehensible. I compare this process to an artist painting a picture or a poet writing a poem. In each case, we are (as Hamlet said) holding a mirror up to nature. However, the imitation itself—the artifact—may vary. Thus, Jan Van Eyck, Claude Monet, and Wassily Kandinsky might all paint one particular scene differently.

Consider John Donne, John Dryden, or Anthony Hecht. Each would create a poem describing a common event[10] but in his own way. The reason for this is that (a) each views the event in an objective way as to the measurement of sounds and colors but (b) each arranges these details somewhat differently according to an order based on a value-laden worldview. The result is an artifact about which the group could come to factual agreement queried in a court of law but which each would describe differently. The significance of the whole and of the way the parts are arranged to make up the whole varies.

---

[10]Obviously, this is a thought experiment. The point of putting people of different styles and historical eras together is to highlight how important the component of worldview is in the way we process empirical data.

Also consider the way different peoples have reacted to the human condition to create religion. If such a reaction were a transparent process of merely translating either a revelation (of God) or a reaction to some common human need, then we would expect that there would be one and only one religion, but this is obviously not the case. The reason is that (as with the painters and the poets) people react to the same revelation or human need differently.[11] Thus, we have various religions in the world (which are almost as numerous as the variety of artistic schools of expression).

These examples express some of the relationships among (a) worldview, (b) empirical events, and (c) other theoretical constructs. Together, I call these *interactions:* integration through the process of dialectical interaction.[12]

This integration has two important manifestations in the way we apply ethical theories. First is the way we integrate empirical events into theoretical categories (dialectical subsumption) given our worldview. Second is the way we match our ethical imperatives with our worldview. Let us discuss each of these briefly and then examine the process of applying an ethical theory.

The first manifestation is the way we integrate empirical events into theoretical categories (dialectical subsumption) given our worldview. Dialectical subsumption is the interactive process by which objects are schematized into our consciousness. The best way to describe dialectical subsumption is to contrast it to mechanical subsumption. In mechanical subsumption, a class, alpha, has certain membership requirements (e.g., possession of trait phi). When any x has phi, it belongs to alpha. The entire process is termed *mechanical* because it is a simple mechanistic process of sorting things where they belong according to some preestablished set of rules. The decision procedure is certain so that the procedure could be performed on a sample space so that it would be exhaustive and complete. This model of mechanical subsumption may be possible in mathematics and computer modeling. It is often used to give fullness to certain theories in some of the social sciences (especially economics!).

Unfortunately, mechanical subsumption is largely a priori in character.[13] This means that instead of interacting with the data in a carefully refining, bootstraping operation, the practitioners intend a simple process of observing whether x possesses phi and, if it does, putting it into alpha.

---

[11]This analogy may be objectionable to advocates of a religion who believe that their particular version is the only one of any true value. They would object to the aesthetic model I am creating here and prefer a more scientific one.

[12]See *Basic Ethics*, Chapter Eight, for an exposition of the various types of dialectical processes relevant here.

[13]Although mechanical subsumption is widely used in diverse fields from legal positivism to econometrics to some theories of zoological systematics, it has been attacked by others as well. The reader is invited to examine some of these in context. Two diverse examples are cited in law by Ronald Dworkin, *Taking Rights Seriously* (Cambridge, MA: Harvard University Press, 1977), chaps. 2 and 3; and in evolutionary biology by Ernst Mayr, *Toward a New Philosophy of Biology* (Cambridge, MA: Harvard University Press, 1988), pt 5.

Dialectical subsumption is more complicated than this. Let us consider two arguments along this line: (a) the ascription of properties to some object is a complicated process involving the worldview of the observer and (b) the manner by which the observer inserts the object into a category is also theory laden (meaning that it is connected to the observer's worldview).

A. First Form.

My first argument is that the ascription of properties is not a simple procedure. Although the painters Cranach and Turner may agree that the sunset is red, they may mean different things by this. Cranach may consider the sunset as a carefully circumscribed aspect of the third ground or background of the painting's composition while Turner may say that there is only one ground and that the sunset affects everything. The "what it is" is intricately connected to the "way it behaves." Thus, the ascription of properties includes more than a simple list of properties in some mechanical, objective manner. Instead, how the properties exist within the entire composition and the interaction of these into some environmental context must be considered. Both of these conditions are necessary to really understand the properties of some object.

An example of the linkage between the object and its activity is the identification of function along with morphology in evolutionary biology. Without function, the shapes, colors, and sizes are not completely described. The what it is is conditioned by the way it behaves. Both are necessary to understand homology in an evolutionary context. This means that the ascription of properties is not a simple, objective procedure without a connection to the observer's worldview. In the examples cited, a person's theoretical dispositions condition the way the person depicts the object itself.

These examples illustrate that the ascription of properties is not as straightforward as the mechanical subsumptionists would have us believe. Dialectical subsumption is a procedure that is informed by an individual's worldview. The way that the observer understands the object is colored by the way the observer understands the object to behave. The way that the object behaves is conditioned by the observer's theoretical assumptions about this object and objects like it. Finally, an individual's theoretical assumption about general laws governing existing entities is a major component of that person's worldview.

B. Second Form.

The manner by which we insert an object into a category is also theory laden (meaning that it is connected to the worldview of the observer). In many ways, this second mode of explaining dialectical subsumption is similar to the first. The second form involves fitting unknown objects into preestablished categories. This contrasts to the first form that seeks to identify objects and to ascribe to them certain traits and properties.

In biology, the second form is called *taxonomy* and the theory governing the process is called *systematics*. A person examining some individual object to determine what group it belongs to ascribes certain traits to it and uses that description to match (or approximate) its membership in some higher class (thus employing the first form). Sometimes this task is rather delicate; often the individual object is not clearly in a single subspecies but may possess traits of two or more subspecies. In these cases, the observer must make a judgment about the physical traits that are most significant, which is relative to the function of the part in question. Thus, the observer is ranking morphological traits based on theoretical assumptions about functional efficacy.

This is just like the first form in which the observer harbored certain more general theoretical assumptions to help form a judgment about what traits an object possessed and how the traits were to be described. In the second form, the observer uses a more general context (i.e., theoretical assumptions, part of the observer's worldview), which is the justification for putting the individual object into this or that taxonomological category.

Thus, both the ascription of properties to the object (the first form) and the act of placing the object into its appropriate category (the second form) are connected to the observer's worldview. This means that the mechanical subsumption model is false.

The alternative to the mechanical subsumption hypothesis is the *dialectical subsumption* thesis. According to it, the observer moves back and forth between the object and his understanding of the object (including all of his theoretical assumptions) until the nature of the object can be determined. When a dissonance occurs between the object as preconceived and the object as dialectically understood, the latter trumps the former.

The second manifestation *is the way we match our ethical imperatives with our worldview*. The dialectical process of matching ethical imperatives with our worldview is outlined in Chapter Eight of *Basic Ethics*. What is the driving force behind this dialectic? What might cause an individual to accept certain courses of action and to reject others? For the answer to these questions, we must return to the Personal Worldview Imperative. This dissonance may occur when a theory suggests that the individual do x, but x is contrary to certain core values that this person holds. Let us examine two examples to see how dissonance occurs.

Example One.

Max is a guard at a Nazi concentration camp. His superiors have given him a directive to shoot a dozen Jewish prisoners because the camp needs fewer prisoners to meet its production requirements. Max marches the prisoners to a corner of the camp that is under repair and from which they could escape if he would turn away. He would never be detected if he shot his gun in the air and allowed them to escape because little attention is paid to the disposal of bodies (since this camp kills hundreds each day).

Max has been taught by his mother that human life is sacred. He knows that these Jews have committed no crimes except being at the wrong place at the wrong time. Therefore, Max believes that killing these people is wrong; he also believes that he has a prima facie duty to obey his superiors. It is a time of war and he has his orders. He is inclined to let the prisoners escape, but the law says that he should not.

Example Two.

Sally is an American woman of European descent who grew up in poverty in Appalachia. She had always been close to her mother, who told her that African Americans and the affirmative action program were responsible for her father losing his job and committing suicide as a result. Sally is now a sergeant in the army and has some African Americans under her command. Military regulations require that all soldiers be treated equally regardless of race. However, she has the opportunity to make the lives of these African Americans in her command very difficult as a payback for what happened to her father. She is inclined to "give them hell," but the regulations say she should not.

These two examples are complementary. In the first case, Max's personal worldview may cause him to disobey the law to do the right thing. In the second case, Sally's personal worldview may cause her to disobey the law to do a bad thing. What are we to make of this?

The first question to be asked is whether the Personal Worldview Imperative has been engaged in either case. If Max and Sally had never examined their convictions, then they will probably act according to some idea of punishment should they break the law. In other words, if both are convinced that the law will not punish them, they will probably follow their worldview. But what of this worldview? How responsible are they for it? Was it not merely handed to them by another?

Socrates' dictum—the unexamined life is not worth living—lies at the heart of the Personal Worldview Imperative. I contend that if Max had examined his worldview as suggested by the Personal Worldview Imperative, he would have assumed ownership for his values. In that case, clearly he would not have performed the dissonant action of killing the prisoners. The conflict would be resolved in favor of the worldview.

Sally's case is more challenging; her worldview is incoherent. If she were to consider everything she believes in, that is, (a) that no biologically significant difference between the races exists, (b) that what happened to her father was an instance of an individual affected by a government policy (which was not established by African Americans), and (c) that no logical link exists between what happened to her father and these people now in her command. Such an introspective inventory would surely cause Sally to change her worldview. According to the Personal Worldview Imperative, we must strive to make our worldview coherent. If Sally accepted this challenge, then she would alter her beliefs.

What if Sally does not alter them? In this case, she would be a pawn of her mother's value system. Her responsibility for her immoral treatment of her subordinates would still fall to her because she failed to examine her life (via the Personal Worldview Imperative). Her real flaw would be living an inauthentic existence as a slave to another (in this case, her mother). All the consequences of this initial choice also may be attributed to Sally. Sally is actually responsible even if the paradigm she used to guide her actions came from another.[14] This is the description of the material conditions of agency. How we treat Sally as to her culpability of action is another issue. We may determine that circumstances influenced her failure to examine her life.

I believe that all immoral worldviews that are examined according to the Personal Worldview Imperative will be revised. This is so because I believe that only moral worldviews will satisfy the conditions of rationality, such as those described in the Personal Worldview Imperative.

In this way, the Personal Worldview Imperative offers a necessary basis for any moral theory. Therefore, I can write this introduction without knowing the moral theory of a practitioner. If she has adopted the Personal Worldview Imperative completely, then it will condition the version of any ethical theory into one that will be serviceable to her or any other agent.

This does not mean that all theories are to be judged as equally correct (see my earlier discussion of painters and poets). No, an individual's worldview will dictate that Deontology, Utilitarianism, Intuitionism, or Virtue Ethics is *the* correct theory. The Personal Worldview Imperative allows this judgment to be made. However, the version of this theory (whichever is chosen) will also be conditioned by the Personal Worldview Imperative. An example of this is the emphasis on both understanding as well as justification (see *Basic Ethics*, Chapter Eight).

In this way, the Personal Worldview Imperative is not a full-blown theory but an important element when considering questions of metaethics, normative ethics, and Applied Ethics. It may offer a bridge between often inaccessible theories and the real lives of people who wish to consider ethical issues.

---

[14]Of course, some would disagree that we really have as much choice as I have portrayed. A pointed rebuttal of my position in this regard has been made by Anita Allen, "Confronting Moral Theories: Gewirth in Context" in Michael Boylan, ed. *Gewirth: Critical Essays in Action, Rationality, and Community* (New York: Rowman and Littlefield, 1999).

V. Decision Making.

Figure 1.1 is a version of the process that I believe should be performed when an individual decides to apply an ethical theory. The process begins when the individual must make a decision that has ethical implications. The process is a rather simplified version of how I believe we should apply any ethical theory.

What can be highlighted about this process is that it emphasizes the sincerity of the individual in following his conscience. *Conscience* means the gathering of

Step One: The person identifies the problematic situation in all its particularity, including any possible ethical issues.

Step Two: The agent identifies relevant moral rules in which he believes.

Step Three: The individual engages in dialectical subsumption of the ethical issues in step one, relating them to the rule identified in step two (see the last section for a discussion of dialectical subsumption).*

Step Four: The operation of step three will produce a provisional action directive (i.e., an ethical imperative for action).

Step Five: The individual matches his provisional action directive from step four with his worldview (as discussed in the last section).

Step Six (a): If the provisional action directive fits with his worldview according to the criteria of the Personal Worldview Imperative, he has an ethical imperative for action.

Step Six (b): If the provisional action directive does not fit with the individual's worldview according to the criteria of the Personal Worldview Imperative, he must return to step three.

Step Seven (a): If the difficulty can be resolved by further dialectical subsumption (following his worldview examination in step five), he has an ethical imperative for action.

Step Seven (b): If the difficulty cannot be resolved by further dialectical subsumption, the individual must return to step five and repeat the process.

Step Eight (a): If the difficulty can be resolved, he has an ethical imperative for action.

Step Eight (b): If the difficulty cannot be resolved, six (b) and seven (b) should be repeated until the problem is resolved or an impasse is reached.

Step Nine: In the event of an impasse, the individual should return to the process of choosing an ethical theory and repeat that process.

*When step three occurs as mechanical subsumption, the model is more similar to logically abstract supreme principle theory models discussed in *Basic Ethics*, Chapter Nine.

Figure 1.1 The Process of Applying an Ethical Theory

a person's exact understandings. This congregation of knowledge is really one form of worldview. Thus, to act according to conscience (in this sense) means to act so that the person's core beliefs are not violated by the proposed action.

It is important to relate the gravity of the proposed action to the primary nature of the core beliefs. For example, if an individual were considering parting his hair from behind or eating a peach, the intended action is clearly rather trivial. If such actions were ethically offensive to the person's core beliefs, then there would be no question that they would be prohibited. Likewise, if the action in question were serious (e.g., Sally's dilemma discussed earlier) and the worldview impediment were relatively trivial, the decision would be easy.[15]

When the ethical issue is serious and the conflicting value is primary (e.g., abortion, the death penalty, euthanasia), the situation is most challenging. When this occurs, the individual must do her best to be true to her conscience/worldview. If the worldview has been carefully crafted according to the steps listed in Figure 1.1, then this touchstone should represent the person's own best approximation of those values that together are most important in life.

If there truly are a right and a wrong in human conduct, we can imagine the four situations shown in Figure 1.2. In the first alternative, the individual has a good motive (one that is fully consonant with his worldview and the relevant ethical principle(s); see steps three and five in Figure 1.1) and a good action.

The second alternative suggests a good motivation with a bad action (the person sincerely believed that what she was doing was correct, but it really was not).[16] The significance of this second alternative contrasts with the third alternative (bad motivation and an accidentally good action). The real issue is engaged at this point. I believe that acting in accordance with one's worldview is the most important criterion. If this means that a person commits a bad action, then at least that person was doing the best s/he could; it was sincerely executed. The possibility that the action might turn out to be the best does not lend any credit to the individual who has acted against her best inclinations.[17]

The basis of this judgment is the Personal Worldview Imperative. When an individual accepts the fact that he must examine his life and develop a single, comprehensive, and internally coherent worldview that he must strive to act out in his life, he has self-consciously agreed that this exercise

---

[15]A further discussion of this type of analysis can be found in each of the accompanying volumes to this series. See the Evaluating a Case Study series of essays.

[16]Whether something is or is not a good action in this context is a thought experiment to make a point about the relationships between conscience/worldview and the act itself. Some would contend that the only way to determine whether an action is right or wrong is to apply the appropriate operational criteria to it. In this case, there is no right or wrong apart from the successful execution of said operation. This point of view could negate the force of my thought experiment unless one were willing to allow the posit that an action was actually right apart from some agent's deliberations on the subject.

[17]For an example of this, see the excerpt from H.G. Wells's *The History of Mr. Polly*, in Michael Boylan, ed., *Perspectives in Philosophy* (New York: Harcourt Brace, 1993), pp. 379–88. Mr. Polly intends to commit suicide and ends up a hero. Was it right to treat him as a hero?

	Motive/Action	
Motive/Action	1. Good/Good	2. Good/Bad
	3. Bad/Good	4. Bad/Bad

FIGURE 1.2 **A Matrix of Actions and Motives**

of autonomy and freedom is what we should do. Such behavior defines us as humans in a more comprehensive way than even saying that we are "rational animals" because the Personal Worldview Imperative specifies the *manner* of executing our rationality. It is more holistic and ties people to abstract, atemporal logic; to an intellectual tradition; and to various cultural and personal values that jointly describe who we are.

As Figure 1.2 illustrates, an individual goes through this process by engaging in both dialectical subsumption (which commits that individual to creating a bridge between the particular action at hand and various principles that enrich and give meaning to her understanding of that action)[18] and in the worldview check. This check is analogous to the procedure of balancing a checkbook. We all do some quick mental arithmetic to estimate what our total should be and then we go through the mechanics of adding and subtracting. If our mechanical total is quite different from our original guess, we suspect a mistake and repeat the procedure. This process is similar to the worldview check, which offers a check and balance against improper calculations. This is so because we live in our worldview, and we accept it as being what we want—even if we do not always fully execute its demands.

We could use the vernacular expression Is this really *me?* to describe this interaction in another way. If it isn't me, then I should not do it—or I should redefine who me is. Thus, the ultimate authority of action is always the subject (the "me") because the me will be responsible. It is the "me" who will have to live with the action taken.

Thus, the short answer to how to apply an ethical theory is that an individual should strive to be (a) true to the moral theory s/he has chosen, (b) as thorough as possible (according to some sort of scale of proportionality of ethical gravity) in her or his application process (especially steps one through five—in Figure 1.1), and (c) as open as possible to altering or changing her or his ethical theory according to the interactions of the *entirety* of her or his worldview. It seems to me that this is what we can and should expect of everyone, no more, no less.

---

[18]This process is also similar to Paul Ricoeur's view of the role of the productive imagination in the A-version of Kant's schematicism.

chapter two

Interview with Edmund D. Pellegrino, M.D.

I. INTRODUCTION.

Dr. Pellegrino has had a distinguished career. He was chairperson of the Department of Medicine at the University of Kentucky Medical Center (1959–1966); vice president of the Health Sciences (dean of the School of Medicine, director of the Health Sciences Center, and professor of medicine) at the State University of New York, Stony Brook (1966–1973); chancellor and vice president for Health Affairs at the University of Tennessee (1973–1975); president and chairman of the Board of Directors and professor of medicine at Yale University Medical Center (1975–1978); president of Catholic University of America as well as professor of philosophy and biology (1978–1982); director of the Kennedy Institute of Ethics at Georgetown University (1983–1989); director of the Center for the Advanced Study of Ethics at Georgetown University (1989–1994); and John Caroll Professor of Medicine and Medical Ethics, director of Clinical Bioethics at Georgetown University Medical Center (1991–1994). He is currently University Professor of Medicine and Medical Ethics at Georgetown University Medical Center.

II. The Structure of the Interview.

The questions in the interview focus on ethical theory and real-life issues in biomedicine, including informed consent, truth telling, privacy and confidentiality, paternalism and autonomy, the termination of life, medical research, and health care in the United States. These subjects follow the structure of the book. Dr. Pellegrino has been a pioneer and prominent practitioner of bioethics. His keen insights should be studied as the thoughts of an accomplished bioethicist. To facilitate an appreciation for his insights, I will offer some advice on how to read this interview.

III. How to Understand the Interview.

From the outset, Dr. Pellegrino's views must be understood from three perspectives:

1. He has a well-reasoned moral theory. Dr. Pellegrino espouses Virtue Ethics as his moral theory of choice. This choice does not mean that he does not also use some maxims from Deontology from time to time, but his primary perspective is grounded in Virtue Ethics. (The student is directed to the Introduction for an overview of Virtue Ethics, and to the exercises—"Evaluating a Case Study—Developing a Practical Ethical Viewpoint"—found at the end of Chapter Three.) One useful exercise would be to go through this interview and highlight sections that make Dr. Pellegrino's Virtue Ethics position evident and note how his position might be different if he were, for example, a utilitarian.

2. Dr. Pellegrino has formulated a view about the professional dimensions of medicine. These have their background in the Oath of Hippocrates (discussed briefly at the beginning of Chapter Four). The professional standards of medicine constitute the purpose or *telos* (Greek for *end* or *purpose*) toward which all practitioners should strive. Another useful exercise would be to search for references to the purpose or *telos* of the profession. Along with ethical principles per se, these professional standards offer strong reasons for action.

3. Dr. Pellegrino understands the practical nuts and bolts of medicine. Throughout his professional career, he has been a healer, caring for patients at all levels: the temporarily ill, the critically ill, and the terminally ill. His is a knowledge built on the particularity of individuals who have lived and died while he cared for them. From this perspective, pay careful attention to the examples that Dr. Pellegrino uses. They demonstrate how he has fulfilled the moral maxims he espouses in practice. One exercise might be to list the examples on a sheet of paper and next to each item identify the moral maxim involved and the way that moral maxim is related to the broader moral principle. In addition to this, see how often examples refer to the purpose (*telos*) of medicine. This is a particularly instructive exercise because it will allow the reader better to integrate ethical theory, the professional standards of medicine, and the particular situation that faces the health care provider. With these prefatory comments, let us go to the interview.

Interview with Edmund D. Pellegrino, M.D.

ETHICAL THEORY

Q: Must we choose one single ethical theory?
A: Ultimately, we must have an ethical theory. We cannot function in the world without one. We all need some basis for moral justification. This is the case because we are called on each day to act in situations that have ethical content, in other words, in which it matters what we choose (there are right and wrong possibilities). We all need to give reasons to explain why we decide as we do. The trouble is that most people are not aware of ethical theory at all because they have not thought about it. One could, like Socrates, approach each of these people and question her in such a way that would stimulate this reflection and this would be the first step in her self-revelation of the theory behind her choices.

However, it is very rare for anyone to use one theory exclusively. Most people rely on a dominant ethical theory while employing other theories as ancillary or alternate justifications, as the situation may demand. The dominant theory supervenes in cases of conflict. Indeed, it is through this supervention that we can identify each person's dominant theory. This is the person's "fall-back" theory—the axiomatic presupposition from which a person's moral justification begins.

Understanding the dynamics of moral choice is important because one of our obligations as individuals is to understand the reasons for our actions. This involves balancing (a) the intent of the agent about to commit the act, (b) the nature of the act itself, (c) the circumstances of the act, and (d) the consequences of the act. All four of these elements are important. But each is treated and will reflect the dominant ethical theory one espouses.

Many modern theories of ethics emphasize one of these elements over the other. For example, if an individual chooses to emphasize the consequences of the act, that person might create a theory that discounts intentions. The result is a sort of behaviorism in which the person views actions as physical movements on the part of individuals that have consequences that can be quantified and put into a cost benefit structure.[1] Others choose to emphasize the moral agent (virtue theorists) or the nature of the act (deontologists). Overemphasis of any one theory to the exclusion of all others puts the four elements of a moral event in a state of imbalance.

For example, a theory such as Consequentialism puts the four-element model out of balance and fundamental distinctions—such as between "killing" and "letting die"—are lost. In my work I have sought a better balance, which can yield a richer response to phenomenological description so necessary in the practice of medicine.[2]

Q: If intention is so important, shouldn't we have a way to judge a good intention from a bad one?
A: Of course, but this requires asking the additional question about the validity of the source of justification. This is a more general inquiry that covers more than just philosophical ethics.

There are currently a variety of candidates for the source of intention, for example (a) divine revelation, (b) human reason, (c) (a) and (b) together, (d) the mechanical/chemical operation of the nervous system operating alone, and (e) culture, history, and intuition. Each of these might claim to be justifications for judging the intention of an act as good or bad. Obviously, which justification one uses makes a tremendous difference. There are advocates for all of them in our society. This creates part of the difficulty we encounter in moral dialogue. When people differ on the fundamental starting points in their moral reasoning, then the entire discussion of intent is open to conflict and confusion.

---

[1] For a discussion of one theory of this type, see the discussion of Utilitarianism in Michael Boylan's *Basic Ethics*, chap. 3.—ED.

[2] For a fuller treatment of this, see Edmund D. Pellegrino and David C. Thomasma, *A Philosophical Basis of Medical Practice* (New York: Oxford University Press, 1981), chap. 2.

Q: **Without such questioning, might a person be unable to respond when he finds himself in personal crisis in which the categories he has been using prove to be inadequate?**
A: Yes. That is one reason that the teaching of ethics is so important—especially ethical theory and metaethics in which the teacher challenges students to come to grips with who they think they are morally—and *why.*

Q: **What do you find appealing and problematic about Intuitionism, Utilitarianism, and Virtue Ethics?**
A: Let me offer a few brief comments on these theories. Every line of reasoning must start somewhere with some axiom or proposition or principle, such as the Principle of Noncontradiction.[3] Grasping an axiom of this sort is intuitive in the sense that it is grasped immediately. These axiom-level principles must be very limited in number. This is why I advocate an economy of intuitions. Once the axioms are laid down, one moves by deduction and evidence rationally to prove other propositions. The problem with Intuitionism occurs when one universalizes it as a sufficient justification for morality.[4] This leads to Subjectivism, Egoism, and Relativism.

Second, is Consequentialism. As I mentioned earlier, consequences are important but are not the only consideration. For example, the Principle of Beneficence is the central ethical imperative in medicine. To know what is in the patient's interests requires calculations about consequences. If a patient complains of a cardiac chest pain, several treatments are possible. The patient could be treated with drugs, surgery, angioplasty, and so on. What treatment course to adopt depends on weighing various benefits and risks associated with each option. This is consequentialist thinking. If the patient were an avid skier, surgery is possibly the best course; for another patient with a sedentary lifestyle, noninvasive treatment might be acceptable. The decision must focus on optimizing the good for that person.

In ethics, however, Consequentialism becomes hazardous if it makes the consequences the sole determinant of moral good, especially if utility is the consequence selected above others. In the utilitarian view, one person's good could be sacrificed for the good of the many. However, as a physician, I must be concerned with the good of the patient before me. (The only exception is when my patient is a harm to others. This might occur if the patient had a contagious disease such as AIDS or tuberculosis.) In ordinary circumstances, the physician is bound by a covenant of trust to act on behalf of the patient he is treating, not on behalf of society, the economy, or the family.

Then there is virtue-based ethics. What makes Virtue Ethics so important is that it recognizes the reality of the moral agent. The character of

---

[3]The Principle of Noncontradiction states that one cannot both assert p and non-p at the same time and in the same respect.—ED.
[4]Compare to level 2 Intuitionism in *Basic Ethics,* chap. 1.—ED.

the physician is often the patient's final safeguard against harm. Many virtues are important to the physician, but the virtue of benevolence is the most important. Other virtues are prudence, fidelity to trust, honesty, courage, and effacement of self-interest. Each of these virtues is essential if the end of medicine—the good of a particular patient—is to be achieved. Thus, the ends of medicine entail certain virtues.

Q: Sort of like the Ring of Gyges?[5]
A: Exactly. One must practice the virtues because they ensure ethical actions, not because someone is watching or is about to bring some lawsuit.

The virtues of medicine are determined with reference to the end or *telos* of that discipline. In the case of medicine, this end is now in dispute among some ethicists. However, I believe we can derive this end by analyzing the phenomena of what it means to be a patient. The moment a person becomes a "patient" because of a medical problem four things happen: (a) the person is vulnerable, (b) she is exploitable, (c) she is dependent on her doctor, and (d) she is anxious about her condition.

The physician (and all health care workers) confronts this patient who is in a state of diminished capacity to act and is dependent on the doctor's knowledge and skill. More is expected of the physician because of the patient's vulnerability and exploitability. The patient puts her well-being in the hands of the physician (and of all health care workers). This is not just metaphorical language. We invite the patient to trust us. We voluntarily offer to help and when we do, we have made a promise to help. Fidelity to trust is therefore a virtue of physicians entailed by the *telos* of medicine.

When the patient confronts us, we must clearly see the *telos* of medicine (i.e., the good of the patient). This is a compound good that the physician must balance in his practice of medicine. I would rank these goods as follows in descending order of importance: spiritual good, the good of the patient as a human, personal good, and the physician's idea of medical good.

Q: So it begins with a situation of trust resulting from the four phenomenological factors?
A: Yes, no matter who you are, you cannot deny that you go to a physician for right and good healing and helping actions and decisions. If this is the proximate *telos* of medicine, then whatever brings it about is good.

---

[5]According to legend, a shepherd named Gyges once served the king of Lydia. One day a great storm and earthquake created an opening in the earth. Gyges descended into this opening where he beheld (among other things) a golden ring that made him invisible. Plato discusses this story in the *Republic*, Book 2 (the standard edition is edited by Jon Burnet. Oxford: Clarendon Press, 1902). Plato's point in bringing up this story is that if one possessed Gyges's ring and became invisible to men and the gods, then one would never be punished for an immoral action. If there were convincing reasons for *still* acting morally under these circumstances, then morality has an intrinsic (as opposed to an extrinsic) justification. [Ed.]

Medicine strives to "heal" (i.e., to make whole again, to restore the balance we call "health").[6] Galen defines health as the state in which we can do the things we want to do with a minimum of pain or discomfort. The *telos* of medicine is to restore a person to a state of health in Galen's sense and, if that is impossible, then to help the person to cope with the new reality of illness, disability, or impending death.

A virtuous health care professional (physician, nurse, and others) must see this *telos* as her mission. If she does not strive to attain this end, she is not being excellent (virtuous) in the execution of her professional duty.

The end of medicine grounds medical ethics and defines its virtue. Medical ethics begins in the phenomenological characteristics of the medical interaction. This factual situation creates normative duties. In this way, the normal "ought" is based on a kind of dialectal necessity. I do not think this perspective commits the error of the naturalist fallacy—neither Hume's or G.E. Moore's.[7] But this is the subject of a more extended metaethical discourse than is suitable here.

REAL-LIFE ISSUES

Q: What about the issue of informed consent? Some would say that there is no real informed consent—especially considering the four categories you cited earlier.
A: Informed consent is a point on a continuum. It is not a yes/no "bright line." As you have suggested, some contend that informed consent is not a realistic goal. But every conscious person can give some degree of informed consent. If the health care provider understands this, then he can optimize the possibilities if he attends to full questions: (a) Is the patient able to communicate? (b) Is the patient able to understand the options and their gravity? (c) Can the patient repeat these options and dangers in her own words? Does the patient understand the *costs* (dangers) as well as the *benefits* of both treatment and nontreatment? (d) Is the patient able to give a reasoned judgment based on her own values—not mine or yours?

The physician must be particularly attentive to avoid subtle forms of coercion. The physician must not take advantage of his position of power even for the "good" of the patient. The patient by the nature of her illness is at a disadvantage in this human interaction, and care must be exerted to protect her vulnerability.

Q: Yes, and the physician can have his own point of view. For example, if you approach an internist about your knee problem, he may suggest physical

---

[6]In ancient medicine, health was defined as the balance among the four humours: blood, phlegm, black bile, and yellow bile. This theory originated with the Hippocratic writers and was further developed by Galen. [Ed.]

[7]The naturalistic fallacy occurs when one mistakes an unnatural object for a natural one. I discuss this in *Basic Ethics*, Chapter One. [Ed.]

therapy and anti-inflammatory drugs while a surgeon might tell you that surgery is the only answer.

A: This is true unless we have good scientific evidence for a measurable difference in outcomes. This is the reason that we must fall back on character. The physician must be as self-critical as possible. This is the only way that the physician can overcome his natural bias. In the end, it comes down to knowing himself as well as his patient. This is very important for informed consent. The physician must be as scrupulous as possible in his attempt to engage the patient in an authentic process of choice.

To try to ensure that consent is indeed morally valid, the physician should make sure that the consent is (a) freely given (i.e., there is no coercion or manipulation), (b) informed (i.e., to the extent that the patient is able to understand the relevant medical information pro and con), (c) cooperative (i.e., the physician and the patient enter into a dialogue about the patient's future and decide together), (d) representative of the values of both the patient and the physician (i.e., the fundamental morals and those values of the parties involved are revealed and enter into the medical decision at hand).

Q: What about truth telling? This has been a knotty question in clinical situations.

A: Yes, it has. But the general rule is that truth must obtain if we seek to serve the ends of medicine as previously discussed. The problems usually occur in the manner in which "bad news" is transmitted. How much should be told? When? How? We must take into account the age, sex, and background of the patient involved. There is no formula for truth telling that will ensure a morally valid consent and consent process. The issue is less truth telling than how, when, and in what manner the truth is told.

Another issue is the rare case of *therapeutic privilege.* In therapeutic privilege, the physician might be justified in withholding the truth if she thought that the truth would do grave harm to the patient. Since the physician must (at the minimum) do no harm, it is clear that if there is good evidence that the patient might commit suicide if he had certain information, then it could be permissible not to give all or part of the information to him.

Q: Could we expand a bit? Say you had a patient who got very discouraged easily but otherwise had a fighting spirit. If you withheld certain information from the patient, you could invoke her fighting spirit and thereby increase her chances of recovery.

A: Yes, that's right. That is another application of therapeutic privilege. Hope is so important for recovery that it could be acceptable to withhold information if the physician believed that he could invoke such an attitude. However, all things considered, I think that I would tell the patient. The physician can keep a fighting spirit alive by telling the patient the facts incrementally and by setting realistic goals for treatment. In actual fact, patients often know the truth but want to approach it in their own way. The effect on the patient's willingness to fight would be disastrous if the patient caught her doctor in deception.

There can be other situations in which truth telling might be modified. In some cultures, it is proper to talk to the family about the circumstances and allow them to find the best way to inform the patient. In such cultures, because of the high importance of the family as the primary unit, this is understood by the patient as well as the family. If the patient asks a direct question, however, he is owed an honest and direct answer.

Q: This is true. Privacy is linked with autonomy, and this plays against community. Certainly autonomy and community are poles with which political philosophers have been wrestling for centuries.
A: True. Physicians are not to reveal what a patient tells them. This relationship is essential to the bond of trust that lies at the heart of medicine's mission. But it is important to emphasize that this bond (like all others in ethics) is not absolute. If my HIV patient is married, I would tell the spouse despite the prima facie obligation of confidentiality. I would give the patient time to do so himself. But I would override his demand for privacy because the patient's claim to autonomy ends when there is clearly identifiable, grave, probable harm to another person as a result of the patient's exercise of his autonomy.

Q: This sensitivity is much appreciated by patients. I have been in the hospital several times, and I have noted that some health care professionals are much more sensitive than others about preserving one's privacy and dignity.
A: It is a very important aspect of Medical Ethics, yet one that is much ignored. All health care professionals should be sensitive to the human dignity of their patients. The "privacy" notion is multidimensional and must be fitted to each patient's preferences, lifestyles, and so on.

Q: What about paternalism and autonomy? How do you weigh in on these two poles relating to patients?
A: Enhancing a patient's decision making and involvement in his medical treatment enhances the patient's dignity. Affirming the dignity of human beings is a prima facie good. Many issues, such as the gravity of the condition, the patient's state of consciousness, his education, his activity, his culture, and so on, may affect autonomy. In serious trauma cases in the emergency room, there is no time to give patients all the facts when split-second decisions may be necessary to save their life. Patients are in a state of diminished capacity when they are seeking treatment. This can impede their decision-making skills. Under these circumstances, a weak form of paternalism is justifiable. But, ordinarily, strong paternalism—even for the patient's good—is not justifiable.

Q: What if the patient had a spouse and children who were absolutely dependent on her and would be destitute were she to die?

A: Now you are getting to the limits of autonomy. Just as truth telling was limited by the entire context of the act, so also is autonomy. I would set out these limitations as follows:

1. Autonomy is limited when its exercise causes harm to an innocent or distant third party. When this harm to others is sufficiently grave, it overrides the principles of autonomy.
2. Autonomy is limited when its exercise violates the physician's personal, moral, or spiritual values. For example, the patient might insist that the physician assist her in suicide. The physician is not obligated to assist the patient in committing an action that is contrary to the physician's personal moral values.
3. Autonomy is limited when its exercise violates the physician's medical conscience. If the patient wants antibiotics for a viral infection or renal dialysis for urinary incontinence, the physician may refuse because antibiotics do nothing to fight viruses nor dialysis anything for incontinence. At the same time, there are negative consequences to these treatments.
4. Finally, autonomy is limited when its exercise creates a conflict of interest. For example, a patient may want to die just so his family can collect his life insurance. Autonomy is so "absolutized" today that patients often want to micromanage the physician's decision in health care. It is not uncommon for a patient to second-guess his physician's decision about where his blood pressure should be or at what rate his intravenous vasopressor should be dripping.

Patients may be quite knowledgeable about their illnesses, but they usually do not know the whole story. Their knowledge can get in the way of good medicine. Even the physician who becomes a patient loses her objectivity about specific details of treatment. There may be some point at which I would have to tell such a patient that although I appreciate her opinion, she must trust me to act in her best interest. That, after all, is why she consulted me in the first place. If the patient insists in a course of treatment I do not think is in her interests, I may suggest that I may not be the best doctor for her.

To be concise: I always invite participation on the part of the patient, but I cannot accept dictation when it is not in the patient's interest. To do so would go against the ethical mission of medicine. I cannot be beneficent unless I am able to act in my patient's behalf according to the best of my abilities.

Q: What about the termination of life? Clearly, this is a controversial issue in medicine. Many hold that termination at the end of life is similar to that at the beginning. What is your view?
A: They are similar only if you accept the position that some have put forward equating a living person with appearance of the cerebral cortex in fetal development. I think this is wrong because it is arbitrary. These two stages in life—death of the brain and appearance of the brain—are not analogous.

My own view is that when two germ cells come together in conception there is created a person in a "state of active potency." In that moment, the developing embryo has all the qualities appropriate to that stage of human life. Unless we interfere with it, it will develop into a living infant. Therefore, its status at any stage is inviolate. To interrupt a pregnancy is to take the life of a human being.

Q: Is this situation like the other cases you have discussed in which the right in question is prima facie and subject to the broader context of the act? I am thinking of cases in which a mother's life or health is threatened by the child.
A: No. The right to life is not simply prima facie. It is an absolute in the sense that it may never deliberately be violated. Choices between mother and fetus rarely occur anymore, but when those cases do occur, it is often the result of bad obstetrics or bad medicine. With all the prenatal diagnostic equipment now available, there is little reason for the so-called textbook case dilemma ever to occur.

But if you press me on such cases, I'd say that under those circumstances, we must act to optimize both lives. We do not want to lose two lives. If we had to act, I believe that the Rule of Double Effect could come into play so that any deleterious consequence would be the unintended result of a positive action on behalf of one or the other.

Q: With euthanasia and the termination of life at the end of life, would you support the distinction between "killing" and "letting die"?
A: Yes. One difference is with the intent. There are those who do not recognize intent. They would deny that a difference exists between killing and letting die. Such writers emphasize a behaviorist set of physical events, such as A removed B from machine C, and B died; therefore, A caused B to die. But this is not the case. The disease or accident caused B to die and unless it was A's intent to kill B (by taking B off machine C against B's wishes or by injecting B with poison), then A cannot be said to have caused B's death.

At the end of life, physical and emotional deterioration is a reality. This does not justify euthanasia, but it does require us to deal with our patients with compassion. Helping someone face death is very much a part of compassionate medicine.

Pain medications must be used in optimum doses. Not to do so is tantamount to moral and legal malpractice. This is a moral obligation even if *unintentionally* it might accelerate death.

Q: Do you believe it is your duty to encourage patients in such situations to come to their own spiritual peace?
A: Yes. When we face death, we confront our own finitude. Any serious illness will pose a spiritual crisis. We have to come to terms with the ending of our lives. This is true of the atheist as well as the theist. Spiritual peace is part of the overall good of the patient. The physician must act beneficently to assist the patient in confronting the spiritual challenge of dying. Physicians should not replace ministers but should seek their help.

Q: **The limits of medical research have been particularly on the minds of people since the cloning of Dolly the sheep. To put the question bluntly, are there areas of scientific research that should not be pursued?**

A: Certainly. Let me name five for you: (a) we should not engage in cloning humans, (b) we should not create human embryos for research purposes, (c) we should not submit four-celled human embryos to various environmental test factors simply to observe what effects will ensue, (d) we should not engage in cross-species fertilization, and (e) we should not fund chemical or biological weapons research.

Q: **What about the atomic bomb, then? Was that an area of research that should not have been pursued?**

A: This is not an easy question to answer. At the time I believed (like many others) that it was justified to end the war, and so on. But now in retrospect I think our decision to drop the bomb was not justified.

Q: **Well, it did violate the "rules of war" in that it was intended to cause high civilian casualties.**

A: Yes, it did violate the "rules of war." What it also did for the first time was to cause destruction to an enormous number of noncombatants, contaminate a large part of a nation for a considerable period of time, and produce long-term effects on those exposed but not killed.

Q: **Getting back to scientific medical research, what should our response be to an unethical research project such as the eugenics research performed by the Nazis?**

A: After the war, data obtained from gruesome experiments on humans were unearthed. Many argued that the data should be used if they helped others. Others said that using the data even for the good of others dishonored the victims.

One solution was to ask the survivors of those experiments and the relatives of those who had perished what to do with the data. What did they want done? Should the data be destroyed or should it be handed over to the scientific community to see whether there was something there that might benefit humankind? The survivors, in my view, have a special relationship to the data and a moral claim on how it should, or should not, be used.

Q: **What do you think about alterations of human genes? When is it permissible?**

A: When the intent is therapeutic and only somatic cells are involved, the beneficial consequences dictate that we should pursue such research. Other things being equal, this type of research would not be very different from other experimental therapies.

When we are dealing with germ cells (those involved in reproduction), however, the situation is different. At present, we have no clear idea of the potential risks for future generations. Also, there is the temptation to believe that we can "improve" the human race by altering the germ line. All the dangers of eugenic engineering of the human species then emerge. Eugenic purposes are not morally licit uses of our genetic knowledge.

Q: What about the morality of using control groups in scientific research? This has been brought to the fore in AIDS research in which continuing clinical trials might mean we are denying life-saving drugs/treatments that may be effective.

A: The methodology of clinical trials is aimed at determining whether a particular drug or treatment is truly efficacious in fighting a disease. If we acted without such a tight and rigorous system, it would be very difficult to ascertain casual connections. Inductive logic requires clinical trials and control groups. Without such trials, we are reduced to anecdotal evidence.

However, it must be said that there should be a proportionate reason for undertaking a controlled clinical trial in the first place. These are some points that bear mentioning:

1. There must be a proportionate reason for the clinical trials.
2. There must be no other way to get the same results.
3. There must be a sound scientific design so that the data are reliable enough to warrant the trial in the first place.
4. There must be truly informed consent on the part of all participants.
5. Once a treatment is shown to be effective, the trial must be ended.

Q: According to that schema, one could dismiss the Tuskegee Case as having violated (1), (4), and (5).

A: That was a horrid incident and showed why we need careful guidelines and monitoring of human experiments. When a treatment becomes effective, the randomized clinical trials must be terminated. There was no possible moral justification for continuation of the Tuskegee experiments once it became apparent that we had an effective treatment for syphilis.

Q: Are there any other issues you wish to raise concerning medical research?

A: Yes, I think that we ought to be considerate of animals as well. The use of animals in medical research should be limited. The criteria I have just outlined apply to animals as well. If we can find the same results without involving an animal, we should do so. And if we must involve an animal, then let it be in a nonpainful way when at all possible.

The Principle of Proportional Respect is useful here. The more advanced the animals on the evolutionary scale, the higher their capacity to perceive pain, the more respect we must show them.

Q: Our last general area of interest is health care in the United States. How do you evaluate our health care system?

A: As presently organized, I think it is unjust. It is not reflective of a good society. This is because (a) health care has been commercialized, (b) there is limited access to those who need it—the poor, the marginally insured, and the uninsured, and (c) quality is still variable.

By making health care a commodity, we have put a price tag on what is priceless: human health. A good society has a moral obligation to provide a system of health care that will be available, accessible, and of equal quality to all its citizens.

Q: What do you think of national health insurance systems that have created a two-tiered system of health care?

A: I am not in favor of two-tiered systems. They tend to destroy the sense of community that is necessary to sustain a fair health care system. There is no such thing as two levels of care. There are only good medicine and bad medicine. Good medicine should be available to all.

Q: Why is there so much reluctance in establishing such a health care system? Does it go back to our discussion on privacy?

A: One factor surely is our emphasis on individualism. When your focus is on each individual person, then the rest of society tends to become invisible. The result is a model in which each person stands or falls individually based on his "merit" alone. On this view, if we are losers in the natural lottery—too bad! None of us stands alone—without others, we cannot survive or thrive. Without healthy citizens, there can be no "healthy society" in the broad sense.

Q: Is this the reason that some in our society view the government as "robbing" them when it assesses taxes to redistribute benefits such as health care?

A: Yes, it is the libertarian view that sees individual autonomy and power as the most important thing. The price we pay for this "liberty" is to ignore those in need. I think that the sick have a moral claim on us. This implies a moral right to health care and a correlative moral duty to provide it.

Q: I would say that the moral right to health care can be justified by its proximity to human action. Without health, our ability to act is severely limited so that we all must claim health care as a right.

A: I agree. Without health care, humans cannot flourish. We cannot pursue life, liberty, and happiness when we are ill, in pain, suffering, or disabled. Illness is a universal phenomenon of our humanity; it afflicts everyone sooner or later, and it bears no fixed relationship to whether or not we are deserving.

chapter three

From Theory to Practice

General Overview. In Chapter Two, we encountered a prominent practitioner of medicine and Biomedical Ethics, Dr. Edmund D. Pellegrino. He offered a combination of Virtue Ethics and his concept of his profession to bridge the gap between theory and practice. Moving from theory to practice is always one of the most troublesome areas in Applied Ethics. Often some people can wax eloquently about the general principles of ethics but are left wanting when they are asked about some particular moral problem. They reply, Well, if we understand x in this way, then we will tell you to do y. But if you understand x in another way, then you must do z. Often the response to their reply is: All of that is fine, but what should I do?

The disconnect between theory and practice is similar to the response to their reply. Professionals in health care demand answers that might assist them in determining how to make decisions in the day-to-day practice of their jobs. Some responses to this real, practical need have been to create codes of ethics and laws to follow. These are important responses, but they beg the question of *why* anyone should follow this prescription over another or this law rather than another.

To bridge this gap, we need certain "linking principles." An example of a linking principle in biomedicine is *precautionary reason* (presented in the following essay by Deryck Beyleveld and Shaun Pattinson). Each professional area has its own linking principle (e.g., business ethics has the Principle of Fair

Competition; see the *Business Ethics* volume in this series). A linking principle is intermediate between a principle of Normative Ethics and an action-guiding directive from Applied Ethics. When we seek to create a linking principle, we must refer both to a normative theory and to a group of moral problems.

In their essay, Beyleveld and Pattinson attempt to define one such linking principle: the Principle of Precautionary Reason. Beyleveld approaches Biomedical Ethics as a philosopher and lawyer who heads a biomedical institute at the University of Sheffield in Britain. Shaun Pattinson's approach is from the perspective of a research student in the Faculty of Law at the University of Sheffield.

The normative moral theory that Beyleveld and Pattinson use is the deontological theory of Alan Gewirth. Gewirth, like Kant, sets out a supreme principle of morality. As you recall from the Introduction, Kant's supreme principle is the *Categorical Imperative.* Gewirth's supreme principle is called the *The Principle of Generic Consistency.* This principle enjoins us to act in accord with the generic rights of our recipient as well as of ourselves. Basically, this principle means that each person can claim for herself certain rights. These rights are connected to the goods of action, such as food, clothing, shelter, and basic education. To be effective agents in any society, we need these goods as a baseline level.

Gewirth sees a connection between having a right to food and society's having a duty to provide that person with food. Thus, he considers rights and duties to be two sides to the same coin. In this way, Gewirth can be seen to follow in the liberal tradition of Locke, Rousseau, and Kant. Individuals have rights, and these rights are stronger as the individuals approach the basic necessities of action. Once rights are established, society has a duty to provide individuals with the good in question.

All linking principles must connect to particular moral problems. How does precautionary reason connect to practical concerns? First, the moral problems in question refer to any action in which the agency of a person is in question. *Agency* means the capacity of a person to perform a conscious, deliberate action. Obviously, agency is most apparent at the extremes of life (in fetuses and aged people). It is also important in other cases, such as in genetic engineering and in life in a persistent vegetative state.

At the heart of Beyleveld and Pattinson's essay is the issue of the level of respect (the duties) that ensue to the agents in question. Gewirth takes the position that duties decrease according to the proportionality of the agent's ability to act. Thus, a fetus at two months has less ability to act than a fetus at six months. Therefore, the six-month fetus deserves a higher gradated rights level (and the ensuing societal duties) than the two-month fetus. Animals also fit into this matrix. A monkey has a higher proportionality of action than a cow; thus, it garners a higher level of respect.

Beyleveld and Pattinson are sympathetic to the need for gradation but believe that Gewirth's solution is not consistent with his own supreme principle of morality (the Principle of Generic Consistency). They contend that the notion of proportional rights is problematic, and that rights do not come to a person in bits and pieces but all at once. Either one is an agent or is not—period—the end.

However, that is not the end of the story. Who is an agent? According to Beyleveld and Pattinson's thesis, we should be very careful whom we exclude from agency. We may have various operational definitions, but we must be very careful about saying that someone is *not* an agent. This relates directly to the philosophical problem of *other minds,* which connects to this problem: Each of us knows, by virtue of being conscious, that we think and are sentient beings. But how can we know that others are, as well? This is a difficult question. Various philosophers from Mill to Ryle have written on this question. Beyleveld and Pattinson are saying that we should be very generous in our assessment of who might be a rational agent with purposes and desires to act since the consequences of being wrong are severe.

Thus, Beyleveld and Pattinson create this linking principle between normative moral theory, that is, Deontology—Gewirth style—and the moral problems concerning who we should consider to be a moral agent. Instead of making a graded scale of agency, Beyleveld and Pattinson make a graded scale of those we should consider to be agents.

If they are correct, their contribution is important because it requires biomedical professionals to be especially generous concerning their attribution of status to a patient brought to them. The Principle of Precautionary Reasoning will affect the way health care professionals view and/or care for their patients.

Precautionary Reason as a Link to Moral Action

Deryck Beyleveld and Shaun Pattinson

INTRODUCTION[1]

In *Reason and Morality* (1978), Alan Gewirth demonstrates[2] that agents and prospective agents[3] deny that they are agents if they do not accept and act in accordance with the Principle of Generic Consistency (according to which all

---

[1]This essay is derived in part from Beyleveld and Pattinson 1998.
[2]See Beyleveld 1991.
[3]An agent acts, i.e., voluntarily pursues its freely chosen purposes. A prospective agent has the capacity and disposition to act. We use "agent" to cover both agents and prospective agents.

agents are required to act in accordance with the "generic rights"[4] of all agents). Since Gewirth's concept of an agent is equivalent to Kant's idea of "a rational being with a will," Gewirth establishes that the Principle of Generic Consistency has the status that Kant claimed was necessary for an imperative to be categorically binding: namely, that it be "connected (entirely *a priori*) with the concept of the will of a rational being as such" (Kant 1948, 62).[5] The Principle of Generic Consistency is, therefore, established as the supreme principle, not only of morality, but of all practical reasoning.

To establish what may or may not be done, what ought or ought not to be done, is, quite simply, a matter of establishing what the Principle of Generic Consistency permits or requires in relation to *agents*.

This, however, is by no means an unproblematic task. The way in which Gewirth defines agency is to be viewed, not as a generalisation about the empirical characteristics of human beings or any other creatures in the world, but as a function of the characteristics that beings must be supposed to have if they are to be regarded, rationally, as subjects and objects of practical precepting. Agents are defined as they are in Gewirthian (and Kantian) theory, because it is only for beings with the capacity to direct their actions voluntarily towards purposes that they have chosen that questions arise about what practical precepts may or should be followed, and it is only to such beings that practical precepts can rationally be directed. However, while this feature renders the premise of Gewirth's argument for the Principle of Generic Consistency immune from objections derived from empirical psychology, it opens the way to an objection of an altogether different kind.

As defined, being an agent involves having a kind of mental attitude (so that the capacities that make up being an agent are, in essential part, mental capacities). Thus, since I (any agent) have direct access to my mental state, I know that I am an agent directly. I do not, however, know that any other being is an agent in this way. The best I (any agent) can do, when trying to determine whether or not some other being "X" is an agent, is to construct a model of the characteristics and behavior to be expected of an agent, and test X's characteristics and behavior against it. However, even if X exhibits all the characteristics and behavior expected of an agent (as most biologically human beings do) and is *ostensibly* an agent, this does not *prove* that X *is* an agent. It is *possible* that X is a programmed automaton without a mind, and no amount of empirical observation of X's characteristics and behavior will be able to prove otherwise. The relevance of empirical evidence cited for X's mental

---

[4]Generic rights are to the generic features of agency (those capacities an agent needs to be able to act at all or with any general chances of success, *whatever its purposes might be*). Interference with, or deprivation of, a generic feature of agency will interfere (or tend to interfere) with an agent's capacity to act or to act successfully, *regardless of what the action envisaged is.*

[5]See Beyleveld 1999a for analysis of the relationship between Kant's derivation of the Categorical Imperative and Gewirth's argument to the Principle of Generic Consistency.

status depends on metaphysical assumptions. In short, the problem of knowing whether or not another being is an agent is a special case of the philosophical problem of other minds.

Thus, a sceptic might concede that Gewirth has, indeed, shown that the Principle of Generic Consistency is categorically binding upon *agents*, but then contend that this has no *practical* significance, because it cannot be demonstrated with the same degree of stringency (to the sceptic—any agent) that there are any other agents. In other words, the Principle of Generic Consistency has categorical application only in the abstract. In relation to objects in the empirical world, it provides no categorically binding criterion for moral action.

In this essay we will first of all respond to the sceptic. We will argue that the categorically binding nature of the Principle of Generic Consistency requires precautionary reasoning to be employed so as to make it a categorically binding requirement to regard all beings that behave as though they are agents *as* agents.

In Part II we will argue that this same reasoning requires agents to recognise duties to various "marginal" groups (such as young children, the mentally deficient, fetuses, and non-human animals), in proportion to the degree to which there is evidence that they might possibly be agents. Gewirth himself has argued that such marginal groups have the generic rights in proportion to the extent to which they approach being agents (see Gewirth 1978, 121–24, 140–45). However, instead of deriving such protection from the epistemic limitations of the Principle of Generic Consistency's empirical application, Gewirth seeks to extend the population to which the principle grants protection in the abstract. In Part III, we argue that Gewirth's attempt to do this fails.

Part IV will focus on Gewirth's analysis of the level of protection to be conferred on fetuses, thereby demonstrating that despite adopting a different rationale, our analysis grants a similar level of protection to marginal groups as Gewirth.

I. Precaution and Ostensible Agents

Given that the sceptic cannot coherently deny that he, she, or it[6] is an agent, there are a number of ways of responding to the sceptic who wishes to deny that the Principle of Generic Consistency has any categorically binding application.

First, this position is virtually impossible to sustain in practice. To sustain it, the sceptic must refrain from prescribing anything to any other being. It cannot impose duties on others, or think that there are any beings against whom it can claim the rights that it must, in the abstract, claim for itself. Indeed, it cannot engage in any discourse of reasons with any being other than itself.

---

[6]We use "it" to avoid implying that all agents are human or are necessarily gendered.

Second, while it might be coherent to consider that there are no other agents, it would certainly be regarded as irrational to do so on the criteria that govern everyday life. To attempt to eschew the practical force of the supreme principle of morality by recourse to solipsistic assertions is still a very high price to pay.

Third, the sceptic's objection does not place the Principle of Generic Consistency at any disadvantage compared with any other practical principle or moral theory, simply because the denial that there are other agents will affect any scheme of practical prescriptions equally.

However, it is possible to do much better than any of this! Everything that our sceptic wishes to assert may be conceded to the point of agreeing (*even where* X, on the basis of its characteristics and behavior, appears to be an agent) that the propositions "X is an agent" and "X is not an agent" are on a par with respect to an ability to demonstrate *the truth* of either. However, it needs to be appreciated that these propositions are not on a par *morally.* If I (any agent) mistakenly presume X to be an agent, then, although this will lead me (mistakenly) to have to restrict my exercise of my rights to some extent, I do not deny my (or any other agent's) status as a rights-holder. But, if I mistakenly presume X not to be an agent, then I deny that X (an agent) is a rights-holder.

Thus, to presume that X is an agent runs no risk of violating the primary injunction of the Principle of Generic Consistency, whereas to presume that X is not an agent, runs this risk. But, given that the Principle of Generic Consistency is categorically binding, there can be no justification under any circumstances whatsoever for violating it. Thus, to risk the possibility of violating the Principle of Generic Consistency, *when this can be avoided,* is itself to violate the Principle. Therefore, it is itself categorically necessary to do whatever one can to avoid this consequence (provided, of course, that the actions taken do not conflict with more important requirements to be derived from the Principle of Generic Consistency).

Where X displays the characteristics and behavior expected of an agent, we might say that X is "ostensibly an agent" or an "ostensible agent." When X is an ostensible agent, by the very nature of the case, it will be possible to treat X as an agent. In this case at least, it is possible to avoid the risk *altogether* of mistakenly denying that X is an agent, by presuming X to be an agent and acting accordingly.

Hence, it follows that agents are categorically required to accept, where X is an ostensible agent, the metaphysical possibility that X might not be an agent, is to be wholly discounted, and X's ostensible agency is to be taken as sufficient evidence that X has the capacities needed to be an agent.

Implicit in the reasoning to this conclusion, which constitutes a moral argument for the recognition of other minds,[7] is the following Precautionary Principle:

---

[7]This argument, of course, is a version of Pascal's Wager operating under the constraints of a categorical moral principle.

If there is no way of knowing whether or not X has property P, then, insofar as it is possible to do so, X must be assumed *to have* property P if the consequences (as measured by the Principle of Generic Consistency) of erring in presuming that X *does not have* P are worse than those of erring in presuming that X *has* P (and X must be assumed *to not have* P if the consequences of erring in presuming that X *has* P are worse than those of assuming that X *does not have* P).[8]

II. Proportional Duties to Apparent Partial Agents Under Precautionary Reasoning

It has been shown that where X exhibits the characteristics and behavior of an ostensible agent, I (any agent) am categorically required to treat that being as an agent. Suppose, however, that X exhibits (and, as far, as I am able to ascertain, only exhibits) capacities of agency to a degree *less than* an ostensible agent. In other words, suppose the evidence is sufficient to infer only that X is a *partial agent*—a being that has some of the characteristics needed to be an agent to at least some degree, without having sufficient of these to the degree needed to be an agent. In such a case, although X is apparently only a partial agent, *precisely because the proposition that an other is an agent is a metaphysical one and human reason is limited in such matters,* I cannot infer that X *is not* an agent. Just as I cannot *know with certainty* that an other being *is* an agent when that being is an ostensible agent, so I cannot *know with certainty* that X *is not* an agent when X is apparently only a partial agent.

So, even where an other being is apparently only a partial agent there remains a risk that—if I suppose that it is not an agent, and act accordingly—it is an agent, and I will have deprived it of the protection of the Principle of Generic Consistency to which it is entitled. Thus, it remains categorically required, all things being equal, to do whatever one can do to avoid this consequence—provided, as always, that my doing so does not violate more important provisions of the Principle of Generic Consistency.

However, where X is apparently only a partial agent, it is not possible to avoid this consequence *altogether.* I can, indeed, refrain from harming (and can assist) X in ways that would safeguard the benefits that it would receive *if* X had rights and chose to exercise them. I can, indeed, recognise duties not to harm (and to assist) X in various ways. However, it must not be forgotten

---

[8]Because of its link to the Principle of Generic Consistency, this principle is categorically binding. The reasoning behind *dicta* such as "innocent unless proven guilty!" or "give the benefit of the doubt" can be subsumed under this principle. Precautionary reasoning, as such, need not take the Principle of Generic Consistency as the yardstick by which to evaluate the consequences of error.

that if X is, in fact, an agent, then the Principle of Generic Consistency requires X (thereby) to be accorded will claim-rights,[9] the benefits of which it may waive. But, by not displaying ostensible agency, X fails to demonstrate (even under precautionary reasoning) that it has the capacities by virtue of which X is able to waive the benefits of what it is entitled to. Thus, the "duties of protection" that I must recognise that I have towards X, where X is apparently only a partial agent, are unavoidably paternalistic, which is at odds with what X is strictly entitled to *qua* agent (should X, in fact, be an agent).

Given that I am categorically required (under precautionary reasoning) to recognise duties of protection to X and Z (who are both apparently only partial agents), what am I required to do if these duties come into conflict?

All other things being equal, such conflicts are to be handled by a criterion of avoidance of more probable harm, according to which, "If my doing y to Z is more likely to cause harm h to Z than my doing y to X (and I cannot avoid doing y to one of Z or X), then I ought to do y to X rather than to Z."

Where y = failing to observe a particular duty of protection and h = mistakenly denying a being the status of an agent, we can infer by this criterion that, "If my failing to observe a particular duty of protection to Z is more likely to mistakenly deny Z the status of an agent than is my failing to observe this duty of protection to X (and I cannot avoid failing to observe this duty to one of Z or X), then I ought to fail to observe my duty to X rather than to Z."

Since I am more likely to mistakenly deny that a being is an agent the more probable it is that the being is an agent, it follows that my duties of protection to those who are more probably agents take precedence over my duties of protection to those who are less probably agents.

The moral status of a being may be measured by the weight to be given to the duties of protection owed to it by an agent. In such terms, it follows that the moral status of beings who are more probably agents is greater than that of beings who are less probably agents. In other words, the moral status of beings is *proportional* to the probability that they are agents.

Given that X's display of the capacities of agency must (under precautionary reasoning guided by the Principle of Generic Consistency) be viewed as sufficient evidence that X is an agent, it follows that if X displays characteristics and behavior to a degree less than that of an ostensible agent, then this must be viewed as less than sufficient evidence (but evidence nonetheless) that X is an agent. In other words, where X is an ostensible agent, the probability that X is an agent must be taken to be 1, and where X is apparently only a partial agent, the probability that X is an agent must be taken to be >0 but <1 in proportion to the capacities of agency that X displays.

---

[9]Claim-rights are justified claims imposing correlative duties on others. There are two principal theories of claim-rights: the benefit (or interest) theory and the will (or choice) theory. The difference between the benefit and will theory is that the latter requires the right-holder to have the capacity to waive the benefit of the right (i.e., be an agent).

Thus, we establish that apparent partial agents are owed duties of protection by agents in proportion to the degree to which they approach being ostensible agents—not *qua* their being partial agents—but *qua* their possibly being agents.[10]

III. GEWIRTH'S USE OF THE PRINCIPLE OF PROPORTIONALITY TO DERIVE GENERIC RIGHTS FOR MARGINAL GROUPS

Gewirth also maintains that the Principle of Generic Consistency grants proportional protection to various marginal groups, such as young children, the mentally deficient, fetuses, and non-human animals (see Gewirth, 1978, 121–24; 140–45). However, Gewirth's reasoning for this conclusion differs significantly from our own. Instead of deriving such protection from the epistemic limitations of the Principle of Generic Consistency's empirical application, Gewirth maintains that the protection granted by the Principle of Generic Consistency's ontology is not confined to agents. Gewirth claims that the "Principle of Proportionality" operates to extend the population to which the Principle of Generic Consistency applies in the abstract.

Gewirth (1978, 121) states the Principle of Proportionality as follows:

> When some quality Q justifies having certain rights R, and the possession of Q varies in degree in the respect that is relevant to Q's justifying the having of R, the degree to which R is had is proportional to or varies with the degree to which Q is had. Thus, if x units of Q justify that one have x units of R, then y units of Q justify that one have y units of R.

At an intermediate step in his argument for the Principle of Generic Consistency, Gewirth shows that agents must (on pain of denying that they are agents) consider their being agents as the sufficient condition for their possession of all of the generic rights (see Gewirth 1978, 10). Consequently, agents deny that they are agents if they do not grant the generic rights equally to all other agents. Thus, the claim that the Principle of Generic Consistency requires agents to grant the generic rights in part to partial agents is to be validated by substituting "being an agent" for Q and "the generic rights" for R in the Principle of Proportionality. In other words, Gewirth wishes to use the Principle of Proportionality in combination with the Principle of Generic Consistency to infer that as one approaches agency, one is accorded proportionally greater generic rights.

---

[10]We do not mean to suggest that the Principle of Generic Consistency requires agents to do everything they possibly can to cater for the possibility that apparently only a partial agent is an agent, as *all things are often not equal*. Analysis of the relative weight of costs derivable from the Principle of Generic Consistency must be left for consideration in future works. For a brief exploration of some of the complexities involved, see Beyleveld 1999b.

According to James F. Hill (1984, 182),

> The agent will hold the Principle of Proportionality presumably on the grounds that it is rational to do so and, in addition, because of the central role it has played in the traditional doctrines of distributive justice.

However, such grounds are too weak if the Principle of Proportionality is to be used to extend the subjects of protection of a categorically binding principle. Gewirth himself claims not merely that the Principle of Proportionality "is a pervasive feature of traditional doctrines of distributive justice (1978, 121) but that it is true and, since Gewirth claims that agents are categorically required to grant the generic rights in part to partial agents, he must be claiming that it is necessarily true.

However, while it is necessarily true that, when having Q justifies having R, and the possession of Q varies in degree in the respect that is relevant to having Q's justifying the having of R, the degree to which R is had is a *function* of the degree to which Q is had, it cannot be inferred (without further conditions being imposed) that having R is *such* a function of having Q that, if having x units of Q justify that one have x units of R, then having y units of Q justify that one have y units of R for *all* values of x and y.

It is also preferable to make explicit the conditions that must be satisfied for possession of Q to vary in degree in the respect that is relevant to having Q justify having R. Thus, with it being understood that R can be any property at all, the Principle of Proportionality should be stated as "When having some quality Q justifies having some property R, and the extent of having Q sufficient to justify having R in full is not necessary to justify having R to any extent at all, the degree to which R is had is a function of the degree to which Q is had."

As we stated above, in the process of arguing for the Principle of Generic Consistency, Gewirth shows that being an agent (defined as having purposes that it acts[11] for) is necessary and sufficient for having the generic rights in full (see Gewirth 1978, 10). While having purposes that one acts for is an *invariant* relational property, to have this relational property, it is necessary to have particular capacities and properties.[12] While agents have these capacities to the degree needed to have this relational property, partial agents (by definition) have the capacities required to be agents to a lesser extent. Gewirth claims that the Principle of Proportionality shows that the degree to which partial agents have the generic rights depends upon the degree to which they have the capacities required to be an agent.

---

[11]See footnote 3.

[12]Gewirth himself refers to the capacities and properties required to be an agent (to have this relational property) as the "practical abilities of the generic features of action" (Gewirth 1978, 122).

This cannot be true, because having the capacities required to be an agent to the degree needed to be an agent is not only necessary (and sufficient) to have the generic rights in full (so that agents with these capacities to degrees greater than that needed to be an agent cannot, thereby, acquire the generic rights to a greater extent), *it is necessary to have any generic rights at all*. This is because, as derived, the generic rights are will claim-rights; i.e., those who have them can always, by their free choice, waive the benefits that exercise of the generic rights entitles them to—provided only that they do not, thereby, neglect or violate their duties to other agents. This is not a function of an arbitrary espousal of the will theory of rights. It derives from the fact that, in the argument to the Principle of Generic Consistency, agents are required to claim the generic rights for themselves, not because they are required to value the generic features of agency for their own sakes, but as instrumental to their pursuit or achievement of their purposes whatever these might be. But, in order to be able to freely waive the benefits of a right, one must have *all* the capacities needed to be an agent. Thus, partial agents cannot have any generic rights.

This objection cannot be evaded by acknowledging that partial agents cannot have any generic rights strictly speaking, and claiming, instead, that the Principle of Proportionality nonetheless shows that partial agents have "quasi-generic rights" (unwaivable protections correlative to duties of agents not to harm partial agents, or to assist them in need) in proportion to their approach to being agents. The Principle of Proportionality can only license inferences about the quantity of predication of a quality; it cannot (by itself) license inferences that alter the quality of what is predicated. To have a quasi-generic right is not to have a generic right to some extent. It is to have a different quality of protection from that granted by a generic right.

IV. Applying Precautionary Reasoning to the Human Fetus[13]

In *Reason and Morality,* Gewirth seeks to apply his Principle of Proportionality (together with the Principle of Generic Consistency) to the human fetus (see Gewirth 1978, especially 142–43). Gewirth claims that together these principles establish

(a) The fetus has generic rights, which do not include a generic right to freedom,[14] but are restricted to rights to the conditions ("well-being") necessary to fulfil its potential to develop into an agent (the chief of which conditions is its life).

---

[13]For a broader picture of the moral status of the human embryo and fetus incorporating the arguments of this paper, see Beyleveld 1999b. For an earlier analysis, see Beyleveld 1998.

[14]Presumably because, not being an agent, the fetus lacks freedom (the capacity to make choices) altogether, and " 'may act' implies 'can act.' "

(b)   The fetus' generic rights

> (i)   are overridden in case of conflict with the generic rights of its mother;
> (ii) are not merely of lesser weight than those of its mother, but minimal in comparison—because the fetus has the capacities required to be an agent in "remotely potential form" only and lacks purposivity altogether;[15] and
> (iii) increase in weight with the length of gestation, because the greater the length of gestation the closer the fetus approaches having the degree of the capacities required to be an agent that an agent has.[16]

Applying the Principle of Proportionality under precautionary reasoning requires agents to accept duties of protection towards the fetus insofar as, and to the degree that, the fetus approaches being an ostensible agent (on the grounds that the closer the fetus approaches to being an ostensible agent, the more likely it is to be an agent). Assuming that the fetus' mother is an ostensible agent, she must be taken to be an agent.[17] On the evidence that precautionary reasoning requires us to accept, it is (very much) less likely that the fetus (at any stage of its development) is an agent than that its mother is. Hence, greater moral status must be granted to the mother than to the fetus: duties to the mother (which must be taken to be correlative to her rights) will outweigh any duties in relation to the fetus in case of conflict. Apart from the fact that we cannot agree with Gewirth's claim that the duties of protection towards the fetus derive from the fetus' generic rights, we can agree with (b)(ii).

With this caveat, using the Principle of Proportionality under precautionary reasoning requires us to agree with (b)(iii) as well. In principle, the longer the gestation of the fetus, the more the agency-related characteristics and behavior it will display (by virtue of which it will get closer to being an ostensible agent), and this means that we must progressively take seriously the possibility that it might be an agent after all, in consequence of which we must treat it with greater precaution (and, hence, greater respect).

---

[15]Evelyn Pluhar maintains that Gewirth's claim that fetuses do not have primitive purposes or memories has "been called into question quite successfully by neurophysiologists and cognitive psychologists" (1995, 252). She cites empirical research that has been interpreted to show that "neural pathways sufficient for pain perception are present well before birth" and asks rhetorically, "Does Gewirth suppose that aversion to pain or unpleasant sensations also springs ex nihilo upon the point of birth?" (ibid.) However, while Gewirth's description of the capacities of the fetus may well be inaccurate, this has no bearing on the *principles* of application involved in Gewirth's analysis.

[16]Gewirth often writes as though "approaching having the capacities required to be an agent" and "having the capacities required to be an agent in part are interchangeable." They are if "approaching having the capacities required to be an agent" is always read as "approaching having the capacities required to be an agent in full."

[17]And even if she does not display this degree of agency-related characteristics and behavior, she is bound to display more of these than the fetus—at any stage of its development.

Gewirth appears to say that the Principle of Proportionality and the Principle of Generic Consistency justify that the fetus has a right to realise its potential to develop into an agent—from which it may be inferred that the fetus has a right to life and the other conditions necessary to realise its potential to develop into an agent.

If so, then we need an explanation of how the Principle of Proportionality can effect the inference from (a) "X is an agent with the generic rights" to (b) "Y (a partial agent with the potential to develop into an agent) has a right to develop into an agent."

We do not know what Gewirth has in mind. However, agents must be granted additive rights—rights to development of their potential (capacities) for action (understood as rights to increase their competence as agents). Since increasing an agent's competence as an agent involves increasing the degree of capacities it has beyond the degree required to be an agent, agents' additive rights are essentially rights to increase the degree of the capacities they have. Perhaps Gewirth reasons that fetuses (as partial agents) must, by the Principle of Proportionality, be granted these same rights to development of the degree of the capacities they possess in proportion to the degree of these capacities they already have. Since the fetus (as a partial agent) cannot yet act, development of its capacity to act can only mean its development into an agent; and, thus, its right to develop its capacity to act will be a right to develop into an agent.

Implicit in the claim that the fetus has a right to develop into an agent is the claim that a partial agent with the potential to be an agent has a right to develop into an agent. So, if the reasoning we have suggested for Gewirth is valid, then an important conclusion follows; viz., a partial agent that is a potential agent has a right to life (and other conditions of its being able to develop into an agent) in proportion to the degree to which its potential is realised (i.e., to the degree to which it approaches being an agent).

However, if this is Gewirth's reasoning, then it is unsound. The fetus (as a potential agent) is still no more than a partial agent, and cannot have any generic rights. So the Principle of Proportionality cannot show that it has the generic rights to develop its potential to act in proportion to the degree of the capacities required to be an agent that it has. Development of this capacity for action up to the level needed to be able to exercise rights is not commensurable with development of this capacity beyond this level.

What if we look at the matter under precautionary reasoning? Under such reasoning, the fetus is to be viewed as a possible agent that does not exhibit the capacities required to be an agent to the degree that requires us to accept that it is an agent. So viewed, if the fetus is an agent, then its failure to display the characteristics and behavior of an ostensible agent is not because it is not an agent; it is because something is preventing it from displaying the qualifying characteristics and behavior (or from displaying it in ways that we can interpret properly).[18]

So, if the fetus is, despite apparently being only a partial agent, an agent, then the proper story to tell is not that, as it approaches being an ostensible agent, its potential to be an agent is being realised, but that as it approaches being an ostensible agent, its potential to express itself as an agent is being realised. Suppose, then, that the fetus is an agent. From this it follows that the fetus does have the generic rights.

Of course, because the fetus is apparently only a partial agent, we cannot treat it as having such rights. But we can protect it as an agent by accepting the duty to allow the fetus' potential to display the capacities required to be an agent to develop (and to assist this development, when necessary). Furthermore, this duty will be subject to proportionality reasoning, because the more the fetus displays as these sort of characteristics and behavior develop (to the point of being an ostensible agent), the more seriously we must take the possibility that it is an agent.

However, we cannot conclude from this that we have a duty to protect the life of a potential agent as such (and other conditions of its being able to develop into an agent) in proportion to the degree to which it approaches being an agent, for the potential that is the basis of our duty to protect the fetus' development of the capacities (required to be an agent) is not the potential of the fetus to be an agent, but the potential of a possible agent unable to display these capacities to develop the ability to do so.

We have already argued that, under precautionary reasoning, agents have a duty to allow the fetus' potential to display the capacities needed to be an agent to develop (and to assist this development, when necessary), and that this duty is subject to proportionality reasoning. However, because evidence that a fetus or embryo (X) is a potential ostensible agent is evidence relevant to the probability that X is an agent, precautionary reasoning also supports the following claims:

(1) Evidence that X is a potential ostensible agent, by itself, requires agents to grant X moral status (in proportion to the strength of the evidence); and

(2) Evidence that X is a potential ostensible agent adds to the moral status secured for X by the degree to which X exhibits the characteristics and behavior associated with possession of the capacities required to be an agent. Thus, if Y is apparently only a partial agent with y moral status (by virtue of Y's degree of the

---

[18]Thus, one way of explaining why we are required to take more seriously the possibility that a fetus is an agent the closer it approaches to being an ostensible agent is that the more the agency-related characteristics and behavior it displays, the less elaborate and fanciful are the metaphysical stories we have to tell to explain why, despite being an agent, it is unable to display the expected characteristics and behavior.

generic capacity for action) but not apparently a potential ostensible agent, and X is apparently a partial agent with y moral status and also apparently a potential ostensible agent, then agents must take more seriously the possibility that X is an agent than that Y is an agent, by virtue of which their duties of protection to X are greater than their similar duties to Y. (And, of course, the degree to which evidence of potential to become an agent adds to X's moral status will be proportional to the strength of this evidence.)

The weakest evidence that one can have that X is a potential ostensible agent is that X is a member of a species S (some of) whose members are known to develop into ostensible agents under specified conditions.[19] To this can be added knowledge of specific characteristics that X has and of correlations between possession of these and development into ostensible agents by members of S. All factors of this kind being equal, the further X develops in the direction of becoming an ostensible agent, the more confident one can be that X will develop the whole way. Thus, considerations of evidence for potential and considerations of evidence of degree of approach to being an agent will not be wholly independent. The precise interactions, however, cannot be stated without a detailed analysis, which must be left for another occasion.

CONCLUDING REMARKS

In the final analysis, despite the fact that he couches this in terms of the having of generic rights, the thesis that Gewirth wants to defend is that various categories of creature that do not display all the necessary characteristics of agents are necessarily accorded moral status by the Principle of Generic Consistency in proportion to the degree to which they approach being ostensible agents. We have argued that this thesis is true.

However, Gewirth's attempt to demonstrate this thesis takes the form of claiming that the Principle of Proportionality grants the generic rights in part to partial agents, in proportion to the degree to which they approach being agents. In so doing, Gewirth is modifying what the Principle of Generic Consistency says. If he is right, then this principle itself should state not just that agents must grant the generic rights equally to all agents, but that agents must grant the generic rights to all beings in proportion to their approach to being agents. This claim affects the ontology of Gewirth's moral theory; the population of the principle's beneficiaries in the abstract terms in which the categorically binding argument is couched. Gewirth's application of the Principle of Proportionality to the Principle of Generic Consistency is part of his

---

[19]Complications, which we will not address here, are created by the fact that these conditions can be specified differently. Thus, the concept of potentiality, like that of a cause (vs. background conditions), is to a degree normative in being dependent on what is taken to be "normal."

argument to the principle itself, rather than an application of the principle to objects in the empirical world.

We have argued that this attempt must fail. Gewirth cannot be right about this without implying propositions that contradict the possible validity of his argument for the Principle of Generic Consistency.

Our own argument does not attempt to extend the principle's ontology, which remains restricted to the population of agents. It is not presented as part of the derivation of the principle at all. It is grounded in an argument about the process that must be gone through to apply the Principle of Generic Consistency to objects in the empirical world. It takes as its basis the fact that application of the Principle of Generic Consistency requires judgments concerning which objects in the world are agents. The key to this argument is the claim that considerations of precaution render agents categorically bound to accept that beings displaying the characteristics and behavior expected of an agent are to be taken to be agents even though it cannot be proven that this is so. The same considerations of precaution, however, render it illegitimate to entirely discount the possibility that a being displaying any of the necessary characteristics of an agent might be an agent. How seriously this possibility must be taken is, however, proportional to how much evidence we have that the being is an agent (which will depend on how much of the behavior sufficient—under precautionary reasoning—to render it necessary to judge that a being is an agent the being displays).

Thus, under precautionary reasoning, proportionality reasoning requires that beings that are apparently only partial agents be granted moral status in proportion to how closely they approach being ostensible agents. Consequently, although our analysis and Gewirth's own are very different theoretically, the practical implications of these analyses (accurately performed) should not be very different.

Thus, in practice, we can say that we have shown that agents owe duties of protection to partial agents in proportion to their approach to being agents. If we do this, however, it must not be forgotten that this is only a shorthand, and that the duties are actually owed to beings that are apparently only partial agents on the basis of their possible status as agents, by virtue of which they are owed not in proportion to the degree of approach to being an agent but in proportion to the degree to which what is apparently only a partial agent approaches being an ostensible agent.[20]

---

[20]This may seem to be an overly subtle point. However, it is arguable (see Copleston 1965, vol. 7, Pt. 1, 22) that the German Idealists inflated the Kantian theory of knowledge into a metaphysics of reality by regarding the categories not as conceptual moulds of human understanding but as categories of existence, and that this was facilitated by Kant's use of ontological locutions such as phenomena and noumena to express theses about the role of the categories in empirical knowledge. In our view, this is not trivial but is responsible for systematically obscuring the major insights of Kant's transcendental philosophy for over two centuries. (See Beyleveld 1980.)

References

Beyleveld, Deryck. 1980. "Transcendentalism and Realism." Paper presented at the Theory Group Meeting of the British Sociological Association, University of Sussex, September. (Available from the author.)

Beyleveld, Deryck. 1991. *The Dialectical Necessity of Morality: An Analysis and Defense of Alan Gewirth's Argument to the Principle of Generic Consistency.* Chicago: University of Chicago Press.

Beyleveld, Deryck. 1998. "The Moral and Legal Status of the Human Embryo." In Elisabeth Hildt and Dietmar Mieth, eds., *In Vitro Fertilisation in the 1990s: Towards a Medical, Social and Ethical Evaluation,* 247–260. Aldershot, London: Ashgate.

Beyleveld, D. 1999a, "Gewirth and Kant on Justifying the Supreme Principle of Morality." In M. Boylan, ed., *Gewirth: Critical Essays on Action, Rationality, and Community,* 97–117. New York and London: Rowman & Littlefield.

Beyleveld, Deryck. 1999b. "The Moral Status of the Human Embryo and Fetus." In Deryck Beyleveld and Hille Haker, eds., *Ethics in Human Procreation, Genetic Diagnosis and Therapy.* Aldershot, London: Ashgate.

Beyleveld, Deryck, and Pattinson, Shaun. 1998. "Proportionality under Precaution: Justifying Duties to Apparent Non-Agents." Unpublished paper. (Available from the authors.)

Copleston, Frederick, S. J. 1965. *A History of Philosophy.* New York: Image Books.

Gewirth, Alan. 1978. *Reason and Morality.* Chicago: University of Chicago Press.

Kant, Immanuel. 1948. *Groundwork to the Metaphysic of Moral.* In H. J. Paton, trans., *The Moral Law.* London: Hutchinson.

Hill, James F. 1984. "Are Marginal Agents 'Our Recipients'?" In Edward Regis, Jr., ed., *Gewirth's Ethical Rationalism: Critical Essays with a Reply by Alan Gewirth,* 180–91. Chicago: University of Chicago Press.

Pluhar, Evelyn B. 1995. *Beyond Prejudice: The Moral Significance of Human and Nonhuman Animals.* Durham, NC: Duke University Press.

EVALUATING A CASE STUDY: DEVELOPING A PRACTICAL ETHICAL VIEWPOINT

Your goal in this book is to respond critically to case studies on various aspects of Medical Ethics. To do this, you must be able to assess the ethical impact of some critical factor(s) in situations that pose ethical problems. One factor in assessing the case is the ethical impact of the project/policy/action. This chapter and Chapters Four through Seven end with an "Evaluating a Case Study" section that focuses on a particular exercise. These sections include case studies to which you can apply the insight you gained from the readings and discussion in the chapter. Because the information presented in these "Evaluating a Case Study" sections is cumulative, you should be able to write a complete critical response to a case study by the end of Chapter Seven.

Macro and Micro Cases.

Beginning with this chapter, each chapter will end with cases for you to consider. The cases section is divided into two categories, macro and micro. Each type of case employs a different point of view.

Macro Case. The macro case takes the perspective of someone in an executive position of authority who supervises or directs an organizational unit. His or her decisions will affect many people and resonate in a larger sociological sphere.

Micro Case. The micro case examines the perspective of someone at the proximate level of professional practice, such as a nurse or doctor actually involved in the art of healing. Obviously, this case applies to more people than does the macro case.

Case Development. This book suggests one way to develop critical evaluations of ethical cases. In the "Evaluating a Case Study" sections, you will be asked to apply a specific skill to the cases presented. At the end of Chapter Seven, you will be able to write an essay concerning the application of an ethical perspective to a specific problem.

Please note that although the cases presented here have fictional venues, they are based on composites of actual biomedical practice.

These end-of-chapter evaluations seek to bridge the gap between Normative Ethics and Applied Ethics. Skill in using Applied Ethics is very important, for this is where the practical decision making occurs. My approach in these essays is to allow you to employ techniques that you have been taught elsewhere in addition to those found in this text. Depending on your background in science or a health care field, you can write a critical response to a case study that demonstrates your professional acumen along with your sensitivity to the ethical dimensions found in the situation you are examining. Classes that have few students with scientific or biomedical backgrounds will deemphasize the fundamental details of science and health care and concentrate instead on a less technical response.

Biomedical personnel often become so enmeshed in the practice of medicine that they lose their ability to discern and react to possible ethical dilemmas, a difficulty experienced in all professions.[1] But this is wrong. The "Evaluating a Case Study" sections will help you analyze both ethical and practical situations. The approach will invoke a technique that rates a proposal as having three levels of complexity: surface, medium, and deep. The level of interaction allows you to see at a glance how the competing areas of interest and ethical value conflict.

The five "Evaluating a Case Study" sections are intended to sequentially lead you to develop the abilities to write a critical response to a case study: (a) Developing a Practical Ethical Viewpoint, (b) Finding the Conflicts (Chapter Four), (c) Assessing Embedded Levels (Chapter Five), (d) Applying Ethical Issues (Chapter Six), and (e) Structuring the Essay (Chapter Seven).

---

[1]For a fuller discussion of this see, *Basic Ethics*, chap. 7.

At the end of Chapter Four through Seven, you will be presented case studies to which you can apply your newfound skills. By the end of the term, you should be able to create an ethical impact statement of some sophistication.

Let us begin first by choosing an ethical theory and then proceed to develop a practical viewpoint. Few people bother to choose an ethical theory; most pick-up a few moral maxims that they apply when the occasion seems appropriate. The manner of this acquisition is often environment dependent, that is, having to do with their upbringing, friends, and the community(ies) in which they live. As such, their maxims reflect those other viewpoints.

The Personal Worldview Imperative enjoins us to develop a single comprehensive and internally coherent worldview that is good and that we will strive to act out in our lives (see Chapter One). One component of this worldview is an ethical theory. Thus, each of us must *develop* an ethical theory. This does not this mean that we must all start from scratch. Those before us have done much good work. But we must personally choose an ethical theory and assume ownership for it as being the most correct theory in existence. It is not enough merely to accept someone else's theory without any active work on our part. We must go through the process of personal introspection and evaluation to determine what we think is best and to be open to ways we can improve the theory (in concept or in practice)

This process of making an ethical theory our own can take years. This course is only a few months. Does this pose a problem? Not really when you consider that part of the process of making an ethical theory our own involves provisional acceptance and testing of various moral maxims. Obviously, this testing has a limit. We should not test whether it is morally permissible to murder by going out and murdering various people. The testing I am advocating is a way to examine various moral commands and evaluate whether their application is consonant with other worldview values we hold. The process will perhaps go back and forth in a progressive dialectic until we have accepted or rejected the commands.

To begin this process of testing, we must identify the most prominent ethical theories and their tenets. Many books survey and evaluate the major ethical theories. In this series of textbooks *Basic Ethics in Action,* I have written one such survey entitled *Basic Ethics.* I would suggest that you refer either to that book or to another like it to obtain enough information to enable you to begin the process of choosing an ethical theory.

For the purposes of this book, I will highlight four major theories: Utilitarianism, Deontology, Intuitionism, and Virtue Ethics. To begin the process, I recommend that you choose a single theory from these four (or from others your instructor may offer) as your critical tool as you prepare for class. You might ask, How do I know which viewpoint to choose? This is a difficult question. It concerns the justification of the various ethical theories.

Many criteria can be used to justify an ethical theory. One criterion is Naturalism. Each theory presupposes a naturalistic or nonnaturalistic epistemological standpoint. Naturalism is complicated, for our purposes, let us describe it as a view that holds that no entities or events are in principle beyond the domain of scientific explanation. Cognitive claims are valid only if they are based on accepted scientific modes.

Ethical Naturalism states that moral judgments are also merely a subclass of facts about the natural world that can be studied scientifically. From this study, we can determine moral correctness as a corollary of certain facts that can be scientifically investigated (e.g., how much pleasure various alternatives will produce for the group). Thus, utilitarians believe that moral judgments *are* judgments about which alternative will be most beneficial to some group's survival.

A utilitarian might point to the scientific study of nature and say that the instinct to seek pleasure is evidenced in all species. Furthermore, an evolutionary advantage seems to exist for those species that act for the benefit of the group that does not exist for those that do not act in this way.

Many sociobiologists make this sort of claim. The main imperative of evoltuionary theory is that a person's own genes be passed on to another generation. If passing on a person's own genes is impossible, the next best thing is to pass on the genes of the individual's relatives. Thus, seemingly altruistic behavior (such as a bird that stays behind in dangerous situations so that the group might survive) is really selfish because helping the group *is* helping the bird to pass on its genes (or those of its relatives).

Sociobiology, of course, is not universally accepted, nor is it necessary for a utilitarian to be a sociobiologist. However, this example does illustrate a type of justification that the utilitarian might make. He could move from the concept of group happiness in animals and extrapolate to humans. The supporting data are scientific; therefore, the theory is naturalistic.

Deontologists may or may not be naturalists. Since Deontology involves a duty-based ethics, the key question to be asked concerns how we know whether a binding duty exists to do such and such. Are all moral "oughts" derivable from factual, scientifically ascertainable "is" statements? If they are, then the deontologist is a naturalist. If they are not, then the deontologist is not a naturalist.

In his book *Reason and Morality,* Alan Gewirth claims to derive ought from is. There is no reference to knowledge claims that are not compatible with the scientific inquiry of natural objects. This would make Gewirth a naturalist. Kant and Donagan are somewhat different. Each refers to supernatural entities that are not scientifically supported. Kant spends considerable effort trying to define these boundaries in the "Transcendental Dialectic" section of his book *The Critique of Pure Reason.* This aside, neither Kant nor Donagan considered that a problem about integrating the factual and the normative existed.

If you are inclined to view reality as an extension of evolutionary biology or to believe that group advantage immediately entails a moral ought, then you are leaning toward Utilitarianism. If you think that people should act from pure duty alone without reference to anything except the rightness of the action, however, then Deontology is probably your preference.

The is-ought problem was sharpened by intuitionist G.E. Moore,[2] who rejected Ethical Naturalism because he believed it contained a fallacy (which he dubbed the *naturalistic fallacy*). This fallacy claims that it is false to define goodness in terms of any natural property. This is so because good is not definable and because good is not subject to scientific examination. This is true because the factual is realm is separate from the normative ought realm. The chasm between the two cannot be crossed.

Good for Moore is a unique, unanalyzable, non-natural property (as opposed, for example, to yellow, which is a natural property). Clearly scientific methods are of no use. Science can tell us things about yellow but can tell us nothing about the meaning of good. Other intuitionists also hold that we understand important moral terms and/or moral maxims by cognitive means that are not scientific. Generally, these are immediate and cannot be justified in factual "is" language.

Intuitionism is therefore a non-naturalistic theory. Still, it has some remote connections to Naturalism. For example, one can point to the *plausibility* of accepting certain common moral maxims—such as a prohibition against murder—by reference to other societies. (In other words, since all societies prohibit murder, the prohibition against murder must be immediately apparent to all.) However, plausibility is not the same thing as exhaustive scientific demonstration. Justification in Intuitionism lies in its alleged unarguable truth that can be grasped in principle immediately by all.

If you are having trouble adopting any of the theories and believe that acceptance or rejection of an ethical theory comes to some sort of brute immediate acceptance, then you will probably want to accept Intuitionism as your ethical theory.

Finally, we turn to Virtue Ethics. This theory seems at first to be naturalistic. Aristotle lends credence to this when he talks about relying on the common opinions of people about what is considered to be a virtue. The common opinions could be gathered and reviewed much as a sociologist or anthropologist might do, and this "scientific" method would yield definitive results. Aristotle believed that some common agreement about a core set of virtues existed.

---

[2]I cannot stress too much the impossibility of completely pigeonholing philosophers. In some important ways, Moore was an intuitionist because "good" had to be accepted as an unanalyzable, unnatural fact. Toward the end of *Principia Ethica*, however, he sounds much like an agathistic utilitarian, one who wishes to maximize the group's good. This mixture of labels among philosophers shows only that labels are limited in what they can do.

Ross and Rawls have deontological and intuitionistic aspects to their theories. Therefore, one label alone cannot adequately capture the spirit of their philosophy. In an introductory text, such as this one, labels are used to simplify—but hopefully not obfuscate—the dynamics present in these thinkers.

Justification, therefore, was not an issue for Aristotle. If we accept a worldview such as Aristotle presents, then we would all agree that everyone considers courage (for example) to be a virtue. The confirming data can be gathered and scientifically studied; ergo, it is naturalistic. The proof depends on the community that values these traits. This emphasis on community makes Virtue Ethics a favorite theory among those who call themselves *communitarians.* The communitarian begins with the group and its institutions and depends on individual members to submit to the authority of the group (or to change the group in ways it accepts).

How does Communitarianism affect today's pluralistic society? Some might argue that consensus about the virtues no longer exists nor does a single community to which we all belong. If there is no consensus as Aristotle envisioned, then what constitutes a virtue may collapse into a form of Intuitionism. For example, I think that X is a virtue. You think Y is a virtue. X and Y are mutually exclusive traits. You and I come from different communities/societies; therefore, we cannot come to an agreement. All each of us can say is I am right and you are wrong. Personal insight (Intuitionism) is all we have to justify our practices (to ourselves and to others).

If you believe that courage, wisdom, self-control, piety, and so forth are virtues in every society, then perhaps you will choose Virtue Ethics as your model.

To help you choose an ethical theory, try this exercise. Examine one or more of the following moral situations and (a) interpret what is right and wrong according to each of the four theories, (b) then give an argument that might be proposed according to each theory, and (c) state your own assessment of the strengths of each theory.

Situation One.

You are the constable of a small, remote, rural town in Northern Ireland. The town is divided into the Catholics (20 percent minority) and the Protestants (80 percent majority). All Catholics live in one section of town on a peninsula jutting into the river just east of the main part of town.

One morning a young Protestant girl is found raped and murdered next to the town green. According to general consensus, a Catholic must have committed the crime. The Protestants form a citizens committee that demands the following of the constable: "We believe you to be a Catholic sympathizer, and we don't think you will press fast enough to bring this killer to justice. We know a Catholic committed the crime. We've sealed off the Catholic section of town; no one can go in or out. If you don't hand over the criminal by sundown, we will torch the entire Catholic section of town, killing all 1,000 people. Don't try to call for help. We've already disabled the telephone."

As you made every effort to find out who did it, but you made no progress. You could not find out. At one hour before sundown, you don't know what to do. Your deputy says, "Why don't we just pick a random Catholic and tell them he did it? At least we'd be saving 999 lives."

"But then I'd be responsible for killing an innocent man!" you reply.

"Better one innocent die and 999 be saved. After all, there's no way the two of us can stop the mob. You have to give them a scapegoat," the deputy responds.

Describe how each ethical theory might approach this situation. Which one is most consonant to your own worldview, and why?

Situation Two.

You are a railroad switcher sitting in a tower and controlling a switch that allows trains to travel over the regular track or switches them to a siding. One morning you face a terrible dilemma. The N.Y. Zephyr is traveling at high speed on the main track, and a school bus filled with children (at least fifty) has stalled on the main track as it crosses Elm Street. The bus driver is trying to restart the engine, but the ignition will not turn over. It is clear to you that the bus will not get off the track in time. On the siding track is a homeless man who has fallen down and caught his foot on a rail tie. It is also clear that he is stuck.

In fifteen seconds, you must decide whether to use the switch to send the train to the siding—thereby killing the homeless man—or to do nothing and allow the train to take its normal course and thereby hit the bus and probably kill most if not all of the fifty school children on board.

Describe how each ethical theory might approach this situation. Which one is most consonant to your own worldview, and why?

Situation Three.

You are on the executive committee of the XYZ organization of health care professionals. Each year the committee gives an award to one of its members who displays high moral character in his or her work. This year you are among the four judges for the award. There is some disagreement among the judges, however, about what constitutes a good person. The judges, besides yourself, are Ms. Smith, Mrs. Taylor, and Mr. Jones. The candidates for the award are Mr. Big and Mrs. Little.

Ms. Smith said that the award should go to Mr. Big because he saved a man from drowning. However, Mr. Jones demurred, saying that Mr. Big's motives are suspect because the man he saved was in the midst of a very big financial deal with Mr. Big. If the man had been allowed to drown, Mr. Big would have lost a lot of money. Ms. Smith said motives are not important but that the goodness of the act counts and the man who was saved runs a big business in town. Many people besides Mr. Big would have been hurt if he had not saved the man.

Mr. Jones said the award should go to Mrs. Little because she performed a kind act of charity in chairing the town's United Way Campaign last year. Surely such an act could not be said to benefit Mrs. Little in any way (unlike Mr. Big).

Mrs. Taylor said that she is somewhat unsure about either Mr. Big or Mrs. Little because both of them have been recommended on the basis of a single good act. Mrs. Taylor believed that it would be better to choose a candidate who has shown over time to have performed many good actions and to be of good character. "After all," she said, "a single swallow does not make a spring." Mr. Jones and Ms. Smith scratched their heads at this remark and turned to you. Who is right?

Describe how each ethical theory might approach this situation. Which one is most consonant to your own worldview, and why?

Choosing an ethical theory is only the first step in developing a practical ethical viewpoint. A link between the normative theory and application of the theory is needed. In Chapter One, I outlined my basic position concerning a personal worldview and how it might be utilized when applying an ethical theory. Deryck Beyleveld and Shaun Pattinson's essay on precautionary reasoning is an example of one way to do this. Beyleveld and Pattison create one such segue in their concept of "precautionary reasoning." According to this concept, a person must arrive at a level of potential agency ascription to fetuses, impaired humans, and nonhumans. Different people will arrive at different base levels at which they think it prudent to ascribe human agency (with all its ensuing rights) to some potential agent. A person may appeal to biological facts—such as the structure and development of the forebrain—for this. Another person may be more operational in evaluating seemingly purposive behavior. Still others may adopt other criteria.

The point is that one important aspect of developing a practical ethical viewpoint is to challenge ourselves to think about and provisionally accept certain tenets necessary to effectively apply ethical principles to practice. These concepts should allow professionals to connect normative theories to the real-life problems that confront them.

Before addressing ethical cases, try first to provisionally accept one moral theory. Then try to determine what connecting principles or concepts are necessary to translate theory to practice. Concentrate your efforts on these connections. They will be very useful to you as you address what you see as the important issues residing in each case.

chapter four

Physician, Nurse, and Patient— The Practice of Medicine

General Overview. This chapter presents a general overview of some key practices that constitute the profession of medicine. To this end, I have divided the chapter into four parts: Paternalism and Autonomy, Privacy and Confidentiality, Informed Consent, and Gender Issues. These four make significant contributions in defining medicine and identifying the issues it must address to improve. Many of these issues overlap because no clean separation exists between each of them. Issues related to one area inevitably influence those of another.

As an introduction to the traditional view of the practice of medicine, I first present the Hippocratic Oath that has been the foundation of the establishment of Medical Ethics. I hope that the reader will spend some time in studying this oath; its influences resonate throughout the book. The version presented here is my own.

The Oath

By Apollo (the physician), by Asclepius (god of healing), by Hygenia (god of health), by Panacea (god of remedy), and all the gods and goddesses, together as witnesses, I hereby swear that I will carry out, inasmuch as I am able and true to my considered judgment, this oath and the ensuing duties:

1. To hold my teacher in this art on a par with my parents. To make my teacher a partner in my livelihood. To look after my teacher and financially share with him when he is in need. To consider him as a brother and his family to be my family. To teach his family the art of medicine, if they want to learn it, without tuition or any other conditions of service. To impart all the lessons necessary to practice medicine to my own sons and daughters, the sons and daughters of my teacher, and to my own students, who have taken this oath—but to no one else.[1]

2. I will help the sick according to my skill and judgment but never with an intent to do harm or injury to another.

3. I will never administer poison to anyone—even when asked to do so. Nor will I ever suggest a way that others (even a patient) could do so. Similarly, I will never induce an abortion. Instead, I will keep holy my life and art.

4. I will not engage in surgery—not even upon suffers from the stone but will withdraw in favor of others who do this work.[2]

5. Whomever I visit, rich or poor, I will concern myself with the well-being of the sick. I will commit to no intentional misdeeds, nor any other harmful action such as engaging in sexual relations with my patients (regardless of their status).

6. Whatever I hear or see in the course of my professional duties (or even outside the course of treatment) regarding my patients is strictly confidential and I will not allow it to be spread about but instead will hold these as holy secrets.

Now if I carry out this oath and not break its injunctions, may I enjoy a good life and may my reputation be pure and honored for all generations. But if I fail and break this oath, then may the opposite befall me.

There are many versions of professional codes of ethics.[3] I thought about including the American Medical Association Code and the codes for various other health professions, but I decided that the Hippocratic Oath set the standard for what a professional code should be. Let us examine a few key

---

[1] In other words, to those who would not be fit to practice medicine. To this day, we maintain an elaborate screening process to eliminate those we do not believe to be academically or otherwise fit to enter into the practice of medicine.

[2] This is a rather odd clause that has disturbed many over the years. Why shouldn't the physician engage in surgery? Is surgery wrong? If so, why not simply prohibit it? To leave it for another to do seems to be passing the buck. Some have suggested that this passage refers to castration. But again, if this is the case, why not prohibit the act itself? Others have suggested that one should not engage in surgery until one is a master physician. In this case, the injunction is directed only toward new physicians who have just taken the oath. The problem with this interpretation is that there is no textual support for this. A final interpretation is that surgery, being rather messy, is not for master physicians but for less talented technicians. Although not totally satisfactory, this seems the best interpretation to me.

[3] The reader is encouraged to turn to my more extensive treatment of this subject in Chapter Seven of *Basic Ethics*.

features of codes to identify elements that indicate why we should accept or reject them.

Let me begin by saying that I think that among professional codes, the Hippocratic Oath is a good one. It balances specific prohibitions such as not administering poison or not having sexual relations with patients with more general principles such as "I will concern myself with the well-being of the sick" and "commit no . . . harmful actions." These general principles are very useful because they do more than simply prohibiting a particular action. These principles are put into the context of medicine's mission.

The first point sets the tone that medicine is an art that is given by the gods. It is an esoteric art that is to be reserved for those who are willing to follow the code. Thus, it is not open to everyone. Its purpose is to do good to others and always avoid harming others.

The code ties itself to the larger moral tradition, "I will commit no intentional misdeeds." Whereas the reference to not committing a "harmful action" has a direct link to the manner in which medicine is practiced, "misdeeds" links the physician to the larger moral tradition. There is no possible hiding in the shared community perspective alone.

Figure 4.1 identifies three factors that are the basis of any good professional code. Codes of professional ethics fail in overemphasizing one of these elements or in ignoring an element entirely. If codes of ethics exist to remedy the "inward perspective" problem described earlier, then they must create links to more general "shared worldviews." Having such links would put them in the realm of common morality.

This is the most important point from my perspective. The "practice" of a profession often defines its excellence in an introspective way so that achieving these functional requirements is all that matters; the profession is divorced from any other visions, that is, moral visions.

In the modern arena, many professional codes have evolved from a legal perspective. The practitioners of the profession do not want to do something that would cause them to go to jail or to be sued. Thus, they create a certain code that will specify acceptable and unacceptable behavior, which protect them from such outcomes. These codes are defensive in nature and are at the

---

Elements of a Good Professional Code

1. A specific listing of common abuses.
2. A few general guidelines that tie behavior to the mission of the profession.
3. A link to general theories of morality.

FIGURE 4.1 **Elements in a Normative Professional Code**

opposite end of the spectrum from the Hippocratic Oath. Their mission is not to set internal standards and create a link to common morality but to maximize an egoistic bottom line at the expense of the pillars of professionalism: one's specialized education and one's mission to serve others.

Any code that takes as its basis a negative approach designed to protect the practitioner from unwanted consequences is fundamentally inadequate. Instead, we should dream about what the profession may be in the best of all possible worlds and create a code that properly reflects this mission.

I. Paternalism and Autonomy.

Overview. How much control should each of us have over our own health care choices? Most of us would reply that we should have as much control as possible. Who would turn over control of his or her life to another? Does autonomy not go hand in hand with the freedom and self-determination that are upheld by most moral theories?

This view has a twofold problem: First, to be autonomous (literally a self-lawmaker), an individual must have adequate knowledge to use to explore and examine all options. This specialized knowledge is beyond the scope of most patients, so that they must rely on others to present the information they lack (often in a simplified version). The professional's judgment is generally superior to that of even an enlightened layperson. Thus, the factual understanding along with the judgment of experience generally puts the physician/nurse into a paternalistic role from the outset. (*Paternalism* refers here to acting in the patient's best interests. It is especially troublesome when the patient does not understand what is in her best interests so that the physician is in the position of ignoring the patient's wishes and acting as he, the physician sees fit.)

In the practice of medicine, patients can (and should) be brought into the decision-making process, but they are rarely able to become full collaborators. Thus, their knowledge and judgment limit patient autonomy.

Second, the patient is often in an impaired state that makes fully deliberative decision making rather difficult at best. The patient is either in pain, emotionally traumatized, or in some way not up to making a fully unemotional, rational decision. To burden a patient with the full weight of being an autonomous partner in the health care decision-making process may be unfair to the patient.

Including the patient in the process as much as circumstances permit has advantages, although the time constraints involved in split-second life-and-death situations often prevent this. By including the patient in the process, the physician/nurse is recognizing and affirming the patient's dignity.

Too often physicians have included only their more intelligent patients in the decision-making process. Also, paternalism can cloak racist or sexist predilections on the part of the physician/nurse. Thus, some form of autonomy seems absolutely necessary.

If both autonomy (in some form) and paternalism (in some form) are inevitable, how should they be balanced? Are there any guiding principles that might be used as linking principles of medical practice? In the following article, Hilary Jones begins the discussion of autonomy and paternalism by engaging in a general discussion of the two terms as they apply to daily life and to the sick. Next, Jones identifies autonomy with the embodiment of a moral principle and depicts paternalism as a form of behavior. If this is true, then the so-called conflict between the two is not a true conflict because each term refers to a different range of entities. By extension, we might infer that it would be better to be "appropriately" paternalistic in behavior and to consider autonomy as an abstract concept that is to be implemented as it can be. As such, the conflict disappears as each is developed on its own terms.

Julian Savulescu argues that conventional defenders of patient autonomy are mistaken because they view the physician as merely a fact provider to the patient, who will then make the decision about what to do about her health. He argues that the physician must be more than a fact provider and must become an "argument" provider. This means that the physician must first determine what he thinks is the best course of treatment and then engage the patient in a Socratic-style dialogue to ensure that the patient really understands what she is doing when she makes a choice about her treatment. This scenario is rational because it engages the physician in a logical, ethical argument but is noninterventional because it does not have seek to override the patient's wishes as its ultimate goal.

Nancy S. Jecker questions whether a physician who refuses to provide futile treatments to a patient who requests them is unjustifiably paternalistic. She begins her investigation with a survey of what constitutes a valid patient wish. Jecker contends that not all denials of a patient's wish constitute unjustified paternalism. What the patient must do is to cite reasons for the request so that they can be examined. When these issues hinge on a moral issue, the reasons cited must include *moral* reasons. If these arguments are not plausible, then Jecker contends that refusal of treatment is not unjustifiably paternalistic.

The last selection in this section reports the actual case of Robert D. Orr, M.D., who was confronted with a medical decision that had to be made immediately. He ascertained that the patient's requests were not in her best interests and by doing so acted in the patient's best interests. Dr. Orr is committed to patient autonomy, but this incident made him believe that his earlier opinions were incomplete. Three letters expressing responses to Dr. Orr's article are also included.

Autonomy and Paternalism: Partners or Rivals?

Hilary Jones

While autonomy and paternalism are part of our everyday lives, they become more of an issue when we fall ill. Professional opinion is divided on the relative merits of these two concepts in health care and the arguments continue to rage.

Definition of Autonomy

Dworkin (1988) advises that there are many definitions of autonomy and warns against the assumption that different authors are all alluding to the same thing when they use the term. He does, however, identify two features common to all definitions: that autonomy relates to persons; and that it is a desirable attribute. There is a third feature which Dworkin fails to mention, perhaps because he considers it axiomatic, i.e. that all definitions contain, or ought to contain, the word 'self', e.g. self-rule, self-determination, self-government.

Tschudin (1989) points out that individuals, while being free agents, are still social beings. Consequently, we influence and are influenced by social factors and therefore the concept of autonomy must be a relative one. Harris (1985) also discusses the relativity of autonomy. He describes it as an 'ideal notion' which is approachable rather than attainable. These ideas are difficult to refute but should be considered with caution, and in perspective. To offer such arguments as reasons for not striving to reach that ideal may, at times, be tempting, but are nonetheless indefensible.

The Popular View of Paternalism

The most commonly quoted definition of paternalism is that of 'doctor/nurse knows best'. Melia (1989) describes it more formally as:

> '. . . where health-care professionals make choices about the treatment of patients or clients which they deem to be in those clients' best interests.'

She suggests that this may be an uncomfortable issue to confront, perhaps because it challenges us to question what nursing really means and to examine our motives for entering a caring profession. When a person for whom we are caring makes an autonomous decision which will result in some self-harm, a conflict arises between the client's right to autonomy and the nurse's duty of care. Often the problem is resolved by the use (consciously or unconsciously) of paternalistic action by nursing and medical staff.

THE AUTONOMOUS PERSON

With these definitions in mind, how are we to regard autonomy and paternalism in our own daily lives, as well as in the lives of others? An instant reaction might be that autonomy is an absolute right—the 'no-one tells me what to do' response. We might think of it as being a basic human right, a priceless commodity which we acquire at birth and take with us when we die. On closer examination, however, this view proves to be false. Apart from the obvious and distressing truth that too often we fail to extend even basic human rights to some individuals, the fact remains that none of us are fully autonomous at all times.

Komrad (1983) cites some situations in which autonomy is severely jeopardized (*Table 1*). The latter, serious illness, poses the greatest threat. Although Komrad gives examples of illnesses and diseases which might result in the most devastating consequences for the affected person, he suggests that:

'All illness represents a state of diminished autonomy.'

His argument is based on the premise that the sick depend upon physicians for treatment, or at least for their expertise. However, he later qualifies this position by admitting that it is an over simplification. He confesses that this interpretation would have us believe that the nonmechanically minded owner of a broken car would not be autonomous at all, while the sick (but qualified) physician would be fully autonomous.

In reality, the car owner might choose to obtain several opinions and then make a truly informed and autonomous choice based on the information

TABLE 1   Situations Which Jeopardize Autonomy

Imprisonment
Pregnancy
Marriage
Political office
Serious illness

Source: Komrad (1983)

received, or the discerning owner might decide to scrap the car and buy a bike. On the other hand, the sick physician's autonomy is not necessarily protected by personal expertise. After all, no physician would be in a position to self-medicate during a myocardial infarction. This does not detract from Komrad's original conclusion that autonomy is reduced by illness, but merely questions the premise upon which it is based. Undeniably, the sick do rely on physicians for treatment, but equally physicians rely on the sick for their raison d'être. However, Komrad does not suggest that a physician's autonomy is diminished by his/her dependence upon the sick.

PATERNALISM IN OUR DAILY LIVES

If we accept that autonomy may be periodically reduced both within and outside the health-care setting, then can paternalism similarly be present in all areas of life? Komrad (1983) believes that paternalism advances as autonomy recedes and vice versa. He describes paternalism and autonomy as 'two inversely varying parameters along a spectrum of independence'. Taken literally, this would imply that the two are mutually dependent and inseparable. We would have to believe that reduced autonomy on every occasion would be compensated for by some paternalistic action. But action by whom, and with what intent? Clearly, there are many instances when no outside agent is involved at all, particularly when what we want conflicts with what we may have. On these occasions paternalism is simply not part of the equation.

Higgs (1985) believes that the paternalistic withholding of information is peculiar to health-care professionals. Admittedly, instances in other professions may not spring readily to mind, but that may be more to do with the covert nature of the practice than with its scarcity. For example, advertisers and educationalists often behave paternalistically, although their actions may be subtle, discreet, and well camouflaged. Undoubtedly, the most blatant example of all is in government where our elected representatives think it a wise and completely justified act to withhold information which, they believe, it would not be in our best interests to have.

PARTICULAR PROBLEMS POSED BY ILLNESS

Having established the naturally dynamic nature of autonomy and paternalism, what factors serve to reduce autonomy dramatically in people who become ill? Brody (1980) highlights the problem of 'social gap'. He notes that physicians provide more information to people in higher social classes than to those in the lower classes. The problem is compounded, he says, by the fact that people in lower social classes often feel intimidated by their physicians.

Rumbold (1986) draws attention to the vulnerability of patients. Illness may cause people to become confused, weak or fearful. When these states interfere with self-advocacy, autonomy is seriously affected. This vulnerability may be made much worse if the attitude of staff towards patients is such that assumptions are made on their behalf. Such assumptions might include a belief that patients do not want to know about their illnesses, or even worse, that they are incapable of understanding.

Rumbold describes how routine regimes can reduce patients' dignity by such acts as:

- Requiring patients to wear night clothes even though it is daytime and they are physically able to be up and about
- The tendency for conversations between professionals and patients to take place when the patient is lying down
- The impression of authority or power which the wearing of uniforms seems to convey.

At the most basic level, it appears that autonomy is reduced the moment any patient walks on to the ward and encounters the first 'uniform'. Naturally, there are some people who do not feel in the slightest way threatened by this ritualistic display of power. Nonetheless, loss of autonomy is virtually assured for one reason or another for anyone entering hospital.

The adoption of the sick role is one of the major contributing factors to both diminished autonomy and a resulting paternalistic response. Parsons (1975, cited in Childress, 1982) puts forward a case for the rights of patients to adopt the sick role if they so wish. This relieves them of the responsibility for their illness and encourages them to seek professional help. However, while agreeing that the adoption of a sick role is sometimes necessary, Burns (1991) stresses that it can cause problems. He also proposes that while the sick role ought to be discouraged it tends, instead, to be strongly reinforced by the attention of nurses.

VULNERABLE PATIENTS

For patients whom others have labelled 'incompetent' all these problems are exaggerated, particularly when these labels are applied, as they sometimes are, on the flimsiest of evidence. For example, Dyer and Bloch (1987) consider that psychiatric patients must be offered paternalistic care since they are unable to exercise free judgment. Parrish (1992) points to the fact that women with learning disabilities are often denied choices in methods of contraception which are always afforded to other women. Undoubtedly, the decisions involved in these examples are made by people whose intentions are entirely honourable; yet they argue that it is necessary to restrict or negate a persons' human rights in order to 'do good'. This is a dubious and debatable case of the ends justifying the means.

PARTNERS, RIVALS OR NEITHER?

To return to the question posed by the title of this article, it seems unlikely that staunch advocates of either position would consider any form of partnership between autonomy and paternalism. Those who adopt a 'middle of the road' approach might conceivably consider the notion more favourably, but they are few and far between.

The autonomy model is rapidly gaining ground. Inevitably, its rate of progress has caused something of a backlash against the concept of paternalism—and an almost feverish desire in some quarters to deny any and all connection with it. There are still those who attempt (arguably without success) to put forward a case for paternalism, e.g. Komrad (1983), Weiss (1985) and Black (1993). Weiss sees the paternalistic model as one in which the physician determines what is in the patient's best interest, while taking into account the patient's views and values. Black considers that, in the past, paternalism took an exaggerated form. He points to the caricature of Sir Lancelot Sprat in the Gordon *Doctor . . .* novels as being typical of the image of the dominant partner in the doctor/patient relationship of the day and one which is no longer valid.

Where the arguments of Weiss and Black fall down is in their false assumptions that things have changed to any great degree. In Weiss' view, doctors must consider their patients' opinions when deciding what course of action to take. However, when that decision is finally made, it will still be made by the doctor. If the patient's values conflict with the physician's, they will not really influence the outcome.

Black's position is slightly different in that he sees paternalism as it was practised in the past as being far less defensible than modern day paternalism. He believes that historically it was carried to excess and resulted in autocracy. Presumably, he believes that autocratic physicians are now extinct—an opinion which, it must be said, is quite astonishing in its credulity.

If some form of partnership is advocated by writers like Komrad, Weiss, and Black, it must surely be a limited one. Autonomy would take the role of a silent partner whose existence would be a mere technicality.

However, can a rivalry between autonomy and paternalism be said to be any more of a reality than a partnership? At first glance it might appear so. All health-care workers receive their training in the context of the prevailing social ethos. Those who trained at a time when social conformity was the norm are likely to continue to act paternalistically. Since they must work alongside doctors and nurses whose training has had a quite different emphasis, there will always be the potential for conflict.

Evidently, the argument relates more often to a set of attitudes more often than to a moral principle. Nurses who act 'in their patients' best interests' are apt to view their more recently qualified colleagues as uncaring or disinterested. Conversely, nurses who adopt the autonomy model may regard their paternalistic colleagues as bombastic and inflexible. The rivalry then, if it exists at all, is actually between contrasting styles in working practice.

It may be reasonable to conclude that neither partnership nor rivalry are realistic concepts. A true comparison can never really be made between autonomy and paternalism because they are essentially different in quality. Autonomy is the embodiment of a principle while paternalism is a form of behaviour. Ultimately, however, the science and art of nursing are also largely concerned with principles and with behaviours and, as such, demand that we remain aware of the issues and are willing to debate them.

References

Black Sir Douglas (1993) Black looks . . . at paternalism, *J R Coll Physicians Lond* 27(1): 6–7
Brody DS (1980) The patient's role in clinical decision-making. *Ann Intern Med* 93: 718–22
Burns RB (1991) *Essential Psychology.* 2nd edn. Kluwer Academic Publishers, Lancaster
Childress JF (1982) *Who should decide? Paternalism in Health Care.* Oxford University Press, New York
Dworkin G (1988) *The Theory and Practice of Autonomy.* Cambridge University Press, Cambridge
Dyer AR, Bloch S (1987) Informed consent and the psychiatric patient. *J Med Ethics* 13:12–6
Harris J (1985) *The Value of Life: An Introduction to Medical Ethics.* Routledge, London
Higgs R (1985) On telling patients the truth. In: Lockwood M, ed. *Moral Dilemmas in Modern Medicine.* Oxford University Press, Oxford
Komrad MS (1983) A defense of medical paternalism: maximising patients' autonomy. *J Med Ethics* 9: 38–44
Melia KM (1989) *Everyday Nursing Ethics.* Macmillan Education, Basingstoke
Parrish A (1992) Promoting health for all. *Nurs Stand* 7(9): 53
Rumbold G (1986) *Ethics in Nursing Practice.* Baillière Tindall, London
Tschudin V (1989) Informed consent. *Surg Nurse* 2(6): 15–7
Weiss GB (1985) Paternalism modernised. *J Med Ethics* 11: 184–7

Rational Non-Interventional Paternalism: Why Doctors Ought to Make Judgments of What Is Best for Their Patients

Julian Savulescu

It is almost universally accepted that doctors ought to make judgments of what is medically best for their patients. However, the view that doctors ought to make judgments of what is, all things considered, best for their patients has fallen into serious disrepute. It is now widely believed that it is up to patients, not their doctors, to judge what they ought to do, all things considered. I will argue that doctors ought to make value judgments about what is best for their patients, not just in a medical sense, but in an overall sense.

In the bad old days of paternalism, doctors did make judgments about what patients ought to do, all things considered. They also compelled patients to adopt what they judged to be the best course of action. Over the last twenty years, this approach has received much criticism. Liberal societies are founded upon a belief that we each have a fundamental interest in forming and acting on our own conception of what is good for us, what direction our lives should take, what is, all things considered, best for us. Forming a conception of what is best for oneself and acting on that conception is being an autonomous agent. By taking away from patients the ability to make and act on conceptions of what they judged was best, paternalists frustrated the autonomy of their patients.

There is a second problem with the old approach. Paternalists were making value judgments (often under the guise of what was 'medically or clinically indicated' (1)) which would have been more properly made by the patients who were going to be affected by the treatment. Consider one example. Joe is about to have an operation to remove a tumour from his diaphragm. An anaesthetist visits him preoperatively to discuss his anaesthetic. She then discusses post-operative analgesia. This, she explains, is very important because the major complication after his operation will be the development of lung collapse and pneumonia. If he does not receive adequate analgesia, and is unable to breathe deeply and cough comfortably, this will be much more likely. She informs him that there are two forms of analgesia available after his operation: thoracic epidural analgesia and intravenous narcotic infusion. The analgesic effectiveness of the thoracic epidural is greater. Joe will more easily be able to cough and breathe deeply, so better preventing the development of pneumonia. She explains that the risk of nerve damage from any epidural is around 1/15,000. There is an additional risk with thoracic epidurals in particular: a very small risk of spinal-cord damage from the procedure (damage from the needle) or complications that arise after it (epidural haematoma or abscess). In some of these cases, spinal-cord damage could result in paraplegia. There have only been isolated case reports of these complications so it is not possible to put a figure on how great the risk is but it is certainly very small. Overall, the risk of nerve damage is very small and the risk of developing pneumonia much greater. The anaesthetist explains the significance of developing pneumonia. In some cases, it results in respiratory failure requiring artificial ventilation. Such infections are sometimes very difficult to treat and patients stand a reasonable chance of dying if they develop respiratory failure. The overall risk of serious morbidity and mortality is greater if one has the narcotic infusion than if one has the epidural. She recommends having a thoracic epidural. (If she had been a paternalist, she would have simply inserted a thoracic epidural at operation.)

Joe, having understood all this information, chooses to have the narcotic infusion. He is an active sportsman and the risk of spinal-cord injury is very significant for him. He also claims that he is willing to put up with more pain, and still attempt to cough and breathe deeply, if in this way he will avoid the potential for harm to his spinal cord.

Two Reasons

In this case, which treatment Joe ought to have is not simply determined by facts related to Joe's health (the medical facts). There are two reasons why Joe's doctor ought not make a decision about what is, all things considered, best for Joe. Each has to do with a different sense of 'value'. Firstly, Joe's decision is based on his values, that is, what he is valuing. It is an essential element of self-determination that people construct a notion of what is important in their lives (their values) and act on these. Joe values independence and an active physical life. His choice reflects these values.

Secondly, the question of whether Joe ought to have the thoracic epidural is a value judgment, a judgment of what is of value. Judgments of what is of value, all things considered, are different from judgments of fact. It is a fact, let us assume, that a thoracic epidural is associated with better analgesia and a lower risk of developing pneumonia, but a greater risk of spinal-cord damage, than a narcotic infusion. However, it is not a fact that this makes thoracic epidural overall better for Joe. That is a value judgment. Value judgments must be based on all the relevant facts. These include the medical facts but also facts about the significance of the medical procedures for Joe's own life, and facts about his values. Since no one but Joe knows his plans, his hopes, his aspirations and his values, the argument goes, Joe is better placed than his doctor to evaluate the significance of the various benefits and complications of each treatment. Joe is in a privileged position to judge what is best, all things considered. Joe's doctor, ill-placed to know these other relevant facts, ought to stick to judgments about the medical facts.

For these reasons, medical practice has moved away from the old paternalistic model of 'Doctor knows best' or 'Doctor's orders' to the currently fashionable 'shared decision-making' model.

'Physicians bring their medical training, knowledge, and expertise—including understanding of the available treatment alternatives—to the diagnosis and management of the patients' conditions. Patients bring a knowledge of their own subjective aims and values, through which the risks and benefits of various options can be evaluated. With this approach, selection of the best treatment for a particular patient requires the contributions of both parties' (2).

On one widely held interpretation of this account, doctors bring medical knowledge, medical facts, to the patient who makes a judgment of what ought to be done on the basis of his or her values. Doctors give up making judgments of what is, all things considered, best for the patient and stick to providing medical facts. This approach has found considerable favour in the literature and in practice. Many informed general practitioners and medical students whom I have taught tell me that doctors ought not make tricky value judgments about their patients' lives.

This model of doctor as fact-provider has some serious shortcomings.

Firstly, it is not clear that doctors *can* avoid making value judgments about what patients ought to do, should do, or what it is best for them to do. Sometimes these value judgments are difficult to spot. Consider the oncologist whose patient has lung cancer. 'Chemotherapy is medically indicated', he says. This appears to be a purely descriptive, factual statement. But it is really also a prescription to have chemotherapy. If we were to ask this oncologist why chemotherapy was medically indicated, he might offer this argument: 1. chemotherapy will prolong your life; 2. longer life is better than shorter life; 3. so you ought to have chemotherapy. Premise 2 is clearly a value judgment.

It is difficult to see how doctors, as persons, could avoid making judgments like 2. The content of these value judgments varies from person to person, but it is difficult to imagine a person with no values. Most people have some norms which they apply to their behaviour. It is also difficult to imagine that these values do not come into play when a doctor is asked to perform a procedure on a patient.

'FRAMING EFFECT'

Perhaps doctors cannot avoid making value judgments, but they should keep these to themselves. According to the fact-provider model, doctors should just provide facts such as, 'Chemotherapy will prolong your life'.

However, it is not clear that facts can be communicated free of value. Psychologists have described how the way information is presented can determine the significance of that information for people. This is called the 'framing effect'. When choice is framed in terms of gain, we are risk-averse. When choice is framed in terms of loss, we are risk-taking (3). For example, lung cancer can be treated by surgery or radiotherapy. Surgery is associated with greater immediate mortality (10 per cent v 0 per cent mortality), but better long term prospects (66 per cent v 78 per cent five-year mortality). The attractiveness of surgery to patients is substantially greater when the choice between surgery and radiotherapy is framed in terms of the probability of living rather than the probability of dying. This effect still occurs whether the evaluator is a physician or someone with statistical knowledge (4).

The manner in which physicians present information is influenced by their values. Surgeons present the probabilities of the outcome of surgery in terms of survival, not death. It is not clear that framing effects can easily be overcome. Even if we present probabilities in terms of both survival and mortality, people are 'loss averse'. They focus myopically on the loss associated with events (5). Subtle nonverbal cues also influence the impact of information. Indeed, information seems ineluctably to bring with it a message. It is not difficult to recognise what someone values, even if they do not tell us. Far better, I think, to bring the practice out into the open, and argue explicitly for what we believe in.

But let's assume that doctors can give up either making value judgments or communicating them. Should they?

Medicine as a practice is founded on commitment to certain values: pain is bad, longer life is usually better than shorter life, and so on. A part of learning to practise medicine is learning to take on these values. These implicit evaluative assumptions rarely surface because they are a matter of consensus. 'Ethical dilemmas' arise when patient values diverge from medical values (6).

Should medicine give up a commitment to certain values? To be sure, we might believe that some of medicine's values are mistaken. Some ought to be changed or refined. But medicine should have a commitment to *some* values. Otherwise what would direct research effort, provide a standard of care or a framework for the organisation of practice? Mass consumer choice, a thin reed which bends to the prevailing winds, is sometimes irrational and even chaotic, at other times immovably apathetic, and seems ill-suited to provide such direction alone. This may be slightly hyperbolic, but it does seem true that medicine needs a set of values, no doubt shaped by informed public attitude, which guides practice. Those values must be more substantial than a commitment to do what every individual patient desires.

MORAL STAKES

The second serious shortcoming of the doctor as fact-provider model is that medicine differs from many other professional practices in that the doctor is often called upon to do very serious things to his patient. In deciding to ablate a patient's bone marrow prior to bone-marrow transplantation, a doctor is going to make his patient very sick. There is unavoidable serious harm associated with medical practice that is far greater than in engineering or tax consultancy. The moral stakes are much higher. Since medical practice involves serious harm to others, as well as benefit, doctors ought to form a judgment of what ought to be done, all things considered. In the extreme case of assisted suicide, a patient asks her doctor to help her die. Should a person do this without making a decision whether it is for the best? Surely not. It is at least generally true that good moral agents reflect upon and form judgments concerning what they ought to do. The same applies to less spectacular, every-day instances of medical practice. Prescribing an antibiotic may cause renal failure. A good doctor must form a judgment about whether prescribing that antibiotic is really justified, even if the patient has an informed desire to have it.

Thirdly, and most importantly, patients can fail to make correct judgments of what is best, just as doctors can. Patients can fail to make choices which best satisfy their own values (7). They can make choices which frustrate rather than express their own autonomy (8). The mere fact that a competent patient makes an informed choice does not imply necessarily that that choice reflects what he values.

Patients can also make incorrect value judgments. They can fail to give sufficient weight to relevant facts, just as the old paternalists did when they concentrated on the medical facts. Consider an example.

Joan is 35 years old and has a one cm cancer of the breast without clinical evidence of lymph node metastasis. Her mother and sisters had cancer of the breast. Her surgeon argues, based on her history and the cytology of the tumour, that she has a very high chance of developing a second carcinoma. He recommends a bilateral mastectomy. This, he argues, will give her the best chance of survival. Joan replies that this will be very disfiguring. She would prefer to have a lumpectomy followed by yearly mammography. This, she argues, will give her a better quality of life.

Joan's surgeon inquires further. It turns out that by better quality of life, she means that she will retain her present physical appearance. Her husband would be shocked if she had a bilateral mastectomy, even if she were to have breast implants. 'He is very attached to my breasts', she says. Her marriage is difficult at present, and she does not believe that it would survive the shock of such operation.

These are of course relevant facts to which the surgeon was not originally privy. Previously, he believed she ought to have a mastectomy. Are these new facts of sufficient importance to cause him to change his judgment? In some cases, they might be. If survival with lumpectomy and mammography was roughly the same as that after mastectomy, then he might change his mind. If Joan's life was really going to be miserable after a mastectomy, and much happier after a lumpectomy, then this would be a good reason not to have the mastectomy.

However, in some cases, the surgeon might retain his original judgment. He might believe that, if the risk of dying from not having the mastectomy was significant, that it was not worth risking death to conform to her husband's and society's expectations of her physical appearance. Moreover, he might believe that if her relationship would be destroyed by her having a mastectomy, it was not likely to survive or was not worth dying for. He might believe, not necessarily without basis, that Joan will be unhappy in her marriage whether she has a lumpectomy or a mastectomy. He might believe that Joan is mistaken in attaching so much weight to her husband's attachment to her breasts. He might continue to believe that she ought to have the mastectomy, despite the revelation of new facts. Indeed, even in the presence of *all* relevant facts, if these could be discovered, he might believe that Joan ought to have a mastectomy. Despite having access to the same facts as Joan, such a doctor might continue to differ with her about what is best and he may continue to try to convince her that she is wrong.

Some value judgments are wrong. To claim that one's life is not worth living because one's bunion is painful is mistaken, no matter how well-informed the judgment. To be sure, doctors make wrong judgments of what is best. But so do patients at times.

It is of course easier to turn the decision over to Joan and just provide some medical facts. It is easier to avoid making an all-things-considered value judgment. It is difficult to discuss with a patient why she holds the views she does. It is difficult to provide an argument for why she is wrong which is convincing to her. But such discussion and argument can help patients to make better decisions for themselves. Good advice, which we should expect from our friends and doctors, consists in more than information.

Shared Decision-Making

There has been a movement away from paternalism. There are, however, two ways of responding to the problems which have thrown paternalism into disrepute. The first is for doctors to give up the practice of making judgments about what is, all things considered, best for their patients. They should stick to providing medical facts to competent patients who then make choices as to what is best based on their values. This is the model of 'shared decision-making'.

The second approach agrees that in the past doctors concentrated too much on medical facts. Other facts are also important in determining what is best. These include facts about the patient, his values, his circumstances and so on. But this approach denies that the patient has sovereign access to the relevant facts, though in many cases she knows them better than anyone else. Doctors can, and ought to, try to discover these other facts and form for themselves an all-things-considered judgment of what is best. Doctors need not give up making value judgments; they can try to make better value judgments. If a doctor's value judgment differs from that of her patient, she ought to engage her patient, find reasons for their differences, and revise her own views. Or, if her view still appears justified, she ought to continue to attempt to convince her patient that she is wrong.

Does attempting to convince a patient that he is wrong in choosing some course threaten his autonomy? It may. One can argue coercively or non-coercively. There are many ways in which a doctor might get a patient to come around to agreeing with him that do not involve rational convergence between the two parties. I am not discussing these ways of arguing. What I am discussing is attempting to convince a patient by rational argument that he is wrong. Far from frustrating a patient's autonomy, this enables a patient to act and choose more autonomously. There are at least three ways in which this is so.

1. To be autonomous, one must be informed. A doctor, in attempting to convince his patient, will appeal to reasons. Some of these reasons will draw attention to relevant facts. He will be asking his patient to reconsider the significance of these facts for her life. Thinking about these facts in a new light, her choice will become more active, more vivid and so more an expression of her autonomy (8).

2. The second point I cannot argue for in detail here. For a choice to be autonomous, one must be informed. But one must not only be informed of the facts, but also of what is of value. (Or, a relevant fact is what other people have rationally valued or thought to be of value.)

3. As a result of a patient rethinking her choice and giving reasons for that choice in the process of arguing for it, that choice will become a more rational choice and one which she really does value.

So a doctor ought not to be merely a fact-provider but also an argument-provider. In this way, he enables his patient to make a more autonomous choice.

Paternalists went wrong not in forming judgments about what was best for their patients, all things considered. They went wrong in concentrating too much on only medical facts. Moreover, they went wrong in *compelling* patients to live according to their, the doctors', evaluations of what was best. That often does violate patient autonomy. If Joan continues to want a lumpectomy despite her surgeon's attempts to convince her that she is wrong, he ought not to compel her to have a mastectomy (though in some cases, he might believe that her judgment is so wrong that he cannot provide what she asks and withdraws from the case). We ought not to compel competent people to do what is best, even if what they desire is substantially less than the best. However, allowing competent people to act on their judgment of what is best for their own lives does not imply that those judgments are right. Nor does it imply that doctors should not form for themselves judgments about what is best. Nor does it imply that doctors should not try to convince their patients by rational argument that what they are advocating is the best course. Indeed, a doctor ought to form such judgments for his own sake as a moral agent and the patient's sake as an autonomous agent. We can retain the old-style paternalist's commitment to making judgments of what is, all things considered, best for the patient (and improve it) but reject his commitment to compelling the patient to adopt that course. This practice can be called rational, non-interventional paternalism. It is 'rational' because it involves the use of rational argument. It is 'non-interventional' because it forswears doing what is best.

Medicine is entering a new era. Doctors are now required not only to have medical knowledge, but knowledge of ethics, of what constitutes a value judgment, of the fact/value distinction, of how to make value judgments and how to argue rationally about what ought to be done. This requires new skills. It is relatively easy to be a fact-provider (though how to present facts itself presents a problem). It is easy to turn decision-making over to patients and say: 'There are the facts—you decide'. It is difficult to find all the relevant facts, to form evaluative judgments, and critically examine them. It is even more difficult to engage a patient in rational argument and convince him that you are right. If doctors are to avoid the shortcomings of being mere fact-providers, if they are to function properly as moral agents, if they are to promote patient autonomy, they must learn these new skills. They must learn these skills for another reason: gone are the days when they could make uninformed judgments of what was best for their patients and act on these. Gone too are the days when they did not have to provide a justification for the position they were advocating. And that justification goes beyond the fiction of a 'purely medical' justification.

References

1. Hope T, Sprigings D, Crisp R. Not clinically indicated: patients' interests or resource allocation? *British Medical Journal* 1993; 306:379–381.

2. Brock D W, Wartman S A. When competent patients make irrational choices. *New England Journal of Medicine* 1990; 322: 1595–1599.

3. Tversky A, Kahneman D. The framing of decisions and the psychology of choice. *Science* 1981; 211: 453–458.

4. McNeil B J, Pauker S G, Sox Jr H C, Tversky A. On the elicitation of preferences for alternative therapies. *New England Journal of Medicine* 1982; 306:1259–1262.

5. Kahneman D, Varey C. Notes on the psychology of utility. In: Elster J, Roemer J E, eds. *Interpersonal comparisons of well-being.* Cambridge: Cambridge University Press, 1991: 127–163.

6. Thanks to one referee for expanding this point.

7. See reference (3), and also: Kahneman D, Tversky A. Choices, values, and frames. *American Psychologist* 1984; 39: 341–350.

8. Savulescu J. Rational desires and the limitation of life-sustaining treatment. *Bioethics* 1994; 8: 191–222. Savulescu J. *Good reasons to die* [doctoral dissertation]. Monash University, Jun, 1994.

Is Refusal of Futile Treatment Unjustified Paternalism?

Nancy S. Jecker

INTRODUCTION

Are physicians who refuse to provide futile treatments guilty of unjustified paternalism? Zawacki answers this question in the affirmative, suggesting that refusing to provide futile treatments to those competent patients who request them is tantamount to treating an adult patient like a child. "The case for futility as a valid ethical category is . . . based on a presumption that 'the doctor knows best'," Zawacki charges. He continues by quoting Childress: "[the paradigm of paternalism has historically] allowed a physician to act 'as a father,' that is, 'benevolent but also treating the patient as a child who cannot be permitted to determine his or her own welfare or the means to it.' " According to this conception, contemporary debates about medical futility represent a misguided backlash against autonomy, a stark reversal of the ethical progress that the field of bioethics has sought and achieved since its inception. As bioethicists committed to the new "'informed-consent' paradigm of medical decision making," we should not turn our backs on years of progress in ethics and law.

   In this article, I will argue that medical futility is wrongly conceived as unjustified paternalism. To the contrary, refusing to use futile treatments is consistent with respect for patient autonomy and with balanced consideration of other values in medicine. Furthermore, heightened awareness of patient autonomy has not replaced beneficence, as the concept of a paradigm shift implies. Instead, autonomy has supplemented beneficence (and other values), thereby enhancing moral complexity.

MEDICAL FUTILITY IS NOT UNJUSTIFIED PATERNALISM

Paternalism refers to "the principle and practice of paternal administration; government as by a father; the claim or attempt to supply the needs of or to regulate the life of a nation or community in the same way as a father does those of his children;" and, "the principle of acting in a way like that of a father toward his children."[1] In medicine, the most general meaning of "paternalism" is benevolently restricting a competent person's freedom. The most common example is to use a beneficial treatment against the wishes of a competent patient and for the patient's good. Yet paternalism also applies more broadly, to both actions and omissions that violate a competent patient's wishes for the purpose of either benefitting or avoiding harm to the patient. Thus, Beauchamp and Childress define paternalism as including any form of "intentional nonacquiescence or intervention in another person's preferences, desires, or actions with the intention of either avoiding harm to or benefitting the person."[2]

Paternalistic behavior becomes a source of *prima facie* moral concern in medical situations only when it violates the autonomous preferences, desires, or actions of a competent patient. It is not a source of moral concern when surrogate decision makers or members of the healthcare profession attempt to act in the best interest of an infant; a profoundly retarded adult; a patient with end-stage Alzheimer's disease; or a healthy but inebriated adult. More precisely stated, paternalism raises moral concern if (1) the patient expresses an autonomous preference or desire, or intends to carry out an autonomous action; (2) another person overrides the patient's preference, desire, or action; and, (3) the other person does so either to promote the patient's good or to avoid harm to the patient.

Many instances in which futile treatments are withheld or withdrawn fail, for obvious reasons, to meet these conditions. For example, withdrawing a ventilator from a patient in a persistent vegetative state who has expressed no prior preferences about what he or she would want in this situation is not paternalistic because conditions (1) and (2) are not met. Nor is it paternalistic when healthcare professionals turn down requests for expensive diagnostic tests that are not medically indicated for the sole purpose of complying with cost-containment policies established by their health-maintenance organizations. In such cases, condition (3) is not satisfied because healthcare professionals are not acting with the intention of promoting the patient's good or avoiding harm to the patient. Likewise, paternalism is not at stake when deciding to withdraw dialysis from a patient with multiple-system organ failure when the futility of dialysis has been explained to the patient and the patient understands and agrees. It is also not paternalistic for a healthcare professional to discontinue cardiopulmonary resuscitation and emergency cardiac care if a patient fails to respond after 30 minutes. In the last case, although the patient had previously expressed that "everything" should be done in such a situation, the requirements of paternalism are not met because the emergency medical technician is not acting with the intention of avoiding harm to or conferring a good to the patient. Instead, the reason for ceasing life-sustaining efforts is to desist in an activity that provides no benefit (or harm) to the unconscious patient.

These examples make evident that even if refraining from futile interventions can sometimes be characterized as paternalistic and disrespectful of patient autonomy, this characterization hardly captures the entire case for futility as a valid ethical category, as Zawacki contends. Are there other cases where refraining from futile treatments more closely resembles the kind of negative paternalism described above?

> Consider the situation of an 85-year-old patient in an intensive care unit who has reached the final stages of a terminal condition, such as pancreatic cancer. The patient expresses a competent request to be a "full code" in the event that she suffers a cardiac arrest. The medical team is uncomfortable meeting this request, believing that aggressive medical measures such as cardiopulmonary resuscitation, insertion of an endotracheal tube, and use of defibrillators, would be a positive harm to the patient, only adding to the patient's pain and discomfort at the end of life. After consultation with the ethics committee, the attending physician decides to override the patient's wishes. This decision is consistent with the hospital's policy of not offering or using futile treatments. The team provides full comfort and palliative measures, doing everything possible to minimize the patient's pain and discomfort.

In this situation, all three of the conditions for paternalism sketched above appear to be met: the patient has apparently expressed an autonomous preference, the physician overrides the patient's wishes, and does so with the goals of benefitting and avoiding harm to the patient.

Yet upon closer examination this apparently straightforward situation becomes less clear. Although overriding a patient's wishes in order to benefit or avoid harm to the patient always raises *prima facie* moral concern, such concern does not necessarily prevail. As others have shown, paternalism is sometimes ethically (and legally) justified.[3] Consider the following series of cases.

1. A patient suffering from multiple sclerosis requests her physician to end her life by lethal injection.
2. A professional athlete wants a prescription for steroids in order to enhance his athletic prowess.
3. A patient with a common cold asks for antibiotics.
4. Believing that a miracle will occur, a patient whose death is imminent repeatedly requests her physician to keep her alive "no matter what."
5. A patient learns that his physician is hosting a dinner party and would like an invitation.

In none of these cases is it unethical for healthcare professionals to override the patient's wishes. In case 1, it is ethically permissible for the physician to refuse to meet a request for euthanasia because the practice of voluntary, active euthanasia runs contrary to ethical standards of medicine. Even those who would like to see ethical standards in this area changed do not favor forcing providers who oppose euthanasia to perform it. In cases 2 and 3 the physician is again justified in denying the patient's request for medical treatment, this time because the treatments in question clearly violate accepted standards of medical practice. A physician who acceded to a patient's wishes in case 2 would be roundly criticized not only for violating professional standards but also for subjecting the patient to serious risks. In case 4, performing miracles is not an obligation that the physician undertakes; the responsible physician explains that medicine's powers to prolong life are limited. In case 5, the patient's request for a social invitation obviously falls outside the scope of the provider-patient relationship.

As these cases attest, not all denials of patients' requests are ethically wrong. The question that must be settled is how to distinguish between justified and unjustified refusals of patients' wishes. To address this question, we should explore the extent to which patients request treatments that providers cannot give without (1) transgressing ethical standards of the profession; (2) using interventions that fall outside the range of medically sound treatment options; or (3) granting wishes that are obviously beyond the scope of medicine or of the provider-patient relationship.

A second set of considerations concerns whether or not the patient's request reflects a truly autonomous choice. The word "autonomy" means, literally, "self-legislation" or "self-rule," implying authorship of the moral laws and rules that are imposed upon oneself. Someone becomes an autonomous agent, not simply by expressing a desire, but by bearing responsibility for decisions and actions. Rather than granting patients unfettered freedom, the ethical principle of respect for autonomy enjoins respect for persons who "engage in self-determination at the deepest level," and are "personally, morally accountable" for their conduct in a way that "could not possibly be ascribed to a being who had no such authorship."[4] In these instances, it is wrong to override a patient's wishes because doing so violates the patient's integrity; it forces the patient to act (or be acted upon) in a manner incompatible with the patient's deepest moral convictions.[5]

These remarks suggest that, for patients' wishes to reflect their genuinely autonomous choices, patients must not only indicate their desires, but must also express some moral reason or principle that justifies their request. To return to the example described above, involving the patient with end-stage pancreatic cancer who wants to be made a "full code," it is impossible to tell offhand whether the patient's request conveys an autonomous choice. We must first engage the patient in conversation to learn more about the considerations leading to this request. As Katz notes,

> mere acceptance of patients' "yes" or "no" responses to a proposed intervention may not express respect for their self-determination, dignity, or integrity. Indeed, blindingly accepting either response may violate their integrity and constitute an act of disloyalty to the person. Either response, if accepted without question, is disrespectful of patients' capacities for reflective thought, which might have led to a different choice more consonant with their own wishes and expectations.[6]

The patient's request carries greater moral weight if the patient cites as a reason to support her request that she wants to try to live long enough to see a relative who is arriving from a distant state or that she needs a few more days to get her affairs in order. By contrast, the patient who can offer no reason for wanting a futile treatment or who requests nonbeneficial interventions on the basis of fear, denial, anger, or gaining control for its own sake, can hardly defend such a request by appealing to patient autonomy. In these and other situations, requests for futile treatments are not evidence of moral forethought and responsibility, as autonomy implies, but instead evidence that the patient (or patient surrogate) is, for example, reacting to the stress of the situation; clinging to unrealistic hopes and expectations; feeling overcome by intense emotions; or succumbing to the pain, discomfort, and physical exhaustion that often accompany serious illness.[7] In these instances, refusing to provide futile treatments does not constitute unjustified paternalism nor does it express the clash of conflicting moral principles implied by the idea of 'overriding patient autonomy'. Instead, refraining from futile interventions in such instances is consistent with thoughtful consideration of, and respect for, genuine patient autonomy.

AUTONOMY HAS NOT REPLACED BENEFICENCE

In the preceding discussion, I have highlighted that the concept of patient autonomy is often misunderstood and that the value of patient autonomy is not absolute. These points are not intended to suggest that the concept of patient autonomy should be abandoned, nor that respect for patient autonomy is a trivial concern. To the contrary, most agree that the greater emphasis on patient autonomy that occurred during the 1960s and 1970s was a much needed correction to the historical abuses associated with medical paternalism. At the same time, it is misleading to characterize this shift of emphasis as the replacement of a "beneficence paradigm" with an "autonomy paradigm." Such language falsely conveys that the value of promoting the patient's good has lost all relevance. Yet both patients and society continue to hold healthcare professionals responsible not merely for offering up a menu of options from which patients may choose, but also for maintaining individual and public health.[8] A more accurate description of the evolution of ethics in medicine holds that the historical emphasis on promoting the patient's good has been supplemented in modern times with greater recognition of the value of patient autonomy. Although healthcare professionals continue to stand in a fiduciary role with respect to patients, they must simultaneously pay attention to the competent patient's wishes. This description portrays the ethics of medicine as increasing in complexity and as irreducible to any single, foundational principle. Rather than finding a single source of moral value, bioethics has historically uncovered the heterogeneity of morality, what Larmore has called, "a motley of ultimate commitments."[9]

Conclusion

In conclusion, although abuses of medical futility undoubtedly occur, sometimes involving unjustified paternalism, this does not suffice to show that all appeals to futility are abusive or involve unjustified paternalism.[10] Instead, potential abuses underscore the urgency of clarifying the meaning of futility; agreeing upon its ethical implications; educating healthcare professionals and patients; and developing policies to ensure more open, consistent, and thoughtful application of this concept.[11]

As demonstrated in recent studies, healthcare professionals are already using "futility" in clinical practice to justify withholding and withdraw life-sustaining treatments.[12] Cost-conscious healthcare organizations are already appealing to the related notions of "medically unnecessary" and "nonbeneficial" to support reducing the use of costly services.[13] To address this reality, we should scrutinize these practices and hold both clinicians and healthcare institutions accountable to sound ethical principles and accepted standards of medical care.[14]

The medical profession has already begun to take the lead in defining futility and reaching a consensus about its ethical implications. Thus, more and more groups have expressed support for limiting futile interventions including the American Medical Association, Canadian Medical Association, American Heart Association, Amercian Academy of Pediatrics, President's Commission, American College of Chest Physicians, Society of Critical Care Medicine, American Thoracic Society, and others.[15] Yet much work lies ahead. As new medical technologies appear, the need to evaluate outcomes, agree upon standards, and forge ethical consensus about the benefit or non-benefit of treatments for different patient groups will not abate. Nor will we ever complete the task of exercising moral judgment in applying general standards of medical futility to particular cases. Futility's meaning and ethical implications will, and should, continue to challenge the ethics of medicine.

Notes

1. *The Compact Oxford English Dictionary,* under the word "paternalism."

2. T. Beauchamp and J. Childress, *Principles of Biomedical Ethics,* 4th ed. (New York: Oxford University Press, 1994), 274.

3. *Ibid.*

4. H. Morreim, *Balancing Act* (Boston: Kluwer Academic Publishers, 1991), 136.

5. N.S. Jecker, J.A. Caresse, and R.A. Pearlman, "Caring for Patients in Cross-cultural Settings," *Hastings Center Report* 25 (1995): 6–14.

6. J. Katz, *The Silent World of Doctor and Patient* (New York: Free Press, 1984), 125.

7. N.S. Jecker and L.J. Schneiderman, "When Families Request that 'Everything Possible' Be Done," *Journal of Medicine and Philosophy* 19 (1994): 261–77.

8. N.S. Jecker and L.J. Schneiderman, "Judging Medical Futility: An Ethical Analysis of Medical Power and Responsibility," *Cambridge Quarterly of Healthcare Ethics* 4 (1995): 21–33.

9. C. Larmore, *Patterns of Moral Complexity* (New York: Cambridge University Press, 1987), xi.

10. L.J. Schneiderman and N.S. Jecker, "Futility in Practice," *Archives of Internal Medicine* 153 (1993): 437–41; N.S. Jecker and L.J. Schneiderman, "Futility and Rationing," *American Journal of Medicine* 92 (1992): 189–96; J.R. Curtis *et al.,* "Use of the Medical Futility Rationale in Do-not-attempt Resuscitation Orders," *Journal of the American Medical Association* 273 (1995): 124–28.

11. L. Stell, "Stopping Treatment on the Grounds of Futility: A Role for Institutional Policy," *Saint Louis University Public Law Review* 11 (1992): 481–97; N.S. Jecker, "Calling It Quits: Stopping Futile Treatment and Caring for Patients," *The Journal of Clinical Ethics* 5 (Summer 1994): 138–42.

12. D.A. Asch, J. Hansen-Flaschen, and P.N. Lanken, "Decisions to Limit or Continue Life-sustaining Treatment by Critical Care Physicians in the United States," *American Journal of Respiratory and Critical Care Medicine* 151 (1995): 288–92; L. Pijnenborg *et al.,* "Withdrawal or Withholding of Treatment at the End of Life," *Archives of Internal Medicine* 155 (1995): 286–92; A.R. Myerson, "Helping Health Insurers Say No," *New York Times,* 20 March 1995.

13. American Medical Association, Council on Ethical and Judicial Affairs, "Ethical Issues in Managed Care," *Journal of the American Medical Association* 273 (1995): 330–35; N.S. Jecker, "Managed Competition and Managed Care: What Are the Ethical Issues? *Clinics of Geriatric Medicine* 10 (1994): 527–39.

14. L.J. Schneiderman and N.S. Jecker, *Wrong Medicine: Doctors, Patients, and Futile Treatment* (Baltimore: Johns Hopkins University Press, in press).

15. American Medical Association, Council on Ethical and Judicial Affairs, "Decisions Near the End of Life," *Journal of the American Medical Association* 267 (1992): 2229–33.

16. American Medical Association, Council on Ethical and Judicial Affairs, "Guidelines for the Appropriate Use of Do-not-resuscitate Orders," *Journal of the American Medical Association* 265 (1991): 1868–71; Canadian Medical Association, "Joint Statement of Resuscitative Interventions," *Canadian Medical Association Journal* 151 (1994): 1176a–76c; American Heart Association, Emergency Cardiac Care Committee and Subcommittees, "Guidelines for Cardiopulmonary Resuscitation and Emergency Cardiac Care," *Journal of the American Medical Association* 268 (1992): 2171–83; American Academy of Pediatrics, Committee on Bioethics, "Guidelines on Foregoing Life-sustaining Medical Treatment," *Pediatrics* 93 (1994): 532–36; President's Commission for the Study of Ethical Problems in Medicine and Biomedical and Behavioral Research, *Deciding to Forego Life-Sustaining Treatment* (Washington, D.C.: Government Printing Office, 1982); American College of Chest Physicians/Society of Critical Care Medicine Consensus Panel, "Ethical and Moral Guidelines for the Initiation, Continuation, and Withdrawal of Intensive Care," *Chest* 97 (1990): 949–58; Society of Critical Care Medicine, Task Force on Ethics, "Consensus Report on the Ethics of Foregoing Life-Sustaining Treatments in the Critically Ill," *Critical Care Medicine* 18 (1990): 1435–39; American Thoracic Society, "Withholding and Withdrawing Life-sustaining Treatment," *Annals of Internal Medicine* 115 (1991): 478–85; Hastings Center, *Guidelines on Termination of Life-sustaining Treatment and the Care of the Dying* (Indiana University Press, 1987); Hastings Center, Guidelines on the Termination of Life-sustaining Treatment and the Care of the Dying (Indianapolis: Indiana University Press, 1987).

Confessions of a Closet Paternalist

Robert D. Orr, MD

The pastor was just beginning to read the scripture when an usher tapped me on the shoulder and whispered that there was an emergency in the rear of the church. As I was directed through the door of the pastor's study, I encountered a scene of semiorderly panic: one person was calling 911; another was bursting through a door on the opposite side of the room shouting, "I know CPR, can I help?" and another was wringing her hands as she stood beside a motionless form lying on her back in the middle of the floor.

I knelt beside a well-dressed elderly woman who was pale, apneic, pulseless, and had a sizeable healing abrasion on her right forehead. My calm professional exterior belied the internal panic I felt at being thrust into a medical emergency with no stethoscope, blood pressure cuff, cardiac monitor, or equipment to measure blood gases. As I began going through the "ABCs" [airway, breathing, circulation], I found that the way she was positioned had caused the tight collar of her red silk blouse to constrict her throat. When I loosened two buttons, she gasped and started slow but unlabored, spontaneous breathing. Within moments there was also a weak and rapid pulse.

On direct questioning, the woman wringing her hands, Mrs McCarthy, reported that this was Mrs Pulaski, aged 93, to whom she gave a ride to church each Sunday. She was under the care of a physician and was on five or six medicines for diabetes, high blood pressure, and a heart condition and was also on a new medicine for "nerves." She lived alone and was quite independent. She had mentioned that morning that she had fallen at home the previous Monday—an explanation for the healing wound on her forehead. She had suddenly slumped over in church without warning, now three or four minutes ago. As this history was gathered, the unconscious woman began to stir. She first mumbled something unintelligible, and Mrs McCarthy recognized that Mrs Pulaski was coming around in Polish. As the four paramedics arrived with several pieces of equipment, she was switching to heavily accented English and was saying she felt fine and wanted to go home.

The paramedics moved in to administer oxygen, check her blood pressure, and apply the cardiac monitor and pulse oximeter. They carefully explained to Mrs Pulaski each intervention as it was applied, and she increasingly resisted each one. While the emergency medical technicians did their job very professionally, I began my differential diagnosis: simple syncope, hypoglycemia, oversedation or drug interaction from her new "nerve" medicine, subdural hematoma causing a seizure, or an arrhythmia that also could have caused the earlier fall. She needed to go to the emergency department at the hospital just six blocks away for further evaluation.

The technician in charge said to Mrs Pulaski, "We would like to put you on the stretcher and take you to the hospital to see your doctor. Is that OK?" I bit my tongue as I thought, Hasn't he been listening? "Is that OK"! Of course it's not going to be OK. She has already said six times that she wants to go home.

An unbalanced conversation ensued. The paramedic was calm and quiet and was trying to explain the need for further evaluation. Mrs Pulaski was loud and irate, not hearing anything he was saying and demanding that she be taken home. She even tried to blame poor Mrs McCarthy with, "This wouldn't have happened if you hadn't brought me to church!" This was going nowhere fast. It was then that my closet door opened, and I heard this authoritative voice from within me say to the paramedic in a tone reserved for wayward children, "Don't ask her permission. Just put her on the stretcher and take her to the ER."

The reason that voice both frightened and surprised me is that I teach clinical ethics to medical students and residents. I emphasize a patient's right to self-determination. I decry paternalistic behavior by physicians—behavior that we say was common in the past, but is much less common today. But here it was alive and well within my professional being. Could I salvage this situation from catastrophe?

I knelt again by her side and said rather firmly, "Mrs Pulaski, it is not normal to fall at home and injure yourself and then to pass out again in church a few days later. Something is wrong. It may be some problem with your medication, or it may be something more serious that needs to be fixed in the hospital. But we don't know now. We are going to take you to the Emergency Department at the hospital and call your doctor to come and sort out the problem. Now we are ready to help you onto the stretcher. Put your hand on my shoulder." She mumbled in Polish, but she put her hand on my shoulder. The ambulance left forthwith.

Rather than return to the middle of the sanctuary to sit with my wife, I took Mrs Pulaski's now-vacant seat in the rear pew. I heard nothing of the sermon. I tried to muster a defense for this paternalistic stranger who lived in my closet. I give a lecture to residents on "Patient Refusal of Physicians' Recommendations." *Patients have a right to self-determination, a right even extending to the refusal of potentially life-sustaining interventions.* Mrs Pulaski's situation was probably not life threatening. The crisis had passed spontaneously, and she was stable within a few minutes. *We must be sure the patient is competent to make decisions, has been adequately informed of the consequences of refusal, and is not being coerced; persuasion is OK, but manipulation and coercion are not.* She appeared to be competent. The emergency technician was trying to give her adequate information, though rather unsuccessfully. The utterance from the stranger in my closet certainly sounded coercive. *There are narrowly defined circumstances when paternalism may be justified. When a competent patient is making a seriously irrational choice that is not consistent with her chosen therapeutic goals and the harm done by overriding her choice is less than the harm done by acceding, it may rarely be ethically permissible to ignore her choice.* Mrs Pulaski's situation did not fit that description. Then what went wrong?

I immediately recalled a Franz Ingelfinger essay in which he says, ". . . the physician should recommend a specific course of action" and "[a] physician who merely spreads an array of vendibles in front of the patient and then says 'Go ahead and choose, it's your life' is guilty of shirking his duty, if not malpractice" (F. J. Ingelfinger: "Arrogance," *The New England Journal of Medicine,* 1980, 303:1507–1511). The utterance in question was born of frustration from watching another medical professional who was being too objective and not being sufficiently "arrogant" in this beneficent sense; one who was failing in his responsibility to give strong professional guidance in a serious situation.

As the pastor pronounced the benediction, I was trying to determine whether the closet door had been opened from the outside or the inside.

CORRESPONDENCE

Medical Paternalism Revisited

TO THE EDITOR: I am writing about the article by Dr Robert D. Orr regarding his confrontation with his own "paternalism" in the March 1995 issue.[1] In my opinion, Mrs Pulaski may have lacked decision-making capacity. She was in a state of crisis—embarrassed, overwhelmed, and possibly disoriented. She did not seem to fully appreciate the gravity of her situation. I wonder if she could have explained what her medical problem was, the possible consequences of refusing treatment, and her reason for refusal.[2] Additionally, treatment refusal did not fit with her previous pattern of medical compliance.

As a consultation psychiatrist and a member of our hospital bioethics committee, I am frequently confronted with the nondemented, nonpsychotic patient who may lack the capacity to make medical decisions because of a functional state. Depression, denial, and lack of maturity all can impair a patient's ability to give informed consent.[3,4] More discussion of this topic would be welcome. I confess that at times I, too, am a closet paternalist.

LORETTA Y. HOWITT, MD
Department of Psychiatry
Kaiser Los Angeles Medical Center
4700 Sunset Blvd
Los Angeles, CA 90027

References

1. Orr RD: Confessions of a closet paternalist. West J Med 1995; 162:279–280

2. Applebaum PS, Grisso T: Assessing patients' capacities to consent to treatment. N Engl J Med 1988; 319:1635–1638

3. Bursztajn HJ, Harding HP Jr, Gutheil TG, Brodsky A: Beyond recognition—The role of disordered affective states in impairing competence to consent to treatment. Bull Am Acad Psychiatry Law 1991; 19:383–388

4. Ganzini L, Lee M, Heintz, R, Bloom J, Fenn D: The effect of depression treatment on elderly patients' preferences for life-sustaining medical therapy. Am J Pyschiatry 1994; 151:1631–1636

* * *

*TO THE EDITOR: Robert D. Orr, MD, is to be commended for allowing the appeal of a spunky old lady to generate a caring that overcame the casuistic catechism of contemporary ethical analysis in medicine.[1] In saying to Mrs Pulaski, "Put your hand on my shoulder," and helping her onto the stretcher, he demonstrated the caring that almost 70 years ago, Peabody lucidly described as at the heart of the care of the patient.[2]

I suggest that the root of the predicament in which Dr Orr found himself, a predicament in which most current ethical discussions leave the physician who is facing a "real live patient," lies in an analysis of the clinical situation in terms of the stance of each individual, patient and physician, vis-à-vis the other, rather than on the human bond that encompasses both. But in the profession's flight from paternalism, the implications of this caring bond, in formal discourse blandly spoken of as the physician-patient relationship, seem to be overlooked in most of the current ethical analyses.

Caring need not be paternalistic, as seen in the way we care for a friend, a respected colleague, or even an admired teacher. With each, we might take an action that overrode their expressed wishes simply because we cared enough to risk the relationship or, in the case of a patient, a lawsuit. There is a difference between beneficence, which entails action in an impersonal spirit of kindness, and caring, where a personal involvement is the crucial determinant of action. As proponents of scientific medicine, have we become so fearful of the personal and subjective that we are unable to recognize this distinction? Do we fear to acknowledge caring because of the personal involvement it might imply? Because of the responsibility it might imply? Must we cite Ingelfinger's argument for a beneficent arrogance (from a paper that can be read in an entirely different manner)[3] to justify an occasional lapse into caring behavior?

---

*The opinions or assertions contained herein are the private views of the author and should not be construed as official or as necessarily reflecting the views of the Uniformed Services University of the Health Sciences or the US Department of Defense. There is no objection to its presentation and/or publication.

Dr Orr's actions reveal him to be a caring physician. His ruminations are a sad commentary on how far we still have to go in understanding Peabody's message.

SIMON AUSTER, MD, JD
Family Practice and Psychiatry
Uniformed Services of the Health Sciences
F. Edward Hebert School of Medicine
Bethesda, MD 20814-4799

References

1. Orr RD: Confessions of a closet paternalist. West J Med 1995; 162:279–280
2. Peabody FW: The care of the patient. JAMA 1927; 88:877
3. Ingelfinger FJ: Arrogance. N Engl J Med 1980; 303:1507–1511

* * *

TO THE EDITOR: The "Lesson From the Practice" by Robert D. Orr, MD,[1] and Mrs Pulaski's situation brought back lessons learned during a three-hour seminar on ethical dilemmas given during the American College of Healthcare Executives Congress in Chicago last month.

We were divided into groups of about eight, and each group considered a different case study. Mine considered the case of an 82-year-old woman whose family wanted to avoid having a pneumoencephalography (PEG) line surgically inserted into her stomach. Despite a few statements to the contrary, the group voted almost unanimously to appeal to the family to permit the surgical procedure; failing that, the hospital would go to court to gain guardianship of the woman, then do the procedure and send her to a nursing home. When these results were offered to all the seminar participants (made up of hospital executives and some clinical people), no one voiced strong objections, and the hospital's need to protect itself from legal liability was again reiterated. A number of comments were made about the irrelevancy of the family's wishes. The hospital's position was likened to "abetting suicide" if it did not insist on the surgery.

I later learned that the actual patient of this case study did get the PEG line—the physician and staff appealed to a son who eventually gave in—and was sent to a nursing home, where she died three months later. When I asked the seminar leader, who knew the woman and her family, if she valued those last three months, he said "No."

I suspect that 93-year-old Mrs Pulaski, by refusing hospital admission, hoped to avoid losing control of her future. She had reason to be concerned.

SUSAN J. ANTHONY
Editor, Healthcare Forum Journal
425 Market St, 16th Floor
San Francisco, CA 94105

Reference

> 1. Orr RD: Confessions of a closet paternalist. West J Med 1995; 162:279–280

* * *

Dr Orr Responds

TO THE EDITOR: Dr Howitt deduces that Mrs Pulaski lacked decision-making capacity and did not appreciate the gravity of the situation. She may well be correct, but my concern, in retrospect, was that I had not adequately assessed her decision-making capacity and had overruled the paramedics' attempts to inform her. Although the ability to give informed consent may be impaired by illness, denial, and other factors, we must take care that we do not revert to the old standard that determined patients to be incompetent if they did not agree with their physician.

I hope that Dr Auster is correct in his implication that Dr Peabody would have interpreted my "paternalistic" action as caring. The "casuistic catechism of contemporary ethical analysis" is not, however, to be completely ignored. Although I might have chosen a different word than arrogance (per Dr Ingelfinger) to characterize a physician's responsibility to make a recommendation, caring (good) can truly become arrogant (bad) in some situations. The caring human bond that Dr Auster describes is probably more operative in an established physician-patient relationship than in a medical crisis confronted by strangers. I am relieved to have my actions perceived as caring rather than arrogant, but disappointed that he found my ruminations to be a sad commentary on medicine and medical ethics.

Ms Anthony's brief case report allows me the opportunity to tell readers that "Mrs Pulaski" had a brief stay in the hospital, a few weeks in a convalescent home, and 18 months ago returned home with a live-in companion. She appears to be glad for my paternalistic intervention, although I have not had the opportunity (nor the courage) to ask her directly.

ROBERT D. ORR, MD
Department of Family Medicine
Loma Linda University Medical Center
Loma Linda, CA 92354

II. PRIVACY AND CONFIDENTIALITY.

Overview. The principle of confidentiality is at least as old as the Hippocratic Oath. Its underlying assumption is that a physician, nurse, or health care worker must know all the facts to be able to treat a patient effectively. If the patient believes that some health facts are embarrassing or otherwise wishes not to disclose them, she will not divulge them unless she knows that these facts will be held in confidence. Failure to disclose pertinent information is a particular problem in the public health field. It affects not only the patient but also people with whom the patient has contact and to whom the patient may have transferred the disease. Because these people may be denied information, they may not receive necessary treatment.

A threat to the privacy and confidentiality issue is the increasing number of databases that record our health information so that insurance companies can assess it to determine medical reimbursement. Alhough these databases strive to be as accurate as possible, anecdotal information leads me to believe that this information is misused. Obviously, the computer age has made information very accessible. But do we want *all* information easily accessible to anyone who wants it? Can this information be used to discriminate against us in our work and in our status in society?

These databases provide some benefits, however. A comprehensive national database could be beneficial. For example, a person new in a community or on vacation might need immediate health care. The ability to obtain the patient's medical history via such a database, might enable the new physician to treat the patient in a more effective manner. Obviously, the erosion of privacy through the advent of information technology has advantages and disadvantages. Sometimes efficiency and equity are in conflict.

In the following article, Paul Cain identifies the basic issues involved in the current debate concerning privacy. He believes, in theory, that confidentiality is based on the concept that information entrusted by one person to another will not be divulged. This model suggests a type of covenant between patient and health care provider. In practice things work differently, however; there may be duties of confidentiality that do not involve any such covenant. In this instance, respect for the patient's confidentiality may entail duties even when no explicit information transaction between patient and health care provider occurs. Thus, the duty of confidentiality comes from two sources.

These duties of confidentiality are restricted only by reference to those whose need and right to know relate to the patient's health care needs. Cain recognizes that such a restriction is not a "line drawn in the sand" but that health care providers work in gray areas, including situations related to issues of patient autonomy (controlling the access of information about himself) and informed consent (knowing who has a need to know about his medical condition).

Katharine Smith and Jan Russell explore privacy issues from the point of view of African American women infected with the human immunodeficiency virus (HIV). How do the concerns of privacy affect these individuals in their day-to-day lives? Obviously, whether to disclose their HIV status is an ethical issue; imbedded within it are the various personal factors that confront these women, such as the "unfairness" of being afflicted with HIV in general and aspects of their self-image. If the ethics of caring requires us to empathize with another's particular circumstance, then appreciation of the needs and concerns of actual people suffering is crucial in being able to treat their medical needs. Thus, gaining trust and building confidence in another is crucial so that the patient will reveal her true health situation.

Carol Ford, Susan Millstein, Bonny Halpern-Felsher, and Charles Irwin test the hypothesis that confidentiality is an essential part of medicine. They report a randomized controlled trial indicating that adolescents are very concerned about confidentiality. They communicate less with physicians and even forgo health care because they are concerned about issues related to confidentiality. This is especially true in sensitive areas such as sexual behavior, drug use, and mental health. Physicians and health care providers who wish to heal their patients must overtly assure them that confidentiality is a part of the practice of medicine.

The final article in this section involves Britain's National Health Service (NHS). The headline "Banks access computer records, foreclose on cancer patients" identifies a problem involving the access to confidential information in our electronic age. I hope that readers will think about the possible downsides of having so much information about patients available on general databases (such as the Medical Information Bureau, MIB). What are the rights of privacy and how should they be protected?

The Limits of Confidentiality

Paul Cain

INTRODUCTION

The issue of confidentiality is recognized as being of great importance in professional work, and has been addressed extensively in the literature.[1-8] In particular, the question of what, morally, is the point at which confidentiality may be broken, has been widely discussed, for example by Ngwena and Chadwick in an earlier issue of this Journal.[5] However, little attention has been given to the question: what is the point at which confidentiality has, as a matter of fact, been broken? As distinct from the moral scope discussed by

Ngwena and Chadwick, at issue here is the conceptual scope of the obligation of confidentiality. It is this that I wish to explore.

The importance of this question of scope is, perhaps, evident, for any discussion of *whether* confidentiality should be breached presupposes a view of *when* it has been breached. It may be useful, here, to highlight the practical relevance of this by reiterating a question that I have posed, but not resolved, in an earlier discussion[9]: is breaking confidentiality (1) telling anyone else what has been told to you in confidence, or (2) telling someone who neither needs nor has the right to know? (It might be added, if not (1) or (2), then what?) To anticipate, I shall conclude that neither (1) nor (2) adequately takes account of the range of situations encountered in health care; as I shall argue, the question of what are the limits of confidentiality does not admit of a simple answer.

What I wish to establish, therefore, is a criterion, or criteria, for the concept of 'breaking confidentiality'. A first step must be to clarify what counts as confidential information, and what constitutes the obligation of confidentiality.

CONCEPTS OF CONFIDENTIALITY

Confidential information is commonly said to be secret information that is disclosed or entrusted on the understanding that it will not be divulged to a third party. (The notion of secrecy is, incidentally, captured in the French term for confidentiality—'le secret professionel'.) It is information that is imparted 'in confidence', and indeed can be referred to as a 'confidence'. This version of confidentiality is displayed in the following quotations: 'Confidentiality, which can be defined as entrusting information to another with the expectation that it will be kept private' (Joseph and Onek, p. 313)[4] and 'confidentiality is the preservation of secret information concerning the user which is disclosed in the professional relationship' (Banks, p. 26).[8]

This version is also, presumably, implicit in Clause 10 of the United Kingdom Central Council for Nursing, Midwifery and Health Visiting (UKCC)[10] *Code of professional conduct,* which lays down that every nurse must 'protect all confidential information concerning patients and clients obtained in the course of professional practice . . .' Here, an obligation of confidentiality derives from a promise or undertaking that the information will not be divulged to a third party.

This is made clear by Gillon (p. 106)[3] who says that one of the conditions necessary 'to create a moral duty of confidentiality' is that a person must 'undertake—that is, explicitly or implicitly promise—not to disclose another's secrets'. In this version, therefore, the notion of trust is fundamental: information is 'entrusted' on the assumption that professionals are trustworthy (i.e. will not break their promise).

The centrality of trust in the account of confidentiality in view is emphasized in the UKCC advisory leaflet[11] explaining the nature of confidentiality:

> Turn to almost any dictionary and you find that the focal word in the defini-
> tions of 'confide', 'confidence' or 'confidential' is 'TRUST'. To trust another per-
> son with private and personal information about yourself is a significant matter.

This account of confidentiality is, clearly, appropriate in contexts such as
individual psychotherapy and the priestly confessional, but it is not at all clear
how it can accommodate the range of contexts and situations that arise in
health care. For example, health care is typically delivered through teams:
hence a promise not to disclose information to a third party would, typically,
be unworkable. Conceptually, this is not a problem, however, since the undertaking not to disclose information to a third party, which, as has been seen,
constitutes the obligation of confidentiality, can be revised to allow for a wider
boundary within which the promise of nondisclosure will be honoured. (Quite
where this boundary should lie is the chief concern of this article.)

Less straightforward in terms of the concept in question is the fact that,
in undertaking home visits, doctors, nurses and health visitors acquire much
information that is not specifically entrusted to them (they may, for example,
simply notice things) but which would, nevertheless, be regarded as confidential. Further, it may not be easy, and probably is in any case not standard
practice, when first meeting a client, to make a clear undertaking regarding
confidentiality. What is the hardest of all to accommodate, within the concept
of confidentiality that I have outlined, is the fact that health care professionals
work with clients who are unconscious, or who are severely demented, or
who have severe learning disabilities. In such contexts, there is no intentional
disclosure, information is not entrusted, and there is no undertaking given
not to disclose information about the client (how could there be when communication is impossible?). Nevertheless, they would hold themselves to be
under a duty of confidentiality.

There is, thus, an apparent puzzle: how to match the widely used *language* of confidentiality to the range of cases that do not conform to a widely
accepted *concept* of confidentiality.

One way out of this is to claim that this wider use of the language of
confidentiality expresses a professional obligation to be discreet, which, in
turn, is based directly in the principle of respect. Respect for clients involves
respect for their ownership of information about themselves, respect, therefore, for their private sphere. This is due (whether the client is unconscious,
dementing or fully autonomous) to the client as a person. Hence professionals,
who have access to this information in virtue, simply, of their professional
role, do not have the right to divulge information to third parties, unless there
is some other, overriding, principle at stake.

The principle of respect requires, therefore, that information acquired
should be treated with discretion. This does not mean, however, that it will not
be passed on, but that, if it is, this will be done responsibly and for good reasons (for example, to protect a child from harm). This does mean, however,

that, rare exceptions apart, information acquired will be treated as confidential (i.e. *as if* it had been entrusted, and *as if* there had been a specific promise not to disclose).

Another way out of the puzzle is to adopt the account of confidentiality endorsed in the *Guidelines for professional behavior* published by the College of Nurses of Ontario.[12] This stipulates that 'all information relating to the physical, psychological, and social health of clients is confidential. Any information collected during the course of providing nursing services is confidential'. Here it would appear that an obligation of confidentiality arises simply *in virtue of the professional role*, rather than from an explicit undertaking not to divulge information. For two reasons, at least, it could be argued that this account of confidentiality should be resisted.

First, it could be argued that not all information acquired in the course of professional practice should be regarded as confidential. This is implied by Clause 10 of the UKCC *Code of professional conduct*,[10] which, in stating that every nurse shall respect 'confidential information', clearly assumes that some information is not confidential. An example of the latter might be this: if a community nurse happened to notice that a child had severe bruising, she would almost certainly not regard this as confidential.

This objection can, however, be met, if, holding to the stipulation that *all* information is confidential, we tolerate the revision to a common way of thinking that this entails (i.e. we allow that bruising to a child, and any other items that, it might be held, should be divulged, *are* confidential). This, however, would not be conceptually problematic, since, in such a case, divulging such information to a third party could be seen to be a breach of confidentiality.

Secondly, it could be argued that the proposed concept lacks two notions that are fundamental to any account of confidentiality, and which were key elements in the sources quoted at the start of this discussion: that of a 'confidence', and that of a promise not to divulge. The notion of a 'confidence' is lacking, since no reference is made to information being specifically entrusted, and the notion of a promise is lacking, since, for this concept to apply, it is sufficient simply to be in a professional role.

This second objection can also, I believe, be met. Clients typically have to trust professionals, and in the case of health care, have to *entrust themselves* to professionals; to entrust oneself is more fundamental than, and therefore embraces, entrusting items of information about oneself. So although reference to particular 'confidences' may be absent from the conception of confidentiality under discussion, a fundamental notion of confiding is retained. Further, since clients have to trust professionals, they have a right to expect that professionals will be *trustworthy*. In relation to information, this means that clients have a right to expect that information they make available will be kept confidential. This rightful expectation is acknowledged in professional codes of practice, and these, arguably, legitimize talk of an *implicit* undertaking in relation to keeping information confidential. The notion of a promise is, therefore, on reflection, not lacking in the conception of confidentiality under discussion, since to be in a professional role, and in particular in the role of a nurse, carries with it an implicit promise to keep information confidential. This notion is in fact specifically endorsed by the College of Nurses of Ontario's Guidelines,[12] which lay down that 'nurses make an implicit promise to maintain confidentiality'.

It seems, therefore, that, in addition to an account of confidentiality that is based directly in the principle of respect, a case can be made for two concepts of confidentiality: according to one, confidential information is specifically entrusted on the basis of an explicit undertaking that it will not be passed on, and the obligation of confidentiality arises from this undertaking; according to the other, confidential information is *any* information acquired in the course of professional practice, and the obligation of confidentiality resides in the basic professional obligation to be trustworthy. (This second concept would entail, incidentally, that, in its reference to 'confidential information obtained in the course of professional practice', Clause 10 of the UKCC *Code of professional conduct*[10] is tautologous.)

The differences between these two concepts suggest that it would be appropriate to talk in terms of a strong and a weak concept. The first is 'strong' in laying down a precise requirement (i.e. that an explicit disclosure of private information is made) and in carrying the moral weight of an explicit promise not to divulge. The second is 'weak', in that there is no explicit promise, and, by comparison, the requirements are less rigorous (i.e. there is not necessarily any explicit disclosure of information, or any explicit request for secrecy).

If this analysis is satisfactory we have, thus, a fuller account of confidentiality, which can accommodate the range of contexts that arise in health care. We are able, therefore, to discuss the question of the limits of confidentiality, that is, the question of criteria for the concept of breaking confidentiality.

The Limits of Confidentiality

When a client has disclosed information on the understanding that this will not be divulged, and an undertaking of nondisclosure has been given, a breach is when that undertaking has not been honoured. A promise has been made, and that promise has been broken. The 'limit' of confidentiality in such a case is whatever has been agreed to be the boundary within which information disclosed will be kept safe. This boundary may be open to review. A case in point would be where the primary health care team find accommodation for a patient who has been mentally ill, and, with his or her agreement, inform the housing association that their client has a volatile history.

When information has not been disclosed on this understanding (for example, because the client is unable to communicate) and there has not been an express undertaking of nondisclosure, identifying the limits of confidentiality is less straightforward. I will explore this by reviewing various possibilities in turn.

1. *The limit of confidentiality is set by what the client would have wished.* What the client would have wished must, clearly, be central to an account of the limit of confidentiality in such cases. This is because of the principle of respect and the obligation to be trustworthy. However, since health care staff do not, generally speaking, have an intimate knowledge of their clients, such that they can confidently judge what the client would have wished, for this criterion to be applicable to practice an account is needed of what it would be *reasonable to suppose* the client would have wished the limit of confidentiality to be, had he or she been in a position to make his or her wishes known. In other words, 'what the client would have wished . . .' has to be given content. Is this content provided by possibility (2)?

2. *The limit of confidentiality is set by reference to who has a need to know.* This is initially attractive, as it allows within the boundary those in the health care team who may share the task of caring for the client. It is, however, too permissive, as the following example illustrates. A client confided in the nurse that he was having unprotected sex with his partner. The nurse knew that he was HIV positive. She was aware, therefore, of a dilemma: not to tell the partner would protect confidentiality, and yet this would also risk harm. In this case, the fact that the situation was felt as a dilemma indicates that telling the partner was perceived as a breach of confidentiality, and yet, undoubtedly, the partner had a need to know. This case suggests that (2) should be replaced by:

3. *The limit of confidentiality is set by those who have a right to know.* However, this is unsatisfactory also, since the fact that her partner was HIV positive is clearly information to which she had a right. She had a right to know, but the nurse, at least in respect of the principle of confidentiality, judged that she did not have a right to tell. She might justifiably have told, but, in that case, there would have been a breach of confidentiality. We therefore need to revise (2) and (3) to read:

4. *The limit of confidentiality is set by reference to those whose need and right to know relate to the health care needs of the client.* This builds in a necessary restriction, and also clarifies the position of the health care team: their right to know derives from their need to know, which in turn derives from the obligation to meet the needs of the client. It also points to a distinction between two kinds of information that may be disclosed, namely, a distinction between what is, and what is not, relevant to the client's health care needs. Only the former, on this criterion, may be passed on to other members of the health care team without a breach of confidentiality.

This last account does, surely, provide a satisfactory way of marking the limit of confidentiality, and so of marking the boundary beyond which we should talk of breaking confidentiality. This is because the only reason that health care workers, in their professional role, acquire information about people, is because these people are their clients and have particular health needs. Given the importance of respect and trust, such information can, therefore, be shared without breach of confidentiality only with those involved in their care.

It is relevant to emphasize that the limit identified in (4) is proposed as a clarification of (1) (i.e. it is proposed as a reasoned account of what a client 'would have wished' the limits of confidentiality to be, had his or her wishes been communicated). It may be, however, that the limit identified in (4) does not apply in all cases. The following situation may be an example. A nurse on a medical ward learnt, in the course of conversation with a newly admitted patient, that he was a keen golfer. She told a patient in a nearby bed (who was also a keen golfer), with a view to promoting a welcoming atmosphere. It would be counter-intuitive to claim this as a breach of confidentiality, even though it appears to fall outside the limit identified in (4), since patients on a ward are not among those 'whose need and right to know relate to the health care needs of the client'. This is not a problem, though, for the overriding criterion is (1): 'what the client would have wished'. It is reasonable to suppose that the nurse's action was in line with what her patient would have wanted her to do. (Golfers have much in common!)

What has not yet been clarified is whether a breach of confidentiality has occurred if a client's case is referred to *anonymously* outside the boundary identified in (4), such that either the client cannot be, or is not, identified. This may occur in a number of ways: nurses on one ward may discuss a patient with colleagues on another ward who are not involved with that patient; a nurse may discuss a patient with her partner, perhaps out of a need to unburden herself; a case history may be written up in a medical or nursing journal; or a case history may be discussed by students, as part of their training.

Should these, and other examples of going beyond the limit identified in (4), be seen as breaches of confidentiality, since, in all such cases, information is disclosed to those who do not have a need or a right to know that arises from involvement in the client's care?

It may be felt that, where there is anonymity and the client either cannot be or is not identified, no breach has occurred; but how can a reasoned account for this view be given? It could be argued that an account emerges from reflection on the implications of criterion (1), which, as I have made clear, is more fundamental than (4), since this is simply an attempt to give content to (1). Criterion (1) lays down that 'the limit of confidentiality is set by what the client would have wished', and the question could be put of why would clients wish that their case should not be discussed anonymously, if, as a consequence, they cannot be, or are not, identified? Underlying this question is the assumption that the point of confidentiality is to protect privacy and to erect a barrier against possible embarrassment, and that, where anonymity ensures this, no breach has occurred.

Against this it could be argued that there is a sense in which clients *own* personal information, and that professionals, whose access to it is only legitimized by their involvement in the client's care, do not have the right to extend 'ownership' beyond the limits of those who are directly involved in that care. Underlying this argument is the assumption that the point of confidentiality, in addition to protecting privacy and ensuring a barrier against possible embarrassment, is to respect autonomy.

Perhaps here we are up against the limits of what can be established by reasoning alone about what a reasonable client's wishes might be. My intuition is that the argument supporting the view that no breach has occurred carries more weight, but I am not clear how this intuition can be shown to be correct. What I think can confidently be said is that the more such anonymous disclosure is *responsible* (i.e. directed to good ends), such as the unburdening of stress or the education of students, the more likely it is to conform to the wishes of the reasonable client, and therefore the less likely it is to constitute a breach of confidentiality.

CONCLUSION

This discussion has been an attempt to clarify the limits of confidentiality, not in the sense of the boundary beyond which confidentiality may *justifiably* be broken, but in the sense of the boundary beyond which it has as a matter of fact been broken. (What would *justify* a breach is clearly another discussion, which, however, presupposes getting clear about where the boundary lies.) I have claimed that the limit is set by the wishes of the client, and that, where these are not known (whether because the client is unable to communicate or because his or her views have not been sought), the limit is set by what the client would have wished. Since the latter is a vague and unworkable notion (for it demands too intimate a knowledge of individual clients), I have attempted to give content to the notion of what the reasonable client would wish. This, I argued, would identify the limit by reference to those whose need and right to know relate to the client's health care needs. An exception to this was, arguably, where information was passed on anonymously in such a way that the client either cannot be, or is not, identified.

What in theory emerges as a simple statement may, in practice, turn out to be less straightforward, for where a client *is* able to make his or her wishes known, this may be in (possibly unavoidable) ignorance of the extent to which information disclosed may have to be shared (for, what the treatment may require may not be precisely known), and, where the client is *not* able to make his or her wishes known, the proposed analysis may not match what he or she would have wished, and this (*ex hypothesi*) is not known. Further, there will be the need for judgement about what the analysis implies; for example, are the surgery receptionist, the hospital porter, or the neighbour, among those who have 'a need and a right to know'?

To note this uncertainty is to draw attention to a commonplace fact, that the 'fit' between concepts and practice is not always exact, and that no amount of theoretical 'fine-tuning' can dispense with the need for individual judgement.

References

1. Bok S. *Secrets: on the ethics of concealment and revelation.* Oxford: Oxford University Press, 1986.

2. Edgar A. Confidentiality and personal integrity. *Nurs Ethics* 1994; **1**: 86–95.

3. Gillon R. *Philosophical medical ethics.* Chichester: Wiley, 1986.

4. Joseph D., Onek J. Confidentiality in psychiatry. In: Bloch, S., Chodoff, P. eds. *Psychiatric ethics.* Oxford: Oxford University Press, 1991: 313.

5. Ngwena, C., Chadwick, R. Confidentiality and nursing practice: ethics and law. *Nurs Ethics* 1994; **1**: 136–50.

6. Shardlow, S. Confidentiality, accountability and the boundaries of client-worker relationships. In: Hugman, R., Smith, D., eds. *Ethical issues in social work.* London: Routledge, 1995: 65–83.

7. Siegler M. Confidentiality in medicine: a decrepit concept. *N Engl J Med* 1982; **307**: 1518–21.

8. Banks, S. *Ethics and values in social work.* Basingstoke: Macmillan, 1995.

9. Cain, P. The ethical dimension. In: Cain, P., Hyde, V., Howkins, E., eds. *Community nursing, dimensions and dilemmas.* London: Arnold, 1995: 91–92.

10. United Kingdom Central Council for Nursing, Midwifery and Health Visiting. *Code of professional conduct,* third edition. London: UKCC, 1992.

11. United Kingdom Central Council for Nursing, Midwifery and Health Visiting. *Confidentiality: an elaboration of Clause 9 of the second edition of the UKCC's* Code of professional conduct for the nurse, midwife and health visitor. London: UKCC, 1987.

12. College of Nurses of Ontario. *Guidelines for professional behavior.* Ontario: College of Nurses of Ontario, 1995: 9.

Ethical Issues Experienced by HIV-Infected African-American Women

Katharine V. Smith and Jan Russell

INTRODUCTION

Human immunodeficiency virus (HIV) and acquired immunodeficiency syndrome (AIDS) have given rise to a variety of ethical problems about 'what is right or what ought to be done'[1] for those infected with the virus, their loved ones, their health care providers, and society. For example, do persons with AIDS (PWA) have the right not to inform past sexual partners of the diagnosis? Do those past sexual partners have a right to be told the diagnosis? Although many authors have addressed such ethical problems on a theoretical level, few have addressed these issues through research. Most research that has addressed HIV-related ethical issues has investigated the ethical problems and/or the attitudes of nurses rather than those encountered by the infected persons themselves.[2-15]

METHOD

Sample

This study was part of a larger project exploring the lives of HIV-infected African-American women; a purposive sample of five women participated. Two were 23 years old, and the others were aged 26, 40 and 42. Two were married. Of the three single participants, two had current partners and one did not. One participant had completed the 11th grade; two had passed the General Education Diploma (GED); one had completed high school and some vocational training; and the fifth had completed two years of college. Only one participant had health insurance; the other four had only Medicare. All of the participants had children. One had two children, one of whom had been killed. Two women each had three living children, ranging from six months old to six years old in one, and from one to nine years old in the other. Another participant had three grown children, one of whom had also been killed. The fifth participant had four children, ranging from 18 months to five years of age. Among the five participants, there was therefore a total of 13 living children and two deceased.

Procedure

To explore the ethical issues faced by these women, each was asked in an audiotaped interview to describe her 'experience as a black woman infected with HIV/AIDS'. No other prompts were given; rather, each woman's story was allowed to unfold in her own words. In a follow-up interview, data from the first interview were validated, and more directed, but again open-ended, questions derived from the literature were asked. Questions focused on their exposure to HIV/AIDS, its effects on their lifestyle, its effects on their family, and the ethical issues (if any) that they dealt with regarding their diagnosis. The data were analysed using Giorgi *et al.*'s[16] method of phenomenological analysis.

FINDINGS

The findings of this study indicate that four broad categories of ethical issues are faced by HIV-infected African-American women, revolving around issues of: diagnosis; disclosure; treatment by, and of, others; and future pregnancies.

Diagnosis

One issue that participants had faced in relation to their diagnosis was the need to be tested. One had learned from friends that a previous partner had died of AIDS. She said:

> I took the tests because someone that I had been with had died from AIDS, a guy I had been with prior to me getting married . . . I came to the clinic and I talked to my doctor and told him that I was told a previous lover had died from AIDS and that I wanted to be tested. So I was and two weeks later I came back for the results and sure enough, I was positive.

Another was tested because she was suspicious of her current partner:

> . . . because I had a good idea that my mate was positive . . . that was another reason I got tested, because he wasn't telling me, you know, the full detail of why he was in the hospital.

Participants discussed the fear associated with being tested for, and potentially being diagnosed with, HIV/AIDS:

[Other people] don't want to get tested because they're scared they are going to say yes. I didn't want to get tested either, but I did. I could still be walking around, right now, today and not be tested. I was scared then, but I still laughed 'cause I didn't think it could happen to me. But it wasn't funny then and it wasn't funny before I laughed. It is serious.

Despite their fears, each woman did make the decision to be tested:

I went down there and I got tested, and I was six months pregnant. They told me that the test that I took was negative and to come back in three months. Well, I delivered in February, February 14, 1993, and I went down there February of 1993 and they told me that my test came back and was positive.

Once the women were tested, they faced ethical issues about the way they were informed of their positive HIV/AIDS status. One participant said:

I went into the treatment centre and I came in, I was laughing and joking. She said, 'Your test results are back.' Well I told her, 'I know I ain't got AIDS.' She said, 'Sit down, you're HIV.' Then I didn't hear anything else she said, I busted down, broke down . . .

Disclosure

Several aspects of disclosure presented ethical issues for these women. The first issue was their partner's disclosure (or lack of disclosure) of his HIV status. Three of the five participants had specifically asked their partners about their status, and all three were assured the partners did not have HIV. These three women later found that their partners had not been honest about their status, and subsequently found themselves to be HIV positive, too, despite their efforts to the contrary. This aspect of disclosure, or the lack of it, illustrates the dilemma of their own right of disclosure versus their partner's right to privacy. One woman stated:

I asked him why he didn't tell me before we did something, you know, and he said, 'Well, I thought you was going to tell somebody.' I told him: 'Well, you put my life in your hands and the kids.' I had three kids when I met him and he didn't tell me until I told him I might be pregnant, we'd been together about six months then and I didn't know nothing about it. He died before I had my baby.

Although these three women did not believe their partners' lack of disclosure was right, none of them expressed anger about it. One woman believed most HIV positive people would not disclose, but she believed she both should and would:

But nine times out of 10, 90%, you know, of the world, they would not tell anybody: 'Hey, I got HIV', but I would, because I don't want nobody to go down that road.

Another said:

Right, we talked about it, and that's when I told him that if he had it to let me know, that we could work something out. But he says that he felt that I would of, you know, he really cared about me, but it was just something that he wasn't ready to tell me because so many people have rejected him . . . and he didn't want that. So, and I guess I would have felt the same way.

Perhaps the participants' own experiences with HIV enabled them to understand their partners' fear of rejection, although all three maintained that they would choose to deal with this issue differently:

But see, if it was me, I would tell somebody and if they didn't want to be bothered, well, you know, I would kind of feel lost behind too. But, I think every person has a right, in this world, to make that decision upon themselves. Because, that is like taking a life.

Deciding that they would deal with this issue of disclosure differently from their partners was one thing, but actually doing it was another. The women who had not contracted HIV/AIDS from their current partners had to decide if they would inform their present partners of their diagnosis. Invariably, these women did. One woman said:

The first day I was diagnosed he was at the clinic with me and I came out and on the way home I told him. I had prepared for a divorce that day after I left the clinic, I got in the car and I had already made up my mind that we would be divorced so he could go on because his came back negative. His is negative and that's okay you know and I just, I couldn't pay him to leave, he has always been there.

Another ethical aspect of disclosing their HIV/AIDS status was *how* to disclose:

It is not something that you can just tell somebody, you know, somebody that you are with 'cause you're going to feel like they're going to kick you off to the side. You know, like kicking you to the curb, you know, not wanting to be bothered. And, it is something that you can't really tell someone: 'Hey, I'm infected with HIV.' I mean it is a hard thing to deal with . . . it depends on the individual.

Although it was hard, these women told their partners in the best way they could; one woman said:

Well, it was right after I had my baby and before I got off the drugs and stopped drinking. I had got, I had already set myself up to tell him, but we'd never been, we hadn't had sex at all . . . because I was pregnant. So, I went and got me some beer and liquor. So I drank it and I drank a fifth, about ten cans of beer, because I wanted to be really, really, really drunk when I told him. And, so I said man, I told him, and it was like he just sat there, like I didn't tell him nothing at all. He really didn't take it too hard and I told him the next morning, well: 'If you want to leave you can leave, you know. I'll understand and everything. I love you . . . and everything'. We've been together ever since.

Besides the issue of disclosure to partners, there was the issue of disclosure to others with whom the participants had sex. Two women specifically stated that they sometimes divulged their diagnosis to sexual partners, but at other times chose not to. They felt no need to disclose if proper precautions were taken, although one woman took those precautions to protect herself:

> Some of them I tell that I got it [HIV/AIDS] and some of them I don't. But I'm not only protecting them, I'm protecting myself too from getting another sexually transmitted disease.

The other woman, however, took those precautions to protect her partner:

> 'Cause, my motto is: You are going to put on everything I tell you or we won't have sex. And if you ask me why I'm doing this and you're serious about this I will tell you. But if you don't ask me why, I won't as long as I know I'm protecting you.

The final disclosure issue for these women was the disclosure of their diagnosis to others, including family, friends and employers. Sometimes the women had a choice about whether to disclose or not:

> A guy that I worked with, that I really cared about, we had an affair and so I told him. I felt like, well I found out and my husband has to have it and this guy has to have it too; these are the only people I have been with.

Sometimes, however, the diagnosis was disclosed by others, against the women's wishes:

> He called my mother and told my mother that I have AIDs and it set my mother through such a shock she went through. Anyway when I called my mother and she told me that he said that I was, I was devastated, so I came over to her house and sat down and talked to her.

Perhaps one of the most important ethical issues these women faced was whether to disclose their positive HIV/AIDS status to their children. They struggled with this issue ('. . . it was just really hard for me to decide if I wanted, you know, to tell them, you know . . .'), and chose to deal with it in different ways. One woman said:

> I tell them that I have HIV and they know and I tell them don't tell everyone, don't discuss this with no one, but I want you two to know that.

In fact, this particular woman said:

> Right now today they are nine and eight, and I'll tell them. I tell them that I'm HIV and I tell them what condoms are, I tell them about AIDS, I try to get tapes. I want them to see them because I don't want them to grow up like that.

Another participant, however, chose not to inform her children:

> I don't want to tell my family what I have, because I don't want my family to tell them [her children] that I'm died of AIDS . . . because it's going to be really hard on them, something that they probably won't be able to accept.

DISCUSSION

[T]his was a particularly difficult area of ethical decision-making because the women did not have to make one decision: to disclose or not to disclose. Rather, they had to make multiple decisions about whether to disclose to this person, or that group, or this employer. Also, when deciding about disclosure, they seemed very cognizant of other people's feelings, needs and rights. This was different to, for example, issues of diagnosis, where the women made one definitive decision either to be tested or not. The decision to be tested, at least in an immediate sense, affected the woman only. After all, she might test negative, in which case the issue stopped with her; it was only after she tested positive that she had to begin to consider others and their need to know of her diagnosis. She then moved into the complex arena of disclosure decisions.

CONCLUSION

This study suggests that HIV-infected African-American women deal with many daily decisions regarding what is right or what ought to be done. As these women described their experiences, they expressed concern regarding diagnosis, disclosure, treatment of and by others, and pregnancies. Perhaps the most fundamental truth of their experience, however, was the conviction that HIV/AIDS, itself, is 'not fair': 'It's [HIV/AIDS] not fair to the kids that are being born; it's not fair to the people who get it; it's not fair to the people who have it.'

Further research must be conducted regarding this most 'unfair' disease, and the ethical issues that its African-American female victims deal with on a daily basis.

References

1. Davis A, Aroskar M. *Ethical dilemmas and nursing practice.* Norwalk, CT: Appleton and Lange, 1991.

2. Alexander R, Fitzpatrick J. Variables influencing nurses' attitudes toward AIDS and AIDS patients. *AIDS Patient Care* 1991; **5**: 315–20.

3. Chubon SJ. Ethical dilemmas encountered by home care nurses. *Home Healthcare Nurse* 1994; **12**(5): 12–17.

4. Forrester DA, Murphy PA. Nurses' attitudes toward patients with AIDS and AIDS-related risk factors. *J Adv Nurs* 1992; **17**: 1260–66.

5. Jemmott JB, Freleicher J, Jemmott LS. Perceived risk of infection and attitudes toward risk groups: determinants of nurses' behavioral intentions regarding AIDS patients. *Res Nurs Health* 1992; **15**: 295–301.

6. Martin DA. Effects of ethical dilemmas on stress felt by nurses providing care to AIDS patients. *Crit Care Nurs Q* 1990; **12**(4): 53–62.

7. Murphy JM, Famolare NE. Caring for pediatric patients with HIV: personal concerns and ethical dilemmas. *Pediatr Nurs* 1994; **20**: 171–76.

8. Prince NA, Beard BJ, Ivey SL, Lester L. Perinatal nurses' knowledge and attitudes about AIDS. *J Obstet Gynecol Neonatal Nurs* 1989; *18:* 363–69.

9. Scherer YK, Haughey BP. Nurses' experiences in caring for patients with AIDS in Erie County. *J NY State Nurs Assoc* 1988; **19** (2): 4–8.

10. Scherer YK, Haughey BP, Wu YB. AIDS: what are nurses' concerns? *Clin Nurse Specialist* 1989; **3** (1): 48–54.

11. Scherer YK, Haughey BP, Wu YB, Kuhn MM. AIDS: what are critical care nurses' concerns? *Critical Care Nurse* 1992; **12** (7): 23–29.

12. Scherer YK, Haughey BP, Wu YB, Miller CM. A longitudinal study of nurses' attitudes toward caring for patients with AIDS in Erie County. *J NY State Nurs Assoc* 1992; **23** (3): 10–15.

13. Scherer YK, Wu YB, Haughey BP. AIDS and homophobia among nurses. *J Homosex* 1991; **21** (4): 17–27.

14. van Servellen GM, Lewis CE, Leake B. Nurses' responses to the AIDS crisis: implications for continuing education programs. *J Continuing Educ Nurs* 1988; **19** (1): 4–8.

15. Webb AA, Bunting S. Ethical decision making by nurses in HIV/AIDS situations. *J Assoc Nurses AIDS Care* 1992; **3** (2): 15–18.

16. Giorgi A, Fischer C, Murray E eds. *Duquesne studies in phenomenological psychology.* Pittsburgh, PA: Duquesne University Press, 1975.

Influence of Physician Confidentiality Assurances on Adolescents' Willingness to Disclose Information and Seek Future Health Care

A Randomized Controlled Trial

*Carol A. Ford, Susan G. Millstein,
Bonnie L. Halpern-Felsher,
and Charles E. Irwin Jr.*

Adolescent patients must seek health care and communicate with physicians regarding sexual behaviors, substance use, and mental health if physicians are to address the major causes of adolescent morbidity and mortality.[1-5] However, adolescents report that concerns about privacy in clinical settings decrease their willingness to seek health care for sensitive health problems[6-8] and may inhibit their communication with physicians.[9] Thus, adolescents may not receive needed health care because of their concerns about confidentiality.

Provision of confidential care to adolescents regarding sexuality, substance use, and mental health issues is supported by professional organization recommendations and legal statutes in many states.[10-12] Professional organizations recommend that physicians discuss confidentiality with adolescent patients and include in these discussions a description of the conditions under which confidentiality must be limited.[11] However, many physicians do not discuss confidentiality with adolescents,[7,13,14] and those physicians who do convey varying messages; 36% who discuss confidentiality with adolescents assure conditional confidentiality, while 64% assure unconditional confidentiality.[14]

This study tests the influence of physician assurances of confidentiality on adolescents' concerns about confidentiality. The following 2 hypotheses were tested: (1) Adolescents who receive an assurance of confidentiality from a physician will be more willing to disclose general information, more willing to disclose sensitive information, more willing to report truthfully, and more likely to consider a return visit than adolescents who are not assured of confidentiality. (2) Adolescents who receive an unconditional assurance of confidentiality will be more willing to disclose general information, more willing to disclose sensitive information, more willing to report truthfully, and more likely to consider a return visit than adolescents who receive a conditional assurance of confidentiality.

METHODS

Study Population

A school-based sample and simulated depictions of clinic visits were used rather than a clinic-based population to include adolescents who might not present to a clinic setting because of confidentiality concerns.[15] The general enrollment of the students in the 3 suburban public high schools in the San Francisco Bay Area participating in this study was 52% male and predominantly white (84% white, 5% Asian, 4% African American, 5% Hispanic, and 2% other); the average daily nonattendance rate was 11.5%. All 679 students enrolled in mandatory "Social Issues" classes were invited to participate in this study, which was described as a study "to learn how teenagers and adults can communicate better."

Parental consent and student assent were obtained according to guidelines approved by the University of California at San Francisco Committee on Human Research and the participating school district administration.

Procedures

This study was conducted in classrooms during the 1994–1995 academic year. All participating adolescents randomly selected an audiotape player containing 1 of 3 taped scenarios. Each scenario was presented by an adolescent narrator and a physician reading a script that was identical except for the experimental manipulation. The narrator invited the adolescent to imagine meeting the physician whose voice was on the tape for a routine medical office visit. After inquiring about routine medical history, the physician explained that the next questions would be about sensitive topics; this explanation was modeled after an example of a transition statement recently published by the American Medical Association.[16] The transition statement contained the experimental manipulation, which was the presence or absence of an assurance of confidentiality and a variation in the content of the confidentiality assurance. In the unconditional confidentiality group, the physician stated, "I want you to understand that when we talk about things that have to do with sex and drugs and your feelings, that it is confidential.

This means that what we talk about is just between you and me and that other people, including your parents, will not find out about it unless you want them to know." In the conditional confidentiality group the physician delivered the identical statement heard by the unconditional confidentiality group, followed by, "One exception to this is if I am concerned someone has abused or hurt you. Another exception is if I am concerned you are planning to commit suicide. In these situations I would have to talk to other adults, but I would talk to you first so we could figure out the best way to handle it." Confidentiality was not mentioned by the physician in the scenario heard by the control group.

The adolescents then turned off the tape and completed an anonymous written questionnaire reporting their willingness to disclose information to the physician depicted in the scenario regarding general issues, sexuality, substance use, and mental health concerns. In addition, students were asked about their willingness to seek future health care from the physician depicted in the scenario for routine and sensitive issues.

Preparation of Audiotape Scenario

The scenario script was written by a panel of clinicians and revised after pilot testing with 31 adolescent reviewers. The voices of the physician in the taped scenarios were selected after pilot testing of 2 female and 2 male clinician voices with similar styles of verbal delivery. A total of 13 male and 12 female adolescents listened to paired recordings of male or female clinicians reading identical scripts and rated their perception of each physician on 13 semantic differential scales describing qualities such as listening skills, caring, and honesty. The male and female voices rated most similar by comparison of scale means were selected for the final taping.

The 2 selected clinicians created final tapes by recording the full script, which contained the text for an unconditional confidentiality assurance followed by the text explaining the conditions under which confidentiality must be limited. The full script was used as the tape for the conditional confidentiality group. Tapes for the unconditional confidentiality group and the control group were created by selectively removing taped sequences, thus assuring otherwise identical tapes.

Because of concerns that physician sex might influence willingness to disclose information and return for visits, 51% of adolescents listened to a same-sex physician and 49% listened to an opposite-sex physician.

Masking

Tape players were number coded to represent the experimental manipulation and sex of the physician represented on the tape secured inside. The coding scheme was concealed from the researchers who distributed and collected tape players by placement in a locked drawer.

Assignment

The adolescents selected tape players from sex-specific boxes that contained equal numbers of randomly distributed tapes representing all experimental conditions with a female or male physician. To avoid repeated patterns of tape distribution, researchers randomly redistributed tape players within sex-specific boxes before each distribution. To detect potential problems with adolescents exchanging tapes, each tape player was opened to verify that it contained a tape with a matching number code at the end of every 3 classroom collection periods; no tape exchanges were identified.

Measures

Sociodemographic Variables.—The sociodemographic variables measured for the participating adolescents included sex, age, and race/ethnicity. Their socioeconomic status (SES) was assessed by the proxy measure of level of maternal education.

Past Experiences.—Adolescents were asked their frequency of physician visits during the past 2 years, time of last routine physical examination, whether specific risk-assessment questions were asked during their last visit for a routine physical examination, and the truthfulness of their responses. They were also asked if, since becoming a teenager, they had ever not seen a physician about a problem because they were worried that their parents might find out, and whether a physician had ever talked to their parents without their permission about things they had wanted to keep private.

General Disclosure.—The Miller Self-Disclosure Index[17] was modified to measure adolescents' willingness to disclose general information to the physician in the scenario. This 10-item scale was introduced by the question, "If this doctor asked about the following topics, would you be willing to discuss them?" Examples of items included "my personal habits," "what is most important to me in life," and "my close relationships with other people." Responses were recorded on a 4-point Likert-type scale ranging from 1 (no, not at all) to 4 (I would discuss completely and fully); Cronbach α was .89.

Disclosure of Sensitive Information.—A 10-item scale was developed to measure willingness to disclose information about the sensitive topics of sexuality, substance use, and mental health and was introduced by the question, "Imagine you were facing the situations listed below and that they came up while this doctor was talking to you. Would you be willing to discuss them?" The items addressing sexuality included sexual decision making, refusal skills, strategies for influencing partners reluctant to use condoms, and issues related to sexual orientation. The items addressing substance use included refusal skills and concerns about excessive alcohol use. The items addressing mental health included deterioration in academic performance, feelings of sadness, and suicidal ideation. Responses were recorded on a 4-point Likert-type scale ranging from 1 (no, not at all) to 4 (I would discuss completely and fully); Cronbach α was .92.

Honesty.—An 11-item scale was developed to measure adolescents' perceptions about how truthful their responses would be to questions that might be asked by the physician in the scenario and was introduced by the question, "Imagine you were experiencing the things listed below and this doctor asked you these questions. How truthfully do you think you would answer?" Examples of the items included "if I had ever had sex," "if I had smoked cigarettes in the past 3 months," and "if I had thoughts of suicide." Responses were recorded on a 4-point Likert-type scale ranging from 1 (I would definitely tell the truth) to 4 (I would definitely not tell the truth); Cronbach α was .90.

Likelihood of Future Visits.—An 8-item scale was developed to assess adolescents' willingness to seek health care from the physician represented in the scenario and was introduced by the question, "Would you want to see this doctor again if you had the following problems?" The items assessing likelihood of a return visit for nonsensitive issues included "if you needed a routine physical" and "if you had a bad cough and fever." Items assessing likelihood of returning for general sensitive issues were "if you had some very private concerns" and "if you needed help with a difficult problem." Items assessing likelihood of a return visit for specific sensitive issues included "if you had a problem you thought was related to sex," "if you were smoking cigarettes and wanted to stop," "if you had a problem related to alcohol," and "if you were thinking of ending your life." Responses were recorded on a 4-point Likert-type scale ranging from 1 (definitely) to 4 (definitely not); Cronbach α was .87.

Statistical Analyses

Statistical analyses were performed using SPSS for Windows Release 6.1 (SPSS Inc, Chicago, Ill). The effects of sociodemographic factors on willingness to disclose general information, willingness to disclose information about sensitive topics, intended honesty, and likelihood of return visits were tested using analysis of variance and linear regression. Sociodemographic factors found to be significantly related to outcome variables were controlled using hierarchical multiple linear regression when examining the effects of confidentiality assurances and content of confidentiality assurances on outcome variables. All statistical significance reporting is based on 2-sided hypotheses testing using linear regression analyses with an α of .05. For ease of reporting, all scales were dichotomized (at 2.5), and logistic regression analyses were performed to determine probabilities. Our achieved sample size (562) provides 95% power, with a 2-tailed α of .05, to detect a standardized effect size of 0.4 (between-group differences of 0.3 on a 4-point Likert-type scale with an estimated SD of 0.75).[18]

RESULTS

Of 679 students enrolled in mandatory "Social Issues" classes, 615 were present on the day of data collection. Of students present, a total of 47 were excluded from participation before randomization for reasons including lack of parental consent (n=32), lack of student assent (n=11), illegible group identification number (n=1), and student disability that prevented participation (n=3). Of the remaining 568 students randomized to 3 groups, 5 were excluded from the study because they did not identify their sex (1 from the control group, 3 from the unconditional assurance group, and 1 from the conditional assurance group), and 1 was excluded because of excessive missing data on questionnaires (from the conditional assurance group). The final sample of 562 adolescents represented 92% of students present on the date of data collection (Figure).

The mean age of participating adolescents was 14.9 years (SD=0.82); 348 (62%) were in grade 9, 180 (32%) in grade 10, and 34 (6%) in grade 11. The sample was predominately white (77% white, 4% Asian, 3% African American, 4% Hispanic, and 11% other) and middle to high SES. Most (62%) had seen a physician for a routine examination within the preceding year, and 97% had visited a physician at least once in the preceding 2 years. No significant differences were found in the sociodemographic variables and past experiences among the 3 experimental groups. As expected, statistically significant differences were found between experimental groups on items assessing adolescents' description of confidentiality assurances heard on the tape (Table 1).

Ninety-six adolescents (17%) reported that they had forgone health care in the past because of concerns that their parents would find out. Of the 540 adolescents who responded to questions about their last routine visit, 41% reported that they were asked if they had sex, 16% if they needed condoms, 41% if they smoked cigarettes, 33% if they drank alcohol, 25% if they had feelings of depression, and 15% if they had thoughts of suicide. Of adolescents who were asked these specific risk-assessment questions, the proportions

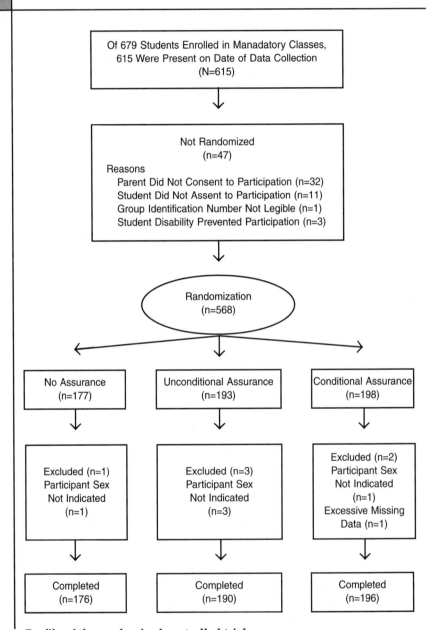

Profile of the randomized controlled trial.

TABLE 1 Adolescents' Sociodemographic Characteristics and Description of Audiotape by Confidentiality Assurance Group*

Variables	No Assurance	Unconditional Assurance	Conditional Assurance	Total
	Sociodemographic Characteristics			
Male sex, No. (%)	82/176 (46.6)	100/190 (52.6)	108/196 (55.1)	290/562 (51.6)
Age, mean±SD, y	14.8 (0.79)	15.0 (0.83)	14.9 (0.83)	14.9 (0.82)
Race/ethnicity, No. (%) white	135/171 (78.9)	139/186 (74.7)	149/192 (77.6)	423/549 (77.0)
Socioeconomic status, No. (%) of mothers with a high school education	165/173 (95.4)	180/188 (95.7)	181/190 (95.3)	526/551 (95.5)
Routine examination within past year, No. (%)	99/170 (58.2)	118/187 (63.1)	125/193 (64.8)	342/550 (62.2)
Physician visit in past 2 years, No. (%)	166/171 (97.1)	180/187 (96.3)	189/193 (97.9)	535/551 (97.1)
	Description of Audiotape			
Same-sex physician, No. (%)	93/176 (52.8)	90/190 (47.4)	104/196 (53.1)	287/562 (51.1)
Questions asked, No. (%) yes				
"Did this doctor talk to you about confidentiality?"	54/176 (30.7)†	153/190 (80.5)	163/194 (84.0)	...
"Did this doctor mention times when they could not keep things confidential?"	16/175 (9.1)	11/190 (5.8)	152/194 (78.4)‡	...

* Denominators may vary because of missing data.
† Significant difference between adolescents not assured of confidentiality and participants assured of confidentiality by x^2 analyses ($P<.001$).
‡ Significant difference between adolescents assured of conditional confidentiality and other experimental groups by x^2 analyses ($P<.001$).

who reported 100% truthfulness in their responses were as follows: 78% for having sex, 67% for needing condoms, 59% for smoking cigarettes, 48% for drinking alcohol, 36% for feelings of depression, and 63% for thoughts of suicide. Seven percent of adolescents reported that, since becoming a teenager, a physician had talked to their parents without their permission about things they had wanted to keep private.

Influence of Sociodemographic Variables on Disclosure and Future Visits

Listening to the female physician was associated with increased willingness to disclose general information . . . for both male and female adolescents. Therefore, physician sex was controlled for in all hypothesis-testing analyses in order to assess the unique effect of confidentiality assurances on the outcome variables, above and beyond the effects of the sex of the physician.

There were no statistically significant interactions between the sex of the physician and the adolescent's sex. However, a trend was noted within each experimental group such that similar proportions of male and female adolescents were willing to disclose sensitive information and return for future visits when a same-sex physician was depicted on the tape; listening to an opposite-sex physician decreased the proportion of female adolescents but increased the proportion of male adolescents willing to disclose and return (Table 2).

Adolescents with higher SES reported more willingness to disclose general information when compared with adolescents of lower SES. . . ; therefore, SES was also controlled for in analyses testing the influence of confidentiality assurances on general disclosure. Adolescents' sex, age, race/ethnicity, and school did not affect outcome variables and were not included in subsequent analyses.

Influence of Confidentiality Assurances on Disclosure and Future Visits

After controlling for physician sex, assurances of confidentiality significantly influenced adolescents' willingness to disclose sensitive information. An average of 46.5% of the adolescents assured of confidentiality reported willingness to disclose sensitive information regarding sexuality, substance use, and mental health, compared with 39% of adolescents who were not assured of confidentiality. No differences were found between the unconditional and conditional confidentiality groups in willingness to disclose sensitive information (Table 3).

Confidentiality assurances also influenced the likelihood of future visits. An average of 67% of adolescents who were assured of confidentiality by

TABLE 2   **Percentage of Adolescents Willing to Disclose Sensitive Information and Return for Future Visits by Confidentiality Assurance Group, Sex, and Physician Sex***

PERCENTAGE WILLING TO DISCLOSE SENSITIVE INFORMATION						
PHYSICIAN SEX	No Assurance, % (n=175)		Conditional Assurance,% (n=194)		Unconditional Assurance, % (n=189)	
	Female	Male	Female	Male	Female	Male
Female physician[†]	40	47	44	51	49	57
Male physician	32	39	36	43	41	48

PERCENTAGE WILLING TO RETURN FOR FUTURE VISIT						
	No Assurance, % (n=175)		Conditional Assurance,% (n=196)		Unconditional Assurance, % (n=190)	
	Female	Male	Female	Male	Female	Male
Female physician[‡]	56	62	64	70	75	79
Male physician	43	49	52	58	64	69

* No statistically significant interactions between physician and adolescent sex by linear regression analysis. Percentages were derived by logistic regression analysis that did not include interaction terms.

[†] Male and female adolescents report increased willingness to disclose sensitive information to a female physician by analysis of variance (F=4.95 [df=1, 556], P=.03).

[‡] Male and female adolescents report increased willingness to return for a future visit to a female physician by analysis of variance (F=10.95 [df=1, 559], P=.001).

a physician reported that they were willing to return to see that physician in the future, compared with 53% of adolescents who heard no mention of confidentiality. When comparing unconditional and conditional groups, assurances of unconditional confidentiality increased the number of adolescents willing to return for a future visit by 10 percentage points, from 62% (122/196) to 72% (Table 3).

Confidentiality assurances did not influence willingness to disclose general information or intended honesty.

Of concern, as noted in Table 1, some adolescents did not accurately recall the experimental manipulation. To determine the impact of adolescents who misidentified their experimental group, repeat hypothesis testing was performed with the subsample of adolescents who reported accurate group identification. In these analyses, confidentiality assurances were found to increase willingness to disclose general information, and the effects of

TABLE 3   Percentage of Adolescents Willing to Disclose and Return
for Future Visits by Confidentiality Assurance Group*

Outcome Variable	No Assurance, No. (%)	Conditional Assurance, No. (%)	Unconditional Assurance, No. (%)
General disclosure[†]	92/176 (52)	118/196 (60)	114/190 (60)
Disclosure of sensitive information	68/175 (39)[‡]	85/194 (44)	93/189 (49)
Honesty	105/175 (60)	121/195 (62)	135/190 (71)
Future visits	93/175 (53)[§]	122/196 (62)[||]	137/190 (72)

    * All percentages adjusted to control for influence of physician sex.
    † Adjusted to control for influence of adolescent's socioeconomic status.
    ‡ Significant difference between adolescents not assured of confidentiality
and adolescents assured of confidentiality by linear regression analyses (β=.10,
P=.02).
    § Significant difference between adolescents not assured of confidentiality
and adolescents assured of confidentiality by linear regression analyses (β=17,
P<.001).
    || Significant difference between adolescents assured of conditional
confidentiality and adolescents assured of unconditional confidentiality by linear
regression analyses (b=.14, P=.001).

confidentiality assurances on willingness to disclose sensitive information
and seek future health care were stronger than those found in analyses with
the entire sample.

COMMENT

Adolescents may communicate less with physicians or even forgo health care
because of concerns about confidentiality,[6–9] resulting in lost opportunities to
receive needed health care. This study shows that assurances of confidentiality by physicians decrease the chance that confidentiality concerns will act as
a barrier to adolescents' receiving health care. Physician confidentiality assurances increase adolescents' willingness to discuss sensitive topics related to
sexuality, substance use, and mental health and increase adolescents' willingness to return for future health care.

    Several points highlight the potential clinical significance of these find-
ings. First, in this study the effects of confidentiality assurances on willingness
to disclose and seek future health care were produced by 2 or 5 sentences
about confidentiality in verbally simulated scenarios. In clinical practice, multiple nonverbal cues could enhance the effect of confidentiality assurances.
Second, this study shows that physicians are more likely to receive thorough
risk-assessment information if they discuss confidentiality with adolescent

patients. This is an important goal since many adolescents reported that in real life they are not openly communicating with physicians who ask standard risk-assessment questions recommended by the American Medical Association, Maternal and Child Health Bureau, US Preventive Services Task Force, and American Academy of Pediatrics as a strategy to better address health issues associated with major causes of adolescent morbidity and mortality.[1-4] Third, concerns about confidentiality prevent many adolescents from seeking health care, as illustrated by our finding that 17% of adolescents had forgone health care in the past at least in part because of privacy concerns. Consistently discussing confidentiality with all adolescent patients may substantially decrease the number of adolescents who forgo health care because of confidentiality concerns. Finally, we do not know the personal behaviors or mental health issues of adolescents most influenced by concerns about confidentiality. If adolescents with higher risks of health problems become more likely to disclose sensitive information and seek future health care from physicians who discuss confidentiality, the clinical importance of our findings would be magnified. This is an important area for future investigation.

Clinicians who discuss confidentiality with adolescents must choose whether they mention the limitations of confidentiality. Although professional organizations recommend that physicians discuss conditional confidentiality,[11,19] most physicians who discuss confidentiality with adolescents assure unconditional confidentiality.[14] Physicians may be reluctant to mention the limitations of confidentiality because of concerns about negative impacts on the patient-physician relationship. When comparing conditional with unconditional confidentiality assurance groups in this study, no significant differences were found in adolescents' willingness to disclose information. However, adolescents assured of unconditional confidentiality were more willing to return for routine health needs than adolescents assured of conditional confidentiality, suggesting that adolescents who learn that there are exceptions to a guarantee of confidentiality may not discriminate between health concerns routinely addressed confidentially and issues that cannot be managed confidentially (such as suicidal ideation or abuse). Future investigation is needed to clarify and minimize potential negative impacts of including a description of the legal limitations of confidentiality in discussions about the privacy of patient-physician relationships.

This report presents the results of hypothesis testing using the entire sample, which includes adolescents who did not accurately recall the experimental manipulation. Although more conservative than results obtained during a separate analysis using only participants who accurately recalled the experimental manipulation, these results are more ecologically valid; in real life some adolescents may not accurately recall a physician's discussion of confidentiality. However, inaccurate recall of the experimental manipulation is interesting. No tape exchanges were identified during frequent systematic checks, making undetected switches in group assignment unlikely. Some adolescents reported hearing messages not presented on the tape. For example, 30.7% of adolescents in the control group inaccurately responded yes to the following question placed near the end of the questionnaire: "Did this doctor talk to you about confidentiality?" Potential explanations include some adolescents not being able to distinguish between information conveyed by the simulated physician on the tape and real physicians in the past, not understanding the question, and misinterpreting something on the tape as a physician addressing the issue of confidentiality (eg, misinterpreting either the narrator explaining that the questionnaire was anonymous or a portion of the physician script that was not the experimental manipulation). Other adolescents did not recall a message that was presented on the tape. One potential explanation for this lack of recall is that the adolescents were not listening to the tape. Other possible explanations include that the adolescents were listening and heard the manipulation but either did not consciously remember hearing the message when queried or did not interpret the message as "about confidentiality"; in these situations, it would be possible for confidentiality assurances to influence likelihood of disclosure and return visits despite the apparent lack of recall of the experimental manipulation.

This research was not designed to address the issue of the sex of the physician and disclosure or return visits. By controlling for the sex of the physician, we have shown that adolescents were more willing to communicate with and seek future health care from both male and female physicians who discuss confidentiality. Yet, 2 findings related to sex are of note. First, the influence of the sex of the physician on reported willingness to disclose and likelihood of future visits we found cannot be explained by differing nonverbal communication, dialogue, or time spent talking with the adolescent, though it is possible that the male and female voices in our scenarios differed in characteristics other than sex. Second, we noted clinically interesting interactions between the sex of the physician and that of the adolescent. However, further investigation is needed before conclusions can be made about the effects of the sex of physicians on adolescents' willingness to disclose information and seek health care.

Several potential limitations of this study should be noted. The extent to which the adolescents' responses to simulated scenarios and their reported willingness to disclose and return for visits would be reflected in real-life situations is unknown. Although adolescents' reported intentions are at least partially predictive of their behaviors,[20] adolescents experiencing a routine health problem or crisis may respond differently than they had anticipated when imagining the same situation. The generalizability of our findings is unknown because our participants were in school, predominately white, and of middle to high SES. Finally, although these are not likely to be major limitations because of random assignment to experimental groups, we did not do the following: the adolescents' personal behaviors were not assessed because of restrictions imposed by the school setting, and the influence on our outcome variables of past confidentiality discussions with actual physicians could not be assessed because the adolescents were queried about their past experiences talking to physicians after they had listened to the audiotape (and may not have been able to distinguish between the simulation and real past physician interactions when responding).

Despite these potential limitations, we believe our findings indicate that even brief discussions of confidentiality increase adolescents' willingness to discuss issues related to sexuality, substance use, and mental health and to seek future health care. Thus, strategies need to be identified to increase the number of physicians who routinely discuss confidentiality with adolescent patients. Furthermore, future investigation is needed to identify ways of discussing the limitations of confidentiality that minimize potential negative effects on adolescents' seeking care in the future for routine and nonreportable sensitive health concerns.

References

1. American Medical Association. *AMA Guidelines for Adolescent Preventive Services (GAPS): Recommendations and Rationale.* Baltimore, Md: Williams & Wilkins; 1994.

2. Green M, ed. *Bright Futures: Guidelines for Health Supervision of Infants, Children, and Adolescents.* Arlington, Va: National Center for Education in Maternal and Child Health; 1994.

3. US Preventive Services Task Force. *Guide to Clinical Preventive Services.* 2nd ed. Baltimore, Md: Williams & Wilkins; 1996.

4. American Academy of Pediatrics. *Guidelines for Health Supervision III.* Elk Grove Village, Ill: American Academy of Pediatrics; 1997.

5. Ozer E, Brindis CD, Millstein SG, Knopf DK, Irwin CE. *America's Adolescents: Are They Healthy?* San Francisco: University of California, San Francisco, National Adolescent Health Information Center, 1997.

6. Marks A, Malizio J, Hoch J, Brody R, Fisher M. Assessment of health needs and willingness to utilize health care resources of adolescents in a suburban population. *J Pediatr.* 1983;102:456–460.

7. Cheng TL, Savageau JA, Sattler AL, DeWitt TG. Confidentiality in health care: a survey of knowledge, perceptions, and attitudes among high school students. *JAMA.* 1993;269:1404–1407.

8. Chamie M, Eisman S, Forrest JD, Orr MT, Torres A. Factors affecting adolescents' use of family planning clinics. *Fam Plann Perspect.* 1982;14:126–139.

This research was supported in part by a grant from the Maternal and Child Health Bureau (MCJ000978) and the Norman Schlossberger Memorial Fund, San Francisco, Calif.

The authors gratefully acknowledge David Bell, MD, Jeanette Broering, RN, MS, MPH, Saul Kanowitz, MPH, Scot Lappa, MD, Anna-Barbara Moscicki, MD, Gian Oddone, Keith Pirl, MD, Joseph Rudek, PhD, and Jeanne Tschann, PhD, for their contributions to this project and Art Evans, MD, MPH, for his helpful review of the manuscript. The authors would like to express sincere appreciation to Diane C. Kirkpatrick and the administration, parents, teachers, and students of Tamalpais Union High School District, Marin County, California, for their support and participation in this project. Technical assistance was provided by Roy Rodriguez, Dulce Mohler, and Ming Lau.

9. Malus M, LaChance PA, Lamy L, Macaulay A, Vanasse M. Priorities in adolescent health care: the teenager's viewpoint. *J Fam Pract.* 1987;25:159–162.

10. English A, Matthews M, Extavour K, Palamountain C, Yang J. *State Minor Consent Statutes: A Summary.* Cincinnati, Ohio: Center for Continuing Education in Adolescent Health; April 1995.

11. Gans JE. *Policy Compendium on Confidential Health Services for Adolescents.* Chicago, Ill: American Medical Association; January 1993.

12. Council on Scientific Affairs, American Medical Association. Confidential health services for adolescents. *JAMA.* 1993;269:1420–1424.

13. Purcell JS, Hergenroder AC, Kozinetz C, et al. Interviewing techniques with adolescents in primary care. *J Adolesc Health.* 1997;20:300–305.

14. Ford CA, Millstein SG. Delivery of confidentiality assurances to adolescents by primary care physicians. *Arch Pediatr Adolesc Med.* 1997;151:505–509.

15. Zabin LS, Stark HA, Emerson MR. Reasons for delay in contraceptive clinic utilization: adolescent clinic and nonclinic populations compared. *J Adolesc Health.* 1991;12:225–232.

16. Levenberg PB, Elster AB. *Guidelines for Adolescent Preventive Services (GAPS): Implementation and Resource Manual.* Chicago, Ill: American Medical Association, Dept of Adolescent Health; 1995.

17. Miller LC, Berg JH, Archer RL. Openers: individuals who elicit intimate self-disclosure. *J Pers Soc Psychol.* 1983;44:1234–1244.

18. Hulley SB, Cummings SR. *Designing Clinical Research.* Baltimore, Md: Williams & Wilkins; 1988.

19. English A. Treating adolescents: legal and ethical considerations. In: Farrow JA, ed. *The Medical Clinics of North America.* Philadelphia, Pa: WB Saunders Co; 1990:1097–1112.

20. Adler NE, Kegeles SM, Irwin CE Jr, Wibbelsman C. Adolescent contraceptive behavior: an assessment of decision processes. *J Pediatr.* 1990;116:463–471.

Patient Data, Confidentiality, and Electronics

Identifiable data should no longer be freely available within the NHS [Editorial]

"Banks access computer records, foreclose on cancer patients."[1] This emotive headline from America in 1993 demonstrated the risks to confidentiality posed by electronic patient records—which are easy to inspect, copy, and transmit without anyone knowing. In Britain, attempts by the medical profession to ensure that such headlines should never be seen here led to fundamental disagreements with the Department of Health. These in turn stalled the already slow development of electronic data handling in the NHS. Only now, with the publication in December of the Caldicott report, is a way forward beginning to emerge.

Shortly after this American headline, the BMA and the Department of Health first discussed confidentiality within the NHS information strategy. The Department of Health (and the NHS Executive) believed all electronically held clinical data should be shared through "the wider NHS family" to facilitate NHS management,[2] but the wider family turned out to be almost anyone in contract with or relating to the NHS, whether clinically involved or not. The BMA felt that patient confidentiality would be so threatened that the only ethical solution was to keep all identifiable clinical data within the clinical domain.[3]

After failing to reach any agreement for several years, the two sides last year agreed to the setting up of a review of the problem of identifiable patient information within NHS information systems under the chairmanship of Dame Fiona Caldicott.[4] The aim was to study flows of identifiable patient data in NHS business to decide whether the inclusion of identifiers was justified and what action could be taken to minimise potential breaches of confidentiality.

Given that the NHS Executive believes that authorised insiders misusing their position represent the most serious threat to confidentiality, it was particularly appropriate that the executive should undertake this review. As an NHS Executive review studying NHS procedures in the light of rules set down by the executive,[2] it is no surprise that all the business flows studied, such as general practitioners' family planning claims and extracontractual referrals, were deemed justified in containing patient identifiers. Nevertheless, the report went on to develop principles of confidentiality and build recommendations on these principles about how the NHS should handle electronically held patient data. These are to apply across the administrative and clinical arms of the NHS and are the start of a continuing process.

The better parts of the report state good practice for NHS electronic health records for the first time; the bad bits will require further negotiation to bring the recommendations back in line with the principles. A particular problem is the idea that the NHS number will act as a "de-identifying" variable in patient data (thereby supposedly enhancing protection of the data). In a computerised NHS, however, the NHS number is actually a better identifier than the patient's name and address. To solve this problem, pilot studies are under way to look at controlling access to the NHS number, and hence clinical records, in active NHS use. Nevertheless, and despite these real problems, the most valuable feature of the report is its promotion of a culture change within the NHS administrative machine. The report insists (and in accepting the report the NHS Executive has accepted) that identified data are no longer freely available for all to see within the NHS.

What does this mean for clinicians? Work—and thought. It is no longer enough to say that data privacy is somebody else's problem, because clinicians are ultimately responsible for the safety of the patient data they commit to electronic transfer or storage.[5] This responsibility is wide and poorly understood. In the same way as paper records require proper care, so must clinical computer systems store data safely, and transmit data only to other appropriate safe havens, usually clinical ones. If clinicians cannot ensure that, they must see that the data have their identifiers removed before being committed to electronic media. This concept is new for many clinicians, and, while relatively easy in general practice, is a problem for most hospitals, which have traditionally been relaxed about care of patient data. This concept poses particular questions about research databases and registers, and the data guardians proposed by Caldicott to effect and enforce the report's principles will require considerable support, education, and training for their role (which the NHS Executive has agreed to finance).

Another American newspaper article recounts how a patient made the reasonable request that his electronic data should be identifiable only on the ward computer terminal.[6] This apparently simple request created enormous problems for the hospital computer system because confidentiality had not been designed in from the start. The risk exists that the same thing could happen in Britain if the residue of the internal market makes clinicians and administrators feel justified in breaking patient confidentiality. Given the advice of the BMA,[3] the Caldicott report, and adequate money now delivered for protecting confidentiality, there is no longer any excuse for either the executive or clinicians to fail to protect patient data adequately.

A peripheral issue the Caldicott report brings in its train is whether the NHSnet confers confidentiality, for the two are often confused. The NHSnet is the developing NHS intranet for exchanging business and clinical electronic messages, and many had hoped it would solve the confidentiality problem for patient data. Unfortunately it does not, being only a set of dedicated telephone wires. Safe carriers are helpful but not an answer, for the risk to patient data is not in transit, but at workstations throughout the NHS where the data are used.

The final question for confidentiality is how the NHS Executive will ensure that it gains informed consent from patients to use their data, a task the Caldicott review declined to tackle. The true sign of how seriously confidentiality is regarded by the NHS will be the action the executive takes to make informed consent the gold standard for handling patient identifiable data.

GRANT KELLY
*Chair, Joint Computing Group of the General Medical Services
Committee and Royal College of General Practitioners*

References

1. RMs need to safeguard computerised patient records to protect hospitals. *Hospital Risk Management* 1993 Sep:129–40.
2. NHS Executive. *The protection and use of patient information.* Leeds: NHS Executive, 1996.
3. Anderson RJ. *Security in clinical information systems.* London: BMA, 1996.
4. Department of Health. *Report on the review of patient identifiable information.* London: Department of Health, 1997. (Caldicott report.)
5. General Medical Council. *Confidentiality.* London: GMC, 1995.
6. Garfinkel S. Computers compromise privacy, cut cost of care. *Boston Globe* 1997:Jun 5.

III. INFORMED CONSENT.

Overview. Informed consent is related to autonomy. The assumption is that a patient provided with all pertinent information will be able to deliberate and determine a course of treatment. The physician in this model acts as a fact provider, and the patient considers various options and then makes a free and unforced choice.

This model is perhaps flawed. To be fully informed, a patient would have to be a physician in that specialty. Obviously, most people cannot fully understand all the relevant information about their conditions. They can get some narrow sense of what is at stake, but this information may easily be contextually misunderstood.

This does not give license for complete paternalism. But one must recognize that "informed" is relative to the capability of the patient. A physician who waters down an explanation to the patient's level is paternalistically making choices in the way he presents alternatives.

Obviously, the choice of what to present can be affected by the physician's personal attitudes. In such cases, the physician or health care professional may decide that because of their race, religion, or gender, certain patients may or may not be capable of understanding their conditions. As a result, the health care provider engages in a diagnosis-treatment discussion that may not engage the patient at the highest level she can comprehend.

The last aspect of informed consent concerns clinical testing. For too long, researchers have not fully disclosed all the known consequences that might befall a clinical test subject. From the Tuskeegee experiment to various tests involving chemical and biological agents, the history of informed consent in scientific research has not been good. We must determine how far we are willing to go to enforce strict standards.

In the following article, Julian Savulescu and Richard Momeyer argue that for consent to be informed, it must be rational. They continue Savulescu's earlier argument by contending that the physician should be more than just a fact provider but also must be a Socratic agent who flushes out false beliefs. Obviously, this action causes the physician to create a set of acceptable beliefs. The authors of this article use an example of a Jehovah's Witness to prove their point.

The next article presents a discussion about the *British Medical Journal's* internal policy about accepting articles that describe research in which the standard of informed consent has not been fully met. The discussion tries to determine the boundaries of privacy and how they interact with informed consent.

Ellen Agard, Daniel Finkelstein, and Edward Wallach present a case in which a woman's informed consent may be unduly influenced by her husband. Because the proposed operation will cause infertility, the hospital staff wants to be sure that "true" informed consent exists. The wild card is that this couple is from a culture in which the husband typically is allowed decision-making power over all the members of his household—including his wife! The issue is whether the hospital staff should determine the wife's true feelings and use those as the basis of informed consent or whether they should bend to the couple's cultural tradition and allow the husband to make the decision.

In the final article, Ronald Bayer takes an entirely different point of view and poses the question of whether the patient should be informed of a health care provider's status vis-à-vis HIV. If the health care provider is competent and poses no known risk to infect patients, does this health care provider owe patients the disclosure of his condition? If being HIV infected has no functional effect, what right does the patient have to know?

Should Informed Consent Be Based on Rational Beliefs?

Julian Savulescu and Richard W. Momeyer

I. INTRODUCTION

Medical ethics places great emphasis on physicians respecting patient autonomy. It encourages tolerance even towards harmful choices patients make on the basis of their own values. This ethic has been defended by consequentialists and deontologists.

Respect for autonomy finds expression in the doctrine of informed consent. According to that doctrine, no medical procedure may be performed upon a competent patient unless that patient has consented to have that procedure, after having been provided with the relevant facts.

We have no quarrel with these principles. We do, however, question their interpretation and application. Our contention is that being autonomous requires that a person hold rational beliefs. We distinguish between rational choice and rational belief. Being autonomous may not require that one's choices and actions are rational. But it does require that one's beliefs which ground those choices are rational. If this is right, what passes for respecting autonomy sometimes consists of little more than providing information, and stops short of assessing whether this information is rationally processed. Some of what purports to be medical deference to a patient's values is not this at all: rather, it is acquiescence to irrationality. Some of what passes for respecting patient autonomy may turn out to be less respect than abandonment. Abandonment of patients has never been regarded as a morally admirable practice.

We will outline three ways in which patients hold irrational beliefs: (1) ignorance, (2) not caring enough about rational deliberation, and (3) making mistakes in deliberation. We argue that it is the responsibility of physicians not only to provide relevant information (which addresses 1), but to improve the rationality of belief that grounds consent (2 and 3).

II. RATIONALITY AND AUTONOMY

II.I True Belief and Autonomy

The word, "autonomy", comes from the Greek: autos (self) and nomos (rule or law).[1] Autonomy is self-government or self-determination. Being autonomous involves freely and actively making one's own evaluative choices about how one's life should go.

It is a familiar idea that it is necessary to hold true beliefs if we are to get what we want. For example, John loves Northern Indian dishes and loathes Southern Indian dishes. Yet he is very confused about which dishes belong to which area. He consistently orders Southern Indian dishes thinking he is ordering Northern Indian dishes. His false beliefs cause him to fail to get what he wants.

However, true beliefs are important for evaluative choice in a more fundamental way: we cannot form an idea of *what* we want without knowing what the options on offer are *like*. Consider a person with gangrene of the foot. She is offered an amputation. In evaluating "having an amputation" she is attempting to evaluate a complete state of affairs: how much pain she will experience, whether she will be able to live by herself, visit her grandchildren, and so on. (Importantly, knowing the name of one's disease and the nature of the operation are less important facts.)

II.II True Belief and Practical Rationality

Practical rationality is concerned with what we have reason to care about and do. Let's distinguish between what there is good reason to do and what it is rational to do. Paul sits down after work to have a relaxing evening with his wife. She gives him a glass of what he believes is wine, but is in fact poison. There is a good reason for Paul not to drink it, even if this is not known to Paul. However, if he believes that it is wine, it is rational for him to drink it.[2] Thus:

> It is rational for a person to perform some act if there would be a good reason
> to perform that act if the facts were as he/she believes them to be.

Thus holding true beliefs is important in two ways: (1) it promotes our autonomy and (2) allows us to see that there is good reason to do. This does not collapse autonomous choice with rational choice. Even holding all the relevant true beliefs, a person may autonomously choose some course which he or she has no good reason to choose. For example, assume that the harms of smoking outweigh the benefits. Jim has good reason to give up smoking. However, he may choose to smoke knowing all the good and bad effects of smoking. His choice is then irrational but his beliefs may be rational and he may be autonomous. His choice is not an expression of his autonomy if he believes that smoking is not only pleasurable, but good for your health.

II.III Coming to Hold True Beliefs

One important way to hold true beliefs is via access to relevant information. For example, one way to get Paul to believe that the wine is poisoned is to provide him with evidence that it is poisoned.

We can never know for certain that our beliefs are true. We can only be confident of their truth. Confidence is the likelihood that a belief is true. Beliefs which are based on evidence (rational beliefs) are more likely to be true than unfounded (irrational) beliefs. The likelihood that our beliefs are true is a function both of how informed they are and of how we think about that information.

Theoretical rationality is concerned with what it is rational to believe.

> It is rational for a person to believe some proposition if he/she ought to believe
> that proposition if he/she were deliberating rationally about the evidence available and his/her present beliefs, and those beliefs are not themselves irrational.

Let's say that a person is "deliberating rationally" if[3]:

1. She holds a degree of belief in a proposition which is responsive to the evidence supporting that proposition. For example, the firmer the evidence, the greater the degree of belief ought to be.
2. She examines her beliefs for consistency. If she detects inconsistency, she ought appropriately to contract her set of beliefs or adjust her degree of belief in the relevantly inconsistent beliefs.
3. She exposes her reasoning to the norms of inductive and deductive logic. Valid logic is important because it helps us to have the broadest range of true beliefs.

Consider the following example. Peter is trying to decide whether to have an operation. Suppose that he is provided with certain information and reasons in the following way.

1. There is a risk of dying from anaesthesia. (true)
2. I will require an anaesthetic if I am to have this operation. (true)

Therefore, if I have this operation, I will probably die.

The conclusion does not follow from the premises. Peter comes to hold an irrational belief because he commits a logical error. Irrational beliefs are less likely to be true than rational beliefs. Since knowledge of truth is elusive for subjective beings like us, the best we can hope for is informed, rational belief.

If we are right that information is important to evaluative choice because of its contribution to a person holding the relevant true beliefs necessary for evaluation, then deliberating rationally is as important as being informed, since this also affects the likelihood that one's beliefs are true. Being fully autonomous requires not only that we are informed, but that we exercise our theoretical rationality.

III. An Example of Irrational Belief: Jehovah's Witnesses and Blood

Jehovah's Witnesses (JWs) who refuse life-saving blood transfusions for themselves are often taken to be paradigm cases of autonomous, informed choice based on different (non-medically shared) values that require respect and deference.

Jehovah's Witnessess refuse life-saving blood transfusions because they believe that if they die and have received blood, they will turn to dust. But if they refuse blood (and keep Jehovah's other laws) and die, they will enjoy eternal life in Paradise.[4]

Jehovah's Witnesses interpret *The Bible* as forbidding the sustaining of life with blood in any manner. They base this belief on passages such as:

> "Every creature that lives and moves shall be food for you . . . But you must not eat the flesh with the life, which is the blood, still in it".[5]

Anyone eating the blood of an animal would be "cut off" or executed.[6] The only legitimate use of animal blood was as a sacrifice to God. Leviticus 17: 11 states:

> ". . . the life of the creature is the blood, and I appoint it to make expiation on the altar for yourselves: it is the blood, that is the life, that makes expiation".[7]

Jehovah's Witnesses believe these views concerning blood were important to the early Christian Church. At a meeting of the apostles and older men of Jerusalem to determine which laws would continue to be upheld in the new Church, blood was again proscribed:

"... you are to abstain from meat that has been offered to idols, from blood, from anything that has been strangled, and from fornication".[8]

Jehovah's Witnesses believe that these passages imply more than a dietary proscription. They attach great symbolic significance to blood: it represents the life or soul. Thus they claim that the exhortation "abstain from blood" applies to all forms of blood, at all times. They argue that there is no moral difference between sustaining life by taking blood by mouth ("eating blood") and taking blood directly into the veins.

Relative to their beliefs, JWs are practically rational. Any (practically) rational person would choose to forgo earthly life if this ensured that one would enjoy a blissful eternal existence in the presence of God. If JWs are irrational, it is because their beliefs are irrational. A failure of theoretical rationality causes them to do what there is good reason not to do and frustrates their autonomy.

We believe that the beliefs of JWs are irrational. One way to show this is to question the rationality of belief in the existence of God or in the truth of some religious version of morality. For argument's sake, we will accept theism. However, the vast majority of those in the Judaeo-Christian tradition have not interpreted these passages from *The Bible* as proscribing blood transfusion. The beliefs of JWs are irrational on at least two counts: their particular beliefs are not responsive to evidence nor are their interpretations of Biblical text consistent. These failures of rationality are shared with other forms of religious "fundamentalism" and so-called "literal" interpretations of religious texts. It is worth noting that many JWs are also Creationists, believing all of Genesis to be literally true. Ignorance of historical context, the diverse intentions and circumstances of Biblical peoples and authors, oral and written traditions in the Middle East, other religious traditions and interpretations of Biblical texts, inconsistencies between different canonised works and the like all help ground an unduly simplistic interpretation of *The Bible*.

Mere ignorance, however, is not to be equated with irrationality. Wilful ignorance is. And wilful ignorance is what lies behind grounding understanding of *The Bible* on faith rather than the kinds of knowledge suggested above. This sort of wilful ignorance cuts across educational levels as it is rooted in dogmatism and closed-mindedness rather than degrees of education.

However, we believe that JWs' beliefs are irrational even in terms that should be acceptable to JWs.

Firstly, their interpretation is inconsistent with other passages of *The Bible* and Christian practices. It is inconsistent with the Christian practice of communion. Communion is the holy ceremony of the Last Supper. At the Last Supper

"Jesus took bread, and having said the blessing he broke it ... with these words: 'Take this and eat; this is my body.' Then he took a cup [of wine], and having offered thanks to God . . . [said] . . . 'Drink from it . . . For this is my blood, the blood of the covenant, shed for many, for the forgiveness of sins'".[9]

Secondly, Paul warns against slavish obedience to law:

"... those who rely on obedience to the law are under a curse ...".[10] "Christ bought us freedom from the curse of the law by becoming . . . an accursed thing".[11]

The answer is not obedience to law but faith.

"... the law was a kind of tutor in charge of us until Christ should come, when we should be justified through faith; and now that faith has come, the tutor's charge is at an end".[12]

Paul himself does not understand *The Bible* to be literally true, as evidenced when he speaks of the story of the origin of Abraham's sons being "an allegory".[13] He goes on to say:

"Mark my words: I, Paul, say to you that if you receive circumcision Christ will do you no good at all . . . [E]very man who receives circumcision is under obligation to keep the entire law. When you seek to be justified by way of law, your relation with Christ is completely severed . . . [O]ur hope of attaining that righteousness . . . is the work of the Spirit through faith . . . the only thing that counts is faith active in love".[14]

If the beliefs of JWs are irrational, why are they irrational?

IV. THREE EXAMPLES OF HOLDING A FALSE BELIEF

In all three of the following cases, the person lacks a true belief which is relevant to choice. We describe how to help a person come to hold true beliefs, drawing out the parallels with patients and JWs.

Case 1. Lack of Information

Arthur 1 is burning rubbish in the garden. The fire grows rapidly. It begins to threaten surrounding buildings. They are not in imminent danger but Arthur wants to douse the fire with water before it gets out of hand. He goes to the shed where he keeps a jerry can of water for just such a situation. He has a high degree of belief that this can contains water. Unbeknownst to him, someone has substituted petrol for water in the can. He throws the liquid on the fire and the petrol ignites, causing an explosion. He is badly burnt. Was Arthur irrational?

We need a more complete description of the state of affairs.

Arthur always locks the shed. There had been no signs of forced entry. There was only one jerry can in the shed. It was in the position where Arthur always kept it, next to the shovel. He had only the previous weekend refilled it with water after using it to put out another garden fire. If Arthur simply had no reason to suspect that the can contained anything but water, it was rational to believe that it contained water. A person who unavoidably lacks relevant information is neither theoretically nor practically irrational.

What should we do if we see Arthur about to throw the liquid onto the fire?

Arthur is rational, but he lacks a relevant true belief that he could have. In this case, the solution is simple. Provide information. Tell him, "Stop. The can contains petrol." If there were no time to provide this information, we ought to grab the can from his hands.

Many patients who hold false beliefs are like Arthur 1: uninformed. What we ought to do is provide them with information. If this is not possible, we should do what is best for them.

Are there any JWs like Arthur 1? Jehovah's Witnesses are remarkably well informed about blood transfusion, the effects of refusing it, and the Biblical context of their belief. But some may be unaware of the conflicting Biblical passages. These ought to be treated like Arthur 1. However, many are not like him. The provision of information is not alone an adequate response. What is required is rational argument.

Case 2. Not Engaging in Rational Deliberation

Arthur 2 is the same as Arthur 1, but in this case Arthur goes to the shed and finds it unlocked. He is not sure whether he left it locked last weekend. He thinks he probably did. The jerry can is next to the lawn mower. Arthur thinks that he normally keeps it next to the shovel. But, again, he is not sure. Is he irrational if he believes the can contains water?

Arthur clearly ought to believe that the door is open and the can is next to the lawnmower. But for these propositions to constitute evidence for the conclusion that the contents of the can are not water, Arthur must believe that the position of the can and door have changed. Should Arthur believe that he left the jerry can next to the shovel? This depends on the degree of belief Arthur has in his recollection of how things were. If he is vague, then there is no evidence.

Arthur may not lack information as much as a context for that information because he fails to remember relevant facts. This may be beyond control. In this case, Arthur 2 is like Arthur 1. But in some cases, a person fails to remember because he fails to think about the issue. And he may fail to think about the issue because he fails to care enough about the truth of his beliefs or the consequences of his actions.

Arthur could be directed to think more carefully about what he sees and of the possible implications of his actions. There may be other evidence he would find, if he looked, for believing the propositions that the door was locked and the can was next to the shovel. He may notice other items in the shed have been moved.

It is often thought that consultation in medicine involves presenting information so that it is understood. But even understanding is not enough. Facts must be assembled to tell a story or to construct an argument which stands in the foreground of deliberation. The arrangement and form of the facts is as important as their content.

Are there any JWs who are like Arthur 2? There is, we are assuming, evidence that their beliefs are false. However, being informed of these facts is not sufficient to cause them to hold the relevant true beliefs. They also need to care about thinking about that information in a rational way. The hallmark of faith is a stubbornness to respond to the evidence for a proposition. While this may be necessary for belief in God, it cannot be the appropriate paradigm for interpretation of God's word. *The Bible,* as a guide to how to live, aims to sanction some ways of living and proscribe others. Faith *in any interpretation* of God's word cannot be acceptable.[15] When interpreting Biblical text, the appropriate paradigm for theists is rationality and not faith. Indeed, the efforts of JWs to argue for their interpretation of *The Bible* indicates that they subscribe to this paradigm. What they are required to do by that paradigm is to care more about the proper exercise of rationality.

Intervention in this case would include trying to persuade JWs to care more about rationality by showing how they themselves appeal to rational argument and why *The Bible* must be interpreted rationally.

We are often like Arthur 2 and some JWs: we fail to care enough about what we believe and what we commit to memory. This failing is at the interface of practical and theoretical rationality: we fail to care enough (a practical failing) about the rationality of our beliefs (a theoretical failing).

Case 3. Theoretical Irrationality

Arthur 3 is the same as Arthur 2 but in this case, Arthur is sure he left the door to the shed locked and sure that the jerry can is in a different position from where he left it. On entering the shed, he smells petrol. He doesn't normally keep petrol in the shed. None the less, he throws the fluid on the fire.

As the evidence mounts up, Arthur becomes more theoretically irrational if he fails to consider the possibility that the can contains petrol. At the limit, if the evidence is overwhelming, he is like a person who believes that p, and that if p then q, but fails to believe that q.

Why might Arthur be theoretically irrational?

He may simply fail to believe that what he smells is petrol. This would be an error of perception.

He may fail to examine his beliefs for inconsistency. He may fail to compare what he believes to what the evidence suggests is the case.

Most importantly of all, Arthur may not be very talented at theoretical reasoning. He may not be good at assembling the evidence and drawing conclusions from it. It is not enough for a person to throw up *any* explanation for evidence presented to him. To move from "I saw a light on the water" to "I saw a ghost at Dead Man's Bluff" is to make an unjustified and irrational leap. Ideally, we should infer to the best explanation.[16]

Physicians, concerned to promote theoretical rationality, may assemble facts in a way which together suggest a conclusion. But patients may still fail to draw the right conclusion. Telling a patient that he has "advanced cancer" may imply that he will die. But the patient may not conclude this. Indeed, even telling a patient that he will die may not convey "the message" that the physician intends to give: perhaps that the patient ought to sort out his affairs, that he will not offer any more curative treatments, and so on.

How would a person who is in a similar epistemic position to Arthur, but who is more theoretically rational than Arthur 3, convince him that the can contains petrol? He would engage Arthur in argument. He would provide reasons. He might say something like, "The can seems to be in a different position from how you left it. That might suggest that someone has used it. I can smell petrol. Perhaps someone has used the can to carry petrol."

The reason why most JWs hold an irrational belief is because they make mistakes in their theoretical reasoning. What is the best way to correct these mistakes? For many, it is a matter of someone versed in the relevant texts taking them through the argument.

In other cases, the route may be more indirect. A JW may be presented with some information, call it, I, which should or would cause him to conclude that C if he also held other beliefs, B. However, he may fail to believe B or utilise B. He may have forgotten B in the urgent search for salvation, or had it drummed out of his head, or failed to see any longer its relevance. Intervention requires that we tap into these other beliefs. For an argument to be convincing for him may require the construction of the appropriate context: to show him that his belief should be rejected in his own terms.

Our object is the beliefs of JWs, not necessarily their choices. In some circumstances, JWs might autonomously choose to reject blood. We can autonomously adopt a course of action with a low probability of success, provided that we hold the relevant rational beliefs. Neither risk-takers nor the exceedingly cautious are necessarily non-autonomous, nor are they necessarily doing what there is good reason not to do.[17]

If JWs were to hold the relevant informed, rational beliefs, they might then autonomously choose to reject blood. But from their revised epistemic position, many would no doubt accept blood.

V. Summary and Implications

Where most rational agents differ from JWs is that they do not hold all of the following beliefs:

1. There is a God.
2. Divinely conferred immortality is possible for human beings after death.
3. God forbids eating blood.
4. Accepting a blood transfusion is no different from eating blood.
5. If one eats blood when alive, one turns to dust upon death.
6. We know 3–5 to be true based on faith that a (selectively) literal interpretation of *The Bible* reveals God's will.
7. If one lives a faithful life in accord with Jehovah's laws, eternal life is assured.

Many health care workers no doubt believe 1 and 2 and some variation on 7; it is 3, 4, 5, or especially 6 that is rejected. But this is a difference not in moral beliefs or values but about the structure of reality. This is a difference of opinion about metaphysics.

Hence if we are to respect JWs' refusals of life-prolonging blood transfusions, it is not on the grounds that we are obliged to respect decision-making that is based on a different value system from ours. Their values are the same as many other theists and atheists. They value earthly life and immortality as much as others do.

We often hear that we should allow people to do what there is no good reason to do out of respect for their nature as autonomous beings, as ends in themselves. But many such instances are something else entirely. They are cases in which people hold irrational beliefs. They are cases of theoretical irrationality. We do not respect autonomy when we encourage people to act on irrational beliefs. Rather, such beliefs limit a person's autonomy.

Rational Deliberation

Our aim has been to expand the regulative ideal governing consent. We have argued that true beliefs are necessary for evaluation. Information is important to choice insofar as it helps a person to hold the relevant true beliefs. But in order to hold the relevant true beliefs, competent people must also think rationally. Insofar as information is important, rational deliberation is important. Just as physicians should aim to provide relevant information regarding the medical procedures prior to patients consenting to have those procedures, they should also assist patients to think more clearly and rationally. They should care more about the rationality of patients' beliefs.

Since holding true beliefs is necessary to be autonomous, we do not respect autonomy when we allow patients to act on irrational beliefs. Should physicians override choices based on irrational beliefs? Should life-saving blood transfusions be given to JWs against their wishes?

When we look at to how informed medical decisions must be, we see that a requirement of informedness functions as an ideal to be striven for, and not as a requirement to be enforced. Society generally accepts that patients should be informed of all the relevant facts, but not that they must be compelled to accept information which they do not want. To force information on a person would be coercive.

The requirements of theoretical rationality should be on a par with requirements of informedness. This raises the question whether we should override both choices made in ignorance of relevant information or on the basis of irrational beliefs. We believe that there are reasons against taking this radical departure from the notion of informed consent as a regulative ideal.

The first reason is consequentialist: if we allow doctors to override choices based on some species of irrationality, then other JWs will be distressed at the thought their decisions will be overridden. The general misery and distrust of medicine that would result would reduce the value of such a policy. In the vast majority of cases, JWs' refusal of blood does not compromise their care. In fact, many may receive better care. Given the small numbers of people who would be saved by such a policy, it is not clear that it would be for the best. As is usually the case, education is better than compulsion.

Secondly, though a practice of allowing people to act out of wilful ignorance or irrationality may not promote their autonomy in the short term, respect for autonomy is not the only ground for non-interference in another person's life. It is surely enough that it is his life, and that he ought to be allowed to do what there is no good reason to do, if he chooses. Respect for persons is not restricted to respect for wholly rational persons.

In some cases, irrationality is so gross that it calls into question a person's competence. In these cases, intervention may be justified. But at lesser degrees of irrationality, we encourage the development of autonomy for all people in the long term by adopting a policy of empowering people to make their own choices.

Thirdly, *requiring* that choice be grounded on rational beliefs before it is respected is fraught with dangers. Those who claim to know Truth with certainty are at least as dangerous as those who claim to know Right and Good with certainty. Dogmatic ideologues of either sort show a lamentable propensity to use their "knowledge" to oppress others, sometimes "benignly" as paternalists, more often tyrannically as authoritarians. Hence a measure of epistemic scepticism about our own rationality or the lack of rationality in others is highly desirable.

In the end, deferral to irrationality, to partial autonomy, to imperfect consent and to unexplored values and metaphysical beliefs in patients may be necessary, even morally required. But before reaching this point, a physician committed to the highest standard of care will exercise her talents as an educator to promote greater rationality in patients. Not to make the effort to promote rational, critical deliberation is to risk a very contemporary form of patient abandonment: abandonment to human irrationality.

Duties as Educators

In important ways, physicians have always been expected to be educators: about how bodies work, do not work, and go awry; about how to care for our bodies in sickness and health; about, in the end, how to live a mortal embodied existence. Our discussion suggests, however, that physician duties as educators are more extensive. For in order genuinely to respect autonomy and patients' values, physicians must be prepared to do more than provide patients with information relevant to making evaluative choices. They must attend to how that information is received, understood and used. Good education is not restricted to providing information. It requires encouraging in others the requisite skills for dealing with information rationally.

If an ethic of respect for persons in contemporary medicine rules out—except in the most extreme cases—coercion as a response to patient irrationality, it also makes more imperative a "critical educator" response to patient irrationality. One caveat, however: effective educators know when to promote critical enquiry. Physicians, whose primary obligations are to the medical wellbeing of patients, will do well to resist the secondary obligation to promote rational criticism of deeply held beliefs at a time when their patients are impaired and suffering greatly. Thus the time to engage a hypothetically irrational JW in a critical enquiry about her convictions on "eating blood" is not the time at which she might benefit from an immediate blood transfusion because her life is in jeopardy.

It may be a very contemporary form of physician abandonment of patients in need to accept wilfulness as autonomy, the mere provision of information as adequate for informed consent, and acceptance of any morally or metaphysically bizarre view held by patients as grounds for not pursuing a medically beneficial course of treatment. But if physicians are to promote autonomy, if they are to respect patients as persons, if they are to help patients to choose and do what there is good reason to do, they should care more about the rationality of their patients' beliefs. Physicians must concern themselves with helping patients to deliberate more effectively and, ultimately, must themselves learn to care more about theoretical rationality. To do any less is to abandon patients to autonomy-destroying theoretical irrationality.

ACKNOWLEDGEMENT

Thanks to Derek Parfit, Michael Lockwood and David Malyon for many helpful comments.

References and Notes

1. Dworkin G. *The theory and practice of autonomy.* Cambridge: Cambridge University Press, 1988:. 12.

2. Adapted from Parfit D. *Reasons and persons.* Oxford: Clarendon Press, 1984: 153.

3. Forrest P. *The dynamics of belief: a normative logic.* Oxford: Basil Blackwell, 1986.

4. Watch Tower Bible and Tract Society of Pennsylvania. *Family care and medical management for Jehovah's Witnesses.* New York: Watch Tower Bible and Tract Society of New York, 1995.

5. *The new English Bible:* Genesis 9:3–4.

6. *The new English Bible:* Leviticus 17: 10, 13, 14; 7: 26, 7; Numbers 15: 30, 31; Deuteronomy 12: 23–5.

7. *The new English Bible:* Leviticus 17: 11.

8. *The new English Bible:* Acts 15: 29.

9. *The new English Bible:* Matthew 26: 26–9.

10. *The new English Bible:* Galatians 3: 10.

11. *The new English Bible:* Galatians 3:13.

12. *The new English Bible:* Galatians 3: 24–5.

13. *The new English Bible:* Galatians 4: 24.

14. *The new English Bible:* Galatians 5: 2–6.

15. Belief in God may be a basic belief: a belief which does not rest on other beliefs. (Swinburne R. *Faith and reason.* Oxford: Clarendon Press, 1981: 33.) A basic rational belief is a belief in a proposition that is (1) self-evident or fundamental, (2) evident to the senses or memory, or (3) defensible by argument, inquiry or performance (Kenny A. *Faith and reason.* New York: Columbia University Press, 1983: 27). Beliefs about eating blood are secondary beliefs. They must be justified in terms of other beliefs. It is precisely this that cannot be rationally done.

16. Armstrong DM. *What is a law of nature?* Cambridge: Cambridge University Press, 1983: 59.

17. Pascal gave a rationalist argument for belief in God: we have more to lose if we do not believe in God, and we are wrong (eternal torment), than we have to lose if we do believe in God, and we are wrong (living under an illusion). So we ought to believe that God exists (Pascal B. *Pensées.* Geneve: Pierre Cailler, 1947: fragment 223). Theoretically rational JWs could give a similar justification for refusing blood.

Changing the *BMJ*'s Position on Informed Consent Would Be Counterproductive

J. S. Tobias

Any author would be gratified by an overwhelming postbag in response to a provocative article—provided, of course, that not all the voices are raised in condemnation. Fortunately, however, it is clear even from the titles of the letters published by the *BMJ* 17 May and 26 July 1997 that a wide variety of views persists. On the one hand, titles such as "Doctors are arrogant to think they need to debate issue of patient consent"[1] and "Lack of respect for patients in medical research may reflect wider disrespect in clinical practice"[2] provide a clear and unambiguous view. But on the other, "Ethics committees and the *BMJ* should continue to consider the overall benefit to patients,"[3] "Consent is not always practical in emergency treatments,"[4] and "Let readers judge for themselves"[5] offer a more relaxed view. As Little and Williamson point out,[3] writing from a department of primary medical care, "adopting an absolute ethical view in open trials ignores the realities of—and would undermine the ability of research to inform—normal practice and thus could ultimately harm patients, including those who agree to take part in trials."

As one of the protagonists of the debate, I am greatly concerned by many of the specific issues raised by correspondents. As well as the problem of, for example, emergency medical situations, the issue of risk of bias raised by a senior statistician[6] is of particular importance since well conducted randomised trials tend to form the most influential basis of today's evidence based medical practice. Added to this, we have a past chairman of a research ethics committee at one of London's most prestigious research hospitals pointing to the wide disagreement as to which clinical situations require trial without fully informed consent—reminding us that "no one can claim to have a monopoly on deciding what is ethical."[7]

Equally difficult is the argument—supported by preliminary data—that many patients may not digest information sufficiently well to permit a genuinely informed level of consent,[8] at the very least, it is clear that many patients in this study by Montgomery et al had no recollection whatever of consenting even to a course of radiotherapy—a consent which, we are assured from the article, had most certainly been given. If, as I believe, fully informed consent can sometimes be needlessly cruel,[9] what is the point of insisting on it in all cases when about a quarter of patients (judging by Montgomery et al.'s study) cannot even recall being told about common side effects of treatment when all had been provided with this information?

As I pointed out when first setting out my stall, one of my chief anxieties concerns the somewhat old fashioned concept of doctoring in its traditional pastoral sense. While applauding the use of evidence based approaches and recognising the need for powerful trials to generate essential information, I do, nevertheless, feel a responsibility of equal importance—to act as patients' adviser, counsellor, advocate, and support. With many sophisticated patients, well informed and willing to enter into a robust two way dialogue, the medical scientist occupying a fair portion (I hope) of my brain can take the lead. For the majority, however—less educated, less well informed, and less able to marshal their arguments—a somewhat more directive or (without being pejorative) "paternalistic" approach will often be far more appropriate, and gratefully received. As Dr. Thurstan Brewin, past chairman of Health Watch points out, "Those who want the *BMJ* to take a rigid view should spend a day in a ward full of elderly people. They would probably find many who, though far from being mentally incompetent, are at times confused and forgetful. What could be more unrealistic than to refuse to recognise this for fear of being called patronising? . . . Some people underestimate the harm that can be done to many sick patients when fully informed consent for every trial is sought, no matter how tense or difficult the situation."[10]

I willingly give Ms Hazel Thornton, chairwoman of the Consumers' Advisory Group for Clinical Trials, the final word.[11] As she clearly explains, her group "works directly with the professions . . . [and] identifies an urgent need to advance public education about clinical trials. Concepts such as randomisation, risk perception, and probability are poorly understood . . . . Such cooperation . . . will create a different attitude to research, which will be seen not as an imposition but as an activity to which we all have a responsibility to contribute." Her letter, entitled "We all have a responsibility to contribute to research," echoes my own view that both doctors and patients have much to gain from this type of partnership and that overzealous directives attempting to monopolise the moral high ground will surely prove counterproductive. The *BMJ* would be unwise to stifle important research by confining too closely the outline, structure, and phraseology of trial consent—details that are far better left to the originators of the studies and their local ethics committees.

References

1. Bratt DE. Doctors are arrogant to think they need to debate issue of patient consent. *BMJ* 1997;314:1477.

2. Sikorski J. Lack of respect for patients in medical research may reflect wider disrespect in clinical practice. *BMJ* 1997;315:250.

3. Little P, Williamson I. Ethics committees and the BMJ should continue to consider the overall benefit to patients. *BMJ* 1997;314:1478.

4. Morley C. Consent is not always practical in emergency treatments. *BMJ* 1997;314:1480.

5. Bland M. Let readers judge for themselves. *BMJ* 1997;314:1477.

6. Chanter DO. Risk of bias may be another reason not to seek consent. *BMJ* 1997;314:1478.

7. Soutter P. No one has a monopoly on deciding what is ethical. *BMJ* 1997;314:1477.

8. Montgomery C, Lydon A, Lloyd K. Patients may not understand enough to give their informed consent. *BMJ* 1997;314:1482.

9. Tobias JS, Souhami RL. Fully informed consent can be needlessly cruel. *BMJ* 1993;307:1199–201.

10. Brewin T. "Blanket" consent to trials would be a good idea. *BMJ* 1997;315:253.

11. Thornton H. We all have a responsibility to contribute to research. *BMJ* 1997;314:1479.

Informed Consent— A Publisher's Duty

Mary Warnock

Informed consent has become a shibboleth: you cannot be a respectable member of the medical research world unless you invoke the concept and accede to its demands, nor can you be a respectable publisher of research papers unless you ensure that your authors have clean hands in this regard. Informed consent is also, and perhaps more urgently, required in the case of medical and surgical procedures; but it is in the context of research requirements that the following remarks are offered.

The concept itself is not wholly simple. Questions may be raised about what counts as full consent or sufficiently informed consent, especially in the case of subjects who may find the idea of randomisation difficult to grasp or who may have problems, as we all do, with the calculation of risk. I believe, however, that we should not make too much of these difficulties, which are inherent in the nature of medical research and which can be minimised by tactful and sympathetic dialogue with potential subjects. The central moral problem, however, is concerned with the possible exploitation of the subjects of research. For research, including clinical research, is aimed, not at the good of the individual patient, but at the production of medical knowledge, which is for the good of society at large (although the individual patient may benefit from it by chance). This is the difference between research and the use even of innovative treatment for an individual patient.

In a research programme the subjects are being used as a means, not as an end in themselves. To treat someone merely as a means is widely agreed to be a moral evil, a breach of the "categorical imperative," on which the very possibility of morality was held by Kant to depend. Philosophy apart, to make use of people, especially when they are not aware of what is going on, is generally agreed to be wrong. This evil is removed if people offer their services voluntarily. They then become willing partners in a joint enterprise rather than mere tools in it. Since they are free to decline to take part, their power of choice has not been overridden. They are being treated as befits a human as opposed to any other animal. The moral principle involved here is often referred to as the principle of autonomy. I prefer the more precise title of the principle of non-exploitation. Since it is especially easy to exploit the helpless and incompetent—those who, though human, seem to have little power of understanding or making a serious choice—the principle ought to be considered scrupulously in the case of such people. However, if research into the very conditions that produce such incompetence, such as Alzheimer's disease, is to continue it may be necessary to resort to consent by proxy. It seems morally important that such consent should be sought.

The principle of non-exploitation has come to seem to many to be by far the most important moral principle that should govern research using human subjects. This is understandable on historical grounds: there are far too many cases, in the second world war and, sadly, more recently, of whole populations of people being damaged or destroyed as victims of research programmes about which they were ignorant or had no choice. The relevance of history is that it causes people to deploy the "slippery slope" argument—if once the principle of non-exploitation is allowed to be breached where will it end? To which the answer implied is that it will end in horrors such as were revealed at Nuremberg.

However, the slippery slope is a weak argument (though it exercises an enormous power over the imagination) in that there is no logical connection between allowing the principle to be breached in some cases and allowing it to be totally forgotten. The argument relies on a poor view of human nature: "Give them an inch and they'll take an ell." Biological and medical scientists are especially suspect these days, and this arises from the power of the slippery slope. It is crucial, therefore, that in this context editors should keep their heads and differentiate between different cases in which the principle has been breached.

There is all the difference in the world between, on the one hand, extending the use of anonymous data, collected for a particular study, to a further, previously unthought of, study and, on the other hand, the randomised testing of drugs in the treatment of a specific disease. In the first case there is no question of harm accruing to the subjects, and thus the use of the word "exploitation" is an exaggeration. It seems to me a misuse of words to suggest that not obtaining informed consent in itself constitutes a harm; sometimes it amounts to exploitation, sometimes it does not. Nor does it seem that the use for research purposes of discarded or unwanted tissue is exploitation—though there exists a lack of clarity about the relation between an individual and his or her body parts, which ought to be remedied. The matter becomes critical when a pharmaceutical company may make vast profits from the use of, say, a spleen that has been removed from the body of an individual. Does the person have property rights over something that was once, in some sense, his or her property but is so no longer?

The conclusion is that editors must try, in the words of a prayer much used in Hertford College Chapel, "to distinguish things that differ." This makes the editorial function hazardous, with editors potentially subject to accusations of failing in their duty to ensure the moral respectability of research. But any other policy seems to me to rely on a dogma—that there are no other principles worth considering in the ethics of research except the principle of non-exploitation—and to rely also on an exceptionally wide and unrealistic view of what counts as exploitation.

Trial Subjects Must Be Fully Involved in Design and Approval of Trials

Lisa Power

Reading the *BMJ* debate about informed consent and publication recently, it seemed to me that there was a basic flaw in the premise. Instead of "Why?" I wanted "How?" If informed consent is about the dignity and empowerment of trial subjects and the genuine participation of patients in our health research, then how can this be maximised throughout the trial process? If we look at the overall issue—the involvement of patients or potential patients—rather than the single aspect of informed consent we can begin to treat the disease rather than arguing over the symptoms.

I do not believe that you can obtain better practice about informed consent merely by making a rule about publication. There will always be some people prepared to obtain such consent technically without any real commitment to its spirit, because all they see it as is a signature at the bottom of a form and not a partnership. This is not to impugn the motives with which they entered research, but lack of time and money and urgency of need can put pressure upon the best of intentions. Of course, there are trials in which informed consent cannot be obtained, as Len Doyal outlined, and any hard and fast rule that the *BMJ* made about publication would probably have to be broken at some point. But the onus of justifying failure to obtain consent should not arise at publication stage for the first time; questions should be being asked far earlier in the process.

To improve the practice of obtaining informed consent wherever possible there must be a number of changes in attitudes. There needs to be a greater emphasis in doctors' education on interpersonal and communication skills, and a greater willingness on the part of some trial investigators to involve nursing staff in communicating with trial volunteers; doctors are not the only people with a voice and a brain. Secondly, there needs to be an understanding that giving patients or potential patients some say in the design and approval of trials is a positive process and not just a hoop to jump through. This involvement can stretch from trial design to writing information sheets and sitting on ethics committees. Thirdly, the onus should be clearly on those designing trials to show, as part of their basic data, their process for subject consent and uptake, rather than on others to challenge them in retrospect.

Placing the subjects of a trial at the centre of the process is not an easy matter. It may need extra finance or education, or other forms of support, and it may take time. Sometimes, I agree, it is not possible because of the nature of the trial, but this should be the exception—the question about informed consent should always be "Why not?" rather than "Why?" In my experience, as a participant in a vaccine trial and as an activist pressing drug companies to talk with us about their trial designs, such involvement is always to the good. I can appreciate that it feels like a nuisance to people who have not had to consider us before, but it leads to better trials with better uptake and, of equal importance, to greater involvement of individuals in their own health.

By fostering debate about informed consent, the *BMJ* has already added more to this process than any simple rule would do. I hope that it continues to do so.

Studies That Do Not Have Informed Consent from Participants Should Not Be Published

Heather Goodare

In his editorial of 12 April 1997 the editor asks, "Should the *BMJ* reject all studies that do not include informed consent?"[1] The simple answer is "Yes." This is the stated policy of others that observe the "uniform requirements for manuscripts submitted to biomedical journals."[2] There is no good reason why the *BMJ* should not follow suit.

It is clear that the Declaration of Helsinki is no longer entirely satisfactory as a standard to which medical journals should adhere. The declaration is a watered down version of the Nuremberg Code, formulated after the trials of Nazi doctors who had experimented on concentration camp inmates during the second world war.[3] The code states unequivocally: "The voluntary consent of the human subject is absolutely essential." But the Helsinki Declaration introduced a section on clinical research which says: "If the doctor considers it essential not to obtain informed consent, the specific reasons for this proposal should be stated in the experimental protocol for transmission to the independent committee" (Clause II.5).

Lack of consent in cancer trials has long been a matter of concern,[4,5] and this clause could have been used as an excuse for not seeking consent from competent patients in recent examples of clinical research.[6–10] There is some evidence that not seeking consent, far from eliminating bias (which is usually the reason given), actually adds to it. Patients who find that others in the same category are receiving different treatment will want to know why.[11] It is best to come clean at the outset: patients who discover they have been deceived lose trust in their doctors.

If the present debate leads to a radical rethink of the way clinical research is conducted, matters may improve. Researchers are ignoring a valuable resource if they do not consult patients in designing their trials in the first place. This can save time and money and lead to better outcomes.[12] Also, "joint ownership of the work being done keeps patients involved, instead of isolating them."[9] There should be no more debate about the need to seek consent from competent patients. There are, however, some grey areas that need further consideration.

The Helsinki Declaration makes provision for cases of legal incompetence, or physical or mental incapacity, though national legislation varies, and there is a case for amending legislation when it is deficient, to make proper provision for proxy responsibility where appropriate. We cannot take it for granted that an unconscious person would have consented to a trial had he or she been conscious: indeed, we have a special duty to respect the rights of those who cannot speak for themselves. If a proxy for the patient cannot be found the research should not proceed. In an emergency the doctor's duty is to do his or her best for the patient in the light of current knowledge. The rights of children, too, need to be respected: in the words of Lisa Hammond, aged 15, "Society should accept people of all types, and respect everyone's right to make their own decisions once they have all the facts, be they adults or children."[13]

There remains the matter of clinical audit and epidemiological research. We cannot assume that patients will not mind their data being used for such purposes. As Doyal observes, "Normally patients should give their explicit consent for their records to be accessed."[14] Moreover, these data must be anonymised: we cannot be sure that patients will not mind if researchers and civil servants (who could well be colleagues in the same office) see their clinical details. Researchers may have overstepped the mark in a recent breast cancer audit,[15] by requiring personal data—including names, dates of birth, and postcodes—not from the patients themselves but from doctors and administrators. This sheds light on the uses to which cancer registries could be put and raises awkward questions.[16] It seems that careful thought needs to be given to this matter, including the possibility of a standard question to patients at the time of treatment asking permission to review their records for research purposes. Some clinicians already follow this procedure.[17] Patients are well aware of the importance of such research, and if it is conducted appropriately they could be enthusiastic participants. But their consent must not be taken for granted.

A further problem occurs with the use of stored human tissue. Donors of blood, organs, or cadavers usually give explicit consent to the use of their bodies for therapeutic purposes, medical education, or research, but patients who provide tissue specimens during the course of their own treatment normally do not. If any use of this material for other purposes is proposed, patients' permission (or that of a responsible relative) should be sought. There have already been examples of commercial exploitation and even attempts to patent such material: any possible profit should be used in accordance with patients' wishes. A moving story is told by Steingraber of the cell line MCF-7, widely used in medical research. The initials stand for Michigan Cancer Foundation, and the 7 for the seventh attempt to establish a self-perpetuating stock of cells from the body of the patient. The woman was a nun, Sister Catherine Frances, who died in 1970.[18] Would she have wished a donation by way of royalty to be made to her convent every time her cells were used? Was she asked?

A breast cancer patient expressed the dilemma to me as: "In Victorian times they got upset about body snatching. Now they steal bits of your body when you're still alive." These issues need further debate, with members of the public and patients themselves taking a full part in the discussion.

Notes

I thank Clare Dimmer, Carolyn Faulder, Andrew Herxheimer, Pamela Goldberg, Ann Johnson, Margaret King, and Charlotte Williamson for helpful comments on an earlier draft. Responsibility for the final version is, however, mine alone.

1. Smith R. Informed consent: the intricacies. *BMJ* 1997;314:1059–60.
2. Writing for the Lancet. *Lancet* 1997;439:1–2.
3. The Nuremberg Code (1947). Declaration of Helsinki (1964). *BMJ* 1996;313:1448–9.
4. Faulder C. *Whose body is it? The troubling issue of informed consent.* London: Virago, 1985.
5. CancerLink. *Declaration of rights of people with cancer.* London: CancerLink, 1990.
6. Research without consent continues in the UK. *IME Bulletin* 1988;July:13–5.
7. Burton MV, Parker RW, Farrell A, Bailey D, Conneely J, Booth S, et al. A randomized controlled trial of preoperative psychological preparation for mastectomy. *Psycho-oncology* 1995;4:1–19.
8. McArdle JMC, George WD, McArdle C, Smith DC, Moodie, AR, Hughson AVM, et al. Psychological support for patients undergoing breast cancer surgery: a randomised study. *BMJ* 1996;312:813–7.
9. All treatment and trials must have informed consent. *BMJ* 1997;314:1134–5.
10. Dennis M, O'Rourke S, Slattery J, Staniforth T, Warlow C. Evaluation of a stroke family care worker: results of a randomised controlled trial. *BMJ* 1997;314:1071–6.
11. Moodie A. Psychological support for patients having breast cancer surgery: reply from dissenting author. *BMJ* 1996;313:362.
12. Bradburn J, Maher J, Adewuyi-Dalton R, Grunfeld E, Lancaster T, Mant D. Developing clinical trial protocols: the use of patient focus groups. *Psycho-oncology* 1995;4:107–12.
13. Hammond L. Deciding about leg-lengthening. *Bull Med Ethics* 1993;92:36.
14. Doyal L. Journals should not publish research to which patients have not given fully informed consent—with three exceptions. *BMJ* 1997;314:1107–11.
15. Scottish Breast Cancer Focus Group, Scottish Cancer Trials Breast Group, Scottish Cancer Therapy Network. *Scottish breast cancer audit 1987 & 1993.* Edinburgh: Scottish Cancer Therapy Network, 1996.
16. Veatch RM. Consent, confidentiality and research. *N Engl J Med* 1997;336:869–70.
17. Pincus T. Analyzing long-term outcomes of clinical care without randomized controlled clinical trials: the consecutive patient questionnaire database. *Advances* 1997;13(2):3–46.
18. Steingraber S. *Living downstream: an ecologist looks at cancer and the environment.* Reading, MA: Addison-Wesley, 1997:121–3.

Cultural Diversity and Informed Consent

Ellen Agard, Daniel Finkelstein, and Edward Wallach

CASE

Mr. and Mrs. R have recently come to the United States from Eastern Europe for medical care. They are a professional couple in their mid-thirties: educated, fluent in English, and financially comfortable. They have no children.

Mrs. R has a history of chronic pelvic inflammatory disease that has not responded well to conservative treatment. A year ago, she had a ruptured ectopic pregnancy that resulted in surgical removal of one ovary and fallopian tube. Since then, she has completed three courses of intravenous (IV) antibiotic therapy. She is admitted to the hospital for further diagnosis and treatment.

In consultation with her attending physician, Mr. R expresses great concern about his wife's pain and poor health. Mrs. R is concerned primarily about her ability to have children. Mr. R wants everything possible done to cure his wife, and asks for a surgical consultation.

The surgeon explains to Mr. and Mrs. R that although surgery might help to clear the infection, he does not recommend it at this time because it might well involve removing Mrs. R's second ovary, leaving her infertile. The couple requests that the surgery be done; Mrs. R signs the consent form, and surgery is scheduled.

On the evening before surgery, Mrs. R says to one of the nurses: "I have always wanted to have children, but my husband says that this has gone on too long; that we must do whatever is necessary for my health, so we can get back to our home and our jobs. He says I have been too sick to be a good wife to him." The nurse offers to talk with Mrs. R about her decision, or to arrange for her to talk it over with her physicians or a social worker. Mrs. R says, "My husband is sure that this is the right thing to do."

The nurse understands that in Mr. and Mrs. R's culture, it is customary for the wife to accede to her husband's wishes, and for the husband to make decisions about his wife's medical treatment. However, based on her conversation with Mrs. R, she is concerned that Mrs. R's decision to have surgery may represent her husband's wishes more than her own. The nurse discusses this concern with the attending physician, and they decide to seek guidance from the hospital ethics committee before proceeding with surgery.

DISCUSSION

A Clinical Perspective

It would be preferable not to proceed with surgery until the options for medical treatment have been exhausted. Continued treatment with IV antibiotics offers the possibility of preserving Mrs. R's remaining ovary, maintaining her normal ovarian function and her fertility. However, if Mr. and Mrs. R understand the implications of this procedure, reach their decision together, and give consent, it is acceptable to proceed with surgery.

A Legal Perspective

Informed consent requires that the physician explain to the patient the nature of her ailment, the procedure to be performed, and its risks, benefits, and alternatives. The discussion with Mrs. R should include information about her chances of conceiving and having a normal pregnancy if the surgery is not done.

Mrs. R has been informed of the proposed procedure and has consented to it. She can always revoke her consent. Because she has expressed concern about the surgery, another discussion with her physician is indicated. In an attempt to keep the consent process free of coercion, this discussion should take place only between Mrs. R and her physician.

A Cultural Perspective

We are told that in Mr. and Mrs. R's culture, the wife accedes to the husband's authority in decisions about medical treatment and having children. However, we cannot determine on the basis of the limited information we have, if Mrs. R is being coerced. In fact, we do not know how the couple has arrived at their decision, or what meaning fertility has for them. Perhaps Mr. R is genuinely concerned about his wife's health. Perhaps Mrs. R is genuinely willing to forgo having children.

We must avoid making assumptions based on our own cultural values or our limited understanding of Mr. and Mrs. R's values. Mrs. R is better able than we are to understand the implications of her decision for her marriage and her future. If we interfere, we are assuming that we can make a better decision for her than she can make for herself.

ANALYSIS

This case and commentary were developed by the authors to foster discussion about the impact of cultural diversity on ethical deliberation. As a composite, the case lacks some of the rich depth and detail that emerge during full ethics committee deliberation. First, Mrs. R's desire for children is made known only in a passing comment to one of the nurses. We do not know how to evaluate the strength or durability of this desire, or how to weigh it against the other preferences, desires, and goals in Mrs. R's life. Second, we do not know what efforts have been made to foster communication among Mr. and Mrs. R and the staff—whether they have talked with a social worker, obtained religious guidance (if appropriate), or talked with a representative from the hospital's international office. Finally, we do not have a final resolution for this case. Instead, we struggle to think through the issues that this case raises within these complex, unsatisfactory, and "real world" limitations.

This case presents a real ethical dilemma. Different decisions, choices, and courses of action are open to the couple and to the staff. These different options are supported by strong but conflicting ethical arguments. When it comes to choosing among them, we must decide which ethical arguments are the more compelling.

The dilemma that the staff confronts is this: is it appropriate to proceed with surgery when (1) Mrs. R's consent appears to reflect her husband's wishes rather than her own, and (2) the procedure to which she has consented places her reproductive capacity at risk? We need to consider whether and/or how to explore the decision for surgery further with this couple.

Respect for Cultural Diversity

In this case, Mrs. R has given written consent for surgery. The staff feels that Mr. R has unduly influenced her decision, and that the decision to proceed with surgery goes against her own desire for children. However, it is not clear whether or not it is appropriate for the staff to "second guess" the couple's decision-making process.

In Mr. and Mrs. R's culture, we are told, the husband traditionally takes a dominant role in making major decisions. If this is so, then Mrs. R's decision represents a decision that is consistent with her own social and cultural context. Furthermore, it represents her own understanding of her relationship with her husband, the options that are available to her, and the value of her fertility relative to other life plans and values. As outsiders to this culture, and to the couple's relationship, we are not in a position to evaluate or judge Mrs. R's own reading of her situation. By overriding her decision, the staff risks imposing their own cultural values on Mrs. R, values that may not be relevant or appropriate for her situation. Such interference would be paternalistic; it would assume that the staff can make a better decision for Mrs. R than she can make for herself.

Over time, our society has developed greater awareness, respect, and tolerance for cultural diversity. We recognize that customs, practices, and values vary greatly among cultures. We respect cultural diversity when, for example, we learn to appreciate various styles of art or cuisine, or learn to understand differing religious beliefs and practices. Occasionally such differences may be confusing or unappealing to us. Even so, it is generally appropriate to respond with tolerance and respect.

In the clinical setting, respecting cultural difference may require us to make accommodation in our ordinary practice. Efforts regularly are and should be made to respect dietary restrictions, religious commitments, and different standards of privacy, particularly between genders. Usually these accommodations can be made without compromising professional ethics or personal integrity. Occasionally, however, cultural differences engage our deeply held moral values, and threaten our deepest personal and professional commitments. When this occurs, it is difficult to discern how we ought to proceed.

Although we are obligated to be respectful and tolerant of values and customs that differ from our own, here we confront a cultural tradition that appears to undermine Mrs. R's choice and consent on a fundamental level. In this case, the stakes are so high that we need to consider our respect for cultural differences in the light of our concern for Mrs. R's right to make her own choices.

Respect for Human Rights and Dignity

The validity of Mrs. R's consent, and the significance of the procedure for which she has given consent, are separate but inter-related concerns. We might be less concerned about the consent process if Mrs. R were undergoing a simple appendectomy or low-risk diagnostic test. In general, our scrutiny of the consent process is influenced by the invasiveness or risks of the procedure involved.

The risk to Mrs. R's fertility is not a critical issue in and of itself; for example, if Mrs. R herself did not desire children, and preferred surgery and a quick recovery, her decision would be far less troublesome. However, we do know that fertility and reproduction have profound meaning across cultures. Without necessarily knowing what they may mean to any particular individual, the risk that this surgery poses to Mrs. R's fertility is a matter for concern.

Although we do not know what value childbearing has for Mrs. R, she has made it known that her fertility is important to her, and that she does not want to lose it. The proposed surgery places at risk something she values. Thus the risk to her fertility raises our scrutiny of the consent process to a very high level, and highlights her lack of full consent as a critical issue.

In Western medical practice, obtaining an individual's informed consent is both an ethical and legal requirement. In requiring that consent for a procedure be fully informed, one ensures that patients make their own decisions about medical interventions that affect their health and well-being. Because this surgery affects Mrs. R in a way that is profoundly important to her, it cannot proceed without her full consent.

A commitment to the fundamental dignity and worth of all human beings provides the foundation for the perspective of human rights. From this perspective, fundamental human rights are universally applicable to all human beings, by virtue of each person's unique and intrinsic moral dignity and worth. As this perspective has gained recognition across cultures, it has been widely recognized that the right to make basic life decisions constitutes such a fundamental human right.

Cultural differences do not provide sufficient grounds for overriding what appears to be Mrs. R's deep desire to preserve her fertility. Knowing that gender inequities diminish the rights of women in many cultural settings, we would choose to question rather than reinforce such inequities in the clinical setting. Thus our reluctance to proceed with surgery represents a reluctance to participate in what can be viewed as a violation of Mrs. R's basic human rights.

RECOMMENDATIONS

A first step in addressing this case is to pursue further discussion with Mr. and Mrs. R, separately and together. Social services, the chaplain's department, and the services for international patients that are offered by many hospitals are significant resources for facilitating such discussion. Every effort should be made to understand and respect the decision-making process of Mrs. R and her husband, as well as the concerns of the clinicians involved in Mrs. R's case. An atmosphere of respect offers an opportunity to explore Mrs. R's decision in light of her own values and preferences, as well as those of her husband.

Such a discussion is needed because the details of this case, as we relate them here, do not allow us to make a clear choice for the claims of human rights over the claims of cultural difference. We argue against interpreting this dilemma too readily as a simple case of cultural difference. If we do this, we run the risk of proceeding with surgery that deprives Mrs. R of her fertility, against her wishes. At the same time, we recognize the risk of undue interference in this couple's decision-making process and final decision.

A discussion with Mr. and Mrs. R needs to include a review of the risks of morbidity and mortality associated with surgery, as well as an exploration of their values and how they make decisions. It is possible that after further exploration, Mr. R will place a different value on his wife's desire to have children. If he persists in preferring surgery, then Mrs. R's clinical team must consider how best to preserve her rights and dignity within the constraints of her culture and her relationship with her husband. It is of paramount importance that the medical team avoid generating conflict within the couple's relationship. An imperfect resolution may be to proceed with surgery, but only after making sure that Mrs. R has every opportunity to act according to her own wishes.

As our healthcare system cares for more and more patients from different healthcare backgrounds, our moral obligation to respond to conflicting value judgments will become increasingly apparent. Our duty to respect each individual's human dignity and worth can be as challenging as the case presented here. Recognizing and responding to such conflicts challenges clinicians to obtain all the consultation available to them in situations where cross-cultural differences raise concerns about human rights.

Discrimination, Informed Consent, and the HIV Infected Clinician

We must ask whether patients' rights to avoid the remotest of risks should override clinicians' rights to practise as long as their skills remain unimpaired

Ronald Bayer

In the middle 1980s a central ethical challenge posed by the AIDS epidemic entailed the issue of whether doctors were obliged to care for patients infected with HIV regardless of the small but ineliminable risk that they might become infected as a result. Without exception, those who considered the issue from an ethical perspective concluded that doctors were morally obliged to provide care even in the face of risk; that professional duty took precedence over personal fear or preference.

It was within that context that a small closed meeting was convened in 1988 at the Hastings Center, a research institute just north of New York, devoted to the study of medical ethics. The aim of the meeting was to examine a related but quite different issue: whether patients have a right to avoid contact with doctors infected with HIV. Two leading advocates of the rights of people with HIV, who were at the same time well known for their defence of patients' rights, were asked to address this issue. To the surprise of many at the session, both concluded, with great difficulty, that clinicians who engaged in invasive procedures had a duty to avoid exposing their patients to even the remotest of risks and should stop practising if they became infected.[1]

Despite this conclusion they adamantly opposed mandatory HIV testing to identify infected health care workers, a position that many suggested was inconsistent with their exclusionary posture. Further confounding the discussion was the observation of a conservative professor of law that the exclusion of HIV infected doctors was an irrational but predictable consequence of a regulatory philosophy that assumed that consumers had a right to be protected from risks that were vanishingly small.

I recall this meeting that occurred almost a decade ago because it may shed light on the complex issues involved in the case of Dr Patrick Ngosa, the British obstetrician recently barred from practising medicine because he delayed being tested for HIV despite suspecting that he was infected. The case has produced a paroxysm of anxiety and calls for mandatory HIV testing of health care workers.[2]

The discussions at the Hastings Center took place before the wave of consternation over the American dentist David Acer, several of whose patients developed HIV infection. The precise mechanism of HIV transmission in that dental office has never been resolved. But it was the near death testimony before Congress of one patient, Kimberly Bergalis, in which she denounced those who had failed to protect her, that forced the issue of infected doctors on to the agenda of AIDS policy.

It mattered little that the estimates from the Centers for Disease Control of the risk of HIV transmission—1/40 000 to 1/400 000 from HIV infected surgeons and 1/200 000 to 1/2 000 000 from HIV infected dentists[3]—were vanishingly small (the risk of a fatal reaction to anaesthesia in surgery is 1/10 000). Infected doctors became a symbol of dread. It was not surprising that those who believed that the struggle against AIDS had been subverted by a cabal of civil libertarians and gay activists used the occasion to call for draconian measures.[4] Nor was it surprising that those who had opposed simple measures like needle exchange for injecting drug users—a policy that might have prevented thousands of infections—suddenly argued that any measure that might prevent even one infection (such as testing all doctors and debarring all those who were seropositive) was morally imperative. What was surprising was that the case of Dr Acer produced a fissure between those who had been allies in the struggle for sound, effective AIDS prevention and in efforts to overcome the shameful pattern of discrimination that had punctuated the history of the epidemic. In that clash we can come to appreciate the most difficult challenge posed by the healthcare worker who is infected with HIV.

Several prominent ethicists argued that the principles of medical ethics, which established the right of informed consent, provided ample grounds for claiming that patients had the right to determine whether they should assume even the remotest of risks of HIV transmission in the course of their treatment. Furthermore, they argued that in the previous 20 years medical ethics had evolved away from an objective standard (determined by doctors) of which pieces of information about risk needed to be shared with patients as part of an informed consent, to a "subjective" or patient centred standard. In short, it was for patients, not the experts, to establish the norms of risk disclosure.

For those who opposed the imposition of practice limits on infected healthcare workers, the picture was very different. They argued that the remoteness of the risk of HIV infection rendered practice limitations unnecessary and the demand for disclosure about HIV an unwarranted invasion of privacy. This perspective was in keeping with the historic effort to protect people with disabilities from irrational discrimination. At its core as a determination to prevent subjective fears from overwhelming objective evaluation of the prospects of injury. Fears about exceedingly remote risks could not justify acts of discrimination in medicine or elsewhere. Hence, given what was known about HIV transmission from healthcare workers to patients, exclusionary policies entailed a profound violation of individual rights. What was needed were practice guidelines, such as the introduction of universal precautions, that would reduce the risk of all nosocomial infections.[5]

Between the logic of informed consent and the logic of antidiscrimination there is a deep conceptual chasm, one that ought not to be papered over. Nevertheless, both perspectives help to illuminate the problems posed by physicians like Dr Ngosa. The central issue is not whether healthcare workers should be subject to mandatory screening. It is whether those who are infected should be deprived of the right to practise medicine. In confronting that question, it is essential that we ask whether the rights of patients to refuse to subject themselves to the remotest of risks should trump the rights of doctors who are confronting their own AIDS related mortality to care for patients as long as their skills remain unimpaired. Quiet and careful deliberation, not noisy clamour, is what is needed.

Notes

1. Gostin L. HIV infected physicians and the practice of seriously invasive procedures. *Hastings Center Report* 1989; Jan–Feb: 32–8.

2. Craft N. Trust me—I'm a doctor. *BMJ* 1997;314:910.

3. Centers for Disease Control. *Estimates of the risk of transmission of hepatitis B virus and human immunodeficiency virus to patients by the percutaneous route during invasive surgical and dental procedures.* Atlanta: CDC, 1991.

4. Tolchin M. Senate adopts tough measures on health workers. *New York Times* 1991 July 19.

5. Glantz LH, Mariner WK, Annos GJ. Risky business: setting public health policy for HIV infected health care professionals. *Millbank Quarterly* 1992;70:43–79.

IV. Gender Issues.

Overview. In the last two decades, much has been written on the developing area of Feminist Ethics. I examine these issues in Chapter Five of *Basic Ethics*. For our purposes here, two points are used as touchstones in Feminist Ethics, especially as they relate to Medical Ethics. The first issue is the status of women as an oppressed group. In the history of medicine, the physicians generally have been men and the nurses were women, and the physicians told the nurses what to do. This patriarchal system (intentionally or not) oppressed women. This situation may be changing; but the change is more rapid from the oppressor group's perspective than from the vantage point of the oppressed group.

The second point is the notion of ethical care. *Care* in this context is a concept that includes a concern for the particularity of human relationships over abstract concepts of justice when the two conflict. This perspective is very important, especially in the health care field.

This section begins with two theoretical articles that present some crucial aspects of Feminist Ethics as applied to biomedicine. I challenge readers to follow these themes throughout the book because I have made some attempt to represent some of these concerns in each of the book's core chapters (four through seven).

Mary Mahowald begins the discussion by using the metaphor of nearsightedness to describe the present state of the medical community. A nearsighted person does not see certain realities because her vision extends only so far and she needs glasses to allow her to see a wider range of phenomena than hitherto had been unclear. Mahowald argues that Biomedical Ethics should go beyond the narrow focus on groups and mere abstractions and focus on individuals as well. Individuals and their personal relationships are just as much the stuff of ethics as are abstract concepts.

In making her argument, Mahowald refers to "standpoint" theory, which has some similarities to my own discussions of worldview. An extension of the feminist standpoint to Medical Ethics involves entering into the particularity of individual cases *for their own sake,* not merely for the generic description that they represent (as in the case of Al Brown). One way to integrate the feminist standpoint into the mainstream is to expand the range of voices heard and recognized. Such a prescription may well alter the *ethos* of biomedical practice.

The second article in this section is an editorial on the issue of women's health in biomedical research by Marcia Angell. The editorial takes the view that clinical research over the years has emphasized men's health needs over women's needs. This position creates differences of opinion as evinced in the following letters to the editor.

Finally, Debra Leners and Nancy Beardslee's article considers which attributes should be emphasized in helping patients make health care choices.

The dichotomy of "justice" choices versus "caring" choices is discussed among nurses. Because we all want to encourage the best ethical decision making, we need to find out how we do this. The authors explore what, in fact, nurses do in clinical situations to emphasize caring. Then they highlight areas in which more work is needed, primarily in nurse-physician interactions. Nurses spend many more hours with the patient than the physician does, but the voice of the nurse (generally female) is often unheard. Why is this? The development of a meaningful dialogue is needed to answer this question.

On Treatment of Myopia: Feminist Standpoint Theory and Bioethics

Mary B. Mahowald

The insights of feminist standpoint theory provide a corrective to the nearsightedness, unselfconsciousness, and arrogance that arise in health care and in bioethics, as in other areas of life and work. A *feminist standpoint* is one that reflects the perspectives of women while challenging the social dominance of men's perspectives. Feminist standpoint *theory* refers to the rationale that supports that standpoint and strategies for implementing it.[1] Although my account focuses on sexism, similar arguments apply to racism and classism, and there is obvious overlap in these applications. The common element is that the differences between groups are the grounds by which one group obtains or maintains advantages or power over another. In defense of inequality or injustice, irrelevant differences may be invoked or relevant differences overlooked. From a feminist standpoint,[2] the ethical criterion for determining the relevance of differences between women and men is gender justice or equality.[3]

In what follows I point out flaws in contemporary health care and bioethics that indicate the need for a feminist standpoint. . . . I argue for a view of care and justice as compatible. The ethical and epistemological strengths of standpoint theory are illustrated through a case that reveals one physician's view of her relationship with patients. As a means of promoting gender justice in health care and bioethics, I conclude with a proposal for utilizing feminist standpoint theory on an ongoing basis.

SOME FLAWS IN CONTEMPORARY
HEALTH CARE AND BIOETHICS

Nearsightedness, unselfconsciousness, and arrogance are related flaws, each reinforcing a natural tendency to construe one's partial perspective as the full picture. By nearsightedness, I mean that none of us, as finite, situated individuals, can see all of the parameters of the decisions we make. This limitation says something positive as well as negative. It allows that we at least see what is near, even though we cannot see what is beyond our range of vision, including the long-range implications of our decisions.

To some degree, nearsightedness is encouraged within health care. Medical specialization and hierarchical (usually patriarchal) distribution of roles increase the propensity to limited vision. Beyond the maximization of health expertise that specialization facilitates, the choice of specialties is often motivated by the higher status of those who focus narrowly on a particular area of medicine. Generalists tend to be less rewarded by income and prestige than their specialist counterparts. Nearsightedness is also encouraged whenever the practitioner's obligations are defined exclusively in terms of the patient or client, ignoring the ripple effect that such decisions have on others.

Bioethicists are nearsighted too. Some view bioethical issues solely from their offices, classrooms, and lecture halls, maintaining their distance from the clinical settings in which the actual issues arise. While some are experts in areas on which their work relies, such as metaethics, ethical theory, medical science, clinical skills, and social science, they cannot be experts in all of these areas. Nearsightedness is also evident in the overall failure of bioethicists to attend to the ethical problems raised by racism, classism, and sexism, including heterosexism. Moreover, those who work in medical schools and hospitals may be co-opted by the values and priorities of the institutions that employ them. Such co-optation suggests the nearsightedness that William James referred to as "a certain blindness" regarding other values and priorities.[4]

Unselfconsciousness is used here to mean the lack of a sense of one's limitations. Some unselfconscious persons assume themselves capable of "point-of-viewlessness," defining their particular views as universal.[5] In contrast, a self-conscious person acknowledges her weaknesses as well as strengths, and acts accordingly. Like Socrates in the *Apology*,[6] the self-conscious person is anxious to avoid having others falsely attribute expertise to her. Socratic wisdom, and the imparting of that wisdom, necessarily includes knowledge of one's own ignorance. In areas of health care that emphasize treating the whole person or even the entire family, such as primary care medicine, family practice, nursing, and social work, there is sometimes a tendency to ignore or forget one's limitations. The clinician may then attempt the god-like feat of single-handedly providing for all of her patient's needs, without drawing on the more focused expertise of others whose involvement might improve her care.

Similarly, health care specialists sometimes pass judgment unselfconsciously on areas of health care about which they have relatively little knowledge in comparison with those practicing in those areas—for example, doctors vis-à-vis nurses, or surgeons vis-à-vis psychiatrists. One group may assert authority over the other, while ignoring the fact that they lack the experience and training of the other. This point applies also to clinicians who are ethicists. Although they may provide ethics consultations at the bedside, their clinical specialization limits the extent to which their clinical advice is appropriate for patients who require treatment by other specialists. Patient care, in all of its complex clinical, social, and ethical dimensions, cannot be optimized without the collaboration of those who are optimally qualified for different aspects of its provision.

Titles, positions, social attitudes, and publicity often promote unselfconsciousness. The public sometimes associates leadership in any area of medicine or philosophy with expertise on ethical issues relevant to medicine. Accordingly, a leader in a particular area of medicine or philosophy may be invited to speak or write on ethical issues about which others have broader and more critical knowledge. If she is selfconscious about her limitation, she will defer to those others, or at least call on them and credit them for their input. If she is unselfconscious, she may accept such invitations under false pretenses regarding her expertise. . . .

While unselfconsciousness ignores limitations, arrogance exaggerates strengths. To some, medicine presents a context in which arrogance serves a useful purpose. Consider, for example, the routine behavior of surgeons. To cut into a human body, to manipulate and remove organs, to place other organs and devices into the body—possibly these procedures could only be done by someone who is arrogant. Moreover, just because invasiveness is overt does not mean that it is more drastic than covert interventions. Psychotherapy, for example, may be more invasive than surgery because it affects people's minds rather than their bodies.[7] In both contexts, arrogance may be necessary for therapeutic effectiveness. Arrogance may also be both essential and problematic in nonmedical specialties or professions such as teaching and politics. Rightly or wrongly, bioethicists who are not clinicians may be just as arrogant as those who are.

The dictionary offers "pride" as a synonym for "arrogance." Pride is sometimes construed as a good thing, and only bad if it constitutes a false assessment of the facts. When it is construed in the latter way, pride is purportedly the principal sin of humankind. As Valerie Saiving maintains, however, the principal sin of women is not pride but "underdevelopment or negation of the self."[8] To be truthful about one's strengths along with one's weaknesses is a form of humility. The arrogance to be avoided involves denial of one's limitations, leading to expressions of power that place others at risk. It is not only possible but crucial for health care practitioners and bioethicists to avoid this kind of arrogance.

To some extent, nearsightedness, unselfconsciousness, and arrogance are inevitable in human life. It is possible and desirable, however, to reduce their negative implications through standpoint theory. Standpoint theory is based on recognition that each one's point of view, expertise, and authority are situated and partial. It implies the need for attention to views that are often neglected, such as those of women. A feminist standpoint serves as a corrective to the overall neglect of women's interests, experience, and insights in contemporary health care and bioethics. . . .

FEMINIST STANDPOINT AND ATTENTION TO RELATIONSHIPS AND CONTEXT

An expanded version of feminist standpoint theory is reinforced by the attention that contemporary bioethics has directed to relationships and context. In health care as in other areas, relationships are often discussed in the context of roles. The dominant and dominating role of the paternalistic physician is often cited, but dominant and dominated roles abound within the health care hierarchy. Historically, nurses have been seen and have even viewed themselves as handmaids of physicians, reflecting gender stereotypes.[9] To the extent that standpoint theory has been incorporated into the health care system, nurses have enriched the epistemological base of clinical judgments. Nonetheless, hierarchical arrangements remain evident not only among the different health care professions, but also within each profession. Like society in general, health care reflects a patriarchal system.

In various models of the physician–patient relationship, the doctor's dominant role is the vantage point from which the relationship is explained and assessed. Obviously, patients also play a role in the relationship, but they are often considered only as the assumed object of beneficence, or in the context of *permitting* them to exercise autonomy. Because patients are generally dominated by doctors, standpoint theory is indispensable to the reduction of nearsightedness, unselfconsciousness, and arrogance on the part of physicians. From a feminist standpoint, this is doubly important because the majority of patients are women and the majority of physicians are still men.[10]

None of the prevailing models of the physician–patient relationship[11] reflects a feminist standpoint, that is, one that considers the experiences of women—whether as individuals, women in general, or members of other nondominant groups—as crucial to the analysis and assessment of that relationship. A feminist standpoint is crucial because it takes account of the embeddedness of the doctor–patient relationship in other relationships, whether these involve dominance or not. When feminist standpoint theory applies to individuals as well as groups, it also takes account, as traditional models of the physician–patient relationship do not, of the mutuality of that relationship, acknowledging that physicians and patients alike have rights and responsibilities vis-à-vis each other.

In their critique of traditional ethics, various versions of feminism insist on considerations of context, that is, the situatedness on which feminist standpoint theory relies. In health care, the consideration of context mainly takes the form of case-based analysis. The clinician's thinking and decision making are usually precipitated by an actual case that raises questions about treatment or nontreatment. The health caregiver attempts to optimize care of a particular patient with whom she has a special relationship that involves a special responsibility. Although the term "care" is often identified with treatment, the caregiver knows that this is sometimes a mistaken identity, that optimal care sometimes means that treatment should be foregone or withdrawn.

Recently, Albert Jonsen and Stephen Toulmin have proposed a revival of casuistry as a method by which case-based analyses may be applied to bioethics. They affirm an extended version of feminist standpoint theory (without calling it that) when they write that *"moral knowledge is essentially particular."*[12] Not surprisingly, this method is broadly supported by clinical ethicists. Except for its neglect of broader social issues, it is also supported by feminist bioethicists.[13] The feminist reservation about the adequacy of casuistry for clinical ethics is that its emphasis on cases provides too limited a sense of context.

THE MEANING OF CARE AND THE PITFALLS OF CARE-BASED REASONING

Taking account of the particularity of individual relationships through an extension of feminist standpoint theory not only shows consistency with the case-based reasoning of clinicians and clinical ethicists, but also with the care-based models of moral reasoning recently developed by Carol Gilligan and Nel Noddings. Both derive their understanding of care from an analysis of women's experience; both insist on the centrality of women's standpoint in women's own ethical judgment, but argue for its relevance to men as well. Gilligan, drawing on her studies of women facing unwanted pregnancy, defines a care ethic as concerned primarily with responsibilities that arise from attachment or ties to others, disregarding the impartiality that traditional ethics demands.[14] Noddings distinguishes between natural and ethical caring, claiming the experience of motherhood as the paradigm for ethical behavior. Ethical caring means deliberate expression of the natural inclination of mothers to be engrossed in concerns about their children and to identify their children's interests with their own.[15]

Despite the emphasis on relationships and women's experience that Gilligan and Noddings elaborate, many feminists have been uneasy about the implications of their views. Women's standpoints, after all, are not always identical with a feminist standpoint. Just as nurses who define their primary responsibility as care for patients experience gender injustice in a patriarchal health care system, mothers who naturally and ethically define their primary responsibility as care for their children are often exploited by being deprived of opportunities equal to their male counterparts. The same is true for women who are the predominant caregivers of the disabled, the sick, and the elderly. Feminists are therefore concerned that those who champion a care-based ethic may reinforce the long-standing practice of exploiting women's natural propensity to care. Through its insistence on critique of the dominant standpoint, feminist standpoint theory attempts to preempt this injustice. It thus argues that considerations of gender justice be joined to those of a care ethic.

One feminist who has argued persuasively for a necessary connection between care and justice is Marilyn Friedman. Her account further illustrates how feminist standpoint contributes to ethical theory and practice.[16] Acknowledging that a gender difference in moral reasoning is empirically disputed, Friedman analyzes the implications of gender differences that are not in dispute. "Even if actual statistical differences in the moral reasoning of women and men cannot be confirmed," she writes, "there is nevertheless a real difference in the moral norms and values culturally associated with gender."[17] This "real difference" leads to what Friedman calls a gender-based "division of moral labor," supported by stereotypically defined differences that may or may not be present in individuals.

According to Friedman, the two categories of care and justice overlap, and if care is morally adequate, it involves justice in personal as well as professional relationships. Similarly, if justice means giving people their due, it demands determination of what constitutes due care for each. The application of this concept to health care is obvious: the health practitioner must recognize and respond to the different health needs of each patient. Discovery and treatment of such needs are impossible without attunement to the patient's standpoint as privileged epistemologically and ethically. . . .

If care is defined broadly enough to encompass justice, it is care in either domain, and if justice is defined broadly enough to accommodate the uniqueness of interpersonal and professional relationships, it is justice in either domain. Defining either locus more narrowly requires recognition that human beings live and act in both contexts, with different roles to play in each. The political context mainly involves the narrower concept of justice, while professional and personal contexts mainly involve the narrower concept of care. Only if the concepts of justice and care are construed broadly are they equally applicable to either context. At that point, neither care nor justice has priority; the two are interchangeable because each entails the other. To the feminist position that the personal is political, we might then add that the political is personal.

Friedman proposes a model of friendship for ethical care.[18] If friendship includes both justice and care, it may serve as an ethical ideal for familial as well as for other interpersonal and professional relationships. Developmentally, we learn to care from those who care for us, and in most instances that means friends as well as relatives. The "caring work" that predominates in women's lives occurs in situations in which relatives or nonrelatives regard each other as friends. According to Ruddick, this "caring work" underlies a feminist standpoint.[19]

But is care in the health setting equivalent to the caring described by Gilligan, Noddings, and Ruddick? For all three authors the meaning of care derives from women's experience of caring. Maternal thinking is care-based because its defining feature is a natural inclination to care for one's child. The thinking involved in this process is particular, partial, and practical.[20] It aims to foster the development of another as a unique individual. Just as a woman first becomes a biological mother by pushing her baby out of her body, so the caring labor of maternal thinking (no matter who undertakes it) consists of pushing people toward independence through fulfillment of their own potential. Similarly, the goal of health care is to render the caregiver unnecessary. If the care provided in the health setting has this goal, it is consistent with the care described by Gilligan, Noddings, and Ruddick.

Unfortunately, however, care in the health setting is often equated with treatment, and treatment is not necessarily caring. It is not caring if it ignores or impedes the thrust toward self-differentiation epitomized in childbirth, which is biologically and psychologically natural in human beings. It is not caring if it fails to respect and support the uniqueness of the other that a loving parental relationship exemplifies. In other words, caring essentially involves attention to differences, whether these apply to groups or individuals.[21] An extension of feminist standpoint theory obviously supports this interpretation of caring.

AN ILLUSTRATIVE CASE

As already suggested, the reasons for extending standpoint theory to individuals are epistemological and ethical. To illustrate this in the context of health care, consider the following case:[22]

> Al Brown is a seventy-three-year-old man with cerebral palsy and severe spastic paralysis in all four limbs. He was admitted to a dependent care facility forty years ago and has lived there ever since. Despite his significant physical impairment and need for assistance with basic life functions, he is cognitively intact.
>
> Several years ago, Mr. Brown was given phenobarbitol for treatment of a seizure disorder. When the threat of seizures subsided, he continued to receive 60 milligrams of phenobarbitol four times a day. Now, each time a new pharmacist or physician is assigned to his unit, phenobarbitol levels are drawn. These invariably run in the 50s in micrograms per milliliter, suggesting to clinicians that his dosage should be reduced. Mr. Brown objects to the reduction, stating that he

is doing fine, has not had any seizures, and "always gets messed up when people fool around with my medications."

   Dr. Ann Joseph, the attending physician for the unit, has a somewhat novel
view of her patients and their claims on her. She calls them "customers," and assumes that "the customer is always right" when there is any medical doubt
about treatment or nontreatment. Although Dr. Joseph has explained to Mr.
Brown the risks reported in the medical literature regarding his level of phenobarbitol, he insists, and she agrees, that these are statistical risks that may not
apply to him. He says he feels well with the 60 milligram dosage and poorly
whenever the dosage is lowered. Dr. Joseph regards his view as privileged and
instructs the house staff not to reduce the "customer's" phenobarbitol level.

Although clinical texts do not support Mr. Brown's phenobarbitol
dosage, Dr. Joseph recognizes that her patient has a uniquely valid standpoint from which to judge whether its administration hurts or helps him.
She thus not only respects his autonomy but credits him with knowledge
about his own condition that textbooks, articles, or even experience with
other patients cannot provide. In other words, she recognizes her own nearsightedness, even when her vision is improved by input from colleagues;
self-conscious about her own limitations, she avoids arrogance. As a patient,
Mr. Brown belongs to a dominated group. By gender Dr. Joseph belongs to
a dominated group, but by profession she belongs to a dominant group.
While dominant in her relationship with Mr. Brown, she realizes that his
standpoint constitutes "an engaged vision of the world opposed and superior to dominant ways of thinking."[23]

   Perhaps it is no accident that Dr. Joseph (whose name I have changed
here) is a woman. Recent studies indicate that female physicians spend more
time than their male counterparts listening to patients.[24] With Ruddick, I believe it is possible and preferable for men as well as women to be "maternal
thinkers," and with Gilligan and Noddings I believe it possible and preferable
for men as well as women to be both care-reasoners and justice-reasoners. But
if care for others involves attention to individual differences, the data obtained
by Gilligan and her colleagues suggest that women are more likely than men
to incorporate an extended version of standpoint theory into their moral, political, and professional judgments. Care as defined by Dr. Joseph goes beyond the maxim of clinical practice: "When in doubt, look at the patient." She
recognizes not only the limitations of theoretical knowledge but also the privileged status of patients' experience and knowledge of their own illness. Care
of patients, for Dr. Joseph, involves the dictum: "Listen to the customer."

   Standpoint-based judgments may be more prevalent among women
than men because women already belong to a group whose standpoint has
been neglected throughout history. They are therefore more likely to challenge what Catharine MacKinnon calls "masculine partiality," the presumption of objectivity and universality that men have generally attributed
to their limited knowledge and experience of the world.[25] Sometimes the

presumption is overt; sometimes it is covert. Women themselves often support the presumption.

It is not difficult to understand why many women accept masculine partiality as definitive. Having been socialized in a sexist culture, the wonder is that there are so many women and men who challenge it. Even among those who reject the presumption, the self-consciousness implicit in feminist standpoint theory is sometimes lacking. Consider, for example, the current tendency to use gender-neutral language in addressing various topics in health care and bioethics. Even beyond reproduction, many issues are not gender-neutral. These include the health implications of the feminization of poverty, the problem of battered women, the high incidence of women who suffer from eating disorders and of those who subject themselves to health risks for the sake of appearance.[26] Recent articles on the Human Genome Project address the entire range of ethical and social questions raised by the project in gender-neutral language.[27] Yet it is women alone who supply ova, gestate, and give birth, and who undergo prenatal diagnosis, pregnancy termination, and fetal therapies. It is mainly women, but need not be mainly women, who are targeted for genetic screening, who are primary caregivers of those who are genetically disabled, and who work in those areas of clinical genetics that are least rewarded.[28] Clearly, then, the Human Genome Project is not gender-neutral in its implications.

Such examples call for attention to differences between the genders rather than gender-neutrality. Inattention to gender differences allows the dominant group, whether deliberately or not, to exclude the nondominant group from the advantages that it enjoys. To promote equality in heath care, which presumably is a goal of bioethics as well as feminism, attention to nondominant standpoints is thus not only useful but necessary. But how can such attention be ensured or promoted? In closing I propose a modest strategy for implementing feminist standpoint theory.

PROPORTIONATE REPRESENTATION AS A REMEDIAL STRATEGY

In American society we are familiar with the concept and strategy of proportionate representation. Despite failures in implementing this strategy, it is potentially a means by which each individual exerts some influence in policy decisions that apply to everyone. At an earlier point in history, direct participation of citizens in town meetings offered a purer form of democracy than we have now; that model ceased to be operable when society became too large and complex for every competent adult to be directly involved in its governance. Proportionate representation remains a mechanism intended to ensure as much democracy as possible under the circumstances.

Democratic process is considered a good not only because it maximizes the participation of individuals, but also because it manifests equal regard for each one's participation. Even within a system of equal voting rights, however, it is hardly true that each one's participation is, or is even considered, equal to everyone else's. A similar discrepancy is observable in health care, where the traditional paternalistic relationship of inequality between practitioner and patient prevails, and the income, prestige, and power of physicians is greater than those of other health practitioners.[29] Since most physicians are white men, their dominance involves the dominance of race and gender as well.

Feminist standpoint theory suggests that a means of countering the inevitable nearsightedness of the dominant class is to ensure that those who are not part of that class are included among the decision or policy makers. If such a strategy were implemented, the voices of women and minorities who disagree with those who are dominant would be heard in Institutional Review Boards and ethics committees at the local level, and in state and national commissions addressing health needs and health care ethics. They would also be heard as teachers of health practitioners, especially physicians and thus members of the dominant group, and as leaders or experts in health care and bioethical decision making. Recent meetings sponsored separately by the National Institutes of Health and The Hastings Center are steps in the direction of expanding the range of voices heard.[30]

Proportionate representation means inviting the input of people with whom members of the dominant class do not themselves identify, whose presence may reduce their level of comfort and whose views may challenge theirs. It also means that tokenism, such as having one woman or minority person on the committee, is not enough, particularly when the group's decisions disproportionately affect those who are not dominant. Truly proportionate representation extends beyond gender, race, and class to differences in sexual orientation, political orientation, physical abilities, and mental abilities. It extends beyond the decision making of formally established groups such as academic committees and centers to the informal contexts of health care teams and clinic management.[31] Ideally, proportional representation also takes account of the fact that the same individual many belong to both dominant and nondominant groups. For example, while I belong to the nondominant gender, I represent the dominant class, race, and sexual orientation. To be fully reflective of the engaged vision of the world that standpoint theory offers requires participation of all the nondominant counterparts to dominance. Accordingly, I ought to be self-conscious about the limitation of vision occasioned by my participation in dominant groups. Moreover, the requirement of proportionate representation is not satisfied by having a single individual represent several nondominant groups—unless her voice and vote are counted additionally for each of the groups she represents.

Unfortunately, situations arise in which too few nondominant persons are available to provide proportionate representation. Sometimes the claim that there are too few is refutable, but sometimes it is not. Self-consciousness is then especially demanded of the dominant individuals who render the representation disproportionate. Minimally, such self-consciousness means acknowledgment of differences between dominant and dominated perspectives and efforts to learn about the latter. With regard to gender differences, it means acknowledgment of a possible sexist bias even by those who consider themselves free of such bias. As Virginia Warren observes, "Sexist ethics would never appear sexist [even to the person practicing it]. It would be clothed in a cloak of neutrality because favoring some group or position would be unthinkable."[32] A similar observation applies to groups distinguishable by race and class, and often to those distinguishable by their mental or physical ability or sexual orientation.

The postmodern insight regarding the inadequacy of categorizations is an important reminder that proportionate representation cannot entirely eliminate nearsightedness because nondominant persons are nearsighted also. Those of us who belong to the nondominant gender need to be self-conscious about this limitation, thereby avoiding or at least reducing arrogance. When we make decisions and formulate policies, our judgments remain fallible. Accordingly, from time to time we need to reconsider and revise our judgments in response to changing circumstances and new insights or critique.

In health care and bioethics as in other areas of life, decisions and policies need to be developed by democratic means, inviting the standpoint of diverse individuals in order to maximize their ethical and epistemological validity. Because feminism is committed to equality and to the moral significance of women's experience, both collectively and individually, it supports this strategy for reducing the flaws of nearsightedness, unselfconsciousness, and arrogance. Because care involves ongoing recognition of the dynamic character of individuals and groups, and the complexity of their relationships, it demands attention to differences. The crucial contribution of feminist standpoint theory to bioethics is the egalitarian critique that it adds to that attention.

Notes

I wish to thank Elizabeth Guonjian, Laura Purdy, Mary Solberg, and Susan Wolf for their helpful comments on earlier versions of this chapter. Thanks too to Rosie Tong for her counsel and encouragement during its final revision.

1. Most of those who have written about feminist standpoint do not use the term "theory" in referring to its rationale or methodology. Some sources represent different versions of feminism, some write from and about a feminist perspective but do not use the term "standpoint," and some write about women's experience or perspective but not about feminism. For examples of all of these approaches, see Donna Haraway, "Situated Knowledges: The Science Question in Feminism and the Privilege of Partial Perspective," *Feminist Studies* 14 (1988): 575–99; Nancy C. M. Hartsock, *Money, Sex, and Power: Toward a Feminist Historical Materialism* (Boston, MA: Northeastern University Press, 1985), 232, and "The Feminist Standpoint: Devloping the Ground for a Specifically Feminist Historical Materialism," in Sandra Harding, ed., *Feminism and Methodology:*

Social Science Issues (Bloomington, IN: Indiana University Press, 1987), 136–62; Dorothy E. Smith, "Women's Perspective as a Radical Critique of Sociology," in Harding, ed., *Feminism and Methodology*, 85–96; Sara Ruddick, *Maternal Thinking: Toward a Politics of Peace* (New York, NY: Ballantine Books, 1989), 127–39; Nel Noddings, "Ethics from the Standpoint of Women," in Deborah L. Rhode, ed., *Theoretical Perspectives on Sexual Difference* (New Haven, CT: Yale University Press, 1990), 160–293; Catharine A. MacKinnon, "Feminism, Marxism, Method, and the State," in Harding, ed., *Feminism and Methodology*, 136–56; Terry Winant, "The Feminist Standpoint: A Matter of Language," *Hypatia* 2 (Winter 1987): 123–48; Alison M. Jaggar, *Feminist Politics and Human Nature* (Totowa, NJ: Rowman and Allanheld, 1983), 369–71, 377–89.

2. Consider "*a* feminist standpoint" as equivalent to "*the* feminist standpoint" described by Hartsock and Winant, note 1, above. I prefer the indefinite article because it suggests that there is more than one feminist standpoint. While different versions of feminism concur in their opposition to the oppression of women, they offer different ways of explaining and rectifying the oppression. This leads to different feminist standpoints. To use a visual image, different feminist standpoints are different points of view located within the common locus in which all feminists stand.

3. I have developed a meaning of "equality" essential to a feminist standpoint in *Women and Children in Health Care: An Unequal Majority* (New York, NY: Oxford University Press, 1993).

4. See William James, in John J. McDermott, ed., *The Writings of William James* (New York, NY: Modern Library, 1968), 629–45.

5. Catharine MacKinnon used the term "point-of-viewlessness" to identify the standard that men have erroneously imputed to their view of the world. See MacKinnon, "Feminism, Marxism, Method, and the State," 137.

6. Recall Socrates's discovery of why the oracle of Delphi considered him wiser than the statesman, who instead was reputed to be wiser: "I am wiser than he is by only this trifle, that what I do not know I don't think I do." See W. H. D. Rouse, trans., *Great Dialogues of Plato* (New York, NY: Mentor Books, 1956), 427.

7. While some surgical procedures affect the brain, even those *may* not affect the mind.

8. Valerie Saiving, "The Human Situation: A Feminine View," *Journal of Religion* 40 (1960): 100–12, 108. See also Judith Plaskow, *Sex, Sin and Grace* (Lanham, MD: University Press of America, 1980).

9. Mary B. Mahowald, "Sex-Role Stereotypes in Medicine," *Hypatia* 2 (Summer 1987): 21–38. Thankfully, this view is rarely supported today.

10. Charlotte F. Muller, *Health Care and Gender* (New York, NY: Russell Sage Foundation, 1992), 7–10.

11. Various labels used for different models include paternalism, covenant, contract, business, beneficence-in-trust, friendship, and collaboration. See, for example, Edmund D. Pellegrino and David C. Thomasma, *For the Patient's Good: The Restoration of Beneficence in Health Care* (New York, NY: Oxford University Press, 1988), 101–06; Melvin Konner, *Medicine at the Crossroads* (New York, NY: Pantheon, 1993), 3–27; Sherwin, *No Longer Patient*, 137–57; and Mahowald, *Women and Children in Health Care*, 28–32. The prevailing models include those that give priority to patient autonomy, to physician beneficence toward the patient, or to some combination of respect for patient autonomy and beneficence toward the patient.

12. Albert R. Jonsen and Stephen Toulmin, *The Abuse of Casuistry: A History of Moral Reasoning* (Berkeley, CA: University of California Press, 1988), 330 (italics theirs).

13. For example, Sherwin, *No Longer Patient*, 78–80.

14. Carol Gilligan, *In a Different Voice: Psychological Theory and Women's Development* (Cambridge, MA: Harvard University Press, 1982), and "Moral Orientation and Moral Development," in Eva Feder Kittay and Diana T. Meyers, eds., *Women and Moral Theory* (Totowa, NJ: Rowman & Littlefield, 1987), 19–33.

15. Nel Noddings, *Caring: A Feminine Approach to Ethics and Moral Education* (Berkeley, CA: University of California Press, 1984), 16.

16. Marilyn Friedman, "Beyond Caring: The De-moralization of Gender," in Marsha Hanen and Kai Nielson, eds., *Science, Morality and Feminist Theory* (Calgary, Canada: University of Calgary Press, 1987), 87–110. See also Michael Stocker, "Duty and Friendship: Toward a Synthesis of Gilligan's Contrastive Moral Concepts," in Kittay and Meyers, eds., *Women and Moral Theory*, 56–58.

17. Friedman, "Beyond Caring," 89.

18. Marilyn Friedman, "Feminism and Modern Friendship: Dislocating the Community," *Ethics* 99 (1989): 275–90.

19. Ruddick, *Maternal Thinking*, 130.

20. I cannot here develop the relationship between particularism and partiality, but see Alan Gewirth, "Ethical Universalism and Particularism," *Journal of Philosophy* 85 (1988): 283–302, and Marilyn Friedman, "Partiality," in Lawrence C. Becker and Charlotte B. Becker, eds., *Encyclopedia of Ethics*, vol. 2 (New York, NY: Garland, 1992), 932–35.

21. Martha Minow, among others, has delineated the importance of attending to gender differences as a means of ensuring that care is maximized on a societal level. For example, see her *Making All the Difference: Inclusion, Exclusion, and American Law* (Ithaca, NY: Cornell University Press, 1990), 216–19. But Minow does not elaborate the import of paying attention to individual differences among women.

22. While the clinical details of this case are accurate, I have changed irrelevant details (including names) to ensure confidentiality.

23. Ruddick, *Maternal Thinking*, 129.

24. Natalie Angier, "Bedside Manners Improve as More Women Enter Medicine," *New York Times*, June 21, 1992, sec. 4, p. 18.

25. Catharine A. MacKinnon, "Feminism, Marxism, Method, and the State: An Agenda for Theory," *Signs* 7 (1982): 515–44, 537.

26. *Diagnostic and Statistical Manual of Mental Disorders*, 3d ed. (Washington, DC: American Psychiatric Association, 1987), 66; Kathryn Morgan, "Women and the Knife, Cosmetic Surgery and the Colonization of Women's Bodies," *Hypatia* 6 (Fall 1991): 30; Ruth Sidel, *Women and Children Last* (New York, NY: Penguin Viking Books, 1986), 158.

27. Consider, for example, Andrea Bonnicksen's description of the options available after prenatal screening has detected an affected fetus: "the *couple* will either terminate the pregnancy . . . or bear a child with the disease." See her "Genetic Diagnosis of Human Embryos," *Hastings Center Report* 22 (July–Aug. 1992): S5–11, S6 (my italics). But see also James D. Watson, "The Human Genome Project: Past, Present, and Future," *Science* 248 (1990): 44–48; Francis S. Collins, "Medical and Ethical Consequences of the Human Genome Project," *Journal of Clinical Ethics* 2 (1991): 260–67; and Thomas H. Murray, "The Human Genome Project and Genetic Testing: Ethical Implications," in *The Genome, Ethics and the Law: A Report of a Conference on the Ethical and Legal Implications of Genetic Testing*, Coolfont Conference Center, Berkeley Springs, West Virginia, June 14–16, 1991, AAAS Publication No. 92-115 (Washington, DC: American Association for the Advancement of Science, 1992), 49–78.

28. For example, women constitute 93.5 percent of masters' prepared genetic counselors. See Deborah F. Pencarinha, Nora K. Bell, Janice G. Edwards, and Robert G. Best, "Ethical Issues in Genetic Counseling: A Comparison of M.S. Counselor and Medical Geneticist Perspectives," *Journal of Genetic Counseling* 1 (1992): 19–30, 22.

29. Mahowald, "Sex-Role Stereotypes in Medicine," 22.

30. For example, in September 1991, NIH sponsored a meeting to plan an agenda for the study of women's health during the coming decade; in November 1991, NIH sponsored a meeting on reproductive genetics. Both meetings were predominantly attended by, and led by, women. Participants in the Hastings Center Project on Feminism and Bioethics were also predominantly women.

31. Although the term "health care team" refers to all of those involved in patient care, the team coach or captain is the attending physician, whose dominance, while justified in terms of his medical expertise, may be influenced also by other dominant but irrelevant factors such as race, gender, and class.

32. Virginia L. Warren, "Feminist Directions in Medical Ethics," *Hypatia* 4 (Summer 1989): 73–87, 74.

Editorials

Caring for Women's Health— What Is the Problem?

In this issue of the *Journal* are three articles about the health of women. Nanette Wenger and her colleagues[1] review what is known about the differences in cardiovascular health between men and women: cardiovascular disease is the leading cause of death among women as well as men, although it occurs later in life; it is less likely to be treated aggressively in women, and the mortality is higher. Ruth Merkatz and others at the Food and Drug Administration (FDA)[2] review the recent reversal of the agency's policy that excluded women of reproductive age from participating in new drug studies; according to these authors, women and men may react to drugs differently, and the fact that there may be special risks to the fetus when pregnant women are treated is all the more reason to include women in early studies. And finally, J. Claude Bennett, writing for the Institute of Medicine's Board on Health Sciences Policy,[3] discusses the issues raised by an amendment recently proposed to the Public Health Service Act; this amendment would require that clinical research sponsored by the National Institutes of Health (NIH) include adequate numbers of women and minorities to permit analysis of whether they respond differently from white men.

These articles reflect a widespread view that clinical research has over the years improperly excluded women. According to this view, women have been discriminated against in three ways: diseases that affect them disproportionately are less likely to be studied; women are less likely to be included as participants in clinical trials; and they are less likely to be senior investigators conducting the trials. In the past three years we have seen major efforts to correct these sources of bias, two of which Merkatz et al. and Bennett describe. In addition, the NIH in 1990 established an Office of Research on Women's Health for the explicit purpose of addressing all three forms of discrimination.[4] Shortly after Bernadine Healy became director of the NIH in 1991, she launched the Women's Health Initiative—a massive 15-year study of 160,000 women that will cost more than $600 million and include the largest clinical trial ever conducted.[5] She also moved aggressively to correct discrimination against female investigators within the NIH itself. On the clinical front, there have recently been calls for the establishment of a new medical specialty in women's health. This proposal was provocatively debated in the new *Journal of Women's Health,* which published its first issue in 1992.[6]

Focusing attention on women's health has clearly involved different sorts of efforts targeted toward different sorts of discrimination. I shall comment here primarily on the issue of research on women's health. Is it true that we have not paid sufficient attention to diseases in women? And what are the merits of requiring that women and minorities be included in nearly all clinical trials in numbers large enough to permit determining whether the results pertain to them?

Whether diseases in women have been inadequately studied is difficult to say. First, we have to decide whether we mean a disease that affects women almost exclusively (such as breast cancer), one that affects women disproportionately (such as gallbladder disease), or one that affects both men and women nearly equally (such as cardiovascular disease). If we mean the last, then there is little doubt that women have been systematically excluded as subjects for study, as Wenger et al. make clear in the case of cardiovascular disease.[1] No one can know with certainty all the reasons that women have been excluded, but a few have been explicitly offered.

Women of reproductive age have often been excluded as participants in clinical trials because of possible risks to a fetus. This has not been just a matter of special concern or paternalism. In addition, it has been a matter of avoiding unnecessary risks of legal liability. Older women have been excluded because they often have multiple health problems that may create risks for them and confuse the results of the trial. And finally, the more kinds of participants enrolled in a trial, the more difficult the analysis and interpretation. Given these problems, as well as the indeterminate contribution of sexism, it is not surprising that most clinical trials have been heavily, if not exclusively, weighted toward men.

The scientific reasons for limiting participation in a clinical trial to one sex—as well as to one age group and one race and one socioeconomic group—warrant some special attention. In a clinical trial of a new intervention, valid interpretation requires that the research subjects be as homogeneous as possible. In fact, all subjects in a clinical trial would ideally be identical, except that only half would receive the intervention under study. If this were the case, then there would be no question of different effects in different groups confusing the findings—that is, confounding variables would be less likely to distort the interpretation of the results. This is why twins are in such demand for clinical research. But what we gain in scientific validity by studying homogeneous groups, we lose in generalizability. We cannot be sure that what works in one group will work the same way in others. The assumption has been, however, that it usually will, even though the size of the effect may vary. For example, if a drug decreases fever in men, it is unlikely to increase it in women. Thus, in some studies of diseases that affect both men and women, such as cardiovascular disease, only men have participated as research subjects, but the conclusions have been implicitly applied to women.

Applying the salient conclusions of clinical research to populations not studied is usually reasonable. Typically, there is no biologically plausible reason to expect the findings to vary greatly with sex or race or any other such grouping. Sometimes, however, there is. This is particularly true when the disease or intervention under study is closely tied to known sex differences— such as average muscle mass or estrogen levels. In such instances, it is necessary either to do a very large study to include enough men and women to analyze the results separately, or to do a second trial to study women (assuming that the first trial was mainly in men, as has too often been the case). In the sequence of clinical research, establishing efficacy in the most efficient and valid way possible has been the goal of initial trials. If the initial studies have yielded important results, questions of generalizability have been addressed in subsequent studies, especially if there were suggestions of differential effects in the early research.

These issues are somewhat different from the more complicated question of whether diseases that mainly affect women receive due attention. Here the evidence is mixed and difficult to interpret. For example, we pay far more attention to breast cancer than we do to prostate cancer, but no one would suggest that we live in a society that systematically favors women. This year, for example, the NIH will spend about $197 million for research on breast cancer (Financial Management Branch, National Cancer Institute: personal communication), a disease that will kill 46,000 women.[7] In the same year, we will spend only $37 million for research on prostate cancer, which will kill 35,000 men.[7] Per life lost, then, we are spending four times as much on breast cancer as on prostate cancer. I suspect that the reason for such discrepancies is more likely to be ageism than sexism. Breast cancer is a disease of middle age; prostate cancer is a disease of old age. Similarly, it may be that the greater attention paid to heart disease in men than in women has more to do with the earlier age at which it occurs in men than it does with sex. These discrepancies may reflect other, more nebulous factors as well, including different levels of concern about particular diseases in men and women. For example, it could be that men fear heart diseases more than women do; women consistently express more concern about breast cancer, despite the fact that heart disease is seven times more likely to kill them. Public concern of this sort rightly influences the attention given to various diseases. And there are also biases on the part of investigators that influence what is studied; some diseases are simply more interesting than others.

Despite these caveats, the evidence is that there has been too little research on disease in women, particularly cardiovascular disease. What is the best remedy? In my view, the proposed amendment to the Public Health Service Act would create worse problems than it would solve. To provide a valid analysis of results in subjects of both sexes and all minorities would require unreasonably large trials of new interventions. It would mean trying to determine efficacy and generalizability in the same study—an inefficient approach, as Bennett points out.[3] Inevitably, there would be attempts to evade the requirements, by devising justifications for excluding women and minorities altogether. We would then lose whatever hints we now have of differential effects in small, early trials that include some women and minority-group members. The requirements also assume that clinically important differences between men and women are the rule rather than the exception—a biologically implausible assumption. Finally, the congressional requirements lead to absurdities. Which of the many minorities are to be included? Should both premenopausal and postmenopausal women be included in all studies? Why not all age groups? How many ways must we slice and dice in the interest of fairness? Scientific research does not lend itself to rigid cookbook rules; there must be some room for common sense and considerations of biologic plausibility. Healy's approach is better.[8] The NIH now requires grant applicants to justify any decision to exclude women and minorities from clinical trials, but they need not include them in numbers large enough to determine differential effects.

In trying to remedy patterns of discrimination against women in health care, we need to step carefully. Yes, women should be included more often in clinical trials, but not according to a formula that would make clinical trials more difficult than ever and probably be counterproductive in terms of learning about differential effects in women. And yes, we do need to educate clinicians better about women's health and the presentation of disease in women. But, as argued persuasively by Harrison,[9] a new women's health specialty is not the answer. It would marginalize the care of women and leave the mainstream to men, where the lack of attention to women's health would then be officially sanctioned. (If there is to be separatism, I would prefer a new specialty of men's health, leaving the mainstream to women.) Most important, in my view, is to continue to bring women into the upper echelons of academic medicine. If women are the teachers of the next generation of doctors and the senior investigators in the next generation of clinical research, women's health will finally get the attention it deserves without the need for special rules.

MARCIA ANGELL, M.D.

References

1. Wenger NK, Speroff L, Packard B. Cardiovascular health and disease in women. N Engl J Med 1993;329:247–56.

2. Merkatz RB, Temple R, Sobel S, Feiden K, Kessler DA. Working Group on Women in Clinical Trials. Women in clinical trials of new drugs—a change in Food and Drug Administration policy. N Engl J Med 1993;329:292–6.

3. Bennett JC. Inclusion of women in clinical trials—policies for population subgroups. N Engl J Med 1993;329:288–92.

4. Pinn VW. Commentary: women, research, and the National Institutes of Health. Am J Prev Med 1992;8:324–7.

5. U.S. health study to involve 160,000 women at 16 centers. New York Times. March 31, 1993:A21.

6. Wallis LA. Women's health: a specialty? Pros and cons. J Womens Health 1992;1:107–8.

7. Boring CC, Squires TS, Tong T. Cancer statistics, 1993. CA Cancer J Clin 1993;43:7–26.

8. Herman R. Healy's legacy at NIH: reversing the brain drain, launching the women's initiative. Washington Post. June 15, 1993:Health Suppl:7.

9. Harrison M. Women's health as a specialty: a deceptive solution. J Womens Health 1992;1:101–6.

Women's Health

To the Editor: In her editorial (July 22 issue),[1] Dr. Angell charges that women have been discriminated against in three key areas; yet, my observations and the evidence she presents do not support the charges.

First, Dr. Angell notes, "diseases that affect [women] disproportionately are less likely to be studied." In the area I am most familiar with—oncology—this assertion is ludicrous. In 1993 the National Cancer Institute budgeted $273 million for research on cancers specific to women, including breast, cervical, ovarian, and uterine cancers, and $41 million for research on cancers specific to men, including prostate and testicular cancers (National Cancer Institute: personal communication). In fact, outlays by the National Cancer Institute for research on breast cancer, which kills 46,000 women a year, exceed those for research on lung cancer, which kills 93,000 men and 56,000 women annually.[2] Moreover, for fiscal year 1993, Congress earmarked $210 million of Department of Defense funds exclusively for breast-cancer studies.

Second, Dr. Angell states, "women are less likely to be included as participants in clinical trials." In another article in the same issue of the *Journal*, Bennett notes that "the literature is inconclusive about whether women have been excluded from or importantly underrepresented in clinical trials."[3] Furthermore, it is not clear that the issue is one of discrimination. Dr. Angell herself raises the obvious issue of legal liability. Unless researchers can have ironclad protection from liability for fetal damage, it is unreasonable to require the inclusion of women with childbearing potential. This is not paternalism; it is a matter of legal and corporate survival.

Third, Dr. Angell states, "[women] are less likely to be senior investigators." This is true, but evidence that it is because of discrimination is not presented.

Finally, I believe that in terms of health and medical care, our society in fact systematically favors women. Women live an average of eight years longer than men, in part because of sex-based cultural and legal factors that are unfavorable to men's health. As examples, occupation-related casualties are much higher among men, and in wartime, only men have been conscripted (willingly or unwillingly) to die for their country. The draft, for better or worse, is an example of blatant sex discrimination, having led to the deaths of over 500,000 American men over the past 50 years. Also, women have an entire medical specialty—obstetrics and gynecology—devoted to their special needs.

ACE ALLEN, M.D.
University of Kansas
Medical Center

References

1. Angell M. Caring for women's health—what is the problem? N Engl J Med 1993;329:271–2.
2. Cancer facts and figures—1993. New York: American Cancer Society, 1993.
3. Bennett JC. Inclusion of women in clinical trials—policies for population subgroups. N Engl J Med 1993;329:288–92.

To the Editor: The difference in expenditures for breast cancer ($197 million) and prostate cancer ($37 million) reflects the effort that the medical profession is making to rectify the lack of clinical research on women's health. If the medical profession knew as much about the causes, course, and treatment of breast cancer as is known about the causes, course, and treatment of prostate cancer, the annual expenditures would most likely be quite different. The bottom line is that women of childbearing age, older women, and members of minority groups have all been excluded from clinical trials. These groups combined represent the majority of people in America.

. . . Dr. Angell's solution to the problem of clinical research on women's health is for the National Institute of Health to continue requiring justification for the exclusion of women and minority groups from clinical trials. With all the justifications she gives, meeting this requirement will not be a hard task at all. Dr. Healy's approach, which is to require that applicants for grants from the National Institute of Health justify the exclusion of women and minorities from trials, may be right.* But if, as a profession, we researchers and clinicians do not police sexism, someone is bound to do it for us.

ROBIN L. ROSS, M.D.
Centers for Mental Healthcare Research
Little Rock, AR 72205

To the Editor: Dr. Angell makes several good points. But her contention that ageism is the reason for the emphasis on breast cancer rather than prostate cancer, and on heart attacks in men rather than heart attacks in women, suggests that Americans really do believe that death is optional.

Death can be postponed but not prevented. Older people deserve good medical care, both supportive and, when possible, curative. But when we try to decide which diseases deserve our research dollars, the age at which people die from those diseases should be an important consideration.

---

* Herman R. Healy's legacy at NIH: reversing the brain drain, launching the women's initiative. Washington Post. June 15, 1993:Health Suppl:7.

I am sure that most people, if asked whether they preferred to die of a given disease at 20, 40, 60, or 80 years of age, would choose the last. And I am sure that if they were forced to choose between treating their own 5-year-old child or their 75-year-old grandmother, the child would win out with the grandmother's blessing. Is this ageism?

LYNN PAYER
720 W. 181st St.
New York, NY 10033

Dr. Angell replies:

Drs. Allen and Ross criticize my editorial from opposite sides. Both make useful points, some of which were in the editorial, but in my opinion both go well beyond the evidence. For example, I doubt that we know more about prostate cancer than we do about breast cancer. And Dr. Allen's contention that women's longer life expectancy stems from "cultural and legal factors that are unfavorable to men's health" is astonishing, especially given the illness, poverty, and neglect that so often mark women's extra years.

I appreciate Ms. Payer's point, which shows how complex these issues really are.

MARCIA ANGELL, M.D.

Suffering and Ethical Caring: Incompatible Entities

Debra Leners and Nancy Q. Beardslee

INTRODUCTION

Nurses today are confronted with increasingly complex ethical dilemmas, given the nature of the health/illness care system, the advancement of technology focusing on quantity of life, and the tremendous emphasis on medical cure.[1-3] The authors implemented research exploring the kinds of ethical problems that nurses face in the traditional clinical setting and how nurses cognitively process decision-making about actions to take in ethical dilemmas. The research was funded by the University of Northern Colorado as a pilot study for a potential

TABLE 1   Attributes of Contrasting Moral Voices

Justice	Caring
Abstract reasoning	Personal values
Rationality	Intuition
Right consequences	Relationship
Right actions	Empathy

programme of nursing ethics research. A particular purpose of the research was to examine how nurses process ethical dilemmas in reality when compared with the theoretical literature. One author was very familiar with the theoretical models of Kohlberg[4] and Gilligan,[5] while the other researcher studied the ethic of caring from the perspective of Noddings[6] and Watson.[7]

The current nursing literature describes two major perspectives which can be contrasted in ethical discussions. The first is the perspective of justice, which dominates traditional medical ethics and focuses on abstract reasoning and rationality. Some justice theories address right consequences (consequentialism) and some address right action (deontology).[8] Caring, as the other perspective, involves looking at problems in context, taking into account personal values. Caring is defined as feeling as nearly as possible what the one who is cared for feels and acting on that person's behalf in an actual situation.[9,10] The focus is on intuition, relationships and empathy, rather than rationality (Table 1).

METHOD

Qualitative research was chosen as the design format in order to understand better the experience of ethical dilemmas and decision-making from nurses' perspective. Ethnographic interviews were conducted with six hospital staff nurses and the data analysed according to the Spradley method of ethnography.[11] The computer program, *The ethnograph,* was used to help to organize and analyse the data. Informants included hospital staff nurses from three units of a 250-bed tertiary hospital in northern Colorado. Two of the nurses were male and four were female; the group contained ranges of age, experience and educational backgrounds (Table 2). An interview guide provided the initial structure for the interviews, although the researcher allowed the interviews to flow spontaneously:

1. How would you define an ethical dilemma?
2. What causes or leads to ethical dilemmas?
3. How do ethical situations affect those involved?

TABLE 2   Informant Demographics (*n* = 6)

	INFORMANT					
	A	B	C	D	E	F
Gender	Male	Female	Female	Female	Male	Female
Age (years)	32	48	37	53	35	25
Experience (years)	7	25	7	2	8	1
Educational level	ADN	Diploma	Diploma	BSN	BSN	BSN
Area of nursing	ICU	ICU	Rehab	Rehab	Paed	Paed

ADN: Associate Degree in Nursing; BSN: Bachelor of Science in Nursing; ICU: intensive care unit; Rehab: rehabilitative nursing; Paed: paediatrics.

4. Is there an ethical problem in which you have been involved?
5. What ethical problem has bothered you most in your nursing experience?
6. Describe how you decide what action to take if an ethical dilemma arises. Can you give an example?
7. Has life experience influenced your ethical decisions?
8. What changes do you think are needed?
9. Do you have any suggestion for educating students about ethics?

This guide was used primarily to initiate conversation, to return from a tangent, or to promote discussion if the conversation waned. One researcher conducted all the interviews.

The constant comparative analysis method was employed to uncover six domains, 17 themes and one overarching theme (of suffering and caring being incompatible entities) that brings all themes and domains together. Themes were kept in the language of the informants and direct quotations are used to explain the essence of what the nurses shared.[12]

RESULTS

An analysis of the data revealed the process that staff nurses use to approach ethical dilemmas. They use intuition and describe their actions by words emphasizing the caring role of the nurse. All six respondents gave examples for questions 4, 5 and 6 of the interview guide, which revolved around pain and suffering for the patient. Six domains were identified:

1. Informant definitions
      Something isn't right
      There must be a reason why this happened

2. Preceding conditions

> Afraid of losing a patient
> Value conflict
> Informal and formal structures
> Experience gives a different view

3. Actions taken

> There is a fine line
> I try to think what would the family want
> What that means is . . .

4. Intervening concepts

> They just don't know
> So much is relative, unless they are suffering

5. Risks and consequences

> Banging your head against a wall
> Gambling with your livelihood
> Getting in the way of revenue

6. Recommendations

> The real clinical world
> Choices and decisions
> Be aware of our power

Informant Definitions

The first domain was identified as 'informant definitions'. The researchers chose to ask the participants to define or explain what an ethical dilemma was from their perspective.

The first theme of this domain was 'something isn't right'. This theme provides insight into the intuitive process inherent in initially recognizing an ethical dilemma. Informants consistently spoke of ethical dilemmas as a situation where 'you just know', 'you just don't feel right', or 'something tells you inside'. It is interesting to note that none of the informants used a theoretical or code-based definition. In addition, none of the informants acknowledged any awareness of a code of nursing ethics.

The second theme was that 'there must be a reason why this happened'. The meaning of experience was often discussed in the process of defining ethical dilemmas. Personal and cultural values and beliefs seemed to play an important part in making sense of an ethical situation. When an ethical dilemma was observed, experienced or felt, the informants tended to seek a philosophical meaning, understanding or reason for the dilemma. For example: '[The client] was put on this earth for a reason; maybe this person fulfilled his or her purpose and life needed to be finished', and 'Look at [this situation]. There must be a reason [why] this happened.' The researchers noticed that if a situation was described where there was suffering or a great deal of pain, the search for meaning and understanding was more prominent.

Preceding Conditions

The second domain was 'preceding conditions'. This captured the elements of clinical situations that seemed to promote or structure the process of dealing with ethical dilemmas.

The first theme, 'afraid of losing the patient', describes situations where, because of an attachment formed by the physician or nurse to the client, the complying with a terminally ill patient's desire for 'no extraordinary measures' was more difficult. The possible loss of the patient was not only connected with the loss of a relationship but also with a sense that the provider had 'failed', particularly for the physician involved. One informant said, 'Too often the doctor wants to keep hanging on. If the patient dies he takes it that he failed.' This fear translated into the reluctance of physicians to order pain medication that could depress respiration or, in a long-term situation, cause addiction. When interviewees were asked to give an example of an ethical dilemma, four of the six gave examples concerning life versus suffering: 'She was in a lot of pain and we wanted to give her more medicine. She was a little girl and had AIDS and not very long to live. His comment was: "I don't want her to get addicted."' Another nurse said, 'Usually the hardest I see are life and death issues—like do you prolong someone's life just for the sake of prolonging it—rendering care when I know it might be very painful?' Some physicians were even noted to encourage unrealistic hope in families because they were 'hung up on preserving quantity of life'. Nurses had greater difficulty in dealing with their own emotional attachment issues when they observed that physicians were not following a patient's wishes or desires.

The second theme, 'value conflicts,' came from discussion by the informants of examples of the problems in deciding what is right and what deviates from what is right. Value conflicts were spoken of in terms of differing values between self, patient, family, physician, other nurses, and institutions. This theme captured the informants' use of *self* in evaluating a situation as ethical or not: 'I wouldn't want that done to me'; 'I've seen what a transplant goes through and I would not go through that myself'; and 'I try to think what would I want done as well as what the patient would want done.' Examples that provoked these thoughts included actions that were against their values: 'doctors—all they want to do is to save everyone . . .'; 'Let's get them home; that's what the patients want. It isn't worth it to have them stay in the hospital for only a 5% improvement.' One nurse stated, 'Doctors have other issues; they have their own criteria. They have to support a family, their offices.'

The third theme, 'informal and formal structures', indicated hospital cultural norms that tend to promote the formation of ethical dilemmas. Formal norms were identified as institutional guidelines, expectations and hospital policy which promoted particular clinical approaches. For example, in the process of referring and transferring patients to specialists, the nurses recognized that the providers were 'shifting the ethical decisions to somebody else'.

One informal norm was that physicians generally made the ultimate decisions in ethical situations. Informants said that if the physicians were approachable and open to nursing input, nurses had less difficulty with ethical situations than if the physician was unreceptive. Another informal norm described was seeking out experienced nurses with whom to discuss ethical concerns: 'If I'm concerned, I go to one of the older nurses and say I'm concerned. If they think I'm right, they make things happen. So there's an informal type of structure.'

The last theme was 'experience gives a different view'. The more experience the nurses had in a particular specialty area, the more clear they were about how to approach an ethical situation: 'I think earlier in my career, I could have just gone along with keeping people alive regardless, but now I question those approaches [that measure only quantity of life].' Informants with less experience readily recognized the need to seek out expert nurses for their advice and input in ethical dilemmas.

Actions Taken

The third domain collapsed data that seemed to explain the actions taken by the nurses in ethical dilemmas. Examples of these actions included communicating, educating and pain management.

The first theme of this domain was: 'There is a fine line.' This theme explains the problem of coming to terms with the limits of what can and/or what should be done in an ethical dilemma. The 'fine line' was specific to the actual and potential degree of suffering (physical, mental and emotional) experienced by clients as a result of ethical decisions made. The nurses were very concerned that the patients should not suffer in any way, regardless of the ethical decision. The observations of suffering or physical pain tended to move the nurses to be active patient and family advocates when this fine line was crossed. If suffering or pain were not apparent, the nurses were more accepting of clinical situations, even if they personally felt the ethical dilemma was not handled appropriately. 'If anyone is in pain, I draw the line'; 'I think I get to the point where I can say, "Well, [the patient] is not suffering", but there is a fine line where I can't accept [just extending life].'

The second theme of this domain was: 'I try to think, "What would the family want?" ' The basis for ethical decision-making was often described in two ways: (1) what would the nurse want if he or she were in the client's place; and (2) what would the clients themselves and/or their families want? The informants tended to employ the adage of 'do unto others' and/or tried to empathize on the part of the client and the family.

The final theme of this domain was 'what that means is . . .'. This theme is representative of the overwhelming data provided by the informants regarding nursing actions in the communication and educational realms of intervention. Although none of the nurses interviewed verbalized that they felt significant in the decision-making process, all gave examples of tremendous amounts of nursing activity involved in communicating with the client, the family and other providers. The informants saw themselves as responsible for interpreting information and communicating these interpretations to doctors, clients, families, other nurses, ancillary providers and all peripheral services. The informants described this role as one of a 'helper' and gave many examples of how they clarified and facilitated communication for all parties involved. Education-based actions included preparing for and clarifying medical procedures. At times, education was also used as a strategy to advocate for or to offer different choices to those the physician had provided to the family and the client. The following are quotations from two of the informants: 'Doctors say, "You need this or that or you're going to die", so [patients] say, "Well, I'll do it."' Nurses explain to patients their rights and help them to explore all their options: 'You can't do anything more sometimes than say, "Have you considered this or that?", and "You do have the right to say no. Don't feel you are being bulldozed into this."'

Intervening Concepts

Intervening concepts that influence ethical decision-making comprise the fourth domain.

The theme 'they just don't know' examined the informants' consistent claim that ethical dilemmas were influenced by the degree to which there was accurate and adequate information sharing among all care providers and the client and the family. One informant said, 'When all of the pertinent information is not known by all parties, you get different expectations of patient care outcomes.' This theme also reflects the informants' concern that patients and families often don't realize that there are other choices beyond 'doing everything possible'. Another informant said, 'I think we forget there is a choice to not have intervention . . . Just because we have [technology] doesn't mean we have to use it in every case.'

The second theme of this domain was 'so much is relative unless they are suffering'. This theme reiterates earlier data about ethical decision-making with patients who are suffering or in pain. Informants communicated that each ethical decision is relative to the diagnosis, prognosis, client and family knowledge base and requests, as well as to the health care providers' recommendations and desires about a particular situation. Quality of life and quantity of life were very relevant to the decision-making process but suffering and pain surfaced as critical aspects to decision-making.

Risks and Consequences

The fifth domain condensed data that spoke of the risks that nurses take in becoming involved in ethical dilemmas: 'risks and consequences of getting involved'.

The first theme was 'banging your head against a wall'. All informants spoke of the negative interpersonal emotional stress associated with ethical dilemmas. Frustration and disgust were expressed if nurses saw themselves as failing in an ethical situation: 'I've tried to question ethical situations in the past and felt as if I've run up against a brick wall. I just don't want to invest the time and energy and become disgusted with myself because I couldn't change things'; and 'It isn't healthy to continue to bang your head against a wall if you can't change things.'

The second theme was 'gambling with your livelihood'. Besides emotional risks, informants said that nurses may risk their jobs by expressing opinions in ethical patient care situations. The employment risks were associated with physician responses to conflicting opinions. Informants spoke of the importance of 'having the physician on your side' to avoid the potential of risking the job: 'If you go against a physician and lose, you're going to pay for it.' In this quotation, 'lose' referred to the nonagreement of the physician to the nurses' requests for treatment modification.

The last theme was 'getting in the way of revenue'. Informants expressed concern that their intervention in ethical decision-making could ultimately effect a lack of revenue for the hospital: 'If we didn't have to worry about losing our job every time we explain to patients their rights that would be one thing. But we don't want to get in the way of the revenue generation.' As nurses are educated more and more about the financial side of care, they recognize that, if technology is not used, patients are downgraded in terms of care needs, or transferred out of the facility, and revenue is lost to the agency. One informant described an experience where she supported a family decision to transfer to another institution: 'The doctor was furious with me and we lost the revenue because the parents went ahead with the transfer. I guess there are times I don't care if I do lose my job or close down the unit.'

Recommendations

The last domain summarized all data regarding the 'informants' recommendations about the difficulties with ethical dilemmas'. This study sought to gain practising nurses' insights into how to prepare nursing students for ethical dilemmas.

The first theme, 'the real clinical world', reflects the informants' suggestions that student nurses should be exposed more to real ethical problems in clinical practice.

The second theme, 'choices and decisions', is tied to data regarding the need for more education about choices in ethical situations. Informants discussed the importance of educating patients to be 'more aware and more self-responsible'. Either how this education was supposed to happen, or who was responsible for the education, was not identified by the informants as a nursing responsibility.

The last theme was 'be aware of our power'. Informants discussed the need for nurses to empower themselves to deal with ethical dilemmas. One nurse advised: 'Nurses need to be kinder to each other and offer each other moral support in difficult clinical situations.' Another spoke specifically about the power nurses could tap into if they wanted to: 'Nurses need to be more aware of how much power we have and the abilities we have to show people better ways to make choices.'

DISCUSSION

Because of the pervasiveness of references to suffering and pain within all of the data analysed, the researchers found in this study an overarching theme: 'suffering and ethical caring: incompatible entities'. Client and/or family suffering and pain were identified as: (1) critical to bringing ethical dilemmas to the forefront; (2) important intervening variables to ethical decision-making; (3) significant motivators for the nursing role as client advocate and a willingness to take risks; (4) crucial to educating patients about choices; and (5) closely connected with the degree to which a nurse takes action on an ethical situation. Informants were adamant that clients and families should experience as little suffering and pain as possible. Being ethical meant minimizing or eliminating the possibility of pain and suffering in the event of poor prognosis.

In the comparison of the data with the theoretical literature,[13–15] the researchers found little in the way of evidence that the nurses used a moral voice of justice. The moral voice of caring, however, was evident, first in the attempt to understand self and the client through the 'do unto others' adage, as well as the use of empathy, and, secondly, in the difficulty and risks of working with clients who have to make hard ethical decisions. The data point to the nurse in the caring relationship: connected, trying to understand, empathic and accepting, but educating about possible options or choices. This supports other researchers' findings.[14,16,17] Holistic ethics may integrate and define new directions for health care ethics.[18]

Since most of the ethical dilemmas reported primarily involved the interaction of nurses and physicians, more research is needed in this area. Although nurses spend significantly more time with the patients, their voice may not be heard.[19,20] Why does this occur? Is there not similar vocabulary or educational curriculum regarding ethics in health care? Joint ethical classes or workshops for nursing and medical students may increase the understanding of all viewpoints.[21]

Problems with undermedication for pain continue to need to be addressed. Greipp[22] feels that this is a major area that needs to be concentrated on to enhance patient care. Affective and cognitive educational programmes are necessary, as the many components of opiophobia need to be addressed for both nurses and physicians.

This study was a pilot to begin the exploration of how nurses are involved with ethical decision making. An entire programme of research is recommended to: (1) expand on the current findings; (2) understand further the expert knowledge base of clinical nurses in ethical situations; (3) explore how ethical decision making may vary in a variety of clinical practice areas; (4) identify nursing roles and actions that are supportive or nonsupportive of ethical situations; and (5) explore the educational needs of student nurses as they study and observe ethical dilemmas.

References

1. Webb C. Caring, curing, coping: towards an integrated model. *J Adv Nurs* 1996; **23**: 960–68.

2. Smith KV. Ethical decision-making by staff nurses. *Nurs Ethics* 1996; **3**: 17–25.

3. Catalano J. Critical care nurses and ethical dilemmas. *Crit Care Nurse* 1991; **1**: 20–25.

4. Kohlberg L. *The philosophy of moral development*, San Francisco, CA: Harper and Row, 1981.

5. Gilligan C. *In a different voice*. Cambridge, MA: Harvard University Press, 1982.

6. Noddings N. *Caring: a feminine approach to ethics and moral education.* Berkeley, CA: University of California, 1984.

7. Watson J. Caring knowledge and informed moral passion. *ANS Adv Nurs Sci* 1990; **13** (3): 15–24.

8. Davis A, Aroskar M. *Ethical dilemmas and nursing practice.* Norwalk, CT: Appleton and Lange, 1991.

9. Benner P, Wrubel J. *The primacy of caring.* Menlo Park, CA: Addison-Wesley, 1989.

10. van Hooft S. Bioethics and caring: *J Med Ethics* 1996; **22**: 90–94.

11. Spradley J. *The ethnographic interview.* New York: Holt, Rinehart and Winston, 1979.

12. Sandelowski M, Davis D, Harris B. Artful design: writing the proposal for research in the naturalist paradigm. *Res Nurs Health* 1989; **12**: 77–84.

13. Parker R. Measuring nurse's moral judgement. *Image J Nurs Scholarship* 1990; **22**: 213–18.

14. Cameron M. Justice, caring and virtue. *J Prof Nurs* 1991; **7**: 206–208.

15. Olsen D. Controversies in nursing ethics: a historical review. *J Adv Nurs* 1992; **17**: 1020–27.

16. Pinch W. Is caring a moral trap? *Nurs Outlook* 1996; **44**: 84–88.

17. Fry S. Toward a theory of nursing ethics. *J Adv Nurs* 1989; **4**: 9–22.

18. Keegan L, Keegan G. A concept of holistic ethics for the health professional. *J Holistic Nurs* 1992; **10**: 205–17.

19. Holm S, Gjersoe P, Grode G, Hartling O, Ibsen K, Marcussen H. Ethical reasoning in mixed nurse-physician groups. *J Med Ethics* 1996; **22**: 168–73.

20. Weber J. Teaching moral reasoning to student nurses. *J Holistic Nurs* 1992; **10**: 263–74.

21. Andre J. Learning to see: moral growth during medical training. *J Med Ethics* 1992; **18**: 148–52.

22. Greipp M. Undermedication for pain: an ethical model. *ANS Adv Nurs Sci* 1992; **15**(1): 44–53.

EVALUATING A CASE STUDY: FINDING THE CONFLICTS

After establishing an ethical point of view (including a segue to application), we are ready to approach cases. The first stage in handling cases effectively is to analyze the situation according to normal practice and potential ethical issues. Obviously, sometimes ethical issues are involved in what one will do, and at other times they are not. It is your job to determine when ethical issues are involved. Let us consider specific cases.

Case 1.

You are a nurse who has an obnoxious patient in room 28. He claims that his medication dosage is wrong and should be reevaluated immediately. This patient has made this complaint many times before. Each time the dosage was checked and was found to be correct. The normal practice with problem complainers is to be slow in responding to their demands. After all, other patients who do not create such a fracas need your time.

Does this case involve any ethical issues? If so, what are they? How do they affect normal practice?

Case 2.

You run a medical research facility at a major university and are testing a drug for one form of cancer. The preliminary results of your research after two years are not promising; in fact, the drug seems to have a deleterious effect in some instances. Your project has been funded for four years. The drug's results could change, but meanwhile people who might have had several more years of life under conventional treatments are dying. If you stop the experiment now, however, you may put people out of work, jeopardize future funding, and affect your entire university's science program.

Does this case involve any ethical issues? If so, what are they? How do they affect prudential (self-interested) concerns?

Checklist for Detecting Ethical Issues

Directions. Read your case carefully. Determine your ethical viewpoint (see "Developing a Practical Ethical Viewpoint," p. 53ff.). Decide which individual's perspective you will develop in your comments. Create one or more detection questions that will identify ethical issues. These detection questions will follow from your own ethical perspective. For example, from my practical ethical perspective, I have chosen the following two detection questions to bring moral issues to my attention. These questions follow from a deontological viewpoint.

1. *Is any party being exploited solely for the advantage of another?* (Exploitation can include instances of lying, injuring, deliberately falsifying, creating an unequal competitive environment, and so forth.)
2. *Is every effort being made to assist and affirm the human dignity of all parties involved?* (Affirming human dignity can include instances of encouraging the fulfillment of legal and human rights as well as taking personal responsibility for results that are consonant with these principles. Thus, you cannot hide behind nonfunctioning rules.)

By asking these questions within the context of the case, I am able better to understand the moral dimensions that exist with other professional concerns.

A few other comments may be useful concerning my detection questions. Question 1 concerns "prohibitions" (i.e., actions that you must refrain from doing). Question 2 concerns "obligations" (i.e., actions that you are required to do). Anything that is not an ethical obligation or a prohibition is a "permission" (i.e., an action that you may do if you choose). Thus, if the case you present does not invoke a prohibition or an obligation, then you may act solely according to the dictates of your professional practice. It is often useful to group your detection questions as prohibitions and obligations, which emphasizes different types of moral duty.

Try creating detection questions and apply them to the earlier two cases. What do they reveal about the moral issues involved in the cases? How do different detection questions emphasize different moral issues? How different are these perspectives? How similar are they?

Once you have completed this preliminary ethical assessment, you can return to the ethical theory you have adopted and determine *how* and *why* the prohibitions and obligations are applicable to this theory.

Read the following macro and micro cases and follow the steps outlined:

A. Identify your practical ethical viewpoint including any linking principles.
B. Determine which character's perspective you will adopt.
C. Identify two or more detection questions that define obligation and prohibition within the ethical theory you have chosen.
D. Apply the detection questions to the cases to bring attention to the ethical issues.
E. Discuss the interrelationships between the dictates of the ethical issues and those of the professional practice. How might they work together? How might they be opposed?

Macro and Micro Cases*

Macro Case 1. The U.S. Senate is about to consider a new patients' bill of rights. The parts of the bill that concern you are three policy directives aimed at paternalism versus patient autonomy. In this case, identify three issues you believe would be controversial regarding federal legislation covering patient autonomy and paternalism (these will be the three policy directives contained within the Senate bill).

After you identify three issues, describe the two sides of each issue. Then write a mock Senate debate in the form of a dialogue between two or more senators discussing your three points from the floor of the Senate. Structure the debate so that it involves moral arguments. Identify a winner of the debate from your own viewpoint.

Macro Case 2. Metropolitan Gotham City (any major U.S. city) needs to share medical information as the result of the creation of a consortium among local hospitals allowing certain ones to specialize in particular areas of treatment that require very expensive medical equipment. Thus, many inter-hospital referrals are made.

The regional consortium has a request for proposals for a new information system that will facilitate this information exchange. Various vendors will submit proposals to a committee appointed by the consortium to evaluate them. Because there is a conflict between privacy protections and efficiency, each vendor must write a proposal that addresses each but supports one side over the other.

You must take the persona of either (a) the vendors (at least two opposing positions) or (b) the selection committee evaluating at least two opposing proposals (which you will create). If you choose the vendor point of view, argue the case for a proefficiency system and a proprivacy system (one vendor will argue one position and another will take the other position). In each instance, be sure to use major ethical theories to make your point.

If you choose the selection committee perspective, you must justify your choice of a system that either emphasizes (a) efficiency or (b) privacy. Again, you must use a major ethical theory to support your eventual conclusion.

Macro Case 3. You are an upper-level male administrator at a large teaching hospital. You have just been to a conference in which a speaker described the female voice within the hospital. The speaker indicated how much better the hospital would function if it listened to that female voice and incorporated it into the institution's operations in fulfilling its mission.

---

*For more on macro and micro cases, see the overview on p. 53ff.

You wonder what would happen if you tried to do this in your hospital. All the senior officers at the hospital are men, and only one female is on the governing board. Making such changes could cause you to be viewed as a trouble maker and could hurt your career. On the other hand, you went into hospital administration to do some good in the world. You agree in theory with what the speaker said, but doing something about it is rather different.

List three areas in which a hospital might benefit by giving more expression to the female voice. Then list all the negative repercussions that might occur if you make incorporating the female voice into the hospital's mission a top-level priority. Finally, if you are in favor of doing this, write a memo to the appropriate person arguing that position. If you are against doing this, write a memo to yourself that you will put into your files detailing why you do not think that you should support this position this time. In either case, refer to a majority ethical theory.

Macro Case 4. You have been appointed chairperson of the governor's task force on health care allocations for the next decade. The state is divided into four large health care regions, but at this moment you are thinking about Region 2, which encompasses a major city.

One of the findings that has interested you is that allocation requests from inner city poverty areas differ from those from affluent suburban areas. Requests from the inner cities are for basic medical supplies for low-tech medical services delivery. This group needs more physicians, subsidized pharmaceuticals (such as medicine for hypertension), and extensive prenatal and pediatric care, along with basic health care information so that patients in this area can make informed health care decisions that will affect their lives.

The suburbs request sophisticated diagnostic and surgical facilities to meet high-tech needs in sports medicine, cosmetic surgery, and less invasive operating procedures.

The committee's decisions must go through the normal political process. At the moment, many on the committee believe that the affluent areas should get the major share of this money. Their reasons are that the affluent people in the suburbs (a) support the society with their taxes and therefore should be cared for first; (b) vote in much higher numbers so that they are more important in political decisions; and (c) have lobbying groups that will support their interests. Because they "put their money where their mouths are," they should be rewarded with funding.

In contrast, the poor in the inner city (a) pay fewer taxes, (b) vote in small numbers and therefore have little influence in political decisions, and (c) are not the movers and shakers of society. They are disproportionately female, black, Hispanic, and native American, and many of them are children. These groups do not have a powerful constituency.

How can you balance the needs of these two groups? What moral principles should be used to guide the allocation of resources? You must write a preliminary report to the governor in three days. Use ethical principles to guide your recommendation of resource allocation.

Micro Case 1. You are a physician in private practice. John Smith and Mary Jones have been your patients for years. During a physical exam, Mr. Smith informs you that he is engaged to be married to Ms. Jones. You ask whether Mr. Smith has disclosed his HIV condition to Ms. Jones. "We've always practiced safe sex," Mr. Smith answers. "She can't possibly be infected."

"But don't you think she has a right to know? *Before* you are married?"

"That's nobody's business but mine," Mr. Smith replies.

Mr. Smith leaves and you begin to consider the situation. You swore an oath of confidentiality when you became a physician. But you also swore an oath to do no harm. Would you be doing harm by not preventing possible harm? Does Mary Jones have a right to know that her husband-to-be is HIV positive? And if he refuses to tell her, should you tell her?

Identify issues involved from the physician's point of view, using a major ethical theory to justify telling Ms. Jones. Be sure to refer to the practice of medicine according to the Hippocratic Oath. (As an optional assignment, list arguments that Mr. Smith and Ms. Jones might make about their own interests in this case. Do these considerations change what the physician should do? Why or why not?)

Micro Case 2. You are a nurse in the maternity section of a suburban hospital. One of your patients, Ms. Younger, has just had her first child. Her health insurance allows her a 48-hour stay, however, Ms. Younger's baby, Sally, is quite jaundiced. You know from your twelve years of experience that such severe cases can easily be treated in two or three days under a bilirubin light. You also know that Ms. Younger is due to be discharged in three hours. The physician in charge took the position of the hospital and the insurance company that patients should be discharged in 48 hours.

When you brought up the jaundice problem to the physician, he replied, "Well, she can put the baby in front of a window to get a similar effect, and if that doesn't work, the insurance company will send out a nurse with a portable bilirubin light. It will work out."

"But you don't know this woman like I do," you answered. But the physician would not change his position. You tried to explain that Ms. Younger is a first-time mother without a car and coming back to the hospital for blood checks would be impossible. In addition, Ms. Younger does not understand the seriousness of her baby's condition.

The physician replied that the hospital and the insurance company had well-conceived procedures for everything. It would all be fine.

You believe, however, that the baby's life is at stake. You believe that the only way to solve the problem is to bring more people into the dialogue so that they might understand the true extent of the situation. If a conversation were enjoined, then surely an effect that was good for all parties would result.

What are the possible options that are open to you? Provide at least three alternatives and then, using this list, outline an action plan based on principles of human relationship and ethical theory to guide your actions. How do principles of justice and care interact in the various options you set out?

Micro Case 3. You are a physician. Your patient, Sam, has heart problems caused by some venal blockage near the heart. You have presented the possible treatment options to Sam: (a) do nothing, (b) use drug therapy to thin his blood, (c) perform angioplasty, or (d) perform by-pass surgery. Sam is a very fearful person and is in favor of the drug therapy.

What Sam fails to account for, however, is that he is at high risk right now. Although drug therapy is the safest treatment (vis-à-vis its side effects alone), it still leaves him with the greatest risk. You try to explain this to Sam: risk of treatment (the risk inherent in the treatment itself) plus resultant risk (one's risk of death after undergoing treatment) = total risk. In a simplified model, you tell Sam that the risk of treatment for the four alternatives ranks as follows (based on an ascending risk scale of 1–10):

A. No therapy: = 0/resultant risk = 9.5/total risk = 9.5
B. Drug therapy: = 0.5/resultant risk = 8/total risk = 8.5
C. Angioplasty: = 1.5/resultant risk = 6/total risk = 7.5
D. By-pass surgery: = 5/resultant risk = 1/total risk = 6.0

Although Sam is not a risk taker, he is making a choice that is really riskier for him. This seems to you to be an irrational choice.

What should you do? Should you try to bully Sam into options C or D? Should you enlist others to help convince Sam that C or D is best? Should you enlist family members to help Sam make the decision? Or should you let Sam make his own decision? After all, it is his life. Write an essay justifying your decision.

Micro Case 4. You are an emergency room physician at an inner city hospital. Mrs. Lopez, a poor first-generation immigrant from Central America, comes to see you since she has no regular doctor. She has a bronchial infection that can be treated with antibiotics. In the course of your examination of Mrs. Lopez, you discover a lump on her right breast. This lump concerns you and you suggest some tests. Through the hospital's interpreter, you inform her of your plan.

Mrs. Lopez does not want tests. She just wants to get her medicine and leave, but you fear that her breast lump may be malignant and that only by prompt treatment can you save her life. Mrs. Lopez does not like talking about her breasts with strangers, and her husband would never allow anyone to cut her in that area of her body.

You feel certain that the reasons that Mrs. Lopez wants to leave and forgo any tests are that she does not fully appreciate the danger she is in and she comes from a cultural tradition in which the husband's likes or dislikes (concerning the appearance of his wife's breasts) are decisive.

Cite at least three alternatives for action. Then show why one of these alternatives is the best. Use a major ethical theory and linking principle to justify your action.

chapter five

Issues of Life and Death

I. EUTHANASIA.

Overview. Euthanasia means "good death" in classic Greek. It also has come to mean mercy killing, which involves taking an *action* that will end a life that is afflicted with a terminal disease and that is characterized by intense suffering. *Passive euthanasia* entails stopping the life-support system or other artificial life-sustaining support of a patient who is terminally ill. The patient or his family may seek this solution. Some due process is generally required before the request can be granted. Although the doctor may be the agent who brings about the patient's death by discontinuing treatment, it is not considered active euthanasia because nothing is administered to cause death. The primary cause of death is the disease itself, which becomes untreated. Whether a legitimate distinction exists between active and passive euthanasia is a topic of some dispute.

An associated concept is assisted suicide in which a physician or another person provides the means necessary for a patient to end his or her own life. Dr. Jack Kevorkian has created an apparatus that can be set up and then manipulated by the patient to effect his own death. Assisted suicide is a form of euthanasia because the patient requesting to die is not in the calm, dispassionate state necessary for free rational choice but likely is in pain, needing help. In such circumstances, it is not unusual for the patient to plead for death. When providing the patient the means to grant this wish, is the doctor or other person acting differently than if he actually administered the death-causing substance to the patient herself?

Opinions concerning euthanasia and assisted suicide are strongly held. Some believe that they are the most compassionate responses to a person who will die anyway and is suffering greatly. Nonetheless, active euthanasia is not legal in most of the world. It is considered to be murder in the United States, Britain, Canada, Australia, and the Philippines. Holland has the most liberal laws affecting euthanasia among the industrialized nations of the world. In 1985 the Royal Dutch Medical Association formed guidelines for a national Commission on Euthanasia. Under these guidelines, if a patient acts voluntarily, makes a well-considered request that is reviewed by the physician's colleagues, has a durable death wish, and suffers to an unacceptable degree, the physician will not be prosecuted for engaging in active euthanasia or assisted suicide.

Assisted suicide is prohibited explicitly by law in twenty-six states in the United States. However, when these laws have been tested, they have rarely been enforced when the death is caused by a spouse or loved one of the deceased. In these cases, it is assumed that compassion is the intent, and good intent is said to be the determining factor. When a physician performs euthanasia or assisted suicide, evidence generally suggests the the patient was exercising autonomy in this decision.

Our discussion highlights two issues related to euthanasia: withholding or withdrawing nutrition or hydration in general and the treatment of newborns with severe congenital abnormalities or very low birth weight. The discussion brings the question of what constitutes euthanasia to a more specific level.

The first issue relates to the care of people who are in a "persistent vegetative state." These individuals do not respond to stimuli in ways that we would say "operationally" exhibit rationality. The issue (using Beyleveld's concept of precautionary reasoning) concerns whether these people should be considered to be capable of reason in a precautionary way (since some philosophers declare in the mind-body debate that it is impossible to measure human thinking fully by scientific means). If this is the case, then the problem of people in a persistent vegetative state becomes more complicated. The advocates of withholding or withdrawing nutrition or hydration base their case on the patient's inability to think. If humans are defined as rational animals, then the inability to think renders them nonhuman. As nonhumans, lives are no longer protected by most moral theories. Thus, the determination of who is and who is not able to think becomes very important.

Currently, we determine this operationally by interaction with the world and by using measurement devices that rely on a model of what a functioning brain ought to be doing. These are our best measures. But are they conclusive? How far should we extend precautionary reasoning in these cases? This is a very important consideration.

The second issue involves infants with severe congenital abnormalities and/or very low birth weights. These infants would usually have died in previous decades. Now, however, modern science has made great strides in treating these infants, but the cost of doing so is very high. Some (especially certain utilitarians) view these costs in an allocation question affecting the entire medical care system. If we could use this money more effectively in prenatal care, for example, might we not save more lives? Would saving more lives promote the general good?

One consideration involves balancing the burden that these infants will place on their parents and on society versus the benefit of saving the lives of infants who may or may not be permanently impaired in some way. Another consideration is the concept that each life is precious and that society should treat every newborn aggressively without regard for cost (limited only by the ought-implies-can dictum).[1] The possible or probable suffering of the infant as it develops should also be considered. This argument is similar to the general argument for active euthanasia. We paternalistically decide how much suffering would be bearable for the infant and then act accordingly.

The following articles present information to enable the reader to create a consistent position on euthanasia.

In the first article, Daniel Callahan argues for a distinction between killing and allowing to die. He bases this argument upon two key premises: (a) the metaphysical premise that thinking that a person's own actions in removal of life support are the sole cause of another's death is arrogant and (b) the moral premise that distinguishes between causing death and being morally responsible for that death. In passive euthanasia, Callahan asserts, one causes death without being ethically responsible for it.

In the second article, Pieter V. Admiraal argues that human suffering is the greatest of evils. Therefore, when a patient is suffering without hope of recovery and meets various other criteria, then the physician may perform euthanasia. Dr. Admiraal has performed euthanasia himself and thinks that the so-called distinction between active and passive euthanasia is specious.

Leon Kass forms his argument based on an examination of the Hippocratic Oath and its injunction against administering a poison. If the Hippocratic Oath defines professionalism and if the physician wishes to be a professional, then she should not administer a poison (i.e., perform active euthanasia or assisted suicide). However, Kass does allow for engaging in passive euthanasia along the lines outlined by Callahan.

In the first article on withholding nutrition and hydration, John Dolan argues that such procedures are tantamount to murder. He bases his argument on the premise that denying any nonterminal patient food and drink (nutrition and hydration) is to cause the death of an innocent, which is murder. Thus, to

---

[1]See *Basic Ethics*, Chapter Four.

cease nutrition and hydration for patients in persistent vegetative state is to murder them. Advance directions or living wills do not change the situation. If this type of euthanasia is allowed to continue, he believes it will lead to the same road the Nazis traveled.

John Jefferson Davis begins his article with a survey of the literature on removing hydration and nutrition, which are termed artificial means of maintaining life. If these artificial means constitute "extraordinary" measures, then this is the same position as passive euthanasia. Davis cites Ed Payne, who suggests that if a person removes a feeding tube, the person must be prepared to feed the patient orally; everyone deserves this. However, if the patient cannot feed herself because she is in a persistent vegetative state, then artificial feeding need not be continued. This distinction when paired with the concept of individual life (which describes the unique preciousness of human life as opposed to mere biological life) are criteria on whether one is permitted to remove a feeding tube.

In the common hypothetical case that both Dolan and Davis write about, Dolan says no and Davis says yes to the removal of Mr. Stevens's feeding tube.

The Hastings Center Newborn Project presents the history of neonatal intensive care decision making as well as some commonly accepted conditions that should be addressed when the discontinuation of treatment to impaired infants is considered. One condition is that we must distinguish between children with abnormalities that will be fatal and children who are merely disabled (with Downs Syndrome or any other condition that society considers a disability). Engaging in passive euthanasia in the first instance (fatal abnormalities) may be acceptable, but surely no justifiable argument can be made for euthanizing those who are merely disabled. (The principal argument that might be put forward for the second case is the inconvenience/cost argument, mentioned earlier).

Nurses Winifred J. Pinch and Margaret L. Spielman provide a feminist perspective to the discontinuation of treatment for infants. Instead of examining the problem as traditional philosophers have by discussing the abstract right and wrong of the ethical positions in a vacuum, they point out that the situations of the parents need to be considered. Parents are traumatized by their child's plight, which can cause them to be divorced from the decision-making process. Only when hospital personnel recognize this natural impairment (because of the parents' intimate relationship with their child) may a more effective means of communication be found. This recognition is termed *medicalization,* and it allows the parents to enter more actively the decision-making process and not depend on the paternalistic choices of the physicians. Only by creating a community between physician, nurse, parent, and child and honestly confronting the range of options confronting the parents can any real progress be made in this regard.

Killing and Allowing to Die

Daniel Callahan

... No valid distinction, many now argue, can be made between killing and allowing to die, or between an act of commission and one of omission. The standard distinction being challenged rests on the commonplace observation that lives can come to an end as the result of: (a) the direct action of another who becomes the cause of death (as in shooting a person), and (b) the result of impersonal forces where no human agent has acted (death by lightning, or by disease). The purpose of the distinction has been to separate those deaths caused by human action, and those caused by nonhuman events. It is, as a distinction, meant to say something about human beings and their relationship to the world. It is a way of articulating the difference between those actions for which human beings can be held rightly responsible, or blamed, and those of which they are innocent. At issue is the difference between physical causality, the realm of impersonal events, and moral culpability, the realm of human responsibility.

The challenges encompass two points. The first is that people can become equally dead by our omissions as well as our commissions. We can refrain from saving them when it is possible to do so, and they will be just as dead as if we shot them. It is our decision itself that is the reason for their death, not necessarily how we effectuate that decision. That fact establishes the basis of the second point: if we *intend* their death, it can be brought about as well by omitted acts as by those we commit. The crucial moral point is not how they die, but our intention about their death. We can, then, be responsible for the death of another by intending that they die and accomplish that end by standing aside and allowing them to die.

Despite these criticisms—resting upon ambiguities that can readily be acknowledged—the distinction between killing and allowing to die remains, I contend, perfectly valid. It not only has a logical validity but, no less importantly, a social validity whose place must be central in moral judgments. As a way of putting the distinction into perspective, I want to suggest that it is best understood as expressing three different, though overlapping, perspectives on nature and human action. I will call them the metaphysical, the moral, and the medical perspectives.

METAPHYSICAL

The first and most fundamental premise of the distinction between killing and allowing to die is that there is a sharp difference between the self and the external world. Unlike the childish fantasy that the world is nothing more than a projection of the self, or the neurotic person's fear that he or she is responsible for everything that goes wrong, the distinction is meant to uphold a simple notion: there is a world external to the self that has its own, and independent, causal dynamism. The mistake behind a conflation of killing and allowing to die is to assume that the self has become master of everything within and outside of the self. It is as if the conceit that modern man might ultimately control nature has been internalized: that, if the self might be able to influence nature by its actions, then the self and nature must be one.

Of course that is a fantasy. The fact that we can intervene in nature, and cure or control many diseases, does not erase the difference between the self and the external world. It is as "out there" as ever, even if more under our sway. That sway, however great, is always limited. We can cure disease, but not always the chronic illness that comes with the cure. We can forestall death with modern medicine, but death always wins in the long run because of the innate limitations of the body, inherently and stubbornly beyond final human control. And we can distinguish between a diseased body and an aging body, but in the end if we wait long enough they always become one and the same body. To attempt to deny the distinction between killing and allowing to die is, then, mistakenly to impute more power to human action than it actually has and to accept the conceit that nature has now fallen wholly within the realm of human control. Not so.

MORAL

At the center of the distinction between killing and allowing to die is the difference between physical causality and moral culpability. To bring the life of another to an end by an injection kills the other directly; our action is the physical cause of the death. To allow someone to die from a disease we cannot cure (and that we did not cause) is to permit the disease to act as the cause of death. The notion of physical causality in both cases rests on the difference between human agency and the action of external nature. The ambiguity arises precisely because we can be morally culpable for killing someone (if we have no moral right to do so, as we would in self-defense) and no less culpable for allowing someone to die (if we have both the possibility and the obligation of keeping that person alive). Thus there are cases where, morally speaking, it makes no difference whether we killed or allowed to die; we are equally responsible. In those instances, the lines of physical causality and moral culpability happen to cross. Yet the fact that they can cross in some cases in no way shows that they are always, or even usually, one and the same. We can normally find the difference in all but the most obscure cases. We should not, then, use the ambiguity of such cases to do away altogether with the distinction between killing and allowing to die. The ambiguity may obscure, but does not erase, the line between the two.

There is one group of ambiguous cases that is especially troublesome. Even if we grant the ordinary validity between killing and allowing to die, what about those cases that combine (a) an illness that renders a patient unable to carry out an ordinary biological function (to breathe or eat on his own, for example), and (b) our turning off a respirator or removing an artificial feeding tube? On the level of physical causality, have we killed the patient or allowed him to die? In one sense, it is our action that shortens his life, and yet in another sense his underlying disease brings his life to an end. I believe it reasonable to say that, since his life was being sustained by artificial means (respirator or feeding tube) made necessary because of the fact that he had an incapacitating disease, his disease is the ultimate reality behind his death. But for its reality, there would be no need for artificial sustenance in the first place and no moral issue at all. To lose sight of the paramount reality of the disease is to lose sight of the difference between our selves and the outer world.

I quickly add, and underscore, a moral point: the person who, without good moral reason, turns off a respirator or pulls a feeding tube, can be morally culpable; that the patient has been allowed to die of his underlying condition does not morally excuse him. The moral question is whether we are obliged to continue treating a life that is being artificially sustained. To cease treatment may or may not be morally acceptable; but it should be understood, in either case, that the physical cause of death was the underlying disease.

MEDICAL

An important social purpose of the distinction between killing and allowing to die has been that of protecting the historical role of the physician as one who tries to cure or comfort patients rather than to kill patients. Physicians have been given special knowledge about the body, knowledge that can be used to kill or to cure. They are also given great privileges in making use of that knowledge. It is thus all the more important that physicians' social role and power be, and be seen to be, a limited power. It may be used only to cure or comfort, never to kill. They have not been given, nor should they be given, the power to use their knowledge and skills to bring life to an end. It would open the way for powerful misuse and, no less importantly, represent an intrinsic violation of what it has meant to be a physician.

Yet if it is possible for physicians to misuse their knowledge and power to kill people directly, are they thereby required to use that same knowledge always to keep people alive, always to resist a disease that can itself kill the patient? The traditional answer has been: not necessarily. For the physician's ultimate obligation is to the welfare of the patient, and excessive treatment can be as detrimental to that welfare as inadequate treatment. Put another way, the obligation to resist the lethal power of disease is limited—it ceases when the patient is unwilling to have it resisted, or where the resistance no longer serves the patient's welfare. Behind this moral premise is the recognition that disease (of some kind) ultimately triumphs and that death is both inevitable sooner or later and not, in any case, always the greatest human evil. To demand of the physician that he always struggle against disease, as if it was in his power always to conquer it, would be to fall into the same metaphysical trap mentioned above: that of assuming that no distinction can be drawn between natural and human agency.

A final word. I suggested [in an earlier discussion] that the most potent motive for active euthanasia and assisted suicide stems from a dread of the power of medicine. That power then seems to take on a drive of its own regardless of the welfare or wishes of patients. No one can easily say no—not physicians, not patients, not families. My guess is that happens because too many have already come to believe that it is their choice, and their choice alone, which brings about death; and they do not want to exercise that kind of authority. The solution is not to erase the distinction between killing and allowing to die, but to underscore its validity and importance. We can bring disease as a cause of death back into the care of the dying.

Euthanasia in The Netherlands

Justifiable Euthanasia

Pieter V. Admiraal

In recent years I have spoken on numerous occasions about various aspects of euthanasia practice in general hospitals. I always limit myself to that group of patients who are in the terminal phase of an incurable, usually malignant disease, and I have always placed emphasis upon the desirability of good terminal supportive care by a team of doctors, nurses, and pastors. At the same time I have repeatedly pointed out that the practice of euthanasia occurs only as a last resort and that the majority of patients die without recourse to euthanasia.

I shall limit myself to just two aspects of euthanasia. First, I wish to discuss what causes a patient to make a request for euthanasia to the doctor who is treating him; and secondly, to address the question of what we are to understand by "passive euthanasia".

WHAT MAKES A PATIENT REQUEST EUTHANASIA

A patient in the terminal phase will only request euthanasia if he considers his suffering to be unbearable and chooses to die rather than to live under these circumstances. I assume that the request is the result of a lengthy decision process by a patient who is fully conscious of the consequences of his request to himself, to his relatives, and to the doctor to whom he directs his request. At the same time I assume that all persons involved are agreed that the suffering of the patient cannot be relieved in any way and that the performance of euthanasia is only and exclusively in the interest of the patient. Euthanasia then becomes the ultimate act of care for the dying.

What brings the patient to the point of requesting euthanasia from his doctor? Which factors cause the suffering of the patient to become unbearable? Objective considerations lead us to distinguish physical and psychological causes which are closely related to each other.

Physical Causes of Requests for Euthanasia

Loss of Strength

Especially in cachectic patients, a serious loss of strength occurs as a result of greatly increased protein breakdown and poor peripheral circulation. As a result, the patient in a terminal phase no longer is capable of any physical exertion. The patient then becomes totally dependent on nursing care both day and night.

Fatigue

The loss of strength practically always is accompanied by extreme fatigue even without any physical effort at all. This fatigue cannot be influenced in any way at all and is experienced as exhausting by the patient.

Pain

Until recently pain was the most important cause of physical and psychological suffering. Nowadays, in most cases, pain can be adequately controlled without the normal psychological functions of the patient being adversely affected.

As examples of pain treatment one can mention pharmacotherapy with the administering of analgesics and psychopharmaceuticals, the continuous epidural application of morphine-like analgesics, and the fixed blocking of the sensitive nerve-paths of the sympathetic nervous system.

Unfortunately, the above methods of controlling pain are not yet known or applicable everywhere. Pain can then become unbearable. In a small number of instances pain cannot be subjected to acceptable control even with the most advanced techniques. One may be compelled to administer morphine and/or psychopharmaceuticals intravenously on a continuous basis in such high doses that it has serious harmful effects on the psychic functioning of the patient.

Shortness of Breath

An increasing shortness of breath and belabored breathing often occurs in the terminal phase. Some of the causes can be:

■ Specific lung aberrations such as inflammations of tumors, which increasingly diminish lung capacity, resulting in the development of dyspnea. But also the growth of small tumors in the lungs, for example in the trachea or in the bronchi, can result in a serious stridor.

■ Growth of tumors in the mouth cavity can cause a serious obstruction to breathing and even result in suffocation.

■ A large quantity of liquid in the lungs as a result of insufficient coughing up due to loss of strength or in consequence of a cardial decompensation.

■ A diminished tissue oxygenation will by reflex action lead to faster breathing which can be experienced as shortness of breath by the patient.

Sleeplessness

Although sleeplessness may occur as a complaint all by itself, it is especially patients who suffer fatigue, shortness of breath, and pain who sleep badly, and this can result in exhaustion. When pain is the cause, one will have to administer an analgesic late in the evening or increase the dosage.

Persistent sleeplessness in patients without pain often necessitates the administering of barbiturates as a result of which the patient may be dull and drowsy during the daytime. Just as in the case of healthy people, waking periods appear to be longer at night than they actually are. Conversely, after a short period of sleep the patient can get the false impression that he has slept a long time, and that can be very disappointing and make the waking period seem even longer.

Nausea and Vomiting

Nausea can be a side effect of analgesics or of cytotoxics. The administering of antiemetics is then indicated, but the effect is often disappointing. In the case of a total blockage of the stomach intestine, vomiting will be continuous, sometimes even when there is continuous suctioning by means of a stomach siphon. Vomiting is exhausting and disorients the patient.

Flow of Saliva

When there is a total blockage of the esophagus or the throat cavity, the saliva produced must be spit out constantly and that is psychically burdensome.

Thirst

Thirst occurs when there is a disturbance of the electrolyte content of the blood and with dehydration. Especially when the patient is being treated at home it can be difficult to administer sufficient liquids by means of an infusion or a stomach siphon. The routine (almost ritual) moistening of the lips does not then offer relief.

Incontinence

There are several causes which can lead to the patient being incontinent with respect to urine or to feces for a shorter or longer period during an illness. Incontinence requires constant intensive nursing care and is experienced by the patient as humanly degrading.

Decubitis

Bedsores will easily develop in patients as a result of bad blood circulation in the skin, and definitely so in the case of cachectic patients who can no longer move themselves because of the loss of strength and the increase of fatigue. If the patient in addition is incontinent, then bedsores can scarcely be averted in intensive nursing. Through tissue deterioration and secondary infections the bedsores are often accompanied by a very penetrating, unpleasant odor.

Miscellany

Some miscellaneous causes are:

- Constipation, especially with the administering of morphine-like analgesics.
- Perspiration
- Hunger
- Itching, especially with jaundice
- Coughing
- Ascites [Dropsy of the abdomen]
- Cystitis with an [implanted] catheter
- Fungi infections of the mouth cavity
- Hiccupping with [organic] processes in the upper abdomen

Side Effects of Therapeutic Treatments

Finally, our therapeutic actions can cause the patient minor or serious side effects for a shorter or longer period of time. Thus, there is the general malaise after major surgical operations or extended X-ray therapy. Repeated cytotoxic treatments cause not only a general feeling of malaise but usually also the loss of body hair which is experienced as something extremely unpleasant, especially by women. As pointed out earlier, patients suffer from nausea for a long time when analgesics and cytotoxics are administered, while painful muscle indurations can occur with the extended administering of intramuscular injections.

The above summation is not intended to suggest the order of frequency in which these problems occur. Fatigue, shortness of breath, nausea, pain, incontinence, and decubitis are in general the biggest problems. But an isolated symptom, like an itch or hiccups can also in the long run be experienced as unbearable by a patient.

Psychological Causes of Requests for Euthanasia

The most important psychic causes are as follows:

Somatic Deviations

This includes psychic suffering as a result of the above described somatic problems. All of the somatic deviations mentioned above can become a serious psychic burden to the patient.

Many of the above deviations last during an extended period of the illness, and almost all of them get increasingly worse, often to the very time of death, which in the long run leads to the psychical exhaustion of the patient, despite all nursing and spiritual care. It is especially incontinence, decubitis, and the loss of all strength which the patient in the end experiences as humanly degrading. Under these circumstances many patients consider this last phase as an affront to human dignity, as suffering without any use or purpose, as undeserved and as the disintegration of their humanness.

Anxieties

Practically every patient is plagued by anxiety during the course of his illness. From the very beginning, from the moment that an unfavorable diagnosis has been made and death is inevitable, many patients develop a fear of pain and grievous suffering. This anxiety is based on hearsay or on one's own experience, and even today is seemingly confirmed by the texts of some obituary announcements. [For example: after long and painful suffering, patiently endured, the Lord called home to his eternal rest, our dearly beloved . . . .] But information provided by lay-persons is often not very encouraging. Whereas, many doctors betray their task as physicians by providing poor information or by falling short in the doctor-patient relationship. Regrettably, many doctors still talk and publish about "the pain of cancer" as something that is worse than any other pain.

Much more difficult to combat or to refute is the anxiety about spiritual and physical decay and deformation. After all, we cannot guard the patient against these. The only help we can give here is the promise to alleviate suffering when possible or if necessary to end it. The same thing holds for the anxiety about needing total nursing care and becoming totally dependent. Loneliness and isolation are also anxious threats and indeed many patients are lonely in long nights of waking, alone with their thoughts and fearful expectations. Isolated nursing in the end phase, however much needed from a nursing perspective, encourages this loneliness at home or in the hospital. Only the experience of a warm shared humanity can afford relief in this situation.

Anxiety about dying itself can have various causes. In dying there comes, of course, the inevitable parting from this life, the world in which one has lived and worked, and from beloved relatives. But there can also be anxiety about the moment of dying, the anxiety that then "something" will happen that is unpleasant and threatening without your having any definite idea of what that might be. It is certain that the theatrical portrayal of dying on the stage, or on the screen, usually is far removed from reality. The death scene in an opera is a flagrant example of this.

Anxiety about what comes after death is culturally and religiously determined and can vary from a vague anxiety about the unknown to a literal deathly fear of punishment, which may or may not be eternal. Fortunately, many persons also die in the firm conviction of another, blessed life, united with those who went before. There are also more and more people who, in consequence of the present Western cultural pattern, no longer believe in a hereafter and consequently do not have any anxiety about the hereafter. Fears about dying can be discussed with both the spiritual counselor and the doctor.

As a result of intoxications from one's own body or from various pharmaceuticals, anxious hallucinations or confusions can occur. It requires competent medical and professional knowledge to prevent or to combat these anxieties.

Grief

However much we all realize that death is inevitable and unbreakably linked to life, the certainty of the approaching end of our lives makes us sorrowful. Grief can be about the loss of family and friends or about the loss of earthly things, the possession of which has now become so useless.

Grief will become worse in the measure that less expression can be given to it. Especially in the beginning of the illness process, when the diagnosis is just received, it often happens that the patient, his family and his friends, conceal their grief from each other; and sometimes, out of fear to show their own grief, they are not open to the grief of the other. Grief is then crowded out and bottled up. Grief then becomes sorrow and it would be better to listen to each other's grief and to give each other the opportunity to cry out one's feelings. Mutual understanding is after all the basis of the saying: "Company in distress, makes sorrow less." Grief becomes unbearable when it is not recognized, and the patient is left alone with it, and not understood [by others].

Grief becomes bitter when the patient poses the question of why this happens to him who does not deserve it, and not to another who does seem to deserve it; also when he asks why this should happen to him now, at this point in his life. We see this especially in young people who see their future cut off and by older persons who, after a life of hard work, anticipated enjoying a well earned rest, or who finally wanted to get at fulfilling their long cherished and long postponed ideals.

Such a grief can easily turn into rancor, revolt, and aggression. There can also be grief about the grief of those left behind or about the uncertain, perhaps even precarious future which confronts those left behind. Cares, for example, about less income when the provider dies, or cares about the further nurturing of children when the mother dies young. Such grief depresses the patient and can easily turn into a serious depression.

Some strict believers can experience their grief as wrong in the sight of God who "proposes and disposes," and they may feel guilty about the fact that they do not accept and cheerfully bear their grief.

Rancor, Resistance, Aggression, and Denial
but also Acceptance and Acquiesence Play
an Important Role in the Terminal Phase

They were clearly described for the first time by Kubler-Ross and it is to her great merit that she prepared the way for meaningful terminal care of the dying. Without in any way minimizing her work, I must point out that her observations are for the most part based on observations of American patients with a different life style and a different cultural pattern from that of the European. The above physical and psychological problems can become unbearable suffering for the patient and create the occasion for a request for euthanasia.

Suffering is specific for each human being: an animal does not suffer in the sense that we mean here. An animal feels pain, a human being suffers pain. Only that person can suffer who is capable of deliberate comparative retrospective and prospective contemplation in which one compares, weighs, and evaluates. Suffering therefore includes grief, depression, concern, and anxiety. But fortunately, there is also hope, acquiescence, and acceptance. These too are specifically human.

The suffering of a human being is strictly individual and is determined by the psychological tension and inner resources of that person in enduring dire distress. The suffering of the other is largely withdrawn from our objective observation and consequently it is difficult to weigh and to judge.

It is therefore just as wrong to admiringly attribute to one heroism or martyrdom and to reproach the other for a cowardly attitude toward life. We must seriously ask ourselves where some among us derive the right to judge the suffering of another to be bearable when that person tells us that his suffering is unbearable.

In my honest opinion, it is the inalienable right of each person to make the judgment that his individual suffering is no longer bearable and to request euthanasia from the doctor who is treating him. But then that doctor may not and cannot refrain from making a judgment about the suffering of the person who requests euthanasia. After all, a request for euthanasia, by itself, does not legalize its application. The doctor must then attempt, on the basis of observable facts and on the basis of feeling his way into the situation of the patient, apart from his own emotions, arrive at a judgment which is as honest as possible. He shall have to try to realize in his own mind why the patient under these circumstances prefers death to life. Above all he will have to ask himself whether the circumstances can be improved. His judgment will become more mature and more balanced as his experience in providing terminal care to the dying increases. He must always remain aware that he continues to bear the final responsibility for his decision. It is therefore desirable and necessary that the doctor seek the counsel and assistance of others so that he may in this way constantly test his opinion against that of others.

It is my opinion that every doctor has the right and the duty after prolonged and thorough deliberation to carry out euthanasia; at the request of the other person and in his interest, knowing that he is responsible to himself, to the other, and to the law. Similarly, every doctor has the unassailable right under any circumstances to refuse to carry out euthanasia, knowing that he is responsible to himself and to the other.

The carrying out of euthanasia can only be based on the acknowledgment of unbearable suffering. Here I wish consciously to pass over the Christian view that suffering purifies or, in a broader sense, that suffering is part of life and therefore must be accepted. Many do not subscribe to these views and I think it absolutely wrong to impose such a value judgment on another person or to make him dependent on it. A doctor can refuse to carry out euthanasia on those grounds, provided he does not block the way for a doctor who is prepared to act on the request of the patient.

It would be wrong to give the impression that the request of a patient who is terminally ill with cancer must always and only be based on the above examples of unbearable suffering. Thus, a patient who has arrived at the point of acceptance and acquiescence may no longer attach any value to his life, his relatives, or to his environs. We then speak of a total detachment, one that is especially difficult for relatives to understand and accept. Such a patient only longs for the end. We see this with some frequency in patients of advanced age who have lost all their relatives and friends. As indicated earlier, the desire for reunion can play a role in believing patients.

CARRYING OUT "PASSIVE EUTHANASIA"

In the Netherlands the political discussion about the legalization of euthanasia is to a large extent controlled by the confessional parties which find themselves confronted with a dilemma: on the one hand the practice of euthanasia is considered acceptable by a large majority of the population, including the confessional part, but on the other hand, the Roman Catholic Church and some Protestant churches forbid the practice of active euthanasia.

In order to get out of this impasse, the term "passive euthanasia" has been introduced in recent years. In general, it is defined as "the discontinuance of life sustaining means or treatment as a result of which the patient dies after a shorter or longer period." This can be clarified by means of two examples:

1. Stopping existing [life support] medications such as antibiotics, cytotoxins, anti-arrythmia's [heart regulating medications], medications for increasing blood pressure, diuretics, cortico-steroids, or insulin.

2. Stopping existing nonmedication treatments such as kidney dialysis, blood transfusions, intravenous or tube feeding, reanimation, physiotherapy, or antidecubitis treatment.

Under passive euthanasia one could also place the carefully considered decision not to begin one of the above treatments or an agreement not to reanimate when breathing is arrested or the heart stops beating.

In passive euthanasia there is therefore a conscious decision by the doctor either to discontinue an existing treatment or not to initiate a possible treatment. Only fifty years ago the problems were not so great. The number of possible treatments was small and just about all were exclusively symptomatic so that the treating physician, already in an early stage of the illness, was compelled and justified in saying to the patient that he, as a doctor, could do no more.

Today it is quite different. Our therapeutic arsenal is very extensive, every year new medicines and methods are discovered so that the number of patients to whom the doctor must say, "I can do nothing more for you," is becoming smaller and smaller.

As we have discussed earlier, a number of these therapies cause so many unpleasant side effects that the continuance of the treatment becomes unacceptable to the patient and he asks his doctor to discontinue the treatment. Obviously in reaching this decision, other factors, for example, the hopeless prospect of symptomatic treatment without any chance of a definite cure, also plays an important role. Whereas in the past, it was a matter of necessity that the doctor himself had to discontinue a treatment, it now will be difficult for many doctors to discontinue a treatment at the patient's request. Indeed, there has been a case where the patient had to sign a declaration demanding the discontinuance of further treatment.

One thing is clear: if the doctor discontinues treatment and does no more the patient will die from the direct consequences of his disease. Using the example cited above, death will be the result of a serious sepsis, cardiac arrest, diabetic or uremic coma, anemia, malnutrition, breathing insufficiency, etc. This means that with passive euthanasia most patients will die only after a long pathway of suffering.

Under these circumstances the word euthanasia is completely mistaken and misleading. This is not at all the "gentle death" which is desired by the patient. The word "passive" here refers altogether to the attitude of the doctor.

Passive euthanasia is nothing but abstention. And abstention, doing nothing, is surely the very last thing a patient making a request [for euthanasia] is entitled to.

Of course, after abstention [nontreatment] it is possible to make dying easier in various ways. But if this occurs with analgesics and psychopharmaceuticals in high doses, then I see no difference at all with active euthanasia. The concept "passive euthanasia" then becomes a cover for the active euthanasia which is not allowed.

Even more dangerous, in my judgment, is the standpoint taken by some church people in the Netherlands who say that there is no euthanasia when a patient dies sooner than normal as a result of high doses of morphine-like analgesics. That opens the door to abuses!

First of all, the number of patients whose pain is untreatable is getting smaller and smaller; and secondly, to carry out euthanasia with morphine in patients who have been treated with morphine for a considerable period of time already, just will not work, because of the swiftly developing tolerance to the breath depressant effect. What must be prevented is that under the guise of controlling pain the lives of patients can be terminated in a wrong and uncontrolled manner without even calling this euthanasia.

In summary, I wish to posit that passive euthanasia is a hypocritical euphemism and not in the interest of the patient who is in a terminal phase.

Why Doctors Must Not Kill

Leon R. Kass

Do you want your doctor licensed to kill? Should he or she be permitted or encouraged to inject or prescribe poison? Shall the mantle of privacy that protects the doctor-patient relationship, in the service of life and wholeness, now also cloak decisions for death? Do you want *your* doctor deciding, on the basis of his own private views, when you still deserve to live and when you now deserve to die? And what about the other fellow's doctor—that shallow technician, that insensitive boor who neither asks nor listens, that unprincipled money-grubber, that doctor you used to go to until you got up the nerve to switch: do you want *him* licensed to kill? Speaking generally, shall the healing profession become also the euthanizing profession?

Common sense has always answered, "No." For more than two millennia, the reigning medical ethic, mindful that the power to cure is also the power to kill, has held as an inviolable rule, "Doctors must not kill." Yet this venerable taboo is now under attack. Proponents of euthanasia and physician-assisted suicide would have us believe that it is but an irrational vestige of religious prejudice, alien to a true ethic of medicine, which stands in the way of a rational and humane approach to suffering at the end of life. Nothing could be further from the truth. The taboo against doctors killing patients (even on request) is the very embodiment of reason and wisdom. Without it, medicine will have trouble doing its proper work; without it, medicine will have lost its claim to be an ethical and trustworthy profession; without it, all of us will suffer—yes, more than we now suffer because some of us are not soon enough released from life.

Consider first the damaging consequences for the doctor-patient relationship. The patient's trust in the doctor's wholehearted devotion to the patient's best interests will be hard to sustain once doctors are licensed to kill. Imagine the scene: you are old, poor, in failing health, and alone in the world; you are brought to the city hospital with fractured ribs and pneumonia. The nurse or intern enters late at night with a syringe full of yellow stuff for your intravenous drip. How soundly will you sleep? It will not matter that your doctor has never yet put anyone to death; that he is legally entitled to do so will make a world of difference.

And it will make a world of psychic difference too for conscientious physicians. How easily will they be able to care wholeheartedly for patients when it is always possible to think of killing them as a "therapeutic option"? Shall it be penicillin and a respirator one more time, or, perhaps, this time just an overdose of morphine? Physicians get tired of treating patients who are hard to cure, who resist their best efforts, who are on their way down— "gorks," "gomers," and "vegetables" are only some of the less than affectionate names they receive from the house officers. Won't it be tempting to think that death is the best "treatment" for the little old lady "dumped" again on the emergency room by the nearby nursing home?

It is naive and foolish to take comfort from the fact that the currently proposed change in the law provides "aid-in-dying" only to those who request it. For we know from long experience how difficult it is to discover what we truly want when we are suffering. Verbal "requests" made under duress rarely reveal the whole story. Often a demand for euthanasia is, in fact, an angry or anxious plea for help, born of fear of rejection or abandonment, or made in ignorance of available alternatives that could alleviate pain and suffering. Everyone knows how easy it is for those who control the information to engineer requests and to manipulate choices, especially in the vulnerable. Paint vividly a horrible prognosis, and contrast it with that "gentle, quick release": which will the depressed or frightened patient choose, especially in the face of a spiraling hospital bill or children who visit grudgingly? Yale Kamisar asks the right questions: "Is this the kind of choice, assuming that it can be made in a fixed and rational manner, that we want to offer a gravely ill person? Will we not sweep up, in the process, some who are not really tired of life, but think others are tired of them; some who do not really want to die, but who feel that they should not live on, because to do so when there looms the legal alternative of euthanasia is to do a selfish or cowardly act? Will not some feel an obligation to have themselves 'eliminated' in order that funds allocated for their terminal care might be better used by their families or, financial worries aside, in order to relieve their families of the emotional strain involved?"

Euthanasia, once legalized, will not remain confined to those who freely and knowingly elect it—and the most energetic backers of euthanasia do not really want it thus restricted. Why? Because the vast majority of candidates who merit mercy-killing cannot request it for themselves: adults with persistent vegetative state or severe depression or senility or aphasia or mental illness or Alzheimer's disease; infants who are deformed; and children who are retarded or dying. All incapable of requesting death. They will thus be denied our new humane "assistance-in-dying." But not to worry. The lawyers and the doctors (and the cost-containers) will soon rectify this injustice. The enactment of a law legalizing mercy killing (or assisted suicide) on voluntary request will certainly be challenged in the courts under the equal-protection clause of the Fourteenth Amendment. Why, it will be argued, should the comatose or the demented be denied the right to such a "dignified death" or such a "treatment" just because they cannot claim it for themselves? With the aid of court-appointed proxy consenters, we will quickly erase the distinction between the right to choose one's own death and the right to request someone else's—as we have already done in the termination-of-treatment cases.

Clever doctors and relatives will not need to wait for such changes in the law. Who will be around to notice when the elderly, poor, crippled, weak, powerless, retarded, uneducated, demented, or gullible are mercifully released from the lives their doctors, nurses, and next of kin deem no longer worth living? In Holland, for example, a recent survey of 300 physicians (conducted by an author who supports euthanasia) disclosed that over 40 percent had performed euthanasia *without the patient's request,* and over 10 percent had done so in more than five cases. Is there any reason to believe that the average American physician is, in his private heart, more committed than his Dutch counterpart to the equal worth and dignity of every life under his care? Do we really want to find out what he is like, once the taboo is broken?

Even the most humane and conscientious physician psychologically needs protection against himself and his weaknesses, if he is to care fully for those who entrust themselves to him. A physician-friend who worked many years in a hospice caring for dying patients explained it to me most convincingly: "Only because I knew that I could not and would not kill my patients was I able to enter most fully and intimately into caring for them as they lay dying." The psychological burden of the license to kill (not to speak of the brutalization of the physician-killers) could very well be an intolerably high price to pay for the physician-assisted euthanasia.

The point, however, is not merely psychological: it is also moral and essential. My friend's horror at the thought that he might be tempted to kill his patients, were he not enjoined from doing so, embodies a deep understanding of the medical ethic and its intrinsic limits. We move from assessing consequences to looking at medicine itself.

The beginning of ethics regarding the use of power generally lies in naysaying. The wise setting of limits on the use of power is based on discerning the excesses to which the power, unrestrained, is prone. Applied to the professions, this principle would establish strict outer boundaries—indeed, inviolable taboos—against those "occupational hazards" to which each profession is especially prone. *Within* these outer limits, no fixed rules of conduct apply; instead, prudence—the wise judgment of the man-on-the-spot—finds and adopts the best course of action in the light of the circumstances. But the outer limits themselves are fixed, firm, and non-negotiable.

What are those limits for medicine? At least three are set forth in the venerable Hippocratic Oath: no breach of confidentiality; no sexual relations with patients; no dispensing of deadly drugs. These unqualified, self-imposed restrictions are readily understood in terms of the temptations to which the physician is most vulnerable, temptations in each case regarding an area of vulnerability and exposure that the practice of medicine requires of patients. Patients necessarily divulge and reveal private and intimate details of their personal lives; patients necessarily expose their naked bodies to the physician's objectifying gaze and investigating hands; patients necessarily expose and entrust the care of their very lives to the physician's skill, technique, and judgment. The exposure is, in all cases, one-sided and asymmetric: the doctor does not reveal his intimacies, display his nakedness, offer up his embodied life to the patient. Mindful of the meaning of such nonmutual exposure, the physician voluntarily sets limits on his own conduct, pledging not to take advantage of or to violate the patient's intimacies, naked sexuality, or life itself.

The prohibition against killing patients, the first negative promise of self-restraint sworn to in the Hippocratic Oath, stands as medicine's first and most abiding taboo: "I will neither give a deadly drug to anybody if asked for it, nor will I make a suggestion to this effect. . . . In purity and holiness I will guard my life and my art." In forswearing the giving of poison, the physician recognizes and restrains a god-like power he wields over patients, mindful that his drugs can both cure and kill. But in forswearing the giving of poison, *when asked for it,* the Hippocratic physician rejects the view that the patient's choice for death can make killing him—or assisting his suicide—right. For the physician, at least, human life in living bodies commands respect and reverence—*by its very nature.* As its respectability does not depend upon human agreement or patient consent, revocation of one's consent to live does not deprive one's living body of respectability. The deepest ethical principle restraining the physician's power is not the autonomy or freedom of the patient; neither is it his own compassion or good intention. Rather, it is the dignity and mysterious power of human life itself, and, therefore, also what the oath calls the purity and holiness of the life and art to which he has sworn devotion. A person can choose to be a physician, but he cannot simply choose what physicianship means.

The central meaning of physicianship derives not from medicine's powers but from its goal, not from its means but from its end: to benefit the sick by the activity of healing. The physician as physician serves only the sick. He does not serve the relatives or the hospital or the national debt inflated due to Medicare costs. Thus he will never sacrifice the well-being of the sick to the convenience or pocketbook or feelings of the relatives or society. Moreover, the physician serves the sick not because they have rights or wants or claims, but because they are sick. The healer works with and for those who need to be healed, in order to help make them whole. Despite enormous changes in medical technique and institutional practice, despite enormous changes in nosology and therapeutics, the center of medicine has not changed: it is as true today as it was in the days of Hippocrates that the ill desire to be whole; that wholeness means a certain well-working of the enlivened body and its unimpaired powers to sense, think, feel, desire, move, and maintain itself; and that the relationship between the healer and the ill is constituted, essentially even if only tacitly, around the desire of both to promote the wholeness of the one who is ailing.

Can wholeness and healing ever be compatible with intentionally killing the patient? Can one benefit the patient as a whole by making him dead? There is, of course, a logical difficulty: how can any good exist for a being that is not? But the error is more than logical: to intend and to act for someone's good requires his continued existence to receive the benefit.

To be sure, certain attempts to benefit may in fact turn out, unintentionally, to be lethal. Giving adequate morphine to control pain might induce respiratory depression leading to death. But the intent to relieve the pain of the living presupposes that the living still live to be relieved. This must be the starting point in discussing all medical benefits: no benefit without a beneficiary.

Against this view, someone will surely bring forth the hard cases: patients so ill-served by their bodies that they can no longer bear to live, bodies riddled with cancer and racked with pain, against which their "owners" protest in horror and from which they insist on being released. Cannot the person "in the body" speak up against the rest, and request death for "personal" reasons?

However sympathetically we listen to such requests, we must see them as incoherent. Such person-body dualism cannot be sustained. "Personhood" is manifest on earth only in living bodies; our highest mental functions are held up by, and are inseparable from, lowly metabolism, respiration, circulation, excretion. There may be blood without consciousness, but there is never consciousness without blood. Thus one who calls for death in the service of personhood is like a tree seeking to cut its roots for the sake of growing its highest fruit. No physician, devoted to the benefit of the sick, can serve the patient as person by denying and thwarting his personal embodiment.

To say it plainly, to bring nothingness is incompatible with serving wholeness: one cannot heal—or comfort—by making nil. The healer cannot annihilate if he is truly to heal. The physician-euthanizer is a deadly self-contradiction.

But we must acknowledge a difficulty. The central goal of medicine—health—is, in each case, a perishable good: inevitably, patients get irreversibly sick, patients degenerate, patients die. Healing the sick is *in principle* a project that must at some point fail. And here is where all the trouble begins: How does one deal with "medical failure"? What does one seek when restoration of wholeness—or "much" wholeness—is by and large out of the question?

Contrary to the propaganda of the euthanasia movement, there is, in fact, much that can be done. Indeed, by recognizing finitude yet knowing that we will not kill, we are empowered to focus on easing and enhancing the *lives* of those who are dying. First of all, medicine can follow the lead of the hospice movement and—abandoning decades of shameful mismanagement—provide truly adequate (and now technically feasible) relief of pain and discomfort. Second, physicians (and patients and families) can continue to learn how to withhold or withdraw those technical interventions that are, in truth, merely burdensome or degrading medical additions to the unhappy end of a life—including, frequently, hospitalization itself. Ceasing treatment and allowing death to occur when (and if) it will seem to be quite compatible with the respect life itself commands for itself. Doctors may and must allow to die, even if they must not intentionally kill.

Ceasing medical intervention, allowing nature to take its course, differs fundamentally from mercy killing. For one thing, death does not necessarily follow the discontinuance of treatment; Karen Ann Quinlan lived more than ten years after the court allowed the "life-sustaining" respirator to be removed. Not the physician, but the underlying fatal illness becomes the true cause of death. More important morally, in ceasing treatment the physician need not *intend* the death of the patient, even when the death follows as a result of his omission. His intention should be to avoid useless and degrading medical *additions* to the already sad end of a life. In contrast, in active, direct mercy killing the physician must, necessarily and indubitably, intend *primarily* that the patient be made dead. And he must knowingly and indubitably cast himself in the role of the agent of death. This remains true even if he is merely an assistant in suicide. A physician who provides the pills or lets the patient plunge the syringe after he leaves the room is *morally* no different from one who does the deed himself. "I will neither give a deadly drug to anybody if asked for it, nor will I make a suggestion to this effect."

Once we refuse the technical fix, physicians and the rest of us can also rise to the occasion: we can learn to act humanly in the presence of finitude. Far more than adequate morphine and the removal of burdensome machinery, the dying need our presence and our encouragement. Dying people are all too easily reduced ahead of time to "thinghood" by those who cannot bear to deal with the suffering or disability of those they love. Withdrawal of contact, affection, and care is the greatest single cause of the dehumanization of dying. Not the alleged humaneness of an elixir of death, but the humanness of connected living-while-dying is what medicine—and the rest of us—most owe the dying. The treatment of choice is company and care.

The euthanasia movement would have us believe that the physician's refusal to assist in suicide or perform euthanasia constitutes an affront to human dignity. Yet one of their favorite arguments seems to me rather to prove the reverse. Why, it is argued, do we put animals out of their misery but insist on compelling fellow human beings to suffer to the bitter end? Why, if it is not a contradiction for the veterinarian, does the medical ethic absolutely rule out mercy killing? Is this not simply inhumane?

Perhaps *inhumane,* but not thereby *inhuman.* On the contrary it is precisely because animals are not human that we must treat them (merely) humanely. We put dumb animals to sleep because they do not know that they are dying, because they can make nothing of their misery or mortality, and, therefore, because they cannot live deliberately—i.e., humanly—in the face of their own suffering and dying. They cannot live out a fitting end. Compassion for their weakness and dumbness is our only appropriate emotion, and given our responsibility for their care and well-being, we do the only humane thing we can. But when a conscious human being asks us for death, by that very action he displays the presence of something that precludes our regarding him as a dumb animal. Humanity is owed humanity, not humaneness. Humanity is owed the bolstering of the human, even/or especially in its dying moments, in resistance to the temptation to ignore its presence in the sight of suffering.

Death by Deliberate Dehydration and Starvation: Silent Echoes of the Hungerhäuser

John M. Dolan

The thesis defended here is that the central question raised by the case under discussion is whether it is ever permissible to arrange deliberately for a disabled person who is not terminally ill to die of thirst and starvation. It is worth recalling that the Phoenicians, who devised the method of execution known as crucifixion, originally employed the technique as a method of killing by deliberate dehydration and starvation.[1]

> The earliest 'cross' was actually just a vertical stake to which the condemned was tied and left to expire from thirst and starvation.[2]

It is remarkable that physicians and laymen are now seriously contemplating adoption of a method of killing that was regarded as particularly cruel and degrading in the ancient world and was, among the Romans, who inherited the technique from the Phoenicians, "reserved for slaves and the worst of criminals."[3]

SHORT ANSWER

The first of the three principles employed in this initial analysis has two versions, one moral, the other legal. The moral version of the principle reads as follows:

(1) A deliberate omission that causes death is morally an act of intentional killing when three conditions are satisfied:

    (i)   it is within the agent's power to supply what is being withheld;
    (ii) the agent has an obligation to supply it; and
    (iii) the agent understands that withholding what is needed is likely to cause death.[4]

The relevant notion of obligation appealed to in clause (ii) is, of course, moral obligation. If one replaces the word *morally*, which occurs earlier in the formulation above, with the word *legally* and reinterprets the obligation in clause (ii) as legal obligation, then one has a legal principle that is valid in a number of legal systems, including our own, namely:

(1) A deliberate omission that causes death is legally an act of intentional killing when three conditions are satisfied:

    (i)   it is within the agent's power to supply what is being withheld;
    (ii) the agent has an obligation to supply it; and
    (iii) the agent understands that withholding what is needed is likely to cause death.[5]

Let us now consider the bearing of this principle (in both of its versions) on the case we are examining. The officers of the nursing home certainly have the capacity to supply nourishment to Mr. Stevens. Further, they assert (correctly, in my judgment) that they have an obligation to supply nourishment to Mr. Stevens (an obligation that is both moral and legal). Finally, they understand clearly that withholding nourishment from Mr. Stevens will certainly result in his death.

It follows from the principle enunciated above (in both of its forms), and from the propositions just stated about the officers of the nursing home, that deliberate withholding of nourishment from Mr. Stevens on the part of those officers would, in the circumstances we are considering, count both morally and legally as an act of intentional killing.

A second principle relevant to the case we are considering reads as follows:

(2) Intentional killing of the innocent always counts as murder.

The term *innocent*, as it figures here, means simply "not harming." Thus, someone who is assaulting another person is *not* innocent in the relevant sense. Someone found guilty of a capital offense by due process of law is also not innocent in the relevant sense. Advocates of euthanasia and abortion differ in their response to this principle. Some acknowledge it but insist either that the particular form of destruction they favor does not count as intentional killing or else that the individuals whose destruction they favor are not persons. In its 1986 statement concerning withholding food and water from patients who are not terminally ill, the American Medical Association (AMA) took the first of these lines, declaring, in effect, that one can deliberately withhold food and water from a patient who is not terminally ill and thereby cause that patient's death without intentionally killing him.[6] A host of other advocates of euthanasia and abortion—e.g., most of the defenders of *Roe v. Wade*[7] speaking of the status of the unborn child, the Nazi theorists Karl Binding and Alfred Hoche on severely retarded persons,[8] and scores of contemporary bioethicists on such severely disabled persons as Karen Ann Quinlan and Nancy Beth Cruzan[9]—choose the second approach, assuring us that the individuals whose destruction they advocate are not persons. Other writers, even more frightening, acknowledge that the euthanasia (or abortion) they advocate does amount to deliberate killing of innocent persons but deny principle (2). Some imagine that the consent of the victim waives the victim's right to be free from lethal assault, thereby exonerating the killer.[10] Others ignore even this weak gesture of justification and confidently assert that destruction even of *unconsentng* innocent persons is perfectly justified under certain circumstances. Judith Jarvis Thomson's defense of abortion[11] falls into this category, as do current proposals to "retrieve" organs from living anencephalic infants and proposals to destroy incompetent patients for their own good. Sounder authors embrace principle (2); indeed, G.E.M. Anscombe invokes (2) as a specification of the central core of application of the concept of murder.[12]

Given the conclusion we have already reached, namely, that the deliberate withholding of nourishment from Mr. Stevens on the part of the nursing home officers would be an act of intentional killing, it follows from principle (2) that such a deliberate withholding would also count as murder.

The upshot of this elementary reasoning is obvious, for we can appeal now to a third principle, which is both basic and wholly uncontroversial:

(3)   Murder is always wrong.

Anyone who undertook to challenge this principle would be challenging moral judgment at bedrock. Some writers suppose that murder can be defined as "wrongful killing." If that view were correct, then challenges to principle (3) would be as silly as challenges to the proposition that all bachelors are unmarried. Correspondingly, in that case, principle (3) would be as empty as the assertion that all bachelors are unmarried. But, as G.E.M. Anscombe and Philip E. Devine both argue in their discussions of murder, the definition of murder as wrongful killing is incorrect.[13] The prohibition of murder is a substantive prohibition; it is not the empty injunction to refrain from carrying out the sorts of killing that you should refrain from carrying out. . . .

Since the deliberate withholding of food and water from Mr. Stevens on the part of the nursing home officers would count as their intentionally killing him and since intentional killing of the innocent always counts as murder and since murder is wrong, we conclude that the officers of the nursing home should continue to supply Mr. Stevens with nourishment and that the court should deny the petition to have that nourishment cut off.

QUESTIONS RAISED BY THE CASE OF MR. STEVENS

Having conducted an initial swift review of the case of Mr. Stevens, we may examine the case at a more leisurely pace. In this less brief analysis, we will investigate the following questions.

1. What are the facts concerning Mr. Stevens's medical condition?
2. Did Mr. Stevens, in effect, give his family an advance directive that bears on his present condition?
3. If Mr. Stevens did give his family the implicit advance directive they attribute to him, was it *rational?*
4. If Mr. Stevens did give an implicit advance directive that was rational, is it one that falls within the constraints of justice and the dictates of law?
5. If Mr. Stevens did give an implicit advance directive that satisfies all of the conditions just mentioned, *where* should the project of effecting his death by malnutrition and dehydration be carried out? Is a nursing home or a hospital an appropriate place to effect death by deliberate withholding of nourishment?

In the sections that follow, we will take up these questions one by one.

What Are the Facts Concerning Mr. Stevens's Medical Condition?

The diagnosis of "persistent vegetative state," cited by family members urging that Mr. Stevens's nutrition be cut off, is contested. The case description mentions both the judgment of his eldest daughter (whose reactions could be colored by wishful thinking) and the (less easily dismissed) consensus among the nursing staff, who believe that Mr. Stevens is "higher functioning" than many other residents in the facility. It would be foolish to disregard this testimony. There are in fact several reasons why one should be extremely cautious about staking a life-and-death decision on the diagnosis that has been assigned to Mr. Stevens. First, and most important, all medical diagnoses and prognoses are subject to uncertainty, and the diagnosis in the present case falls into an area of considerable shakiness.[14] Second, quite apart from the circumstance that the label "persistent vegetative state" makes discriminatory use of the adjective *vegetative* (implicitly encouraging the already virulent tendency to label certain disabled persons as "vegetables"), it is also enormously crude. There is a vast range of degrees of damage to the brain that could result in prolonged or, in some cases, permanent unconsciousness.[15] A careful clinician would be loath to lump all of those different injuries and medical conditions under a single crude label, particularly in a moral climate under which patients assigned the label are sometimes targeted for death. Third, the specific cause of Mr. Stevens's injuries, namely, head trauma, is more likely than anoxia (oxygen deprivation) to result in a prolonged period of unconsciousness from which the patient has a chance of recovering. Conceding the reliability of the diagnosis in Mr. Stevens's case is not at all a trivial matter.

Did Mr. Stevens, in Effect, Give His Family an Advance Directive That Bears on His Present Condition?

But let us waive all questions and doubts about the diagnosis and prognosis Mr. Stevens has been accorded. Let us address another question. The family, at any rate Mr. Stevens's wife and three of his children, believe that Mr. Stevens gave them an implicit advance directive. They understand him to have said, in effect: "If ever I am in a persistent vegetative state, I authorize you to withhold food and water from me in order to bring about my death from malnutrition and dehydration." Is this belief of theirs correct?

The evidence that Mr. Stevens gave such an implicit advance directive is actually shaky and rests on a number of hypotheses and conjectures, each of which is open to question. First, when he said at the death of his wife's father that the man had been "released from the prison of his own useless body," he may have been speaking without thought, filling a void, saying something, anything, because *something* had to be said. If this was the case, it would be grotesque to base any serious act on his remark, much less an act intended to cause his own death.

Second, even if he had thought a bit about what he was saying, it is possible that his words were chosen more to console his wife than to express any considered judgment on his part concerning the value of his father-in-law's life in a semi-comatose state. Once again, it would be grotesque to appeal to the remark as a justification for embarking on a course of action intended to cause his death.

Third, even if his remark did express a considered judgment on his part concerning the value of life in a semi-comatose state, nothing whatever follows about his willingness to *sanction actions deliberately aimed at causing the death of a semi-comatose person*. . . .

It tells us a great deal also about our current moral climate that a physician might draw the inference drawn by the physician attending Mr. Stevens, for that physician's reaction is scarcely anomalous but, rather, reflects a strong current trend in the medical world. Just how strong that trend is and just how far things have gone was dramatically illustrated in May of 1989. In that month, Dr. Pieter Admiraal, who may be the best-known living medical killer in the world,[16] visited Minneapolis and met with a large group of local physicians, bioethicists, and hospital ethics committee members in a conference room at one of our region's leading hospitals.[17]

What was most striking about that meeting, apart from the circumstance that it was taking place at a prestigious hospital, was the disturbing fact that Dr. Admiraal turned out to be more conservative and respectful of innocent human life than most of the Americans present. It emerged that there are three things a number of our American medical people advocate and practice that Dr. Admiraal thinks are dead wrong. The assembled physicians and bioethicists found this particularly infuriating. The three points of contention:

1. Some Americans advocate (and practice) euthanasia by means of withholding nourishment, but Dr. Admiraal found this a cruel and unacceptable method of killing people. Admiraal said: "You're doing the same thing I am; you're just playing games with words when you describe what you're doing."

2. Some Americans advocate (and practice) euthanasia in the case of incompetent persons, but Dr. Admiraal found this morally unacceptable, insisting that he would never kill a patient who was not both lucid and requesting euthanasia. This was a source of particular discomfort to our local practitioners, who insisted concerning the incompetent: "But they're the ones that suffer the most!"

3. Some Americans advocate (and to a limited extent practice) euthanasia based on instructions in living wills, but Dr. Admiraal said that he refuses "to kill someone on the basis of a piece of paper lying around in a drawer somewhere."[18]

Apart from the disturbing fact that the admitted killer Dr. Admiraal turned out to be more respectful of life than most of the American medical people assembled to meet him,[19] it was interesting to discover that Admiraal was paying attention to linguistic devices by which our advocates of euthanasia mask from themselves the character of the practices they propose. "You're doing the same thing I am; you're just playing games with words." The euphemized, debased vocabulary that is commonly employed in these cases and similar ones is worth careful attention.[20]

The euphemisms employed include those that implicitly falsify the facts. Thus, you will find people discussing cases like that of Mr. Stevens as though such a case poses the question whether the patient should be "allowed to die." But Mr. Stevens is not even terminally ill, much less on the verge of death.[21] Therefore, speaking of "allowing him to die" can only be a euphemism for speaking of *killing him*. It is worth noticing that one can read whole volumes by the advocates of euthanasia and never once encounter the words *kill* or *killing*. Thus, in the "Final Report of the Netherlands Commission on Euthanasia: An English Summary,"[22] a typical page contains the phrases *terminate life* and *termination of life* six times but does not contain the word *kill* even once.[23] Indeed, the word *kill* does not appear at all in the entire document. (Advocates of abortion also routinely employ the phrase *terminate pregnancy* in preference to *abortion* and never, under any circumstances, speak of *destroying unborn children*.) One scholar reports that he examined "tens of thousands" of Nazi documents without once encountering the German word for *killing* before, finally, after some years, coming upon that word in reference to an edict concerning dogs.[24]

One phrase favored by those who promote death by deliberate dehydration and starvation is "withholding hydration and nutrition." What a wonderfully clinical sound. How reasonable and sensible. Nothing of the ugliness of "withholding food and water" and certainly none of the even worse ugliness of "denying food and water." But, observe, even if we speak of "withholding food and water," we are still engaging in an important form of euphemism, what we might call euphemism by omission. For this phrase omits the central feature of the contested cases: namely, that the persons who are being denied food and water are persons who are not terminally ill, much less on the verge of death. To withhold food and water from a person who will die shortly anyway and whose death will not be caused by withholding the food and water is one thing. But to withhold food and water from a person who is not dying and whose death will be caused by the denial of food and water is quite another. Thus, the phrase "withholding hydration and nutrition" misleads in two respects: it masks the circumstance that it is denial of food and water that is at issue, and it entirely ignores the fact that the denial in question will kill the person undergoing our twentieth-century version of crucifixion. . . .

If Mr. Stevens Did Give an Implicit Advance Directive That He Was to Be Starved to Death in His Present Condition, Was That Directive Rational?

Let us forget, for now, the use of debased idiom that facilitates the movement toward euthanasia and other unspeakable practices. Let us agree to put to one side the grave doubts that attach to the claim that Mr. Stevens left his family with implicit instructions to bring about his death through thirst and starvation if he ever fell into a state of apparently irreversible unconsciousness. Let us imagine, for the moment, that there is not the shadow of a doubt attaching to the diagnosis that has been assigned to Mr. Stevens, and let us imagine that his family is wholly justified in believing that he left them with implicit instructions to kill him through starvation and dehydration if he ever became permanently unconscious. Let us now examine the possible rationality of an advance directive to have oneself killed by means of thirst and starvation. This question brings us to the heart of the mentality that drives the euthanasia movement.

To see what is going on here, consider other logically possible advance directives. For example:

> If ever I'm unable to feed myself and the probability of my being restored to full functioning and health is less than 95%, I direct my caregivers to withhold all nutrition and hydration. I understand that, if they act upon this directive, the probability is that I will die from malnutrition and dehydration rather than from my underlying disease or disability.

How likely is it that anyone would find that a rational directive? How likely is it that anyone would judge it an informed and considered decision on someone's part? This directive instructs us to kill by means of deliberate starvation and dehydration even when there is as much as a 94% chance that the patient will be restored to full functioning and health. No one would judge the directive rational. However good the evidence that a particular person did indeed leave behind such a directive, we would not act on it; indeed, it is clear that we *should* not act on it.

Now consider a bundle of other possible advance directives:

> If ever I'm unable to feed myself and it is the considered judgment of my attending physician that I will never recover
>
> > [my ability to solve differential equations],
>
> I direct my caregivers to withhold all nutrition and hydration in order to bring about my death. I understand that, if they act upon this directive, the probability is that I will die from malnutrition and dehydration rather than from my underlying disease or disability.

Here we might also consider five other possible advance directives, each of which can be obtained from the one just given by replacing the bracketed phrase with one of the following:

- my vision
- my ability to walk
- my bladder control
- my ability to play the violin
- my rational faculty

Imagine any one of these six possible advance directives given in writing, signed by the person issuing the directive, duly notarized by a notary public, and witnessed by three persons (none of whom is an heir of the person issuing the directive). Now ask: "How likely is it that we would find the directive rational?"

It is not likely that any of us would find the first five directives rational. Perhaps a particular mathematician would find life not worth living if he could no longer solve differential equations. We might empathize with him, share his sorrow at having to abandon work from which he derived profound satisfaction. But it is not likely that we would deem it rational of him to want to have himself destroyed if he could no longer pursue mathematics. And it is even more unlikely that we would follow his instructions to bring about his death by deliberate dehydration and starvation.

No one stands ready to withhold nourishment from Mr. Stevens simply because he asked us to do so, though undoubtedly many would be prepared to destroy him on the basis of the sixth advance directive given above, the one that takes effect when the person signing it has lost the possibility of recovering his or her rational faculty. Those who are prepared to arrange Mr. Stevens's destruction by starvation on such a basis are willing to do so not because he asked us to do it, but because, in *their* opinion, the degree of disability from which he now suffers is one with which no reasonable person would want to live.[25] This is the heart of the alleged impulse to honor the autonomy of a severely disabled person.

It is not an impulse to honor autonomy. It is, rather, a reaction of horror to certain forms of disability, an instinctive feeling that life would not be worth living under certain circumstances, that certain people are better off dead. And if that is the heart of the impulse, there is absolutely no reason to believe that deliberate starvations will be reserved only for those who ask for them, nor for those whose disabilities are as severe as those of Mr. Stevens. The proposal to withhold nourishment from him is, finally, a proposal to withhold nourishment from anyone as severely disabled as he is, whether that person has requested our version of Phoenician crucifixion or not. Inevitably, it is a proposal that we withhold nourishment from many other persons less severely disabled than he is. . . .

If Mr. Stevens Did Give a Rational Implicit Directive to Stop Assisted Feeding in the Present Circumstances, Is That Directive One Which Falls within the Constraints of Justice and the Dictates of the Law?

At this point, we are waiving doubts about Mr. Stevens's diagnosis, accepting without question the hypothesis that he requested death by starvation and dehydration in the event of permanent unconsciousness, and assuming that his request was fully informed and rational. We now address a quite different question. Assuming all of the foregoing, is the project of causing someone's death by dehydration and starvation one that falls within the constraints of justice and the law?

Here we can be brief. The principles set out in the first section of this article answer the present question. The crucial principle is the second presented in our initial analysis: Intentional killing of the innocent always counts as murder. Is Mr. Stevens innocent? Clearly, he is. Will cutting off his food and water kill him? Clearly, it will. Can one cut off his food and water without intending to kill him? Clearly, one cannot. One cannot stop his feeding and then claim after he is dead that his death from dehydration and starvation was merely a foreseen but unintended consequence of one's action, and one cannot do that even if one has good reason to believe that Mr. Stevens would have wanted to die given the degree of disability from which he was suffering.

Thus, since one cannot cut off Mr. Stevens's food and water without intentionally killing him, and since intentional killing of the innocent always counts as murder, one cannot cut off his food and water without murdering him. Further, since, by our third principle, murder is always wrong, it follows that it is wrong to cut off Mr. Stevens's food and water.

Neither the law nor morality conditions its protection of persons on standards of fitness and well-being. The most frail and disabled person is as entitled to their protection as the most vigorous and flourishing. In fact, as emphasized at the outset of this article, it is precisely in the case of the most vulnerable persons that the protection of the law is most urgent and the demands of justice most rigorous.

If Mr. Stevens Did Give an Implicit Advance Directive That Satisfies All of the Conditions Just Mentioned, Where Should the Project of Effecting His Death by Malnutrition and Dehydration Be Carried Out?

The further we proceed with this exercise, the more we are forced to strain credulity. At this point, we must imagine that there is no doubt concerning the diagnosis that has been made of Mr. Stevens's condition, that without question he instructed his family to kill him by starvation and dehydration if he should ever become permanently unconscious, that this advance request for Phoenician crucifixion was entirely rational, and that this advance directive is entirely consistent with all of the requirements of the law and justice. One is tempted to say that, if all of these (increasingly wilder) assumptions are correct, then anything goes, and there is nothing further to discuss. But there does remain a further point of substance. Grant, for the sake of argument, all of the improbable assumptions just enumerated. Now ask: "*Where* should the project of bringing about Mr. Stevens's death by dehydration and starvation be carried out?"

Since we are imagining that it is within the constraints of justice and the law for some persons under some circumstances to bring about deliberately the death of a disabled person by thirst and starvation, the question we must now consider is this: are the officers of a nursing home persons who can qualify for the lethal role under discussion? . . .

The courts so far have an uneven record with respect to their treatment of the claim by administrators that Phoenician crucifixion is incompatible with their professional obligations; in some cases, e.g., *Bouvia*[26] and *Gray,*[27] they have actually ordered facilities to carry out the dehydration and starvation of patients; in others, e.g., *Brophy*[28] and *Jobes,*[29] they have respected the administrators' claims to the extent of ruling that the patients be transferred to facilities whose administrators were willing to carry out the lethal project; in still other cases, e.g., *O'Connor*[30] and *Cruzan,*[31] they have struck down requests for deliberate dehydration and starvation without explicitly ruling on this claim by administrators. Nonetheless, the *moral* correctness of the judgment that the officers of a nursing home or hospital have an obligation to feed the people whose care they have undertaken is unassailable and cannot be touched by the rulings of any court.

If the officers of a nursing home were to undertake the lethal project of bringing about death by deliberate starvation and dehydration, they would be acting in violation of their professional obligations. Therefore, they cannot venture on the undertaking. And it follows that a nursing home is certainly not the place at which the project of Phoenician crucifixion can be undertaken. But there is an important further point that deserves to be mentioned.

Even if the lethal project the family of Mr. Stevens has in mind were not in conflict with the traditional responsibilities and goals of the nursing home administrators, there would be still further reasons for their refusing to undertake it. For, even if it were not in conflict with those goals and responsibilities, it would still, at the very least, constitute the carrying out of a task that is distinct from those nursing home administrators are professionally required to perform. And there would be two very good further reasons why such officers should not carry out death by thirst and starvation. First, it is essential for every profession to have a clearly defined goal and to direct all its efforts toward that goal, for, even when a goal is sharply and clearly stated, there will be many obstacles to achieving it. But if professionals are asked to aim at several (possibly competing) marks, they are likely to end up hitting none of them. The second reason why nursing home officers should not undertake bringing about death by starvation and dehydration is simply this. They cannot assume that it would be possible to carry out the lethal project in utter secrecy. Nor can they assume that everyone who learns of what they did will conclude that the person killed by thirst and starvation actually wanted to die such a death. Thus, if a given nursing home were the first in its community to take on the new sort of lethal project, its officers would have to anticipate that some hidebound traditionalists in the community and even some trendy modernists would be unwilling to entrust frail relatives to the home's care. If all nursing homes made it a routine practice to carry out such killings, more than a few people would be wholly unwilling to place relatives in them.

In sum, the two additional reasons are these: revising our practices so that nursing homes could assume the project of killing by thirst and starvation would create confusion by multiplying the goals of the homes, and it would undermine trust in them, thus interfering with their ability to carry out their traditional mission of care. Recall the widespread distress over the campaign by certain drug companies to encourage physicians to add the role of drug vendor to their traditional undertakings. One article devoted to the controversy describes the incentive held out to physicians:

> Physicians have always had the right to sell or give away medicine . . . at present, only about 5 per cent of the nation's doctors are selling drugs. But the repackagers . . . have a very inviting message: doctors can earn as much as $40,000 a year in extra income.[32]

But critics charge that, at the very least, the practice of having doctors engage in the sale of drugs may create the appearance of a conflict of interest. Thus,

Arnold Relman, editor of the *New England Journal of Medicine,* writes: "Trust in one's physician is an essential but fragile ingredient of medical care. It may not withstand the conversion of physicians into vendors of drugs for profit."[33]

If there is good reason to believe that assuming the role of drug vendor can result in a substantial conflict with the traditional commitments of the physician, there is clearly much more reason to believe that neither the physician nor the nursing home administrator can assume the role of killer without *violent* conflict with the traditional commitments of his or her office. And there is equally good reason to believe that *neither profession* can assume the lethal project of Phoenician crucifixion *without undermining* the trust essential to its own form of care.

It does not require profound insight to recognize that the lethal project of causing death by deliberate dehydration and starvation stands in violent contrast with the traditional goals and standards of nursing homes or hospitals. Whatever one may think of causing a vulnerable person's death through deliberate dehydration and starvation, one must acknowledge that such undertakings are not what nursing homes and hospitals were set up to accomplish and that nursing homes and hospitals could not incorporate such undertakings into their practice without defeating their primary purposes.

CONCLUSION

The questions we have considered are inextricably linked to other important ones. There is, for example, the question as to who has full moral standing. Who counts as a full-fledged member of our moral community? Who is entitled to the full range of protections each of us routinely expects in his or her own case? To whom do we owe our devotion and respect and care?[34]

The tendency to think that an unconscious patient like Mr. Stevens has somehow, in virtue of his disability, lost his full moral claim on us seems to be rather widespread. Even some people who recognize the central importance of our treatment of the defenseless and the vulnerable nonetheless feel a certain uneasiness about defending an unconscious patient's right to nourishment. They join the defense of that right somewhat reluctantly and only because they fear that allowing the deliberate starvation of an unconscious person like Mr. Stevens might one day lead to the deliberate starvation of real persons, persons like you and me, persons with an authentic, unproblematic right to protection and care. Viewed from this perspective, the sort of argument I've been elaborating here is deliberately over-stringent. A remark by Kierkegaard is pertinent:

> Most people really believe that the Christian commandments, for example, to love one's neighbors as oneself, are intentionally a little too severe, like putting the clock a half hour ahead to make sure that one will not be late in the morning.[35]

But the present defense of Mr. Stevens is no more deliberately overstated than are the commandments to which Kierkegaard refers. To care for Mr. Stevens, to provide him with cleanliness and warmth and nourishment, is not to engage in extraordinary or heroic activity. Mother Teresa once remarked: "We do no great things—only small things with great love."[36] If the meaning of each individual life is fathomless and inexhaustible, and there is in every individual human existence something unique and inexpressible, something that inevitably transcends our powers of analysis, something that mocks "quality of life" criteria, then we must acknowledge that a comatose person like Mr. Stevens is a real person, as much a person as you or I, as worthy of protection and respect, and as precious in the eyes of God. . . .

Concerning one of the German hospitals at which euthanasia was performed, U.S. Supreme Court Justice Robert H. Jackson, the man who served as the U.S. Chief Counsel for the Nuremberg Trials, wrote as follows:

> To begin with, the [euthanasia at Hadamar] involved only the incurably sick, insane, and mentally deficient patients of the Institution. It was easy to see that they were a substantial burden to society, and life was probably of little comfort to them. It is not difficult to see how, religious scruples apart, a policy of easing such persons out of the world by a completely painless method could appeal to a hard-pressed and unsentimental people. But 'euthanasia' taught the art of killing and accustomed those who directed and those who administered the death injections to the taking of human life. Once any scruples and inhibitions about killing were overcome and the custom was established, there followed naturally an indifference as to what lives were taken. Perhaps also those who become involved in any killings are not in a good position to decline any further requests. If one is convinced that a person should be put out of the way because, from no fault of his own, he has ceased to be a social asset, it is not hard to satisfy the conscience that those who are willful enemies of the prevailing social order have no better right to exist. And so Hadamar drifted from a hospital to a slaughterhouse.[37]

The silent echoes of the Hungerhäuser can now be heard here. There are a number of gravestones on which we can read the names of defenseless and incompetent persons who never refused food or water but who, nonetheless, died slow deaths of thirst and starvation; these gravestones stand in states from Massachusetts to California; they contain such names as: Paul Brophy, Ella Bathurst, Nancy Ellen Jobes, Anna Hirth, Marcia Gray, Nancy Cruzan, and others. The ghastly scene encountered by Gerhard Schmidt when he assumed the directorship of Eglfing-Haar may be less distant than we would like to think. Schmidt found ninety-four survivors on the two starvation wards. In his words: "Huge, dark halls . . . silent. No noise. Nothing. . . . The people showed no sign of life. A few stood. They said nothing. Like half-corpses."[38]

We have already commented on the role of euphemism and other debased language in the debate over euthanasia. It is worth noticing a specific euphemism that performs a useful role for those who promote death by deliberate dehydration and starvation. Such individuals routinely discuss cases like the present one as though the question at issue were whether *"artificial feeding"* should be continued. It suits the advocates of euthanasia to describe a case like Mr. Stevens' in this way. To continue or discontinue *artificial* feeding—who could reasonably oppose cutting off *fake* feeding? But it is important to recognize that there is nothing artificial about the feeding in question. That the nourishment is said to be artificially administered does not in any way imply that it is artificial nourishment. It is *real feeding,* supplying *real nourishment,* accomplishing exactly what it is supposed to accomplish. And indeed that is precisely why advocates of euthanasia want to stop the feeding.

Mr. Stevens is a living human being. His severe disability prevents him from feeding himself, but not from digesting and metabolizing the nourishment he receives. Mr. Stevens is not terminally ill. He is not dying. The question whether we can withhold nourishment from such a person is not a test of our mercy; it is a test of our justice. It is, finally, a test of our moral intelligence. "Feed the man dying of hunger, because if you have not fed him, you have killed him."[39]

Notes

1. PANATI, *supra* note 1, at 139.
2. *Id.*
3. *Id.*
4. Compare this principle with one attributed to Aquinas by G.E.M. Anscombe: "The principle by which such harm [by omission] is voluntary was stated succinctly by St. Thomas Aquinas: It was both possible and necessary for the agent to act, and he did not." THE LINACRE CENTRE, EUTHANASIA AND CLINICAL PRACTICE: TRENDS, PRINCIPLES AND ALTERNATIVES 33 (1982) [hereinafter EUTHANASIA AND CLINICAL PRACTICE].
5. It is a commonplace of legal theory that, where there is a legal obligation to act, a deliberate omission is legally equivalent to a positive act that brings about the result achieved by the omission. For relevant discussion, see, for example, W. PROSSER & W. KEETON, PROSSER AND KEETON ON THE LAW OF TORTS sec. 56 (5th ed. 1984).
6. *See* AMERICAN MEDICAL ASSOCIATION, CURRENT OPINIONS OF THE COUNCIL ON ETHICAL AND JUDICIAL AFFAIRS OF THE AMERICAN MEDICAL ASSOCIATION 12–13 (1986) (2.18 - Withholding or Withdrawing Life-Prolonging Medical Treatment: "Even if death is not imminent but a patient's coma is beyond doubt irreversible . . . it is not unethical to discontinue all means of life-prolonging medical treatment. Life-prolonging medical treatment includes . . . artificially . . . supplied . . . nutrition or hydration." *Id.*)
7. 10 U.S. 113 (1973).
8. *See* K. BINDING & A. HOCHE, THE RELEASE OF THE DESTRUCTION OF LIFE DEVOID OF VALUE (1920) (English translation published privately by Robert L. Sassone, Library of Congress No. 75-7723 (1975)) [hereinafter K. BINDING & A. HOCHE (Sassone)]. Their frequently cited monograph is one of the seminal documents in the literature of Nazi ideology.
9. *See, e.g.,* Buchanan, *The Limits of Proxy Decision-Making,* in PATERNALISM 153 (R. Sartorius ed. 1983). Discussing such severely disabled persons as Karen Ann Quinlan, Allen E. Buchanan writes: "In sum, it appears that a coherent theory of decision-making for patients in an irreversible vegetative state requires a concept of the death of a person more refined than that of the Harvard Criteria (footnote omitted). . . . A cognitivist or higher-brain-function concept of death would allow us to replace the question 'How can this person's right of self-determination be exercised?' with the question 'What rights and interests do the family and the state have in determining what may be done with the mortal remains of what was formerly a person, and how are these rights and interests affected by the rights and interests of a living person in determining what is

to be done with his remains when he dies?'" *Id.* at 164. Binding and Hoche also introduce a notion of a "mentally dead" person that, like Buchanan's "higher-brain-function concept of death," classifies as dead a large number of persons with disabilities whom the rest of us recognize as living human beings. K. BINDING & A. HOCHE (Sassone), *supra* note 14, at 37.

10. Interestingly, even Binding and Hoche, ready as they are to declare various human beings as nonpersons and to authorize their destruction on that ground, subscribe to the widespread fallacy of supposing that a person can waive the right to be free of lethal assault. Thus, Binding writes in his section of their joint monograph: "The killing of a consenting person does not break down the will to life of the killed person. By contrast, the force exercised against the life of an unconsenting victim characterizes the seriousness of regular unconsented killing. This is why we have to consider the killing of a consenting person objectively to be less serious." K. BINDING & A. HOCHE (Sassone), *supra* note 14, at 15.

11. *See* Thomson, *A Defense of Abortion*, 1 PHIL. & PUB. AFF. 47 (1971).

12. "We cannot offer a sharp and simple definition of murder. But there is a central part of what the term covers which can be reasonably well-defined, namely *the intentional killing of the innocent.* Whenever this is done by rulers, soldiers, terrorists or other violent men, reference is made, in reporting it, to the murder of innocent victims. This gives us a stereotype of the murderer, and constitutes the hard core of the concept." EUTHANASIA AND CLINICAL PRACTICE, *supra* note 10, at 25.

13. *See* EUTHANASIA AND CLINICAL PRACTICE, *supra* note 10; P. DEVINE, THE ETHICS OF HOMICIDE (1978). In conversation, G.E.M. Anscombe has reported to me a beautiful counter-example devised by Dr. Mary Catherine Geach to refute the proposed definition. The example concerns a man employed as an executioner who carries out his lethal assignment in a case in which the condemned man is his own father and is known by him to be his own father at the time he executes him. Our clear moral intuition tells us that what the executioner is doing in this case is wrong. Our intuition speaks in this way even for those of us who may be of the opinion that capital punishment is morally admissible. Yet, our intuition tells us also that the executioner, in this case, is not a murderer (even if the practice of capital punishment is wrong). Thus, the counter-example presents a case of wrongful killing that is not a case of murder.

14. The experience of a neurologist at the Hennepin County Medical Center in Minneapolis dramatically illustrates the hazards of medical prognosis. A police officer, David Mack, who was injured in the line of duty and entrusted to the neurologist's care, was declared to be in a "persistent vegetative state" by the neurologist. More than a year later, an observant nurse at the long-term care facility to which David Mack had been sent, noticed that he was "there" (fully conscious), and after a period of rehabilitation, Mack was able to communicate by means of a letter board and to return to his family. *See In re* Torres, 357 N.W.2d 332, 335 n.1 (Minn. 1984); PRESIDENTS COMMISSION FOR THE STUDY OF ETHICAL PROBLEMS IN MEDICINE AND BIOMEDICAL AND BEHAVIORAL RESEARCH, DECIDING TO FOREGO LIFE-SUSTAINING TREATMENT 179 n.22 (1983).

15. For valuable instruction concerning the clinical crudity of the term ("persistent vegetative state"), I am indebted to Prof. James Moriarty, M.D., Department of Neurology, University of Minnesota.

16. The adjective *living* is crucial here, since, for all his notoriety, Dr. Admiraal, the leading exponent and practitioner of active euthanasia in the Netherlands, has nowhere near the name recognition of Dr. Karl Brandt or Dr. Josef Mengele. So far, his body count is puny when measured by the standards set by Brandt and Mengele, if one restricts one's count to those persons Dr. Admiraal freely acknowledges having killed with his own hands. If one attempted to take into account those persons who were killed as a result of Dr. Admiraal's having instructed various persons in methods of medical murder or killed as a result of the climate Dr. Admiraal has helped to create through his advocacy of euthanasia, then Dr. Admiraal's total body count would begin to be respectable by Nazi standards. In any case, one should bear in mind that this physician is alive and practicing medicine in accordance with his own deranged conceptions. Despite his heavy schedule of speaking engagements, it is unlikely that he has killed his last patient, and in any event, when he does give up the practice of medical murder, he can do so secure in the knowledge that a number of other physicians, inspired by his example, will continue to kill patients with the same unballasted conviction of righteousness that has marked his own work.

17. I am indebted to Mary Krumholz, R.N., who produced a careful thirteen-page handwritten transcription of the proceedings. I am also indebted to one of the physicians in attendance at the meeting who confirmed the accuracy of the transcription. Since there is more than

one reason that the physician in question might not welcome acknowledgment here, I extend my private thanks to him.

18. *Id.*

19. Observe that a certain amount of self-selection operated here. Physicians and nurses who practice recognizably Hippocratic medicine and would never dream of making a "quality of life" judgment concerning a patient entrusted to their care, much less of engaging in a lethal assault on a patient, are unlikely to attend a talk by a medical killer. In fact, organizers of such a talk are likely not even to extend invitations to physicians or nurses who are powerfully dedicated to the traditional goals of medicine—thus, Mary Krumholz, who is well-known in our community for her commitment to those goals, had not been invited to the meeting but attended in the spirit of a field anthropologist.

20. The *locus classicus* for the analysis of debased language in the service of unspeakable practices is George Orwell's *Politics and the English Language*, in 4 THE COLLECTED ESSAYS, JOURNALISM AND LETTERS OF GEORGE ORWELL 127 (S. Orwell & I. Angus eds. 1968). Orwell writes: "In our time, political speech and writing are largely the defence of the indefensible. Things like the continuance of British rule in India, the Russian purges and deportations, the dropping of the atom bombs on Japan, can indeed be defended, but only by arguments which are too brutal for most people to face, and which do not square with the professed aims of political parties. Thus political language has to consist largely of euphemism, question-begging and sheer cloudy vagueness." *Id.* at 136.

21. I am indebted to Charles Geach for calling to my attention the linguistic blunder involved in the phrase "imminently dying," which is commonly employed in such contexts as the present one.

22. *Final Report of the Netherlands Commission on Euthanasia: An English Summary*, 1 BIOETHICS 163, 174 (1987).

23. *Id.* at 163–174.

24. NAZI DOCTORS, *supra* note 25, at 445 (citing Hilberg, *Confronting the Moral Implications of the Holocaust*, 42 SOC. EDUC. 272, 275 (1978)).

25. G.E.M. Anscombe writes: "So far, most propaganda for euthanasia assumes it should be voluntary. Like the first justifications for induced abortion, this is only a way-station. But it impresses, because it strikes people as not wronging someone to kill him if he wills it. However, it needs pointing out that they would still think it was wronging him, but for the accompanying judgment that his condition is so irremediably wretched that it is fortunate for him 'to die.'" EUTHANASIA AND CLINICAL PRACTICE, *supra* note 10, at 28.

26. Bouvia v. Superior Court (Glenchur), 179 Cal. App. 3d 1127, 225 Cal. Rptr. 297 (Cal. Ct. App. 1986).

27. Gray v. Romeo, 697 F.Supp. 580 (D.R.I. 1988).

28. Brophy v. New England Sinai Hospital, Inc., 398 Mass. 417, 497 N.E.2d 626 (1986).

29. *In re* Jobes, 108 N.J. 394, 529 A.2d 434 (1987).

30. *In re* Westchester County Medical Center (O'Connor), 72 N.Y.2d 517, 531 N.E.2d 607, 534 N.Y.S.2d 886 (1988).

31. Cruzan v. Harmon, 760 S.W.2d 408 (Mo. banc 1988), *aff'd sub nom.* Cruzan v. Director, Missouri Dep't of Health, 110 S. Ct. 2841 (1990).

32. Holcomb, *The Druggist's Crucial New Role*, N.Y. Times, Apr. 17, 1988, sec. 6, Part II (Magazine), at 39, 61.

33. *Id.* at 61–62.

34. Richard J. Neuhaus ably addresses this line of inquiry. See R. Neuhaus, The Way They Were, The Way We Are (May 19, 1989) (a paper delivered at a conference entitled "The Meaning of the Holocaust for Bioethics," held at the University of Minnesota).

35. Exact source unknown.

36. D. Hunt, ed., LOVE: A FRUIT ALWAYS IN SEASON—MEDITATIONS BY MOTHER TERESA OF CALCUTTA, 121 (1987).

37. R. Jackson, THE HADAMAR TRIAL, FORWARD (1949), *cited in* K. BINDING & A. HOCHE (Sassone, *supra* note 14, at 2).

38. *Quoted in* NAZI DOCTORS, *supra* note 25, at 99.

39. SECOND VATICAN COUNCIL, THE SIXTEEN DOCUMENTS OF VATICAN II AND THE INSTRUCTION ON THE LITURGY 513, 587 n.69 (Pope Paul VI, *De Ecclesia in Mundo Huius Temporis*, promulgated Dec. 7, 1965) (St. Paul eds.).

Concerning the Case of "Mr. Stevens"

John Jefferson Davis

The case presented for consideration concerns a "Mr. Stevens," a forty-nine year old man who received a severe head wound in an automobile accident. Various medical tests have been performed in the two-year period since the accident, and recent results indicate that a portion of Mr. Stevens's cerebral cortex has atrophied and has been replaced by cerebrospinal fluid. The remainder of his brain and brainstem appear to be intact and capable of functioning normally.

Recent examinations by consulting neurologists have led these physicians to diagnose Mr. Stevens as being in a "persistent vegetative state" (PVS). He is being maintained in an intermediate care nursing facility, expenses being paid from damages awarded to him as a result of the accident. Three months after the accident a gastrostomy tube was inserted into his stomach to supply food and fluids. The physician described Mr. Stevens's ability to swallow at that time as "unsophisticated and reflexive," and there was concern that without the tube food or fluids could enter his lungs and cause further complications. The examining physicians agree that Mr. Stevens could live indefinitely in his present condition so long as artificial feeding and hydration are provided.

Mr. Stevens's wife has now petitioned a trial court to authorize the discontinuation of artificial feeding and hydration. She and three of the children agree that he "would not wish to live indefinitely in this way." They invoke in support of this request statements made in reference to his father-in-law, who died after a long illness, lingering for some time in a semi-comatose state somewhat similar to Mr. Stevens's present condition. Stevens had made the comment, heard by the entire immediate family, that it would be better for his father-in-law to "die now rather than linger endlessly in some mindless state." Afterward Mr. Stevens further commented that death had released his father-in-law "from the prison of his own useless body."

One year prior to his own accident Mr. Stevens had orally consented to the withholding of "heroic" treatment from his own father, who was almost totally incapacitated by Alzheimer's disease. Mr. Stevens's father continues to live and is able to receive food and fluids by mouth.

At the time of his accident Mr. Stevens was teaching high school English and history. His accident occurred as he was driving to a local university, where he was taking graduate courses in pursuit of a Ph.D. in English, with a view toward teaching English at the college level. His own immediate family and his present and former students all agree that he considered the "life of the mind" as requisite to the "fullest human existence."

The resolution of the case is complicated by the fact that Mr. Stevens's eldest daughter, who visits him as often as three times a week, is opposed to the removal of the feeding tube. She believes that it would be "wrong to starve her father to death" and that her father would "never want them to do something that was wrong." The nursing staff also objects to the discontinuation of artificial feeding, believing that Mr. Stevens is "higher functioning" than many of the other residents of the facility. In spite of the neurologists' diagnosis of a persistent vegetative state, both the eldest daughter and members of the nursing staff testify that Mr. Stevens appears to interact with them to some degree.

Given the incompetency of Mr. Stevens to make decisions concerning his own medical treatment, the trial court must resolve the dispute between Mrs. Stevens and the three children on the one hand, and the eldest daughter and the nursing staff on the other, both as to a matter of *fact*—the state of Mr. Stevens's consciousness—and a matter of *interpretation*—that is, the proper interpretation of what Mr. Stevens's wishes might be relative to his medical treatment, were he competent to make such a decision.

Several questions of clarification arise naturally in this case. Just how extensive is the damage to his cerebral cortex? Can the extent of the damage be quantified? Does Mr. Stevens show signs of *any* consciousness, however minimal, or does the diagnosis of PVS accurately reflect *total* absence of any self-awareness? It will become apparent during the course of the analysis that the distinction between even *minimal* sapience and total lack of any potential for present or future sapience can in fact make a significant moral difference in the decisions reached in Mr. Stevens's case.

It is the limited purpose of this article to clarify some of the ethical and theological issues that are involved, not to address the related legal issues of "substituted judgment" or the medical issues related to the reliability of the diagnostic criteria for PVS. Certain assumptions and conclusions from these fields will be utilized during the course of the study but, due to limitations of space and the author's competence, will not be extensively discussed.

HISTORY OF THE DISCUSSION

The case of Nancy Beth Cruzan[1] has given much visibility to the matter of maintaining patients by artificial food and hydration, but discussions of such matters by ethicists and moral theologians long antedates the *Cruzan* case. As early as 1950, in an important article titled *The Duty of Using Artificial Means of Preserving Life,*[2] Fr. Gerald Kelly, S.J., specifically addressed the question of patients in a state of coma:

I am often asked whether such things as oxygen and intravenous feeding must be used to prolong the life of a patient, already well prepared for death, and now in a terminal coma. In my opinion, the circumstances of this case make it obvious that the non-use of artificial life sustainers is not the same as mercy killing; and I see no reason why even the most delicate professional standard should call for their use. In fact, it seems to me that, apart from very special circumstances, the artificial means not only need not but should not be used, once the coma is reasonably diagnosed as terminal. Their use creates expense and nervous strain without conferring any real benefit. It must be kept in mind, however, that it is for the physician to decide when the coma is terminal.[3]

Kelly is aware that in these circumstances a decision to discontinue artificial feeding might be construed as mercy killing but clearly believes that this is not actually the case. In the case he discusses, artificial feeding of the dying, comatose patient is seen as a useless treatment that confers no real benefit and hence is not morally obligatory. It should be noted, however, that Kelly addresses the case of the imminently *dying*, comatose patient; Mr. Stevens, on the other hand, may be irreversibly comatose but is not imminently dying.

In a 1958 doctoral dissertation at the Gregorian University in Rome, Daniel A. Cronin, the present Roman Catholic bishop of Fall River, Massachusetts, reviewed some fifty moral theologians from Aquinas to those writing in the early 1950s in his study titled "The Moral Law in Regard to the Ordinary and Extraordinary Means of Preserving Life."[4] Cronin concluded that Catholic teaching in such matters exhibited a consistent pattern: "Even natural means, such as taking of food and drink, can become optional if taking them requires great effort or if the hope of beneficial results (*spes salutis*) is not present."[5] In Cronin's conclusion the concept of "benefit to the patient" comes to the fore.

In 1962 John P. Kenny, O.P., professor of philosophy at Providence College in Providence, Rhode Island, addressed the issue of discontinuation of medical treatment for unconscious patients.[6] Would it be ethically permissible to remove a respirator from an unconscious patient who has shown no improvement after prolonged treatment? Kenny states his conclusion in the following way:

In a case of deep unconsciousness when the patient has received extreme unction, the physician may remove the artificial respiration apparatus before the blood circulation has come to a complete stop. . . . The continued attempt at resuscitation is an extraordinary means to which the patient, and the doctor is not obliged. Moreover, the rights and duties of the family depend, in general, upon the presumed will of the unconscious patient. The proper duty of the family usually obliges only to the use of ordinary means . . . when the continuance of resuscitation constitutes a definite burden for the family they can lawfully insist that the doctor should discontinue these attempts. . . .[7]

Kenny concludes that in such cases the use of a respirator for an (irreversibly) comatose patient is an extraordinary and nonobligatory treatment, presumably because it confers no real benefit to the patient and may impose financial or emotional burdens on the family. In the context of a Roman Catholic hospital, discontinuation of such treatment would presuppose the patient's spiritual preparation for death through the administration of the sacraments.

In the sixth edition (1967) of his widely used text on medical ethics[8] Charles McFadden, O.S.A., addresses the specific case of a patient who has lapsed into what the physicians are convinced is a "terminal coma":

> If the patient, while conscious, was not spiritually prepared for death, there would, of course, be the strict obligation to continue intravenous nourishment—hoping and praying that the person may come out of the coma at least long enough to make his final peace with God. If, however, the person has been spiritually prepared for death, and there is no reasonable expectation that consciousness will ever be regained, it would appear morally permissible to cease intravenous nourishment.[9]

It should be noted that the case McFadden has in mind is that of a patient in a "terminal coma," by which he evidently means an imminently dying patient who is irreversibly comatose. In a related but distinct issue, that of an imminently dying but not comatose cancer patient suffering from a great deal of pain and being fed intravenously, McFadden held that while it might be theoretically justifiable to remove artificial feeding as an "extraordinary" and disproportionate means, in actual medical practice he would be opposed to the withdrawal of such means for fear of scandalizing the family and possibly setting a precedent that could be misconstrued as condoning euthanasia.[10] As will later become apparent, this analytical tension between a course of action that has theoretical justification with respect to the patient per se and a course of action considered with respect to its possible social consequences has considerable relevance in the case of Mr. Stevens.

In 1970 the Protestant moralist Paul Ramsey, professor of religion at Princeton University, addressed the issue of patients in deep and irreversible comas in the Beecher Lectures at Yale. In a finely nuanced essay, "On (Only) Caring for the Dying,"[11] Ramsey articulated the principle that caring for the patient was always in order and that the patient should never be abandoned. And yet in some exceptional circumstances, the patient may be beyond the ability to receive human care:

> If there are cases of neglect and defect of care for the dying, there may also be . . . a now useless extension of care. Acts of charity or moving with grace among the dying that now communicate no presence or comfort to them are now no longer required. If it is the case that a wife is tragically mistaken when she takes twitches of the eyes to be a sort of language from her husband irreversibly comatose for seven years . . . then . . . it is no longer care for him. It is no contradiction to withhold what is not capable of being given and received.[12]

Ramsey's premise in such a case appears to be that continuation of artificial feeding would represent useless and futile treatment. There is, in effect, no sapient "patient" who can experience benefit from the proffered care.

Thomas J. O'Donnell, S.J., in a 1980 review of Catholic perspectives on prolonging life decisions,[13] speaks of "minimal means" that he believes are appropriate in all treatment situations:

> Because this concept of relatively ordinary or relatively extraordinary means of prolonging life ranges across a wide spectrum of personal assessment and decision, sometimes on behalf of others, subsequent reflection has suggested to me the necessity of identifying a category of care for the totally helpless terminal patient which might be called "minimal means" (such as customary hygienic and nutritional support) and which must always be used because, given the nature of the human composite, the neglect of such minimal care would be tantamount to an act of positive destruction.[14]

O'Donnell does not specifically address the issue of nondying patients in a persistent vegetative state supported by artificial feeding and hydration, but his remarks appear to indicate that he would consider such to be "minimal means" in this context and that termination of artificial feeding would be tantamount to "positive destruction" or euthanasia.

Benedict Ashley, O.P., and Kevin O'Rourke, O.P., writing in a 1982 medical ethics text[15] published by the Catholic Health Association of the United States, do not directly address the problem of patients in persistent vegetative states but do raise a critical issue in the debate, namely the fundamental spiritual purpose of human life itself:

> In maintaining that one is free to make a judgment not to prolong life because a grave burden would result, even though prolonging life is possible, we are affirming that, while human life is a great good, it is not the greatest good. The greatest good is friendship with God, charity. Thus, if prolonging life would seem to interfere with friendship with God, directly or indirectly, life need not be prolonged. This is the practical meaning of the word burden: making it difficult for one to attain the purpose of life.[16]

The authors cite the 1957 statement of Pius XII that "[l]ife, health, all temporary activities are in fact subordinated to spiritual ends."[17] As subsequent discussion will show, the current debate reflects, among many other considerations, lack of agreement as to whether a patient in an irreversible persistent vegetative state and being artificially maintained can be understood to be fulfilling the spiritual purposes of human life.

In a 1983 article Joanne Lynn and James F. Childress addressed the question "Must Patients Always Be Given Food and Water?"[18] They wrote in the wake of vigorous public discussions generated by the May 1981 case in Danville, Illinois,[19] and the April 1982 case in Bloomington, Indiana,[20] concerning nontreatment decisions for disabled newborn children. Lynn and Childress took the position that there should be a presumption in favor of providing nutrition and fluids but that this presumption could be rebutted in particular cases. In the case of patients in a persistent vegetative state, such artificial feeding produces no real benefit to the patient:

> Some patients can be reliably diagnosed to have permanently lost consciousness. This unusual group of patients includes those with anencephaly, persistent vegetative state, and some preterminal comas. In these cases, it is very difficult to discern how any medical intervention can benefit or harm the patient. These patients cannot and never will be able to experience any of the events occurring in the world or in their bodies. When the diagnosis is exceedingly clear, we sustain their lives vigorously mainly for their loved ones and the community at large . . . if the parents of an anencephalic infant or of a patient like Karen Quinlan in a persistent vegetative state feel strongly that no medical procedures should be applied to provide nutrition and hydration, and the caregivers are willing to comply, there should be no barrier in law or public policy to thwart the plan.[21]

The authors also discuss related cases where artificial feeding and hydration could represent "futile treatment" in the case of the imminently dying or a "disproportionate burden" when such means could cause nausea, mental confusion, or other negative side effects.[22]

In a 1987 article published in *America*,[23] John J. Paris, S.J., and Richard A. McCormick, S.J., review the Catholic tradition on the use of nutrition and fluids and comment in particular on a 1986 amicus curiae brief submitted by the bishops of the New Jersey Catholic Conference in the case of Nancy Jobes.[24] This case involved a request by the family to have a feeding tube removed from their thirty-one year old daughter who had been in a persistent vegetative state for five years. The bishop's brief had taken the position that "nutrition and hydration, which are basic to human life, and as such distinguished from medical treatment, should always be provided to the patient."[25] Paris and McCormick, however, argued against this view, noting that until "such highly charged cases as Quinlan's there was little ambiguity or hesitancy about ending artificial feeding for dying patients."[26] According to these authors, "to count mere vegetative existence as a patient benefit—is to let slip one's grasp on the heart of the Catholic tradition in this matter."[27] In such cases, the authors reasoned, these treatments are futile and confer no real benefit to the patient.

In their 1987 article, "Feeding and Hydrating the Permanently Unconscious and Other Vulnerable Persons,"[28] William E. May and nine co-authors argued that both morality and the law should recognize a strong presumption in favor of artificial feeding and hydration in the case of such seriously debilitated but nondying patients, where such means are not excessively burdensome or expensive.[29] Human bodily life, they argued, is inherently good, not merely instrumental to other (spiritual) goods; the omission of nutrition and hydration could be an act of euthanasia by omission; such treatments are not in most cases excessively burdensome to the patient, and "remaining alive is never rightly regarded as a burden"; dying of thirst and starvation can be painful and disfiguring; maintaining artificial feeding and hydration can nurture in the caregivers such qualities as mercy and compassion.[30]

In a September 21, 1989, letter to the Diocese of Camden, New Jersey, Bishop James T. McHugh gave pastoral guidance to priests and parishioners in the wake of the Nancy Jobes case.[31] According to Bishop McHugh, even in the case of the irreversibly unconscious patient, feeding is not useless because it sustains a human life. Furthermore:

> If the withholding or withdrawing of nutrition is *intended* to cause or hasten death, the intention then is euthanasia and the withholding or withdrawing is morally impermissible . . . in such cases discontinuing nutrition and hydration does not simply allow the patient to die from some existing pathology, but introduces a new cause of death, that is, starvation and dehydration.[32]

According to McHugh, removal of artificial food and hydration in such circumstances is an act of euthanasia by omission.

In their 1989 amicus curiae brief on behalf of the Value of Life Committee, Inc.,[33] attorneys Walter Weber and Thomas Cornell argued, in the case of Nancy Beth Cruzan, then pending before the U.S. Supreme Court, that Nancy Beth Cruzan, despite her disability and lack of consciousness, was a person with rights to life, liberty, and equal protection of the law under the Fourteenth Amendment. The framers, they argued, made no distinction between "human beings" and "persons," and the inseparable union of humanity and personhood is fundamental to the unique value of human life.[34]

In a 1989 article[35] Germain Grisez, professor of Christian ethics at Mt. Saint Mary's College in Emmitsburg, Maryland, reversed an earlier position[36] and argued that artificial feeding should ordinarily be provided even for irreversibly comatose patients. A number of considerations led the author to change his mind, among them being the serious difficulty in making diagnoses in cases of coma and persistent vegetative states; the fact that artificial feeding in most instances is neither burdensome nor expensive; and the fact that artificial feeding confers the important benefits of keeping the patient alive and maintaining the bonds of human solidarity between the patient and the caregiver.[37] At the core of Grisez's argument is the conviction that a dualism of "biological" human life and "personal" human life is indefensible. Bodily life is an intrinsic good, not a merely instrumental good, and this bodily life, even apart from consciousness, does not, according to Grisez," cease to be good when one no longer can enjoy a degree of cognitive-affective function or attain other values."[38]

In a 1989 companion article to the one by Grisez immediately above, Kevin O'Rourke, O.P., argues for the contrary view.[39] When no potential for attaining the spiritual ends of life is present, it would seem that artificial means are ineffective and futile. O'Rourke poses the question: "There is no attempt to prolong the life of anencephalic infants; why then prolong the life of people whose cerebral cortex will never again function?"[40] To view the indefinite prolongation of life in a persistent vegetative state as a great "benefit" is to make (biological) human life an "absolute" good, something clearly contrary to the mainstream of Catholic teaching.[41]

In a brief commentary made January 1990[42] on the Nancy Beth Cruzan case, Ed Payne, M.D., refers to the question of euthanasia in relation to the discontinuation of artificial feeding:

> Suppose that the feeding tube is removed and she is able to swallow. What then? Her parents' intent will become clear. If they do not make the attempt to feed her orally (by mouth), then they intend euthanasia. If, however, they are making the choice simply to stop a medical treatment, then they will have her fed orally. . . . In this case, they would not intend euthanasia. *The provision of food and water by mouth should not be denied anyone, since it is not medical care.*[43]

Payne's "thought experiment" is a way of answering the question: "Is cessation of artificial feeding an act of euthanasia by omission?" The willingness to feed by mouth subsequent to withdrawal of artificial means is evidence of nonintent to commit euthanasia by omission. In Payne's view feeding by mouth is obligatory ordinary care, while artificial feeding is a form of medical treatment.

By way of summary at this point, this review of the history of the discussion has shown the existence of a substantial body of opinion in both Catholic and Protestant traditions that artificial feeding of irreversibly comatose patients may, in many instances, confer no real benefit on the patient. The discussion of the nondying comatose patient, however, a matter made more prominent since the 1976 case of Karen Quinlan, has produced less substantial agreement. In a post-*Roe v. Wade* (1973)[44] political environment, and in the wake of the "Baby Doe" cases of the 1980s,[45] discussions have also been impacted by concerns that decisions to discontinue artificial feeding even in "hopeless" cases could open the door to euthanasia as a broader social policy. Such social and political considerations make the ethical analysis of cases such as that of Mr. Stevens more problematic than they might otherwise be in a society with a broader consensus on basic moral values relating to the value of human life.

ANALYSIS OF KEY TERMS AND CONCEPTS

In reviewing the literature in this area, it becomes apparent that the resolution of the issue brings a number of terms and concepts to the fore, of which the following seem to be crucial: With respect to the matter of feeding, is a gastrostomy tube more analogous to *medical treatment* or to the *ordinary care* of feeding by mouth? Is the human person best understood in a *holistic* or *dualistic* fashion—that is to say, is there a legitimate distinction between human *biological* life and human *personal* life? And, perhaps most fundamentally, is human life, considered especially with regard to its bodily, physiological dimensions, an *intrinsic good* in itself, or rather an *instrumental* good in relation to a higher spiritual purpose?

With respect to the first question, it is apparent that a gastrostomy tube is more analogous to medical treatment than to the ordinary care of feeding by mouth. While it is true that the effect of both means of feeding may be the same—the delivery of food and fluids to the patient—it is also the case that the two means differ in several important respects. In the first place, they differ as to their *preconditions of use.* The insertion of a gastrostomy tube is a surgical procedure requiring professional medical skills; ordinary feeding by mouth requires no such specialized medical skills and is an ordinary human action. In the second place, the two means differ as to the *conditions of reception.* Ordinary feeding by mouth presupposes a conscious patient who can interact socially with the caregiver, experience personally the reception of food, and actively cooperate in the process of receiving the nourishment offered. In this case the experience of human solidarity associated with the physical and symbolic aspects of sharing food is a bilateral and mutually participatory process. In the case, however, of a tube-fed patient in a persistent vegetative state, the reception of food is a passive process and not a bilateral, mutually interactive process. The patient has no conscious experience of social interaction. As in the case of surgery, the medical personnel may deliver some "benefit" to the patient, but the patient is not aware of it at the time. The point of these observations, then, is that feeding a patient by gastrostomy tube or other artificial means is a form of medical treatment, and like other forms of medical treatment its initiation, continuation, or withdrawal should be considered in relation to the burdens and benefits of use in any particular case. This perception is in keeping with recent trends in the law, which have tended to see artificial feeding as more analogous than not to artificially maintaining a patient with a respirator.

With respect to the second set of issues, it would seem that there is a legitimate distinction between human life in its biological and personal dimensions. While there has been a noticeable tendency in theological scholarship in this century to claim a "holistic" view of man as the "biblical" view, and to deny any "dualism" in this area, more recent scholarship has shown this tendency to be misplaced. In his definitive monograph in this area,[46] Robert H. Gundry has carefully analyzed the relevant biblical and theological literature and summarizes his conclusions as follows: "We conclude that Paul, along with most Jews and other early Christians, habitually thought of man as a duality of two parts, corporeal and incorporeal, meant to function in unity but distinguishable and capable of separation."[47]

This conclusion is in keeping with the teachings of traditional Christian theology—Roman Catholic, Orthodox, and Protestant—which has held from the earliest centuries that while it is true in a sense that man is a "psychosomatic unity" of body and soul, it is nevertheless also the case that body and soul are distinguishable and capable of separation. The most obvious case in point is the "intermediate state" between the individual's death and the final resurrection, where, in the Christian scheme of things, the soul is in the presence of God (or purgatory), while the body awaits the final resurrection and its reuniting with the soul.

The point of these observations is that from the perspective of traditional Christian theology, it is quite legitimate to recognize a distinction between body and soul, between human life in its physiological and personal dimensions. From this perspective it is quite possible to envision a situation in which a human body and its organ systems exhibit signs of physiological life and yet from which the soul has departed. The observations of the Old Testament scholar Hans Walter Wolff are germane at this point:

> In order to define the borderline between life and death in any given case, we need to be able to define death and life. The Old Testament answer was that for the whole of life man passes into death at the precise moment when the praise of God falls silent. . . . It is therefore possible for a dead man to be survived by all the organs of his body . . . when man is beyond the possibility of praising God, he is truly 'in death,' 'in real objective fact.'[48]

From the biblical perspective man is created for the purpose of praising the Creator and experiencing a conscious personal relationship with God. When this possibility no longer exists, then man has passed—at the personal level—from life into death, even though bodily organs may still function.

Bodily life is an *expression* of the person, but it does not *exhaust* the personal dimension, nor is it identical with the person in his or her totality. A patient in an irreversible persistent vegetative state, who has no present or future potential (in this life) for experiencing conscious relationships with other persons is, from the perspective of the biblical data as understood by Wolff, already in the realm of death, personally considered, even though the bodily organs continue to function. It seems pointless to construe continued organ function as a "benefit" to the patient, when there is no conscious subject who has any reasonable possibility now or in the (temporal) future of actually *experiencing* these benefits.

These considerations are not unrelated to the third set of issues, namely, whether bodily life is to be understood as an intrinsic or an instrumental good. It is apparent that in the present case such a distinction can make a significant moral difference. The position taken here is that human bodily life is an instrumental good in relation to the personal and spiritual purposes for which man was created (in the Christian scheme of things). It might be noted that this view is implicit, in the Christian tradition, in the recognition that in certain circumstances martyrdom is morally praiseworthy and even morally obligatory. Human bodily life is a relative and not an absolute good, and one may sacrifice one's bodily life in obedience to God or for the greater good of the community. It is obvious, of course, that the case of Mr. Stevens does not involve martyrdom, but nevertheless the point remains that in certain instances human bodily life is not to be preserved at all costs.

The basis for construing bodily life as a good instrumental to higher spiritual or personal purposes reflects the view that human life is fundamentally life-in-relationship: life in community, life in relationship to God and other persons. When, as in the case of a patient in an irreversible persistent vegetative state, there is no reasonable present or future potential for conscious relationships with other living persons, then the patient's organs may be functioning, but the "person" is no longer present; he or she is beyond the reach of human interaction, and maintaining such a state of affairs indefinitely would seem to be a futile enterprise.

If it were to be argued, on the contrary, that bodily life is an (almost absolute) intrinsic good, in and of itself, irrespective of any potential for relationship, then consider the following question and thought experiment. If it were possible, hypothetically, to maintain with cryogenic technology a PVS patient indefinitely—since bodily life per se is an inherent good—how long should such a state of affairs be continued? Ten years? Twenty-five? Seventy-five? Two hundred? A thousand years? Should the body be maintained for a hundred years in hopes that a cure will be found? Would the patient find awakening to a changed world from which his family and friends had long since passed away an unmixed blessing? These questions are only hypothetical, of course, but they nevertheless suggest that a "bodily life at any cost" perspective can lead to a reductio ad absurdum.

There is understandable concern that the position here argued could easily slide over into a "quality of life" ethic that would open the door to euthanasia as a social policy. I would suggest, however, that there is an important moral distinction between a so-called quality of life ethic and one which recognizes that there are minimal physiological preconditions for personal life as it is usually understood. The diagnosis of irreversible brain damage and/or persistent vegetative state is a *medical* judgment that has moral implications for *personal* decisions—but the judgment is, in the first instance, based on medical and physiological criteria, not social ones. The line may be a fine one, but nevertheless a distinguishable line can be drawn between the anencephalic newborn and the irreversibly PVS patient on the one hand and the Alzheimer's patient and the profoundly mentally retarded person on the other. In the former cases, there is no reasonable present or future potential (in this life) for even minimal cognitive awareness; in the latter cases this potential, however minimal or impaired, still exists.

CONCLUSION

In conclusion, I believe the trial court may ethically grant the petition of Mrs. Stevens to have artificial feeding and hydration withdrawn from her husband. This conclusion reflects a judgment that artificial feeding and hydration is a form of medical treatment more analogous to the use of a respirator than to ordinary feeding by mouth. It further judges that Mrs. Stevens and the other children have more accurately understood the values and wishes of Mr. Stevens than has the eldest daughter. Continuation of artificial feeding and hydration confers no real benefit on the patient, since there is no reasonable present or future prospect (in this life) that Mr. Stevens will regain consciousness and so be able to pursue and experience the interpersonal and spiritual purposes of human life. Both law and morality should carefully distinguish between cases of *minimal* and *severely impaired* consciousness (e.g., advanced Alzheimer's disease, profound retardation) and cases of *nonexistent potential* for present or future consciousness (e.g., anencephaly, irreversible PVS), in order to guard against the encroachment of euthanasia as a social policy.

Notes

1. Cruzan v. Director, Mo. Dep't of Health, 110 S.Ct. 2841 (1990).
2. Kelly, *The Duty of Using Artificial Means of Preserving Life,* II THEOLOGICAL STUDIES 203 (1950).
3. *Id.* at 219–220.
4. *Quoted in* Paris & McCormick, *The Catholic Tradition on the Use of Nutrition and Fluids,* AMERICA, May 2, 1987, at 356, 360.
5. *Id.* at 360.
6. J. KENNY, PRINCIPLES OF MEDICAL ETHICS (1962).
7. *Id.* at 126.
8. C. MCFADDEN, MEDICAL ETHICS (1967).
9. *Id.* at 246.
10. *Id.* at 244–46.
11. P. RAMSEY, THE PATIENT AS PERSON (1970).
12. *Id.* at 162.
13. O'DONNELL, *A Catholic Historical Perspective on Prolonging Life Decisions, in* THE NEW TECHNOLOGIES OF BIRTH AND DEATH: MEDICAL, LEGAL AND MORAL DIMENSIONS 162 (1980).
14. *Id.* at 168.
15. M. ASHLEY & D. O'ROURKE, HEALTH CARE ETHICS: A THEOLOGICAL ANALYSIS (2d ed. 1982).
16. *Id.* at 383.
17. *Id.* at 384.
18. Lynn & Childress, *Must Patients Always Be Given Food and Water?* HASTINGS CENTER REP., Oct. 1983, at 17.
19. *In re* Mueller (Vermilion County Ill. Cir. Ct., Juv. Div., July 19, 1981).
20. *In re* Treatment and Care of Infant Doe, No. GU 8204-004A (Monroe County Cir. Ct. Apr. 12, 1982).
21. Lynn & Childress, *supra* note 18, at 18.
22. *Id.* at 18–19.
23. Paris & McCormick, *supra* note 4, at 356.
24. *In re* Jobes, 510 A.2d 133 (N.J. Super. Ch. 1986).
25. Paris & McCormick, *supra* note 4, at 357.
26. *Id.* at 360.

27. *Id.* at 361.

28. May, Barry, Griese, Grisez, Johnstone, Marzen, McHugh, Meilaender, Siegler & Smith, *Feeding and Hydrating the Permanently Unconscious and Other Vulnerable Persons,* 3 ISSUES IN LAW & MED. 203 (1987).

29. *Id.* at 209.

30. *Id.* at 204–206.

31. *In re* Jobes, 529 A.2d 434 (N.J. Super. Ch. 1986).

32. McHugh, *Principles in Regard to Withholding or Withdrawing Artificially Assisted Nutrition/Hydration,* Letter from the Office of the Bishop, Diocese of Camden, N.J., at 3, 4 (1989).

33. Brief of the Value of Life Committee As Amicus Curiae In Support of Respondents, *In re* Cruzan, (U.S. S. Ct. Oct. 1989) (No. 88-1503).

34. *Id.* at 7–8.

35. Grisez, *Should Nutrition and Hydration Be Provided to Permanently Unconscious and Other Mentally Disabled Persons?* 5 ISSUES IN LAW & MED. 165 (1989).

36. Grisez, *A Christian Ethics of Limiting Medical Treatment: Guidance For Patients, Proxy Decision Makers, and Counselors,* 2 POPE JOHN PAUL II LECTURE SERIES IN BIOETHICS 35, 49–50 (1986).

37. Grisez, *supra* note 35, at 168, 172.

38. *Id.* at 173.

39. O'Rourke, *Should Nutrition and Hydration Be Provided to Permanently Unconscious and Other Mentally Disabled Persons?* 5 ISSUES IN LAW & MED. 181 (1989).

40. *Id.* at 189.

41. *Id.* at 192.

42. Payne, *The Nancy Beth Cruzan Case,* 1 BIBLICAL REFLECTIONS ON MODERN MED. 1 (1990).

43. *Id.* at 2.

44. Roe v. Wade, 410 U.S. 113 (1973).

45. *In re* Treatment and Care of Infant Doe, No. GU 8204-004A (Monroe County Cir. Ct. Apr. 12, 1982), Weber v. Stony Brook Hosp., 456 N.E.2d 1186, 60 N.Y.2d 208 (1983).

46. R.GUNDRY, SOMA IN BIBLICAL THEOLOGY WITH EMPHASIS ON PAULINE ANTHROPOLOGY (1976).

47. *Id.* at 154.

48. H. WOLFF, ANTHROPOLOGY OF THE OLD TESTAMENT 110–11 (1974).

The Hastings Center Newborn Project

Section 1: A History of Neonatal Intensive Care and Decisionmaking

Cynthia B. Cohen, Betty Levin, and Kathy Powderly

While there has been no shortage of claims in the literature about the way in which Americans have dealt with children born with impairments in the past, the evidence offered in support has been scanty. It is, therefore, essential to understand the historical context within which current professional and public attitudes and norms have evolved.

The use of technology in the treatment of infants born prematurely, diseased, or with anomalies is a relatively recent phenomenon. At the beginning of this century, most babies were born at home, and sick infants were generally cared for and either lived or died at home. Most care to newborns was delivered by general practitioners, midwives, or obstetricians. The general philosophy of care was to protect the premature infant from infection and provide support with as little interference and handling as possible.

This noninterventionist philosophy began to change as physicians applied to infants newly developed techniques that were proving successful in adults. The most significant technological developments in neonatal care occurred after World War II. Clinicians realized that most of the infants who died were low birthweight, premature babies. Special units were established to care for these infants, and technology developed for war, such as plexiglass and plastics, and new medical advances, such as antibiotics, dramatically changed their treatment. During the late 1940s and '50s, babies began regularly to be fed with indwelling tubes and to be given high concentrations of oxygen, and neonatal surgical techniques were developed, for example, to shunt fluid from the ventricles of infants who had hydrocephalus.

Even with the development of such techniques, however, capabilities were still very limited by today's standards. In 1963, for example, First Lady Jacqueline Kennedy gave birth by cesarean section to Patrick Bouvier Kennedy five and one half weeks before his due date. He weighed 2100 grams (4½ pounds) and died, despite every effort to save him, of respiratory distress syndrome on the second day of his life.

Since the mid-1960s, the care of critically ill infants has improved dramatically. The use of respirators, electronic monitoring, analysis of small blood samples and the development of specialized staffs of highly trained nurses that characterize intensive care have all contributed to the survival of smaller and smaller infants. Regional networks have been organized to coordinate services for obstetrical and newborn care, and regional tertiary care centers developed services specializing in high risk births and the care of sick infants. Neonatology became a Board Certified subspecialty in 1975.

With the improvements in medical care, mortality rates for sick newborns fell dramatically, especially for very premature infants. Infants born before twenty-eight weeks of gestation, previously considered "nonviable" fetuses, began to be treated successfully. But as these technologies advanced, some specialists viewed impaired babies as part of a group of cases for which newly developed techniques did more harm than good. Whereas previously an isolated practitioner and/or family might have privately decided to allow an individual baby to die, practitioners at various regional centers began to discuss certain treatment decisions as part of a new problem brought on by technological advances.

In the late 1970s and early 1980s the debate concerning nontreatment had two main dimensions: 1) questions of substance (Should all babies be treated? If not, which babies should live?) and 2) questions of procedure (Who should decide?). Seminal articles were contributed by clinicians who debated the prognosis for infants with various conditions, by philosophers and others who debated the ethical principles guiding treatment choice, and by lawyers and those who debated the legal ramifications of parental and caregiver decisions not to provide aggressive treatment. Many academic discussions at Johns Hopkins featured a nationally distributed film that portrayed the decision of doctors to respect the refusal of surgery by parents of an infant born with Down's syndrome and a surgically correctable, life-threatening anomaly.

In a number of cases, physicians went to court when parents refused to give consent to treatment. For example, in 1974, Baby Boy Houle was born with malformations that included no left eye, a rudimentary left ear, and a tracheoesophageal fistula (necessitating intravenous feedings and allowing fluid to enter the lungs, bringing about pneumonia). Brain damage was suspected. When the parents refused to give consent for surgery, the physicians initiated a neglect case. A judge ordered surgery saying, "the existence of the child herein gives the court equitable jurisdiction to fulfill the responsibility of government in its character as *parens patriae* to care for infants and protect them from neglect." Despite the surgery, the baby died the next day.

The issue of nontreatment of catastrophically ill newborns began to receive national media attention in 1981 following reports of a decision to withhold treatment from conjoined (Siamese) twins born in Danville, Illinois. When the twins were delivered, joined with a single trunk below the waist, sharing three legs as well as internal organs, the obstetrician decided not to resuscitate; the parents concurred. The twins started to breathe spontaneously. An order, "Do not feed in accordance with the parents' wishes," was written on the medical chart.

An anonymous caller reported the case to the Illinois Department of Children and Family Services. The department filed a petition of neglect against the parents, temporary custody was granted to Family Services, and the children were moved to another hospital for evaluation. The parents and the attending physician were charged with conspiracy to commit murder. When a hearing was held, no witnesses were willing to give testimony linking the parents and physician directly to the order to withhold food from the twins and the charges were dismissed.

Four months later, custody of the twins was returned to the parents and they were brought home. Although they were expected to live only for a few months, they were later successfully separated; one survived for four years and the other is still alive. To this date, no parents or clinicians have been successfully prosecuted criminally for withholding treatment from a catastrophically ill newborn.

The issue of appropriate treatment for newborn infants with severe impairments reached a level of intense public discussion with the birth in Bloomington, Indiana in 1982 of an infant who came to be known as Baby Doe. The baby had Down's syndrome and a surgically correctable gastrointestinal malformation. The infant's parents, after receiving conflicting opinions from physicians, decided not to consent to surgery to correct the malformation.

The hospital contested this decision in the Indiana courts. The parents' right to decline surgery for their infant was upheld by the Supreme Court of Indiana without a written opinion and the record of the case was sealed. The infant died at six days of age. The decision not to treat him, however, led to a series of federal regulations and legislation designed to require treatments for handicapped infants.

In 1983, the Department of Health and Human Services issued new regulations that became known as the "Baby Doe Directives." These regulations required signs to be hung in prominent places in nurseries, obstetrical units, and pediatric units stating that failure to provide food or medically beneficial treatment to a handicapped infant solely because of his or her handicap was a violation of the Rehabilitation Act of 1973. A telephone system—a "Baby Doe Hotline"—was set up to receive anonymous reports of discriminatory denials of treatment. A federal court invalidated these regulations as a result of a suit claiming that they had been issued without complying with the required procedures for administrative rule making.

After following the requisite procedures, the federal government reissued similar regulations, which, like the first, asserted that failure to provide treatment was discrimination and that a federal presence in investigation and enforcement was appropriate. These rules were in effect only for a short period of time before they were invalidated by a federal court of appeals on grounds that the Rehabilitation Act was never intended by Congress to apply to medical decisions about newborns. The court concluded that the Act was directed toward handicapped persons who could benefit from services despite their handicap, rather than persons whose handicap itself was the subject of services.

The Supreme Court, in a review of this decision, agreed with the lower court's invalidation of the "Baby Doe" regulations. It noted that treatment decisions are traditionally left by state law to concerned parents and attending physicians or, in exceptional cases, to state child welfare agencies.

However, the holding was *not* that parents have a right to refuse treatment for their handicapped children, but that, ordinarily, review of such parental decisions belongs to the states. Moreover, the court did not indicate whether the Rehabilitation Act could be invoked legitimately by Health and Human Services if the department developed an adequate factual record to support regulations governing hospitals' decisions to accept parental refusals without bringing the situation to the attention of state authorities.

In 1984, in what was viewed as "compromise legislation," Congress passed amendments to the Child Abuse and Neglect Prevention and Treatment Act. These amendments focused on withholding "medically indicated" treatment from an infant as a form of child abuse and neglect rather than discrimination. Pursuant to these amendments, federal regulations then set criteria that each state must meet to receive federal grants for its child abuse program.

The criteria require child abuse agencies to establish procedures for responding to reports of medical neglect of infants from whom medically indicated treatment is withheld. Under the amendments, medically indicated treatment is defined by federal law to mean: "treatment (including appropriate nutrition, hydration and medication) which, in the treating physician's . . . reasonable medical judgment, will be most likely to be effective in ameliorating or correcting all such (life-threatening) conditions. . . ." There are three exceptions: (1) for infants who are irreversibly comatose; (2) for infants for whom such treatment would merely prolong dying, not correct all of the infant's life-threatening conditions, or be useless in ensuring the infant's survival; or (3) for infants for whom such treatment would be "virtually futile" and its provision would be inhumane.

The amendments have been taken to indicate that all infants who are born with impairments, such as Baby Doe, should receive treatment for life-threatening conditions, while infants whose immediate prognosis is dismal and for whom treatment would be inhumane need not be treated. Thus, although there is considerable debate about the reach of the federal law and the kinds of sanctions that could be brought against parents, physicians, and child abuse agencies that do not adhere to these standards, federal regulations support a strong ethos in favor of treatment of almost all newborn infants with "state of the art" medical care.

Section 7: Conclusion

Arthur Caplan

The work of The Hastings Center Newborns Project has been to open a new conversation rather than to close off prior discussion. Our exchange of ideas and opinions led not to uniformity or unanimity but to judgments based on certain features of an at least partially shared moral framework. We have endeavored to articulate the grounds of our conclusions and to suggest directions for future investigations. We present the following summary as a product of this distillation:

■ It is clear that parents, health care providers, courts, and governmental officials have legal and ethical responsibilities toward children with disabilities. Congenital anomalies such as Down's syndrome, uncomplicated instances of spina bifida, blindness, or other mildly to moderately disabling conditions provide no moral basis for either withdrawing or withholding treatments. Disabilities, in and of themselves, do not provide a basis for failing to accord children born with them the same access to medical and social services that would be given to any other child afflicted with a problem requiring medical intervention.

■ Recent debates about the morality of the treatment of imperiled newborns have narrowly focussed on dilemmas raised by children born with significant congenital anomalies. The questions surrounding premature newborns or those born with injuries as a result of the birth process need much greater attention: How should physicians and nurses cope with uncertain prognoses for extremely premature infants in the neonatal intensive care unit? How ought research and innovative interventions to be distinguished from efficacious therapies in dealing with a child who has suffered asphyxia or a traumatic injury? What ethical norms ought to guide the continuation of treatment efforts once they have been initiated in an intensive care unit?

■ There has been a great deal of discussion and debate about the need to assure that no infant is the victim of discrimination, abuse, or neglect at birth. There has not been a corresponding discussion of the moral responsibility that families and the community have to assure that infants with special needs, whether present at birth or not, do not become the victims of discrimination, abuse, or neglect by the community. The focus of moral discussion must reflect issues of treatment and care that extend beyond the boundaries of the neonatal intensive care unit.

■ Discussion must begin to focus on the treatment decisions that confront professionals and parents after the newborn period. Decisions may be more painful after there has been time to form powerful emotional bonds with a child, either in the hospital or in the home, but if it becomes clear that further treatments may prove futile or terribly burdensome, then painful decisions must be confronted. To make decisions earlier in life in order to decrease the emotional burden is to sacrifice the interests of the infant to the emotional needs of others.

■ A moral framework acknowledging the centrality of quality of life considerations as reflected in a concern for protecting the best interests of children is appropriate for guiding decisionmaking for children with severe disorders and diseases that prove unresponsive to medical interventions. The President's Commission for the Study of Ethical Problems in Medicine advocated a "best interest" standard that focuses exclusively on the interests of imperiled children, not the interests of their families or of the community as a whole. This is the most appropriate moral norm to utilize when attempting to decide whether treatment ought to be withdrawn or withheld. In special circumstances, the "best interest" standard is inapplicable and a "relational potential" standard may be substituted.

Federal and state laws and regulations incorporate a sanctity of life or "vitalistic" standard for guiding decisions where newborns are concerned. However, recent court decisions in many states acknowledge the appropriateness of a "best interest" standard for the same set of treatment decisions for adults. We can find no legitimate reason for supporting such an asymmetry and believe that the interests of children with chronic diseases and disabilities would best be served by reconciling any such differences in existing laws and regulations.

■ Despite the claims of some commentators to the contrary, active killing conflicts with standards protecting the best interests of children. In addition, arguments for active euthanasia frequently turn upon considerations of the interests and welfare of society, factors that are simply not appropriate as variables to guide the decisions of medical professionals or family members. Moreover, the possibilities for error and abuse inherent in the legalization of active euthanasia, when combined with the onus placed upon health professionals to violate their existing professional moral strictures against any involvement with procedures that actively hasten death, make the enactment of any public policy that would countenance the active killing of either children or adults morally repugnant.

■ Most decisions concerning treatment for children are best handled by informed, open, and frank discussions among health care professionals and the families of children with medical needs. A newly evolving procedural mechanism, infant ethics committees, has been created in many institutions to help enhance the possibilities for communication at times of great emotional crisis. These committees ought to be available to and utilized by both health care professionals and families.

Mandatory prospective review by ethics committees should not generally be necessary in making decisions about the course of treatment that any patient, child or adult, might receive. However, routine retrospective review of decisions to withhold or withdraw care is highly desirable for both the education of health care providers regarding their responsibilities and options and in order to maintain public confidence that close scrutiny is given to each and every decision to withdraw or forgo care.

■ Much greater attention needs to be given to educating the health professions and the public about the kinds of medical problems and disorders that can occur at birth or during infancy. Government agencies, schools, professional societies in health care, and religious organizations must endeavor to do a better job than is presently being done to communicate clearly with the general public about the possibilities and problems that are associated with disability and disease in infancy. Greater efforts must be mounted to educate those of childbearing age about the risks imposed by unhealthy behaviors upon the developing fetus. Open and frank discussion should be encouraged among pregnant women and their physicians concerning the possibility of congenital disorders or chronic diseases and the options available for detecting them *in utero* and for coping with them should they be present in a newborn.

Finally, we believe that society is not presently fulfilling its clear obligation to assist infants and children with disabilities. The moral duty to provide such assistance rests upon the twin foundations of the presence of clear and self-evident need on the part of many children and their families and the obligation society has to insure that all citizens have an equal opportunity to fulfill their abilities and potentials. The moral claims of children with medical needs, of whatever etiology, should receive the highest priority among competing claims for social resources.

SELECTED REFERENCES

Section 1

Raymond S. Duff and A.G.M. Campbell, "Moral and Ethical Dilemmas in the Special-Care Nursery," *NEJM*, 289:17 (1973), 890–94.

James M. Gustafson, "Mongolism, Parental Desires, and the Right to Life," *Perspective in Biology and Medicine* 16:4 (Summer 1973), 529–57.

John Lantos, "Baby Doe Five Years Later: Implications for Child Health," *NEJM* 317:7 (1987), 444–47.

John Lorber, "Results of Treatment of Myelomeningococele: An Analysis of 524 Unselected Cases, with Special Reference to Possible Selection for Treatment," *Developmental Medicine & Child Neurology* 13:3 (1971), 279–303.

Dorothy Pawluch, "Transitions in Pediatrics: A Segmental Analysis," in *The Sociology of Health and Illness: Critical Perspectives,* P. Conrad and R. Kern, eds. (New York: St. Martin's Press, 2nd ed., 1986).

William A. Silverman, "Incubator-Baby Side Shows," *Pediatrics* 64:2 (1979), 127–41.

Henry S. Spaulding, *Moral Principles and Medical Practice* (New York: Benziger Brothers, 1921).

Federal Register, April 15, 1985, 45 CFR 1340, DHHS Part IV; Child Abuse and Neglect Prevention and Treatment Program; Final Rule.

Bowen v. American Hospital Association, 54 LW 4579 (U.S. Sup. Ct., June 9, 1986), affirming *American Hospital Association v. Heckler,* 585 F. Supp. 541 (S.D.N.Y.).

The Parents' Perspective: Ethical Decision-Making in Neonatal Intensive Care

Winifred J. Pinch and Margaret L. Spielman

HIGH RISK NEWBORN

Mistakes in nature and human error combine to provide the driving force that has created a specialized area of care, the high risk newborn. Issues within high-risk newborn care have been themes in ethical debate for many years now. A report by Duff & Campbell in 1973 first created widespread dissonance as they discussed special-care nursery deaths (299) including 14% related to withholding treatment. Decisions were reached in those cases through active dialogue between health professionals and parents until resolution was reached (Duff and Campbell 1973). A multidisciplinary national conference in 1976 provided an early sounding board for debate about ethical issues in neonatal care relative to withdrawing life-sustaining treatment and the responsibility for decision-making (Jonsen & Garland 1976). In a more recent project, experts continued their struggle with the controversies surrounding imperiled newborns (Caplan & Cohen 1987).

The 'Baby Doe' quandary of more recent years placed treatment decisions for high-risk newborns on the front page and the plight of newborns, parents and health professionals on public display. Society rocked with shock that some parents would elect not to treat their newborn, and Federal legislation to prevent neglect of handicapped infants was born out of that response (Annas 1983, Steinbock 1984, Murray 1985).

Related Literature

The theme of ethics and newborn treatment echoes over the years between 1973 and the more current 'Baby Doe' incidents; it extends beyond, continuing into the present. The focal point of dilemmas for health professionals in a majority of cases can be categorized under the general rubric of decision-making. These dilemmas frequently revolve around quality of life decisions (Klitsch 1983, Bailey 1986, Sims-Jones 1986, Kuhse & Singer 1987, Marchwinski 1988). The advanced technologies available to sustain life in the neonate can dictate the protocol of care the decisions to use these technologies are compounded by concern for the dependent nature of the infant, the iatrogenic effect of therapy, the cost of care, and the definition of a reasonable length of time to attempt a particular therapy (Ragatz & Ellison 1983, Martin 1985, Ellison & Walwork 1986, Reedy *et al.* 1987, Berseth 1987).

The actual role of parents in ethical decision-making has been notably under-represented in the literature. Health professionals and other interested individuals tend to write *about* parental participation in the ethical dimension of high-risk newborn care, rather than to report on dialogue *with* parents (Cohen 1976, Callahan 1979, Strong 1983a, 1983b, 1984, Rue 1985, Penticuff 1988). Few, if any, have developed a systematic report of the parental perspective (Ellis 1984, Gortner 1985, Ketefian 1988). Some parents' viewpoints have been dramatically represented by singular, outraged cries for involvement and autonomy (Stinson & Stinson 1981, Lyon 1985, Barthel 1985, Harrison 1986, Preemies 1988).

What is the best approach to ethical dilemmas in the care of high-risk newborns? It would seem imperative to ask this question of those for whom the decision has the most intimate and long-term implications—*the parents.* It is necessary to know the responses of parents in order to provide anticipatory guidance, preventive measures and follow-up care based on a foundation of reliable knowledge.

METHOD

A phenomenological approach was utilized for this study in order to describe systematically the perception of ethical decision-making by families with an infant in the neonatal intensive care unit (NICU), an area that heretofore had not been investigated (Benoliel 1984). The goal included the development of an understanding of the experience from the parents' perspective based on the delineation of major themes or concepts that represented the families' viewpoints (Knafl & Howard 1984).

Sample

The 32 families of newborns in a Level III neonatal intensive care unit (NICU) were interviewed prior to the infant's discharge. The sample included all mothers, two grandmothers (who had primary care giving responsibilities), and 21 fathers who were interviewed over a period of 12 months. Merenstein & Gardner's (1985) criteria for a high-risk newborn were used to determine admission to the study (see Table 1 for a description of the infant status). A convenience sample was formed as staff nurses utilized the neonate criteria to invite parents to participate. Parents were provided with a research information sheet. Informed consent was obtained by an investigator. Hospital records, were utilized to document the status of the newborn after all predischarge interviews were completed.

Procedure

A semistructured interview guide, based on material from Lyons (1983) for her investigation of moral reasoning, provided the initial questions. Theoretically, Lyons' study was based on an integration of the research of Kohlberg (1958, 1973, 1975, 1981, Kohlberg *et al.* 1983) and Gilligan (1977, 1979, 1982a, 1982b) which accommodated the expression of masculine and feminine modes of moral reasoning when exploring a chosen ethical dilemma. The circumstances and the decision-making were probed to explore sources of conflict, events the parents experienced, and their thoughts and feelings about these issues relative to the moral dimension of their situation. A pilot study was conducted with families of high-risk infants in the community health setting to affirm the ability of families to respond to the proposed interview.

TABLE 1   Summary of Infant Status (*n* = 42)

Days in NICU:	Low = 1 day (expired)
	< 30 days = 18
	30–60 = 8
	61–90 = 5
	91–120 = 7
	> 120 = 3
	High = 235 days
	Missing = 1
Birth weight:	Low = 540 g
	600–999 g = 15
	1000–1599 g = 8
	1600–2999 g = 7
	2100–2499 g = 4
	*Criteria = < 2500 g
	> 2500 g = 6
	Missing = 1
Gestational age:	Low = 24 weeks
	24–26 weeks = 7
	27–30 weeks = 14
	31–34 weeks = 15
	35–37 weeks = 4
	*Criteria < 37 weeks
	> 37 weeks = 2
APGAR 1" 5"	Low 0 1
	21 below 5 at 5"
	*Criteria = < 5
	18 above 5 at 5"
	Missing = 2
Bilirubin high	Low = 3 ml/dl
	*Criteria = > 15 ml/dl
	3 above 15 ml/dl
	High = 25.9 ml/dl
	Missing = 1
Diagnosis and treatments	*Criteria = Presence of surgical interventions and/or birth anomalies
	90 Different diagnoses
	61 Different treatments

*Criteria for high risk status as presented by Merenstein & Gardner (1985).

After the collection of demographic data including the parents' impression of the status of the newborn, parents were asked to describe the event that was most outstanding for them as they looked back over the pregnancy, birth and subsequent experiences in the intensive care nursery. Using that event as a reference point, the parents and an investigator explored the experience to determine the presence of any sense of conflict. As the interview progressed, the parents were led specifically to the events surrounding their infant in the NICU if they did not initially volunteer this portion of their experience as the most outstanding. After identifying a conflict situation, regardless of the time of its occurrence, the parents were asked what they did, their thoughts about whether it was the right thing to do, and how they knew it was right. Confirmation of the NICU experience as one with or without moral conflict, was probed in depth with the parents during the interview. As more interviews showed a lack of perception of an ethical conflict, very specific questions were developed and included to probe possible ethical dilemmas related to the infant's status or treatment. Possible dilemmas included the use of a ventilator, iatrogenic effects of therapy, possible negative outcomes for the infant, and experimental treatment. Interviews were conducted in the parents' room in the acute care setting or in the parents' home and were recorded on audio tape. Field notes were recorded on the tape immediately after the interview.

ANALYSIS OF DATA

During the process of gathering data from the families, both investigators continually examined the interview questions, the results, and additional means to probe the areas of investigation utilizing the tapes and the hard copies of the transcripts. Although interview data began to appear to be repetitious beginning about the tenth interview, additional families were contacted for two major reasons. Firstly, the investigators has some doubts about the severity of the condition of the infants of these families and wanted to be sure to access the most critically ill infants admitted to the NICU. Secondly, the long-range goal of the project included interviewing the families longitudinally to document changes in the families' perceptions over time (Swanson-Kauffman 1986, Knafl & Webster 1988).

Interview data were coded independently by each investigator and then compared. Printouts of the coded data by category were examined and data were subcategorized, and evaluated on an on-going basis as the team conducted the study. In addition, an experienced qualitative researcher reviewed randomly selected transcripts to provide interrater reliability by evaluating the match between category names and the transcript data. Also a nurse clinician with experience both in the NICU and with high-risk families in the community reviewed the description of the results and randomly selected transcripts to validate the match of data between the investigators' categories, the informants' dialogue and her own clinical experience. Finally, parents with a high-risk infant reviewed the study results to validate the report, based on that family's experience (Swanson-Kauffman 1986, Knafl & Webster 1988).

FINDINGS

Analysis of the interviews led the investigators to identify several themes that appeared in a majority of the individual discussions: conflict naming, content of decision-making, context of decision-making, information sharing, and perception of high-risk newborn status. These themes, taken together, were seen to describe a concept that was named the medicalization of parenting. Parental characteristics are summarized in Table 2.

Medicalization of Parenting

Overall, informants in this study appeared to have adopted a passive role in decision-making responsibility, including the ethical dimension of new-born care. It is important to note that this was an acceptable situation for most of them. Parents cited the presence of stress, lack of comprehension of the technological details, or a capitulation to the health professionals' expertise as rationale for their behaviour.

Most families felt disconnected from the child and expressed feelings of emptiness and lack of fulfilment, even depression when the nursery at home remained unoccupied. They described their interactions with the infant as limited. However, ethical decisions were made relative to the care of the high-risk infant and when parents were not making those decisions, then the health professionals were making them in conjunction with all of the other care they provided.

Conflict Naming

Decision-making was introduced by asking parents to describe a circumstance during the pregnancy, birth or NICU experience for their newborn, in which they were not sure what was the right thing to do. For several teenage mothers, whether or not to keep the baby was a consideration uppermost in their thinking. Other families identified the amniocentesis, use of preterm labour medications, transport from rural facilities, Caesarian sections, and specific signs and symptoms such as vaginal bleeding, as instances when they were distraught. No direct infant concerns were raised by the initial posing of the questions. With probing, a few infant-related issues were identified such as the use of surfactant, the decision to circumcise, and whether or not to breast-feed. The general flavour of responses indicated that decisions for the baby would not have to be made until he/she came home.

Parents, when specifically asked about their role in treatment decisions for the neonate, stated that there was no decision-making required or that they were not involved in the process of decision-making in the majority of the situations. They were very aware of the need to sign informed consents for treatment, but they discussed this as a perfunctory permission-granting

TABLE 2   Summary of Parental Characteristics for the 32 Families

Relationship to baby	Mother	32	
	Father	18	
	Grandmother	2	
Marital status	Married	26	
	Single	6	
		M	F
Age in years	20 and under	4	0
	21–25	3	2
	26–29	9	7
	30–39	15	9
		M	F
Ethnic identification	Caucasian	24	16
	Black	5	2
	Mixed	1	0
	Oriental	1	0
	Hispanic	1	0
		M	F
Educational level (highest or current)	< High school	5	0
	High School (graduated)	9	5
	> High School	14	12
	College (graduated)	3	2
	> College	1	1
		M	F
Occupation*	Blue collar	5	9
	White collar	14	8
	Business/professional	4	1
	None	9	0
		M	F
Religious preference	Catholic	10	7
	Protestant	19	9
	Buddhist	1	0
	None	2	2
Financial status**	Adequate	18	
	Inadequate	8	
	Missing data	6	
Health care benefits	Had coverage	21	
	No coverage	5	
	Missing data	6	

M = Mother; F = Father (data presented from those who participated in interview).
*Categorizations based on Friedman (1981); **Categorizations based on Geismar & La Sorte (1964).

activity for them. It did not involve conflict nor did it pose a dilemma under most circumstances. They articulated the view that if the health professionals needed to implement a procedure, it should be done. There were few negative feelings shared relative to decision-making and its ethical dimensions but rather in the majority of the families, acceptance and gratefulness characterized their perception of the situation.

Dependence was recognized as families cited their lack of medical knowledge. A number of families interjected their reliance on religious faith and its relationship to their infant's needs. Most families focused on their own emotional state during the conflict they elected to discuss. One parent shared her contemplation of suicide. Parents discussed events associated with the pregnancy and birth initially, rather than the course of the newborn's life in the NICU.

Content of Decision-Making

Nutrition, cleanliness and sleep were selected by parents for discussion of concerns related to the infant. The domain of normal newborn care appeared to be the focus parents preferred, not the technical aspects of high-risk care. These were familiar areas for parents who may have felt more secure and comfortable in this domain. Parents addressed such areas as diaper size, the time that a baby was allowed to suck, the choice of breast milk versus formula, waking the baby to feed or give medications, and positions for sleep. Although parents expressed this concern, they also expressed feelings of little control over decisions made in these more familiar areas.

Treatment decision-making encompassing such issues as the viability of extremely low birth weight infants, use of surfactant, iatrogenic effects from antibiotics, oxygen and ventilators, the need for multiple invasive procedures, and pain in the neonate are just a few of the ethical concerns apparent in the literature. The content of decision-making for families of neonates in this study did not generally include these concerns. It certainly was not a priority item in any case and it clearly did not encompass moral conflict. It was striking by its absence yet the decision-making in these areas was critical in terms of the infant's status and prognosis.

Context of Decision-Making

In the discussion of the decision-making in which they were involved, parents addressed their recollection of the circumstances surrounding their experience. The reminiscence accompanied decision-making in pregnancy and at birth, for few initially addressed any decision-making pertaining to the infant. Many of the mothers mentioned their physical and mental status as limiting their ability to concentrate or make rational choices. The sheer number of permissions was also a factor. Again, the stress, the feeling of being overwhelmed by the rush of premature events, might have changed their ability to cope with these extraordinary circumstances.

Several parents requested more scheduled time with health professionals, particularly the physician in charge. The parents wanted to be reassured that changing house staff were familiar with the current status of their infant.

Parents especially noted that they did not want this dialogue to occur through the nurses, nor did they want the discussion to transpire in public places.

Information Sharing for Decision-Making

Responsible decision-making cannot occur without first acquiring the knowledge necessary to make an informed choice. The nurses were frequently mentioned as sources of information. Parents with some background or experience in health care were better able to articulate information about the entire perinatal period. Technical information, including both procedures and medications were a problem for several families to name even. The use of surfactant was an area of common knowledge. The knowledge level may be attributed to a hospital-based research project with surfactant. Some parents were intimidated by the staff and indicated their observation of the NICU as busy and without sufficient nursing staff; consequently they were reluctant to intrude on the nursery routine to get information.

High-Risk Newborn Status

Parents were asked directly the diagnosis of their infant(s). When parents were unable to respond to this question, they were queried relative to their understanding of the rationale for the newborn's admission to the intensive care nursery. As viewed from the parents' perspective, few serious problems ever existed among the group of babies in these families. Some parents simplistically viewed the infants' need to grow, weight gain, or the inability to nourish themselves as rationale for admission to the NICU, with little understanding of the associated pathology or medical problems that could threaten life itself. At this point in the study, as seen through the eyes of the parents, there was little evidence that complex technologies or sophisticated treatment central to ethical debate in neonatal care, were utilized for these high-risk infants.

The babies of these families did *not* represent an unusual group of marginally-ill neonates, as subsequently documented in the discharge summaries of the hospital record (see Table 1). The most profound evidence relates to the number of babies who underwent extensive, invasive and complex treatment during this residence in the NICU; however, these were seldom addressed by the parents. A significant disparity existed between the parents' description of the near discharge status of their infant and the documentation in the charts of the infants who went home with significant residual problems. Some may require extensive intervention in the future; others are blind, severely deaf and/or mentally retarded. Their parents seldom addressed these areas as ones of concern, of ethical decision-making, or in which any kind of problem might reside.

This does not imply that parents were not informed. Documentation existed in the hospital record to validate information sharing and teaching. These interview results serve to emphasize that either parents do not remember the aforementioned events, deny their existence, or have chosen not to discuss them in the course of this dialogue, even with probing.

DISCUSSION

A chasm apparently exists between the health professional's perspective of the ethical dimension of neonatal care and the parents' perspective of ethical issues. The agonizing struggle for a sound, moral direction of neonatal care while implementing highly invasive or potentially iatrogenic-producing treatments was not articulated by most of these parents. Only two families addressed their grief related to termination of treatment and expressed their ownership of the responsibility for this ethical decision.

Other individuals have theoretically supported the medicalization of parenting phenomenon. Steinfels (1978) focused on the technology of pregnancy and childbirth and described a conflict of values between professionals and patients over a decade ago. She critically examined the imposition of the medical model upon these events and the enforced sick role of the patient (mother), which led to decision-making based on assumptions that changed childbirth from a family event to a medical event. Mitchell (1986) built on this medical model view and described her perception that medicalization also occurred in instances of prematurity or neonatal injury. She voiced concern that nurses were now in charge of a hospital-centred crisis instead of a mother in charge of a family event. The nurse occupies a powerful position that may influence family functioning far into the future.

The rationale for the distancing that these parents created or were led to develop relative to the ethical decision-making dimension of care for their newborns is unclear. At the predischarge stage, responsibility for ethical decision-making has been abdicated by most parents, if it was ever owned, and they appear to fail to present themselves first as parents of their newborn on this issue. The average length of stay for these infants (42) was 55 days, yet parents elected to focus on pregnancy and birth, rather than the infant and their experiences with the child. The need for mothers to discuss the pregnancy and birth experience is recognized. However, in this context, the focus reflected their free choice despite the fact that their role as parents of a high-risk infant was discussed as the rationale for their invitation to participate in the research project.

Replication Needed

Future replications of this study are necessary before global generalizations of the results are applied. The study was conducted with a majority of families from one Level III nursery in the Midwest and these parents' responses may not be representative of most families of high-risk newborns. Despite the general milieu of contentment that appears to exist within this group of parents relative to treatment decisions and the ethical implications for their high-risk newborns, it must be remembered that the infants had not been discharged. Parents of chronically ill and handicapped infants do express their astonishment at the implications of treatment decisions later, when the full realization of the depth and breadth of child care impacts them. Long-term follow-up of these families is planned to document changes should they occur, in perceptions of ethical decision-making.

Parents continue to be the majority of individuals who live with the outcomes of high-risk neonate interventions. Further credence for their responsibility and their role in ethical decision-making is required in future deliberations. For those families who are able to accept the status quo, no changes may be required. For parents who object to their divorce from treatment decisions, a solution is required (Stinson & Stinson 1981, Bridge & Bridge 1981, Barthel 1985). Currently, even the 'Baby Doe' regulations sanction society's legitimate intervention in the care of the high-risk newborn and the implied philosophical position that parents do not always know best. It is imperative to delineate between the two groups—those who desire involvement and those who do not—at an early stage and to monitor the outcomes of ethical decisions for the families of both groups.

Acknowledgments

This study was supported by a grant from the Health Future Foundation Incorporated, Omaha, Nebraska.

This article is dedicated to the parents of newborns, who so freely gave of their time to participate in the study. The authors also want to acknowledge the assistance provided by the nurses in the NICU who informed the parents of our study and referred them to us. In addition, we extend a generous thank you to Linda Pickham BSN RNC and Kathryn Moore Koehler MSN RN at AMI/Saint Joseph's Hospital; Joan F. Norris PhD RN, Associate Dean, Director of the Graduate Program, Joan M. Lappe MS RN, Catherine O. Wellman MS RN and Patricia Nilsson MS RN, all at Creighton University; Sheri Lyons RN and Susan E. Reinarz BSN RN, at the University of Nebraska Medical Center, for their support during the project or in the preparation of this manuscript.

References

Annas G. (1983) Disconnecting the Baby Doe hotline. *Hastings Center Report* **13**(3), 14–16.
Bailey C.F. (1986) Withholding or withdrawing treatment on handicapped newborns. *Pediatric Nursing* **12**(6), 413–416.

Barthel J. (1985) His name is Jimmy: Should he have been allowed to live? *McCall's* **113**, 110–111, 156–161.

Benoliel J.Q. (1984) Advancing nursing science: Qualitative approaches. *Western Journal of Nursing Research* **6**(3), 1–9.

Berseth C.L. (1987) Ethical dilemmas in the neonatal intensive care unit. *Mayo Clinical Proceedings* **62**, 67–72.

Bridge P. & Bridge M. (1981) The brief life and death of Christopher Bridge. *Hastings Center Report* **11**(6), 17–19.

Callahan S. (1979) An ethical analysis of responsible parenthood. *Birth Defects: Original Article Series* **15**(2), 217–238.

Caplan A. & Cohen D. (1987) *Ethics and the Care of Imperiled Newborns: A Report by the Hastings Center's Research Project on Ethics and the Care of Imperiled Newborns.* The Hastings Center, Briarcliff Manor, NY.

Cohen M.A. (1976) Ethical issues in neonatal intensive care: Familial concerns. In *Ethics of Newborn Care* (Jonsen A.R. & Garland M.J. eds), University of California, Berkeley, CA, pp. 54–63.

Duff R.S. & Campbell A.G.M. (1973) Moral and ethical dilemmas in the special-care nursery. *New England Journal of Medicine* **289**, 890–894.

Ellis R. (1984) Philosophic inquiry. In *Annual Review of Nursing Research* (Werley H.H. & Fitzpatrick J.J. eds), Springer, New York, pp. 211–227.

Ellison P. & Walwork E. (1986) Withdrawing mechanical support from the brain-damaged neonate. *Dimensions of Critical Care Nursing* **5**(5), 284–293.

Friedman M.M. (1981) *Family Nursing: Theory and Assessment.* Appleton-Century-Croft, New York.

Geismar L.L. & La Sorte B. (1964) *Understanding the Multiproblem Family.* Association Press, New York.

Gilligan C. (1977) In a different voice: Women's conceptions of self and morality. *Harvard Educational Review* **47**(4), 481–517.

Gilligan C. (1979) Woman's place in man's life cycle. *Harvard Educational Review* **49**(4), 431–446.

Gilligan C. (1982a) *In a Different Voice: Psychological Theory and Women's Development.* Harvard University Press, Cambridge, MA.

Gilligan C. (1982b) New maps of development: New visions of maturity. *American Journal of Orthopsychiatry* **52**(2), 199–212.

Gortner S.R. (1985) Ethical inquiry. In *Annual Review of Nursing Research* (Werley H.H. & Fitzpatrick J.J. eds), Springer, New York, pp. 193–214.

Harrison H. (1986) Neonatal intensive care: Parent's role in ethical decision making. *Birth* **13**(3), 165–175.

Jonsen A.R. & Garland M.J. (1976) *Ethics of Newborn Intensive Care.* Institute of Governmental Studies, Berkeley, CA.

Ketefian S. (1988) *Moral Reasoning and Ethical Practice in Nursing: An Integrative Review.* National League of Nursing, New York.

Klitsch M. (1983) Mercy or Murder? *Family Planning Perspectives* **15**(3), 143–146.

Knafl K.A. & Howard M.J. (1984) Interpreting and reporting qualitative research. *Research in Nursing and Health* **7**, 17–23.

Knafl K.A. & Webster D.C. (1988) Managing and analyzing qualitative data: A description of tasks, techniques, and materials. *Western Journal of Nursing Research* **10**(2), 195–218.

Kohlberg L. (1958) The development of modes of moral thinking and choice in the years ten to sixteen. Unpublished doctoral dissertation. University of Chicago, Illinois.

Kohlberg L. (1973) *Collected Papers on Moral Development and Moral Education.* Moral Research Education Foundation, Harvard University, Cambridge, MA.

Kohlberg L. (1975) The cognitive developmental approach to moral education. *Phi Delta Kappan* **56**, 670–679.

Kohlberg L. (1981) *The Philosophy of Moral Development.* Harper & Row, San Francisco.

Kohlberg L., Levin C. & Hewer A. (1983) *Moral Stages: A Current Formulation and a Response to Critics.* S. Karger AG, Basel, Switzerland.

Kuhse H. & Singer P. (1987) Severely handicapped newborns: For sometimes letting- and helping-die. *Law, Medicine & Health Care* **14**(3–4), 149–153.

Lyon J. (1985) *Playing God in the Nursery.* W.W. Norton, New York.

Lyons N. (1983) Two perspectives: On self, relationships, and morality. *Harvard Educational Review* **53**(2), 125–145.

Marchwinski S. (1988) The dilemma of moral and ethical decision making in the intensive care nursery. *Neonatal Network* **6**(5), 17–20.

Martin D. (1985) Withholding treatment from several handicapped newborns: Ethical–legal issues. *Nursing Administrative Quarterly* **9**(4), 47–56.

Merenstein F.B. & Gardner S.L. (1985) *Handbook of Neonatal Intensive Care.* C.V. Mosby, St Louis.

Mitchell C. (1986) Ethical issues in neonatal nursing. In *Perinatal Nursing: A Clinical Handbook* (Angelini D.J., Knapp C.M.W. & Gibes R.M. eds), Blackwell Scientific, Boston, pp. 429–437.

Murray T.H.E. (1985) The final anticlimactic rule on Baby Doe. *Hastings Center Report* **15**(3), 5–9.

Penticuff J.H. (1988) Neonatal intensive care: Parental prerogatives. *Journal of Perinatal and Neonatal Nursing* **1**(3), 77–86.

Preemies (1988) *Newsweek* **111**(20), 62–68 +.

Ragatz S.C. & Ellison P.H. (1983) Decisions to withdraw life support in the neonatal intensive care unit. *Clinical Pediatrics* **22**(11), 729–735.

Reedy N.J., Minogue J.P. & Sterk M.B. (1987) The critically ill neonate: Dilemmas in perinatal ethics. *Critical Care Nursing Quarterly* **10**(2), 56–64.

Rue V.M. (1985) Death by design of handicapped newborns: The family's role and response. *Issues in Law & Medicine* **1**(3), 201–225.

Sims-Jones N. (1986) Ethical dilemmas in the NICU. *The Canadian Nurse* **82**(4), 24–26.

Steinbock B. (1984) Baby Doe in the Courts. *Hastings Center Report* **14**(1), 13–19.

Steinfels M.O. (1978) New childbirth technology: A clash of values. *Hastings Center Report* **8**(1), 9–12.

Stinson R. & Stinson P. (1981) On the death of a baby. *Journal of Medical Ethics* **7**, 5–18.

Strong C. (1983a) Defective infants and their impact on families: Ethical and legal considerations. *Law, Medicine & Health Care* **11**(4), 168–181.

Strong C. (1983b) The tiniest newborns. *Hastings Center Report* **13**(1), 14–19.

Strong C. (1984) The neonatologist's duty to patient and parents. *Hastings Center Report* **14**(4), 10–16.

Swanson-Kauffman K.M. (1986) A combined qualitative methodology for nursing research. *Advances in Nursing Science* **8**(3), 58–68.

II. Abortion.

Overview. Abortion is currrently one of the most controversial ethical issues in the United States. It has always been a topic of biomedical interest. Hippocrates advocated strenuous dancing to induce a spontaneous abortion. Galen suggested jumping off a wall.

In recent times, the United States Supreme Court decision in *Roe v. Wade*[1] declared unconstitutional a Texas law that restricted legal abortions to cases affecting the life of the mother. This decision had the effect of legalizing abortion in the United States. The ruling established three guidelines affecting abortion legislation: (a) until the end of the first trimester, the decision to have an abortion is completely up to the woman; (b) after the first trimester, the state may regulate abortion health; and (c) when the fetus is viable (in the third trimester), the state may regulate or prohibit abortion except when the mother's life is at stake.

In the years since *Roe v. Wade,* the debate has continued. Abortion foes have organized marches, supported prolife political candidates, and picketed

---

[1]410 US 113, 93 S, Ct. 705, 1/22/73.

clinics that perform abortions. Extremists have even resorted to terrorist tactics in clinic bombings and murders of physicians. Abortion supporters have organized marches and supported candidates favoring their position. Each side has tended to demonize the other, and little constructive discourse has resulted.

This section presents two very influential essays in the history of this debate and a new article that I have written. John Noonan reviews various criteria concerning the criteria of biological personhood. For Noonan (and many foes of abortion), the definition of when an organism becomes human is crucial to the abortion debate (since to kill an innocent human at will is generally thought to be a definition of murder). He looks for biological events that might be taken as significant in the creation and development of a fetus. He chooses a model that describes chances of survival. Before conception, the potential fetus (as viewed from the probability of conception) is less than 1 in 200 million. After conception, the odds drastically change to 4 in 5. Noonan takes this change in probability to indicate a change in the biological status of the fetus that is so significant that he believes it confers personhood.

Judith Jarvis Thomson accepts the premise that the fetus may be a person (for the purpose of discussion). Her argument is that the killing of an innocent is sometimes permissable. In other words, it is not tantamount to murder (killing in self-defense is an example of this). She suggests that there is no absolute right to life for any innocent. This is especially true in pregnancy during which the fetus depends on the pregnant woman's body for its well-being. If a person has absolute control over her body and is not obliged to put her life or well-being at risk, then the woman who allows a pregnancy to develop makes a choice that is entirely a moral permission, not an obligation. She may or may not allow the pregnancy to develop since her body will be used in the process.

Thomson argues that those who go beyond their moral duties to help others are called Good Samaritans. Being a Good Samaritan may be the decent thing to do, but it is not obligatory. In the same way, bringing a pregnancy to term (especially one that began voluntarily) may be a decent thing, but it is not obligatory.

My article proposes a middle ground by recognizing the truth and falsehood of both positions. I believe that by using the methodology of the Personal Worldview Imperative, we can enter into the worldviews of both sides and understand what compels them to hold their various positions. From there the antiabortion foes are shown to be wrong because the status of the fetus and even the postbirth infant does not confer dialectically necessary rights. Using the notion of precautionary reasoning suggested by Deryck Beyleveld and Shaun Pallinson,[2] I create levels of proportional respect owed to the fetus beginning at the end of the first trimester. I then integrate this position with the

---

[2]For a discussion of precautionary reasoning see Chapter Three of this text.

Aristotelian sense of potentiality that also relates to the moment of conception until the end of the first trimester. The sense of respect due the embryo at this basic level is proportionally diminished but not absent entirely. I also show the proabortion position to be wrong because it does not differentiate levels of threat that motivate a pregnant woman to seek an abortion. Not all levels are equal. It is important to differentiate these levels and compare them to the levels of respect due to the embryo and to identify when in pregnancy to act.

This model of the Personal Worldview Imperative seeks to create a new context through which advocates of both sides can justify their positions and gain an understanding of the opposing side. This is not a position of relativism, but it does open the door for dialogue.

An Almost Absolute Value in History

John T. Noonan Jr.

The most fundamental question involved in the long history of thought on abortion is: How do you determine the humanity of a being? To phrase the question that way is to put in comprehensive humanistic terms what the theologians either dealt with as an explicitly theological question under the heading of "ensoulment" or dealt with implicitly in their treatment of abortion. The Christian position as it originated did not depend on a narrow theological or philosophical concept. It had no relation to theories of infant baptism.[1] It appealed to no special theory of instantaneous ensoulment. It took the world's view on ensoulment as that view changed from Aristotle to Zacchia. There was, indeed, theological influence affecting the theory of ensoulment finally adopted, and, of course, ensoulment itself was a theological concept, so that the position was always explained in theological terms. But the theological notion of ensoulment could easily be translated into humanistic language by substituting "human" for "rational soul"; the problem of knowing when a man is a man is common to theology and humanism.

If one steps outside the specific categories used by the theologians, the answer they gave can be analyzed as a refusal to discriminate among human beings on the basis of their varying potentialities. Once conceived, the being was recognized as man because he had man's potential. The criterion for humanity, thus, was simple and all-embracing: if you are conceived by human parents, you are human.

The strength of this position may be tested by a review of some of the other distinctions offered in the contemporary controversy over legalizing abortion. Perhaps the most popular distinction is in terms of viability. Before an age of so many months, the fetus is not viable, that is, it cannot be removed from the mother's womb and live apart from her. To that extent, the life of the fetus is absolutely dependent on the life of the mother. This dependence is made the basis of denying recognition to its humanity.

There are difficulties with this distinction. One is that the perfection of artificial incubation may make the fetus viable at any time: it may be removed and artificially sustained. Experiments with animals already show that such a procedure is possible. This hypothetical extreme case relates to an actual difficulty: there is considerable elasticity to the idea of viability. Mere length of life is not an exact measure. The viability of the fetus depends on the extent of its anatomical and functional development. The weight and length of the fetus are better guides to the state of its development than age, but weight and length vary. Moreover, different racial groups have different ages at which their fetuses are viable. Some evidence, for example, suggests that Negro fetuses mature more quickly than white fetuses. If viability is the norm, the standard would vary with race and with many individual circumstances.

The most important objection to this approach is that dependence is not ended by viability. The fetus is still absolutely dependent on someone's care in order to continue existence; indeed a child of one or three or even five years of age is absolutely dependent on another's care for existence; uncared for, the older fetus or the younger child will die as surely as the early fetus detached from the mother. The unsubstantial lessening in dependence at viability does not seem to signify any special acquisition of humanity.

A second distinction has been attempted in terms of experience. A being who has had experience, has lived and suffered, who possesses memories, is more human than one who has not. Humanity depends on formation by experience. The fetus is thus "unformed" in the most basic human sense.

This distinction is not serviceable for the embryo which is already experiencing and reacting. The embryo is responsive to touch after eight weeks and at least at that point is experiencing. At an earlier stage the zygote is certainly alive and responding to its environment. The distinction may also be challenged by the rare case where aphasia has erased adult memory: has it erased humanity? More fundamentally, this distinction leaves even the older fetus or the younger child to be treated as an unformed inhuman thing. Finally, it is not clear why experience as such confers humanity. It could be argued that certain central experiences such as loving or learning are necessary to make a man human. But then human beings who have failed to love or to learn might be excluded from the class called man.

A third distinction is made by appeal to the sentiments of adults. If a fetus dies, the grief of the parents is not the grief they would have for a living child. The fetus is an unnamed "it" till birth, and is not perceived as personality until at least the fourth month of existence when movements in the womb manifest a vigorous presence demanding joyful recognition by the parents.

Yet feeling is notoriously an unsure guide to the humanity of others. Many groups of humans have had difficulty in feeling that persons of another tongue, color, religion, sex, are as human as they. Apart from reactions to alien groups, we mourn the loss of a ten-year-old boy more than the loss of his one-day-old brother or his 90-year-old grandfather. The difference felt and the grief expressed vary with the potentialities extinguished, or the experience wiped out; they do not seem to point to any substantial difference in the humanity of baby, boy, or grandfather.

Distinctions are also made in terms of sensation by the parents. The embryo is felt within the womb only after about the fourth month. The embryo is seen only at birth. What can be neither seen nor felt is different from what is tangible. If the fetus cannot be seen or touched at all, it cannot be perceived as man.

Yet experience shows that sight is even more untrustworthy than feeling in determining humanity. By sight, color became an appropriate index for saying who was a man, and the evil of racial discrimination was given foundation. Nor can touch provide the test; a being confined by sickness, "out of touch" with others, does not thereby seem to lose his humanity. To the extent that touch still has appeal as a criterion, it appears to be a survival of the old English idea of "quickening"—a possible mistranslation of the Latin *animatus* used in the canon law. To that extent touch as a criterion seems to be dependent on the Aristotelian notion of ensoulment, and to fall when this notion is discarded.

Finally, a distinction is sought in social visibility. The fetus is not socially perceived as human. It cannot communicate with others. Thus, both subjectively and objectively, it is not a member of society. As moral rules are rules for the behavior of members of society to each other, they cannot be made for behavior toward what is not yet a member. Excluded from the society of men, the fetus is excluded from the humanity of men.[2]

By force of the argument from the consequences, this distinction is to be rejected. It is more subtle than that founded on an appeal to physical sensation, but it is equally dangerous in its implications. If humanity depends on social recognition, individuals or whole groups may be dehumanized by being denied any status in their society. Such a fate is fictionally portrayed in *1984* and has actually been the lot of many men in many societies. In the Roman empire, for example, condemnation to slavery meant the practical denial of most human rights; in the Chinese Communist world, landlords have been classified as enemies of the people and so treated as nonpersons by the state. Humanity does not depend on social recognition, though often the failure of society to recognize the prisoner, the alien, the heterodox as human has led to the destruction of human beings. Anyone conceived by a man and a woman is human. Recognition of this condition by society follows a real event in the objective order, however imperfect and halting the recognition. Any attempt to limit humanity to exclude some group runs the risk of furnishing authority and precedent for excluding other groups in the name of the consciousness or perception of the controlling group in the society.

A philosopher may reject the appeal to the humanity of the fetus because he views "humanity" as a secular view of the soul and because he doubts the existence of anything real and objective which can be identified as humanity. One answer to such a philosopher is to ask how he reasons about moral questions without supposing that there is a sense in which he and the others of whom he speaks are human. Whatever group is taken as the society which determines who may be killed is thereby taken as human. A second answer is to ask if he does not believe that there is a right and wrong way of deciding moral questions. If there is such a difference, experience may be appealed to: to decide who is human on the basis of the sentiment of a given society has led to consequences which rational men would characterize as monstrous.

The rejection of the attempted distinctions based on viability and visibility, experience and feeling, may be buttressed by the following considerations: Moral judgments often rest on distinctions, but if the distinctions are not to appear arbitrary *fiat*, they should relate to some real difference in probabilities. There is a kind of continuity in all life, but the earlier stages of the elements of human life possess tiny probabilities of development. Consider for example, the spermatozoa in any normal ejaculate: There are about 200,000,000 in any single ejaculate, of which one has a chance of developing into a zygote. Consider the oocytes which may become ova: there are 100,000 to 1,000,000 oocytes in a female infant, of which a maximum of 390 are ovulated. But once spermatozoon and ovum meet and the conceptus is formed, such studies as have been made show that roughly in only 20 percent of the cases will spontaneous abortion occur. In other words, the chances are about 4 out of 5 that this new being will develop. At this stage in the life of the being there is a sharp shift in probabilities, an immense jump in potentialities. To make a distinction between the rights of spermatozoa and the rights of the fertilized ovum is to respond to an enormous shift in possibilities. For about twenty days after conception the egg may split to form twins or combine with another egg to form a chimera, but the probability of either event happening is very small.

It may be asked, What does a change in biological probabilities have to do with establishing humanity? The argument from probabilities is not aimed at establishing humanity but at establishing an objective discontinuity which may be taken into account in moral discourse. As life itself is a matter of probabilities, as most moral reasoning is an estimate of probabilities, so it seems in accord with the structure of reality and the nature of moral thought to found a moral judgment on the change in probabilities at conception. The appeal to probabilities is the most commonsensical of arguments, to a greater or smaller degree all of us base our actions on probabilities, and in morals, as in law, prudence and negligence are often measured by the account one has taken of the probabilities. If the chance is 200,000,000 to 1 that the movement in the bushes into which you shoot is a man's, I doubt if many persons would hold you careless in shooting; but if the chances are 4 out of 5 that the movement is a human being's, few would acquit you of blame. Would the argument be different if only one out of ten children conceived came to term? Of course this argument would be different. This argument is an appeal to probabilities that actually exist, not to any and all state of affairs which may be imagined.

The probabilities as they do exist do not show the humanity of the embryo in the sense of a demonstration in logic any more than the probabilities of the movement in the bush being a man demonstrate beyond all doubt that the being is a man. The appeal is a "buttressing" consideration, showing the plausibility of the standard adopted. The argument focuses on the decisional factor in any moral judgment and assumes that part of the business of a moralist is drawing lines. One evidence of the nonarbitrary character of the line drawn is the difference of probabilities on either side of it. If a spermatozoon is destroyed, one destroys a being which had a chance of far less than 1 in 200 million of developing into a reasoning being, possessed of the genetic code, a heart and other organs, and capable of pain. If a fetus is destroyed, one destroys a being already possessed of the genetic code, organs, and sensitivity to pain, and one which had an 80 percent chance of developing further into a baby outside the womb who, in time, would reason.

The positive argument for conception as the decisive moment of humanization is that at conception the new being receives the genetic code. It is this genetic information which determines his characteristics, which is the biological carrier of the possibility of human wisdom, which makes him a self-evolving being. A being with a human genetic code is man.

This review of current controversy over the humanity of the fetus emphasizes what a fundamental question the theologians resolved in asserting the inviolability of the fetus. To regard the fetus as possessed of equal rights with other humans was not, however, to decide every case where abortion might be employed. It did decide the case where the argument was that the fetus should be aborted for its own good. To say a being was human was to say it had a destiny to decide for itself which could not be taken from it by another man's decision. But human beings with equal rights often come in conflict with each other, and some decision must be made as whose claims are to prevail. Cases of conflict involving the fetus are different only in two respects: the total inability of the fetus to speak for itself and the fact that the right of the fetus regularly at stake is the right to life itself.

The approach taken by the theologians to these conflicts was articulated in terms of "direct" and "indirect." Again, to look at what they were doing from outside their categories, they may be said to have been drawing lines or "balancing values." "Direct" and "indirect" are spatial metaphors; "line-drawing" is another. "To weigh" or "to balance" values is a metaphor of a more complicated mathematical sort hinting at the process which goes on in moral judgments. All the metaphors suggest that, in the moral judgments made, comparisons were necessary, that no value completely controlled. The principle of double effect was no doctrine fallen from heaven, but a method of analysis appropriate where two relative values were being compared. In Catholic moral theology, as it developed, life even of the innocent was not taken as an absolute. Judgments of acts affecting life issued from a process of weighing. In the weighing, the fetus was always given a value greater than zero, always a value separate and independent from its parents. This valuation was crucial and fundamental in all Christian thought on the subject and marked it off from any approach which considered that only the parents' interests needed to be considered.

Even with the fetus weighed as human, one interest could be weighed as equal or superior: that of the mother in her own life. The casuists between 1450 and 1895 were willing to weigh this interest as superior. Since 1895, that interest was given decisive weight only in the two special cases of the cancerous uterus and the ectopic pregnancy. In both of these cases the fetus itself had little chance of survival even if the abortion were not performed. As the balance was once struck in favor of the mother whenever her life was endangered, it could be so struck again. The balance reached between 1895 and 1930 attempted prudentially and pastorally to forestall a multitude of exceptions for interests less than life.

The perception of the humanity of the fetus and the weighing of fetal rights against other human rights constituted the work of the moral analysts. But what spirit animated their abstract judgments? For the Christian community it was the injunction of Scripture to love your neighbor as yourself. The fetus as human was a neighbor; his life had parity with one's own. The commandment gave life to what otherwise would have been only rational calculation.

The commandment could be put in humanistic as well as theological terms: Do not injure your fellow man without reason. In these terms, once the humanity of the fetus is perceived, abortion is never right except in self-defense. When life must be taken to save life, reason alone cannot say that a mother must prefer a child's life to her own. With this exception, now of great rarity, abortion violates the rational humanist tenet of the equality of human lives.

For Christians the commandment to love had received a special imprint in that the exemplar proposed of love was the love of the Lord for his disciples. In the light given by this example, self-sacrifice carried to the point of death seemed in the extreme situations not without meaning. In the less extreme cases, preference for one's own interests to the life of another seemed to express cruelty or selfishness irreconcilable with the demands of love.

Notes

1. According to Granville Williams (*The Sanctity of Human Life*, p. 193), "The historical reason for the Catholic objection to abortion is the same as for the Christian Church's historical opposition to infanticide: the horror of bringing about the death of an unbaptized child." This statement is made without any citation of evidence. [As previously argued], desire to administer baptism could, in the Middle Ages, even be urged as a reason for procuring an abortion. It is highly regrettable that the American Law Institute was apparently misled by Williams' account and repeated after him the same baseless statement. See American Law Institute, *Model Penal Code: Tentative Draft No. 9* (1959), p. 148, n. 12.

2. Thomas Aquinas gave an analogous reason against baptizing a fetus in the womb: "As long as it exists in the womb of the mother, it cannot be subject to the operation of the ministers of the Church as it is not known to men" (*In sententias Petri Lombardi 4.6* 1.1.2).

A Defense of Abortion[1]

Judith Jarvis Thomson

Most opposition to abortion relies on the premise that the fetus is a human being, a person, from the moment of conception. The premise is argued for, but, as I think, not well. Take, for example, the most common argument. We are asked to notice that the development of a human being from conception through birth into childhood is continuous; then it is said that to draw a line, to choose a point in this development and say "before this point the thing is not a person, after this point it is a person" is to make an arbitrary choice, a choice for which in the nature of things no good reason can be given. It is concluded that the fetus is, or anyway that we had better say it is, a person from the moment of conception. But this conclusion does not follow. Similar things might be said about the development of an acorn into an oak tree, and it does not follow that acorns are oak trees, or that we had better say they are. Arguments of this form are sometimes called "slippery slope arguments"—the phrase is perhaps self-explanatory—and it is dismaying that opponents of abortion rely on them so heavily and uncritically.

I am inclined to agree, however, that the prospects for "drawing a line" in the development of the fetus look dim. I am inclined to think also that we shall probably have to agree that the fetus has already become a human person well before birth. Indeed, it comes as a surprise when one first learns how early in its life it begins to acquire human characteristics. By the tenth week, for example, it already has a face, arms and legs, fingers and toes; it has internal organs, and brain activity is detectable.[2] On the other hand, I think that the premise is false, that the fetus is not a person from the moment of conception. A newly fertilized ovum, a newly implanted clump of cells, is no more a person than an acorn is an oak tree. But I shall not discuss any of this. For it seems to me to be of great interest to ask what happens if, for the sake of argument, we allow the premise. How, precisely, are we supposed to get from there to the conclusion that abortion is morally impermissible? Opponents of abortion commonly spend most of their time establishing that the fetus is a person, and hardly any time explaining the step from there to the impermissibility of abortion. Perhaps they think the step too simple and obvious to require much comment. Or perhaps instead they are simply being economical in argument. Many of those who defend abortion rely on the premise that the fetus is not a person, but only a bit of tissue that will become a person at birth; and why pay out more arguments than you have to? Whatever the explanation, I suggest that the step they take is neither easy nor obvious, that it calls for closer examination than it is commonly given, and that when we do give it this closer examination we shall feel inclined to reject it.

I propose, then, that we grant that the fetus is a person from the moment of conception. How does the argument go from here? Something like this, I take it. Every person has a right to life. So the fetus has a right to life. No doubt the mother has a right to decide what shall happen in and to her body; everyone would grant that. But surely a person's right to life is stronger and more stringent than the mother's right to decide what happens in and to her body, and so outweighs it. So the fetus may not be killed; an abortion may not be performed.

It sounds plausible. But now let me ask you to imagine this. You wake up in the morning and find yourself back to back in bed with an unconscious violinist. A famous unconscious violinist. He has been found to have a fatal kidney ailment, and the Society of Music Lovers has canvassed all the available medical records and found that you alone have the right blood type to help. They have therefore kidnapped you, and last night the violinist's circulatory system was plugged into yours, so that your kidneys can be used to extract poisons from his blood as well as your own. The director of the hospital now tells you, "Look, we're sorry the Society of Music Lovers did this to you—we would never have permitted it if we had known. But still, they did it, and the violinist now is plugged into you. To unplug you would be to kill him. But never mind, it's only for nine months. By then he will have recovered from his ailment, and can safely be unplugged from you." Is it morally incumbent on you to accede to this situation? No doubt it would be very nice of you if you did, a great kindness. But do you *have* to accede to it? What if it were not nine months, but nine years? Or longer still? What if the director of the hospital says, "Tough luck, I agree, but you've now got to stay in bed, with the violinist plugged into you, for the rest of your life. Because remember this. All persons have a right to life, and violinists are persons. Granted you have a right to decide what happens in and to your body, but a person's right to life outweighs your right to decide what happens in and to your body. So you cannot ever be unplugged from him." I imagine you would regard this as outrageous, which suggests that something really is wrong with that plausible-sounding argument I mentioned a moment ago.

In this case, of course, you were kidnapped; you didn't volunteer for the operation that plugged the violinist into your kidneys. Can those who oppose abortion on the ground I mentioned make an exception for a pregnancy due to rape? Certainly. They can say that persons have a right to life only if they didn't come into existence because of rape; or they can say that all persons have a right to life, but that some have less of a right to life than others, in particular, that those who came into existence because of rape have less. But these statements have a rather unpleasant sound. Surely the question of whether you have a right to life at all, or how much of it you have, shouldn't turn on the question of whether or not you are a product of a rape. And in fact the people who oppose abortion on the ground I mentioned do not make this distinction, and hence do not make an exception in case of rape.

Nor do they make an exception for a case in which the mother has to spend the nine months of her pregnancy in bed. They would agree that would be a great pity, and hard on the mother; but all the same, all persons have a right to life, the fetus is a person, and so on. I suspect, in fact, that they would not make an exception for a case in which, miraculously enough, the pregnancy went on for nine years, or even the rest of the mother's life.

Some won't even make an exception for a case in which continuation of the pregnancy is likely to shorten the mother's life; they regard abortion as impermissible even to save the mother's life. Such cases are nowadays very rare, and many opponents of abortion do not accept this extreme view. All the same, it is a good place to begin: a number of points of interest come out in respect to it.

1.

Let us call the view that abortion is impermissible even to save the mother's life "the extreme view." I want to suggest first that it does not issue from the argument I mentioned earlier without the addition of some fairly powerful premises. Suppose a woman has become pregnant, and now learns that she has a cardiac condition such that she will die if she carries the baby to term. What may be done for her? The fetus, being a person, has a right to life, but as the mother is a person too, so has she a right to life. Presumably they have an equal right to life. How is it supposed to come out that an abortion may not be performed? If mother and child have an equal right to life, shouldn't we perhaps flip a coin? Or should we add to the mother's right to life her right to decide what happens in and to her body, which everybody seems to be ready to grant—the sum of her rights now outweighing the fetus's right to life?

The most familiar argument here is the following. We are told that performing the abortion would be directly killing[3] the child, whereas doing nothing would not be killing the mother, but only letting her die. Moreover, in killing the child, one would be killing an innocent person, for the child has committed no crime, and is not aiming at his mother's death. And then there are a variety of ways in which this might be continued. (1) But as directly killing an innocent person is always and absolutely impermissible, an abortion may not be performed. Or, (2) as directly killing an innocent person is murder, and murder is always and absolutely impermissible, an abortion may not be performed.[4] Or, (3) as one's duty to refrain from directly killing an innocent person is more stringent than one's duty to keep a person from dying, an abortion may not be performed. Or, (4) if one's only options are directly killing an innocent person or letting a person die, one must prefer letting the person die, and thus an abortion may not be performed.[5]

Some people seem to have thought that these are not further premises which must be added if the conclusion is to be reached, but that they follow from the very fact that an innocent person has a right to life.[6] But this seems to me to be a mistake, and perhaps the simplest way to show this is to bring out that while we must certainly grant that innocent persons have a right to life, the theses in (1) through (4) are all false. Take (2), for example. If directly killing an innocent person is murder, and thus is impermissible, then the mother's directly killing the innocent person inside her is murder, and thus is impermissible. But it cannot seriously be thought to be murder if the mother performs an abortion on herself to save her life. It cannot seriously be said that she *must* refrain, that she *must* sit passively by and wait for her death. Let us look again at the case of you and the violinist. There you are, in bed with the violinist, and the director of the hospital says to you, "It's all most distressing, and I deeply sympathize, but you see this is putting an additional strain on your kidneys, and you'll be dead within the month. But you *have* to stay where you are all the same. Because unplugging you would be directly killing an innocent violinist, and that's murder, and that's impermissible." If anything in the world is true, it is that you do not commit murder, you do not do what is impermissible, if you reach around to your back and unplug yourself from that violinist to save your life.

The main focus of attention in writings on abortion has been on what a third party may or may not do in answer to a request from a woman for an abortion. This is in a way understandable. Things being as they are, there isn't much a woman can safely do to abort herself. So the question asked is what a third party may do, and what the mother may do, if it is mentioned at all, is deduced, almost as an afterthought, from what it is concluded that third parties may do. But it seems to me that to treat the matter in this way is to refuse to grant to the mother that very status of person which is so firmly insisted on for the fetus. For we cannot simply read off what a person may do from what a third party may do. Suppose you find yourself trapped in a tiny house with a growing child. I mean a very tiny house, and a rapidly growing child—you are already up against the wall of the house and in a few minutes you'll be crushed to death. The child on the other hand won't be crushed to death; if nothing is done to stop him from growing he'll be hurt, but in the end he'll simply burst open the house and walk out a free man. Now I could well understand it if a bystander were to say, "There's nothing we can do for you. We cannot choose between your life and his, we cannot be the ones to decide who is to live, we cannot intervene." But it cannot be concluded that you too can do nothing, that you cannot attack it to save your life. However innocent the child may be, you do not have to wait passively while it crushes you to death. Perhaps a pregnant woman is vaguely felt to have the status of house, to which we don't allow the right of self-defense. But if the woman houses the child, it should be remembered that she is a person who houses it.

I should perhaps stop to say explicitly that I am not claiming that people have a right to do anything whatever to save their lives. I think, rather, that there are drastic limits to the right of self-defense. If someone threatens you with death unless you torture someone else to death, I think you have not the right, even to save your life, to do so. But the case under consideration here is very different. In our case there are only two people involved, one whose life is threatened, and one who threatens it. Both are innocent: the one who is threatened is not threatened because of any fault, the one who threatens does not threaten because of any fault. For this reason we may feel that we bystanders cannot intervene. But the person threatened can.

In sum, a woman surely can defend her life against the threat to it posed by the unborn child, even if doing so involves its death. And this shows not merely that the theses in (1) through (4) are false; it shows also that the extreme view of abortion is false, and so we need not canvass any other possible ways of arriving at it from the argument I mentioned at the outset.

2.

The extreme view could of course be weakened to say that while abortion is permissible to save the mother's life, it may not be performed by a third party, but only by the mother herself. But this cannot be right either. For what we have to keep in mind is that the mother and the unborn child are not like two tenants in a small house which has, by an unfortunate mistake, been rented to both: the mother *owns* the house. The fact that she does adds to the offensiveness of deducing that the mother can do nothing from the supposition that third parties can do nothing. But it does more than this: it casts a bright light on the supposition that third parties can do nothing. Certainly it lets us see that a third party who says "I cannot choose between you" is fooling himself if he thinks this is impartiality. If Jones has found and fastened on a certain coat, which he needs to keep him from freezing, but which Smith also needs to keep him from freezing, then it is not impartiality that says "I cannot choose between you" when Smith owns the coat. Women have said again and again "This body is *my* body!" and they have reason to feel angry, reason to feel that it has been like shouting into the wind. Smith, after all, is hardly likely to bless us if we say to him, "Of course it's your coat, anybody would grant that it is. But no one may choose between you and Jones who is to have it."

We should really ask what it is that says "no one may choose" in the face of the fact that the body that houses the child is the mother's body. It may be simply a failure to appreciate this fact. But it may be something more interesting, namely the sense that one has a right to refuse to lay hands on people, even where it would be just and fair to do so, even where justice seems to require that somebody do so. Thus justice might call for somebody to get Smith's coat back from Jones, and yet you have a right to refuse to be the one to lay hands on Jones, a right to refuse to do physical violence to him. This, I think, must be granted. But then what should be said is not "no one may choose," but only "*I* cannot choose," and indeed not even this, but *I* will not *act*" leaving it open that somebody else can or should, and in particular that anyone in a position of authority, with the job of securing people's rights, both can and should. So this is no difficulty. I have not been arguing that any given third party must accede to the mother's request that he perform an abortion to save her life, but only that he may.

I suppose that in some views of human life the mother's body is only on loan to her, the loan not being one which gives her any prior claim to it. One who held this view might well think it impartiality to say "I cannot choose." But I shall simply ignore this possibility. My own view is that if a human being has any just, prior claim to anything at all, he has a just, prior claim to his own body. And perhaps this needn't be argued for here anyway, since, as I mentioned, the arguments against abortion we are looking at do grant that the woman has a right to decide what happens in and to her body.

But although they do grant it, I have tried to show that they do not take seriously what is done in granting it. I suggest the same thing will reappear even more clearly when we turn away from cases in which the mother's life is at stake, and attend, as I propose we now do, to the vastly more common cases in which a woman wants an abortion for some less weighty reason than preserving her own life.

3.

Where the mother's life is not at stake, the argument I mentioned at the outset seems to have a much stronger pull. "Everyone has a right to life, so the unborn person has a right to life." And isn't the child's right to life weightier than anything other than the mother's own right to life, which she might put forward as ground for an abortion?

This argument treats the right to life as if it were unproblematic. It is not, and this seems to me to be precisely the source of the mistake.

For we should now, at long last, ask what it comes to, to have a right to life. In some views having a right to life includes having a right to be given at least the bare minimum one needs for continued life. But suppose that what in fact *is* the bare minimum a man needs for continued life is something he has no right at all to be given? If I am sick unto death, and the only thing that will save my life is the touch of Henry Fonda's cool hand on my fevered brow, then all the same, I have no right to be given the touch of Henry Fonda's cool hand on my fevered brow. It would be frightfully nice of him to fly in from the West Coast to provide it. It would be less nice, though no doubt well meant, if my friends flew out to the West Coast and carried Henry Fonda back with them. But I have no right at all against anybody that he should do this for me. Or again, to return to the story I told earlier, the fact that for continued life that violinist needs the continued use of your kidneys does not establish that he has a right to be given the continued use of your kidneys. He certainly has no right against you that *you* should give him continued use of your kidneys. For nobody has any right to use your kidneys unless you give him this right— if you do allow him to go on using your kidneys, this is a kindness on your part, and not something he can claim from you as his due. Nor has he any right against anybody else that *they* should give him continued use of your kidneys. Certainly he had no right against the Society of Music Lovers that they should plug him into you in the first place. And if you now start to unplug yourself, having learned that you will otherwise have to spend nine years in bed with him, there is nobody in the world who must try to prevent you, in order to see to it that he is given something he has a right to be given.

Some people are rather stricter about the right to life. In their view, it does not include the right to be given anything, but amounts to, and only to, the right not to be killed by anybody. But here a related difficulty arises. If everybody is to refrain from killing that violinist, then everybody must refrain from doing a great many different sorts of things. Everybody must refrain from slitting his throat, everybody must refrain from shooting him— and everybody must refrain from unplugging you from him. But does he have a right against everybody that they shall refrain from unplugging you from him? To refrain from doing this is to allow him to continue to use your kidneys. It could be argued that he has a right against us that *we* should allow him to continue to use your kidneys. That is, while he had no right against us that we should give him the use of your kidneys, it might be argued that he anyway has a right against us that we shall not now intervene and deprive him of the use of your kidneys. I shall come back to third-party interventions later. But certainly the violinist has no right against you that *you* shall allow him to continue to use your kidneys. As I said, if you do allow him to use them, it is a kindness on your part, and not something you owe him.

The difficulty I point to here is not peculiar to the right of life. It reappears in connection with all the other natural rights, and it is something which an adequate account of rights must deal with. For present purposes it is enough just to draw attention to it. But I would stress that I am not arguing that people do not have a right to life—quite to the contrary, it seems to me that the primary control we must place on the acceptability of an account of rights is that it should turn out in that account to be a truth that all persons have a right to life. I am arguing only that having a right to life does not guarantee having either a right to be given the use of or a right to be allowed continued use of another person's body—even if one needs it for life itself. So the right to life will not serve the opponents of abortion in the very simple and clear way in which they seem to have thought it would.

4.

There is another way to bring out the difficulty. In the most ordinary sort of case, to deprive someone of what he has a right to is to treat him unjustly. Suppose a boy and his small brother are jointly given a box of chocolates for Christmas. If the older boy takes the box and refuses to give his brother any of the chocolates, he is unjust to him, for the brother has been given a right to half of them. But suppose that, having learned that otherwise it means nine years in bed with that violinist, you unplug yourself from him. You surely are not being unjust to him, for you gave him no right to use your kidneys, and no one else can have given him any such right. But we have to notice that in unplugging yourself, you are killing him; and violinists, like everybody else, have a right to life, and thus in the view we were considering just now, the right not to be killed. So here you do what he supposedly has a right you shall not do, but you do not act unjustly to him in doing it.

The emendation which may be made at this point is this: the right to life consists not in the right not to be killed, but rather in the right not to be killed unjustly. This runs a risk of circularity, but never mind: it would enable us to square the fact that the violinist has a right to life with the fact that you do not act unjustly toward him in unplugging yourself, thereby killing him. For if you do not kill him unjustly, you do not violate his right to life, and so it is no wonder you do him no injustice.

But if this emendation is accepted, the gap in the argument against abortion stares us plainly in the face: it is by no means enough to show that the fetus is a person, and to remind us that all persons have a right to life—we need to be shown also that killing the fetus violates its right to life, i.e., that abortion is unjust killing. And is it?

I suppose we may take it as a datum that in a case of pregnancy due to rape the mother has not given the unborn person a right to the use of her body for food and shelter. Indeed, in what pregnancy could it be supposed that the mother has given the unborn person such a right? It is not as if there were unborn persons drifting about the world, to whom a woman who wants a child says "I invite you in."

But it might be argued that there are other ways one can have acquired a right to the use of another person's body than by having been invited to use it by that person. Suppose a woman voluntarily indulges in intercourse, knowing of the chance it will issue in pregnancy, and then she does become pregnant; is she not in part responsible for the presence, in fact the very existence, of the unborn person inside? No doubt she did not invite it in. But doesn't her partial responsibility for its being there itself give it a right to the use of her body?[7] If so, then her aborting it would be more like the boys taking away the chocolates, and less like your unplugging yourself from the violinist— doing so would be depriving it of what it does have a right to, and thus would be doing it an injustice.

And then, too, it might be asked whether or not she can kill it even to save her own life: If she voluntarily called it into existence, how can she now kill it, even in self-defense?

The first thing to be said about this is that it is something new. Opponents of abortion have been so concerned to make out the independence of the fetus, in order to establish that it has a right to life, just as its mother does, that they have tended to overlook the possible support they might gain from making out that the fetus is *dependent* on the mother, in order to establish that she has a special kind of responsibility for it, a responsibility that gives it rights against her which are not possessed by any independent person—such as an ailing violinist who is a stranger to her.

On the other hand, this argument would give the unborn person a right to its mother's body only if her pregnancy resulted from a voluntary act, undertaken in full knowledge of the chance a pregnancy might result from it. It would leave out entirely the unborn person whose existence is due to rape. Pending the availability of some further argument, then, we would be left with the conclusion that unborn persons whose existence is due to rape have no right to the use of their mothers' bodies, and thus that aborting them is not depriving them of anything they have a right to and hence is not unjust killing.

And we should also notice that it is not at all plain that this argument really does go even as far as it purports to. For there are cases and cases, and the details make a difference. If the room is stuffy, and I therefore open a window to air it, and a burglar climbs in, it would be absurd to say, "Ah, now he can stay, she's given him a right to the use of her house—for she is partially responsible for his presence there, having voluntarily done what enabled him to get in, in full knowledge that there are such things as burglars, and that burglars burgle." It would be still more absurd to say this if I had had bars installed outside my windows, precisely to prevent burglars from getting in, and a burglar got in only because of a defect in the bars. It remains equally absurd if we imagine it is not a burglar who climbs in, but an innocent person who blunders or falls in. Again, suppose it were like this: people-seeds drift about in the air like pollen, and if you open your windows, one may drift in and take root in your carpets or upholstery. You don't want children, so you fix up your windows with fine mesh screens, the very best you can buy. As can happen, however, and on very, very rare occasions does happen, one of the screens is defective, and a seed drifts in and takes root. Does the person-plant who now develops have a right to the use of your house? Surely not—despite the fact that you voluntarily opened your windows, you knowingly kept carpets and upholstered furniture, and you knew that screens were sometimes defective. Someone may argue that you are responsible for its rooting, that it does have a right to your house, because after all you could have lived out your life with bare floors and furniture, or with sealed windows and doors. But this won't do —for by the same token anyone can avoid a pregnancy due to rape by having a hysterectomy, or anyway by never leaving home without a (reliable!) army.

It seems to me that the argument we are looking at can establish at most that there are *some* cases in which the unborn person has a right to the use of its mother's body, and therefore *some* cases in which abortion is unjust killing. There is room for much discussion and argument as to precisely which, if any. But I think we should sidestep this issue and leave it open, for at any rate the argument certainly does not establish that all abortion is unjust killing.

5.

There is room for yet another argument here, however. We surely must all grant that there may be cases in which it would be morally indecent to detach a person from your body at the cost of his life. Suppose you learn that what the violinist needs is not nine years of your life, but only one hour: all you need do to save his life is to spend one hour in that bed with him. Suppose also that letting him use your kidneys for that one hour would not affect your health in the slightest. Admittedly you were kidnapped. Admittedly you did not give anyone permission to plug him into you. Nevertheless it seems plain to me you *ought* to allow him to use your kidneys for that hour—it would be indecent to refuse.

Again, suppose pregnancy lasted only an hour, and constituted no threat to life or health. And suppose that a woman becomes pregnant as a result of rape. Admittedly she did not voluntarily do anything to bring about the existence of a child. Admittedly she did nothing at all which would give the unborn person a right to the use of her body. All the same it might well be said, as in the newly amended violinist story, that she *ought* to allow it to remain for that hour—that it would be indecent of her to refuse.

Now some people are inclined to use the term "right" in such a way that it follows from the fact that you ought to allow a person to use your body for the hour he needs, that he has a right to use your body for the hour he needs, even though he has not been given that right by any person or act. They may say that it follows also that if you refuse, you act unjustly toward him. This use of the term is perhaps so common that it cannot be called wrong; nevertheless it seems to me to be an unfortunate loosening of what we would do better to keep a tight rein on. Suppose that box of chocolates I mentioned earlier had not been given to both boys jointly, but was given only to the older boy. There he sits, stolidly eating his way through the box, his small brother watching enviously. Here we are likely to say, "You ought not to be so mean. You ought to give your brother some of those chocolates." My own view is that it just does not follow from the truth of this that the brother has any right to any of the chocolates. If the boy refuses to give his brother any, he is greedy, stingy, callous—but not unjust. I suppose that the people I have in mind will say it does follow that the brother has a right to some of the chocolates, and thus that the boy does act unjustly if he refuses to give his brother any. But the effect of saying this is to obscure what we should keep distinct, namely the difference between the boy's refusal in this case and the boy's refusal in the earlier case, in which the box was given to both boys jointly, and in which the small brother thus had what was from any point of view clear title to half.

A further objection to so using the term "right" that from the fact that A ought to do a thing for B, it follows that B has a right against A that A do it for him, is that it is going to make the question of whether or not a man has a right to a thing turn on how easy it is to provide him with it; and this seems not merely unfortunate, but morally unacceptable. Take the case of Henry Fonda again. I said earlier that I had no right to the touch of his cool hand on my fevered brow, even though I needed it to save my life. I said it would be frightfully nice of him to fly in from the West Coast to provide me with it, but that I had no right against him that he should do so. But suppose he isn't on the West Coast. Suppose he has only to walk across the room, place a hand briefly on my brow—and lo, my life is saved. Then surely he ought to do it, it would be indecent to refuse. Is it to be said, "Ah, well, it follows that in this case she has a right to the touch of his hand on her brow, and so it would be an injustice in him to refuse"? So that I have a right to it when it is easy for him to provide it, though no right when it's hard? It's rather a shocking idea that anyone's rights should fade away and disappear as it gets harder and harder to accord them to him.

So my own view is that even though you ought to let the violinist use your kidneys for the one hour he needs, we should not conclude that he has a right to do so—we should say that if you refuse, you are, like the boy who owns all the chocolates and will give none away, self-centered and callous, indecent in fact, but not unjust. And similarly, that even supposing a case in which a woman pregnant due to rape ought to allow the unborn person to use her body for the hour he needs, we should not conclude that he has a right to do so; we should conclude that she is self-centered, callous, indecent, but not unjust, if she refuses. The complaints are no less grave; they are just different. However, there is no need to insist on this point. If anyone does wish to deduce "he has a right" from "you ought," then all the same he must surely grant that there are cases in which it is not morally required of you that you allow that violinist to use your kidneys, and in which he does not have a right to use them, and in which you do not do him an injustice if you refuse. And so also for mother and unborn child. Except in such cases as the unborn person has a right to demand it—and we were leaving open the possibility that there may be such cases—nobody is morally *required* to make large sacrifices, of health, of all other interests and concerns, of all other duties and commitments, for nine years, or even for nine months, in order to keep another person alive.

6.

We have in fact to distinguish between two kinds of Samaritan: the Good Samaritan and what we might call the Minimally Decent Samaritan. The story of the Good Samaritan, you will remember, goes like this:

> A certain man went down from Jerusalem to Jericho, and fell among thieves, which stripped him of his raiment, and wounded him, and departed, leaving him half dead.
>
> And by chance there came down a certain priest that way: and when he saw him, he passed by on the other side.
>
> And likewise a Levite, when he was at the place, came and looked on him, and passed by on the other side.
>
> But a certain Samaritan, as he journeyed, came where he was; and when he saw him he had compassion on him.
>
> And went to him, and bound up his wounds, pouring in oil and wine, and set him on his own beast, and brought him to an inn, and took care of him.
>
> And on the morrow, when he departed, he took out two pence, and gave them to the host, and said unto him, "Take care of him; and whatsoever thou spendest more, when I come again, I will repay thee." (Luke 10:30–35)

The Good Samaritan went out of his way, at some cost to himself, to help one in need of it. We are not told what the options were, that is, whether or not the priest and the Levite could have helped by doing less than the Good Samaritan did, but assuming they could have, then the fact they did nothing at all shows they were not even Minimally Decent Samaritans, not because they were not Samaritans, but because they were not even minimally decent.

These things are a matter of degree, of course, but there is a difference, and it comes out perhaps most clearly in the story of Kitty Genovese, who, as you will remember, was murdered while thirty-eight people watched or listened, and did nothing at all to help her. A Good Samaritan would have rushed out to give direct assistance against the murderer. Or perhaps we had better allow that it would have been a Splendid Samaritan who did this, on the ground that it would have involved a risk of death for himself. But the thirty-eight not only did not do this, they did not even trouble to pick up a phone to call the police. Minimally Decent Samaritanism would call for doing at least that, and their not having done it was monstrous.

After telling the story of the Good Samaritan, Jesus said, "Go, and do thou likewise." Perhaps he meant that we are morally required to act as the Good Samaritan did. Perhaps he was urging people to do more than is morally required of them. At all events it seems plain that it was not morally required of any of the thirty-eight that he rush out to give direct assistance at the risk of his own life, and that it is not morally required of anyone that he give long stretches of his life—nine years or nine months—to sustaining the life of a person who has no special right (we were leaving open the possibility of this) to demand it.

Indeed, with one rather striking class of exceptions, no one in any country in the world is *legally* required to do anywhere near as much as this for anyone else. The class of exceptions is obvious. My main concern here is not the state of the law in respect to abortion, but it is worth drawing attention to the fact that in no state in this country is any man compelled by law to be even a Minimally Decent Samaritan to any person; there is no law under which charges could be brought against the thirty-eight who stood by while Kitty Genovese died. By contrast, in most states in this country women are compelled by law to be not merely Minimally Decent Samaritans, but Good Samaritans to unborn persons inside them. This doesn't by itself settle anything one way or the other, because it may well be argued that there should be laws in this country—as there are in many European countries—compelling at least Minimally Decent Samaritanism.[8] But it does show that there is a gross injustice in the existing state of the law. And it shows also that the groups currently working against liberalization of abortion laws, in fact working toward having it declared unconstitutional for a state to permit abortion, had better start working for the adoption of Good Samaritan laws generally, or earn the charge that they are acting in bad faith.

I should think, myself, that Minimally Decent Samaritan laws would be one thing, Good Samaritan laws quite another, and in fact highly improper. But we are not here concerned with the law. What we should ask is not whether anybody should be compelled by law to be a Good Samaritan, but whether we must accede to a situation in which somebody is being compelled—by nature, perhaps—to be a Good Samaritan. We have, in other words, to look now at third-party interventions. I have been arguing that no person is morally required to make large sacrifices to sustain the life of another who has no right to demand them, and this even where the sacrifices do not include life itself; we are not morally required to be Good Samaritans or anyway Very Good Samaritans to one another. But what if a man cannot extricate himself from such a situation? What if he appeals to us to extricate him? It seems to me plain that there are cases in which we can, cases in which a good Samaritan would extricate him. There you are, you were kidnapped, and nine years in bed with that violinist lie ahead of you. You have your own life to lead. You are sorry, but you simply cannot see giving up so much of your life to the sustaining of his. You cannot extricate yourself, and ask us to do so. I should have thought that—in light of his having no right to the use of your body—it was obvious that we do not have to accede to your being forced to give up so much. We can do what you ask. There is no injustice to the violinist in our doing so.

7.

Following the lead of the opponents of abortion, I have throughout been speaking of the fetus merely as a person, and what I have been asking is whether or not the argument we began with, which proceeds only from the fetus's being a person, really does establish its conclusion. I have argued that it does not.

But of course there are arguments and arguments, and it may be said that I have simply fastened on the wrong one. It may be said that what is important is not merely the fact that the fetus is a person, but that it is a person for whom the woman has a special kind of responsibility issuing from the fact that she is its mother. And it might be argued that all my analogies are therefore irrelevant—for you do not have that special kind of responsibility for that violinist, Henry Fonda does not have that special kind of responsibility for me. And our attention might be drawn to the fact that men and women both *are* compelled by law to provide support for their children.

I have in effect dealt (briefly) with this argument in section 4 above; but a (still briefer) recapitulation now may be in order. Surely we do not have any such "special responsibility" for a person unless we have assumed it, explicitly or implicitly. If a set of parents do not try to prevent pregnancy, do not obtain an abortion, but rather take it home with them, then they have assumed responsibility for it, they have given it rights, and they cannot *now* withdraw support from it at the cost of its life because they now find it difficult to go on providing for it. But if they have taken all reasonable precautions against having a child, they do not simply by virtue of their biological relationship to the child who comes into existence have a special responsibility for it. They may wish to assume responsibility for it, or they may not wish to. And I am suggesting that if assuming responsibility for it would require large sacrifices, then they may refuse. A Good Samaritan would not refuse—or anyway, a Splendid Samaritan, if the sacrifices that had to be made were enormous. But then so would a Good Samaritan assume responsibility for that violinist; so would Henry Fonda, if he is a Good Samaritan, fly in from the West Coast and assume responsibility for me.

8.

My argument will be found unsatisfactory on two counts by many of those who want to regard abortion as morally permissible. First, while I do argue that abortion is not impermissible, I do not argue that it is always permissible. There may well be cases in which carrying the child to term requires only Minimally Decent Samaritanism of the mother, and this is a standard we must not fall below. I am inclined to think it a merit of my account precisely that it does *not* give a general yes or a general no. It allows for and supports our sense that, for example, a sick and desperately frightened fourteen-year-old schoolgirl, pregnant due to rape, may *of course* choose abortion, and that any law which rules this out is an insane law. And it also allows for and supports our sense that in other cases resort to abortion is even positively indecent. It would be indecent in the woman to request an abortion, and indecent in a doctor to perform it, if she is in her seventh month, and wants the abortion just to avoid the nuisance of postponing a trip abroad. The very fact that the arguments I have been drawing attention to treat all cases of abortion, or even all cases of abortion in which the mother's life is not at stake, as morally on a par ought to have made them suspect at the outset.

Second, while I am arguing for the permissibility of abortion in some cases, I am not arguing for the right to secure the death of the unborn child. It is easy to confuse these two things in that up to a certain point in the life of the fetus it is not able to survive outside the mother's body; hence removing it from her body guarantees its death. But they are importantly different. I have argued that you are not morally required to spend nine months in bed, sustaining the life of that violinist; but to say this is by no means to say that if, when you unplug yourself, there is a miracle and he survives, you then have a right to turn round and slit his throat. You may detach yourself even if this costs him his life; you have no right to be guaranteed his death, by some other means, if unplugging yourself does not kill him. There are some people who will feel dissatisfied by this feature of my argument. A woman may be utterly devastated by the thought of a child, a bit of herself, put out for adoption and never seen or heard of again. She may therefore want not merely that the child be detached from her, but more, that it die. Some opponents of abortion are inclined to regard this as beneath contempt—thereby showing insensitivity to what is surely a powerful source of despair. All the same, I agree that the desire for the child's death is not one which anybody may gratify, should it turn out to be possible to detach the child alive.

At this place, however, it should be remembered that we have only been pretending throughout that the fetus is a human being from the moment of conception. A very early abortion is surely not the killing of a person, and so is not dealt with by anything I have said here.

Notes

1. I am very much indebted to James Thomson for discussion, criticism, and many helpful suggestions.

2. Daniel Callahan, *Abortion: Law, Choice and Morality* (New York, 1970), p. 373. This book gives a fascinating survey of the available information on abortion. The Jewish tradition is surveyed in David M. Feldman, *Birth Control in Jewish Law* (New York, 1968). Part 5, the Catholic tradition in John T. Noonan, Jr., "An Almost Absolute Value in History," in *The Morality of Abortion,* ed. John T. Noonan, Jr. (Cambridge, Mass., 1970).

3. The term "direct" in the arguments I refer to is a technical one. Roughly, what is meant by "direct killing" is either killing as an end in itself, or killing as a means to some end, for example, the end of saving someone else's life. See note 6, below, for an example of its use.

4. Cf. *Encyclical Letter of Pope Pius XI on Christian Marriage,* St. Paul Editions (Boston, n.d.), p. 32: "However much we may pity the mother whose health and even life is gravely imperiled in the performance of the duty allotted to her by nature, nevertheless what could ever be a sufficient reason for excusing in any way the direct murder of the innocent? This is precisely what we are dealing with here." Noonan (*The Morality of Abortion*, p. 43) reads this as follows: "What cause can ever avail to excuse in any way the direct killing of the innocent? For it is a question of that."

5. The thesis in (4) is in an interesting way weaker than those in (1), (2), and (3): they rule out abortion even in cases in which both mother *and* child will die if the abortion is not performed. By contrast, one who held the view expressed in (4) could consistently say that one needn't prefer letting two persons die to killing one.

6. Cf. the following passage from Pius XII, *Address to the Italian Catholic Society of Midwives:* "The baby in the maternal breast has the right to life immediately from God.—Hence there is no man, no human authority, no science, no medical, eugenic, social, economic or moral 'indication' which can establish or grant a valid juridical ground for a direct deliberate disposition of an innocent human life, that is a disposition which looks to its destruction either as an end or as a means to another end perhaps in itself not illicit.—The baby, still not born, is a man in the same degree and for the same reason as the mother" (quoted in Noonan, *The Morality of Abortion,* p. 45).

7. The need for a discussion of this argument was brought home to me by members of the Society for Ethical and Legal Philosophy, to whom this paper was originally presented.

8. For a discussion of the difficulties involved, and a survey of the European experience with such laws, see *The Good Samaritan and the Law,* ed. James M. Ratcliffe (New York, 1966).

The Abortion Debate in the Twenty-First Century

Michael Boylan

Very few conversations in the public arena have had such a long life with so little agreement to show for it as the abortion debate. This essay does not intend to settle the issue in a manner that everyone will accept but to outline a way to view the problem so that each person may develop a universal moral theory and a linking principle to resolve this problem.[1] I suggest that the means for doing so lies in the Personal Worldview Imperative: "All people must develop a single comprehensive and internally coherent worldview that is good and that we strive to act out in our daily lives."[2]

To this end, I present my argument in the following way. First, I review some of the history of the debate. Next, I critically examine the key premises in a version of the arguments from each side. Finally, I suggest a way to think about the problem that does not force a single solution on the reader but suggests a way to frame the problem so that each reader might determine his or her own universal maxim.

THE HISTORY OF THE DEBATE

One can summarize the debate over abortion as being between two camps, proabortion and antiabortion.

THE PROABORTION POSITION[3]

1. A woman's body is her own—assertion.
2. Whatever is one's own is under her discretion to dispose of at will—fact.

---

[1]I define a *linking principle* as one that follows from a moral theory but that is "action guiding" in its application. One example of a linking principle is precautionary reason presented in the article by Deryck Beyleveld and Shaun Pattinson (p. 39).

[2]An argument for the Personal Worldview Imperative is given in the Introduction of *Basic Ethics* and in an abbreviated form in Chapter One of this volume.

[3]Obviously, no single argument represents either position entirely. There are, in fact, many distinct arguments for the conclusion that abortion is or is not permissible. My reconstructions here are meant to represent my opinion about the strongest version of each argument in a simple, generic form.

3. A woman's body is under her discretion to dispose of at will—1, 2.
4. The fetus is wholly dependent on the woman's body (at least through most of the first two trimesters of pregnancy)—fact.
5. That which is wholly dependent on one's body is (baring any other intervening duties) wholly under one's discretion to dispose of at will—assertion.
6. The fetus inside a woman is hers to dispose of at will—3–5.
7. To abort a fetus is to remove it from one's body—fact.
8. Removing a fetus from a mother's body will, in most cases, cause it to be biologically nonfunctional—fact.
9. To abort a fetus is to cause it to be biologically nonfunctional—7, 8.
10. Removing something from one's body (which is at one's disposal, at will) is permissible—2, 3.

---

11. Removing the fetus from a woman's body is permissible even if such removal renders the fetus biologically nonfunctional—6, 9, 10.

THE ANTIABORTION POSITION

1. From the moment of conception, there is a person—assertion.
2. All persons should be accorded full human rights—fact.
3. To kill an innocent human agent at will is impermissible—fact (generally accepted by most moral theories).
4. A fetus is an innocent human agent—assertion.
5. To kill a fetus is impermissible—1–4.
6. All morally impermissibly acts should be sanctioned by society as impermissible—fact.
7. Abortion kills the fetus—fact.

---

8. Abortion is impermissible and should be considered by society as impermissible—5–7.

Obviously, a tremendous gap exists between these two arguments. To properly review an ethical argument, I believe that we must assess the worldview(s) of those who make such arguments. Let us examine some aspects of the worldviews to which each side subscribes and then turn to key premises in the preceding arguments and other classic renditions of the argument. To make the worldview of each group understandable and sympathetic, I adopt the persona of an advocate of each as I encourage each of you to explore these worldviews to evaluate what positive and negative points they offer.

The Worldviews of Proabortionists

I believe that much of the power of proabortionists' argument is tied to (1) the unequal consequences that women face in sexual relations, (2) the issue of personal autonomy, and (3) the general societal repression of women. Let us examine these in order.

1. A consequence of a woman engaging in sexual intercourse is the possibility of a pregnancy. A man can engage in intercourse as often as he chooses, but he will never become pregnant. He can (if he is a purely egoistic sort of fellow) walk away when his sexual partner becomes pregnant. Although the consequence of their action is just as much his responsibility as it is hers, only she will have to bear the physical results of their joint behavior. This is unfair. If both the man and woman engaged in an action *jointly*, then they should have to bear the consequences jointly. History has shown, however, that has not always been the case. In fact, some have speculated that the entire institution of marriage evolved solely to protect women from this brute inequality.

Why should men not have to suffer the consequences? The large number of single mothers around the world who must raise families is a testament to the brute inequality of the biological scenario that some sociobiologists have termed a battle of genetic strategies, which suggests that all organisms have a single biological imperative: to send their genes into future filial generations. The best strategy for a man is to inseminate as many women as possible, hoping that some of these actions will result in pregnancies and thus fulfill his biological imperative.

The best strategy for a woman is to be very selective and to try to obtain a commitment from the biological father to assist her because a pregnant woman loses a proverbial step or two in competing for food and shelter. Also, when the child is born, the woman needs to nurse it for at least six months and needs some protection.

If this scenario has any truth to it, the brute biological reproductive strategies of men and women clearly differ. For thousands of years, a mistake on the part of women in the execution of their strategy has had far more deleterious consequences than any failures on the part of men.

Many women often see as a curiosity the fact that some of the most vocal critics of women and their reproductive decisions are men (who bear no biological consequences for their actions: "It is easy for *you* to say . . .").

Thus, I believe that it is fairly clear why women would want the same *option* as men have to be able to walk away from an unfortunate sexual relationship.

Some critics say that men and women ought to face equal consequences. However, how are such consequences to be enforced? Even in the United States (which aspires to be a nation under law), we have not been able to make divorced fathers and men who abandon their reproductive partner pay legally sanctioned child support. How can we ever realistically aspire to make men pay the same price that women pay for the consequences of sexual intercourse?

2. The issue of autonomy relates to the ownership of one's own body. All things equal, it is difficult to know who would own your body except yourself.[4] This means that whatever you own is yours (unless some intervening duty can be proven). If you want to tattoo yourself, put piercing rings in various places, or cut off a limb, it is your privilege to do so because whatever is entirely yours is at your disposal. Thus, if you do not choose to use your body as a growth chamber for an embryo, you need not do it. It is your body to do with as you wish.

3. The general station of women in this society, as in most societies in history, has been as a repressed and enslaved group. This is a broad, sociological statement. This does not mean that there are not individual men who are sensitive and nurturing of their spouses, daughters, and women in general. One need only engage in some volunteer work with women's shelters and other facilities that deal with those in need, however, to recognize the truth of this generalization. Despite all our laws and aspirations as a society, women are treated differently from men. This difference is an added hurdle that women must overcome but that men do not face.

To make the point more clearly, women are the oppressed gender. For men to say to women that they must abide by laws enacted by men that constrict their reproductive freedom (so that they might not be as free as men) is an act of political enslavement. In this way, *freedom of choice* is essential, not the actual execution of an act of abortion. Most women would never want to have an abortion and will never have an abortion. Many women will even carry an impaired infant to term rather than abort it. Nonetheless, despite the fact that most women will never take advantage of the right of abortion (within the United States and a number of other countries), it is important to maintain the freedom of choice.

This freedom of choice is a cornerstone in the edifice that stands against gender enslavement. The struggle of oppressed women demands that they

---

[4]There are at least two objectors to this position. First, to say that one "owns" one's body splits the person in two. There is no proper distinction between one's self and one's body; they are one and the same. Thus, all metaphors of ownership are faulty and do not fit legal notions of ownership. For a statement of this position, see Hugh V. McLachlan, "Bodies Rights and Abortion," *Journal of Medical Ethics,* 23, no. 3 (1997): 176–80. Second, those who accept a theology that posits an all powerful creator God—such as Judaism, Christianity, and Islam (a sizable portion of the world's population)—will demur on this point since it is dogma that God created everything and therefore "owns" what she/he/it has created. In this case, one's body is not one's own but God's. This tenet can have an effect on the argument.

not be subjected to the will of men on something so essential to their biological nature as their reproductive equality. The ability to choose to terminate a pregnancy is merely one part of a very large structure. Not very long ago women who had to pay for the outcomes of their loving relationships were relegated to unlicensed physicians who used dirty tools and whose rates of sepsis was exceeded only by their blood-alcohol levels.[5]

The image of a woman alone, abandoned by her partner and by society, resonates with most women (even if they feel that such a situation will never happen to them). It is a there but for the grace of God, go I scenario. For this reason, most women feel solidarity for their sisters in need and strive to protect them from a solitary journey into hell.

The freedom of choice is an important symbol as a balance against gender oppression.

The Worldviews of Antiabortionists

The second group views reality much differently. To begin with, this group has a very strong belief in relatively unencumbered free will. Each person can act as she pleases without much real perturbation. This means all consequences are deserved. The idea that one gender is oppressed is viewed in several ways by different sides.

1. First, the group believes that this issue revolves around the female sex, which is already protected and is given more than ample opportunities in society. This group might say that a woman today has advantages in job searches over men because all she needs to have is a skill level that approaches a man's level and she will be automatically hired.

2. This group believes that sexual intercourse is an activity given by God for the creation of children. When people go against the laws of God, they must be prepared to accept the consequences. They consider abortion to be an easy way out. This group might say that living with a few more unfortunate consequences in life would be good for most of these unrelated young people.

3. The third perspective held by this group is more profound. It asserts that human life is precious and that everything should be done to preserve the life of the unborn, which cannot protect themselves.

When someone is impaired, s/he needs the protection and support of others. A fetus is in a similar position, but the impairment is not due to a defect

---

[5]For a description of these times, see Leslie J. Reagan, *When Abortion Was a Crime: Women, Medicine, and Law in the United States, 1867–1973* (Berkeley CA: University of California Press, 1997).

in the genotype or in development but is a natural consequence of the current biological stage of this individual. All other things being equal, this embryo will become a human agent capable of reason and of action. This is an acceptance of the normal process of nature.

According to the doctrine of *novus actus interveniens*, the normal process of nature is taken to be the standard. This doctrine, which is well entrenched in the law,[6] states that a person who interferes with the normal operation of nature is responsible for all the ensuing consequences. For example, John is robbing a bank and says to the teller, "If you move, I'll shoot." The teller moves slightly as she presses the alarm button with her foot. The bank robber shoots, and his bullet ricochets off one of the iron bars of the teller's cage and lodges in the neck of a person standing in line behind the gunman.

Who caused the person to be shot? If one holds the inciting incident theory of causation (which is often considered definitive in the philosophy of science), then the teller is to blame. But this is ridiculous. The gunman put the teller into an abnormal situation. The gunman with his gun and his demands had changed the natural order. Thus, according to the doctrine of *novus actus interveniens*, the gunman, not the teller, is at fault for the bullet in the customer's neck because the gunman charged the natural order, and thus all ensuing events (in an appropriately fashioned action description) can be attributed to him.

How does this apply to abortion? The natural order would have the fetus grow and develop in the normal process. Any action that stops this process is considered to be causally responsible for the fetus's demise. If the fetus is a person, then the action is murder. Thus, abortion is murder.

If you were part of a society that institutionalized murder and did nothing to change the situation, then you would be considered an accessory to the murder. Thus, to live in a society that permits abortion and to do nothing to stop it is to be like someone who lived in the societies of Hitler, Stalin, or Pol Pot or in the world at large and could have reacted in some meaningful way to these dictators' actions but did not.

We in the United States have created a society that legalizes the continued killing of thousands of fetuses every year. If these fetuses are humans, are we not then guilty of mass murder? Is our society comparable to the murdering societies of history? Is this not cause enough to prohibit abortion now?

A CRITICAL EXAMINATION OF THE PREMISES OF EACH SIDE

The preceding section presented a version of the pro and con arguments and explored in brief the worldviews of each side. Let us begin here by defining what I mean by *abortion*, which is the removal of a fetus from the female by

---

[6]H.L.A. Hart and A.M. Honoré, *Causation in the Law* (Oxford: Clarendon Press, 1959), pp. 129 ff.; compare with 127, 292–96.

natural or artificial means. The natural abortion is called *spontaneous abortion* and occurs in 20 to 25 percent of all pregnancies (depending on how one frames the data). Most spontaneous abortions, also called miscarriages, occur during the first trimester of pregnancy generally because the developing embryo is malformed. The miscarriage is nature's way of ensuring that potential children with no real chance of survival are given an exit at the beginning of life's journey.

Artificial abortion is the removal of a fetus from the female by medical means. The process of abortion does *not* kill that fetus. As a matter of fact, many embryos removed from the female do die. They do not die just because they are removed from the mother. If equipment such as an artificial womb were available, an embryo removed from a woman could continue to gestate, and would not necessarily die. All this is to say that if there is a right to abortion, it is a right to remove the fetus from a woman's body. But killing the fetus is not a right. If the fetus, for example, were able to be preserved, abortion would be a separate issue from that of what to do with that fetus.[7] One could remove the fetus and allow it to develop without any further contact with its biological mother. The right to abortion, *simpliciter,* is a right to remove a fetus from one's body. This follows from the sample argument and the worldview enhancement necessary to accept that argument. Therefore, the abortion issue changes drastically after the point of viability. In theory, one might be able to remove the fetus from the female and raise it separately. In this case, removing a fetus would not be tantamount to causing it to die.

Having clarified the definition of abortion, let us turn to a few key premises in the arguments on each side. First is the proabortion position as represented by the generic argument I presented. The argument given the worldview background is very persuasive. Detractors are likely to focus on premise 5: That which is wholly dependent on one's body is (baring any other intervening duties) wholly under one's discretion to dispose of at will—assertion.

The logical move is from autonomy over one's own body part to sovereignty over entities dependent on one's body. This is an argument that Judith Jarvis Thomson elaborates in her famous article.[8] Deontologists might object to a blanket endorsement of this position. It seems to violate the "duty

---

[7]In this case, the state would enter the equation as an interested party to govern the interests of the newly born, premature infant.

[8]Judith Jarvis Thomson, "A Defense of Abortion," *Philosophy and Public Affairs* 1 (1971): 47–66. This article has had enormous response. Some of the most interesting of these include Robert N. Wennberg, *Life in the Balance: Exploring the Abortion Controversy* (Grand Rapids, MI: Eerdmans, 1985); John T. Wilcox, "Nature as Demonic in Thomson's Defense of Abortion," in *The Ethics of Abortion: Pro-Life vs. Pro-Choice,* ed. Robert M. Baird and Stuart E. Rosenbaum, rev. ed. (Buffalo, NY: Prometheus, 1993): 212–25; Mary Anne Warren, "On the Moral and Legal Status of Abortion," in *Arguing about Abortion,* ed. Lewis M. Schwartz (Belmont, MA: Wadsworth, 1993), pp. 227–34; Keith J. Pavlischek, "Abortion Logic and Paternal Responsibility: One More Look at Judith Thomson's 'A Defense of Abortion,' " *Public Affairs Quarterly* 7 (1993): 341–61; David Boonin-Vail, "A Defense of 'A Defense of Abortion': On the Responsibility Objection to Thomson's Argument," *Ethics* 107 (January 1997): 286–313.

to rescue," which is a moral obligation to aid another when the other person's basic goods of agency are threatened so long as doing so does not cause the rescuer to risk his or her own basic goods of agency.[9] The duty to rescue is supported by Kant, Gewirth, and Donagan.[10] For example, in the case of Kitty Genovese (which Thomson cites), the apartment dwellers watching her being attacked and killed could have screamed from their windows at the attacker or called the police or both. I can attest from personal experience that this is an effective way to thwart a criminal in the inner city. Thus, if a person can aid another whose basic goods of agency are being threatened without risking his own basic goods of agency, then he is obliged to do so. This is a little different from the depiction given by Thomson. She says that a person is not obliged to go out and confront the attacker but that a person who does is a Good Samaritan. This implies that there are only two responses to the Kitty Genovese case—either fight or flight. This is too simple, however. Surely everyone is obliged to aid another when doing so does not risk his or her own basic goods of agency. But what of abortion?

Is abortion properly analogous to one of these options in the Kitty Genovese example: (a) calling the police and yelling from their windows or (b) leaving the apartment complex to physically stop the assailant? Option (a), involves merely fulfilling a moral duty, which does not deserve praise but a mere statement of gratitude. Option (b) involves risking basic goods of agency, which could result in death. People choosing option (b) are heroes. Is the woman who chooses to carry a fetus to term more like the person doing her duty or the hero? The answer to this question can be an important component in evaluating this argument.

Returning to premise 5, we can also note that what one does to one's own body and what one does to entities that are not part of one's body are different. We pay no mind to eliminating bacteria, viruses, cysts, and growths. They are not of our body and have no intrinsic worth, nor would a reasonable interpretation of precautionary reasoning dictate that they have any worth.[11]

---

[9]The reason for this caveat is that a person is not *obliged* ever to risk his or her own basic goods of agency for the sake of another. To do so would be to admit that the other person has more of a right to the basic goods of agency than the rescuer. This would entail the other person being better *qua* an agent than the rescuer. There is no support for such an assertion under the deontological theories I am citing since all agents are equally entitled to the basic goods of agency simply by being human beings alive on this earth. Those who choose to risk their own basic goods of agency for the sake of others go "above and beyond" their moral duty (i.e., they are heroes). But one who fulfills only his or her duty to save another when his or her basic goods of agency are not at risk is only an ordinary person doing his or her duty.

[10]Immanuel Kant, *Grundlegung zur Metaphysik der sitten*, vol. 4, Prussian Academy edition (Berlin: G. Reimer, 1903), p. 421; Alan Gewirth, "Replies to My Critics," in *Gewirth's Ethical Rationalism: Critical Essays with a Reply by Alan Gewirth*, ed. Edward Regis Jr. (Chicago: University of Chicago Press, 1984), pp. 228–29; Alan Donagan, *The Theory of Morality* (Chicago: University of Chicago Press, 1977), pp. 154ff.

[11]Derek Beyleveld and Shaun Pattinson, "Precautionary Reasoning as a Link to Moral Action," p. 41ff.

A fetus is certainly different, however; it will, all things being equal, develop into a moral agent who has absolute rights to freedom and well-being. Thus, the argument for potentiality is not wholly without merit. Although the fetus is not actually a person in the strong sense of the word, it is a *potential* person. This potentiality of personhood is not trivial and cannot be dismissed.

Next, let us examine the antiabortion position as represented by the generic argument as I presented it. Given its worldview background, the argument is very persuasive. Detractors are likely to focus on premise 3: To kill an innocent human agent at will is impermissible—fact (generally accepted by most ethical theories). Some would want to discuss the nature of "innocence." Is the word an absolute term (i.e., in no way deserves to die) or relative to the action description at hand (i.e, is in no way threatening the life of any other agent—knowingly or unknowingly).[12] The first sense is rather silly as depicted because it presupposes many unstated propositions that would need to be argued and defended. The second sense, on the other hand, has merit. *Innocent* in this reading implies that a person is not materially involved in the loss of fundamental rights of agency for another (intended or otherwise).

For example, consider the deer hunter who shoots another person thinking she was a deer. That person being shot at could justifiably kill the person who is shooting at her. (We assume that the only way to stop the shooting is to use lethal force.[13]) Under this reading, the unwitting hunter is not innocent but is materially guilty because he jeopardizes the life of another.

Under this definition, a person may be innocent only if she is not materially threatening the life of another.[14] Thus, killing a fetus that threatens the life of its mother is not a case of killing an innocent.

Let us explore the word *threatens,* which has many meanings. One meaning is a danger to the mother's life. A fetus (without motive) may be the cause of its mother's death. Another meaning refers to ripping apart the worldview in which the pregnant woman lives. This threatens her because it challenges everything that she holds as precious in her life plan (stated or only imagined). This is not trivial. People kill themselves for as much because threats to one's worldview are very serious. Contained within one's worldview is the very ground of personal well-being. A threat to worldview, in this fundamental interpretation, can be ranked after life itself as the most potent of threats. Thus, when an individual engages in protecting her fundamental worldview, she is entitled to use extreme measures. This can include

---

[12]I discuss what I mean by "action description" in the Introduction to *Basic Ethics.*

[13]The proportionality of "threat" to "minimal response necessary to alleviate the threat" is very important in cases of self-defense. However, in the instance of abortion, the response (abortion) will have a fixed effect (the death of the fetus) until near the end of the second trimester. In this case, the only variable is the level of threat. After viability, of course, the situation changes if there is a policy to use an abortion procedure that seeks to preserve the fetus's life.

[14]Alan Donagan makes a similar distinction; see *The Theory of Morality* (Chicago: University of Chicago Press, 1977), pp. 87ff.

harming materially innocent agents in order to protect this fundamental worldview.

The story is not so simple, however. One's worldview is comprised of various elements—not all of which are of equal importance and weight. This means that the level of threat is variable as is the appropriate response to the threat. Is this a question of balance?

It is always a question of balancing. The difference between theories that explicitly balance—Utilitarianism, Intuitionism, and Virtue Ethics—and those that are often depicted as nonbalancing (such as deontology) is that the former group balances at the back end, that is, at the moment of decision.

Deontological theories also balance, but they aspire to balance at the front end, that is, in the depiction of the act to be judged. An individual seeks balance in judging what type of action is involved. Forming an action description is not value neutral but involves balancing competing understandings of what is happening (i.e., what is relevant). Thus, there is always balancing. The issue is what drives the decision making. I suggest that what drives the decision making ought to be the Personal Worldview Imperative. The consistency portion of this imperative requires a person to treat all cases alike and create rules that do not contradict each other and fulfill the aspirations of that ethical theory.

Thus, one must define what "threatens" his worldview. For example, when I was a track runner, a very talented runner in our club had the potential to be an Olympic runner. He had joined the club because it had four other runners who were favorites to make the 1976 Olympic team. The only problem was that this runner never finished a race in the four years I ran with the club. Something would always get in the way. Either his splits were not exactly as he had wanted them to be, a black bird flew over the track (he hated black birds), he thought he heard someone yelling something at him, or the humidity suddenly changed, and so forth. Surely, although these distractions were real and important to him, the rest of us ultimately viewed them as trivial. The same is true for some meanings of *threaten*. What is a legitimate meaning of the word? To make this point more effectively, let me contrast seven reasons for an abortion that women might consider threats to themselves.[15]

A. Ms. A is pregnant. It has been determined that if she were to bring this fetus to term, she will die. She feels threatened because her life is in danger.

---

[15]These cases are not meant to be comprehensive but merely suggestive of certain levels of threat. The cases assume only willing sexual intercourse. I would characterize all nonvoluntary acts of sexual intercourse (such as rape or incest) as creating a very high sense of threat for the woman, which might be characterized as being between "A" and "B." In this case, carrying the fetus (as innocent as it may be) constantly reinforces the horror and degradation of the initial act. This humiliation is a primary threat to human action and well-being so that the woman would be fully within her rights to remove the fetus from her body at any time.

B. Ms. B is pregnant. She is a married mother of five children with very little financial means. If she carries this fetus to term, her other five children will be pushed over the edge of starvation. Ms. B feels threatened because the lives of her other children are at stake.

C. Ms. C is pregnant. She is married, and her obstetrician has told her that the baby she is carrying has a fatal disease that will kill the child by the age of six. The death will be painful. Medical science might find a cure for this disease, but probably not in time to save her child. Ms. C feels threatened on behalf of her unborn child.

D. Ms. D is pregnant. She is "thirty-something," single, and in a career that is just about to take off. Her profession is so competitive and limited that it is reasonable to assume that if she misses this opportunity, she will never have another one. Ms. D feels threatened because her career and personal life plan are at stake.

E. Ms. E is pregnant. She is a high school senior who has been admitted to a very selective college. Her college admission might not be renewable if she does not attend this fall. Her parents would be furious if they knew she is pregnant. Her whole future is at stake, her plans did not include a pregnancy. She could not be a good mother at this point in her life. Ms. E feels threatened because her future and her reputation are at stake.

F. Ms. F is pregnant. She is married and has decided that she would like to have a boy and a girl. She already has the girl and amniocentesis has indicated that this fetus is also a girl. She and her husband do not want to have more than two children because it is not part of their life plan. Ms. F feels threatened because she has a girl within her when she wanted a boy.

G. Ms. G is pregnant. She is married and has decided that she would like a male child who is intelligent and has the physical features that she believes represent the perfect child: blonde hair, blue eyes, 6 feet in height, and intelligence capable of scoring 1,500+ on the SATs. Assume that a battery of tests can predict a genotype that is most compatible with the desired phenotype/developmental end product. Ms. G's test results indicate that her fetus is deficient in several areas: several shades of brown hair seem likely, brown eyes, height of slightly less than 6 feet, and intelligence capability of scoring only 1200 on the SAT. Ms. G feels threatened because she has a fetus that will not meet her standard for the child she really wants.

Each of these scenarios illustrates a threat on a sliding scale. If a person is entitled to kill an otherwise innocent agent who is materially guilty because it threatens her, then it is important to create a line that separates acceptable threats from unacceptable threats.

Case A involves a pure sense of self-defense. Case B may be said to be an act of self-defense on behalf of another (the other children), although this case is somewhat more difficult because it has several contingencies. These contingencies include calculations on whether the family *will* starve or whether intervening events—such as better employment prospects or higher crop yields—might alter the situation. Other possible scenarios could also be constructed, but the point of this example is to illustrate self-defense on behalf of another. In Case C, the situation is similar to one addressed in active euthanasia. The decision maker is paternalistically acting on behalf of another's best interest. The mother may think that she knows that this child will not want to die so early and with so much suffering. She may also think that she cannot face the trial of caring for another knowing that the future is both fixed and fatal.

Cases D and E are similar except for the age of the women. The age issue can work both ways. One might give greater latitude to the younger woman because she is not fully mature and responsible for her actions. Or one might give greater latitude to the older woman because as one ages, doors of opportunity close. The consequences to the older woman are probably more severe than to the younger. Each case uses *threaten* in the context of "very disruptive to my life plan."

Cases F and G are similar because they indicate a sense of eugenics. In fact, a large number of abortions are performed in the world because of the sex of the fetus. Thousands of female fetuses have been aborted because the mother desired a son. Case G involves a science fiction scenario in which people desire to have "designer babies." This is a desirable future to some but a nightmare to others.

More will be said about these meanings of *threaten* in the next section of this essay.

The other aspect of premise 3 concerns the definition of an agent. This issue has been much discussed in the literature with few definitive results.[16] I would like to preface my remarks by referring to the essay on precautionary reasoning by Deryck Beyleveld and Shaun Pattinson.[17] Beyleveld makes the point that *full human rights*, that is, those that confer absolute respect for freedom and well-being, become operative only when there is an agent who clearly meets the criteria of being a prospective, purposive agent. His point would not be evident without objection until some time in a child's second year of life.[18] If we grant this, all infants less than 30 months of age have no dialectically necessary claim to agency. Q.E.D., these infants have no dialectically necessary claim to life (one of the aspects of well-being).

This standard is certainly very high. Surely it does not mean that we are entitled to kill at will all infants under the age of 30 months. Precautionary reasoning indicates that various actions such as walking and feeding oneself indicate that the infant may be more cognizant than we can scientifically

---

[16]For a discussion of this literature, see Bonnie Steinbock, *Life Before Birth: The Moral and Legal Status of Embryos and Fetuses* (Oxford: Oxford University Press, 1992).

[17]See page 39.

[18]This is a troubling point because it invokes both methodologies and measurements. Some may want to push the point back a bit, but the ultimate measure in this case is whether the child has shown that she or he has a sense of self and that the sense of self deliberates and carries out action. Thus, walking or beginning to speak might count. *Wherever* one wishes to set this point will be well past birth.

document. Many other animals also are able to perform these actions,[19] yet we do not ascribe to them the rights we afford to human agents. To determine why this is so, we need to turn back to the Personal World Imperative.

THE PERSONAL WORLDVIEW AND ABORTION

According to the Personal Worldview Imperative, all people must develop a single comprehensive and internally coherent worldview that is good and that they strive to act out in their daily lives. It enjoins each of us to create both a comprehensive and internally coherent vision of life. One aspect of this is to be able to will ourselves to have actions performed on us without violating the laws of nature as we understand them.[20] This is similar to the Kantian notion of imperfect duties.[21]

A fetus cannot will its own demise (i.e., being aborted) without contradicting the natural law that says that ceteris paribus all humans act for their own preservation and happiness.

What if we could not will? Certainly, this situation may occur when we are at the beginning of life. The fetus does not act; and because *willing* is a precondition to action, the fetus does not will. This seems to be an exception to the Kantian interpretation of the Personal Worldview Imperative referred to earlier. However, some might claim that this situation should be judged as we would assess a person who is asleep (to use Aristotle's example—the fetus is not willing *now* but will be in the position to will in the near future).[22] This argument is a form of precautionary reasoning.

The essence of this doctrine (as I choose to use it) is to make precautionary reasoning a form of Aristotelian potentiality that holds open the possibility that the individual in question may be more empowered than we can scientifically determine. At some time, we must determine a point beyond which it is impossible (from the worldview perspective of the speaker) for the

---

[19]In most cases, human infants go through many developmental stages more slowly than do infants of other species. Thus, on this alone, one would afford more proportional status to puppies or to baby lizards than to humans. Obviously, we do not afford this status because we employ precautionary reasoning.

[20]This interpretation of the Personal Worldview Imperative comes about through the sense of consistency. It would be inconsistent to view ourselves as being outside nature's laws. Therefore, to will exceptions for ourselves is irrational (because it is inconsistent).

[21]The Kantian notion of imperfect duties is here taken to be positive duties requiring action on the part of the agent. One of these duties is the requirement that we aid others whenever we can do so without risking our basic goods of agency. For a discussion of my view of Kantian imperfect duties, see Michael Boylan, *Basic Ethics* (Upper Saddle River, NJ: Prentice Hall, 2000), Chapter Four.

[22]Aristotle believes that a person may have the power of sight even when he is asleep and has his eyes shut. The idea is that when the person is awakened, he will be able to see. The fact that while asleep, this power is only potential does not diminish the claim that he will soon be able to see. Aristotle, *The Metaphysics: Text and Commentary*, W.D. Ross (Oxford: Clarendon University Press, 1924), 1048b 1–6.

individual in question to be afforded the moral rights of agency—even using precautionary reasoning. Does this mean that past the point of affording the fetus proportional rights[23] through precautionary reasoning we are entitled to give the fetus no consideration at all and thus be entitled to kill it at will? The answer is no because I have linked "precaution" with a sense of Aristotelian potentiality. Under this interpretation of *pre*cautionary reasoning, we must give some level of respect to any fetus, no matter how immature. On the principle of proportionality that I have been espousing, we would give more respect to a 13-week fetus than to a 4-week fetus because the 13-week fetus is closer to enjoying precautionary reasoning than is a 4-week fetus. The pregnant woman must determine just how much respect, vis-à-vis various threats that face her.

In this process, a person must first establish the floor of precautionary reason; this requires judgment. Personally, I would put the floor at the end of the first trimester of pregnancy (13 weeks). Before this point, the brain and spinal cord are not connected; therefore, according to my own best understanding, it would be impossible for the fetus to deliberate, plan, and act. Others may disagree with me and put the floor in either direction (i.e., earlier or later in pregnancy).

Second, each individual must determine the limit of respect to accord a fetus who is neither (a) an actual agent nor (b) a possible agent (even under a liberal sense of precautionary reasoning). The agent in question is *potentially* a possible agent. As a potentially possible agent, the fetus is accorded some respect because, baring intervention, it will become a possible agent (protected by precautionary reason) and eventually a full-blown agent (protected by most theories of morality).

This interpretation invalidates the given form of the proabortion argument because it suggests that the at-will provision is incorrect. A person may eliminate some entity at will only when the entity receives no justifiable respect. Under the interpretation just outlined, some level of respect is always due to potentiality tied to precautionary reasoning; the agent involved must determine the *level of respect*. This is a personal assessment, but to say so does not imply relativism. Instead, this expression is the proper expression of the Personal Worldview Imperative in which a person legislates a universal interpretation of reality (which would include valuing this level of respect).

---

[23]The notion of proportional rights stems from the individual's best assessment of the possible degree of agency that *may* exist. This goes well beyond any demonstrated agency (which may be as late as 30 months after birth). This attribution of rights is given not because of demonstrated capacity on the part of the fetus but because it seems possible that an individual may possess attributes that confer agency, that is, a sense of inductive and deductive logic along with the capacity to deliberate about action (even in a very minimal way) *before* this is operationally evident to some observer. Therefore, out of precaution, we act as if the individual has these capacities (even though there is no demonstrable evidence for this). As a result, we confer precautionary rights of agency. These differ from full rights of agency only in the fact that they are not *dialectically necessary* (Gewirth) or *apodeitically necessary* (Kant). They are, in fact, contingently necessary (contingent because they are based on the assessment of the person making the attribution).

I do not believe that a woman may abort a fetus at will. I believe that the fetus must represent a threat that supersedes the level of respect the woman has assigned to the fetus. I would say that the threats represented by F and G in the preceding examples do not meet this standard. Thus, abortion on the basis of the baby's sex or some eugenic desire is impermissible at any stage of pregnancy. The level of respect due the fetus as a mere potential possible agent is greater than the level of maternal threat.

I assess cases A through E in the examples as meeting this standard of threat that supersedes the level of respect for the fetus during the first trimester of pregnancy. Others might demur because they would quarrel with me about balancing of threats. I view case A as meeting a sufficient standard of threat throughout the pregnancy.[24] In third-trimester abortions, however, the opportunity to remove the fetus without destroying it may exist. The right to an abortion is not a right to have the embryo destroyed but merely a right to have it removed from the mother's body.

Cases B, C, D, and E form two units that have similar themes (self-defense for the sake of another and severe disruption to one's personal life plan, respectively). Since averting death is more disastrous to agency than mere roadblocks (no matter how disruptive), I assess B and C as being higher-order threats than D and E. This differentiation must be considered in different stages of pregnancy in which an abortion may be permissible. For example, I lean toward D and E as being permissible only during the first trimester but B and C as being permissible during the first two trimesters.

The general principle in operation is how to weigh threat and response. In Cases D and E the nature of the response changes as the fetus develops. Thus, a response to a fetus in the first trimester is different from a response in the second trimester is different from a response in the third trimester. This is so because in the first trimester one has merely the principle of potentiality by which to refer.

After the first trimester, I believe that the principle of precautionary reason becomes operative and proportionally more relevant until the minimal stages of operationally verifiable agency are evidenced (30 months after birth—or less). After 30 months (or whatever time is chosen), killing the entity is absolutely impermissible unless it were materially threatening the life of the mother.[25]

---

[24]As well as those cases between A and B—as per footnote 15 (covering rape and incest—and all other cases of involuntary sex that has resulted in a pregnancy).

[25]Such a situation would be bizarre and a person would have to stretch her imagination to identify a plausible case. Unfortunately my volunteer work experience has taught me that all too frequently adults feel threatened by children. They cry too much, they keep needing to have their diaper changed, or they drive me nuts with their fussiness are among adults' responses to children. Too often the threat threshold is far too low for these adults. Beating, abusing, and even killing infants is justified in the minds of these adults because the infants' needs interfered with the adults' life plans (as per F and G in the examples). Such a response to a perceived threat is far too great and is therefore morally impermissible.

CONCLUSION.

In this essay, I have aspired to be suggestive rather than definitive on the question of abortion. To this end, I have suggested criteria that different people can use to set the universal limits of permissibility and impermissibility. This variation is due to the variation in personal worldviews in which one may weigh maternal threats and fetal respect differently. Instead of focusing on the definition of personhood or the expression of autonomy, I suggest that focusing on maternal threats versus fetal respect is more productive.

This approach suggests that three levels should be considered when evaluating how much respect anyone deserves: (a) full personhood (at some time in the first few years of development), (b) possible personhood (protected by precautionary reason from some base level to personhood; I put this moment at the end of the first trimester of pregnancy), and (c) potential possible personhood (from the moment of conception to possible personhood).

Full moral rights obtain necessarily to those enjoying full personhood (since they are actual deliberating agents). Something proportionally approaching full moral rights may be claimed for the possible agent, and some proportionally lower level of respect (with its associated rights) should be granted to those on the lowest level of personhood.

In contrast to the traditional antiabortion position that generally argues for full moral rights for the fetus from conception, my theory creates three levels of respect that move well past birth to be complete. In contrast to the traditional proabortionist position that generally argues for the right of abortion at will, my theory denies abortions at will. It requires the demonstration of a level of maternal threat that is greater than the level of respect we ought to give the developing (though not yet actual) person.

The levels that an individual sets for threats versus respect follow from his complex web of values that I call the *worldview*. Through a dialectical interaction between the abortion question and this person's values emerges personal ownership of a universal theory dealing with if, when, and under what conditions an embryo may be separated from its biological mother.

The question of abortion has been in the public forum so long because it addresses many key issues related to the rights of others versus our own individual expressions of autonomy. I believe that total consensus on this issue will never occur in the present framework because consensus is a derivative property of each person's worldview. And because worldviews differ, so will the imperatives they endorse. This is not a statement of relativism but a factual description of various people working on a common problem (each believing that she or he has *the* correct answer).

On the optimistic side, however, I believe that viewing the abortion question from the Personal Worldview Imperative will at least create increased understanding of (a) the other side's position and (b) a vocabulary that is structured so that it does not prejudge the issue (for example, the vocabulary of maternal threat versus fetal respect). This type of understanding will be essential if any real progress in the public debate on abortion is to be made.

EVALUATING A CASE STUDY: ASSESSING EMBEDDED LEVELS

The goal in this series of exercises is for you to be able to write an essay that critically evaluates a biomedical problem involving ethical issues. Your essay should include an examination of aspects of medical practice as well as the ethical dimensions. In Chapter Four, we discussed how to bring the ethical dimensions to the fore through the use of detection questions. These were put side by side the principles of professional practice.

In this chapter, we compare these two types of issues. This comparison can be accomplished in multiple ways; the one offered here invokes a technique that rates professional practice as having three levels of complexity: surface, medium, and deep. The level of interaction allows you to see at a glance how professional practice issues and ethical issues conflict.

You need a model of some type to evaluate the professional practice issues and ethical issues that may conflict. When ethical issues and professional issues conflict, you do not *automatically* choose either. Some ethical problems can be solved easily and do not require forgoing the dictates of the professional practice. At other times, an ethical problem must be solved in such a way that professional practices must be overridden.

You need a methodology for comparison. The *embedded concept model* is one such methodology. I illustrate how this works with several examples that employ a chart to clarify the ways the concepts conflict. You may also want to use this technology if you have access to one of the popular computer spreadsheet programs, but the use of a spreadsheet is not necessary. A more conventional approach is to discuss these differences. The spreadsheet is no substitute for solid narrative description, but at the very least it simplifies and makes visual the model I propose.

Case 1.

You are a senior hospital administrator and you have learned that dissatisfaction has been expressed concerning the manner in which staff members explain the consent forms patients must sign before their surgical procedures can be performed. Although your hospital's practice is within the law and the existing procedures used by other hospitals, your hospital serves an immigrant population with low education levels. To explain the medical procedure and its possible outcomes in more detail would require additional time and would involve additional hospital expenditures, and money is tight (as always). What should you do?

Professional Practice Issues

1. A professional is required only to follow the law and the guidelines of its professional association.
2. Implementing a new system could require additional costs.
3. Going beyond the law and the association's guidelines could be perceived as raising the standard that other hospitals would be required to follow. Meeting this additional standard could require the use of funds that had not been budgeted.

Ethical Issues

1. Physical health is crucial to every person because it is essential to purposive action. What is most important to a rational purposive agent should be within that agent's sphere of autonomy.
2. *Informed* consent is necessary for autonomous decision making.

In this simple case, the ethical guidelines override those of the professional practice guidelines. That means the ethical guidelines are "easier" to solve. When a great disparity exists between the imbeddedness of one alternative as opposed to the other (meaning deep as opposed to surface), that direction should drive the decision. One should implement the other side as it is possible. For example, in this case, the hospital administrator should implement a program to explain medical procedures and their outcomes to patients so that they can better understand the health care decisions they must make. Other professional practice considerations should be addressed in the context of the action to enhance patient understanding, which takes precedence.

Analysis of Consent Practices at Mercy Hospital

	SURFACE	MEDIUM	DEEP
Professional Practice Issues			
A professional is required to follow only the law and the professional association's guidelines	x		
The hospital may be accused of raising the standard	x		
Implementation costs		x	
Ethical Issues			
One's personal health decisions should be within one's sphere of autonomy			x
Only a truly *informed* consent satisfies the conditions of autonomy			x

Case 2.

This case is not so simple. You are a regional director at the World Health Organization. One of your duties is to supervise the distribution of birth control devices to women in less-developed countries. The product of choice has been the intrauterine device (IUD) that has proved to be effective and inexpensive. The problem is that in the United States, several hundred users of the IUD have contracted pelvic inflammatory infections that have been linked to use of the IUD. As regional director, you must decide whether to continue to supply IUDs to women in less-developed countries.

Professional Practice Issues

1. As a professional in the public health field, your responsibility is to choose public policy that maximizes the health and minimizes the health risks in the general population.
2. Sexual activity without birth control in less-developed countries will lead to an increasing population that, in turn, will lead to severe poverty and mass starvation.
3. Mass starvation kills millions; pelvic inflammatory infections kill hundreds. Thus, it is better to save the many (in the spirit of the profession's mission).

Ethical Issues

1. Each person's life is precious.
2. The end of saving more lives does not justify the means of sacrificing others.

This case differs from Case 1 because the ethical and professional guidelines are equal. In this case, the dictates of the ethical imperative must be followed because it is more deeply imbedded in a person's worldview than is

Analysis of Population Control in the Third World

	Surface	Medium	Deep
Professional Practice Issues			
Public health mission to preserve the health of as many as possible			x
Sexual activity without birth control leads to mass starvation			x
The end justifies the means			x
Ethical Issues			
Human life is precious			x
The end does not justify the means			x

the imperative of professional practice. The components of ethics enter the worldview generically as a feature of a person's humanity. The imperatives of professionalism enter the worldview as one of many modes of personal fulfillment.

As with scientific theories, the dictates of a universally binding imperative founded on generic structures trump those of a particular person's individual interests. More details on this appear in the "Evaluating a Case Study" section in Chapter Six.

In this essay, the main concern is the ability to assess the levels of imbeddedness. Some common mistakes that my students have made in performing this assessment follow:

1. *Not giving the imperatives of professional practice their due.* Remember that whether you assess imbeddedness via a spreadsheet or through discursive paragraphs, you are working from your original analysis of the problem. A failure to uncover all the important facets will be reflected in your depiction of imbeddedness. You will notice gaps in the reasoning and will feel that something is missing. If this happens, go back over the issues lists. Rewrite the case in your own words; expand or recast the case in some way. By doing this, you become the author and are forced to recognize key elements in the case as presented.

2. *Seeing everything at the same level of imbeddedness.* You need to view imbeddedness as a way to describe the degree to which the professional practice or ethical issue is essential to the case. A less essential issue should be given less consideration. To better understand the essential structure of a professional practice, prepare short justifications of your choice of that element as an issue in the case. As you prepare your justifications, think about each element in its relation to the whole. If that relation could not be different without seriously altering the whole, then it is essential. If you can find substitutes that would work just as well, the relation is incidental.

3. *Listing too many professional and ethical issues.* This is the flip side to step 1. You have given too much detail that is not essential to the case at hand, or you are listing one issue in a number of different ways. In either event, preparing an essential description of your elements (as in step 2) can help you shorten your issue list to only those required for your evaluation.

Good solid work avoiding these mistakes will enable you to create a more satisfactory result in the argumentative stage, in which you may finally apply your ethical theory to your annotated imbeddedness charts.

Macro and Micro Cases*

Macro Case 1. You are the senior administrator of a national chain of nursing homes. At your recent annual meeting with the directors, a problem among the nursing staff was identified. A sizable number of inhabitants of your nursing homes are in great pain and voice a will to die. The nurses are seeking a policy that will allow them some discretion in dealing with these patients, vis-à-vis allowing nature to take its course. The nurses would like to know the company's position if they delay certain treatments or if they actually hasten death by administering overdose injections in severe cases.

Anecdotal evidence suggests that the relatives of these individuals would not pursue costly lawsuits if this "informal" policy were carried out (although that is always a possibility). In fact, the same evidence indicates that family members long for closure on what seems to be inevitable.

You know that state laws explicitly prohibit active euthanasia. You want to do the right thing, and you must make the decision in a memo to the chairperson of your board of directors. What will you say? What policy direction will you advocate and for what reasons? Make explicit reference to some moral theory as the basis of your decision and linking principle to action.

Macro Case 2. You are an ethicist on a panel at the National Institutes of Health that is studying guidelines for physicians nationwide concerning allowing feeding tubes to be removed from intensive care infants. These infants are in intensive care because they have some blockage that prevents them from receiving conventional nutrition. A simple operation can solve this problem, but some parents prefer to avoid the operation and to discontinue the use of the feeding tube.

The panel is currently split over several issues: (a) Should parents be allowed to make this decision, or should the state assume a paternalistic position and decide? (b) If the state should step in, then how much weight should be given to the wishes and circumstances of the parents? (c) Because the parents would normally want very aggressive treatment for their child, infants in these situations must either have a fatal disease or a serious disability. Should the state treat these instances differently? If the parents are allowed to choose, should they treat these instances differently? (d) Is there a difference in rationale for failing to save an impaired infant due to concerns over the pain it will undergo in an eventual death when it is older against the pain the parents will undergo in caring for a disabled child? (e) Do children who have a short life expectancy deserve the opportunity to live for the amount of time they have? (f) Do mentally and/or physically handicapped children

---

*For more on macro and micro cases, see the overview on p. 53.

deserve the opportunity to live? (g) Do parents of impaired infants have a right not to be encumbered by the extraordinary commitments (emotional, financial, etc.) such situations entail?

You are highly regarded by other members of the panel, and your opinion will carry significant weight. Write a position paper describing your views and defending them using an established ethical theory and linking principle.

Macro Case 3. You are a member of the United States Supreme Court. The Court is about to review a fast-track case concerning so-called defective infants. In this particular case, *Smith v. New York,* Ms. Jane Smith is suing to be able to remove her newborn son from a feeding tube that is keeping him alive. Ms. Smith wants the feeding tube removed because the baby has a blockage that prevents him from receiving nutrition under ordinary means. This blockage can be removed by minor surgery, but Ms. Smith does not want her son to have this operation because he is mentally retarded. She does not want a mentally retarded child. She believes that she has the right to let her child die. Why should she have to devote the rest of her life to caring for this child (either directly or by paying for his care in some type of home)?

The key question here is whether to consider this child to be defective (generally understood to be in unrelievable pain and/or with a terminal condition) and thereby subject to rules and regulations regarding defective children (who are allowed to die) or whether this child is merely handicapped, in which case federal law requires doing everything possible to save him. You want to view this question first from an ethical perspective before considering the legal aspects of the issue (not a part of this essay). Therefore, write an essay identifying the ethical issues involved and use an ethical theory to support your position.

Macro Case 4. You are the incoming administrator of the World Health Organization. The organization's policies about funding for countries that practice (a) infanticide (generally of female infants), (b) gender-based abortion, and (c) family planning–based abortion are being challenged. Some donor nations are upset because they believe the organization's standards are ambiguous. You are charged with clearing up this ambiguity. Some of your aides suggest that you opt for a political/pragmatic solution, but you believe that only an ethical solution will be accepted. Therefore, your task is to determine whether the World Health Organization should support countries that engage in any or all of these practices. What ethical issues are involved? What linking principles would you employ? Do the three different issues demand different responses? Why or why not?

Micro Case 1. Your husband is a nationally recognized journalist. He was severely injured three years ago in an automobile accident while on assignment and has been in an irreversible coma since then. As a result, he lost his reflex for swallowing and is connected to a feeding tube. Health care workers report that occasionally he sits bolt upright, utters a string of words, and then lies down again.

Your husband left no clear statement as to his wishes in such a situation. It is clear to you that he will not come out of the coma. You want to do what is right and to be able to justify your decision to your children as well as to the courts. You also want to get on with your own life. You are thirty-eight years old and have a great deal of your life ahead of you. Write an essay defending one of these positions: (a) leaving things as they are or (b) disconnecting the feeding tube.

Micro Case 2. You are a pregnant teen-aged female. You did not intend to become pregnant; obviously, you were not as careful as you should have been. Your blueprint for life includes college, graduate school, and a fulfilling job but not a child now. Having a baby will not work out with your plans.

You have missed your second period and learned at the family planning clinic that you are in the late stage of the first trimester of your pregnancy. This situation totally unnerves you. You consider suicide. Why should you bear this by yourself? Your partner, Alex, is in the state finals of the baseball championships. You have not told him; you could try to drag him into the situation, but that would not be fair to him. But is this fair to you?

Write an essay based on an ethical theory that justifies what *you* would do.

Micro Case 3. You are an eighty-two-year-old man whose wife of fifty-two years is dying of cancer. She is in great pain despite her treatments and is living in the hospice section of a nursing home. Everyone in this unit is terminal. When you visit your wife, she implores you to give her a lethal dose of her pain-killing medication. Your love her, and seeing her suffer in this way causes you considerable pain. Can killing someone be an act of love? Or is it really an act of escape so that *you* will not have to see her in this condition until the bitter end. You are perplexed. You could give in to your wife's demands, or you could leave things as they are. You could ask the physician to keep her permanently sedated, but even that could not guarantee that your wife would not endure pain and suffering.

You explore this question in your diary. Examine this question using an established ethical theory and linking principle as your guide. Make a decision as to what to do.

Micro Case 4. You are the medical representative on a mountain climbing expedition, and you have lost much of your medical gear. Your group of four has had terrible luck; it was hit by a sudden blizzard that has knocked out all communications with the base camp. Mary, one of the climbers, has been badly injured; she suffered a deep gash on her leg.

The problem is that food is running out fast. Your food supply will last little more than one day. Rescue parties could not make it in this weather, and helicopters could not land in this terrain even in perfect weather. Hope for a rescue is not realistic. You could go for help, which would probably be a three-day trip, but the food supply is a concern. Mary's leg appears to be afflicted by gangrene, and she is in great pain. You have plenty of pain killer left—more than enough for her pain. Mary knows that there is little hope for rescue and implores you to give her a lethal dose of the pain killer. You demur. She says she can inject herself if you make it available for her.

You are conflicted. Should you give Mary a lethal dose or should you make one available for her to give herself? Should you carry on and hope for a miracle? Answer this problem using a moral theory to support your argument.

chapter six

Genetic Engineering

Overview. Genetic therapy is highly controversial. One of the key issues concerns somatic therapy (that affects only the person involved) versus germ-line therapy (that will extend into the person's reproductive capacities and therefore future generations). Another issue concerns the way to introduce the new genes into the cells. The biomechanisms that carry out this function are called vectors. These vectors are often viruses that insert the desired changes into the cells of the patient. Obviously, the type of viruses involved (such as a "deactivated" AIDS retrovirus) can cause concerns.

The first approved gene therapy in the United States occurred on September 14, 1990, at the National Institutes of Health. The patient was a four-year-old girl, Ashanti DeSilva, whose own blood was altered and infused back into her bloodstream to treat a rare genetic deficiency in her immune system.[1] The effects were temporary (i.e., the procedure needed to be repeated), but the treatment allowed her to resume a normal lifestyle. Such is the ideal for patients who are treated by genetic therapy.

---

[1]Larry Thompson, "Should Dying Patients Receive Untested Genetic Methods?" *Science* 259 (January 1993): 452.

Germ-line therapy treats either the unfertilized or the fertilized egg before implantation into the uterus. Advocates say that this is just an additional technique of the *in vitro* fertilization process.

The articles in this chapter discuss issues involved with gene therapy and the logical extension of this process in cloning. The first is an interview with Kevin Brown, M.D., Ph.D., who is a visiting scientist doing research in genetic engineering at the National Institutes of Health. Dr. Brown comments about points made in the readings in this chapter. This discussion by a researcher in the field on articles written by people both in and out of the field is instructive.

Next, Nils Holtug presents an overview of the general issues involved in gene therapy. He refers to the protocols of the European Commission (see the Position Paper on Human Germ Line Manipulation at the end of the chapter) and then examines various motives for genetic engineering.[2] He believes that the permissibility of genetic engineering depends on its purpose, to treat a disease or to enhance the body in some way. The latter motive is less viable and is more associated with germ-line therapy and therefore is more suspect than somatic treatments.

Edward Berger and Bernard Gert frame the issue in terms of *eugenics*, meaning "good births," which has a rather negative connotation in the history of biology. Starting with Francis Galton in 1883 and continuing through the Nazi era,[3] eugenics has been associated with an underlying hatred of heterogeneity. In the mind of the eugenic practitioner is a template for a "perfect" example of a human being. The belief in this perfect template is sometimes called Essentialism, which holds that there is an emblematic depiction of the perfect human. Essentialism is contrary to the basic tenets of evolutionary biology that hail diversity within a species as increasing fitness over a wide range of potential environments. (It is also ridiculous to all of us who have taken classes in taxonomy. No field specimen ever fits the template, which means that the templates—not the specimens—are fictions.)

If human gene therapy is no more than eugenics, then strong arguments against it could be made. To this end, Berger and Gert draw a distinction between positive and negative gene therapy. In positive gene therapy the goal is enhancement of a person in some way, while negative gene therapy attempts

---

[2]I will use the term *genetic engineering* to refer generally to all forms of genetic manipulation. *Genetic therapy* will refer to a more narrow domain in which genetic manipulation is used specifically for the sake of curing some disease or physical disorder. Thus all instances of genetic therapy will be instances of genetic engineering, but not all instances of genetic engineering will be instances of genetic therapy.

[3]Francis Galton, *Essays in Eugenics* (reprinted New York: Garland, 1985); Stefan Kühl, *The Nazi Connection: Eugenics, American Racism, and German National Socialism* (New York: Oxford University Press, 1994); Benno Müller-Hill, *Murderous Science: Elimination by Scientific Selection of Jews, Gypsies and Others, Germany 1933–1945* (Oxford: Oxford University Press, 1988).

to cure genetic diseases that are often fatal. If positive gene therapy is really eugenics, and if eugenics is an evil never to be repeated, *and* if negative gene therapy can lead to positive gene therapy, then both sorts of genetic therapy should be rejected. (Berger and Gert also discuss several other issues dealing with evolutionary consequences of gene therapy.)

Kathleen Nolan believes that the line between somatic and germ-line therapy is not so sharp as others have stated. She suggests that the real issues may lie in the reason for seeking this therapy and the amount of paternalism allotted to parents and physicians in these procedures.

The next three essays deal with cloning. In the first, Dorothy Nelkin and M. Susan Lindee imaginatively explore what cloning could mean to our worldview. Because I am such an advocate of the worldview approach, I believe that this somewhat humorous article is deeper than it appears.

In the second, Søren Holm discusses the argument about the place of an f-2 cloned person with relation to her parent. Does the person live in the shadow of his or her progenitor? Since nature has an input even in development, how would differences be evaluated? Would this be an undue burden to bear?

The final article is a dissenting note from John Harris, who believes that much of the dissent against cloning is the result of prejudice. He finds that a person predetermines her position and then declares whether it is "disturbing" or not based on unsubstantiated reasons. Such reactions have been common in the history of science when new technologies and/or theories have been advanced. Therefore, a person ought only to acknowledge claims that have a logically grounded basis. No aesthetic or random religious objections should be used.

Interview with
Kevin Brown, M.D., Ph.D.

GENE THERAPY

Q: Do you accept the distinction that is sometimes made between somatic gene therapy and germ-line therapy?
A: Yes, I do. Somatic gene therapy is the use of gene therapy to directly alter an individual's genetic makeup in some, but not all, of the patient's cells. As such, it will directly affect only the individual in question, not his or her descendants. In contrast, germ-line therapy is directed at altering the genetic composition in the germ cells (eggs and sperm) either by direct modification of germ cells or by manipulation of embryo cells so that the genetic content of all cells in the body will be modified. Germ-line therapy thus has the potential to affect not only the first-line descendants but also future generations.

Let me say a little bit about the risks and rewards of both approaches. First, all genetic therapy may carry various dangers, both known and unknown. Let's divide these dangers into three affected groups: (a) to the person receiving therapy, (b) to the public at large, (c) to future generations.

First, there are the dangers to the person receiving therapy. These risks are not that dissimilar to the risks involved in any novel treatment intervention. This person probably has some serious and possibly fatal disease. In light of this, the risks involved with experimental somatic gene therapy must be viewed on a risk/reward basis. If the risk of the therapy is 0.9 and if the chances of survival without therapy are 0.1, then one has a statistical "push," but with the hope that the intervention will help. More often, the odds are more in favor of the patient risking the experimental therapy. Thus, the risks

The opinions expressed in this article are solely those of the author and do not necessarily reflect the views of the National Heart, Lung, and Blood Institute or the National Institutes of Health.

of the therapy in this sense have to be viewed in the context of people for whom this is the *only* hope. If they don't accept *this* risk, then they will have greater or equal risk from the disease from which they are suffering.

Second, with genetic therapy using modified viruses as vectors to "carry" the DNA into the cells to be modified, there is also a potential danger to the public at large. Although these viruses are incomplete viruses, there is always the risk that they could recombine with complete or natural viruses and produce a modified infectious virus. So far there is no evidence of recombination happening in humans, and a great deal of work is in progress ensuring that such recombinations—if they occur at all—will be extremely rare.

Third, genetic therapy has the potential for both adverse and beneficial effects on the genetic makeup of future generation. It is sometimes argued that germ-line gene therapy should not be undertaken because it has the potential of altering the human "gene pool" (see Berger and Gert, p. 350). However, the gene pool is already being altered by medical intervention, with individuals who would previously not have survived beyond childhood now not only living into adult life but also reproducing and sending those genes into future generations. It could be argued that medical intervention is already leading to a lowering of genetic fitness in the community, and somatic gene therapy would contribute to that development. In contrast, germ-line therapy has the potential to reverse this trend by eliminating these genes.

Q: What are our duties to these future generations?

A: It is a tricky balance. On the one hand, there probably is a prima facie duty to future generations. But, on the other hand, this duty must be weighed against the rights of people to receive treatment now. When they receive treatment, they may very well be sending defective genes into the gene pool and affecting future generations. But we don't know whether that would be "hurting" future generations, do we? And presumably if we were able to treat the initial patient, similar or better treatment would be available for his or her descendants. I think that we should definitely tilt toward treating the ill patient in front of us through somatic gene therapy. Let's leave the "future generation" speculations for germ-line options.

Q: What is the purpose of vectors?

A: The purpose of vectors is to get DNA into the cells of the patient and, for long-term expression or for germ-line therapy, to get the new DNA integrated into the chromosome. Currently, the most efficient way to get DNA into the cells of the patient is by using modified viruses, although naked or liposome-encapsulated DNA is also being tried. There are three main viral-based delivery systems: (1) retroviruses, (2) adenoviruses, and (3) adeno-associated viruses (AAV). Each vector strategy has its own associated strengths and weaknesses, but they all share one common problem: the inability to insert the modified DNA at precise site-specific locations within the chromosomal DNA. This can be an enormous problem because when the modified DNA is inserted at random into the chromosome, it may disrupt other critical genes or gene control sequences at that site. Depending on what genes are interrupted or modified, the "cure" could have more deleterious effects than the disease being treated. Ideally, one would like to directly target the DNA to a "safe" site in the chromosome, or even better, to insert the corrected gene at the correct site in the chromosome. When these consequences directly affect the subject only (in the case of somatic therapy), one might be inclined to view it as a by-product of the risk/reward calculus in which many terminally ill patients engage. But when we are engaged in germ-line therapy, the consequences may become apparent only many decades after the original intervention and may affect many future generations. This situation is much more serious, and many would argue that we should not even be considering germ-line therapy until we can do this (Holtug, pp. 331–332).

Q: Isn't it dangerous to use viruses such as retroviruses for gene therapy?
A: You are referring, of course, to the fact that the most notorious retrovirus is the AIDS virus, HIV, and that retroviruses including modified lentiviruses (the family to which HIV belongs) are being tried as possible virus vectors for gene therapy. As I mentioned previously, there is a theoretical concern that any of the deactivated viruses that are used as vectors could combine with natural viruses and be reactivated. Obviously, this is of very great concern when viruses such as HIV are being considered as possible vectors.

Q: Is there a difference in strategic plans between "knocking out" deleterious genes and inserting "corrective" genes?
A: I think you are asking two different questions here. At one level, we do not have the ability with gene therapy to "knock out" genes, but all therapy so far is designed to add back functional or corrected genes. The hope is that we may one day be able to correct nonfunctional genes *in situ*, but so far we cannot do that. So, from that stance, all our current strategy is based on inserting "corrected" genes. If we could do it, the assumption is made that knocking out bad genes is less dangerous than inserting new good genes. But this may be specious; whenever you knock something out, you change the equilibrium, and there may be systemic balances we do not fully understand. Thus, when we eliminate something that we do not want, other consequences may occur. Those of us who have tried to delete a computer program without using an uninstall software package can attest that there can be connections about which we are ignorant.

On a second level, is there a difference between plans to correct deleterious genes and to insert advantageous genes? Yes, I think there is, but I am not sure it is as definitive as is sometimes implied in discussions of negative and positive gene therapy, a point that is made in the articles by Holtug (p. 335ff) and by Berger and Gert (p. 349). Discussions of positive gene therapy often are associated with the negative connotations of eugenics, but insertions of genes to prevent high cholesterol levels or reduce the risk of cancer would be examples of positive gene therapy that many people would consider beneficial.

Q: What are the upsides and downsides to germ-line therapy?
A: The perceived upside would be to eliminate deleterious genes that cause fatal or chronic disease not only from an individual but also from the individual's entire family line. The major downside is whether we can effectively do it at all. Effective germ-line therapy assumes that we can put the genes we want to replace exactly where we want, or that we can correct the defective gene *in situ*.

Q: The site-specific problem again?
A: Exactly. At present, we do not have the capability of doing either of these. But if we assume that this were possible (to insert the gene where we want and not affect other genes), then we would be in a position to affect a great many people. We would affect not only the person receiving treatment but also his or her children and all their children's children. This is no small thing we are contemplating here.

Q: How many people do you think might opt for such germ-line therapy?
A: It will probably not be a question of *choice* so much as it will be *opportunity*. Most of the world's population is too poor for such treatment, and even in the wealthier countries, gene therapy will be targeted initially to those in certain disease groups. Thus, there may not be a wholesale change in the genetic makeup of *homo sapiens*, but in time there could be pockets of affected populations among the wealthy in industrialized nations.

Q: Creating genetic drift?
A: Possibly, but unlikely to have the consequences envisioned in popular literature.

Q: What are the key ethical questions that you believe are being raised by germ-line therapy?
A: The ethical questions are rather stark. First, can one make decisions for his or her grandchildren? What gives one that right? What may be a "defect" to some may be a desirable trait to others, and who makes those decisions? Eradicating sickle cell anemia by correcting the abnormal gene is fine for environments without malaria, but the presence of the sickle cell trait (heterozygous, or one copy of the abnormal gene) is advantageous for malaria-infested environments.

The second question concerns when life begins. If it is at conception, then the research that will be necessary to perfect germ-line therapy will be performed on fetuses that will then be destroyed when the experiment is over. If the fetus is at some stage a living person, then such experimentation is similar to the gruesome experiments that the Nazis conducted. These issues are explored further in the euthanasia section of Chapter Five.

The third question concerns whether the perceived benefits of gene therapy could be achieved by other methods, an issue that Holtug explores in his section "Is Germ-Line Therapy Superfluous?" (pp. 334–335). His argument is that while germ-line therapy involves the use of *in vitro* fertilization, "it seems that most of what we could and would want to do in terms of corrective gene therapy could be done by means of selective implantation," an argument that should be taken seriously before we rush headlong into germ-line therapy.

Some of these issues are discussed further in other readings that have been selected for this chapter. Kathleen Nolan looks at the issue of the relationship between an individual and his or her germ cells (i.e., their sperm or ova). Do these belong to those who bear them, or is the relationship different than with other (somatic) cells? She argues that the way we think about these matters will affect the way we "do" gene therapy.

The articles by Nils Holtug and by Berger and Gert look at gene therapy from the perspective of altering humans and the long-term consequences of these changes. Is gene therapy, either somatic or germ-line therapy, an example of "playing god"? And what genes should be corrected and/or improved? Both articles also consider which genes should be targets for gene therapy and explore the distinction between negative and positive eugenics.

Human Cloning

Q: Let's move on to the subject of human cloning. This has been much in the popular media since the Dolly cloning.
A: Quite.

Q: One underlying assumption that is not often discussed is the principle that whatever can be known should be known. Do you agree with this assumption?
A: I'm not sure I agree with it myself, but it is certainly a dogma in the scientific community.

Q: Some would say that there is a difference between knowing and acting on what we know. Do you agree?
A: There is an abstract, definitional difference, but I am not sure that there is any practical difference. Once we knew how to make the atomic bomb, it was only a matter of time before we made one and then used it. Robert Oppenheimer, for one, questioned whether we should have ever moved beyond knowing to acting on what we know. Although it might have been a more authentic gesture if it had come before the atomic bomb was utilized, the fact that he raised the issue reinforces that this is a deep ethical dilemma in scientific research.

Q: This is a link into our discussion about human cloning.
A: Of course. Once we think we can clone a human, it will only be a matter of time until someone tries to do it. Although many countries already have

bans on attempting human cloning, this is not universal, and there has been much debate in the United States as to whether there should be a similar prohibition for publically funded laboratories.

Q: Who will do the research on human cloning if the public laboratories are not permitted to do so?
A: It's a good point. In today's world, ethical committees and institutional review boards strive to ensure that some of the blatant excesses of the past will not be repeated in publicly funded laboratories. But these regulations do not cover all laboratories. According to a recent article in *Science,* scientists have developed embryonic stem cell lines from human embryo cells.[1] This research has great potential not only for understanding fetal development but also as a source of cells for tissue transplantation because these cells have the potential to develop into all types of cells, given the right growth conditions and factors. However, this type of research could not be done at U.S. public-funded laboratories including NIH (because of the U.S. moratorium on the use of public funds for research on tissues derived from human embryos), but it could be done (and was done) by private industry and/or in other countries, where the lure of making money on this new technology drives the entire process and they are not "encumbered" by such strict ethical committees.

Similarly for gene cloning, if it is perceived that there is money to be made in gene cloning—and the industry already has very sophisticated scientific labs that seek to make a profit—these labs may be the ones that will work (and profit) in areas that ethicists deem out of bounds for publicly funded laboratories. Similarly, not all countries have similar ethical standards, and although such research may be banned in some countries, unless there is a worldwide moratorium, stopping research being conducted somewhere in the world will be difficult.

Q: What do you believe is the most important misconception about human cloning?
A: Probably that the cloned person is somehow going to be a xerox copy of the parent, and that the parent will in some way own the clone and live through it. These views are faulty on a number of grounds. First, take the case of identical twins, nature's example of cloning. Even though they are genetically identical, they are not the same person. Although they may look similar, they don't look exactly the same and they certainly don't act exactly the same. This is because their environments are different as well as the way their particular bodies and personalities react to those environments. In contrast to popular belief, and beautifully explored in the article by Nelkin and Lindee, humans are very much more than the sum of their genes. And in the same

---

[1]J.A. Thomson, J. Itskovitz-Eldor, S. Shapiro, M.A. Waknitz, J.J. Swiergiel, V. S. Marshall, and J.M. Jones (1998). Embryonic stem cell lines derived from human blastocysts. *Science* 282: 1145–1147.

way that identical twins are not copies of each other despite having identical genotypes, neither will clones be copies of the parent.

Second, the techniques being employed for cloning now actually involve at least two people (the DNA donor, usually thought of as the parent, the donor of the egg in which the cloned DNA is inserted), and often a third person (the owner of the uterus used to incubate the fetus), let alone those responsible for the upbringing of the child after birth. Thus, although the chromosomal DNA will be from the parent, the mitochondrial DNA, which we are discovering also has biological implications and is responsible for some diseases, will be from the egg donor. So the differences between a parent and clone will be much more marked than the diversity already found in natural identical twins.

Third, once people see that what is being cloned is *not* an exact copy of the parent, the allure of cloning may pass. It is true that since the beginning of time people have wanted to live forever. Some try to become immortal through their work and others through the people they know—children and friends. Surely, these will remain a surer bet than cloning. Once people find that their cloned children may be quite different from them (in looks as well as in personality), this primal allure will pass.

Q: Then what are the upsides and downsides to cloning?

A: Cloning of human embryos may enable us to learn more about the early stages of embryonic and fetal life, and cloning could, of course, be used to provide a source of perfectly matched tissue and organs for transplantation purposes. However, I think many people would consider the idea of creating a new person just to have a source of transplant tissues abhorrent (and what if the clone, or even the egg donor, refuses to give consent) and a prime example of "instrumentalization" (see Harris, pp. 371–374). And I agree with the arguments of Søren Holm (pp. 367–370) on the ethics of trying (albeit I think unsuccessfully) to create a copy of another human.

There is always potential for animal cloning, both as agribusiness seeks to find new products for us to consume and for biomedical research. Already strains of mice have been inbred for years to obtain colonies of mice with identical genetics for research purposes; cloning will speed up this process. Increasingly, scientists have been trying to modify animal tissues, either to produce biomedical products (i.e., hormones) or organs that could be used for human transplantation without being recognized as animal by the immune system, and once it becomes more efficient than the method used to produce Dolly, cloning will allow herds of similar animals to be produced. Already, this has been used to produce more than 50 cloned mice.[2]

---

[2]T. Wakayama, A.C.F. Perry, M. Zuccotti, K.R. Johnson, and R. Yanagimachi (1998). Full-term development of mice from enucleated oocytes injected with cumulus cell nuclei. *Nature* 394: 369–374.

Between these two areas, genetic engineering and human cloning, I believe that the first is really more important, with the potential of real benefits to humankind, but also (and especially in the case of germ-line therapy) requires due diligence on the part of everyone in order to avoid serious consequences that could affect us all. In addition, both cloning and germ-line therapy involve manipulations of human eggs and embryonic cells, with the attendant ethical issues of when life begins and what is and what is not acceptable to do with such tissues.

Altering Humans—The Case For and Against Human Gene Therapy

Nils Holtug

INTRODUCTION

The case in favor of gene therapy is quite simple. Gene therapy is likely to improve the health and well-being of some people that are among the worst off in society, namely patients with painful and life-threatening diseases. However, two types of objection have been raised.

According to one type gene therapy is in itself wrong, irrespective of its overall ability to promote human well-being and other values. This type of objection can be seen as a constraint on when we may (or are obliged to) promote the good (in this case, the health and well-being of human individuals), and is therefore a deontological objection.[1] According to the other type of objection gene therapy will or is likely to have very bad consequences—e.g., in terms of human well-being—and the badness of these consequences outweighs the benefits. This is a consequentialist objection.

In this paper, then, I shall consider how deontological and consequentialist objections apply to somatic, germ-line, and enhancement gene therapy, and whether they provide overall reasons not to perform one or several of these kinds of therapy.

How will gene therapy promote human well-being? It is expected to enable doctors to cure some painful and life-threatening diseases that were previously incurable, or at least to ameliorate the conditions of patients with these diseases. Somatic gene therapy has already been performed on some children with Severe Combined Immunodeficiency with good results, and among the next candidates for diseases to be targeted are cystic fibrosis, hemophilia B, cancer, and AIDS.[2,3] It is yet uncertain how successful a treatment gene therapy will be for these (and other) diseases, but there seems to be little doubt that it will prove a much better treatment than anything that is now available for at least some patients.

Both somatic and germ-line gene therapy aim to benefit patients. But whereas somatic therapy will only benefit the recipient, since only somatic cells are modified, germ-line therapy has the potential for benefiting an indefinite number of people since the genetic modification appears in the germ cells of the recipient and so can be passed on to his or her children.

However, in order for the modification to be passed on to all offspring, it will probably be necessary to either delete or turn off the disease-causing gene(s) (if not, the disease-causing and the corrective gene(s) would (often) come apart during genetic recombination[4]), or to correct the harmful mutation. Apart from that, it will be necessary to be able to target the inserted gene (or DNA sequence) on the chromosomes in order for the technology to be sufficiently safe. We do not yet know whether (or when) these techniques will be available. The question I shall ask concerning germ-line therapy is therefore whether, *if* it does become available, we should proceed with this kind of therapy in the healthcare system.

In the light of the potential benefits, might there nevertheless be moral reasons not to use these kinds of gene therapy? I shall consider first somatic and then germ-line therapy. Finally, I shall consider whether gene therapy for enhancement is a morally legitimate further development.

Somatic Gene Therapy

Playing God?

It is sometimes argued that gene therapy is an instance of 'playing God,' and therefore morally wrong. This argument comes in different versions: man is literally doing what is God's prerogative, or man is doing something that is unnatural, or man is making decisions on inappropriate grounds (e.g., on quality of life assessments), or man is fiddling with things he cannot properly predict the consequences of.[5] According to the first two versions gene therapy is wrong in itself, whereas the fourth version holds that it is wrong only on the further assumption that bad consequences in terms of human health and/or well-being can or are likely to follow. As we shall see, the third version may amount to either a deontological or a consequentialist objection. I shall consider these versions in turn.

Is it God's prerogative to determine the genetic make-up of humans? If it is God's prerogative, then it seems that every time a couple chooses to have a child they are violating it. Of course, it may be part of God's plan that they should have this child (with these genes), but then again it may also be part of God's plan that we should learn to perform gene therapy in order to be able to cure severe diseases.

Might gene therapy instead be considered unnatural and therefore wrong? This claim raises several problems. First, any specification of what is meant by 'unnatural' seems unable to avoid the following trilemma: either it will fail to apply to gene therapy, or it will cover a large scope of technologies we are already practicing and all accept, or it will be hopelessly *ad hoc*. For instance, it seems more than difficult to find a plausible specification of 'unnatural' that applies to gene therapy but not to the vaccination of our children or to organ transplants (which also involve inserting new genes into individuals).

Second, we shall need to know why, according to the favored specification, what is unnatural is also immoral, particularly since the labeling of certain practices as 'unnatural'—e.g., homosexuality—has traditionally been a dominant method of oppression. I have yet to see a plausible explanation of this link between unnatural and immoral.[6,7]

Would the decision to perform gene therapy be made on inappropriate grounds, e.g., on quality of life judgments? Making decisions on the basis of quality of life judgments may be considered just plain wrong. Quality of life judgments may also be claimed to be suspect either because they are considered epistemically inadequate, or because it is held that making important decisions in the healthcare system on this basis is dangerous. In the latter case the argument amounts to a consequentialist objection to gene therapy. I believe that none of these three reservations is well founded, but need not argue the point here. The purpose of gene therapy does not have to be formulated in terms of quality of life, but may be formulated in terms of restoring health. Surely anyone who believes in the value of healthcare will not find such a purpose illegitimate.

Finally, consider the consequentialist version of the 'playing God' argument, according to which gene therapists cannot properly predict the consequences of what they are doing. Since we do not have God's omniscience, we should not embark on projects that may have disastrous consequences for human well-being. However, this requirement is too rigorous. Many of the things we do may have such disastrous consequences, but if the probability that they will is very low, these acts may be legitimate, nevertheless. Whether we ought to abstain from doing them depends on the undesirability of the possible harm and its probability, and on the expected benefits. For instance, research aimed at curing AIDS could possibly result in a disaster (the HIV virus might accidentally be caused to mutate and become more likely to infect), but presumably this does not mean that it is wrong to carry out the research, considering both the probability of this happening and also the expected benefits.

Of course, if the risks involved in somatic gene therapy outweigh the expected benefits, we should not allow it, but, at least until now, it seems that this is not the case. I conclude, therefore, that the 'playing God' argument is not a good argument against somatic gene therapy.

Discrimination

In discussions, I have sometimes heard people espouse the view that gene therapy either discriminates against the individual under treatment, or is likely more generally to trigger a discriminatory attitude toward people who are disabled. This objection is similar to the objection sometimes raised against selective abortion, according to which an abortion on genetic grounds either discriminates against the aborted fetus or against people who already exist and have the disability in question.[8–10]

The point may be that acts of discrimination are in themselves wrong, and that since gene therapy constitutes discrimination, *it* is wrong. Or the point may be that acts of discrimination have harmful consequences, e.g., in terms of lowering the self-esteem and general well-being of the individuals discriminated against. So I need to address both whether gene therapy does in fact constitute an act or practice of discrimination, and how it will affect the people allegedly discriminated against.

It is important to note that gene therapy differs from selective abortion in several respects. Most importantly, gene therapy aims to benefit the recipient by ensuring that she will not have a severe disease. Therefore, it is hard to see why it should be considered an instance of discrimination *against her*, or why she should feel that it was. Therapy will imply that she will be spared a lot of misery, and it is hoped, live as long as other people do.

Does gene therapy discriminate against other people who are disabled, e.g., people who will not or cannot be cured? Since gene therapy reflects the view that certain diseases or disabilities are unwanted, might people who have these diseases but are not treated themselves start to feel unwanted? It is, of course, with gene therapy as with other medical treatments extremely important to distinguish between the disease, which is unwanted, and the individuals who have the disease who are certainly not unwanted. Once this distinction is made, it becomes clear that the performance of gene therapy does not reflect the view that people with disabilities are less important or less worthy of respect than other people. The purpose gene therapy serves is to help the disabled, not to discriminate against them.

Maybe the objection to gene therapy should be interpreted in a subtler way. When gene therapy and other advanced technologies are used in trying to eradicate each and every disease around, this process tends to narrow our conception of what is considered 'normal.' We become much less willing to accept abnormalities in ourselves and others than we were when there really was not anything we could do about them. Arguably, people who cannot meet these high standards are thereby stigmatized in society; furthermore, our focus on technology sometimes gives them false hopes about what medicine has to offer.

I think that this objection has something to be said for it, but that its impact on the question of the acceptability of gene therapy should not be exaggerated. First of all, it is not an objection *specifically* aimed at gene therapy; it will tell against all advances in healthcare. Are we really willing to give up these advances—possible treatments for cystic fibrosis, for AIDS, or for cancer? The fact that there may be some drawbacks does not justify abandoning the entire enterprise regardless of its benefits. Second, the technologies alone do not stigmatize, people's attitudes do. Such attitudes should of course be fought wherever they occur, and it is the duty of governments, schools, and individual citizens to see to it that they are. But I cannot see why it should not be possible to aim both at an advanced healthcare system *and* at a society in which we respect each other and ourselves regardless of disability. It may be something we shall have to work for, but it is well worth working for. Finally, health care personnel and researchers should be careful not to give people false hopes about what is currently possible.

It may be argued that this is all very well as long as we are considering gene therapy for severe diseases, but that this is only the first step. Once we engage in gene therapy, we are on a slippery slope to uses that are morally much more dubious. I have discussed this argument at length elsewhere,[11] so here I can be brief. If there are certain uses of an otherwise very beneficial technology we want to exclude, and there undoubtedly are, we should introduce regulations that will protect us from these uses, rather than exclude the technology. This is what we do concerning other medical technologies (e.g., surgery), and this is also what we should do in the case of gene therapy.

It seems, then, that somatic gene therapy is well worth pursuing.

GERM-LINE GENE THERAPY

The germ-line may be modified in either of two ways: a fertilized egg or very early embryo may be modified, or an egg or sperm (or both) may be modified before fertilization. Whether one of these techniques is superior to the other, e.g., in terms of posing a slighter risk of an undesirable outcome for the resulting individual, can be very difficult to predict today. Therefore, I shall not try to differentiate their moral implications.

It should be noted that these techniques are probably only realistic in the context of in vitro fertilization.

Why Germ-Line Gene Therapy?

Whereas somatic therapy is most commonly considered a legitimate extension of practices already employed within the healthcare system, a vast majority of the reports from governments, councils, and ethics committees, etc., on germ-line therapy disapprove of this option.[12] For instance, in a joint statement from eleven European medical research councils it is said that "The insertion of genes into fertilized eggs or very early embryos is fundamentally different [from somatic therapy] because these genes would be passed on to the off-spring in subsequent generations. Germ-line gene therapy should not be contemplated."[13]

However, an increasing number of scientists and (perhaps particularly) ethicists suggest that such a categorical rejection of germ-line therapy is premature.[14-25] Several considerations speak in favor of germ-line therapy: germ-line therapy is more efficient than somatic therapy because the disease is not passed on from the recipient to her children;[26] some genetic diseases may be treatable only by means of germ-line therapy (e.g., because the blood-brain barrier makes certain cells inaccessible to somatic therapy, or because all cells in the body will have to be treated—this may be the case with muscular dystrophies);[27,28] since fortunately more and more people with severe diseases survive until adulthood (and longer), it seems plausible that this will tend to increase the proportion of disease-causing genes in the human gene pool (and somatic therapy will contribute to this development); and some couples may not want embryos destroyed after IVF even if preimplantation diagnosis reveals that they carry disease-causing genes.[29,30] This last concern, however, would have less weight in cases where the disease could be treated equally well by somatic therapy. Nevertheless, in the light of these potential benefits of germ-line therapy, what might the objections be?

Playing God—Again

Does the 'playing God' objection apply better to germ-line than to somatic therapy? Bishop Finis Crutchfield is reported as objecting to germ-line therapy on the grounds that "efforts to modify the work of the Creator constitute 'pride, the deadliest of all sins.' "[31] But might we not also say that somatic therapy is an attempt to modify the work of the Creator, and is thus equally objectionable? I cannot really see that this objection adds anything new to the versions of the argument I have discussed and dismissed in the context of somatic therapy.

Nor does germ-line therapy seem to be more 'unnatural' than somatic therapy. After all, what some people intuitively find objectionable is that the genes of a human being (or what will become a human being) are modified, and in this respect, the two technologies do not differ. Of course, in the case of germ-line therapy, more people may be affected, but if, as I have argued, it is not unnatural in an objectionable sense to alter one person (with somatic therapy), it is hard to see why it would be objectionably unnatural if we were to alter more (with germ-line therapy). Finally, even if we did find out that there was a sense in which germ-line but not somatic therapy was unnatural, it would still have to be argued that this difference was morally relevant.

Genetic Integrity

The European Community has expressed certain reservations about germ-line therapy. In a human genome analysis program it is held that the right to a genetic identity forms part of the integrity and the dignity of an individual.[32] However, it is difficult to know what to make of this right. Everyone—genetically altered or not—has a 'genetic identity'. But maybe the point is that a person has a right to her *natural* (i.e., unaltered) genetic identity.

Furthermore, it is quite unclear how a person's (natural) genetic identity is supposed to constitute part of her integrity and dignity. According to one interpretation, a person's integrity is violated if her genes are modified, irrespective of whether this is against her interest and/or against her will (or, in the case of germ-line therapy, the interests and will she will later have). However, it is more than difficult to see what the *rationale* for such a right would be. Normally, the purpose a right serves is to protect the individual. But what kind of disvalue to the person would be involved in violating this right, if violating it involved furthering the interests and respecting the autonomous will of the person?

In fact, the terms 'integrity' and 'dignity' suggest instead a Kantian (deontological) concern that persons should be treated as ends in themselves and not as mere means. Presumably, then, a person's integrity and dignity are respected if her interests and/or autonomy are not set aside. How would these values be affected by germ-line therapy?

Germ-line therapy would aim to prevent severe diseases and thus to prevent much suffering and premature death. If the technology became sufficiently safe, this would certainly seem not to be against the interests of future persons, who would avoid having the relevant diseases. In fact, it would seem to be *in* their interest.

There is, however, a problem of identity here. In most cases, the (numerically) *same* individual(s) will not come into existence if germ-line therapy is performed as will if it is not. This follows from a plausible claim made by Kripke, namely that a person would not have existed had she not originated from the sperm and egg from which she in fact originated,[33] and from some facts about the alternatives to germ-line therapy.

Presumably germ-line therapy would be performed on a fertilized egg or early embryo or on one or both gametes before fertilization, and then the embryo(s) would be implanted. Suppose, then, that a specific couple decide to have IVF performed, and if the embryo(s) carries the disease-causing gene, to have germ-line therapy performed. Suppose furthermore that as a result they have a child with a modified genome—call her A. If they had not had the option of germ-line therapy and decided to use it, it is very likely that A would not have existed. Either because they had then not opted for IVF, and so even if they had a child nonetheless, it is extremely likely that it would not be A, since it is extremely unlikely that the same sperm would have fertilized the same egg. Or because, even if they had opted for IVF, it is likely that the embryos would be tested for whether they carried the disease-causing gene, and embryos that were carriers would not be implanted, and so A would not have come into existence.

So the alternatives for A would (most likely) not be existence with or without a modified genome, but existence with a modified genome or nonexistence. This, however, does not undermine the claim that a sufficiently safe kind of germ-line therapy would not be against her interests, nor, more generally, against the interests of future generations. It would indeed be strange to say about A that she has had her right to her genetic identity violated (in a morally objectionable sense), when not violating that right would have meant that she would never exist. To see this, we must consider the value of coming into existence.

Suppose, first that we believe that existence and nonexistence cannot be compared evaluatively.[34] Then it would not make sense to say that coming into existence with a modified genome is against an individual's interests (remember, the relevant alternative is nonexistence). Suppose, instead, that existence and nonexistence can be compared evaluatively, as I have argued elsewhere that they can.[35] Then only in very rare cases would it be worse for an individual to come into existence with a modified genome that meant that she would be healthy, than not to come into existence. In most cases, it would *benefit* people to come into existence in this condition. And, on average, it is likely that it would benefit them (and their descendents) more than it would benefit people with unmodified disease-causing genes (and their descendents) to come into existence.[36] So it is difficult to see that a sufficiently safe kind of germ-line therapy can be opposed by appealing to a concern for the people directly affected.

I suppose it could be argued instead that gene therapy could alienate a child from her parents, if it meant that she had genes or DNA-sequences that did not originate from them.[37] But since presumably she would at most differ in one or two genes (out of a total of somewhere between fifty and one hundred thousand), this does not seem a serious cause for alarm. In any case, the expected benefits to her seem to outbalance quite a lot of (maybe ill-founded) unease she may feel about her heritage.

It seems, then, that the alleged right to one's (natural) genetic identity cannot be justified by appealing to one's interests. But maybe the point is not that germ-line therapy would set aside people's interests, but that it would set aside their autonomy. Although this may be what is meant by referring to the right to one's genetic identity, it is not really a point that focuses on whether persons have an important and inviolable 'genetic identity' or 'genetic integrity,' but rather on the value of deciding for oneself.

The Argument from Autonomy

Germ-line therapy would necessarily involve reshaping the genetic make-up of future persons without their (informed) consent.[38,39] This may be considered a morally objectionable violation of the autonomy of future persons.[40] The

problem with this claim is that future persons are not *now* autonomous individuals. In cases where decisions have to be made concerning individuals
that are not (now) able to make up their own minds, we should act according
to what we expect to be in their best interest. For instance, it seems perfectly
legitimate that surgery is sometimes performed on babies although they cannot themselves consent to the treatment. The relevant concern here seems not
to be autonomy, but acting in the affected party's interest. It should also be remembered that *none* of us has actually chosen our genes and, at least until
now, it has not been considered a moral problem.

Maybe we should interpret the Argument from Autonomy differently. A
more charitable interpretation would be the following: We should make the
decisions that we can expect that future generations (in due time) will want
us to have made. Of course, in most cases this obligation and the obligation
to act in the *interest* of future generations will recommend the same acts.

On this interpretation of the Argument from Autonomy, it can be pointed
out that it may be very difficult to predict the traits future generations will
prefer.[41] Although this is of course true for many traits, there do seem to be
clear exceptions. Presumably no one has ever found nor will ever find Huntington's chorea or Lesch-Nyhan syndrome really desirable. This is just as
predictable as the fact that future generations probably will not particularly
enjoy having skin cancer (and this is of course one of the main reasons for
trying to limit the damage to the ozone layer).

I think that Ulla Wessels has illustrated this inadequacy of the Argument from Autonomy against germ-line therapy beautifully: "Suppose the
medical techniques were at your disposal; suppose you had refused to use
them and your daughter has therefore been born with a serious, now incurable defect that you knew could have been avoided. 'Mummy', she will ask
one day, 'why did you prefer my being ill to my being healthy?' 'Respect for
your self-determination, my love'."[42]

There is also a more fundamental problem with the argument. I have already pointed out that a couple's decision about whether to opt for germ-line
therapy is very likely to affect the (numerical) identity of the individual that
comes into existence. So whose autonomy should they respect? By opting for
germ-line therapy they will be bringing one individual into existence and he
will want them to have done just that, but had they chosen not to have therapy performed, they would have brought a different individual into existence,
and unless his disease is very severe, chances are that he would have wanted
them to have done just *that*.

The Long-Term Risks

Since none of the objections I have considered support the view that germ-line
therapy is inherently wrong, let us now turn to the consequentialist objections.
One of the main reasons for preferring germ-line therapy to somatic therapy
is, of course, that the genetic modification is passed on to future generations,

who will then not need to be treated themselves (unless new harmful mutations occur). However, this fact also gives rise to a problem because it can be very difficult to predict the long-term consequences of germ-line therapy. How will it affect the well-being of people in the distant future?[43–45] Furthermore, errors might be multiplied through each new generation, unlike with somatic therapy, where any error would be restricted to the recipient.[46]

Indeed, no matter how far our knowledge advances, we will never be able to predict the exact consequences of performing germ-line therapy. But this is true for any medical technology. I have already pointed out that research on the AIDS virus could conceivably cause a catastrophe. But the fact that it *could* does not in itself justify that we give up trying to find a cure for AIDS and thus just condemn AIDS patients to a certain and painful premature death. It is of course true that the predictable risks involved in germ-line gene therapy may turn out always to outweigh the expected benefits. But then again, it may also turn out that we acquire enough knowledge to justify the claim that the expected benefits outweigh the predictable risks. I'm not suggesting that this is probable, merely that the possibility cannot be ruled out in advance.

However, maybe the problem with germ-line therapy is rather that we do not *know* the size of the risks, i.e., that we are unable to predict all the possible outcomes and to assign reliable probabilities. But again, I do not think that we can rule out in advance the possibility of the technology progressing to a stage where the knowledge we possess is sufficient to justify progressing slowly with the first trials.

It may still seem that not engaging in germ-line therapy should be recommended because we would then be 'playing safe.' But although it is sometimes assumed that doing nothing is always the safe option, this assumption is in fact quite unwarranted. Bad consequences may ensue both from acting and from omitting, and there appears to be no reason to think that they are more likely to follow from actions. So whether germ-line therapy should be judged to involve unacceptable risks should be determined by weighing these risks against the expected benefits, and comparing with alternative courses of action (or inaction).[47] Therefore an appeal to risks will not justify a rejection of germ-line therapy once and for all: technology may advance such that one day the risks are outweighed by the expected benefits. However, no one—as far as I know—is suggesting that this day has come, and indeed it may not be implausible to suggest that it will probably never come.

The Argument from Evolution

This argument can be considered a version of the former argument, although with a special focus. It is sometimes pointed out that genetic variation is an evolutionary advantage for our (or indeed any) species. This variation is what allows us to adapt to new circumstances in our environment, and so any reduction of genetic variability would involve a risk to us as a species. Since germ-line therapy would involve eradicating certain genes from the human gene pool (namely some disease-causing genes), it would leave us more vulnerable to environmental changes.[48–50]

The force of this argument depends on the nature of the gene therapy employed. As it is practiced today, gene therapy involves inserting genes, not deleting them or turning them off. So gene therapy does not reduce genetic variation. Instead, gene therapy has the potential for *increasing* genetic variation. (Might this prove advantageous in trying to cope with our environment after a nuclear catastrophe or heavy pollution?)

However, in order for germ-line therapy to have the desired effect, it would probably be necessary to delete or turn off the disease-causing gene(s) or to correct the mutation, as I have already pointed out. Nevertheless, even if gene therapy in the future should involve deleting or turning off genes or correcting mutations (this may also be necessary in order to treat diseases that are caused by dominant genes, such as Huntington's chorea), the somewhat hypothetical evolutionary disadvantage involved in deleting a few genes would seem to be outweighed if the benefits were substantial, as they would be if painful and life-threatening diseases could be prevented.[51]

What Else Do Disease-Causing Genes Do?

It is sometimes pointed out that disease-causing genes may not just be carriers of disease, they may also have a positive impact on human health. For instance, people who are heterozygous carriers of the sickle-cell trait are less likely to die from malaria.[52,53] It may be guessed that other so-called genetic 'defects' have equally beneficial effects. The problem with this suggestion is that we do not really know whether, and, if so, to what extent different genetic 'defects' confer benefits on us. It is sometimes suggested that this would explain why these genes have survived in the human gene pool. But again, we would have to weigh the expected benefits against the risks. Even in the case of sickle-cell disease it would seem reasonable to try to eradicate the genes that cause such a debilitating and life-threatening disease for which there exists no effective treatment, while fighting malaria by attacking malaria-carrying mosquitoes and using the efficient drugs that are already available.[54–56]

Controlling Pregnancies?

Would germ-line therapy really enable us to delete some of the genes responsible for severe diseases from the human gene pool? It would seem to require that society had a large measure of control of pregnancies. One strategy would be to screen couples in advance, and if they were carriers, IVF and if necessary subsequent gene therapy would be performed. Other efficient strategies seem to require just as much control.

There would probably be couples who would not feel comfortable with screening or who would object to germ-line therapy for moral reasons. It would hardly be considered legitimate to *force* them to comply, because this is an objectionable violation of parental autonomy and/or because it is counterproductive in terms of well-being. Although there may be exceptional cases in which society ought to intervene when couples make irresponsible choices on behalf of their children, as a rule choices—including reproductive choices—are best left to the couple. Therefore, society could not legitimately exercise the degree of control that would seem necessary to delete specific genes from the human gene pool. Another problem is, of course, that presumably germ-line therapy is only a realistic option in some parts of the world.

True as this may be, it does not undermine the rationale for germ-line therapy. To do that, we would also have to believe that if we cannot benefit everyone, we should benefit no one. The rationale for germ-line therapy is not in itself to delete genes from the human gene pool, but to the highest extent possible to prevent people from getting severe diseases. If germ-line therapy can help in this respect we have a moral reason to perform it, although of course other things would also have to be true. It is to some of these other things I turn next.

Is Germ-Line Therapy Superfluous?

In the light of the risks involved in germ-line therapy, we should consider whether the same results could be reached by other and safer means. In fact, a serious objection to germ-line therapy is that it is superfluous: the same results can be reached at slighter risk through preimplantation diagnosis and selective implantation, or by prenatal diagnosis and if necessary selective abortion.[57–59]

Although offering prenatal diagnosis and selective abortion to couples or women does mean that fewer children are affected with genetically determined diseases, it may not be an acceptable solution to all couples. In couples where both parties are homozygous for the same recessive disease, or where one or both parties are homozygous for a dominant disease, selective abortion is not an option because all fetuses would be affected, but of course such couples are rare. A more serious problem is that some couples would have to go through several abortions before they had a child without the disease. Furthermore, selective abortion would not be an acceptable option for couples who are opposed to abortion or to selection. Finally, selective abortions could actually increase the incidence of disease-causing genes in the human gene pool, thus raising the incidence of future abortions since more children who are merely carriers, and thus more likely to have children themselves, will be born.

Selective implantation has several advantages compared to selective abortion in that abortion is avoided and the incidence of children that are heterozygous carriers of genes for recessive diseases can be brought down rather than increased. However, to most couples, having babies by means of good old-fashioned sex is preferable to IVF, because hormone treatments are avoided and because of the relatively low success rate and high cost of IVF, as well as, of course, for sentimental reasons.

Since presumably germ-line therapy would also involve IVF, it seems that most of what we could and would want to do in terms of corrective gene therapy could be done by means of selective implantation. There would of course be cases where enough unaffected embryos could not be produced. But since they would be very rare, it seems that the existence of such cases cannot justify the investments necessary to make germ-line therapy a viable option.

If, however, germ-line therapy developed to a stage where it no longer required IVF, this situation would change. Then there would be a significant advantage in germ-line therapy. For us to be justified in applying it, we would still have to be able to predict the long-term consequences reasonably accurately. It would also have to be true that the risk was outbalanced by the expected benefits (and more so than in any alternative). It is not implausible to claim that these requirements will never be met, or that germ-line therapy without IVF will never become technically possible. In fact, I have no idea what kind of technique would make it possible. However, it may be premature to *rule out* the development of such a technique in advance.

Another option has to be considered. It is possible and could be considered desirable to improve the genetic make-up of humans by introducing fundamentally new genes into the human gene pool, i.e., introducing genes that do not occur 'naturally' in humans. Such improvements could not be achieved by more traditional means such as selective abortion or implantation. The question raised here, however, is more a question of the moral legitimacy of enhancement engineering than that of germ-line therapy, and it is therefore to enhancement engineering I turn next.

GENE THERAPY FOR ENHANCEMENT

Shopping in Nozick's Genetic Supermarket

Gene therapy for enhancement may be the most perplexing challenge that genetic engineering faces us with. Robert Nozick imagines a future genetic supermarket in which prospective parents could shop genes coding for traits they would want for their children, e.g., a specific sex or eye color.[60] As we have seen, we might even imagine changes that are more radical than this. Traits that humans have not previously possessed could be engineered into people. Both kinds of therapy would be enhancement engineering in the sense that they would aim at making 'normal,' 'healthy' individuals *better* (according to some set of values) by enhancing some characteristic.[61] Both somatic and germ-line therapy could make such changes possible.

There is no doubt that most of us intuitively reject enhancement genetic engineering. I think the main reason for this is that we immediately think of practices such as genetic engineering for intelligence or looks (perhaps Aryan style), practices that seem to have an air of 'playing God' and Nazi eugenics to them. These intuitions are further boosted by science fiction stories in which hi-tech experiments get out of hand (*Frankenstein*) or a new breed of humans is designed in the light of an evil ideology (*The Boys From Brazil*). Certainly we are justified in being opposed to such new designs. But consider instead a different kind of practice:

> Suppose that twenty years from now AIDS has spread all over the world, and many millions are dying. Furthermore, no cure has been found but it has recently become possible to perform gene therapy on teenagers that are not yet infected, securing that they will never catch AIDS, and there are no undesirable side-effects. These teenagers are perfectly 'normal', their genes are those of the average person (if there is any such thing, genetically speaking). Performing gene therapy could save thousands, maybe millions; should we do it?[62]

Performing gene therapy here would be enhancement engineering, but I think that our intuitions concerning this case are quite different from what they are concerning engineering for intelligence or beauty. Performing gene therapy here seems analogous to giving our children injections so they will not catch the flu or severe diseases such as meningitis. These intuitions can be explained in terms of important moral values such as well-being and fairness; using genetic engineering to ensure that young people do not die from AIDS would be very valuable because it would mean avoiding a lot of suffering and avoiding that young people were deprived of the greater part of their lives, something most of us find particularly unfair.

Might enhancement engineering nevertheless be considered inherently wrong, such that a deontological constraint could be justified? The problem is that it is difficult to explain *why*, in itself, it should be considered wrong, or even bad. Surely it is not wrong to vaccinate our children, even though this makes them better than they are naturally (by improving their ability to fight disease). So it cannot be enhancement, in itself, that is wrong. Nor did the previous discussion reveal anything inherently wrong in gene therapy, such that a constraint against effecting the enhancement by means of this technology could be justified.

Instead, consequentialist objections may be mounted. But, at least in the example cited above, none of the consequences seem to be bad, and some of them are clearly very good. So in some cases enhancement engineering might actually be morally permissible. However, as I said, this sort of gene therapy seems quite close to practices already in use in the health care system. What about much more ambitious alterations of human nature?

Making the World a Better Place

It is at least conceivable that enhancement engineering could involve making the world a much better place. Here is a somewhat ironical Jonathan Glover:

> It is easy to sympathize with opposition to the principle of changing our nature. Preserving the human race as it is will seem an acceptable option to all those who can watch the news on television and feel satisfied with the world. It will appeal to those who can talk to their children about the history of the twentieth century without wishing they could leave some things out.[63]

It is difficult not to feel that people would have been justified in doing almost anything to avoid the Nazi atrocities. Of course, any consequentialist will be committed to making the world a better place, no matter by what means. But anyone with some respect for human life and well-being must feel that it is very important to avoid the wars, torture, and oppression that our species has forced upon itself.

Suppose, surely all too simplistically, that we could remove the 'aggressive gene.' It would be possible for us to mold human nature so that our drive to resolve conflicts through war and oppression was eliminated. We might even imagine that the 'aggressive gene' could be replaced with an 'altruistic gene.' This gene would make us much more sensitive to the needs of other people, especially those people that are much worse off than ourselves, such as the 40,000 children who die from malnutrition and related health problems every day in developing nations. It seems that there would be a strong case for effecting such improvements to the human species.

When moral questions of this kind are brought into play, they are often dismissed as building on pure science fiction, all too fantastical to be taken seriously. And indeed, it is quite unlikely that we have an 'aggressive gene' or an 'altruistic gene.' However, it is not at all implausible that aggressive or altruistic traits have a significant genetic component, hidden in our DNA. So although it may be technically very difficult to take out or insert the genetic foundation for these traits, at least in principle, it need not be impossible.

Also, we should be very careful about ruling out such possibilities in advance. The following examples explain why:

> Even in the short term, predictions of technical developments are often wrong: the atomic bomb exploded a decade after Rutherford ruled out the possibility of any practical application of atomic energy.[64]

> Human gene therapy has arrived much sooner than Haldane, for example, predicted: in 1963, he stated that it would be millennia before the human genome could be manipulated.[65]

It took history merely a decade to prove Rutherford wrong, and three to prove Haldane wrong.

Finally, even *if* enhancement engineering of the sort considered should never become possible, related genetic interventions may, and it would be an advantage to have thought about possible moral benefits and drawbacks *before* these techniques are developed.

What might we say on the other side, i.e., what are the possible disadvantages of adopting a scheme of improving the species? I can think of the following questions that would have to be answered satisfactorily before embarking on such a scheme:

- What should we think of the long-term risk?
- What kind of confidence can we have in the ideals according to which *we* want to shape human nature?
- What reasons do we have for believing that enhancement engineering will in fact be used for beneficent purposes?
- How will enhancement engineering affect our views and values?

I have already considered the question of risk in relation to corrective somatic and germ-line therapy. But while we may have a pretty good idea about what will happen if we perform corrective therapy (because we know how people with the 'normal' genes function), our predictions of what new genes or combinations of genes will do are bound to be much less accurate. For instance, we might want to know what else 'aggressive genes' do, besides (perhaps) forcing us into ridiculous wars. Maybe there is an evolutionary advantage in being aggressive, i.e., aggressive individuals tend to survive. We would want to know more about how the loss of this trait might leave us, individually or collectively, more vulnerable.

This gives rise to a further problem. Presumably the 'aggressive gene' would have to be deleted in the very early stage of the embryo or before. And it is not clear that prospective parents, wanting to act in the interest of their child, would want a child that was too altruistic. This is because it does not seem implausible that aggressiveness (or some degree of egoism) is part of what makes for a successful career in many lines of work (and perhaps other areas of life as well). Many prospective parents would not want their child to miss out on such opportunities, and maybe rightly so. Now, it would hardly be legitimate to coerce couples into joining the altruistic program, and the mere fact that many did not join would probably keep yet more out, because they would not want their child to be a 'sucker' ('sucker' is a game-theoretic name for an individual who cooperates with cheats that just take advantage of him).

Concerning the second question, the problem is that we shall be shaping future individuals according to *our* ideals (if therapy is performed on the germ-line). The problem is not that we shall be violating the autonomy of future individuals. I have already argued that regarding future individuals, our moral obligation is to act in their *interest*.[66] So is it plausible to claim that the sort of enhancement engineering we would perform would be in the interest of future generations? According to Glover, John Mackie once said that "... if the Victorians had been able to use genetic engineering, they would have aimed to make us more pious and patriotic."[67] How can we be sure that *our* ideals are any better?

I think that the correct answer to this question is that "In general, we can't." Many values seem to be dependent on culture and history. But as I have already argued, this does not mean that all values are. No-one finds skin cancer a good thing. But apart from severe diseases and intense suffering, what else does everyone agree is really bad?

Acting only insofar as we were *sure* that we were acting in the interest of future people would be setting our standards too high. Many of our acts have consequences for future people, and most of the time all we have to go on is certain expectations as to how future people will be affected. If we required certainty, we could never act (which, in turn, would also have consequences for future people). So the right question to ask seems to be what we can rationally expect to be in the interest of future people. And making the world a place in which war, torture, and oppression do not occur seems to qualify in this respect. This, however, does not mean that we should forget Mackie's point. Many 'interventions' into human nature might turn out merely to reflect present prejudices, rather than to constitute improvements. We should always be aware of this.

The third question to be answered is which reasons we have to expect that enhancement engineering will in fact be used for beneficent purposes. Glover does not want to rule out using genetic engineering to make humans more altruistic, because humans are now to a large extent selfish and aggressive. Of course, if we knew in advance that genetic engineering would be used to change human nature to the better, there might not be a problem. But how can we know this? What reasons does Glover have to be optimistic about the changes we would make in human nature, given his pessimism about human nature? If we accept Glover's view on human nature, we should expect the opposite: that enhancement engineering will be abused.

This objection could be directed against almost all scientific developments (and indeed it is), and we must not let it overwhelm us.[68] But this does not mean that we should assign *no* or only little weight to this possibility. Again, a reasonable policy would involve weighing the expected benefits against the risks.

The fourth and last question is probably the most difficult one to answer. Would enhancement engineering somehow trigger elitism and intolerance in society, as some people fear? Would humans feel a loss in terms of identity if they became too different from what humans used to be?

Whether elitism would come about would probably depend both on the purpose with which genetic engineering was undertaken, and on how fairly the genetic advantages were distributed. If, e.g., the genetic advantage was inserted into everyone, elitism would not be a problem, because everyone would belong to the elite. But, of course, in many cases it is more than probable that such an advantage would not be distributed fairly, at least if we presuppose the standards of our present society.

Concerning a possible 'loss' of identity, the extent of the alteration brought about seems crucial. The human species is and always has been subject to evolution through natural selection, and this means that our genome is altered all the time. There is no fundamental set of genes that constitutes human beings and defines their genetic identity once and for all. Changes are 'natural'. Therefore some alterations through genetic engineering would not seem to make much of a difference. But if the phenotypic impact was severe enough, children might have a hard time identifying with their parents, and vice versa. This is a legitimate worry.

The discussion of the four questions listed above has revealed that there are significant reasons to be *extremely* cautious when or if considering enhancement engineering. It may not be implausible that it would *never* be responsible to engage in such activities. However, the above discussion cannot justify the conclusion that we can rule out this possibility forever, although the only clear-cut examples I can think of are the scenario in which we can prevent young people from dying of AIDS and scenarios that are close to this.

CONCLUSIONS

Presumably somatic gene therapy will be introduced in hospitals in many (more) countries during the next ten years, and granted the argument of this article, this is a good thing. Germ-line therapy and therapy for enhancement are not just around the corner, but it is nevertheless important to try to sort out the ethical questions before technology advances to a point where decisions have to be made. The case for germ-line therapy seems rather weak unless it can be performed without requiring IVF or there are clear (overriding) reasons for enhancing certain human qualities, and somatic therapy is not a reasonable option.

Whether there are such reasons depends on the (long-term) expected benefits and the risks involved, according to the conclusions reached above. The best policy may be never to introduce such therapies, although this will have to be assessed as science progresses and in the light of the confidence one can have in the political and moral standards of the relevant society. Here, as in many other areas of human conduct, it is important to be well aware of our fallibility and of our unfortunate tendency to let our own interests outweigh the interests of future people.

ACKNOWLEDGMENTS

I should like to thank Jens Peter Hjort, Nunni Rømer, Per Sandberg, Peter Sandøe, Peter Singer, and an anonymous reviewer for valuable comments on an earlier version of this paper. Thanks are also due to the Danish Research Councils for financial support.

Notes

1. Some people believe that deontological constraints have a threshold, such that if enough is at stake, it is permissible (or obligatory) to violate a constraint. However, since I shall reject the deontological objections to gene therapy, it doesn't really matter in the present context whether constraints have a threshold.

2. Anderson WF. Editorial: end-of-the-year potpourri—1993. *Human Gene Therapy* 1993;4:701–2.

3. Anderson WF. Human gene therapy. *Science* 1992;256:808–13.

4. Danks DM. Editorial: germ-line gene therapy: no place in treatment of genetic disease. *Human Gene Therapy* 1994;5:152.

5. For an analysis of the different versions of the 'playing God' argument, see Chadwick R. Playing God. *Bioethics News* 1990;9:38–46.

6. For a good discussion of the relation between unnaturalness and morality, see Singer P, Wells D. *The Reproduction Revolution: New Ways of Making Babies.* Oxford: Oxford University Press, 1984:36–41.

7. For a theological analysis to the effect that gene therapy is not unnatural in any morally problematic sense, see Porter J. What is morally distinctive about genetic engineering? *Human Gene Therapy* 1990;1:419–24.

8. For discussions of this objection, see Chadwick R. The perfect baby: Introduction. In: Chadwick R, ed. *Ethics, Reproduction and Genetic Control.* London: Routledge, 1992:110–1. Also see notes 9 and 10.

9. Glover J. Future people, disability and screening. In: Laslett P, Fishkin JS, eds. *Justice Between Age Groups and Generations.* New Haven: Yale University Press, 1992:133–4.

10. Harris J. Is gene therapy a form of eugenics? *Bioethics* 1993;7:180–4.

11. Holtug N. Human gene therapy: down the slippery slope? *Bioethics* 1993;7:402–19.

12. de Wachter MAM. Ethical aspects of human germ-line gene therapy. *Bioethics* 1993;7:167–9.

13. European Medical Research Councils. Gene therapy in man. *The Lancet* 1988;June 4:1271.

14. Anderson WF. Human gene therapy: scientific and ethical considerations. *Journal of Medicine and Philosophy* 1985;10:275–91.

15. Engelhardt HT. Human nature technologically revisited. *Social philosophy & Policy* 1990;8:180–91.

16. Fletcher JC. Ethical issues in and beyond prospective trials of human gene therapy. *Journal of Medicine and Philosophy* 1985; 10:293–309.

17. Glover J. *What Sort of People Should There Be?* Harmondsworth: Penguin, 1984.

18. Harris J. *Wonderwoman and Superman: The Ethics of Human Biotechnology.* Oxford: Oxford University Press, 1992.

19. Hoose B. Gene therapy: where to draw the line. *Human Gene Therapy* 1990;1:299–306.

20. Munson R, Davis LH. Germ-line gene therapy and the medical imperative. *Kennedy Institute of Ethics Journal* 1992;2:137–58.

21. Resnik D. Debunking the slippery slope argument against human germ-line gene therapy. *Journal of Medicine and Philosophy* 1994;19:23–40.

22. Walters L. The ethics of human gene therapy. *Nature* 1986;320:225–7.

23. Wessels U. Genetic engineering and ethics in Germany. In: Dyson A, Harris J, eds. *Ethics and Biotechnology.* London: Routledge, 1994:230–58.

24. Wood-Harper J. Manipulation of the germ-line. In: Dyson A, Harris J, eds. *Ethics and Biotechnology.* London: Routledge, 1994:121–43.

25. Zimmerman BK. Human germ-line therapy: the case for its development and use. *Journal of Medicine and Philosophy* 1991;16:593–612.

26. See note 22. Walters 1986:227.

27. See note 22. Walters 1986:227.

28. See note 25. Zimmerman 1991:594.

29. See note 20. Munson, Davis 1992:140.

30. See note 12. de Wachter 1993:170.

31. Ostling RN. Scientists must not play God. *Time* 1983;June 20:37.

32. Commission of the European Community. *Adopting a Specific Research and Technological Development Programme in the Field of Health: Human Genome Analysis.* Brussels, November 1989.

33. Kripke S. *Naming and Necessity.* Oxford: Basil Blackwell 1980:113.

34. As argued by e.g. David Heyd. See Heyd D. *Genethics: Moral Issues in the Creation of People.* Berkeley and Los Angeles: University of California Press, 1992.

35. Holtug N, Sandøe P. Who benefits?—Why personal identity does not matter in a moral evaluation of germ-line gene therapy. *Journal of Applied Philosophy* 1996;13:157–66. In this article, we also argue that even if the gene therapy itself was to affect the identity of the resulting individual (because of the genotypic or phenotypic impact), this would be irrelevant for a moral assessment of germ-line therapy.

36. However, as I shall argue later, IVF and preimplantation diagnosis could be used to prevent disease-causing genes from being passed on to future generations instead, at a slighter risk.

37. See note 8. Chadwick 1992:125–7.

38. Lappé M. Ethical issues in manipulating the human germ line. *Journal of Medicine and Philosophy* 1991;16:628.

39. Moseley R. Commentary: maintaining the somatic/germ-line distinction: some ethical drawbacks. *Journal of Medicine and Philosophy* 1991;16:642–3.

40. Although autonomy is typically a value defended by deontologists, it is sometimes defended by consequentialists as a value to be promoted.

41. Tauer CA. Does human gene therapy raise new ethical questions? *Human Gene Therapy* 1990;1:414.

42. See note 23. Wessels 1994:239.

43. Dixon P. *The Genetic Revolution.* Eastborne: Kingsway Publications, 1993:178–9.

44. Jonas H. *Technik, Medizin und Ethik.* Frankfurt am Main: Suhrkamp, 1987:197.

45. See note 38. Lappé 1991:630–1.

46. Suzuki D, Knudtson P. *Genethics: The Ethics of Engineering Life.* London: Unwin Hyman, 1989:191.

47. Even if one accepts the Doctrine of Doing and Allowing, and so believes that the risks involved in acting are morally more important than the risks involved in omitting, one would still have to weigh these weighted risks (and benefits) against each other. Of course, it is possible to hold that even the slightest risk involved in acting trumps even the largest risk involved in omitting, but this view is so implausible that it must be considered a nonstarter.

48. Berger EM, Gert BM. Genetic disorders and the ethical status of germ-line gene therapy. *Journal of Medicine and Philosophy* 1991;16:675–7.

49. British Medical Association. *Our Genetic Future.* Oxford: Oxford University Press, 1992:186.

50. See also note 46. Suzuki, Knudtson 1989:188.

51. Adherents of the Argument from Evolution must also consider selective abortion and genetic counseling dubious. For some reason, these worries are seldomly articulated.

52. Nolan K, Swenson S. New tools, new dilemmas: genetic frontiers. *Hastings Center Report* 1988;18:(6)43.

53. See also note 46. Suzuki, Knudtson 1989:84–6.

54. See note 18. Harris 1992:165.

55. Incidentally, it is expected that new progress will be made in fighting malaria by means of genetic engineering; see note 43. Dixon 1993:24. Also see note 56.

56. Seventeenth International Congress of Genetics. *Genetics and the Understanding of Life,* National Centre for Biotechnology Education, University of Reading, 1994:11.

57. See note 49. British Medical Association 1992:187–8.

58. See note 43. Dixon 1993:176–7.

59. For discussion of the argument as presented by the British Medical Association, see Harris J. Biotechnology, friend or foe? Ethics and controls. In: Dyson A, Harris J, eds. *Ethics and Biotechnology.* London: Routledge, 1994:224–5.

60. Nozick R. *Anarchy, State and Utopia.* Oxford: Basil Blackwell, 1990:314–5.

61. The terms 'normal' and 'healthy' are of course quite vague.

62. See note 11. Holtug 1993:407.

63. See note 17. Glover 1984:56.

64. See note 17. Glover 1984:14.

65. Gardner W. Can human genetic enhancement be prohibited? *Journal of Medicine and Philosophy* 1995:20:65–84, at 68.

66. Even if our aim is to make the decisions they will want us to have made, acting in what we believe to be their interest is the best bet.

Of course, it may be in the interest of future people that they are able to exercise their autonomy maximally. If this were the case, it would not provide us with an argument against enhancing these people, but maybe with a duty to enhance their capacities for autonomy. (Max Charlesworth defends the view that autonomy in this sense is the relevant criterion when making decisions about enhancement engineering; see Charlesworth M. *Life, Death, Genes and Ethics.* Crows Nest: Australian Broadcasting Corporation, 1991:93–5.)

67. See note 17. Glover 1984:149.

68. See note 11. Holtug 1993.

Genetic Disorders and the Ethical Status of Germ-Line Gene Therapy

Edward M. Berger and Bernard M. Gert

INTRODUCTION

Over 20 years ago geneticists invented procedures for isolating single, identifiable genes, and for 'splicing' those genes into a foreign chromosome. In its new environment the inserted gene would not only become duplicated, along with the other resident genes of the chromosome, but it could acquire biological function. As the methodology of gene cloning became more refined, business interests began investing heavily in the speculated commercial application of recombinant DNA technology to such areas as agriculture, energy and pharmaceuticals. A new industry, loosely dubbed genetic biotechnology burgeoned.

It became apparent that the same genetic technology would inevitably be applied in order to correct hereditary defects in humans. Major concerns arose that gene therapy, although a worthwhile goal in medicine, would pave the way for the non-medical use of genetic engineering in humans, toward such goals as "reshaping our physiques or our personalities, cloning favored adults, or creating subhuman hybrids" (Davis, 1983). Indeed visions of a Brave New World, or worse, aroused private and public concern and soon led to the establishment of both Presidential and Congressional committees to discuss the issues (Culliton, 1982; Norman, 1983).

In this article we consider several of the ethical issues that have been raised by the application of recombinant DNA technology to humans. We attempt to focus on the application of technology which is currently available but also discuss technology which has some likelihood of becoming available in the near future. Qualitative advances in the field of genetics are made regularly so that interventions which seem 'distant or impossible' today are likely to be considered 'imminent of feasible' in a year. Thus, it is naive and in a sense risky to exclude from consideration the application of techniques that are now on the drawing board.

THE STATE OF THE ART

In humans many traits or phenotypes, such as all of the various blood types, are determined by a single gene. In most cases geneticists discover that these traits are determined by a single gene by first recognizing discrete differences between individuals and then showing that the differences are inherited in a simple, predictable and what has come to be called, a Mendelian fashion. Often, the phenotypic variation is ubiquitous and has no significant consequences for the individual. Whether someone has an O or B blood type, or is able or unable to taste phenylthiocarbamide (PTC) are good examples of unimportant variation. However, certain phenotype variants are rare and represent serious genetic disorders in the medical sense. Hemophilia A, for example, is the result of having only a defective form of a gene whose normal function is to produce a blood protein for clotting.

Variants for traits such as size, or skin color in humans, do not appear in the form of discrete alternatives, but rather show a continuous range in the species. This pattern of continuous variation is based on the interaction of many different genes and the pattern of inheritance for a trait such as size is very complicated. Although polygenic inheritance may be involved in several medically serious disorders, such traits will generally not be considered as likely candidates for gene therapy.

Geneticists have identified and physically isolated a functional allele of several human genes which when present only in a mutated form in an individual, produces a rare but serious genetic disorder. They have also been able to reproduce, or clone these alleles in order to do further research on the disorder related to these genes. These include disorders such as sickle cell anemia, thalassemia, hemophilia, muscular dystrophy, cystic fibrosis, and Lesch-Nyhan syndrome. In a number of cases the precise molecular defect in the abnormal allele has been identified.

As the number of human genes that have been cloned increases, methods become available for introducing those genes into somatic (body) cells and into gametes, in particular eggs. These procedures are generically termed DNA mediated gene transfer. There is ample evidence that these introduced genes can become efficiently integrated into the nuclear chromosomes of the cells. Most important these integrated genes can then become functional: when this happens the cell or organism is said to have become genetically 'transformed'. The genetic transformation of somatic cells is now a fairly routine laboratory procedure for many invertebrate and vertebrate species, including humans (Watson *et al.*, 1982). The genetic transformation of unfertilized or fertilized eggs and preimplantation embryos is more limited at the moment. It has been carried out with the fruit fly, *Drosophila,* mice and several other plant and animal species. The "Mighty Mouse" experiments are the best known examples (Palmiter *et al.*, 1982, 1983, 1986; Hammer *et al.*, 1984). In these cases the gene for a growth hormone, isolated from a rat or from a human, was used to genetically transform a mouse embryo. The gene was expressed resulting in a mouse twice normal size. Equally significant, the integrated growth hormone gene became a heritable element of the mouse. That is, the trait for large size was passed on to Mighty Mouse's offspring.

THE ISSUES RAISED

It is generally agreed that gene therapy for recognized genetic disorders, involving gene transfer into somatic cells, poses no new ethical problems. One important reason for this is that it is simply an extension of commonly used medical procedures. Diabetics who are unable to produce normal amounts of insulin because of a specific gene defect are therapeutically provided this missing gene product by daily injection. If, instead of injecting insulin, therapy could be administered by injecting the insulin gene the effect would be the same, except that gene therapy provides lifetime relief. But the same permanence results if the diabetic receives a tissue or organ transplant, in this case Islet cells of the pancreas, so that no new moral problem seems to arise in somatic cell gene therapy. Although the first application of somatic cell gene therapy led to a great deal of controversy (see Wade, 1980, 1981; Kolata and Wade, 1980), more recent studies on non-human animal models (Belmont *et al.*, 1988; Bodine *et al.* 1989; Dzierzok *et al.*, 1988; Hughes *et al.*, 1989; Millert *et al.*, 1983; Palmer *et al.*, 1987, Sorge *et al.* 1987; Wilson *et al.* 1988), and two NIH approved clinical trials using human patients suffering from ADA deficiency (see Verma, 1990), or malignant melanoma (Rosenberg *et al.*, 1990; Verma, 1990) have clearly demonstrated the feasibility and importance of this approach.

However, gene therapy of gametes, fertilized eggs, or early embryos leads to germ-line transformation (see Behringer *et al.*, 1989; Cavard *et al.*, 1988; Chen *et al.*, 1988; Choo *et al.*, 1987; Friedmann, 1989; Kentoff *et al.*, 1987; Kohn and Anderson, 1989; Pursel *et al.* 1989). The therapeutic effect is permanent, not only in the lifetime of the individual, it is also heritably transmitted to subsequent generations. Individuals who would ordinarily die for genetic reasons now survive and transmit their newly acquired genetic trait to offspring who might otherwise have never existed.

The concern associated with germ line transformation, specifically aimed at therapeutically curing serious genetic disorders, fit into two major categories, which are mentioned now and discussed later. The first major concern is that no clear cut distinction can be made between negative eugenics, the systematic elimination of undesirable genes and positive eugenics, the systematic improvement or perfection of the gene pool. So many genetic conditions have borderline status, that we won't know when to stop. As Rifkin (1983) puts it: "Once we decide to begin the process of human genetic engineering, there is really no logical place to stop. If diabetes, sickle cell anemia and cancer are to be cured by altering the genetic makeup of an individual, why not proceed to other disorders, myopia, color blindness, left handedness? Indeed, what is to preclude a society from deciding that a certain skin color is a disorder"?

A second major concern is that "eliminating so-called 'bad genes' will lead to a dangerous narrowing of diversity in the gene pool" and attempts to "cleanse the germline over tens or hundreds of years will lose traits that we later realize are important" (Rifkin, 1983). In essence, the claim is that we are not now capable of determining the future value of diversity lost by the use of gene therapy. The conclusion that is drawn from this argument is that the human genotype is inviolable and should not be tampered with no matter what the potential benefit.

GENETIC DISORDERS AS MALADIES

Conditions such as ADA deficiency, Tay-Sachs disease, sickle cell anemia, cystic fibrosis, hemophilia, and Lesch-Nyhan Syndrome are serious, in the medical sense, and because of the pain, disability and mortality associated with them they fit together with disorders such as cancer, multiple sclerosis, muscular dystrophy, emphysema and arthritis. All are chronic and demand extensive medical supervision. The link is tightened by recent findings which show that certain forms of cancer (retinoblastoma, acute myelogenic leukemia), muscular dystrophy (the DuChenne type), and arthritis (juvenile form) are genetically based, and that the predisposition to developing emphysema and certain cancers has a genetic basis as well. What is important about these conditions and others is that they show a simple pattern of inheritance, involving a recessive mutation at a single gene leading to the formation of a non-functional allele, and are therefore likely to be early candidates for gene therapy. Most important, they all belong to the generic class of conditions termed malady.

According to Culver and Gert (1982), "A person has a malady if and only if he has a condition, other than his rational beliefs and desires, such that he is suffering, or at increased risk of suffering, an evil (death, pain, disability, loss of freedom or opportunity or loss of pleasure) in the absence of distinct sustaining cause". Human genetic conditions, then, would be classified as maladies when they fulfil these definitional criteria and gene therapy for these maladies would constitute negative eugenics.

We would like here to point out several features of the argument. Death, pain, disability, and the loss of freedom or pleasure are universal evils that we all seek to avoid, unless there is an adequate reason not to (see Gert, 1988). This avoidance of evils, unless there is a reason, does not seem to depend on any particular culture, politics, or personal preference, but seems to be generally universal. The existence of such evils provide explicit objective criteria that we may apply in distinguishing maladies from non-maladies. To the extent that they reflect human values, they are clearly universally accepted values. Thus, in incorporating values into the account of malady we are not thereby giving up its objectivity. The absence of idiosyncratic social value judgements from the definition of malady, and the identification of elements common to all conditions which deserve to be deemed maladies are important aspects of the definition.

The notions of 'distinct sustaining cause' and increased risk are also important. While it is normal for many humans to feel discomfort at high altitude, the distress associated with low oxygen pressure continues and worsens when individuals afflicted with sickle cell anemia are returned to sea level. Similarly, the majority of individuals receiving minor lacerations bleed briefly and then recover, while the hemophiliac faces increased distress as blood loss continues. Both the sickle cell anemic and the hemophiliac are at increased risk of suffering pain and disability because their response to transient insult is abnormal, and because episodes may occur spontaneously. Hemophiliacs may reduce their risk of suffering by living in more controlled environments, although the episodes of spontaneous bleeding would continue. However, in doing so they lose certain freedoms and opportunities.

The concept of malady developed earlier by Culver and Gert has been used here to determine whether or not specific genetic conditions qualify as maladies. According to these definitional criteria genetic disorders such as those mentioned above clearly are maladies. Do these genetic disorders have comparable status using other independent accounts or definitions of disorder or disease, or is there a bias in the definition of malady that we are using?

Taylor (1975) in discussing illness provides a medical approach. He states that "The class of patients can be distinguished from the class of non-patients (disregarding borderline patients) by the intension (attribute complex) of morbidity which is composed of attributes that arouse therapeutic concern". Since each of the genetic conditions discussed above arouses "therapeutic concern" their status as illnesses seems unambiguous.

In King's (1954) analysis: "Disease is the aggregate of those conditions which, judged by the prevailing culture are deemed painful or disabling and which, at the same time, deviate from either the statistical norm or from some idealized status". Here again the criteria of pain or disability are incorporated in the definition and are fulfilled in the cases listed. The requirement that the condition "deviate from the statistical norm or from some idealized status" is clearly met by conditions such as Lesch-Nyhan, Tay-Sachs, hemophilia, and cystic fibrosis. They are all rare conditions, although they are rarer in some ethnic groups than in others. In the case of sickle cell anemia, the incidence of the condition in some Black African populations may be as high as 3/100 births. This is equivalent to the frequency of births carrying the AB blood type. The explanation for the high incidence of sickle cell births in certain Black African populations has been known since 1954 (Allison, 1954).

In considering the definitions of illness provided by Margolis (1976) and Boorse (1975, 1977) we find essentially the same situation. Margolis reasons that: "The body is composed of certain structured systems each of which has an assignable range of normal functions. Defect or disorder of such a system relative to such functioning constitutes as sufficient condition of disease: illness then is relatively palpable disease . . . Disease is whatever is judged to disorder, in the relevant way, the minimal integrity of body and mind relative to prudential functions". Prudential functions to Margolis include the avoidance of death, prolongation of life and restriction of pain. In this sense each of the genetic conditions listed would qualify as a disease.

For Boorse, who wishes to embrace a value free science of health by defining illness with reference to physiological medicine alone, there is the notion of "natural design". He states that: "The state of an organism is theoretically healthy, insofar as its mode of function conforms to the natural design of that kind of organism. The crucial element in the idea of biological design is the notion of natural function". Natural function is related to what is desirable, that is, what most people want. For Boorse the "apical goals" include survival, reproduction, and the ability to "engage in those particular activities, such as eating and sex, by which these goals are typically achieved". Boorse's "apical goals" appear intimately related to Margolis' "prudential values". It appears then, that all of the genetic conditions discussed fulfill the criteria of illness established by Margolis and Boorse. To the afflicted individual the disorder interferes with achieving both Boorse's "apical goals" of survival and reproduction and Margolis's "prudential functions".

Five separate accounts, or definitions of malady, illness and disease have been considered, for several prominent genetic conditions. By all accounts and definitions hemophilia, Tay-Sachs, Lesch-Nyhan, cystic fibrosis and sickle cell anemia fit into a category which would include cancer or tuberculosis. The use of the definitional criteria of malady in considering genetic conditions, then, introduces no bias. It does provide an objective criterion for distinguishing between gene therapy that would be classified negative eugenics and that which would be called positive eugenics. It offers a definition of genetic disorder.

DISTINGUISHING BETWEEN NEGATIVE AND POSITIVE GENE THERAPY

The first argument against gene therapy is that if we use the procedures to cure sickle cell anemia and other genetic disorders, we will be unable to draw the line against using gene therapy to improve our species. This is an example of what is known as a 'slippery slope' argument. The argument involves denying that a non-arbitrary line can be drawn between negative and positive eugenics, and therefore to protect against positive eugenics, we should not even start with negative eugenics. The position taken here is that one can draw such a line; that genetic conditions like those described, share all of the relevant features of conditions such as cancer and multiple sclerosis, so that they should be classified together. By establishing definitional criteria based on those shared features, an objective and culture free distinction can be made between genetic conditions which count as maladies and those which do not. These definitional criteria should not be met by any genetic condition which is obviously not a malady, such as blue eyes or pattern baldness, but must account for all those which obviously are, such as hemophilia and Lesch-Nyhan. We propose that cancer, hemophilia, Lesch-Nyhan, etc. are all 'maladies', because they share all of the essential features of this concept.

The malady concept is objective and non-technical so that it will have a general appeal. While some genetic conditions will fall into a grey area, in terms of gene therapy, we suspect that the number will be small and the ambivalence will not be due to any ambiguity in the definition of malady. Rather, borderline conditions will be maladies which are simply not serious in the medical sense. Further, as we shall argue in the final section, we need not worry about borderline cases, because only those maladies which are serious are legitimate candidates for germ-line gene therapy.

We have tried to maintain objectivity in the sense that our consideration of gene therapy has dealt only with making an unambiguous distinction between positive and negative eugenics. We have not dealt with the ethical status of positive eugenics. In the end it may turn out that the use of gene therapy to enhance humans, for example, make individuals smarter, or to add special attributes, such as resistance to toxic chemicals found in the environment, is acceptable or even desirable. Or, it may turn out that gene therapy for even the most severe genetic disorder is morally unacceptable. As in most other genuine cases of moral controversy, it is the morally relevant facts that will determine the matter, e.g., what are the real world risks of germ-line gene therapy.

EVOLUTIONARY CONSIDERATIONS

A second type of argument against gene therapy is that those alleles which will be systematically eliminated from the human gene pool may be of potential benefit to the species. For example, the trend in agricultural crop management during this century has been toward the development of highly inbred, genetically uniform strains selected for specific features, such as high productivity. In two instances the appearance of a new pathogen (a stem-rust in the case of macaroni wheat in 1954, and a blight fungus in the case of corn in 1969) destroyed over half the American crop. New genetic strains, resistant to the pathogen, had to be selected from a collection of seeds derived from outbred strains and maintained in a 'gene bank'. Had there been no effort to maintain the natural genetic variability of corn and wheat lost during selection, the two species could have gone extinct. The lesson learned here is that the genetic variation of any species provides the evolutionary potential to adapt to new conditions. In terms of human gene therapy, the argument is that it is risky to eliminate a mutant allele such as that responsible for sickle cell anemia, which is or was of benefit.

This argument is false, for two different reasons. The first reason reflects a peculiar misunderstanding about what actually causes a recessive genetic disorder. It is a misunderstanding shared by many geneticists. The second reason is based on a misunderstanding about what gene therapy can and cannot achieve. The first important point is that a genetic disorder, such as Tay-Sachs, is not caused by the presence of two-recessive mutant alleles. Rather the disorder is a consequence of the absence of a functional allele. It does not really matter how many Tay-Sachs alleles are present in an individual, in terms of having the malady, what matters is that a functional allele is absent. Although a non-functional allele can provide a benefit in heterozygous condition (such as the sickle cell anemia allele) it is extremely uncommon. Even with the non-functional allele for sickle cell there is no additional advantage in being homozygous.

The second and more important reason that the evolutionary argument is false is that unlike the situation with selective breeding in crops where genetic variation is lost by inbreeding, gene therapy in its current form does not result in a loss of any allele variation. In fact, just the opposite occurs. To illustrate this point consider how germ line transformation is done.

Several methods of introducing genes into cells have been developed. These include mechanically injecting or 'shooting' cloned genes into a cell or into the nucleus itself. Alternatively, the cell is bathed in a solution containing cloned genes under conditions which favor the cell's internalizing the exogenous DNA. Finally, procedures have been developed which allow the geneticist to package the cloned gene in a defective virus particle, known as a retrovirus, which is subsequently used to infect the cells. Regardless of the mechanism of introduction, or target cell type, in order for the cloned gene to function properly it must find its way into the nucleus and become physically incorporated into the cell's chromosomes, by a mechanism not presently understood. Essentially, the present technology which would be applied to human gene therapy only allows us to add genes. All of the resident genes present in the cell prior to therapy remain in the cell.

Thus, given the present state of technology, there is no analogy between selective germ line breeding, which systematically eliminates genes, and gene therapy which only adds them. Since gene therapy can only add new genes and not replace others already present, nothing is lost. It is of interest to recognize that our current version of gene therapy is of no help with genetic disorders based on dominant, mutant alleles or those due to chromosome abnormalities. It is not yet possible to actually replace a dominant gene in humans with a non-harmful allele. Were gene replacement therapy to become feasible serious consideration of its evolutionary effect would be warranted, however, for the reasons given below, we believe that even were it possible, the number of people involved would be so small as to have no evolutionary effects.

It seems unlikely that any serious attempt to eliminate a deleterious allele from the human gene pool could be successful, using gene replacement therapy, even if it were possible and highly desirable to do so. The technology, when developed for humans, will be very expensive, probably comparable to the cost of in vitro fertilization: the so-called test tube baby procedure. It will be applied on an individual basis, and would have fairly limited accessibility. Being a surgical procedure it would be done only in a hospital setting, on a voluntary basis, and it is likely that a large number of individuals who qualify for the procedure would choose not to participate. As a consequence, clinical ethics associated with standard practices in medical genetics would certainly apply (Fowler *et al.*, 1989).

ADDITIONAL RISKS OF GERM-LINE GENE THERAPY

Germ-line gene therapy would be carried out in order only to prevent the evils associated with genetic disorders that qualify as severe maladies, (thus carrier status would not make one a candiate for gene therapy). Ostensibly, then, germ-line gene therapy provides benefit to some future person who is at risk, and to their potential offspring. Since a future person cannot give consent for gene therapy, or more important, deny consent, the ethical principle of informed consent has no direct application. If germ line gene therapy involved no risk of evil there would be no problem. However experimental results from two kinds of research have established that germ line gene therapy carries with it medical risk. In both studies the problem involves the effect of integrating DNA or genes in new locations in the chromosome.

In the first study, by a group from the Fox Chase Cancer Center in Philadelphia (Wagner *et al.*, 1983), a human growth hormone gene was microinjected into the pronucleus of fertilized mouse eggs. In the experiment reported, six mice were born that contained foreign DNA integrated into their chromosomes. In two of the six cases the inserted DNA behaved as a recessive, embryonic lethal mutation in subsequent generations. In other words, a mouse homozygous for a chromosome carrying the integrated growth hormone gene died prenatally. Insertional mutations, as these are termed, probably involve the disruption of some native gene function(s) by the integration of foreign DNA.

A second and related discovery is that cancers may develop as a result of the movement of normal cellular genes to new locations (Marx, 1982). In several cases aberrant chromosomes of cancer cells turned out to contain a misplaced gene. The obvious implication is that germ line gene therapy could produce the overexpression of some protooncogene and lead to cancer in the patient or his or her offspring as a result of introduced genes becoming integrated in specific regions of the chromosome.

These and more recent findings (Allison *et al.*, 1988; Behringer *et al.*, 1988; Carlson *et al.*, 1989; Doi *et al.*, 1988; Lang *et al.*, 1987; Xiang *et al.*, 1990) clearly point out an urgent need to carry out work that leads to a more precise targeting of gene integration. This research might lead to the development of plasmid or viral vectors that would permit insertion of foreign genes into 'safe' sites in the chromosome. The work would also emphasize techniques that insure stable and permanent integration. That is, once inserted, the foreign genes would remain as stably integrated as any native gene. Ideally, a technique utilizing genetic recombination would be developed in which the detective gene is actually replaced by a normal form. The major point raised by this discussion is that even if germ-line gene therapy is viewed as acceptable, there must be specific guidelines that reflect the limitations of the technology. Thus, there are strong reasons for limiting the use of germ line gene therapy, as it exists today, to treating diseases caused by recessive alleles. These reasons also support avoiding introducing new genes in heterozygous form which might cause serious problems unless we are curing or preventing very serious maladies, e.g., early life threatening disorders, such as those discussed earlier. This gives even stricter standards for the use of germ-line gene therapy, and is further objection to the slippery slope argument.

As the technology which leads to the capability for germ-line gene therapy develops, so will new alternatives. Somatic gene therapy has been discussed. Genetic screening procedures which incorporate recombinant DNA techniques are becoming refined enabling the rapid and reliable identification of carriers. Similar progress in pre-implantation embryo and fetal screening will provide parents an even greater opportunity to choose normal children. It is quite likely that the proposed mapping and sequencing of the human genome, scheduled over the next fifteen years, will produce totally novel opportunities and alternatives in this context.

REAL WORLD CONSIDERATIONS

All that we have said in this paper assumes that everyone involved in germ-line gene therapy accepts the analyses that we have provided and that they would be willing to limit germ-line gene therapy to those cases of severe maladies where there was no less radical way to achieve the same goal, e.g., by pre-implantation screening. However, past experience has shown that exciting new technology, including medical technology, generates pressures for its use. Thus, it is quite likely that if germ-line gene therapy were allowed, it would be used inappropriately. There would be pressure to use it when the same result could be accomplished in a less risky way, or there would be claims that the risks are less than they really are, e.g., inadequate consideration would be given to the risks associated with the gene not being in its normal place.

If we thought that everyone involved in these matters were appropriately thoughtful, we would not hesitate to advocate germ-line gene therapy for those few cases where it might be the therapy of choice. However, at the present time, we do not see enough potential benefit in germ-line gene therapy to human beings to warrant the real world risks that would inevitably follow from its application. We think that the fact that one will be affecting the genetic make-up of an unlimited number of people provides sufficient reason to make any responsible researcher who has thought about these matters to limit such therapy to those cases in which the benefits to the person receiving the initial therapy is so great that it outweighs the risks not only for him but also for all of his descendents. But we do not believe that all researchers are sufficiently responsible to limit their use of this exciting new technology in the appropriate way. Thus, we believe that unless we have almost certain knowledge about the risks involved in germ-line gene therapy, we think that it is extremely unlikely that any benefit to a small number of persons outweighs the risk to an unlimited number of other people.

Before such therapy should be allowed, we think it is necessary to show not merely that some very small number of people might be helped who could not be helped in some less radical way, but that there are a significant number of people for whom germ-line gene therapy would be the treatment of choice. If there are not a significant number of people who are going to be spared serious suffering, then it is not worth the real world risk of developing a kind of therapy which will affect unlimited numbers of people. This is particularly true because we know that in the real world researchers will overestimate their knowledge of the risks involved and hence will be tempted to perform germ-line gene therapy when it is not justified.

Our argument is not that human beings are not capable of using any powerful technology successfully, although present problems with toxic wastes, nuclear wastes, etc., indicate that this argument has some force. Nor do we hold that it is simply inappropriate for mere human beings to shape the future of their species, regardless of the cost-benefit ratio. Rather we hold that any technology which has the potential for causing great harm to very many, cannot justifiably be used in order to provide benefits, even great benefits, for a very few. We do not believe that any impartial rational person would allow untold numbers of people to be put at significant risk of harm in order to benefit a small number of people.

We believe that there is no theoretical reason for not using germ-line gene therapy. We have provided arguments that show the flaws in the slippery slope argument and the mistakes involved in the evolutionary argument against germ-line gene therapy. We have, however, provided arguments that would lead one to severely limit the use of germ-line gene therapy. We think that we have given arguments that might even be used to argue against developing procedures for germ-line gene therapy in human beings. These arguments are not theoretical, they appeal to our knowledge that exciting new technologies tend to get over used, and that given this fact, no such technology should be developed which has great risks for many unless it is needed to prevent great evils for many. We are simply making the case against arrogance and for humility in a situation where a great number of people may be put at significant risk.

ACKNOWLEDGMENTS

This work has been supported in part by funds from the EVIST Program (NSF/NEH) and by the NIH (HG00130). The opinions expressed in this article are solely those of the authors and do not necessarily reflect the views of the granting agencies.

References

Allison, A: 1954, 'Protection afforded by sickle cell trait against subtertian malarial infection', *British Medical Journal* 1, 290.

Allison, J., Campbell, I.L., Monahan, G., *et al.*: 1988, 'Diabetes in transgenic mice resulting from over-expression of class I histocompatability molecules in pancreatic beta cells', *Nature* 333, 529.

Behringer, R.R., Mathew, L.S., Palmiter, R.D., *et al.*: 1988, 'Dwarf mice produced by genetic ablation of growth hormone expressing cells', *Genes Dev.* 2, 453.

Behringer, R.R., Ryan, T.M., Reilly, M.P., *et. al.*: 1989, 'Synthesis of functional human hemoglobin in transgenic mice', *Science* 245, 971.

Belmont, J.W., MacGregor, G.R., Wagner-Smith, K., *et al.*: 1988, 'Expression of human adenosine deaminase in murine hematopoietic cells', *Molecular Cell Biology* 8, 116.

Bodine, D.M., Karlsson, S., and Nienhuis, A.W.: 1989, 'Combination of interleukins 3 and 6 preserves stem cell function in culture and enhances retrovirus mediated gene transfer in hematopoietic stem cells', *Proceedings of the National Academy of Science*, U.S. 86, 8897.

Boorse, C.: 1975, 'On the distinction between disease and illness', *Philosophy and Public Affairs* 5, 49.

Boorse, C.: 1977, 'Health as a theoretical concept', *Philosophy of Science* 44, 542.

Carlson, J.A., Rogers, B., Silfers, R.N., *et al.*: 1989, 'Accumulation of PI2 alphal 1-antitrypsin causes liver damage in transgenic mice', *Journal of Clinical Investigation* 83, 1183.

Cavard, C., Grimber, G., Dubois, N., *et al.*: 1988, 'Correction of mouse transcarbanylae deficiency by gene transfer into the germ here', *Nucleic Acids Research* 16, 2099.

Chen, X.S., Yan, J.S., and Wagner, T.E.: 1988, 'Enhanced viral resistance in transgenic mice expressing the human B-1 interferon', *Journal of Virology* 62, 3883.

Choo, V.A., Raphael, K., McAdam, W., *et al.*: 1987, 'Expression of active human blood clotting factor IX in transgenic mice: Use of a cDNA with complete mRNA sequence', *Nucleic Acids Research* 15, 871.

Culliton, B.J.: 1982, 'Gore proposes oversight of genetic engineering', *Science* 218, 1098.

Culver, C., and Gert, B.: 1982, *Philosophy in Medicine*, Oxford University Press, New York.

Daks, P.M., Allan, J., and Anderson, C.M.: 1965, 'A genetic study of fibrocystic disease of the pancreas', *Annual of Human Genetics* 28, 323.

Davis, B.D.: 1983, 'The two faces of genetic engineering in man', *Science* 219, 495.

Doi, T., Striker, L.J., Qualfe, C., *et al.*: 1988, 'Progressive glumeruloschlerosis develops in transgenic mice chronically expressing growth hormone and growth hormonereleasing factor but not in those expressing insulinlike growth factor-1', *American Journal of Pathology* 131, 398.

Dzierzak, E.A., Papayannopolou, T., and Mulligan, R.C.: 1988, 'Lineage-specific expression of a human beta-globin gene in murine bone marrow transplant recipients reconstituted with retrovirus-transduced stem cells', *Nature* 331, 35.

Fowler, G., Juengst, E.T., and Zimmerman, B.V.: 1989, 'Germ-line gene therapy and the clinical ethics of medical genetics'. *Theoretical Medicine* 10, 151.

Friedman, T.: 1989, 'Progress toward human gene therapy', *Science* 244, 1275.

Gert, B.: 1988, *Morality*, Oxford University Press, New York.

Hallet, W.Y., Knudson, A.G., and Massey, F.J.: 1965, 'Absence of detrimental effect of the carrier state of the cystic fibrosis gene', *Annual Review of Respiratory Disease* 92, 714.

Hammer, R.E., Palmiter, R.D., and Brinster, R.L.: 1984, 'Partial correction of murine hereditary growth disorder by germline incorporation of a new gene', *Nature* 311, 65.

Hughes, P.F., Eaves, C.J., Hogge, D.E., and Humphries, R.K.: 1989, 'High-efficiency gene transfer to human hematopoietic cells maintained in longterm marrow culture', *Blood* 74, 1915.

Kantoff, P.W., Gillio, A.P., *et al.*: 1987, 'Expression of human adenosine deaminase in nonhuman primates after retroviral mediated gene transfer', *Journal of Experimental Medicine* 166, 219.

King, L.S,: 1954, 'What is disease?', *Philosophy of Science* 21, 193.

Kohn, D.B., and Anderson, W.F.: 1989, 'Gene therapy for genetic diseases', *Cancer Investigations* 7, 179.

Kolata, G.B., and Wade, N.: 1980, 'Human gene treatment stirs new debate' *Science* 210, 407.

Lang, R.A., Metcalf, D., Cuthbertson, R.A., *et al.*: 1987, 'Transgenic mice expressing a hemopoietic growth factor gene (GM-CSF) develop accumulations of macrophages, blindness and a fatal syndrome of tissue damage', *Cell* 51, 675.

Margolis, J.: 1976, 'The concept of disease', *Journal of Medicine and Philosophy* 1, 238.

Marx, J.L.: 1982, 'The case of the misplaced gene', *Science* 218, 983.

Miller, A.D., Jolly, D.J., Friedman, T., and Verma, T.M.: 1983, 'A transmissible retrovirus expressing human hypoxanthine-phosphoribosyltransferase (HPRT): Gene transfer into cells obtained from humans deficient in HPRT', *Proceedings of the National Academy of Science, U.S.* 80, 4709.

Norman, C.: 1983, 'Clerics urge ban on altering germline cells', *Science* 220, 1366.

Palmer, T., Hock, R., Osborne, W., and Miller, A.D.: 1987, 'Efficient retrovirus-mediated transfer and expression of a human adenosine deaminase gene in diploid skin fibroblasts from an adenosine deaminase-deficient human', *Proceedings of the National Academy of Science*, U.S. 84, 1055.

Palmiter, R.D., Brinster, R.L., Hammer, M.E., et al.: 1982, 'Dramatic growth of mice that develop from eggs microinjected with metallothioneingrowth hormone fusion genes', *Nature* 300, 611.

Palmiter, R.D., Norstedt, G., Gelinas, R.E., *et al.*: 1983, 'Metallothioneinhuman GH fusion genes stimulate growth of mice', *Science* 222, 809.

Palmiter, R.D., and Brinster, R.L: 1986, 'Germline transformation of mice', *Annual Review of Genetics* 20, 465.

Pursel, V.G., Pinkert, C.A., Muller, K.F., *et al.*: 1989, 'Genetic engineering of livestock', *Science* 244, 1281.

Rifkin, J.: 1983, *Algeny,* The Viking Press, New York.

Rosenberg, S.A., Aebersold, P., *et al.*: 1990, 'Gene transfer into humans—Immunotherapy of patients with advanced melanoma, using tumor infiltrating lymphocytes modified by retroviral gene transduction', *New England Journal of Medicine* 323, 570.

Sorge, J., Kuhl, W., West, C., *et al.*: 1987, 'Complete correction of the enzymatic defect of type 1 Gaucher disease fibroblasts by retroviral mediated gene transfer', *Proceedings of the National Academy of Science,* U.S. 84, 906.

Taylor, F.K.: 1976, The medical model of the disease concept', *British Journal of Psychiatry* 128, 588.

Verma, I.: 1990, 'Gene therapy', *Scientific American* 172, 68.

Wade, N.: 1980a, 'UCSD gene splicing incident ends unresolved', *Science* 209, 1494.

Wade, N.: 1980b, 'UCSD gene therapy racked by friendly fire', *Science* 210, 509.

Wade, N.: 1981, 'Gene therapy caught in more entanglements', *Science* 212, 24.

Wagner, E.F., Covarrubias, L., Stewart, T.A., and Plints, B.: 1983, 'Prenatal lethalities in mice homozygous for human growth hormone sequences integrated in the germ line', *Cell* 36, 647.

Watson, J.D., Tooze, J., and Kurtz, D.T.: 1983, *Recombinant DNA: A Short Course,* Scientific American Books, W.H. Freeman and Co., New York.

Wilson, J., Johnston, P., Jefferson, D., *et al.*: 1988, 'Correction of the genetic defect in hepatocytes from the Wantanable heritable hyperlipidemic rabbit', *Proceedings of the National Academy of Science,* U.S. 85, 4421.

Xiang, X., Benson, K.F., and Chada, K.: 1990, 'Mini-mouse: Disruption of the pygmy locus in transgenic insertional mutant', *Science* 247, 967.

Commentary: How Do We Think About the Ethics of Human Germ-Line Genetic Therapy?

Kathleen Nolan

For many people, the bright ethical line separating somatic and germ-line genetic therapy has begun to erode. Perhaps it always was a bit of a mirage. Still, it seemed to make sense, historically, to separate genetic manipulations ('treatments') of an individual's somatic tissues and cells from genetic manipulations of germ-line tissue. Somatic cell interventions could be placed in simple analogy to other, standard, medical interventions: mechanical repair of damaged *structures* (e.g., setting broken bones), replacement of failing *organs* (e.g., kidney transplant), and support for injured *tissues and cells* (e.g., grafting of burned skin and administration of antibiotics for pneumonia). In fact, the use of some antiviral agents, and most forms of chemotherapy, could be seen as early instances of relatively crude somatic cell 'genetic' therapy, directed at damaged or dysfunctional *RNA and DNA* (e.g., in infected or malignant cells).

Germ-line genetic manipulations seemed in theory quite different. First, because reproductive genes are involved, the locus of disease was not seen to be in the adult patient but instead in the potential offspring, not-yet-existing 'patients' whose moral claims on us are generally cast in terms of their extreme vulnerability. Moreover, because germ-line changes would generally be expected to affect the genetic make-up of *all* tissues and cells in the developing offspring, instead of isolated structures or systems, as well as the genetic make-up of all subsequent generations, such interventions raised the prospect of previously unimaginable individual and societal horrors. Surrounded by the evocative imagery of eugenics, germ-line genetic therapy appeared to pose unique threats to the integrity of the basic stuff of life, a person's original—aboriginal—DNA.

Thus, amidst the struggle between those who strongly favored pursuing genetic therapy and those who vehemently opposed it, a compromise path seemed to present itself. Ethically, (and the cynic would add, politically), support for somatic cell therapy could be more easily garnered. Each patient could give individual consent, and the consequences of the research would be contained within the treated population (absent any escape of mutant or contaminated genetic vectors). No destructive 'experimentation' with embryos would be involved, and the prospects for eugenic exploitation would be negligible. Proponents of germ-line genetic therapy soon came to be seen as pariahs, as the germ-line approach was increasingly portrayed as unnecessary, technically cumbersome, and ethically suspect. Many policy statements by important national and international groups concerned with genetic advances therefore sharply distinguished between somatic cell genetic therapy (acceptable) and germ-line genetic therapy (unacceptable) (Nature, 1986).

The recent erosion of this longstanding great divide has both empirical and theoretical origins. Empirically, research in mammalian and other species over the last few years has yielded startling evidence that some forms of germ-line intervention (i.e., those that involve manipulating early embryos) may be no more difficult than somatic cell techniques. In some cases they may even turn out to be far easier. This would be particularly true for the large class of genetic diseases that are not well-suited to a somatic cell approach, for example, those affecting multiple systems and those with onset very early in development.

Another factor has been the enhanced ability of clinicians to offer innovative prenatal medical and surgical interventions for problems arising *in utero*. In a social climate that increasingly encourages diligence in promoting antenatal well-being (note recent legal efforts to enforce abstinence from alcohol and other drugs during pregnancy), fetuses have become new-found patients. By implication, early embryos can also be viewed as patients, allowing germ-line interventions to be offered more legitimately as a potential therapeutic, rather than eugenic, tool.

These empirical realities have spurred new approaches to analyzing the ethics of germ-line genetic therapy. Advocates of pursuing germ-line techniques can now point to the possibility of responding to otherwise untreatable conditions, or of responding to genetic conditions in a more effective and definitive fashion (Walters, 1986; Zimmerman, 1991). One interesting line of argument goes so far as to posit the germ-line effects of early embryonic treatment as an entirely secondary, even unintended, consequence of efforts to provide effective somatic-cell therapy (Cook-Deegan, 1990; Lappé, 1991).

What is most interesting about these arguments is their inadvertent tendency to incorporate latent ambiguities about the moral and clinical status of early embryos. For, despite the ostensible goal of providing therapy for these 'patients', most of these advocates seem quite comfortable with pursuing germ-line genetic research that would itself entail substantial destruction of embryonic life. Does it not seem awkward to argue for the development of these therapies on the basis of their clinical (i.e., individual) merit while at the same time accepting with equanimity research that involves destroying developing embryos in order to assess the effects of our interventions? What is it that makes the embryo (individual?) worth protecting in one instance and not in the other?

To argue from the perspective of direct patient benefit to the embryo as the ground for proceeding with germ-line approaches thus seems to require a reappraisal of pediatric research ethics and embryonic research practices. Under standard formulations of pediatric research ethics, a clinical trial should proceed only if an honest null hypothesis (or more precisely, 'clinical equipoise') attains between all possible treatment options, including the option of non-treatment (Levine, 1986; Freedman, 1987). That is, the risk/benefit ratio of all options in an ethically designed clinical trial will be approximately equivalent.

If the affected embryo is viewed as an antenatal patient, a trial of genetic therapy would therefore seem to be justified only if the following conditions held: (1) the risk of treatment were no greater than the risk of being born with the given condition, or of being destroyed prior to implantation (the non-treatment options); (2) no other treatment were available that offered a superior risk/benefit ratio; (3) the purely research components of the trial did not themselves pose substantial risk; and (4) consent had been obtained from an appropriate guardian (Nolan, 1990). Under this formulation, embryonic destruction to clarify scientific understanding of the treatment process would be clearly illicit, since it would be a blatantly harmful research procedure.

To avoid this difficulty it might be argued that it is not the embryo *per se* but instead the future child that warrants protection. Early embryonic genetic interventions would then represent efforts at prevention rather than therapy (Zimmerman, 1991). From this perspective, however, screening and selective implantation of unaffected embryos would seem to offer a much better risk/benefit ratio, since any risk to the future child from the attempted therapy would be avoided (Fowler *et al.*, 1989).

Some have also argued that the patients in germ-line genetic therapy are actually the prospective parents, whose right to reproductive privacy generates a sphere of autonomy around the care and treatment of their offspring, which would include the right to pursue germ-line genetic therapies (Zimmerman, 1990). This approach fits neatly with traditional models of genetic screening and counseling, in which the role of the clinician is to provide information and support for parental reproductive decisionmaking, and it would allow for attempts at germ-line therapy for parents who might reject selective screening and implantation. However, research on normal embryos would remain problematic, as would the scope of parental authority, particularly regarding requests for 'unnecessary' genetic interventions (e.g., enhancement therapies or treatment of trivial conditions such as the inability to roll the tongue).

What is it that generates our discomfort with giving parents total discretion over the genetic management of early embryos? To respond by noting that requests for treatment of non-pathological conditions falls outside the realm of medical intervention (Anderson, 1989; Juengst, 1989) leaves the *basis* for restricting parental desires to the strictly medical realm still unaddressed. If genetic modifications of sperm, ova, and early embryos were possible, why could a prospective parent not request any reasonably safe modification that he or she desired?

The difficulty with unlimited parental discretion is that it implies that embryos, and sperm and ova, belong to those who bear them. Yet, the relationship that we have with 'our own' sperm, ova, and embryos seems quite distinct from any notion of 'ownership'. It is more akin to the sense of identity that we have with our own bodies, which we do not *own* but *are*. However, this formulation, too, is problematic. Requests for germ-line changes clearly seem to be of a different order than requests for cosmetic surgery, for example. Moreover, seeing this difference as simply a matter of the consequences of germ-line interventions extending beyond the adult patient who makes the request may underestimate the conceptual and emotional importance of the simultaneous identity and non-identity that we have with our germ cells and offspring.

After all, what is it, other than shared genetic, physical, and psychosocial identities, that forms the basis of familial bonds and parental authority? A child shares half of its genetic identity with each parent, a fetus constitutes itself from the nurturing body of its mother, and a family shares psychological and social interactions that make it a functional unit with an identity separate from other families within the larger cultural nexus.

Part of the highly charged quality that attends reproductive issues results from this sense of shared identity that we have with our offspring. Although the nature of the social relationships of prenatal beings is extremely murky, embryos and germ cells clearly share a genetic identity with their prospective parents. Hence, parents may naturally wish to extend their sphere of personal autonomy to include their reproductive cells and their genetic heirs.

But even this genetic identity is not complete: haploid germ cells are distinct from an individual's diploid somatic cells, and embryos result from a special commingling of the cells of the two different genetic parents. Sperm, ova, and embryos are very like ourselves and yet they are not ourselves. The uniqueness of these cells, their strange dissimilarity from our other cells, thus gives credence to those who would question the unlimited extension of parental authority. When the physical 'identity' between germ cells and embryos and their genetic parents is disrupted, as in *in vitro* manipulations of sperm and ova or in *in vitro* fertilization, these challenges become even stronger.

Of course, similar notions of a separate identity for germ cells and embryos have grounded early objections to germ-line genetic therapy, especially from prolife advocates. It seems wrong, somehow, to change the basic identity of these unique cells and developing beings. Yet, notice the irony here: the same 'individuality' that generates this protective impulse should also generate sympathy for attempts to provide therapy. As long as small amounts of DNA are involved, and phenotypic changes involve only diseased cells, tissues, and organs (and not more basic traits or personality and behavior), the threat to the "individual" involved is relatively minor, and genetic interventions can themselves be portrayed as protective.

Oddly enough, the 'great divide' of germ-line genetic therapy may therefore prove to offer common ground for genetic researchers and prolife advocates, especially if the language of clinical benefit and therapeutics remains dominant. However, a logical corrollary of this approach is that research with embryos should be conducted within the framework of clinical trials with human subjects. Retreat to the language of parental autonomy and reproductive privacy obviates the need to provide benefit for individual embryos as a basis for genetic intervention but does not totally resolve issues related to the grounds and limits of parental discretion. Moving to the language of social good and public health would obviously risk reintroducing fears of eugenic abuses and devaluation of disabled and handicapped individuals.

How, then, are we to think about the ethics of germ-line genetic therapy? The answer, of course, is *carefully* and *honestly.* This means, foremost, that we trace out in detail the implications of our concepts and language, so that we do not deceive ourselves about what we are intending and doing. 'Genetic healing' can easily become a slogan rather than an acceptable goal within a solidly constructed ethical framework. As our excitement about germ-line genetic therapy grows, we must therefore exercise increasing diligence in our efforts to anticipate its myriad personal and social meanings.

ACKNOWLEDGMENTS

Partial support for preparation of this paper was provided by grants from the National Center for Human Genome Research (1 RO1 HG00418-01) and from the Ruth Mott Fund.

References

Anderson, W.F.: 1989, 'Human gene therapy: Why draw a line?', *Journal of Medicine and Philosophy* 14(6), 681–693.

Cook-Deegan, R.M.: 1990, 'Human gene therapy and congress', *Human Gene Therapy* 1, 163–170.

Fowler, G., Juengst, E.T., and Zimmerman, B.K.: 1989, 'Germ-line gene therapy and the clinical ethos of medical genetics', *Theoretical Medicine* 10, 151–165.

Freedman, B.: 1987, 'Equipoise and the ethics of clinical research', *New England Journal of Medicine* 317(3), 141–145.

Juengst, E.: 1989, 'Prenatal diagnosis and the ethics of uncertainty', in J. Munagle and D. Thomasma (eds.), *Medical Ethics*, Aspen Books, Rockville, Maryland, pp. 12–24.

Lappé, M.: 1991, 'Ethical issues in manipulating the human germ line', *Journal of Medicine and Philosophy* 16, 621–639.

Levine, R.J.: 1986, *Ethics and Regulation of Clinical Research*, Urban & Schwarzenberg, Baltimore, Maryland.

Nature (editorial): 1986, 331,100.

Nolan, K.: 1990, 'AIDS and pediatric research'. *Evaluation Review* 14(5), 464–481.

Walters, L.: 1986, 'The ethics of human gene therapy', *Nature* 320, 225–227.

Zimmerman, B.: 1991, 'Human germ-line Therapy: The case for its development and use', *Journal of Medicine and Philosophy* 16, 593–612.

Cloning in the Popular Imagination

Dorothy Nelkin and M. Susan Lindee

Dolly is a lamb that was cloned by Dr. Ian Wilmut, a Scottish embryologist. But she is also a Rorschach test. The public response to the production of a lamb by cloning a cultured cell line reflects the futuristic fantasies and Frankenstein fears that have more broadly surrounded research in genetics and especially genetic engineering. Cloning was a term originally applied to a botanical technique of asexual reproduction. But following early experiments in the manipulation of the hereditary and reproductive process during the mid-1960s, the term became associated with human biological engineering. It also became a pervasive theme in horror films and science fiction fantasies. Appearing to promise both amazing new control over nature and terrifying dehumanization, cloning has gripped the popular imagination.

Underlying the fascination with cloning is the idea that human beings in all their complexity are simply readouts of a powerful molecular text. In *The DNA Mystique: The Gene as a Cultural Icon*, we called this idea "genetic essentialism," a deterministic tendency to reduce the personality and behavior—the very identity of individuals—to their genes.[1] Exploring the popular appeal of genetic essentialism, we tracked its manifestations in the mass media—in television programs, advertising and marketing, newspaper articles, films, and magazines. And we documented the public fears—or hopes—that geneticists will soon acquire the awesome power to determine the human future.

The responses to the Dolly phenomenon mirrored those we found in the popular culture reactions to the Human Genome Project and its mapping of the genes. The very first responses to the news about Dolly's creation were facetious. Dolly and cloning were immediately the subject of jokes on late-night talk shows and Internet web sites. Their humor depended largely on the pervasive assumption that human identity is contained entirely in the sequences of DNA in the human genome: Why not clone great athletes like Michael Jordan, or great scientists like Albert Einstein, or popular politicians like Tony Blair, or less popular politicians like Newt Gingrich, or wealthy entrepreneurs like Bill Gates? There were also anxious scenarios in the popular press, including futuristic stories about making new Frankenstein monsters, or creating Adolf Hitler clones, or producing "organ donors" only to harvest their (fully compatible) viscera.[2]

The dire consequences of cloning have long captured the popular imagination, expressed in numerous novels and science fiction films. Real research projects associated with cloning invariably evoke horror. In 1993, scientists from George Washington University "twinned" a nonviable human embryo in an experiment intended to create embryos for in vitro fertilization. Newspapers, magazines, and talk shows covered the experiment as if it had yielded a cloning technology for the mass production of human beings.[3] Stories about the research envisioned selective breeding factories, cloning on consumer demand, the breeding of children as organ donors, a cloning industry for selling multiples of human beings, and even a freezer section of the "biomarket."[4] Journalists anticipated a "Brave New World of cookie cutter humans,"[5] and they asked if the GWU scientists were playing God.

Similarly, the cloning of Dolly evoked extravagant scenarios that often expressed prevailing social and political tensions. While cloning could theoretically make both sexes irrelevant to reproduction, the technology appeared as a threat to the male of the species—men will no longer be necessary! It also held a promise of creating perfect cows, sheep, and chickens, or perhaps even perfect people. If sperm banks (as portrayed in some women's magazines) were a place to "shop for Mr. Good genes,"[6] why not use cloning to produce and reproduce perfect babies? They could, after all, be dependable reproductive products with proven performance.

Some writers lauded cloning as a way to assure immortality. Again and again media stories predicted that cloning will allow the resurrection of the dead (bereaved parents, for example, might clone a beloved deceased child). Or the technology could provide life everlasting for the deserving (narcissists could arrange to have themselves cloned). Sociobiologist Richard Dawkins, author of the popular book, *The Selfish Gene,* confessed his own desire to be cloned: "I think it would be mind-bogglingly fascinating to watch a younger edition of myself growing up in the 21st century instead of the 1940s."[7] Indeed, in a *New York Times* interview, psychiatrist Robert Coles suggested that the very idea of cloning "tempts our narcissism enormously because it gives a physical dimension to a fantasy that one can keep going on through the reproduction of oneself."[8]

Not surprisingly, in the United States, where demands and desires are frequently framed in terms of rights, cloning too was defined as a "right." The technology spawned not only Dolly but an association called "Cloning Rights United Front." Its members insisted that cloning is part of the reproductive rights of every human being, and, in tune with the political sentiments of the 1990s, they wanted "the government to keep out."[9]

Various professions had something to say about the implications of cloning for their fields.[10] A divorce lawyer predicted the doubling of his business. Historians wondered if the founding fathers could be cloned for display in a "living history" exhibit in a theme park: they suggested that the park might be called "Clonial Williamsburg." Some facetious policy commentators announced that cloning experiments could be developed to solve social problems: the race problem could be resolved by manipulating the balance between melanin and IQ genes. The age-old nature-nurture dispute could be definitively settled by creating clones and raising them systematically in different environments.

Religious ethicists and theologians had a lot to say about the cloning experiment.[11] One writer quipped that cloning offered a "second chance for the soul." If you sin the first time, try again. But a theologian, Rabbi Mosher Tendler, a professor of medical ethics at Yeshiva University in New York, warned that "whenever man has shown mastery over man, it has always meant the enslavement of man." Other theologians, long concerned about the implications of genetic engineering, worried that the scientists who experimented with cloning were "playing God" and "tampering with God's creation."[12] A less reverent wag wondered about the implications of cloning the Pope: Would they both be infallible? And what if they disagree?

In his scientific paper itself, Dr. Wilmut fussed over the problem of whether "a differentiated adult nucleus can be fully reprogrammed." He called the lamb in question 6LL3 rather than Dolly, and made it clear, in diagrams and illustrations of gels, that there is some question about the precise genetic relationship between Dolly and the "donor."[13] Somatic DNA, which was the source of Dolly's genes, is constantly mutating. Dolly, in fact, may not be genetically identical in every way to her "mother," a point that is of some importance for the possible agricultural uses of cloning techniques.

For writers in the popular press, however, such technical details were less important than symbolic associations. The cloning of a lamb was immediately set in a context of other fears about genetics and genetic manipulation, and even in a context of more general fears about science and its applications. One journalist compared cloning to weapons development. Another worried that the shortage of organs for transplantation would be resolved by cloning anencephalic babies (who are born without a brain but are otherwise normal), so that their organs could be harvested for patients in need.

Dolly has also evoked an amazing range of humor—some silly, some funny—about the implications of cloning. Poems, cartoons, one-liners, and puns about cloning appeared almost immediately on the Internet and in mainstream publications. Jokes can reveal cultural fault lines and social tensions, for their humor often plays on the contradictions and ironies of familiar contexts, events, or situations. Dolly jokes were no exception.

Writer Wendy Wasserman wondered what you would say to your shrink if you are your own mother.[14] An Internet inquirer wondered: "If I have sex with my clone, will I go blind?" A cartoonist in the London *Guardian* depicted a women comforting a cab driver who had just run over her husband: "That's alright, I have another one upstairs." Even the issue of scientific fraud became a source of cloning humor. "What if the cloning experiment was in fact a fraud? Well, they really would have pulled the wool over our eyes."

Meanwhile, a journalist predicted a new action movie called "Speed Sheep" in which thousands of cloned sheep clogged Interstate 95. Headlines of cloning stories revelled in puns: "An udder way of making lambs," "Send in the clones," "Little Lamb, who made thee?" "Will there ever be another ewe?" and "Getting stranger in the manger." And inevitably there was the anticipation of "Double Trouble."

More pointed jokes—as well as serious commentaries—expressed the growing tensions over commercial control of biotechnology and its implications for the commodification of the body. Just as the GWU experiment evoked images of a cloning industry and breeding factories, so Dolly evoked cynical references to "test tube capitalists," and sardonic queries about a market for genetic "factory seconds" and "irregulars." A World Wide Web site called Dreamtech advertised a commercial service to create either "custom clones" or "designer clones." The company would clone various celebrities for a range of licensing fees, depending on the anticipated value of the product. The advertisement also offered a personal extraction kit, surrogate services, rapid delivery, and a back-up embryo.[15] Meanwhile, *Business Week* anticipated "The Biotech Century" in which cloning animals is just the beginning: "It's all happening faster than anyone expected."[16] And in an apparently serious sales effort, a company named Valiant Venture Ltd. formed a service called "Clonaid" to provide assistance to would-be parents wanting to have a child cloned. The cost: $200,000.[17] In a casual but revealing conversation during a television interview with one of the authors, a camera technician quipped, only half in jest: "I used to be a person, then I became a social security number. Now I am just a bar code—just a commodity like the cloned sheep."

The messages evoked by Dolly have ranged from promises of progress to portents of peril, from images of miracles to visions of apocalypse. There were many calls for regulation and for a moratorium on cloning experiments. As political and social pressures began to grow, scientists responded, defending the importance of the work. Media images were "selling science short." The calls for regulations and restrictions, they argued, ignored the medical benefits that could follow from cloning experiments and their potential contribution to the development of lifesaving treatments and the testing of new drugs.[18] We are not interested in playing God, said James Geraghty, president of the biotechnology firm Genzyme, but in "playing doctor."[19] Mammalian cloning could help to generate tissue for organ transplantation and encourage transgenics experimentation. And certainly research using cloning would enhance scientific knowledge about cell differentiation. The politicians who sought a ban on cloning research, said the scientists, were "shooting from the hip."[20]

But political pressures continued, reflecting popular mistrust of science and fear that the outrageous possibilities suggested by a cloned sheep will eventually, perhaps inevitably, be realized. News reports and media headlines suggested that science cannot be controlled: "Science fiction has become a social reality." "Whatever's Next?" And, of course, "Pandora's Box."

Dolly, after all, is only a lamb and she is depicted again and again as cuddly and cute, if a bit overweight. But as a symbolic site for the exploration of identity, heredity, destiny, and the social meaning of science, she is a spectacular beast. She is one more step in a series of dreams about science—evoking, for some, euphoric fantasies; for others, horrible nightmares and the fear of science out-of-control. She offers up the possibility of hyper-rationality in the management of bodies and of complete genetic control of cows, sheep, and humans as well. She offers the specter of technical decisions that will turn all bodies (human and animal) into intentional products, manufactured and designed "on purpose." She evokes a way of thinking about bodies as little more than efficient mechanisms for the production of "value"—be it milk, or meat, or creative imagination. Dolly can thus be regarded less as a lamb than as a microcosm of the entire history of science, a symbol of the rich interconnections between animals and human beings, of the struggles between technological changes and moral tenets, of the tensions between the advance of scientific knowledge and demands for political expediency.

Popular speculations about science and its terrors have often been dismissed as based on journalistic ignorance of science, sensationalism, or willful misinterpretation for the sake of making news. But media messages matter. Widely disseminated images and narratives have real effects, regardless of their relationship to the technical details of the scientific work. They shape the way people think about new technologies, assess their impacts, and develop ways to control them. The popular responses to Dolly are especially important because they convey meanings that extend well beyond the single experiment. Dolly has become far more than a biological entity; she is a cultural icon, a symbol, a way to define the meaning of personhood, to describe social issues, and to express concerns about the forces shaping our lives. She provides a window on popular beliefs about human nature and the social order, on public fears of science and its power in society, and on concerns about the human future in the biotechnology age. She is a stunning image in the popular imagination.

Notes

1. Nelkin D, Lindee MS. *The DNA Mystique: The Gene as a Cultural Icon.* New York: W.H. Freeman, 1995.

2. Langreth R. Cloning has fascinating, disturbing potential. *Wall Street Journal* 1997; Feb 24.

3. See, for example, the report on the George Washington University experiment in Dewitt PE. Cloning: where do we draw the line? *Time* 1993;Nov 8;64–70.

4. Some of the scenarios appeared in a review of the media coverage of human embryo cloning in the *Newsletter* of the Center for Biotechnology Policy and Ethics of Texas A & M, 1 January 1994.

5. See note 3, Dewitt 1993.

6. For a review of the commercial metaphors in popular magazines see note 1, Nelkin, Lindee 1995:97.

7. Richard Dawkins, quoted in Butler D, Waldman M. Calls for cloning ban sell science short. *Nature* 1997;386(March 6):9. Dawkins called himself a "closet clone" in an interview with the *Evening Standard* 1997;Feb. 25.

8. Robert Coles, quoted in Neibuhr G. Suddenly religious ethicists face a quandary on cloning. *New York Times* 1997;Mar 1.

9. Reported in the *New York Times Magazine* 1997;May 25:18.

10. Some of the quips that follow in this paper come from the Oracle Service List on the Internet: oracle-list@synapse.net, 30 April 1997. Others are from the Internet and talk shows; still others from jokes repeated through personal conversations. I have selected them from many jokes and stories repeated in popular sources to suggest the range of concerns and issues raised in popular culture.

11. For a review of religious views, see note 8, Niebuhr 1997.

12. Articles in evangelical magazines such as *Christianity Today* have regular articles opposing genetic engineering as "tampering with genes." See, for example, Kroll P. The gene healers, *The Plain Truth* 1990;55:3–8. Pope John Paul II has taken a position on genetic manipulation, arguing that: "All interference in the genome must be done in a way that absolutely respects the specific nature of the human species, the transcendental vocation of every being and his incomparable dignity . . .". Address to the Pontifical Academy of Science, 8 October 1994. Quoted in *Family Resource Center News* 1996;Winter:1.

13. Wilmut I, Schneike AE, McWhir J, Kind AJ, Campbell KHS. Viable offspring derived from fetal and adult mammalian cells. *Nature* 1997;35:810–2.

14. Quoted in *New York Times* 1997;27 Feb.

15. Dreamtech, http://www.D-B.Net/DT1/Intro2.HTML.

16. *Business Week* 1997;March 10:cover.

17. It advertises on the Internet at http://www.clonaid.com/.

18. Threatened bans on human cloning research could hamper advances [Medical News and Perspectives] *JAMA* 1997; 277:1023. Also see statement from a group from the International Academy of Humanism, Defense of cloning and the integrity of scientific research, quoted in *Science* 1997;276:1341.

19. Geraghty J. Quoted in *Genetic Engineering News* 1997;Apr 1:10.

20. Brigid Hogan, Professor in cell biology, quoted in Wadman M. Politicians accused of "shooting from the hip on human cloning." *Nature* 1997;386:97.

A Life in the Shadow: One Reason Why We Should Not Clone Humans

Søren Holm

INTRODUCTION

One of the arguments that is often put forward in the discussion of human cloning is that it is in itself wrong to create a copy of a human being.

This argument is usually dismissed by pointing out that a) we do not find anything wrong in the existence of monozygotic twins even though they are genetically identical, and b) the clone would not be an exact copy of the original even in those cases where it is an exact genetic copy, since it would have experienced a different environment that would have modified its biological and psychological development.

In my view both these counterarguments are valid, but nevertheless I think that there is some core of truth in the assertion that it is wrong deliberately to try to create a copy of an already existing human being. It is this idea that I will briefly try to explicate here.

THE LIFE IN THE SHADOW ARGUMENT

When we see a pair of monozygotic twins who are perfectly identically dressed some of us experience a slight sense of unease, especially in the cases where the twins are young children. This unease is exacerbated when people establish competitions where the winners are the most identical pair of twins. The reason for this uneasiness is, I believe, that the identical clothes could signal a reluctance on the part of the parents to let each twin develop his or her individual and separate personality or a reluctance to let each twin lead his or her own life. In the extreme case each twin is constantly compared with the other and any difference is counteracted.

In the case of cloning based on somatic cells we have what is effectively a set of monozygotic twins with a potentially very large age difference. The original may have lived all his or her life and may even have died before the clone is brought into existence. Therefore, there will not be any direct day-by-day comparison and identical clothing, but then a situation that is even worse for the clone is likely to develop. I shall call this situation "a life in the shadow" and I shall develop an argument against human cloning that may be labeled the "life in the shadow argument."

Let us try to imagine what will happen when a clone is born and its social parents have to begin rearing it. Usually when a child is born we ask hypothetical questions like "How will it develop?" or "What kind of person will it become?" and we often answer them with reference to various psychological traits we think we can identify in the biological mother or father or in their families, for instance "I hope that he won't get the kind of temper you had when you were a child!"

In the case of the clone we are, however, likely to give much more specific answers to such questions. Answers that will then go on to affect the way the child is reared. There is no doubt that the common public understanding of the relationship between genetics and psychology contains substantial strands of genetic essentialism, i.e., the idea that the genes determine psychology and personality.[1] This public idea is reinforced every time the media report the finding of new genes for depression, schizophrenia, etc. Therefore, it is likely that the parents of the clone will already have formed in their minds a quite definite picture of how the clone will develop, a picture that is based on the actual development of the original. This picture will control the way they rear the child. They will try to prevent some developments, and try to promote others. Just imagine how a clone of Adolf Hitler or Pol Pot would be reared, or how a clone of Albert Einstein, Ludwig van Beethoven, or Michael Jordan would be brought up. The clone would in a very literal way live his or her life in the shadow of the life of the original. At every point in the clone's life there would be someone who had already lived that life, with whom the clone could be compared and against whom the clone's accomplishments could be measured.

That there would in fact be a strong tendency to make the inference from genotype to phenotype and to let the conclusion of such an inference affect rearing can perhaps be seen more clearly if we imagine the following hypothetical situation:

> In the future new genetic research reveals that there are only a limited number of possible human genotypes, and that genotypes are therefore recycled every 300 years (i.e., somebody who died 300 years ago had exactly the same genotype as me). It is further discovered that there is some complicated, but not practically impossible, method whereby it is possible to discover the identity of the persons who 300, 600, 900, etc. years ago instantiated the genotype that a specific fetus now has.

I am absolutely certain that people would split into two sharply disagreeing camps if this became a possibility. One group, perhaps the majority, would try to identify the previous instantiations of their child's genotype. Another group would emphatically not seek this information because they would not want to know and would not want their children to grow up in the shadow of a number of previously led lives with the same genotype. The option to remain in ignorance is, however, not open to social parents of contemporary clones.

If the majority would seek the information in this scenario, firms offering the method of identification would have a very brisk business, and it could perhaps even become usual to expect of prospective parents that they make use of this new possibility. Why would this happen? The only reasonable explanation, apart from initial curiosity, is that people would believe that by identifying the previous instantiation of the genotype they would thereby gain valuable knowledge about their child. But knowledge is in general only valuable if it can be converted into new options for action, and the most likely form of action would be that information about the previous instantiations would be used in deciding how to rear the present child. This again points to the importance of the public perception of genetic essentialism, since the environment must have changed considerably in the 300-year span between each instantiation of the genotype.

WHAT IS WRONG ABOUT A LIFE IN THE SHADOW?

What is wrong with living your life as a clone in the shadow of the life of the original? It diminishes the clone's possibility of living a life that is in a full sense of that word his or her life. The clone is forced to be involved in an attempt to perform a complicated partial re-enactment of the life of somebody else (the original). In our usual arguments for the importance of respect for autonomy or for the value of self-determination we often affirm that it is the final moral basis for these principles that they enable persons to live their lives the way they themselves want to live these lives. If we deny part of this opportunity to clones and force them to live their lives in the shadow of someone else we are violating some of our most fundamental moral principles and intuitions. Therefore, as long as genetic essentialism is a common cultural belief there are good reasons not to allow human cloning.

FINAL QUALIFICATIONS

It is important to note that the 'life in the shadow argument' does not rely on the false premise that we can make an inference from genotype to (psychological or personality) phenotype, but only on the true premise that there is a strong public tendency to make such an inference. This means that the conclusions of the argument only follow as long as this empirical premise remains true. If ever the public relinquishes all belief in genetic essentialism the 'life in the shadow argument' would fail, but such a development seems highly unlikely.

In conclusion I should perhaps also mention that I am fully aware of two possible counterarguments to the argument presented above. The first points out that even if a life in the shadow of the original is perhaps problematic and not very good, it is the only life the clone can have, and that it is therefore in the clone's interest to have this life as long as it is not worse than having no life at all. The 'life in the shadow argument' therefore does not show that cloning should be prohibited. I am unconvinced by this counterargument, just as I am by all arguments involving comparisons between existence and nonexistence, but it is outside the scope of the present short paper to show decisively that the counterargument is wrong.

The second counterargument states that the conclusions of the 'life in the shadow argument' can be avoided if all clones are anonymously put up for adoption, so that no knowledge about the original is available to the social parents of the clone. I am happy to accept this counterargument, but I think that a system where I was not allowed to rear the clone of myself would practically annihilate any interest in human cloning. The attraction in cloning for many is exactly in the belief that I can recreate myself. The cases where human cloning solves real medical or reproductive problems are on the fringe of the area of cloning.

Note

1. Nelkin D, Lindee MS. *The DNA Mystique: The Gene as a Cultural Icon.* New York: W.H. Freeman and Company, 1995.

Cloning and Human Dignity

John Harris

The panic occasioned by the birth of Dolly sent international and national bodies and their representatives scurrying for principles with which to allay imagined public anxiety. It is instructive to note that principles are things of which such people and bodies so often seem to be bereft. The search for appropriate principles turned out to be difficult since so many aspects of the Dolly case were unprecedented. In the end, some fascinating examples of more or less plausible candidates for the status of moral principles were identified; central to many of them is the idea of human dignity and how it might be affected by human mitotic reproduction.[1]

Typical of appeals to human dignity was that contained in the World Health Organization statement on cloning issued on 11 March 1997:

> WHO considers the use of cloning for the replication of human individuals to be ethically unacceptable as it would violate some of the basic principles which govern medically assisted procreation. These include respect for the dignity of the human being. . . .

Appeals to human dignity are, of course, universally attractive; they are also comprehensively vague. A first question to ask when the idea of human dignity is invoked is: whose dignity is attacked and how? If it is the duplication of a large part of the human genome that is supposed to constitute the attack on human dignity, or where the issue of "genetic identity" is invoked, we might legitimately ask whether and how the dignity of a natural twin is threatened by the existence of her sister and what follows as to the permissibility of natural monozygotic twinning? However, the notion of human dignity is often linked to Kantian ethics and it is this link I wish to examine more closely here.

A typical example, and one that attempts to provide some basis for objections to cloning based on human dignity, was Axel Kahn's invocation of this principle in his commentary on cloning in *Nature*. Kahn, a distinguished molecular biologist, helped draft the French National Ethics Committee's report on cloning. In *Nature* Kahn states:

> The creation of human clones solely for spare cell lines would, from a philosophical point of view, be in obvious contradiction to the principle expressed by Emmanuel Kant: that of human dignity. This principle demands that an individual—and I would extend this to read human life—should never be thought of as a means, but always also as an end. Creating human life for the sole purpose of preparing therapeutic material would clearly not be for the dignity of the life created.[2]

The Kantian principle, invoked without any qualification or gloss, is seldom helpful in medical or bioscientific contexts.[3] As formulated by Kahn, for example, it would surely outlaw blood transfusions. The beneficiary of blood donation, neither knowing of, nor usually caring about, the anonymous donor uses the blood (and its donor) exclusively as a means to her own ends. The blood in the bottle has after all less identity, and is less connected with the individual from which it emanated, than the chicken "nuggets" on the supermarket shelf. An abortion performed exclusively to save the life of the mother would also, presumably, be outlawed by this principle.

INSTRUMENTALIZATION

This idea of using individuals as a means to the purposes of others is sometimes termed "instrumentalization," particularly in the European context. The advisers to the European Commission on the ethical implications of biotechnology, for example, in their statement on ethical aspects of cloning techniques use this idea repeatedly.[4] Referring to reproductive human cloning, paragraph 2.6 states:

> Considerations of instrumentalization and eugenics render any such acts ethically unacceptable.

Applying this idea coherently or consistently is not easy! If someone wants to have children in order to continue their genetic line do they act instrumentally? Where, as is standard practice in IVF, spare embryos are created, are these embryos created instrumentally?

Kahn responded in the journal *Nature* to these objections.[5] He reminds us, rightly, that Kant's famous principle states: "respect for human dignity requires that an individual is *never* used . . . *exclusively* as a means" and suggests that I have ignored the crucial use of the term "exclusively." I did not, of course, and I'm happy with Kahn's reformulation of the principle. It is not that Kant's principle does not have powerful intuitive force, but that it is so vague and so open to selective interpretation and its scope for application is consequently so limited that its utility as one of the "fundamental principles of modern bioethical thought," as Kahn describes it, is virtually zero.

Kahn himself rightly points out that debates concerning the moral status of the human embryo are debates about whether embryos fall within the *scope* of Kant's or indeed any other moral principles concerning persons; so the principle itself is not illuminating in this context. Applied to the creation of individuals who are, or will become autonomous, it has limited application. True, the Kantian principle rules out slavery, but so do a range of other principles based on autonomy and rights. If you are interested in the ethics of creating people, then, so long as existence is in the created individual's own best interests, and the individual will have the capacity for autonomy like any other, the motives for which the individual was created are either morally irrelevant or subordinate to other moral considerations. So that even where, for example, a child is engendered exclusively to provide "a son and heir" (as is often the case in many cultures) it is unclear how or whether Kant's principle applies. Either other motives are also attributed to the parent to square parental purposes with Kant, or the child's eventual autonomy and its clear and substantial interest in or benefit from existence take precedence over the comparatively trivial issue of parental motives. Either way the "fundamental principle of modern bioethical thought" is unhelpful.

It is therefore strange that Kahn and others invoke it with such dramatic assurance or how anyone could think that it applies to the ethics of human cloning. It comes down to this: Either the ethics of human cloning turn on the creation or use of human embryos, in which case as Kahn himself says "in reality the debate is about the status of the human embryo" and Kant's principle must wait upon the outcome of that debate; or, it is about the ethics of producing clones who will become autonomous human persons. In this latter case, as David Shapiro also comments,[6] the ethics of their creation are, from a Kantian perspective, not dissimilar to other forms of assisted reproduction, or, as I have suggested, to the ethics of the conduct of parents concerned exclusively with producing an heir, or preserving their genes, or, as is sometimes alleged, making themselves eligible for public housing. Debates about whether these are *exclusive* intentions can never be definitively resolved.

Kahn then produces a bizarre twist to the argument from autonomy. He defines autonomy as "the indeterminability of the individual with respect to external human will" and identifies it as one of the components of human dignity. This is, of course, hopeless as a definition of autonomy—those in persistent vegetative state (PVS) and indeed all newborns would on such a view have to count as autonomous! However, Kahn then asserts:

> The birth of an infant by asexual reproduction would lead to a new category of people whose bodily form and genetic make-up would be exactly as decided by other humans. This would lead to the establishment of an entirely new type of relationship between the "created" and the "creator" which has obvious implications for human dignity.

Kahn is, I'm afraid, wrong on both counts. As Robert Winston has noted: "even if straight cloning techniques were used, the mother would contribute important constituents—her mitochondrial genes, intrauterine influences and subsequent nurture."[7] These, together with the other influences, would prevent exact determination of bodily form and genetic identity. For example, differences in environment, age, and *anno domini* between clone and cloned would all come into play.

Lenin's embalmed body lies in its mausoleum in Moscow. Presumably a cell of this body could be denucleated and Lenin's genome cloned. Could such a process make Lenin immortal and allow us to create someone whose bodily form and genetic makeup, not to mention his character and individuality, would be "exactly as decided by other human beings?" I hope the answer is obvious. Vladimir Ilyich Ulyanov was born on 10 April 1870 in the town of Simbirsk on the Volga. It is this person who became and who is known to most of us as V.I. Lenin. Even with this man's genome preserved intact we will never see Lenin again. So many of the things that made Vladimir Ilyich what he was cannot be reproduced, even if his genome can. We cannot recreate prerevolutionary Russia. We cannot simulate his environment and education; we cannot recreate his parents to bring him up and influence his development so profoundly as they undoubtedly did. We cannot make the thought of Karl Marx seem as hopeful as it must then have been; we cannot, in short, do anything but reproduce his genome and that could never be nearly enough. It may be that "manners maketh man" but genes most certainly do not.

As we know from monozygotic twins, autonomy is unaffected by close similarity of bodily form and matching genome. The "indeterminability of the individual with respect to external human will" will remain unaffected by cloning. Where then are the obvious implications for human dignity?

When Kahn asks: "is Harris announcing the emergence of a revisionist tendency in bioethical thinking?" the answer must be, rather, I am pleading for the emergence of "bioethical *thinking*" as opposed to the empty rhetoric of invoking resonant principles with no conceivable or coherent application to the problem at hand.

Clearly, the birth of Dolly and the possibility of human equivalents have left many people feeling not a little uneasy, if not positively queasy at the prospect. It is perhaps salutary to remember that there is no necessary connection between phenomena, attitudes, or actions that make us uneasy, or even those that disgust us, and those phenomena, attitudes, and actions that there are good reasons for judging unethical. Nor does it follow that those things we are confident *are* unethical must be prohibited by legislation or controlled by regulation. These are separate steps that require separate arguments.

MORAL NOSE

The idea that moral sentiments, or indeed, gut reactions must play a crucial role in the determination of what is morally permissible is tenacious. This idea, originating with David Hume (who memorably remarked that morality is "more properly felt than judg'd of"), has been influential in the work of a number of contemporary moral philosophers.[8] In particular, Mary Warnock has made it a central part of her own approach to these issues. Briefly the idea is:

> If morality is to exist at all, either privately or publicly, there must be some things which, regardless of consequences should not be done, some barriers which should not be passed.
> What marks out these barriers is often a sense of outrage, if something is done; a feeling that to permit some practice would be indecent or part of the collapse of civilisation.[9]

A recent, highly sophisticated and thoroughly mischievous example in the context of cloning comes from Leon R. Kass. In a long discusssion entitled "The Wisdom of Repugnance" Kass tries hard and thoughtfully to make plausible the thesis that thoughtlessness is a virtue:

> We are repelled by the prospect of cloning human beings not because of the strangeness or novelty of the undertaking, but because we intuit and feel, immediately and without argument, the violation of things that we rightfully hold dear.[10]

The difficulty is, of course, to know when one's sense of outrage is evidence of something morally disturbing and when it is simply an expression of bare prejudice or something even more shameful. The English novelist George Orwell once referred to this reliance on some innate sense of right and wrong as "moral nose," as if one could simply sniff a situation and detect wickedness.[11] The problem, as I have indicated, is that nasal reasoning is notoriously unreliable, and olfactory moral philosophy, its theoretical "big brother," has done little to refine it or give it a respectable foundation. We should remember that in the recent past, among the many discreditable uses of so-called "moral feelings," people have been disgusted by the sight of Jews, black people, and indeed women being treated as equals and mixing on terms of equality with others. In the absence of convincing arguments, we should be suspicious of accepting the conclusions of those who use nasal reasoning as the basis of their moral convictions.

In Kass's suggestion (he disarmingly admits revulsion "is not an argument") the giveaway is in his use of the term "rightfully." How can we know that revulsion, however sincerely or vividly felt, is occasioned by the violation of things we rightfully hold dear unless we have a theory, or at least an argument, about which of the things we happen to hold dear we *rightfully* hold dear? The term "rightfully" implies a judgment that confirms the respectability of the feelings. If it is simply one feeling confirming another, then we really are in the situation Wittgenstein lampooned as buying a second copy of the same newspaper to confirm the truth of what we read in the first.

We should perhaps also note for the record that cloning was not anticipated by the Deity in any of his (or her) manifestations on earth; nor in any of the extant holy books of the various religions. Ecclesiastical pronouncements on the issue cannot therefore be evidence of God's will on cloning, and must be examined on the merits of the evidence and argument that inform them, like the judgments or opinions of any other individuals.

Notes

1. For a more comprehensive account of the ethics of human cloning generally see Harris J. Goodbye Dolly? the ethics of human cloning. *Journal of Medical Ethics* 1997;23(6).

2. Kahn A. Clone mammals . . . clone man. *Nature* 1997;386:119.

3. Harris J. Is cloning an attack on human dignity? *Nature* 1997;387:754.

4. GAEIB. *Opinion of the group of advisers on the ethical implications of biotechnology to the European Commission*, No. 9. 28 May 1997.

5. See note 2, Kahn 1997.

6. Shapiro D. Letter. *Nature* 1997;388:511.

7. Winston R. *British Medical Journal* 1997;314:913–4.

8. David Hume in his *A Treatise of Human Nature* 1738. Contemporary philosophers who have flirted with a similar approach include Stuart Hampshire; see, for example, Hampshire S. *Morality & Pessimism: The Leslie Stephen Lecture.* Cambridge: Cambridge University Press, 1972; and Bernard Williams in Against utilitarianism. In Williams B, Smart JCC. *Utilitarianism For and Against.* Cambridge: Cambridge University Press, 1973. I first discussed the pitfalls of olfactory moral philosophy in my *Violence and Responsibility.* London: Routledge & Kegan Paul, 1980.

9. Warnock M. Do human cells have rights? *Bioethics* 1987;1(1):8.

10. Kass LR. The wisdom of repugnance. *The New Republic* 1997;Jun 2:17–26. The obvious erudition of his writing leads to expectations that he might have found feelings prompted by more promising parts of his anatomy with which to entertain us.

11. Orwell G. Letter to Humphrey House (11 April 1940). *The Collected Essays, Journalism and Letters of George Orwell,* vol.1. Harmondsworth: Penguin, 1970:583. See my more detailed discussion of the problems with this type of reasoning in Harris J. *Wonderwoman & Superman: The Ethics of Human Biotechnology.* Oxford: Oxford University Press, 1992.

Report of the Council on Ethical and Judicial Affairs

American Medical Association

The Council on Ethical and Judicial Affairs submits the following opinions to the House of Delegates for its information, and recommends that this report be filed.

GENE THERAPY

Gene therapy involves the insertion of a normally functioning gene into cells in which an abnormal or absent element of the gene has caused disease, with the goal of restoring normal cellular function. The replacement gene may be inserted into target cells either in situ or outside the body for later reimplantation.

Two types of gene therapy have been identified: (1) somatic cell therapy, in which human cells other than germ cells are genetically altered, and (2) germ line therapy, in which a replacemnt gene is integrated into the genome of human gametes or their precursors, resulting in expression of the new gene in the patient's offspring and subsequent generations. The fundamental difference between germ line therapy and somatic cell therapy is that germ line therapy affects the welfare of subsequent generations and may be associated with increased risk and the potential for unpredictable and irreversible results.

The goals of both somatic and germ line therapy is to alleviate human suffering and disease by remedying disorders for which available therapies are not satisfactory. This goal should be pursued only within the ethical tradition of medicine, which gives primacy to the welfare of the patient whose safety and well-being must be vigorously protected. To the extent possible, experience with animal studies must be sufficient to assure the effectiveness and safety of the techniques used, and the predictability of the results.

Moreover, gene therapy should be utilized only for therapeutic purposes. Efforts to enhance "desirable" characteristics through the insertion of a modified or additional gene, or efforts to "improve" complex human traits—the eugenic development of offspring—are contrary not only to the ethical tradition of medicine, but also to the egalitarian values of our society and should not be pursued.

In summary, somatic cell and germ line therapy should:

1. conform to the Council on Ethical and Judicial Affairs' guidelines on clinical investigation and genetic engineering;
2. adhere to stringent safety considerations; and
3. be utilized only for therapeutic purposes in the treatment of human disorders—not for the enhancement or eugenic development of patients or their offspring.

Position Paper on Human Germ Line Manipulation

Presented by Council for Responsible Genetics, Human Genetics Committee, Fall, 1992

THE POSITION OF THE COUNCIL FOR RESPONSIBLE GENETICS

The Council for Responsible Genetics (CRG) strongly opposes the use of germ line gene modification in humans. This position is based on scientific, ethical, and social concerns.

Proponents of germ line manipulation assume that once a gene implicated in a particular condition is identified, it might be appropriate and relatively easy to change, supplement or otherwise modify the gene by some form of therapy. However, biological characteristics or traits usually depend on interactions among many genes, and these genes are themselves affected by processes that occur both inside the organism and in its surroundings. This means that scientists cannot predict the full effect that any gene modification will have on the traits of people or other organisms. In purely biological terms, the relationship between genes and traits is not well enough understood to guarantee that by eliminating or changing genes associated with traits one might want to avoid, we may not simultaneously alter or eliminate traits we would like to preserve. Even genes that are associated with diseases that may cause problems in one context can be beneficial in another context.

Two frequently destructive aspects of contemporary culture are linked together in an unprecedented fashion in germ line gene modification. The first is the notion that the value of a human being is dependent on the degree to which he or she approximates some ideal of biological perfection. The second is the ideology that all limitations imposed by nature can and should be overcome by technology. To make intentional changes in the genes that people will pass on to their descendants would require that we, as a society, agree on how to identify 'good' and 'bad' genes. We do not have such criteria, nor are there mechanisms for establishing them. Any formulation of such criteria would necessarily reflect current social biases.

Moreover, the definition of the standards and the technological means for implementing them would largely be determined by the economically and socially privileged. By implementing a program of germ line manipulation these groups would exercise unwarranted influence over the common biological heritage of humanity.

WHAT IS "GERM LINE MANIPULATION"?

The undifferentiated cells of an early embryo develop into either germ cells or somatic cells. *Germ* cells, or reproductive cells, are those that develop into the egg or sperm of a developing organism and transmit all its heritable characteristics. *Somatic* cells, or body cells, refer to all other cells of the body. While both types of cells contain chromosomes, only the chromosomes of germ cells are passed on to future generations.

Techniques are now available to change chromosomes of animal cells by inserting new segments of DNA into them. If this insertion is performed on specialized or *differentiated* body tissues, such as liver, muscle, or blood cells, it is referred to as *somatic cell* gene modification, and the changes do not go beyond the individual organism. If it is performed on sperm or eggs before fertilization, or on the undifferentiated cells of an early embryo, it is called *germ cell* or *germ line* gene modification, and the changes are not limited to the individual organism. For when DNA is incorporated into an embryo's germ cells, or undifferentiated cells that give rise to germ cells, the introduced gene or genes will be passed on to future generations and may become a permanent part of the gene pool.

Deliberate gene alterations in humans are often referred to as 'gene therapy'. The Council for Responsible Genetics (CRG) prefers to use the terms 'gene modification' and 'gene manipulation' because the word 'therapy' promises health benefits, and it is not yet clear that gene manipulations are beneficial.

WHY MIGHT GERM LINE MODIFICATION BE ATTEMPTED IN HUMANS?

If one or both partners carry a version of a gene that could predispose their offspring to inherit a condition they want to avoid, genetic manipulation may appear to be a potential way to prevent the undesired outcome. The earlier during embryonic development the targeted gene or genes are replaced, the less likely is the resulting individual to be affected by the unwanted gene. But while the immediate goal of such a modification might be to alter the genetic constitution of a single individual, modifications made at the early embryonic stages would incidentally result in germ line modification, and so all the offspring of this person would have and pass on the modification.

Alternatively, germ line modification may be the intended consequence of the procedure. One goal might be to 'cleanse' the gene pool of 'deleterious' genes. For example, Daniel E. Koshland, Jr., a molecular biologist, and the editor-in-chief of *Science,* has written, "keeping diabetics alive with insulin, which increases the propagation of an inherited disease, seems justified only if one ultimately is willing to do genetic engineering to remove diabetes from the germ line and thus save the anguish and cost to millions of diabetics." (1) Another goal of germ line manipulation may be to avoid multiple treatments of somatic gene modification that would be required under proposed treatment protocols for certain conditions such as cystic fibrosis.

Some people may also look forward to the possibility of introducing genes into the germ line that can 'enhance' certain characteristics desired by parents or other custodians of the resulting offspring. In the article referred to above, Koshland raises the possibility that germ line alterations could be perceived to meet future 'needs' to design individuals "better at computers, better as musicians, better physically."

The attempt to improve the human species biologically is known as *eugenics,* and was the basis of a popular movement in Europe and North America during the first half of this century. Eugenics was advocated by prominent scientists across the entire political spectrum, who represented it as the logical consequence of the most advanced biological thinking of the period. In the U.S., eugenic thinking resulted in social policies that called for forced sterilization of individuals regarded as inferior because they were 'feeble minded or paupers.' In Europe, the Nazis took up these ideas, and their attempts at implementation led to widespread revulsion against the concept of eugenics. Today public discussion in favor of influencing the genetic constitution of future generations has gained new respectability with the increased possibility for intervention presented by in vitro fertilization and embryo implantation technologies. Although it is once again espoused by individuals with a variety of political perspectives, the doctrine of social advancement through biological perfectibility underlying the new eugenics is almost indistinguishable from the older version so avidly embraced by the Nazis.

It is important to recognize that the dream of eliminating 'harmful' genes (such as those associated with cystic fibrosis or Duchenne muscular dystrophy) from the entire human gene pool could be realized only over time scales of thousands of years, and then only with massive, coercive programs of germ line manipulation. Such a program would be neither feasible nor morally acceptable. As a practical matter then, any presumed beneficial effects of germ line modification would pertain to individual families, not to the human population as a whole. This is in contrast to harmful effects, which would be widely disseminated.

Furthermore, parents who carry a gene which they would not want a child of theirs to inherit could arrange to have unaffected, biologically-related offspring *without* germ line modification. If a gene is well enough characterized to consider gene manipulation, there will always be a diagnostic test available to identify a fetus that carries that gene and parents, if they choose, may then terminate the pregnancy. Given that there are alternatives for avoiding the inheritance of unwanted genes, the main selling point of germ line modification techniques over the long term would appear to be the prospect of enhancement of desired traits.

WHAT IS THE FEASIBILITY OF MODIFYING THE GERM LINE OF HUMANS?

Both somatic and germ line modification are widely performed on laboratory animals for research purposes. Somatic gene modifications have already been performed on humans and additional experimental protocols are being approved by the National Institutes of Health in increasing numbers.

No published reports have yet appeared on germ line modification in humans, but there appear to be no technical obstacles to such experiments, and articles proposing these procedures are becoming more and more common in the literature (2,3,4). Germ line gene modification has actually proved technically easier than somatic modification in mice and other vertebrate animals which have been employed as 'models' for human biology in the past, because the cells of early embryos incorporate foreign DNA and synthesize corresponding functional proteins more readily than most differentiated somatic cells. A widely-reported example of the successful experimental use of the germ line technique was the introduction of an extra gene that specified growth hormone into fertilized mouse eggs. In the presence of the high levels of growth hormone produced, the mice grew to double their normal size. Germ line techniques are also being used in attempts to modify farm animals, with stated goals of increasing yields or enhancing nutritional quality of meat and other animal products.

Given what has been accomplished in animals, the only remaining technical requirements for germ line gene modification in humans are procedures for collecting a woman's eggs, fertilizing them outside her body, and implanting them in the uterus of the same or another woman, where they can be brought to term. These are already well established procedures for humans and are widely used in in-vitro fertilization clinics.

WHAT ARE THE TECHNICAL PITFALLS?

Current methods for germ line gene modification of mammals are inefficient, requiring the microinjection of numerous eggs with foreign DNA before an egg is successfully modified. Moreover, introduction of a foreign gene (even if there is a copy of one already present) into an inappropriate location in an embryo's chromosomes can have unexpected consequences. For example, the offspring of a mouse that received an extra copy of the normally present *myc* gene developed cancer at 40 times the rate of the unmodified strain of mice. (5)

Techniques to introduce foreign DNA into eggs, however, are constantly being improved and eventually will be portrayed as efficient and reliable enough for human applications. It may soon be possible to place a gene into a specified location on a chromosome while simultaneously removing the unwanted gene. This will increase the accuracy of the procedures, but does not eliminate the possibility that gene combinations will be created that will be harmful to the modified embryo, and its descendants in future generations. Such inadvertent damage could be caused by technical error, or more importantly, by biologists' inability to predict how genes or their products interact with one another and with the organism's environment to give rise to biological traits. it would have been impossible to predict, *a priori*, for example, that someone who has even *one* copy of the gene for a blood protein known as hemoglobin-S would be protected against malaria, whereas a person who has *two* copies of this gene would have sickle cell disease.

This unpredictability applies with equal force to genetic modifications introduced to 'correct' presumed disorders and to those introduced to enhance characteristics. Inserting new segments of DNA into the germ line could have major, unpredictable consequences for both the individual and the future of the species that include the introduction of susceptibilities to cancer and other diseases into the human gene pool.

WHAT ARE THE SOCIAL AND ETHICAL IMPLICATIONS OF GERM LINE MODIFICATION?

Clinical trials in humans to treat Adenosine Deaminase Deficiency—a life threatening immune disorder—and terminal cancer with somatic gene modification are already in progress and experiments to treat diabetes and hypertension are under development. It is important to distinguish the ethical problems raised by these protocols from the additional, and more profound questions raised by germ line modification. While the biological effects of somatic manipulations reside entirely in the individual in which they are attempted, such treatments are not strictly analogous to other therapies with individual risk. Radiation, chemical or drug treatment can be withdrawn if they prove harmful to the patient, while some forms of somatic modification cannot. Thus, somatic gene modification requires a person to forfeit his/her rights to withdraw from a research study because the intervention cannot be stopped, whether harmful or not. Valid objections have also been raised to the fact that the first somatic gene modification experiments, involving Adenosine Deaminase Deficiency, were carried out on young children who were not themselves in a position to give informed consent. While it appears that somatic gene modification techniques will be used increasingly in the future, the CRG urges that they be used with greatest caution, and only for clearly life-threatening conditions.

Germ line modification, in contrast, has not yet been attempted in humans. The Council for Responsible Genetics opposes it unconditionally. Ethical arguments against germ line modification include many of those that pertain to somatic cell modification, as well as the following:

- Germ line modification is not needed in order to save the lives or alleviate suffering of existing people. Its target population are 'future people' who have not yet even been conceived.
- The cultural impact of treating humans as biologically perfectible artifacts would be entirely negative. People who fall short of some technically achievable ideal would increasingly be seen as 'damaged goods.' And it is clear that the standards for what is genetically desirable will be those of the society's economically and politically dominant groups. This will only reinforce prejudices and discrimination in a society where they already exist.
- Accountability to individuals of future generations who are harmed or stigmatized by wrongful or unsuccessful germ line modifications of their ancestors is unlikely.

In conclusion, the Council calls for a ban on germ line modification.

References

1. Koshland Jr., Daniel E., "The Future of Biological Research: What is Possible and What is Ethical?", *MBL Science*, v. 3, no. 2, pps. 11–15, 1988.

2. Walters, Leroy, "Human Gene Therapy: Ethics and Public Policy", *Human Gene Therapy,* v. 2, pp. 115–122, 1991.

3. Working Group on Genetic Screening and Testing, *Report of Discussions in Genetics, Ethics and Human Values,* XXIVth CIOMS Conference, Tokyo and Inuyama, Japan, 24–26 July 1990.

4. Buster, John E. and Carson, Sandra A., "Genetic Diagnosis of the Preimplantation Embryo", *American Journal of Medical Centers,* v. 34, pp. 211–216, 1989.

5. Leder, A. et al, "Consequences of Widespread Deregulation of the c-myc Gene in Trangenic Mice: Multiple Neoplasms and Normal Development," *Cell,* v. 42, p. 485, 1986.

EVALUATING A CASE STUDY: APPLYING ETHICAL ISSUES

You are finally at the last stage of the process of evaluating case studies. By this point, you have (a) chosen a practical ethical viewpoint (including the choice of an ethical theory and practical linking principles, whose point of view you will adopt), (b) listed professional and ethical issues, and (c) annotated the issues lists by examining how imbedded each issue is to the essential nature of the case at hand. What remains is the ability to come to an action decision once these three steps have been completed. The final step is to discuss your conclusions.

To do this, you must enter an argumentative phase. In this phase, I suggest that you create brainstorming sheets headed by the possible courses of action open to you. Prepare an argument on each sheet to support that particular course of action utilizing the annotated charts you have already prepared. Then compare what you believe to be the pivotal issues that drive each argument. Use your chosen ethical theory to decide which issue is most compelling. Be prepared to defend your outcomes/action recommendation.

Let us return to the case of contraception in the less-developed countries. As you may recall, the case was as follows.[1] You are a regional director at the World Health Organization. One of your duties is to supervise the distribution of birth control devices to less-developed countries. The product of choice has been the intrauterine device (IUD), which has proved to be effective and inexpensive.

The problem is that in the United States, several hundred users of the IUD have contracted pelvic inflammatory infections that have been linked to use of the IUD.

As regional director, you must decide whether to continue to supply IUDs to women in less-developed countries.

Remember that in this case, the professional practice and the ethical issues were both deeply imbedded, which creates an intractable conflict; there is no simple way to justify one instead of the other.

---

[1]I have heard that many of the structural problems with the IUD that caused pelvic inflammatory infection have not been rectified. I am not competent to comment on this; nevertheless, for this case, let us assume that these problems still obtain.

What you must do is (a) consult your worldview and see what it dictates that you do, and (b) consult the ethical theory of your deepest convictions and see what it would dictate that you do. Is there a synonymy between these? If not, then engage in a dialogue between your worldview and the professional practice. Let each inform on the other. In the end, you should be able to come to some resolution.

One step in this direction is to examine the arguments that support each. What are the critical premises in these arguments?[2] In any argument, there is a conclusion. If you want to contrast two arguments, you must begin by contrasting two conclusions. Conclusions are supported by premises that (logically) cause the acceptance of the conclusion. Therefore, what you must do is to create at least two arguments that entail different conclusions. To do this, create brainstorming lists on the *key issue(s)* involved in the argument. The key issue is that concept that makes the difference. This case has a number of key issues. Let us try to construct arguments that are both for and against the position.

Sample "Pro" Brainstorming Sheet for the Position

Position to be supported.   Continue to sell IUDs in less-developed countries.

Key Thoughts on the Subject

1. As a public health professional, you are enjoined to benefit the greatest number of people possible in your health policy.
2. It is a fact that in less-developed countries, millions die of starvation each year. The simple cause of starvation is too many people for the available food. When you decrease the number of people (given a level food source), more people can eat.
3. There are "blips" to any project. In this case, it is a few hundred or so cases of pelvic inflammatory infection. These casualties pale when compared to the number who will benefit from continuing to provide IUDs.
4. Utilitarian ethical theory dictates that the general good supersedes any individual's good.
5. In less-developed countries, the general good is advanced by continuing to distribute IUDs since more people (by far) benefit than are hurt.

Argument

1. In countries that have a limited amount of food that would feed only a certain population (n), increases in population ($n + x$), will result in x not having enough food to live—fact.

---

[2]See my book, *The Process of Argument* (Englewood Cliffs, NJ: Prentice Hall, 1988; rpt Lanham, MD: University Press of America, 1995) on the details of this process.

2. Many less-developed countries experience the condition mentioned in premise 1—assertion.

3. In many less-developed countries, x increase in population will result in x number of people starving to death—1, 2.

4. Many children who are born are not planned—assertion.

5. If one subtracts the number of unplanned births from the total birth rate, the number of births decreases significantly—assertion.

6. If all children were planned, the number (more than x) of births would decrease significantly—assertion.

7. If all children were planned, less-developed countries would not experience starvation (given constant crop production)—3–6.

8. The IUD is the most effective birth control device in the less-developed countries—assertion.

9. The imperative of professional conduct in public health is to help as many people as possible—fact.

10. Public health professional standards dictate that the IUD should be provided to women in less-developed countries—7, 8.

11. The IUD poses potential health risks to some women (less than 5 percent)—fact.

12. The ethical imperative of Utilitarianism dictates that the right ethical decision is to advance the cause of the common good—fact.

13. Distributing IUDs helps more people in less-developed countries than it hurts—fact.

14. Utilitarianism dictates that the IUD should be provided to women in less-developed countries—11–13.

15. The regional director must continue the distribution of IUDs to less-developed countries—10, 14.

Sample "Con" Brainstorming Sheet Against the Position

Position to be supported. Stop selling IUDs in less-developed countries.

Key Thoughts on the Subject

1. As a public health professional, you are enjoined to benefit the greatest number of people possible in your health policy.

2. It is a fact that in less-developed countries, millions die of starvation each year. The simple cause of starvation is too many people for the available food. When you decrease the number of people (given a level food source), more people can eat.

3. There are "blips" to any project. In this case, it is a few hundred or so cases of pelvic inflammatory infection. These casualties pale when compared to the number who will benefit from continuing to provide IUDs.

4. Human life is precious. No amount of practical gain that can weigh against one human life.

5. Ends do not justify the means. One may have a very good end in mind, but unless the means to that end are just, the end cannot be willed.

Argument

1. In countries that have a limited amount of food that would feed only a certain population (n), increases in population ($n + x$) will result in x not having enough food to live—fact.

2. Many less-developed countries describe the conditions mentioned in premise 1—assertion.

3. In many less-developed countries, x increase in population will result in x number of people starving to death—1, 2.

4. Many children who are born are not planned—assertion.

5. If one subtracts the number of unplanned births from the total birth rate, the number of births decreases significantly—assertion.

6. If all children were planned, the number (more than x) of births would decrease significantly—assertion.

7. If all children were planned, less-developed countries would not experience starvation (given constant crop production)—3–6.

8. The IUD is the most effective birth control device in less-developed countries—assertion.

9. The imperative of professional conduct in public health is to help as many people as possible—fact.

10. Public health professional standards dictate that the IUD should be provided to women in less-developed countries—7, 8.

11. The IUD poses potential health risks to some women (less than 5 percent)—fact.

12. The ethical imperative of Deontology dictates that knowingly jeopardizing the essential health of any person is absolutely impermissible no matter what the practical advantage—assertion.

13. It is absolutely ethically impermissible to provide IUDs to women in less-developed countries when the devices have been shown to be deleterious to the health of Americans—10, 11.

14. In cases of conflict, an absolute ethical imperative trumps an absolute professional standards imperative—assertion.

---

15. The director must halt the distribution of IUDs to less-developed countries—10, 13, 14.

Obviously, the crucial difference in these two arguments is the choice of an ethical theory and the way each is interpreted. Thus, whether a person takes a pro or con position is a function of the underlying value system that person holds. The way a person chooses a value system and the broader practical viewpoint is through the person's worldview and its accompanying baggage.

You must determine how to apply your practical ethical viewpoint. This requires careful attention to the theory and the linking principles you have chosen and the way they affect your evaluation of actual cases. To be an authentic seeker of truth, you must engage in this dialectical process. To do less is to diminish yourself as a person.

You are now ready to evaluate a case study.

Macro and Micro Cases*

Macro Case 1. You are the head of a major state university's genetic research facility. A large multinational company, Perfecta, Inc., has contacted you about a grant related to developing a germ-line therapy to promote growth. Simply put, this therapy would turn families with genes for short adults into families with genes for tall adults. "Think of the market," the president of Perfecta said. "We'll make billions! We also have plans for gene therapy to correct 'imperfect noses' and other undesirable features. The sky is the limit on this one," the president added.

The facts are these. Your laboratory could do the work that Perfecta wants, and a segment of the public will buy genetic enhancement for their future children. You will not be breaking any laws (at least in the way Perfecta has the research setup). Research monies are difficult to obtain, and you are responsible for obtaining grant funding. If you turn down the grant for any reason, other laboratories will do the work and take the money that is now offered to you.

You must respond to Perfecta in three days in the form of a report that will be copied to the president of the university and the chairperson of the board of trustees. What will you say? How will you defend your position?

Macro Case 2. You hold an endowed professorship at an important school of agriculture and are the head of the school's planning committee that is reviewing the school's strategic direction for the future. To be an outstanding research and graduate program, the school must be at the cutting edge of developments. An issue facing the school is cloning, not of sheep but of cattle. People in the United States have been turning away from beef as a staple food over the last decade because of concerns about fat and cholesterol. Now there is the opportunity to create a new breed of cattle that will be more healthy to eat and be more disease free (no more "mad cow disease!").

Such a project would entail a partnership between the school of agriculture and the university's biological research facilities. You have talked with the head of the genetic program, and she made several observations. If you are successful and the industry link (one of the largest in the world) is able to sell the new technique, the school will have made a significant impact on the cattle industry in the United States and around the world. Such success will bring

---

*For more on macro and micro cases, see the overview on p. 53.

the university (especially the biological research program and the school of agriculture) tremendous amounts of money, which can allow them to extend their mission and their programs. It is also possible, she notes, that moving ahead on this project before more preliminary tests have been conducted to determine the consequences to future filial generations could create a number of negative outcomes, such as a decrease in the genetic diversity in the cattle population that could render them less fit for environmental changes. Also, they might become susceptible to new disorders and/or diseases that had been held in check by mechanisms that this project would change. Other possible threats to the equilibrium of the cattle population could, in time, threaten their very existence (because all mechanisms of genetics and how they operate are not fully understood).

These comments are important to you because you want to help lead your school in the right direction for the future. No one wants to be accused of rushing and thereby causing great harm to cattle and humans alike. Likewise, no one wants to be too timid to boldly move forward when an opportunity exists. One of your teachers once said to you, "What can be known, should be known." This is very suggestive to you—yet you are also bothered by some of the things your colleague shared with you. However, you know that agriculture schools have worked on selective breeding for years in an effort to produce the perfect cow. How is this proposal any different?

The time to make your recommendation to the planning committee is at hand. As head of the committee, you are a *very* influential member. Should you recommend accepting or rejecting the project? Write a report stating your decision and presenting your reasons for it.

Micro Case 1. You are a single woman with no intention of ever marrying. However, you like children and have often thought about either adopting a child or conceiving a child through artificial insemination. The problem for you with both of these alternatives is that you never know about the genetic material of the parents (in the case of adoption) or of the father (in the case of artificial insemination). This lack of control on such a crucial point has always bothered you to the point of preventing you from moving forward.

Now you have been contacted by a friend of a friend who knows your dilemma. Your contact is about to work on cloning humans on an island laboratory in the Caribbean. He wants to use a technique to activate one of your eggs and then to implant that egg into your uterus so that you will go through a normal pregnancy and bear your own child who will be genetically identical to you.

This satisfies a number of worries that you have had about "undesirable" genes from other people. Now you can be in total control. Your baby will be genetically identical to yourself. You are inclined to go ahead with the project but want to seek some advice before proceeding.

Write a dialogue between yourself and another person. In this dialogue, explore issues in favor of and opposed to proceeding. Conclude by making a choice and presenting your reasons for it.

Micro Case 2. You are a physician meeting with a couple expressing concerns about starting a family. First, both the man and the woman come from families of short people. Being short has always been a problem for them; they feel that society discriminates against them because of their size. They would like something better for their children. They have heard that a new company, Perfecta, Inc., now offers a procedure that promotes height. They know that the procedure is still experimental and may have some unforeseen effects.

Basically, what this couple wants is advice. The man and woman want to have children, and they want their children to have every opportunity to succeed in this world (and it is their opinion that being tall could help).

Your task as a physician is to advise them about the benefits and risks of such a procedure. What should you tell them and why? What responsibilities do you have toward these people in your professional capacity? What are your ethical duties?

chapter seven

Health Care Policy

I. THE RIGHT TO HEALTH CARE.

Overview. Many people contend that the right to health care is an artifact of our modern technological age. Locke and Rousseau, the great philosophers on rights, do not mention health care as a right, nor do the framers of the Declaration of Independence and the Constitution of the United States. Does this mean that there is no right to adequate health care?

One of the earliest statements about a universal right to decent health care came in 1946 from the World Health Organization when it declared that "the enjoyment of the highest attainable standard of health is one of the fundamental rights of every human being."[1] The United Nation's Declaration of Human Rights (1948) also states that "everyone has a right to a standard of living adequate for the health and well-being of himself and his family, including . . . medical care."[2]

---

[1]World Health Organization, "Preamble to the Constitution" in *The First Ten Years of the World Health Organization* (Geneva: The Organization, 1958), p. 459.
[2]United Nations, "Universal Declaration of Human Rights, Article 25, 1948." *Bulletin of the Pan American Health Organization* 24:4 (1990), p. 625.

A number of nations have a government-run national health system that provides basic health care to all its citizens. Obviously, in these countries a rationing principle is used (since no government could afford to give everyone exactly what he or she wanted). This rationing principle requires patients to apply to a waiting list for expensive procedures. (This ties into the second section of this chapter, which deals with the organ allocation problem.) While waiting for the procedure, his illness might worsen, and he could die. But the procedure works the same way (in theory) for everyone. The rich in these countries (as in the United States) can use their wealth to obtain more comprehensive benefits.

In the first essay of this chapter, I introduce the current health care system in the United States and present some background on it. Then I sketch an ethically based argument that supports universal health coverage for all. Finally, I examine the ought-implies-can caveat.

In the second essay, Charles Fried takes a more libertarian and market-based approach. In his view, the answer to providing health care for more people is health care management. He believes that placing medical personnel of various levels of training in different stages of our medical system will enable us to more effectively utilize our personnel. He suggested that HMOs in the last decade have done just that with various levels of nurses and physician's assistants.

The Universal Right to Health Care

Michael Boylan

Most of us will need health care at some time in our lives. In one sense, it is an invisible commodity because it is not really apparent to us until we need it. With the advances in medical science in the last seventy-five years, modern medicine is increasingly able to do for us, but this has a staggering price tag. Not all Americans have actual access to health care. (*Actual access* means the ability to utilize appropriate health care providers to remedy health problems.) This lack of actual access generally occurs because people have no health insurance, which is not inexpensive. Therein is the genesis of the problem. If comprehensive health care is a right, then it is a right not at present actually accessible to all.

Because health care costs represent more than 15 percent of the GNP in our economy (thus constituting a cluster of businesses in themselves) and because virtually every business is confronted with providing health insurance to its employees, careful thinking on these issues is important. The purpose of this essay is to (a) outline the strengths and weaknesses of the current health care system, (b) sketch the ethical arguments concerning human rights to health care, and (c) argue that everyone has a right to health care consistent with the ought-implies-can doctrine.

STRENGTHS AND WEAKNESSES OF THE PRESENT SYSTEM

When my grandfather was in medical school around the turn of the twentieth century, classes still used Galen (a Greek physician from the ancient world) as their basis. I am a great admirer of Galen, but the medical world that he knew depicted the physician as a person who set broken bones, helped deliver babies, prescribed diet and exercise, and suggested herbs to balance the four humors of the body.

With the beginning of the twentieth century, Galenic medicine became a thing of the past. Medicine advanced rapidly on two fronts, pharmacology and surgery. The former was stirred by advances in specialized medical research and the latter by advances in technique (including ways to keep the patient alive both during and after an operation) and biomedical technology (including prosthetics, improved surgical equipment, and monitoring apparati). This "new medicine" enabled procedures to be performed that were considered impossible in my grandfather's medical school days.

With the new medicine came a higher price tag, most of which was associated with hospitalization. To enable people to be able to afford expensive hospitalization, medical insurance was promoted. Originally, health insurance was designed for catastrophes. (Insurance often works best when it protects its policyholders against an unlikely catastrophe, as homeowners' insurance protects against catastrophes of fire, theft, and so on.)

In the post–World War II period, health insurance gradually added coverage for costs related to pregnancy and childbirth, office visits, and prescription drugs. At the same time, medical advances were increasing rapidly. Hospitals bought new and expensive machines that had to be paid for by all patients who entered the door, whether they needed those services or not. Medical accountability also became an issue as society became more litigious. Increasingly, when medical outcomes "went badly," someone had to be at fault, and malpractice suits were brought to assess blame. This situation created a climate in which both physicians and hospitals had to establish careful guidelines (i.e., standards of professional practice) about what the "prudent" practitioner would do in specific situations. Anyone who varied from this practice was liable for malpractice. Hospitals had to add layers of administrative staff to comply with the demands of high accountability—resulting in an increasingly higher price tag for medical services.

Insurance companies, which had routinely paid bills presented to them in the 1950s and 1960s began to audit bills more carefully for mistakes and fraud, which also increased the costs of insurance.

The good news is that health care in the United States has enabled people to live longer lives. The bad news is that this aging population has greatly increased health care needs. Medicare was established to help meet these needs, but it pays only a fraction of the actual cost of procedures on the open market.[1] This means that younger patients (and their insurance companies) have been forced to subsidize the difference in costs incurred by older patients. This subsidy is an invisible tax.

During the late 1980s, an explosion of health insurance costs was caused by a rise in health care costs. More people, for example, were having knee and back operations instead of hobbling around as their parents had. Americans were using their health insurance as they never had because it enabled them to improve the quality of their lives. By the 1990s, health insurance had become too expensive for many Americans. Family coverage was often as costly as the rent or mortgage. Americans were not used to paying such a high percentage of their income on health insurance. Many had no choice; they could not afford the high premiums and went without coverage. This gamble worked so long as these Americans did not need to go to the hospital. But if they did, they were forced to go to overcrowded public hospitals that often lacked the latest medical equipment.

Medicaid is available for the very poor (although "welfare reform" has limited it). Eligibility varies according to each state, but like Medicare, Medicaid does not reimburse medical providers at the market rate. The difference is made up by "paying customers," people with insurance.

Health Insurance Coverage in the United States

The following is a brief introduction to different types of health insurance.

1. *Traditional indemnity insurance.* The policyholder pays an annual deductible and then is reimbursed for payments for covered claims under a coinsurance arrangement with the insurance company (usually 80 percent for the

---

[1]This situation is evidenced by the recent wave of insurance companies that have left the Medicare HMO marketplace. Companies cannot make money on Medicare patients unless they engage in the practice of skimming (meaning that they take only the healthiest patients) or they have a very large client base that includes enough health patients to compensate for those who need care the most. It has been said that in the last months of life, a typical patient may require a cost outlay equal to the medical costs during his or her entire life. Thus, private insurance companies shy away from Medicare patients unless forced to do so by legislation.

insurance and 20 percent for the policyholder). When the policyholder's expenses reach a certain limit, the company pays 100 percent up to the limits of the policy (usually $1 million to $5 million). Coverage is available primarily for accidents or illness (pregnancy is generally treated as any other illness). In many cases, preventative care is not covered. This type of health insurance is quickly becoming obsolete and is being replaced by the following plans.

2. *Health Maintenance Organizations* (HMOs). Started in the early 1970s, HMOs are set up as full service centers (such as Kaiser Permanente) or networks of physicians (such as individual practice associations, IPAs). In either case, the patient generally has no deductible except a small office payment (usually $5 to $20). Routine coverages are broader under an HMO than with traditional indemnity insurance. HMOs cover claims that indemnity plans generally cover and offer preventative care as well.

In return for expanded routine coverages, the patient gives up some control of health care choices. The primary care physician decides whether the patient needs to see a specialist. If that primary care physician decides that a specialist is not necessary, the HMO will not pay for the service. This "managed care" feature makes HMOs more economical than indemnity plans, but the consumer must balance this economy and broader coverage against less control over his health care decisions.

HMOs also place some restrictions on whom the insured sees for treatment. The insured *must* see a physician participating in that particular HMO. This is another distinction from the traditional indemnity plans that allow the insured to choose any person licensed to practice medicine.

Finally, HMOs generally restrict the services it will provide. Many exclude organ transplants, most have annual caps on the amount of prescription drugs they will cover. The patient must pay costs above this limit. In a survey I did of twenty HMOs in the Washington, D.C., area, the average prescription drug cap was $3,000 per year. A substantial number of physical afflictions require more than this amount.

To offer a real incentive for cost containment, many HMO primary care physicians are given a budget that varies according to the number of patients they treat. If they are under their budget, they receive all or some of the difference. Thus, the physician has a financial interest in holding down the cost of a patient's tests and procedures.

3. *Preferred Provider Organization (PPO).* The PPO is a variation of the traditional indemnity plan. The PPO provides a list of participating physicians (much like the IPAs and HMOs outlined earlier). However, no primary care physician is identified. Participating physicians agree to charge PPO patients predetermined prices. In return, they are listed in the directory and presumably attract more patients. The insurance company knows in advance what its costs will be, resulting in lower outlays. Thus, a PPO is more economical than the traditional indemnity plan but is not so economical as an HMO.

Like the traditional indemnity plan, the PPO does not cover preventative care, but it does offer more treatments than HMOs, and has a preexisting condition clause.

Virtually all choices for medical treatment lie in the patient's hands. Like the HMO, the PPO generally has no deductible except for a modest copayment for an office visit.

4. *Point-of-Service Plans.* Because patient empowerment/autonomy is popular with consumers, many HMO and PPO plans now have an "opt-out" feature. Policyholders who choose to do so can opt out of the plan and change to a traditional indemnity plan. This means that they pay a deductible and co-insurance in order to see any physician they choose (just like the traditional indemnity plans).

To encourage policyholders to use the HMO or PPO, insurance companies often add some restrictions concerning the opt-out option. This is important to the insurance companies so that they can avoid "adverse selection," which occurs when two or more plans exist and sicker members of the population have incentives to utilize one plan to the exclusion of the others.

Health Insurance Coverage in Other Countries

The following plans are the most popular health care in foreign countries.

1. *Government-Run Health Plans.* Many countries offer government-run health plans. Under these plans, physicians are actually employees of the government. They must serve a quota of patients and see people on their list when those people need health care.

Government-run health plans have a number of attractive features: (a) universal, comprehensive coverage, (b) essential elimination of the litigious malpractice climate, and (c) physicians' ability to concentrate on practicing medicine because they are not distracted with running a business.

Government-run health plans have some disadvantages. First, because physicians are government employees, their salaries are far lower than those of physicians in private practice. Some say that this is a disincentive for the best and brightest to enter medicine and practice in the government health service (if high compensation is assumed to be a critical incentive for people to enter medicine as a career). Most countries with a government health service allow physicians to see fee-paying clients. If the compensation incentive is correct, then a country with a government-run health plan will have less able physicians than countries that rely on private practice physicians.

Second, to lower their costs, many physicians have large practices, which can lead to long waits to see them. This clinic atmosphere may discourage some from going to the doctor, even when they need to.

Third, most countries with government-run health plans also have private practice physicians whose patients are the rich. This creates a two-tier health system. Average persons may rightly perceive that they receive a different level of care than the rich.

2. *Single Payer Plans.* The single payer model maintains private practice physicians who are paid by insurance. The government is the only insurance company. With one payer, there is only one set of regulations and guidelines. Subunits of the country (provinces or states) are given health care budgets (much like the budgets mentioned for the HMOs). Once a budget has been exhausted, extreme pressure is placed on the physician to limit further services (though additional services are never completely cut off). If money remains in the budget at the end of the year, the health care community may share it. Like a planned economy, the single payer system has the advantages of central control. Health policy can be uniform. Most theories of distributive justice promote treating similar cases in the same way. Also similar to a planned economy, the single payer system has the disadvantages of central control, particularly less efficiency. Many view the single payer system as having the advantages of government-run health care (such as comprehensive universal coverage) without the drawbacks.

Ethical Arguments on Human Rights and Health Care

Obviously, one important aspect of the health care debate is whether a citizen of a country has a right to health care. If this is so, then it is the government's correlative duty to provide this good to the individual.[2] Thus, if all citizens have a right to health care, then the government has the correlative duty to provide it.

Therefore, whether individuals have a right to health care is an important question. This brief exposition does not attempt to explore this issue fully but merely to identify some important issues and suggest ways the question might be answered. To this end I will outline two theories for the basis of human rights: deongologically based rights theory and community-based rights theory. In each case, I contend that one can derive a strong right to health care. In the final section of this essay, I discuss a limitation of this right (the ought-implies-can caveat).

---

[2]This idea of correlative rights is derived from Wesley N. Hohfeld, *Fundamental Legal Conceptions* (New Haven, CT: Yale University Press, 1919). In that work Hohfeld describes a "claims right." A claim is a right with a specific correlative duty of the form "x has a right to y against z in virtue of p." In this case, x and z are individuals; z has a duty to give x some good, y, because of p (some institution that validates the transaction). Thus, if x lends $10 to z, because of the institution of paying debts, x has a right to that $10 from z at some specified time. In this way, rights and duties are correlative. A right of one agent is identified as the duty of some other agent. A right is a duty seen from another standpoint.

Deontologically Based Rights Theory

Deontologically based rights theory has a number of versions. Many follow from a natural rights tradition.[3] What concerns us here is a form of the theory that states that all people possess some characteristic that justifies their claim to a good as a right. They claim this good solely on the basis of their status as human beings (or in some cases as adult human beings).

The persuasive writers in the natural rights tradition began with John Locke (if not earlier). For our purposes, let us borrow from a deontologist, Alan Gewirth, who uses contemporary action theory to create a dialectically necessary argument to support the claim that all people have the rights to freedom and well-being (see my discussion of Gewirth in *Basic Ethics*).[4] In short, this argument contends that each person must claim freedom and well-being for herself or himself in order to act. The person must logically recognize that he does not differ in this respect from other humans. Thus, in claiming this right for himself, he also claims it for all other humans as well.

The question then becomes whether health care is an essential good of well-being. Using a type of Kantian reasoning, this question could be rephrased as Can I will myself not to have adequate health care coverage without violating a universal law of nature?[5] The answer seems to be no. If a person were to

---

[3]The following are articles to note on this controversy: H.L.A. Hart, "Are There Any Natural Rights?" *Philosophical Review* 64 (1955): 176–77; W.W. Buckland, *A Text-Book of Roman Law from Augustus to Justinian* (Cambridge: Cambridge University Press, 1963), p. 58; *Elementary Principles of the Roman Private Law* (Cambridge: Cambridge University Press, 1912), pp. 9, 61–62; *A Manual of Roman Private Law* (Cambridge: Cambridge University Press, 1925), p. 155; Michel Villey, *Lecons d'histoire de la philosophie du droit* (Paris: Vrin, 1957), chaps. 11 and 14; S.I. Benn and R.S. Peters, *Social Principles and the Democratic State* (London: George Allen and Unwin, 1959); Michael Boylan, "Seneca and Moral Rights," *The New Scholasticism* 53, no. 3 (1979): 362–74; A.I. Melden, *Rights and Persons* (Berkeley, CA: University of California Press, 1977); Jacques Maritain, *Les droits de l'homme et la loi naturelle* (New York: Editions de la Maison Français, 1942); Roscoe Pound, *Jurisprudence* (St. Paul, MN: West Publishing, 1959); Beth Singer, "Community, Mutuality, and Rights" in *Gewirth: Critical Essays on Action, Rationality, and Community*, ed. Michael Boylan (New York: Rowman and Littlefield, 1999). See also Jeffrey Reiman's commentary on Singer's article in the same volume.

[4]It is not my desire to discuss this argument at length but to use it only as an example of a natural rights theory. For a thorough discussion of Gewirth's argument, see Deryck Beyleveld, *The Dialectical Nature of Necessity* (Chicago: University of Chicago Press, 1991); a shortened version of this justification occurs in the article by Beyleveld and Shaun Pattinson (p. 39).

[5]This is intended to be an application of the so-called imperfect duties; see Immanuel Kant, *Groundwork of the Metaphysics of Morals*, tr. H.J. Paton (New York: Harper Torchbooks, 1964), p. 421: "Act as if the maxim of your action were to become through your will a universal law of nature." See also Kant's examples 3 and 4 (p. 423). For a discussion of this puzzling distinction of perfect and imperfect duties, see Paton, p. 31; R. Chisholm, "Supererogation and Offence" *Ratio* 5 (1963): 4; and Alan Donagan, *The Theory of Morality* (Chicago, University of Chicago Press, 1977), pp. 154–55. The duty is "imperfect" because there are multiple ways one might fulfill it. For an argument on this interpretation, see Marcia Baron, "The Alleged Moral Responsibility of Acting from Duty," *Journal of Philosophy* 81 (1984): 197–220; for a different view of the contrast between perfect and imperfect duties, see David Cummiskey, *Kantian Consequentialism* (Oxford: Oxford University Press, 1996), chapt. 6.

deny herself such a good, she would be willing her misfortune and/or destruction, and to do that is to violate a universal law of nature.

In this compressed analysis, I *must* claim the right to adequate (i.e., comprehensive) health care coverage. Because I must claim the good (as an essential element of my well-being), I must acknowledge that everyone can claim it. Because everyone can legitimately claim comprehensive health care for themselves (since it is essential for their well-being in a way that is proximate to action), such claims become claims rights. Every morally justified claim for a good of well-being is dialectically necessary for action. A person cannot deny the possession of such a good for himself or for others.

Thus, everyone has a morally based claims right to adequate (comprehensive) health care coverage. This right is against all other citizens in the society and is constrained only by the ought-implies-can doctrine. Health care is included with other basic goods of well-being such as food, clothing, and shelter. It supersedes various additive goods such as buying a new car and nonsubstractive goods such as one's bank account balance.

Under the Gewirthian/Kantian interpretation, all people have a moral claims right to the most extensive health care that any society can provide (given the limitations of the ought-implies-can doctrine).

Community-Based Rights Theory

Community-based rights theory may have its origin in Hegel and has recently been advanced by Michael Sandel.[6] Beth Singer has presented another contemporary version of the argument.[7] I focus my comments on her version of Communitarianism. Under her theory, we can characterize rights as operative or not operative. This means that a human community recognizes the rights or does not recognize them. According to this view, the rights relation is a social institution governed by the attitudes of a normative community. It is, in one sense, an empty question to ask what rights one has that are not exhibited because "having" and "taking" are different modes. Rights that are not already possessed (by being recognized in the human community) must be "taken" to be operative. This is a political, sociological, and historical truism. The discussion of rights—not operative—must turn on *how* and *by what means* they will, in the future, be "taken." Once taken, these claims are in the repertoire of rights recognized by the community.

---

[6]See G.W.F. Hegel, *The Philosophy of Right*, tr. T.M. Knox (Oxford: Clarendon Press, 1942); see also Michael Oakeshott, *Rationalism in Politics* (London: Methuen, 1962). The sociological angle is developed by George Herbert Mead in *Mind, Self, and Society* (Chicago: University of Chicago Press, 1934). The contemporary communitarian slant has been championed by Michael J. Sandel in *Democracy's Discontent: America in Search of a Public Policy* (Cambridge, MA: Belnap Press, 1996), and *Liberalism and the Limits of Justice*, 2d ed. (Cambridge: Cambridge University Press, 1998).

[7]Beth Singer, *Operative Rights* (Albany: SUNY Press, 1993).

Clearly citizens in the United States do not now have universal, comprehensive health care. Thus, they have no right to universal, comprehensive health care until such time as the reciprocal attitudes of the individual and the community change on this subject.

The process of making health care an operative right in this society can become a question of justice as well as of rights.[8] Justification in terms of distributive justice could take several approaches. Not all of these choose a rights viewpoint to frame the solution. Since right has an individual perspective associated with it, some might argue in terms of group-oriented criteria such as "maximizing freedom" or "maximizing the general utility," and so on. Since this essay intends to prove its argument in terms of rights, the justice argument justified in other terms will not be developed.[9]

Justice for the Singer-style communitarian must show that establishing a universal right to health care is in the community's interest. This could be done in a homogeneous community via Ethical Intuitionism. That is, everyone simply *immediately grasps* the justification for the right to health care. More popular for communitarians is an appeal to Virtue Ethics. This argument might appeal to the virtue of benevolence (for example) and the shared commitment to the consequences that benevolence would entail for community health care.

Utilitarianism could also be cited in support of a communitarian argument if it could be shown that the public utility would be demonstrably improved by initiating a program of universal health coverage in the United States. Surely the United States would be a stronger country if all citizens knew that they had basic health coverage, no matter their employers did or did not offer. (A similar approach was tried by President and Mrs. Clinton in the early 1990s without legislative success.)

I believe that the most effective argument from the communitarian standpoint is the Virtue Ethics approach as one tries to knit together various

---

[8]See James Drane's discussion of health care in terms of justice in "Justice Issues in Health Care Delivery," *Bulletin of the Pan American Health Organization* 24, no. 4 (1990): 566–78. Others who have made a similar approach include James Sterba, "Justice," in *Encyclopedia of Bioethics,* ed. Warren T. Reich (New York: Simon and Schuster Macmillan, 1995), pp. 1308–15; Norman Daniels, *Just Health Care* (Cambridge: Cambridge University Press, 1985); and Alan Gibbard, "The Prospective Pareto Principle and Equity of Access to Health Care," *Milbank Memorial Fund Quarterly/Health Care Society* 59, no. 4 (1982): 399–428.

[9]I should note that not everyone who views the problem in terms of rights agrees with a firm right to health care. See, for example, Tom L. Beauchamp and Ruth Faden, "The Right to Health and the Right to Health Care," *Journal of Medicine and Philosophy* 4, no. 2 (1979): 118–131, conclude that "the major issues about right to health and health care turn on the justifiability of social expenditures rather than on some notion of natural, inalienable, or preexisting rights." Others argue for interpretations that are consistent with the one I advocate; see Charles Dougherty, "The Right to Health Care: First Aid in the Emergency Room," *Public Law Forum* 4, no. 1 (1984): 101–28 and Rashi Fein, "Entitlement to Health Services Reappraised" *Bulletin of the New York Academy of Medicine* 66, no. 4 (July–August, 1990): 319–28.

constituencies and their understandings of what benevolence as a virtue would mean to them and the larger whole (the United States as a country). People would admit that communities *should* support at some basic level those who are not covered by the present system. Regardless of the moral theory employed, I believe that a case can be made to create an operative communitarian right to health care (although the communitarian argument must, of necessity, be subject to the descriptive forces that govern the enactment of any law or entitlement).

The Right to Health Care

Depending on the theory you have chosen to depict human rights, you have two different answers to whether a right to health care exists. I choose a deontological justification of a right to health care according to my adaptation of Kant and Gewirth. I believe I have sketched out the basis of a right to comprehensive universal health care in a dialectically necessary way in my deontological approach.

The community rights viewpoint suggests that there is not a *right* to health care (yet) but that there still may be good reasons for citizens to band together to convince the society that such a right should be recognized (probably using a Virtue Ethics model as a foundation).

Although I believe a dialectically necessary moral claims right can be established for universal health care via a deontological argument following Gewirth and Kant (and good reasons for establishing an operative right via a communitarian argument), one issue still must be addressed. This is the Kantian doctrine that ought implies can.[10] Under this doctrine, no one can be said to have a binding moral duty to perform something that it is practically impossible for him to do. This maxim is important to Kant for without it, his theory is doomed to inconsistency.[11] Thus, the question may be whether the United States can institute comprehensive universal health care. If it can, then it should.

What lies behind this *can?* Does it mean logically possible, practically possible, comfortable to implement, may be implemented without raising taxes or cutting other programs, or politically easy to bring about? Obviously, these interpretations of *can* are different. There lies a large part of the practical implementation of any health care reform.

---

[10]This doctrine has its own controversies. For a discussion, see Christine Korsgaard, "Kant's Formula of the Universal Law," *Pacific Philosophical Quarterly* 66 (1985): 24–47.

[11]The inconsistency is this: a person may have a duty to do x, but it is impossible to do x. Thus the individual has a moral dilemma. No matter what the person does, she is immoral. If she tries to do her duty and fails (which must happen if doing this duty is impossible), she is immoral. If she ignores her duty, she is immoral.

For a discussion of the consequences of moral inconsistency for Kant (or similar systems) see Alan Donagan, *The Theory of Morality* (Chicago: University of Chicago Press, 1977), chapter five.

ASSESSING THE OUGHT-IMPLIES-CAN RESTRICTION ON COMPREHENSIVE UNIVERSAL HEALTH COVERAGE

Important practical impediments must be overcome before a comprehensive universal health care system can be established in the United States. It is not difficult to identify some of them. First, vested interests will be disturbed, including hospitals, doctors, pharmaceutical companies, insurance companies, and the myriad of medical support facilities. It is a political fact that entrenched interests are difficult to overcome in a democracy. This is one aspect of the *can* described in the last section.

A second element of the *can* equates to *economically afford.* This, in turn, requires a specification of *afford.* Clearly, this word implies a value system that ranks alternatives. If comprehensive universal health care is put at the top of the list of alternatives, the United States can certainly afford it. Much of the current dissatisfaction with health care revolves around its *cost.* Although Americans seem reluctant to put it very high on the list of priorities, many of them want the best available care, but at the same time do not want to pay for it. Unless there is a will to rank health care high, comprehensive universal health care coverage will never occur because it is very costly. Its cost is difficult to determine, but in a peacetime economy it is likely to be the largest single item in the federal budget (after payment on the national debt).

Few people really believe that comprehensive coverage can be obtained without either raising taxes significantly or cutting existing programs. This latter alternative is appealing, but each of us has a different idea of programs to cut. We think that those programs that do not benefit us personally should be the ones to be cut.

The establishment of political will is a job for politicians (and is reminiscent of the focus of the communitarian argument). Unless the American people accept that comprehensive universal health coverage is important, legislation providing it will never pass, no matter how "right" it is.

The third sense of *can* involves the type of health care we want. Do we desire everyone to have access to the best available care, or will we settle for a rationing formula? If so, what sort of formula should we choose? If the formula is too restrictive, it may not be an improvement over what we presently have. Again, the *can* requires people to make a conscious decision about whether they believe that the best available care is an integral part of their well-being (or at least a more integral part of their well-being than a second car, a boat, or a summer home).

The last sense of *can* involves who will pay for it. At the end of the twentieth century, the most popular candidate is business. When health care was inexpensive, it became a standard fringe benefit offered by most employers. As health insurance has become more and more costly, employees have paid an increasingly larger share of their premiums. People often have a false sense that if payment for some good does not come directly out of their pockets, then they are not paying for it. Thus, government and big business are thought to be able to provide fringe benefits free of cost to the average person. This, of course, is untrue. The government depends on taxes for its revenue and business passes on its expenses to consumers. We all pay.

Some have suggested that we take the mechanism of health insurance out of the workplace and make it like car insurance, which is privately purchased but mandatory in most states. Owners of small businesses have been most vocal for this option, citing the thin margins on which they work and the limited reserve capital they have at any given time. Indeed, these businesspeople have been the greatest critics of comprehensive universal coverage because they believe it will put them out of business.

It is difficult to assess their claim. If it is true, then some accommodation must be made for small business. Consider sole proprietors, who have no employees and make up a large percentage of the present uninsured population. How can these people be monitored so that they are compelled to purchase health insurance? These hardworking individuals—be they painters, carpenters, consultants, or accountants—have often made the choice not to purchase health insurance. What makes us think that they will purchase health insurance under a different scenario? They will say they have no money left after rent, food, and clothing to purchase insurance. Tax write-offs are not significant to people with little money coming in and no appreciable savings. This argument is another dimension of the ought-implies-can dilemma.

A considerable number of difficulties are associated with establishing comprehensive universal health care coverage in the United States. The task will not be easy but large changes never are. It seems to me that the moral ought supports the change. There are many candidates for this "ought" being overridden by practical problems (the *can*). I do not believe these practical difficulties are definitive.

Therefore, I believe that the moral ought derived from the universal dialectically necessary right for health care creates a duty. Either through business, government, or a combination of these, I believe that the United States ought to go forward with comprehensive universal coverage in some form.

Equality and Rights in Medical Care

Charles Fried

In this article I present arguments intended to support the following conclusions:

1. *To say there is a right to health care does not imply a right to equal access, a right that whatever is available to any shall be available to all.*
2. *The slogan of equal access to the best health care available is just that, a dangerous slogan which could be translated into reality only if we submitted either to intolerable government controls of medical practice or to a thoroughly unreasonable burden of expense.*
3. *There is sense to the notion of a right to a decent standard of care for all, dynamically defined, but still not dogmatically equated with the best available.*
4. *We are far from affording such a standard to many of our citizens and that is profoundly wrong.*
5. *One of the major sources of the exaggerated demands for equality are the pretensions, inflated claims, inefficiencies, and guild-like, monopolistic practices of the health professions.*

I. BACKGROUND

The notion of some kind of a right to health care is not likely to be found in any but the most recent writings, not to mention legislation. After all, even the much more well-established institution of free, universal public education has not achieved the status of a federal constitutional right, is not a constitutional right by the law of many states, and stands as a right more as an inference from the practices and legislation of states, counties, and municipalities. The federal constitutional litigation regarding rights in that area has been restricted to the provision *equally* of whatever public education is in fact provided. So it should not be surprising that the notion of a right to health care is something of a novelty. Moreover, it is only fairly recently that health care could deliver a product which was as unambiguously beneficial as elementary schooling. Nevertheless, if one looks to the laws, practices, and understandings of states, counties, and municipalities, one sees growing up through the last century, and certainly in the twentieth century, an understanding which might be thought of as the inchoate recognition of a right to health care. Indeed, there are those who might say that such an inchoate recognition might be discerned as far back as Elizabethan England.

As one considers this progress, one should not misrepresent history, for in that history lies an important lesson. For the progress may represent not simply a progress in our ideas of social justice, but a progress in what medicine could do. The fact is that the increasingly general provision of medical care may be correlated as well with what medical care could accomplish as with any changing social doctrines. What could medicine accomplish a hundred or even fifty years ago? It is well known that the improvements in health that were wrought in those days were largely the result of improved sanitation, working conditions, diet, and the like. Beyond that, specifically medical ministrations could do very little. They could provide ease, amenities, relief, but rarely a cure. So society may be forgiven if it did not provide elaborate medical care to the poor until recently, since provision of medical care in essence would have meant simply the provision of amenities and placebos. And since society appeared little concerned to assure the amenities to its poor generally, it is no great surprise that it had scant inclination to provide these amenities to the sick poor.

The detailed history of the extension of medical care to the poor, and indeed to those who were not poor but lived in out-of-the-way places, has yet to be written. The emergence of a notion of a right to health care and the embodiment of such a notion in legislation and court decisions must also await difficult historical research. Nevertheless, it is worth noting that, at least in American public discourse, the idea of a right to medical care developed into something which had the appearance of inevitability only recently, in what might be called the intermediate, perhaps golden, age of modern medicine. This was a period when advances in treating acute illness, advances such as the antibiotics, could really make a large difference in prolonging life or restoring health; but the most elaborate technologies which may make only marginal improvements in situations previously thought to be hopeless had not yet been generally developed. In this recent "Golden Age" we could unambiguously afford a notion of a general right to medical care because there were a number of clear successes available to medicine, and these successes were not unduly costly. Having conquered the infectious diseases, medical science has undertaken the degenerative diseases, the malignant neoplasms, and the diseases of unknown etiology; and one must say that the ratio between expense and benefit has become exponentially more unfavorable. So it is really only now that the notion of a right to health care poses acute analytical and social problems. It is for that reason that neither history nor legal analysis will much illuminate our future course. What we do now will be a matter of our choosing, and for this reason careful analysis of the notion of a right to health care is crucial.

II. Equality and Rights: Analytical Distinctions

First, something should be said by way of at least informal definition of this term "right." A right is more than just an interest that an individual might have, a state of affairs or a state of being which an individual might prefer. A claim of right invokes entitlements; and when we speak of entitlements, we mean not those things which it would be nice for people to have, or which they would prefer to have, but which they must have, and which if they do not have they may demand, whether we like it or not. Although I would not want to say that a right is something we must recognize "no matter what," nevertheless a right is something we must accord unless ____ and what we put in to fill in the unless clause should be tightly confined and specific.

This notion of rights has interesting and not altogether obvious relations to the concept of equality, and confusions about those relations are very likely to lead to confused arguments about the very area before us—rights to health care and equality in respect to health care.

First, it should be noted that equality itself may be considered a right. Thus, a person can argue that he is not necessarily entitled to any particular thing—whether it be income, or housing, or education, or health care—but that he is entitled to equality in respect to that thing, so that whatever anyone gets he should get, too. And this is a nice example of my previous proposition about the notion of rights generally. For to recognize a right to equality may very well be—I suppose it often is—contrary to many other policies that we may have, and particularly contrary to attempts to attain some kind of efficiency. Yet, by the very notion of rights, if there is a right to equality, then granting equality cannot depend on whether or not it is efficient to do so.

Second, there is the relation between rights and equality which runs the other way, too: to say that a class of persons, or all persons, have a certain right implies that they all have that right equally. If it is said that all persons within the jurisdiction of the United States have a constitutionally protected right to freedom of speech, whatever that may mean, one thing seems clear: that this right should not depend on what it is one wants to say, who one is, and the like. Indeed, if the government against whom this right is protected were to make such distinctions, for instance, subjecting to constraints the speech of "irresponsible persons," that would be the exact concept of denial of freedom of speech to those persons.

These relations between the notion of right and of equality suggest the great importance of being very clear and precise about how a particular right is conceived: confusions in this regard are rampant in respect to health, and are the source of much pointless controversy. But because the point is quite general, let me first take an example from another area. If we were sloppy in our thinking about what the right of freedom of speech is—and many people are as sloppy about that as they are about their definition of the rights in the area which is our immediate concern—if we were sloppy about that definition, we might, for instance, consider that there has been a denial of right because some people have access to radio or television in getting their ideas across, while others have only the street-corner soapbox to broadcast their views. Indeed, there are those who might find it unjust that even on the soapbox the timid or inarticulate are much less effective than the bold or eloquent. All of these disparities, of course, may or may not be regrettable but they have nothing to do with freedom of speech as a right, given the premise that there is a right to free speech and that this right must be an equal right. It seems clear to me that it is very different from the right to be heard, believed, admired, and applauded. The right to speak freely is just that: a right to be free of constraints and impositions on whatever speaking one might wish to do, should you be able to find someone to listen.

Now this analogy is offered as more than a distant irrelevance. Is it not very similar to many things that are said in the area of health? For analogous to the claim that the right to freedom of speech really implies a right to be heard by the multitude, is the notion that whatever rights might exist in respect to health care are rights to health, rather than to health *care*. And of course the claim is equally absurd in both instances. We may sensibly guarantee that all will be equally free of constraints on the speaking they wish to do, but we should not guarantee that all will be equally effective in getting their views across. Similarly, we may or may not choose to guarantee all equality of access to health care, but we cannot possibly guarantee to all equality of health.

Consider how these clarifications operate upon the historical development I alluded to at the beginning of this analysis. The right whose recognition might be said to have been implicit in social practices throughout the past hundred years was a right not to health care as such, nor yet a right to health, but rather a right to a certain standard of health care, which was defined in terms of what medicine could reasonably do for people. It is this notion which has become so difficult in our present situation, where the apparatus of medicine has become so much more elaborate, pretentious, and costly than it was in earlier times.

Bringing together the historical and the analytical sides, we might conclude that our present dilemma comes from the fact that there are very many expensive things that medicine can do which might possibly help. And if we commit ourselves to the notion that there is a right to whatever health care might be available, we do indeed get ourselves into a difficult situation where overall national expenditure on health must reach absurd proportions—absurd in the sense that far more is devoted to health at the expense of other important social goals than the population in general wants. Indeed, more is devoted to health than the population wants relative not only to important social goals—for example, education or housing—but relative to all the other things which people would like to have money left over to pay for. And if we recognize that it would be absurd to commit our society to devote more than a certain proportion of our national income to health, while at the same time recognizing a "right to health care," we might then be caught on the other horn of the dilemma. For we might then be required to say that because a right to health care implies a right to equality of health care, then we must limit, we must lower the quality of the health care that might be purchased by some lest our commitment to equality require us to provide such care to all and thus carry us over a reasonable budget limit.

Consider the case of the artificial heart. It seems to me not too fanciful an assumption that such a device is technically feasible within a reasonable time, and likely to be hugely expensive both in terms of its actual implantation and in terms of the subsequent care required by those benefiting from the device. Now if the right to health care is taken to mean the right to whatever health care is available to anybody, and if this entails that it is a right to an equal enjoyment of whatever care anyone else enjoys, then what are we to do with respect to the artificial heart? Might we decide not to develop such a device? Though the development and experimental use of it involves an entirely tolerable burden, the general provision of the artificial heart would be an intolerable burden, and since if we provide it to any we must provide it to all, therefore perhaps we should provide it to none.

This solution seems to me to be both uncomfortable and unstable. For surely there is something odd, if not perverse, about foregoing research on such devices, not because the research might fail, but because it might succeed. Might not this research then go on under some kinds of private auspices if such a governmental decision were made? Would we then go further and forbid even private research, rather than simply refusing to fund it? I can well imagine the next step, where artificial heart research and implantation would become like abortion or sex change operations in the old days: something one went to Sweden or Denmark for. Nor is a lottery device for distributing a limited number of artificial hearts likely to be more stable or satisfactory. For there, too, would we forbid people to go outside the lottery? Would it be a crime to cross national boundaries with the intent of obtaining an artificial heart? The example makes a general point about instituting an all-inclusive "right to health care," with the necessary concomitant of an equal right to whatever health care is available. For if we really instituted such a right and limited the provision of health care to a reasonable level, we would have to institute as well a degree of stringent state control, which it is both unlikely we can achieve and undesirable for us even to try to achieve. There is something that goes very deeply against the grain about any scheme which prohibits scientists from making discoveries which no one claims are harmful as such, but which will cause trouble because we can't give them to everybody. There is something which goes against the grain in a system which might forbid individual doctors to render a service, not because it is harmful, but because its benefits are not available to all.

Or take a much less dramatic case—dental care. It is said that ordinary basic prophylactic care is so lacking for tens of millions of our citizens that quite unnecessarily they do not have their own teeth while still in their prime. I take it that to provide the kind of elaborate dental care deployed on affluent suburban families to rural populations, and to all even poorer urban dwellers, would be a prodigiously expensive undertaking, one that would cost each of us quite heavily. But if we followed the slogan, "The best available made available to all," that is what is meant. My guess is the American people would not want to bear this burden and that as a form of transfer payment the poor would prefer just to have the money to spend on other things. But this shows the dangerousness of slogans, for perhaps the greatest part of the dental damage could be remedied at far less cost by fluoridation and by relatively routine care provided by a type of modestly trained person who is only now beginning to exist. Care of this sort can be afforded and should be provided. But this would mean abandoning the concept of equality and accepting the fact that the poor would be getting less elaborate care than those who are not poor.

Now it might be said that I am exaggerating. The case put forward is the British National Health Service, which is alleged to provide a model of high level care at reasonable costs with equality for all. But I would caution planners and enthusiasts from drawing too much from this example. The situation in Great Britain is very different in many ways. The country is smaller and more homogeneous. Moreover, even in Great Britain there are disparities between the care available between urban and rural areas; there are long waits for so-called "elective procedures"; and there is a small but significant and distinguished private sector outside of National Health which is the focus of great controversy and rancor. Finally, Great Britain is a country where a substantial portion of the citizenry is committed to the socialist ideal of equalizing incomes and nationalizing the provisions of all vital services. Surely this is a very different situation from that in the United States. Indeed, it may be that the cry for equality of access to health care bears to a general yearning for social equality much the same relation that the opposition to fetal research bears to the opposition to abortion. In each case it is a very large ideological tail wagging a relatively small and confused dog.

My point is analytical. My point is that apart from a rather general commitment to equality and, indeed, to state control of the allocation and distribution of resources, to insist on the right to health care, where that right means a right to equal access, is an anomaly. For as long as our society considers that inequalities of wealth and income are morally acceptable—acceptable in the sense that the system that produces these inequalities is in itself not morally suspect—it is anomalous to carve out a sector like health care and say that *there* equality must reign.

III. TOWARDS A BETTER DEFINITION OF THE RIGHTS INVOLVED

After all, is health care so special? Is it different from education, housing, food, legal assistance? In respect to all of these things, we recognize in our society a right, whose enjoyment may not be made wholly dependent upon the ability to pay. But just as surely in respect to all these things, we do not believe that this right entails equality of enjoyment, so that whatever diet one person or class of persons enjoys must be enjoyed by all. The argument, put forward for instance by some members of the Labor Party in Great Britain, that the independent schools in that country should be abolished because they offer a level of education better than that available in state schools, is an argument which would be found strange and repellent in the United States. Rather, in all of these areas—education, housing, food, legal assistance—there obtains a notion of a decent, fair standard, such that when this standard is satisfied all that exists in the way of *rights* has been accorded. And it is necessarily so; were we to insist on equality all the way up, that is, past this minimum, we would have committed ourselves to a political philosophy which I take it is not the dominant one in our society.

Is health care different? Everything that can be said about health care is true of food and is at least by analogy true of education, housing, and legal assistance. The real task before us is not, therefore, I think, to explain why there must be complete equality in medicine, but the more subtle and perilous task of determining the decent minimum in respect to health which accords with sound ethical judgments, while maintaining the virtues of freedom, variety, and flexibility which are thought to flow from a mixed system such as ours. The decent minimum should reflect some conception of what constitutes tolerable life prospects in general. It should speak quite strongly to things like maternal health and child health, which set the terms under which individuals will compete and develop. On the other hand, techniques which will offer some remote relief from conditions that rarely strike in the prime of life, and which strike late in life because something must, might be thought of as too esoteric to be part of the concept of minimum decent care.

On the other hand, the notion of a decent minimum should include humane and, I would say, worthy surroundings of care for those whom we know we are not going to be able to treat. Here, it seems to me, the emphasis on technology and the attention of highly trained specialists is seriously mistaken. Not only is it unrealistic to imagine that such fancy services can be provided for everyone "as a right," but there is serious doubt whether these kinds of services are what most people really want or can benefit from.

In the end, I will concede very readily that the notion of minimum health care, which it does make sense for our society to recognize as a right, is itself an unstable and changing notion. As my initial historical remarks must have suggested, the concept of a decent minimum is always relative to what is available over all, and what the best which is available might be. I suppose (to revert to my parable of the artificial heart) that if we allowed an artificial heart to be developed under private auspices and to be available only to those who could pay for it, or who could obtain it from specialized eleemosynary institutions, then the time might well come when it would have been so perfected that it would be a reasonable component of what one would consider minimum decent care. And the process of arriving at this new situation would be a process imbued with struggle and political controversy. But since I do not believe in utopias or final solutions, a resolution of the problem of the right to health care having these kinds of tensions within it neither worries me nor leads me to suspect that I am on the wrong track. To my mind, the right track consists in identifying what it is that health care can and cannot provide, in identifying also the cost of health care, and then in deciding how much of this health care, what level of health care, we are ready to underwrite as a floor for our citizenry.

IV. PRACTICAL PROPOSALS

Although the process of defining the decent minimum is inherently a political process, there is a great deal which analysis and research can do to make the process rational and satisfactory. Much of this is a negative service, clearing away misconceptions and fallacies. For instance, as I have already argued, to state that our objective is to provide the best medical care for all, regardless of the ability to pay, must be shown up for the misleading slogan that it is. But there are more subtle misconceptions as well. The most pervasive of these deal with the situation of the medical profession.

Many observers look at the medical profession, its history of resistance to social change, and the fact that doctors as a profession enjoy the highest incomes of any group in the nation—somewhere around $50,000 a year on the average—and they draw their own conclusions. They draw the conclusion that therefore what is needed is necessarily more regulation. They look at the oversupply of surgeons in this country. They note the obvious fact of over-recourse to surgery which seems to result, and they conclude that what is needed is more government regulation. For instance, the problems of supply would be met by a kind of doctors' draft, requiring service in underserved rural areas. Now I would, for a moment, suggest that we consider some alternative explanations and alternative reforms. Perhaps, after all, the irrationalities in the supply of medical personnel, together with the high incomes earned, are the result not of market forces run wild, but the result of a guild system as tight and self-protective as any we know. It is, perhaps, an irony that the medical profession, having persuaded the public of the necessity of strictly limiting entry into the profession, having persuaded the public of the indispensability of highly trained specialists, is now faced with the threat of a kind of doctors' draft to make these rare specialists available to all. Perhaps clearer thinking might indicate that many of the things which highly paid and highly trained doctors do might be done by an army of less pretentious persons.

It is well known, of course, that doctors' fees as such represent the smaller portion of the total health care budget, so it might be thought that I am taking aim at an obvious, vulnerable, and somewhat irrelevant target. Yet this is not so. Though the fees of doctors represent the smaller portion of the medical budget, doctors themselves control almost all of the decisions—from the decision about hospitalization, to the decision whether to prescribe drugs by brand or generic name—which do influence the total cost of medical care. And it is in this respect that doctors have resisted most attempts to make their behavior rational and cost-effective. In general, it is said that this is because no doctor would sacrifice the individual interests of his patient, and this may be a sincere claim. But a certain skepticism is in order. What choice do the patients have to choose more economical systems of delivery? What doctor, for that matter, even gives his patient the choice between a brand and a generic prescription drug?

But it is in the choice of delivery systems themselves that the consumer is most restricted. Most consumers do not have the choice between a variety of delivery systems from prepaid group plans to the present individual fee-for-service system, with each plan costing what it really costs. If the consumer did have this choice, we might soon find out whether the alleged advantages of the fee-for-service system were something the consumer was willing to pay for. But of course we will never find this out if we are committed to underwrite, out of general revenues, the cost of this most expensive possible delivery system. "The best available to all." That is what we tend to do today for those groups whose medical care we do underwrite. The result is that we are trying to drive down the cost of this most expensive delivery system not by changing its organization but by bureaucratic control. What if, instead, each person were assured a certain amount of money to purchase medical services as he chose? If the restrictive practices of the profession itself could be avoided, would this not help a vast variety of delivery systems to grow up, all competing for the consumer's federally assured dollar? And then those who would want what might be considered as fancier or more individualized services could get them, provided only that they were willing to pay more for them.

Finally, there is a feature of our modern situation which is responsible for the present crisis in health care, and for the impossible dilemma posed by the promise of a right to health care. This is a feature of the society and the culture as a whole. I refer to our culture's inability to face and cope with the persistent facts of illness, old age, and death. Because we are little able to come to terms with the hazards which illness proposes, because the old are a burden and an embarrassment, because we pretend that death does not exist, we employ elaborate ruses to put these things out of the ambit of our ordinary lives. The reason why we hospitalize so much more than is rationally required surely goes beyond the vagaries of the health insurance system. Is it not also the result of the fact that the ill are an embarrassment to us, and that we seek to put them away, so we do not have to care for them, while assuaging our consciences that those "best qualified" to care for them are doing so? And in order that the ruse will work, we greatly overstate what it is that these "qualified" people can do for the ill. Needless to say, they are our willing accomplices in this piece of deception. So it is with the mentally retarded, the aged, and the dying. All of these persons are defined as having an abnormal condition not only justifying but requiring their isolation from us and their care in the hands of "specialists." Perhaps it is time that we recognize that this is part of the neurosis of our age. And of course, those whom we hire to perform our proper human role toward the sick, the old, and the dying can get away with charging a very high price for relieving us of our ordinary human obligations. But is this medical care?

Finally, to avoid misunderstanding, a general theoretic point must be made. My argument must sound harsh and callous—unfeelingly, if not unerringly economic. I have elsewhere argued that it is of the essence of the physician's role and of the patient's expectations that the doctor faced with the patient's need will do everything in his power to alleviate that need.[1] I believe that. I believe that for the individual physician to do less than his best because of some economic calculation of equity or efficiency is a breach of trust. The doctor in his dealings with his patient must not act like a bureaucrat, policy maker, or legislator. But policy makers, voters, and legislators must think in different terms. It is monstrous if an individual doctor thinks like a budget officer when he cares for his patient in need; but it is chaotic and incoherent if budget officers and voters making general policy think like doctors at the bedside.

Note

1. In my book, *Medical Experimentations: Personal Integrity and Social Policy* (Amsterdam and New York: Associated Scientific Publishers/Elsevier, 1974).

II. THE ORGAN ALLOCATION PROBLEM.

Overview. Before 1984, when regulations were established governing the allocation of human organs for transplantation, organs were given to the surgeon who could pass them on to his patients who needed them. To create a more equitable system, the U.S. Congress passed the National Organ Transplant Act of 1984 that created the United Network for Organ Sharing (UNOS). Since 1986, UNOS and its sixty-six regional organ procurement organizations have carried out the intentions of the 1984 act.

The list of organs that can be transplanted is always increasing, but transplanted kidneys head the list followed by hearts, pancreases, livers, hearts-lungs, lungs, and intestines. Not every regional transplant center transplants every organ; most handle kidneys but limit other organs to their specialty. Obviously, the scarcity of donor organs along with their perishable life means that the life-and-death decisions concerning their allocation must be well conceived.

Various people have suggested different standards to apply. The two essays in this section refer to most of these approaches. Rosamond Rhodes's article presents the standard position of seeing organ allocation as an instance of distributive justice. The principle of allocation is based on the greatest need for the longest time. Rhodes also discusses whether free riders (those who have not elected to be organ donors themselves) are entitled to a transplant. She also discusses the "right" to new organs.

Brian Smart takes a different approach. He suggests that a principle of rectificatory justice be adopted. Under this system, a person who has not taken care of her body would be penalized in placement on the waiting list. In this case, Smart takes pains to argue that his system is not against people who have mistreated their bodies but is for those who have led healthy lifestyles.

A Review of Ethical Issues in Transplantation

Rosamond Rhodes

Traditional medical practice cleaves to the principles of doing no harm, acting for the good of patients, and caring for all who come in need. The ethical practice of organ transplantation sometimes requires the thoughtful surgeon to violate each of these central moral tenets. From this alone it is clear that the moral conflicts raised by organ transplantation are complex, compelling, and deserving of especially careful consideration. Unavoidable characteristics of the transplant surgeon's practice require difficult moral judgments which are peculiar to this field. The two major areas of moral quandary are organ procurement and organ allocation. This paper outlines the key ethical issues in transplantation and draws attention to some of the recent literature that argues these issues in greater detail (1–5).

ORGAN PROCUREMENT

Obviously, an organ for transplantation must be harvested from either a recently dead cadaver or a living donor. Taking organs from a cadaver violates certain traditional religious and social attitudes which require us to show respect for the dead by not mutilating the corpse. Taking an organ from a living donor violates the medical dictum "do no harm." Removing a vital organ from a healthy person puts the donor at risk of serious harm from anesthesia, intraoperative complications, and postsurgical complications. The procedure itself is also certain to harm the donor with disfigurement.

The preservation or the significant enhancement of life can justify overriding the moral imperatives that would otherwise prohibit dismembering corpses and harming healthy individuals. However, even though we may decide that organ transplantation can be a morally acceptable practice, we still have to answer many weighty ethical questions about organ harvesting. How should death be defined? What other criteria must be met before organs can be taken from a corpse? Must the consent of families be obtained? Can cadaver organs be purchased from the family of the deceased like other inherited property? Should we allow people to sell their own duplicate organs? When can a living donation be accepted? Can we use organs from the nearly dead or the hardly human?

Brain Death and Cortical Death

There has been a religious and historical tradition of identifying death with a permanent cessation of heart beat and the absence of respiration. But now there are artificial means for keeping hearts beating and lungs working. The technology that makes it possible to keep alive those who would otherwise be dead leaves us with uncertainty about when someone can be called dead. This becomes a crucial issue in transplantation because transplant organs must be kept viable until harvested by keeping the donor body on life support until the organs are removed. Yet it is immoral to kill someone in order to transplant his or her organs. So, if discontinuing life support is killing, then the organs cannot be harvested from those who are on life support.

Brain death has been used as a new medical standard for defining death. According to the new criteria, when brain function has terminated, death is declared, and organs may be taken even though heartbeat and respiration continue. Does this new criterion reflect what is in fact ethically permissible? Brain death has not been accepted as the standard in Japan, so no cadaveric transplants can be performed there. Is brain death too broad a standard, or is it actually too narrow? Perhaps confirmation of the death of the cerebral cortex is a sufficient moral standard for declaring that artificial life support could be discontinued and that organs could be taken for transplantation. Only if cortical death were the accepted standard could the organs of anencephalic new borns and also of those in persistent vegetative states be used (6–10).

Arguments about the acceptability of the brain-death standard reflect broader moral positions on personhood and life. Someone who holds life itself to be sacred is inclined to resist any laxity in the death standard. Those who associate personhood or autonomy with the demand for respectful treatment readily accept the new standard because, once the brain is dead, the individual can no longer make choices or act with deliberation or from principles as an autonomous person could. According to those with a commitment to autonomy, we do not have obligations to the brain dead that we do have to those who can still think and autonomously make choices for themselves (11, 12).

Required Request, Presumed Consent, and Required Donation

Regardless of whether brain death or cortical death is the accepted standard, decisions will have to be made about whether other criteria have to be met before usable organs can be removed from the deceased for transplantation. Currently in the United States we follow the "required request" policy. The next of kin must be asked to donate the organs of the deceased, and their consent must be given before organs can be removed. Some other countries function under a "presumed consent" rule. On this model it is assumed that viable organs will be used for transplantation, although families are given the right to refuse. A third approach (employed for example in Austria) treats the corpse as property of the state and takes all viable organs for transplantation.

Because of the serious shortage of transplant organs, many in the United States have argued for moving from "required request" to "presumed consent" or even to required donation. Although the latter two policies are expected to make more organs available for transplantation, defenders of the "required request" status quo argue that the other policies conflict with our historical commitments to individual liberty and religious freedom and cannot be accepted in our society because the population does not sufficiently trust the medical establishment. Following our present policy leaves about two thirds of those who need transplants without organs and so increases the impetus for accepting organs from living donors (13–17).

Using Living Organ Donors

Physicians consider that they should act for the good of, and should avoid harm to, their patients. If they also consider the psychological benefit to a donor from saving a loved one, or significantly improving a beloved's quality of life, or avoiding the guilt of not trying to help, it will be apparent that donating an organ could be good for the donor. From this perspective, even though subjecting someone to the risks of surgical complications and the certainty of mutilation can never be good, in the context of the totality of what is being achieved, accepting an organ from a living donor could be better than the alternative.

In accepting someone as an organ donor, the most crucial considerations are the seriousness of the recipient's need, the likelihood of avoiding serious complications for the donor, and the quality of the donor's consent. The more pressing the need of the recipient, the greater the reason to do some harm to another. The slimmer the chance of serious harm to the donor and the more autonomous the donor's choice, the greater the acceptability of the donation.

Autonomous donor consent is a basic consideration in taking an organ from a donor because it would be an assault to take an organ from someone without her or his consent. Furthermore, in light of the clear harms that will be done, unless the person declares that the donation would be an overall good, there is no reason to presume that it will be. However, since respect for autonomy is one of the most crucial moral imperatives, cooperating with someone's autonomous choice to give provides a prima facie reason for accepting her or him as an organ donor (18).

Unfortunately, the one who can donate an organ for transplantation—who has an organ that suits the recipient's needs—may not be autonomous. Small children, the demented, and the insane cannot make such decisions for themselves. The autonomy of other prospective donors (including adolescents and those who are being pressed to donate by family members) may be questionable. When you are acutely aware of the moral dimension of taking an organ from a living donor, the ethical acceptability of each prospective donor must be carefully assessed. Furthermore, because the ethical acceptability of living donation relates directly to the likelihood of taking the organ without causing serious harm, the minimum requirement is that each prospective donor must have her or his own medical advocate who is committed to considering the donation only from the perspective of the good of the donor (19–22).

Organ Sales

If organs for transplantation can be taken from dead and also from living donors, can organs be sold? The marketplace serves as an incentive. Since we need more transplant organs to save and improve lives, is it permissible to allow the market to operate and thus increase the available pool?

One argument against organ sales has been that it would result in unjust distribution of organs—the rich would be able to buy what they needed and the poor would be left without. However, a system could easily be devised to avoid this problem. The United Network for Organ Sharing (UNOS), the national organ distribution network, could be the only buyer and could continue allocation of what would be a more adequate supply, following principles that would not discriminate against the poor. If the distribution of purchased organs were just, would organ sales be acceptable? Those still opposed argue that body parts are the kinds of things that should be given and not sold, that using money as the incentive would deprive people of the opportunity to be generous, and that offering money for organs would offend more people than it would inspire. Furthermore, they point out that offering a financial incentive would be unjust to the poor because it would be more likely to coerce them than to affect the decisions of the well-heeled.

Those in favor of allowing organ sales to increase the supply of transplantable organs claim that taking organs from the deceased without financial reimbursement is unfair to the family that might be happy to receive some compensation (for instance, burial costs) for their property. It is also argued that refusing to allow the living to sell their own duplicate organs fails to respect their autonomy by refusing to allow people to act on the choices they think are best for them. Those who argue against a prohibition on organ sales point to the inconsistencies in our attitudes. We do allow people to take much greater risks for financial compensation (boxing, playing football), and we do allow and even praise people who donate without compensation for taking the same risk (23–33).

ORGAN ALLOCATION

Once transplant organs are obtained, careful consideration must be given to how they should be allocated. Meeting the needs of all patients is impossible because there are not enough organs for everyone who needs one. And whenever someone is chosen to receive an organ, those who are passed over and have to wait longer are being harmed as they get sicker and in some cases die. Justice and fairness must be considered in the distribution of the limited supply, but the allocation that would be just and fair is not obvious. Complex issues are subtly interrelated, making theoretical answers hard to reach and harder still to spell out in the individual cases that must be addressed (34).

Distributive Justice

Should everyone who needs a vital organ to live or to live a significantly better life be treated the same way, or are there some considerations that need to be given special weight in distribution? Should social grounds be taken into account, or only medical factors? Which factors should be counted, and how much? Should people be given no more than one organ? Two? Three?

In organ allocation, UNOS—the national distribution system—now gives priority to urgency of need and then to length of time on the list. However, if urgency is always and without qualification the primary consideration, people with the least likelihood of surviving, including some in serious danger of losing a transplanted organ, are the most likely to receive a transplant. But because fewer patients would survive transplantation if such a policy were adopted, some alternative scheme would better maximize the effective use of organs.

In listing potential recipients, transplant centers typically pay most attention to the medical features of gravity and the likelihood of long-term success. Including benefit in their focus improves the overall utility of the distribution system. However, we can still ask whether it is just to overlook considerations like the patient's previous contribution to society or the patient's future prospects of depleting or contributing to the stock of social resources. If the supply of transplant organs does not increase, and if the demand for organs continues to increase, we will be pressed to justify not paying more attention to such social considerations in organ distribution (35–38).

Free Riders

Beyond these most obvious considerations about the characteristics of individual organ recipients, a host of questions arise about whether certain categories of individuals should be excluded from the pool of possible organ recipients. Should free riders—those who are not eligible to donate and those who would not be willing to donate—be denied access to the limited supply of transplant organs? Or should free riders be allowed to benefit from the kindness of strangers without being willing or able to give anything in return? For example, should foreign nationals or those with religious convictions that would rule out donations be eligible to receive organs through UNOS (39)?

Duties and Debts

The discussion of justice in organ allocation can be understood as an attempt to understand who has a right to transplantation. However, rights are often associated with duties. If some people have the right to a transplant, what does "the system" owe them? In other words, when a society declares its commitment to providing transplantation as one form of medical therapy, what are patients entitled to expect? What are the duties of the system to the recipient?

By creating, regulating, and funding UNOS, and by funding the research that has made organ transplantation into a viable therapy for organ failure, our government has implicitly proclaimed its acceptance of an obligation to provide this therapy. Since government's support is drawn from the common pool of social resources, and since the cadaveric organs are donated through a national distribution network, all (citizens, taxpayers, residents) should have equal access to the beneficial therapy. According to this argument, those without the financial wherewithal to pay for transplantation nevertheless have the right to equal access because they are part of the society that has supported its development. Furthermore, because organ harvesters would not refuse cadaveric organ donations from those without health insurance and financial means, monetary considerations should also be irrelevant in organ distribution. So far our society has not acknowledged its obligation to provide for equal access to transplantation; some people cannot get organs because they cannot pay. Unless there is an argument to show why it is just for the poor, who can give organs and who may vote their support of transplantation research, to be ethically denied the opportunity to get organs, we must respect everyone's right to equal access.

Besides the government, individual health care facilities also have duties to their transplant patients.

Certainly the institution is obligated to have facilities and staff adequate for performing the surgery and managing the postsurgical care. They should also have the ability to provide pretransplant and posttransplant education and necessary psychological and social support. A transplant program is also obliged to treat patients with respect by providing sufficient information about the institution's policies, the usual experience of living with a transplanted organ, and about the particular complications of their individual case, so as to allow patients to make autonomous choices about their own lives.

As in other areas of doctor-patient communication, the extent of "informing" that counts as satisfying the obligation to inform is imprecise. Before transplantation, must a patient be informed about the policies of the institution, particulars of the donor's age, life, and death, the cold ischemia time, the condition of the organs, the sources of blood for transfusion, the surgical experience of members of the transplant team, and other details? What must patients be told about their own case shortly after the surgery and then throughout the complications that ensue? The rule of respect for autonomy requires patients to be given all of the information which would be relevant to their immediate and future decisions. Thoughtful and imaginative assessment must go into determining the parameters of that requirement (40, 41).

Since special rights usually come with special duties, do those who get the right to an organ transplant also get special obligations? In other words, once people are accepted as organ recipients, do they then owe anything to "the system"? To get an organ, must you also be willing to donate your transplantable organs if you should die? Must you be willing to commit yourself to acting as an advocate for others to donate organs? Must you be willing to authorize an autopsy if your transplant should fail, so that something might be learned to help others who come later? Although no center demands that patients fulfill these duties, potential recipients should be made aware of them and encouraged to pay their moral debts.

Research

Research raises other questions about organ allocation. Should the goals of improving transplantation success in the current patient population or extending the treatment to patients who are currently considered untreatable be a consideration in organ allocation? If likelihood of success is an important consideration in distribution, is there a place for trying new or modified therapies on patients for whom success is now not likely? Given the generally accepted duty of medicine to pursue new therapies, research that could produce new medical knowledge would justify some overriding of considerations of utility, benefit, and need. The competing concerns of maximizing effective organ use and advancing transplantation must be prudently balanced in allocating transplant organs. An increasing degree of scarcity may impose increasingly strict limitations on those research projects designed to extend the treatment to a greater pool of patients and, at the same time, relax the restrictions on research that would hold a promise of somehow augmenting the organ supply, including split liver transplantation (42), xenografts (43), procuring organs from non-heart-beating donors (44).

SUMMARY AND CONCLUSIONS

Organ transplantation can save and improve lives. So physicians who are obliged to try to save lives and to act for the good of their patients are morally committed to offering this valuable treatment option to those who can benefit from it. Unfortunately, the serious shortage of organs for transplant leaves our society and the medical community to map out and navigate the obscure moral terrain of ethically procuring and allocating organs. The task in this time of organ scarcity is to draw the moral lines with creative and thoughtful consideration of all those who need transplantation, so that those who must decide can courageously go to the edge in trying to do the right thing. And because of the ethical complexity of the situation, those who must act in this uncomfortable moral position must often remember to ask themselves, "Did we do the right things?"

References

1. Childress JF. Ethical criteria for procuring and distributing organs for transplantation. J Health Politics Policy Law 1989; 14(1):87–113.
2. Diethelm AG. Ethical decisions in the history of organ transplantation. Ann Surg 1990; May:505–520.
3. Singer PA. A review of public policies to procure and distribute kidneys for transplantation. Arch Int Med 1990; 150:523–527.
4. Annas GJ. The transplant odyssey. Second Opinion 1989; 12:33–39.
5. Thomasma DC. Ethical issues and transplantation technology. Cambr Q Healthcare Ethics 1992; 1(4):333–344.
6. Rothenberg LS. The anencephalic neonate and brain death: an international review of medical, ethical, and legal issues. Transplantation Proc 1990; 22(3):1037–1039.
7. Churchill LR, Pinkus RLB. The use of anencephalic organs: historical and ethical dimensions. Milbank Q 1990; 68(2):147–169.
8. Berger DH. The infant with anencephaly: moral and legal dilemmas. Issues Law Med 1989; 5(1):67–85.
9. Davis A. The status of anencephalic babies: should their bodies be used as donor banks? J Med Ethics 1988; 14:150–153.
10. Cutter MAG. Moral pluralism and the use of anencephalic tissue and organs. J Med Philosophy 1989; 14:89–95.
11. Veatch RM. The impending collapse of the whole-brain definition of death. Hastings Center Rep 1993; 23(4):18–24.
12. Olick RS. Brain death, religious freedom, and public policy: New Jersey's landmark legislative initiative. Kennedy Institute of Ethics J 1991; 1(4):275–292.
13. Prottas JM. The organization of organ procurement. J Health Politics Policy Law 1989; 14(1):41–55.

14. Spital A. Sounding Board—The shortage of organs for transplantation: where do we go from here? N Engl J Med 1991; 325(17):1243–1246.

15. Veatch RM. Sounding Board—Routine inquiry about organ donation—an alternative to presumed consent. N Engl J Med 1991; 325(17):1246–1249.

16. Caplan AL, Virnig B. Is altruism enough? Required request and the donation of cadaver organs and tissues in the United States. Crit Care Clin 1990; 6(4):1007–1018.

17. Ross SE, Nathan H, O'Malley KF. Impact of required request law on vital organ procurement. J Trauma 1990; 30(7):820–824.

18. Kluge EHW. Designated organ donation: private choice in social context. Hastings Center Rep 1989; 19(5):10–15.

19. The Partnership for Organ Donation. The American public's attitudes toward organ donation and transplantation. Princeton, NJ: The Gallup Organization, 1993.

20. Tomlinson T. Infants and others who cannot consent to donation. Mt Sinai J Med 1993; 60(1):41–44.

21. Rhodes R. Debatable donors: when can we count their consent? Mt Sinai J Med 1993; 60(1):45–50.

22. Hunter J. Consent for the legally incompetent organ donor: application of a best-interest standard. J Legal Med 1991; 12:535–557.

23. Rhodes R, Burrows L, Reisman L. The adolescent living related donor. Healthcare Ethics Committee Forum 1992; 4(5):314–323.

24. Essig B. Legal aspects of the sale of organs. Mt Sinai J Med 1993; 60(1):59–64.

25. Dworkin G. Markets and morals: the case for organ sales. Mt Sinai J Med 1993; 60(1):66–69.

26. Altshuler JS. Financial incentives for organ donation: the perspectives of health care professionals. JAMA 1992; 267(15):2037–2038.

27. Peters TG. Life or death: the issue of payment in cadaveric organ donation. JAMA 1991; 265(10):1302–1305.

28. Pellegrino ED. Families' self-interest and the cadaver's organs: what price consent? JAMA 1991; 265(10):1305–1306.

29. Harvey J. Paying organ donors. J Med Ethics 1990; 16:117–119.

30. Dickens BM. Human rights and commerce in health care. Transplantation Proc 1990; 22(3):904–905.

31. Brecher B. The kidney trade: or, the customer is always wrong. J Med Ethics 1990; 16:120–123.

32. Brecher B. Buying human kidneys: autonomy, commodity and power. J Med Ethics 1991; 17:99.

33. Sloan FA. Organ procurement: expenditures and financial incentives. JAMA 1993; 269(24):3155–3156.

34. American Medical Association Council on Ethical and Judicial Affairs. Report 49: Ethical considerations in the allocation of organs and other scarce medical resources among patients. Code of Med Ethics Reports 1993; 4(2):140–173.

35. Rhodes R, Miller C, Schwartz M. Transplant recipient selection: peacetime vs. wartime triage. Cambridge Q Healthcare Ethics 1992; 1(4):327–332.

36. Veatch RM. Allocating organs by utilitarianism is seen as favoring whites over blacks. Kennedy Institute of Ethics Newsletter 1989; 3(3):1–3.

37. Cohen C, Benjamin M. Alcoholics and liver transplantation. JAMA 1991; 265(10):1299–1301.

38. Moss AH, Siegler M. Should alcoholics compete equally for liver transplantation? JAMA 1991; 265(10):1295–1298.

39. Davis DS. Those who don't give. Mt Sinai J Med 1993; 60(1):59–64.

40. Schanzer H. Child-donor kidneys. Mt Sinai J Med 1993; 60(1):52.

41. Moros D. Cases and doubts: panel discussion. Mt Sinai J Med 1993; 60(1):55–58.

42. Serge M, et al. Partial liver transplantation from living donors. Cambridge Q Healthcare Ethics 1992; 1(4):305–326.

43. Nelson JL. Transplantation through a glass darkly. Hastings Center Report 1992; 22(5):6–8.

44. Younger SJ, Arnold RM. Ethical, psychosocial and public policy implications of procuring organs from non-heartbeating cadaver donors. JAMA 1993; 269(21):2769–2774.

Fault and the Allocation of Spare Organs

Brian Smart

There has been much useful discussion over the allocation of spare resources between patients who are not at fault for the scarcity of healthy organs. The debate here has been over the criteria for the fair distribution of such resources. Should the choice between those who are to receive spare organs and those who are not to receive them be made by lot, by social usefulness, by quality adjusted life years (QALYS) or by appeal to the 'good innings' criterion (1)? For our present purposes I shall assume that we have an answer in the 'distributive justice criterion' (DJC). The DJC gives us an order of priority between innocent parties. The question is: should the DJC be restricted to allocations involving innocent parties or should it apply to those responsible for the scarcity too? Should the allocation of spare organs ignore all questions of fault, or should considerations of rectificatory justice enter when at least one of the patients in need is responsible for the scarcity? Rectificatory justice covers both punishment and reparation for wrongs, and in law is to be found both in the criminal and civil law, for example in torts and contract (2).

HISTORICAL FAULT

There are those who hold that the DJC should command all allocation simply on the ground that the question of responsibility never arises. Michael Lockwood, for example, expresses scepticism about free will: '. . . we are all of us victims of our genetic inheritance, upbringing and so forth, and . . . it is not true that people who bring certain kinds of health care needs on themselves—for example by driving dangerously, overeating, smoking or abusing drugs or alcohol—really *could*, in the final analysis, have acted any differently' (3). This is not the place to discuss the issue of free will and responsibility. But, whether we believe in free will or not, we need to discuss its *implications*, and Lockwood has not addressed these. Our everyday practice of morality and law certainly does distinguish between people who are at fault and those who are not. The cloth out of which that everyday practice weaves culpability is made up of intention and foresight, knowledge of right and wrong, rationality, control over one's actions and emotions, beliefs about the circumstances of the action and a capacity to exercise reasonable care about others. For those who wish to reserve judgement on free will our question still stands: *if* a person is responsible for a shortage of healthy organs, should their access be determined wholly by distributive criteria or should rectificatory justice (punishment or reparation) be involved?

In a recent article proposing a complete criterion of allocation, Michael J Langford distinguishes between past fault, which his proposed criterion excludes as ground for allocation, and a present or future condition, for example alcoholism, which could ground allocation 'if it rendered the medical prognosis poor' (4). However, he does not provide any reason why past fault should be excluded. Now for our purposes it may just be the case that Langford has successfully delineated *the* DJC. Indeed, exclusion of historical fault would be definitionally required, for it would exclude questions of rectificatory justice. But it would plainly beg the question arbitrarily to exclude rectificatory criteria from a complete criterion of allocation: that requires argument.

It is, however, possible to reconstruct a line of reasoning that may have influenced Langford. He believes that a principle of equality should govern his criterion, and, he claims 'that certainly looks like a deontological principle' (4), by which he means 'one that relates to rights and duties that are alleged to apply regardless of the consequences' (5). However, it emerged that he is not defending a deontological principle since he is elaborating a principle to which deontologists, utilitarians (who are interested in only the consequences) and those uncommitted to an ethical theory may subscribe (4). But there is no such neutral principle. It is only utilitarianism which, at base, wholly rejects the moral significance of the past. It is only utilitarianism which would find no possible role for historical fault in a complete principle of allocation: deontology and ordinary morality commonly base judgements of desert, entitlement and liability on past fault of one of the parties involved.

It might also be the case that Langford believes that including rectificatory criteria turns scarce resource allocation into punishment. To that argument I now turn.

A NON-PUNITIVE PRINCIPLE OF RESTITUTION

The idea that historical fault should play a key role in the allocation of health care is vigorously rejected by John Harris. He writes:

> 'We all, of course, have a duty to encourage and promote morality, but to do so by choosing between candidates for treatment on moral grounds is to arrogate to ourselves not simply the promotion of morality but the punishment of immorality. And to choose to let one person rather than another die on the grounds of some moral defect in their behaviour or character is to take upon ourselves the right not simply to punish, but capitally to punish, offenders against morality' (6).

We need to distinguish here between at least two different ways of choosing between people for treatment on moral grounds. The first way is where we give preference to one on grounds of her superior moral character or behaviour, but where neither party is in any way responsible for the scarcity of resources. To decide in this way is to include morality in the DJC: it is not addressed to rectifying any wrong, for the problem of scarcity is neither party's fault. Harris may be right not to include morality in the DJC, but that is another matter. The second way of choosing between people for treatment on moral grounds is where the need to choose is the fault of one of the parties in need of treatment. However, the most obvious cases of such choices are not cases of punishment at all, but cases of self-defence and other-defence.

Consider a case of other-defence in which an unprovoked attack has been launched on Kurt by Charles. Kurt cannot retreat or restrain Charles but you have the power, at no risk to yourself, of intervening by killing Charles. Suppose you do this on the ground that Charles is at fault for causing the dilemma. There is a scarcity of resources, since you do not have the power to save *both* Kurt *and* Charles, only the power to save *either* Kurt *or* Charles. A just case of other-defence would be one in which you choose between these two on moral grounds, not on grounds of general character blemishes but on the ground that Charles is at fault for causing the scarcity of resources and so should bear the cost. This ground needs elaboration. Kurt is not at fault, and so not only should he not have to bear the cost, but Charles *should be forced to make restitution* to Kurt: in other words, Charles should be forced to restore Kurt to the position he rightfully enjoyed before Charles's attack endangered his life (7).

Here we have all the ingredients of a preferential choice between lives on moral grounds. But does it constitute the punishment of immorality, or, in this case, capital punishment? I suggest not. First of all, there is no account of punishment which licenses the treatment justified by self-defence. If Charles is killed for launching an unsuccessful attempt on Kurt's life, that is not because it is a suitable punishment but because it is the minimal reasonable force to defend Kurt: as punishment it would exceed even the harsh limits imposed by the *lex talionis* (an eye for an eye . . .). If all that was needed to defend Kurt was for you to give Charles a slap on the cheek or a harsh frown then that would hardly be a punishment to fit the crime of attempted murder, but it would be all that would be licensed by other-defence. In cases of self-defence and other-defence where the aggressor survives, we can distinguish more clearly between the treatment licensed by defence and the treatment licensed by punishment: the question of punishment obviously does arise in cases of unsuccessful murder even when the aggressor has received the harm that was minimally necessary for a successful defence of the victim.

Self-Inflicted Harm Is Not a Crime

A second reason for rejecting preferential treatment as punishment lies in the fact that self-inflicted harm is not a crime. Damaging one's own heart or lungs by smoking is not forbidden by law: it would be legal paternalism if it were. So the justification, if there is one, for discriminating against a smoker when only one healthy spare set of heart and lungs is available must be non-punitive. And that justification lies in restitution. For suppose that what the smoker who is at fault must do is to restore to others what was rightfully theirs before the commission of the fault. True, the smoker has inflicted harm on only himself. But this ceases to be true if he does not forfeit equality of entitlement to a spare set of heart and lungs. For example, if there is no forfeiture of equality then, the one non-smoker in need of a transplant has a 1/2 chance of acquiring the spare set rather than a 1/1 chance. Without differential treatment according to fault the nonsmoker would be denied his rightful opportunity. By forfeiting his own right to equality the smoker restores the nonsmoker to her rightful *status quo.*

Interestingly, much of this argument applies to someone who damages another's healthy heart or who vandalises one of the two healthy spare sets of organs available (8). The obvious difference is that a crime has now been committed—harm to the person or damage to property: punishment is a matter for the criminal courts. But, in addition to the crime, we have the same kind of situation that arose with self-inflicted harm: there is a scarcity of resources. By harming another's heart, or by vandalising a spare set of organs on their way to the theatre, the person at fault has forfeited his right to equal priority with the innocent patient. The innocent patient is owed restitution of his 1/1 chance of access to healthy organs that he possessed before the fault occurred. Restitution and reparation is a matter either for the civil courts or may be settled out of court.

It might be thought that self- and other-defence are sufficiently unlike choice between lives caused by a shortage of resources to provide a useful insight into the nature of that choice. After all, self- and other-defence involve an aggressor who is a current threat to the victim. For this reason, Langford's distinction between historical fault and current condition might explain why he could justify self- and other-defence. And it might also explain why Harris might want to assimilate preferential treatment against a patient at fault to punishment: for it would involve an historical and not an ongoing fault.

The Threat May Be Current

But historical fault may be found in self-defence. The threat may be current, but the fault may be historical (9). Imagine the aggressor has pushed his trolley to the crest of the hill and has now tied himself in it so that he cannot jump

out: you are tied to the track down which the trolley is heading and fortunately you can operate by remote control a bulldozer which, at the flick of the
switch, will straddle the track, protect you but kill the aggressor when his
trolley smashes into it. The fault is historical in the sense that after the trolley
has crested the hill, the aggressor can do nothing more about it, and flight or
effective threats are not open to the victim. This is unlike the current fault of
an aggressor who is trying to strangle you and in whose power it is to desist
right up to the moment of the victim's death. In this case both the threat and
the fault are current. But the burden of restitution is the same in both cases.
Indeed, it is not inappropriate to ask, in the present tense, 'Who *is* responsible?' in both cases of historical and current fault.

   We now have a non-punitive principle of restitution. It properly belongs
to rectificatory, not distributive justice, since it requires those at fault to restore those endangered or harmed to their rightful *status quo*. It is not punishment, since it is like paying damages in a civil libel suit.

PRIORITY OF NON-SMOKERS OVER SMOKERS IN ACCESS TO SPARE ORGANS?

What are the implications of this principle of restitution? Should medical practitioners supplement the DJC with a fault criterion that prioritises the innocent? Notoriously in ethics, as in economics and physics, there is a large gap
between the enunciation of a sound principle and its practical application.

   First of all, it is unclear who should apply the DJC supplemented by a
rule of restitution. We have ruled out criminal courts since forfeiting priority
of access to scarce resources is not a matter for punishment. But the application of the principle does introduce a dimension not covered by the DJC: assessing degrees of culpability. So expertise for assessing fault is required on
any panel that is involved in the allocation: assessing fault is not a medical
skill. It is to be hoped that the composition of any panel would, like juries, introduce more democracy and in some way involve consultation with those
needing a transplant or with their representatives. One crucial reason for this
is that if restitution is owed to another party, it does not follow that the restitution has to be made. For it is always open to the person who has the right
to restitution *to waive* that right. This is not peculiar to debts of restitution, but
a more general feature of obligations. After all, I do not have to pay you back
the £10 I promised to repay you if you waive your right to repayment. You are
morally sovereign over whether I will be held to that promise or not.

   If, as law and ordinary morality suggests, it is an empirical matter
whether individuals are at fault, there are undoubtedly difficulties in identifying particular cases. For example, the problem with many cases of self-
inflicted heart or lung disease is that it may be caused by addiction to nicotine.
Addiction as such does not rule out fault. For someone may have taken up

smoking or drinking quite freely, but foreseen that he would not be able to give it up once he was addicted (10). On the other hand, a large proportion of smokers become addicted in their early teens and so, because of immaturity, are not responsible for their addiction. Nor should we ignore the stress-related conditions that might cause much smoking in adults: unemployment, inability to keep up mortgage repayments and broken relationships are familiar examples of such causes. Fault is either negated or much reduced by such causes. But it would be a mistake to exaggerate the difficulties of assessing culpability. Let us grant that many complex cases are impossible to resolve and that many others may be resolvable only by the ratified skills of trained lawyers. Because of the constraints of time such cases would be beyond the scope of the allocation of scarce medical resources. Such cases may be contrasted with those in which the relevant histories of the parties are known and which present good, and non-conflicting, evidence of the culpability of one of them. We would insist on this if other-defence were to be justified.

We must now distinguish between being responsible for a condition and being at fault or culpable for that condition arising. For there to be a fault there must be a wrong committed as well as there being responsibility for that wrong. A miner or fireman chooses freely to subject himself to greater risk of harm or disease than is met with in most occupations. And, on the special assumption that if he were not to make that choice nobody would fill his place, it may be true that he causes a shortfall in spare healthy organs. But, because of the social value placed upon such occupations, we are not tempted to say that such a shortfall is the *fault* of the miner or the fireman. Since there is no fault there can be no case for saying that miners should have less priority than those who have no responsibility for their condition. But why should the social value of the occupations involving these risks mean that no fault occurs? The justification lies in fairness. In this case the value is one of social need: the society needs firemen and miners for its welfare. To ask people to take an extra risk (which may be rewarded by danger money) and then to give them lower medical priority than any ordinary member of the public would simply be unfair: indeed there is a case for giving them a higher medical priority in addition to danger money.

One qualification should be made here. The society asks people in dangerous occupations to take only the risks that are reasonable in the circumstances. Negligence can incur harm that was reasonably avoidable. Society did not ask the miner to harm himself in that way.

DANGEROUS SPORTS

Dangerous sports such as rock-climbing and paragliding are not pursued out of social necessity since they do not contribute to social welfare. Society does not ask people to engage in rock-climbing or paragliding. If people freely engage in these sports should they not pay all the extra costs such activities risk and so receive a lower priority in access to spare organs? The argument with smoking is that it is unfair to spread the extra risks of this self-indulgence to those who prefer not to impose an extra risk on themselves. Should not the same apply to dangerous sports? A strong case can be made here for the social value of such sports, providing they are not too dangerous, and providing they are practised nonnegligently. The value does not belong to social welfare, it is not socially necessary as has been stated. But these sports do enhance lives as well as endanger them. Their value is both intrinsic and extrinsic. Intrinsically, skills of a very high order can be acquired, with an accompanying feeling of achievement; but even beginners find the activity exciting and challenging. Yet it is also a spectator sport, in the sense that it can be followed with binoculars or cameras and be read about. Extrinsically, the activity is character-forming as well as being able to provide the best exponents with a living. Activities of this kind thus become a part of our culture and their value contributes to a worthwhile life. After all, social welfare is not an end in itself: it simply enables us to choose and pursue a worthwhile life.

MORAL COMPLICITY

Do dangerous sports differ in important respects from smoking or hard drinking? I think it is easy to show that our society delivers a mixed message on this issue. On the one hand, it permits advertising and sponsorship which may target children, and which presents smoking and drinking as appendages to a glamorous life-style. And, on the whole, it does not restrict smoking very seriously in public places, even when the dangers of passive smoking are well known. Such a policy seems to countenance the sharing of risks between smokers and the general public. On the other hand, government health warnings are compulsory on packets and advertisements. I think the upshot of this is that our society may be charged with moral complicity in the tobacco companies' operations and in the smokers' self-infliction of harm. Part of the message is that there is no fault: the other part of the message is that the activity is dangerous. When combined, these messages are compatible with the claim that smoking is a valuable (chic, cool) way of living in which it would be fair that we should all, smokers and non-smokers alike, bear the costs equally in the case of access to medical care: it would be unjust if non-smokers were given priority.

The claim that smoking is socially valuable should be challenged. One familiar way of doing this is to point out that its value is an illusion created by advertisers, an illusion which can affect young people at an impressionable and vulnerable phase in their lives. We have remarked on how it can be seen as a part of stylish living: this claim might be sustainable if we could substitute a substance that had no deleterious effects on our health. But in the light of its probable effects, the illusion can be sustained only by screening off or ignoring those probable effects. Also, safer remedies are available for removing the stress that smoking can remove (for example exercise or alcohol in moderate quantities). It may be rightly claimed that smoking causes private pleasure while not harming anyone else if practised privately. But that is a reason why people's right to smoke in private should be defended, provided they are aware of the risks. It is not a reason why those risks should be shared with the general public and so reduced for the participants themselves: if the activity lacks social value then the risks should be borne by the participants alone.

So far as smoking is concerned this paper is deliberately hedged about with qualifications. A society which banned the advertising of tobacco and attached no social value to smoking would share no fault with those who smoked of their own free will. In such circumstances, it would be fair to give a lower priority to smokers in the allocation of spare organs.

The argument for this conclusion has been deontological and has been based on a principle of restitution for an historical fault. Yet deontological thinking is only part of our moral thought: we must be sensitive to the consequences of our actions. It is therefore worth remarking that it is likely that the consequences of introducing a restitutive principle would be beneficial. Now that might appear doubtful if we consider Michael Lockwood's observation about one likely consequence of adopting a rule of priority according to fault:

> '. . . there might be good welfarist reasons for according the claims of [smokers] on health care resources a relatively low priority, if the fact were to be widely publicized and could act as an effective deterrent to such irresponsible behaviour. But I doubt whether it would. Someone who is undeterred by the prospect of seriously damaging his health is hardly likely, in my opinion, to be deterred by the prospect of less than ideal health care thereafter' (11).

Lockwood may be right about this particular consequence, at least in the vast majority of cases. Few are likely to be made *more responsible* by a rectificatory response to their fault. But he ignores the possibility that a system of equal access for all alike might induce many to become *more irresponsible* about their health. This is a phenomenon that occurs in the field of safety measures (12). For example, if seat belts are made compulsory there is a tendency for drivers to drive faster and so restore the former accident rates.

To conclude: rectificatory but non-punitive justice has in principle a role to play in the allocation of scarce medical resources. However, this would be just only within a framework of robust preventive medicine: this would mean effective health education and the elimination of cigarette advertising and sponsorship.

References and Notes

1. For the most recent account of a sophisticated allocative criterion see Langford M J. Who should get the kidney machine? *Journal of medical ethics* 1992; 18: 12–17.
2. For the introduction of this distinction see Aristotle, *The Nicomachean ethics* bk 5: 1130a 22–1132a 27.
3. Lockwood M. Quality of life and resource allocation. In: Bell J M, Mendus S, eds. *Philosophy and medical welfare*. Royal Institute of Philosophy, Lecture Series 23. Cambridge: Cambridge University Press, 1988: 49.
4. See reference (1) 13.
5. See reference (1) 16.
6. Harris J. *The value of life*. London: Routledge and Kegan Paul, 1985: 108.
7. For a detailed account see Smart B J. Understanding and justifying self-defence. *International journal of moral and social studies* 1989; 4, 3: 231–244.
8. For such a hypothetical see Wasserman D. Justifying self-defense. *Philosophy and public affairs* 1987; 16, 4: 367, fn 29.
9. David Wasserman wrongly attempts to dissociate an aggressor from his current threat where the fault is historical and the point of no return has been passed. See reference (8) 371–372. For a fault principle characterised as distributive rather than retributive or restitutive see Montague P. The morality of self-defense. *Philosophy and public affairs* 1989; 18, 1: 88.
10. See reference (2): bk 3: 1114a 15–21.
11. See reference (3): 49.
12. See Trammell R L *et al*. Utility and survival. *Philosophy* 1977; 52: 336.

EVALUATING A CASE STUDY: STRUCTURING THE ESSAY

In previous sections, you have moved from adopting an ethical theory to weighing and assessing the merits of deeply imbedded cost issues and ethical issues conflicts. The process involves (a) choosing an ethical theory (whose point of view you will adopt), (b) determining your professional practice issues and ethical issues lists, (c) annotating the issues lists by examining how imbedded each issue is to the essential nature of the case at hand, (d) creating a brainstorming list that includes both key thoughts on the subject and arguments for and against the possible courses of action, (e) comparing pivotal premises in those arguments using ethical considerations as part of the decision-making matrix, (f) making a judgment on which course to take (given the conflicts expressed in d and e, (g) presenting your ideas in an essay. The essay is your recommendation to a professional review board about what to do in a specific situation.

This section represents stage (g) in this process. If we continue with the IUD case, your essay might be something like the following.

Sample Essay

Executive Summary. Although my profession would advocate my continuing to distribute IUDs to women in less-developed countries, it is my opinion that to do so would be immoral. Human life is too precious to put anyone at risk for population control. If IUDs are too dangerous to be sold in the United States, then they are too dangerous for women in poor countries as well. People do not give up their right to adequate health protection just because they are poor. For this reason, I am ordering a halt to the distribution of IUDs until such a time that they can be considered safe again. Furthermore, I will step up efforts to distribute alternate forms of birth control (such as the birth control pill) with better packaging that might encourage regular use.

The Introduction. In this case study, I have chosen the point of view of the regional director. This means that I must decide whether to continue distributing IUDs in less-developed countries despite a health hazard to 5 percent of the women who use this form of birth control. I will argue against continuing the distribution based on an argument that examines: (a) the imperatives of my profession, public health; (b) the imperatives of ethics; and (c) the rights of the women involved. I will contend that after examining these issues, the conclusion must be to cease IUD distribution in less-developed countries until IUDs no longer pose a significant problem to women's health.

The Body of the Essay. Develop paragraphs along the lines indicated in the introduction and executive summary.

The Conclusion. Although the dictates of the normal practice of public health would seem to suggest that IUD distribution continue, the ethical imperatives that human life is individually precious and that each woman has a right to safe medical attention overrule the normal practice of the profession. For these reasons, my office will suspend distribution of IUDs until they no longer pose a health risk to the general population.

Comments on the Sample. The sample provides an essay structure that contains a brief epitome and the essay itself. I often encourage my students to come in with their epitome, key issues, arguments for and against, and brainstorming sheets before writing the essay itself. This way I can get an "in-progress" view of the process of composition.

Obviously, the preceding sample represents the briefest skeleton of an essay proposing a recommendation. The length can vary as can any supporting data (charts, etc.) for your position. Your instructor may ask you to present your outcomes recommendation to the entire class. When this is the assignment, remember that the same principles of any group presentation also apply here including any visual aid that will engage your audience. It is essential to include your audience in your argument as it develops.

Whether it is a written report or a group presentation, the methodology presented here should give you a chance to logically assess and respond to problems that contain moral dimensions.

The following are some general questions that some of my students have raised about writing the essay, that is, the ethical outcomes recommendation.

> *What if I cannot see the other side?* This is a common question from students. They see everything as black or white, true or false, but truth is never advanced by prejudice. It is important as rational humans to take every argument at its face value and to determine what it says, determine the objections to the key premises, determine the strongest form of the thesis, and assess the best arguments *for* and *against* the thesis.
>
> *What is the best way to reach my assessment of the best alternative?* The basic strategy of the essay is to take the best two arguments that you have selected to support the conflicting alternatives and then to focus on that single premise that seems to be at odds with the other argument. At this point, you must ask yourself, Why would someone believe in either argument 1 or argument 2?" If you do not know, you cannot offer an opinion—yet.
>
> The rational person seeks to inform herself by getting into the skin of each party. You must understand why a thinking person might think in a particular way. If you deprecate either side, you lessen yourself because you decrease your chances to make your best judgment.
>
> The rational individual seeks the truth. You have no need to burden your psyche with illogical beliefs. Therefore, you will go to great lengths to find the truth of the key premises that you wish to examine.

In the your final essay, you will focus on one of the argument's premises and find the following:

> A: The demonstrated truth of the conclusion depends on the premises that support it.
>
> B: If those supporting premises are false, then the conclusion is not proven.
>
> C: Since we have assumed that the premises are all necessary to get us to the conclusion, if we refute one premise, we have refuted the conclusion.

> *What if I place professional practice issues or ethical issues too highly in my assessment of the outcome?* The purpose of preparing an imbedded issues analysis is to force you to see that not all ethical issues are central to the problem. Some issues can be solved rather easily. If this is the case, then you should do so. When it is possible to let professional practice issues determine the outcome without sacrificing ethical standards, it is your responsibility to do so. Clearly, some ethical principles cannot be sacrificed no matter what the cost. It is *your* responsibility to determine just what these cases are and just which moral principles are "show stoppers."

Are ethical values the only values an individual should consider? Each person holds a number of personally important values that are a part of his or her worldview. These must be taken into account in real situations. Often they mean that although you cannot perform such and such an act, it is not requisite that the organization forgo doing whatever the professional practice issues dictate in that situation. For example, you may be asked to perform a task on an important religious holy day. Since your religion is important to you, you cannot work on that day, but that does not mean that you will recommend the company abandon the task that another person who does not share your value could perform.

What happens when you confuse professional practice issues and ethical issues? This happens often among managers at all levels. The problem is that one set of issues is neglected or is too quickly considered to be surface imbeddedness. Stop. Go through the method again step-by-step. It may restore your perspective.

Macro and Micro Cases*

Macro Case 1. You are a powerful member of the United States Senate. You have decided not to run for reelection and want to leave a piece of legislation on U.S. health care policy that will be the highlight of a distinguished career in public service. You sense that there is an interest in legislation that will set the health care landscape for the next fifty years. You want to mark that terrain.

Your staff has four alternatives before you. The first is universal health care financed by industry (existing voluntary program) with the government creating a pool of last resort that will provide basic coverage for those who cannot afford to purchase health insurance (although the coverage is not as extensive as many privately funded programs). On a scale of 1 to 10, this plan has a cost of 7.5. The second alternative is a universal health care program that is a single payer system similar to the one in Canada. This alternative has a cost of 6. The third option is a patient's bill of rights plan that only refines our present system by fixing annoying glitches that bother us all. This alternative has a cost of 0.5. The final alternative is government-run universal health care similar to the British system. This alternative has a cost of 10 (including the creation of basic benefits, which are not as extensive as many privately funded plans as is true for the first alternative).

Your job is to create a policy statement to share with your staff advocating any of these four plans for another plan that you create. Since this is the crowning point of your career, be sure to justify your decision in both practical and ethical terms.

---

*For more on macro and micro cases see the overview on p. 53.

Macro Case 2. You are the chief administrator of a hospital in a major U.S. city. This hospital must review its procedures for accepting charity patients who arrive at the hospital via ambulance. According to accepted professional practice, many hospitals send these patients to the nearest charity hospital designated to receive such patients. That hospital receives special funds to make its charity mission possible. Your hospital receives no such money, yet in the past it has treated any patient whose condition might be worsened by a move to another hospital. You can treat such patients only by charging *all* patients with insurance more.

If you let this practice continue without restraint, the private physicians who use your hospital might leave because various managed care companies that would find your hospital costs too high would not approve a procedure scheduled there.

This is a real problem. You would like to continue your hospital's practice of seeing these charity cases because you know that sending these emergency admissions elsewhere can often mean that they could be harmed medically. (In one study, moving such patients increased mortality by 27 percent.) But you also know that hospitals cannot act in a vacuum. All the good intentions in the world will be of no avail if your hospital closes its doors.

Tomorrow you will address the hospital's governing board. You must prepare an argument that will combine practical and ethical arguments to convince the board to pursue a course of action.

Macro Case 3. You are a powerful adviser to the president of the United States and have been chosen to head a commission on the allocation of transplant organs (and other related policies). Your committee is deadlocked as to which option to choose. The first is to allocate according to need (the sickest person gets the organ). The second option is to allocate according to an ordered pair (desert, need). In the ordered pair formula, people who have abused their bodies will be considered only after others who have not abused their bodies have received their transplants. The third proposal suggests that those who have not agreed to be organ donors (usually by a declaration on their driver's license) should be put at the end of the list.

Your vote is key for the majority. As chairperson, you will write the majority's recommendation. What will you recommend? Why?

Macro Case 4. You are the chief administrator at a major hospital. A famous person has been admitted to your hospital in need of a liver transplant. The average waiting time for a liver in your section of the country is 385 days. This person's name is a "household word." Your board of governors knows that this hospital depends on contributions from famous people who organize various charity drives and events. In fact, this particular person organized a charity auction that raised $12 million for the hospital only two years ago.

You have some discretion in allocating vital organs, especially ones that originate from deaths in the hospital. Allocation according to need is somewhat subjective, and you could put this celebrity at the top of the list above seven others who have been waiting for a liver transplant. All things being equal, the rules say that the celebrity should not receive the liver. But you, as chief administrator can tip the balance. What do you do? Why?

Micro Case 1. You work at a major health insurance company in its public relations department. The president of the United States has proposed legislation for universal health insurance that will severely hurt your company. Your own personal values support universal health insurance. Your company is launching a campaign to sabotage this piece of legislation by promoting half-truths and outright lies about the president's plan. You are to play a major part in this campaign. Your company is asking you to do your best to promote these half-truths and lies to defeat a policy initiative that you believe in. What should you do? Good jobs are not easy to obtain, and this is a well-paying job with numerous benefits. You are confused and decide to list the reasons you should and should not promote the company's campaign. Once you decide, how do you justify your decision?

Micro Case 2. You are a recently graduated physician from a poor rural region of the United States. Where you come from, the region's doctor has no set fee schedule and charges people what they can afford (even if it is barter, such as a chicken or a good car wash). This model of serving everyone and the community feelings that it generated were what made you first want to become a doctor. However, when you did your residency, your work was so outstanding that a prominent clinic that caters to the affluent has offered you a high-paying job. This facility is also on the cutting edge of many new medical techniques. This offer would certainly make your life more comfortable, yet you think about all of those folk from where you came and who inspired you to go into medicine.

When you talk this over with others, however, they think you are crazy even to consider the needs of these rural people. "You should take account of your own needs," they say, "both your financial and intellectual requirements." You hear what they are saying, but you are unsure about what to do. It is time to write a letter to your mother to tell her of your decision and to justify it.

Micro Case 3. You are a woman who works for Mr. Alvarez, who is a very fine boss and one of the kindest people you have ever met. He is a widower with one child. You are happily married with two children. There is no romantic relationship between you and Mr. Alvarez; however, you do consider him to be your closest friend (aside from your husband), and he has helped your career and has given you time off when your children were born and when one of them was severely ill.

Mr. Alvarez's kidneys are failing. He has been on dialysis, but even that is failing him. Nothing short of a kidney transplant will save his life. A co-worker distributed a description of the criteria for a prospective donor to everyone in the building. Privately, you decided to be tested to see whether you could be a match for him and found that you could be a match. Now you must decide whether you should offer your kidney to him. To rationally discuss this with your husband, you must list the competing interests at stake and then determine what to do. What will be your choice? Why?

Micro Case 4. You are a nurse at a regional transplant center. In your care are patients who are very ill and awaiting transplant organs. One day you discover that the patient in bed 4 has cheated the system to get ahead on the list. You discovered this information by listening behind a drawn curtain around the bed when the patient had a visitor. The patient was discussing with the visitor how he had "jumped the list."

You are uncertain about what to do. On the one hand, you feel a duty to the other patients awaiting donor organs who have played by the rules. If you follow this line of thinking, you would report the patient's behavior to the hospital's organ allocation review board. The consequences for the patient in bed 4 might be severe. On the other hand, revealing what you heard might be construed as violating the patient's privacy and your oath of confidentiality. Write an essay detailing the issues involved and then recommend a course of action.

Further Readings

Paternalism and Autonomy

Annas, George J. "The Emerging Stowaway: Patient's Rights in the 1980s." In *Value Conflict in Health Care Delivery*. Ed. Bart Gruzalski and Carl Nelson. Cambridge, MA: Ballinger, 1982, pp. 89–100.

Bassford, H.A. "The Justification of Medical Paternalism." *Social Science and Medicine* 16, no. 6 (1982), pp. 731–39.

Beauchamp, Tom L. "The Promise of the Beneficence Model for Medical Ethics." *Journal of Contemporary Health Law and Policy* 6 (Spring 1990), pp. 145–55.

Childress, James F. *Who Should Decide? Paternalism in Health Care.* Oxford: Oxford University Press, 1982.

———, and Mark Siegler. "Metaphors and Models of Doctor-Patient Relationships: Their Implications for Autonomy." *Theoretical Medicine* 5 (1984), pp. 17–30.

Coleman, Lee. *The Reign of Error.* Boston: Beacon Press, 1984.

Dworkin, G. *The Theory and Practice of Autonomy.* Cambridge: Cambridge University Press, 1988.

Hope, T., D. Springings, and R. Crisp. "Not Clinically Indicated: Patients' Interests or Resource Allocations." *British Medical Journal* 306 (1993), pp. 379–81.

Luna, Florencia. "Paternalism and the Argument from Illiteracy." *Bioethics* 9, no. 3/4 (July 1995), pp. 283–90.

Mahowald, Mary B. "Against Paternalism: A Developmental View." *Philosophical Research Archives* 6, 1386 (1980).

Pinkus, Rosa. "The Evolution of Moral Reasoning." *Medical Humanities Review* 10 (Fall 1996), pp. 20–44.

Sulmasy, Daniel. "Managed Care and the New Paternalism." *Journal of Clinical Ethics* 6, no. 4 (Winter 1995), pp. 324–26.

Wicclair, Mark R. "Patient Decision-Making Capacity and Risk." *Bioethics* 5 (April 1991), pp. 91–104.

Wulff, Henrik. "The Inherent Paternalism in Clinical Practice." *Journal of Medicine and Philosophy* 20, no. 3 (1995), pp. 299–311.

Privacy and Confidentiality

Appelbaum, Paul S., et al. "Confidentiality: An Empirical Test of the Utilitarian Perspective." *Bulletin of the American Academy of Psychiatry Law* 12, no. 2 (1984), pp. 109–16.

Bok, S. *Secrets: On the Ethics of Concealment and Revelation.* Oxford: Oxford University Press, 1984.

Cohen, Elliot D. "Confidentiality, Counseling, and Clients Who Have AIDS." *Journal of Counseling and Development 68* (January/February 1990), pp. 282–86.

Dowd, Steven. "Maintaining Confidentiality: Health Care's Ongoing Dilemma." *Health Care Supervisor* 15, no. 1 (1996), pp. 24–31.

Edgar, A. "Confidentiality and Personal Integrity." *Nursing Ethics* 1 (1994), pp. 86–95.

Farber, Neil. "Confidentiality and Health Insurance Fraud." *Archives of Internal Medicine* 157, no. 5 (March 10, 1997), pp. 501–4.

Frawley, Kathleen. "Secretary of HHS's Recommendations Regarding Confidentiality of Individually Identifiable Information." *Journal of AHIMA* 68, no. 10 (1997), pp. 14, 16, 18.

Furlong, Mark. "Reconciling the Patient's Right to Confidentiality with the Family's Need to Know." *Australian and New Zealand Journal of Psychiatry* 30, no. 5 (1996), pp. 614–22.

Glen, Sally. "Confidentiality: A Critique of the Traditional View." *Nursing Ethics* 4, no. 5 (September 1997), pp. 403–6.

Harrington, Cullen. "Disclosure of Child Sexual Abuse." *British Medical Journal* (July 18, 1998), pp. 208–9.

Maclin, Ruth. "HIV-Infected Psychiatric Patients: Beyond Confidentiality." *Ethics and Behavior* 1 (1991), pp. 3–20.

Martin, D.A. "Effects of Ethical Dilemmas on Stress Felt by Nurses Providing Care to AIDS Patients." *Critical Care Nursing Quarterly* 12, no. 4 (1990), pp. 53–62.

Mitchell, Peter. "Confidentiality as Risk in the Electronic Age." *Lancet* 349, 9065 (May 31, 1997), p. 1608.

Informed Consent

Capron, Alexander. "Informed Consent in Catastrophic Disease Research." *University of Pennsylvania Law Review* 123 (1974), pp. 340–438.

Cowles, Jane. *Informed Consent.* New York: Coward, McCann and Geoghegan, 1976.

DeVille, Kenneth. "Treating a Silent Stranger." *Healthcare Ethics Committee Forum* 10, no. 1 (March 1998), pp. 55–70.

Drane, James F. "Competence to Give Informed Consent: A Model for Making Clinical Assessments." *Journal of the American Medical Association* 252, no. 7 (August 17, 1984), pp. 925–27.

Faden, Ruth R., and Tom L. Beauchamp. *A History and Theory of Informed Consent*. New York: Oxford University Press, 1986.

Flax, Robert. "Silicone Implants: Two Stories," *Biolaw* 2, no. 9 (1997), pp. 311–30.

Furrow, Barry R. "Informed Consent: A Thorn in Medicine's Side? An Arrow in Law's Quiver?" *Law, Medicine and Health Care* 12, no. 6 (December 1984), pp. 268–73.

Gaylin, Willard, and Ruth Macklin, eds. *Who Speaks for the Child: The Problems of Proxy Consent*. New York: Plenum Press, 1982.

Geller, Gail. "Informed Consent Regarding Breast Cancer." *Hastings Center Report* 27, no. 2 (1997), pp. 28–33.

Kotva, Joseph. "Was This Consent Informed?" *American Journal of Nursing* 97, no. 5 (May 1997), p. 23.

Lidz, Charles W., Paul S. Appelbaum, and Alan Meisel. "Two Models of Implementing Informed Consent." *Archives of Internal Medicine* 148 (June 1988), pp. 1385–89.

Marwick, Charles. "Exceptions to Informed Consent." *Journal of the American Medical Association* 278, no. 17 (November 5, 1997), pp. 1392–93.

Morrissey, M.M., Adele D. Hoffmann, and Jeffrey C. Thrope. *Consent and Confidentiality in the Health Care of Children and Adolescents: A Legal Guide*. New York: Free Press, 1986.

Rosoff, Arnold J. *Informed Consent: A Guide for Health Care Providers*. Rockville, MD: Aspen, 1981.

Gender Issues

Baier, Annette C. *Postures of the Mind: Essays on Mind and Morals*. Minneapolis, MN: University of Minnesota Press, 1985.

Card, Claudia. "Gender and Moral Luck." In *Identity, Character, and Morality: Essays in Moral Psychology*. Ed. Owen Flanagan and Amélie Rorty. Cambridge, MA: M.I.T. Press, 1990.

Collins, Patricia Hill. *Black Feminist Thought: Knowledge, Consciousness, and the Politics of Empowerment*. New York: Routledge, Chapman and Hall, 1991.

Friedman, Marilyn. "Beyond Caring: The De-Moralization of Gender." In *Science, Morality and Feminist Theory*. Ed. Marsha Hanen and Kai Nielsen. Calgary: University of Calgary Press, 1987.

———. "The Social Self and the Partiality Debates." In *Feminist Ethics*. Ed. Claudia Card. Lawrence, KS: University of Kansas Press, 1991.

Gilligan, Carol. *In a Different Voice: Psychological Theory and Women's Development*. Cambridge, MA: Harvard University Press, 1982.

———. "Moral Orientation and Moral Development." In *Women and Moral Theory*. Ed. Eva Feder Kittay and Diana T. Meyers. Totowa, NJ: Rowman and Littlefield, 1987.

Held, Virginia. *Feminist Morality: Transforming Culture, Society, and Politics*. Chicago: University of Chicago Press, 1993.

———, ed. *Justice and Care: Essential Readings in Feminist Ethics*. Boulder, CO: Westview Press, 1995.

Holmes, Helen Bequaert, and Laura M. Purdy, eds. *Feminist Perspectives in Medical Ethics*. Bloomington, IN: Indiana University Press, 1992.

Jaggar, Alison. *Feminist Politics and Human Nature.* Totowa, N.J.: Rowman and Allan-held, 1983.

Noddings, Nel. *Caring: A Feminine Approach to Ethics and Moral Education.* Berkeley, CA: University of California Press, 1984.

O'Brien, Mary. *The Politics of Reproduction.* London: Routledge, 1983.

Rorty, Amélie, ed. *Explaining Emotions.* Berkeley, CA: University of California Press, 1980.

Ruddick, Sara. *Moral Thinking Toward a Politics of Peace.* Boston: Beacon Press, 1989.

Tannen, Deborah. *You Just Don't Understand: Women and Men in Conversation.* New York: Ballantine Press, 1991.

Thomas, Lawrence. "Sexism and Racism: Some Conceptual Differences." *Ethics* 90 (1980), pp. 239–50.

———. *Living Morally: A Psychology of Moral Character* (Philadelphia: Temple University Press, 1989).

Williams, Patricia J. *The Alchemy of Race and Rights.* Cambridge, MA: Harvard University Press, 1991.

Wolf, Susan. *Feminism and Bioethics: Beyond Reproduction.* New York: Oxford University Press, 1996.

Euthanasia

Angell, Marcia. "Euthanasia." *New England Journal of Medicine* 263, no. 9 (March, 1990), pp. 1348–49.

Annas, George J. "At Law—Killing Machines." *Hastings Center Report* 21, no. 2 (March/April 1991), pp. 33–35.

Anonymous. "It's Over, Debbie." *Journal of the American Medical Association* 259, no. 2 (January 8, 1988), p. 272. Letters. *Journal of the American Medical Association* 259, no. 14 (April 8, 1988), pp. 2094–98.

Callahan, Daniel. *Setting Limits: Medical Goals in an Aging Society.* New York: Simon and Schuster, 1987.

———. "On Feeding the Dying." *Hastings Center Report* 13, no. 5 (October 22, 1983), pp. 30–32.

———. "'Aid-in-Dying': The Social Dimensions." *Commonweal* 118, no. 14 (August 9, 1991), pp. 12–16.

Dessaur, C.I., and C. J. Rutenfrans. "The Present Day Practice of Euthanasia." *Issues in Law and Medicine* 3, no. 4 (Spring 1988), pp. 399–405.

Engelhardt, H. Tristram Jr. "Death by Free Choice: Modern Variations on an Antique Theme." In *Suicide and Euthanasia: Historical and Contemporary Themes.* Ed. Baruch A. Brody. Vol. 35, *Philosophy and Medicine.* Dordrech, The Netherlands: Kluwer Academic, 1989, pp. 251–80.

Fairman, R. Paul. "Withdrawing Life-Sustaining Treatment: Lessons from Nancy Cruzan." *Archives of Internal Medicine* 152, no. 1 (January 1992), pp. 25–27.

Fletcher, Joseph. "The Courts and Euthanasia." *Law Medicine and Health Care* 15, no. 4 (Winter 1987/88), pp. 223–30.

———. "Abortion, Euthanasia, and Care of Defective Newborns." *New England Journal of Medicine* 292, no. 2 (January 1975), pp. 75–78.

———. "Attitudes Toward Defective Newborns." *Hastings Center Studies* 2, no. 1 (January 1974), pp. 21–32.

Gillet, Grant. "Euthanasia, Letting Die and the Pause." *Journal of Medical Ethics* 14, no. 2 (June 1988), pp. 61–68.

Gomez, Carlos. "Consider the Dutch." *Commonweal* 118, no. 14 (August 9, 1991), pp. 5–8.

Grisez, Germain. "Should Nutrition and Hydration Be Provided to Permanently Unconscious and Other Mentally Disabled Persons?" *Linacre Quarterly* 57, no. 2 (May 1990), pp. 30–43.

Husebo, Stein. "Is Euthanasia a Caring Thing to Do?" *Journal of Palliative Care* 4, no. 1/2 (May 1988), pp. 111–14.

Jecker, Nancy S. "Giving Death a Hand: When the Dying and the Doctor Stand in a Special Relationship." *Journal of the American Geriatrics Society* 39, no. 8 (August 1991), pp. 831–35.

Lynn, Joanne. "The Health Care Professional's Role When Active Euthanasia Is Sought." *Journal of Palliative Care* 4, no. 1/2 (May 1988), pp. 100–2.

Musgrave, Catherine F. "Terminal Dehydration: To Give or Not to Give Intravenous Fluids." *Cancer Nursing* 13, no. 1 (February 1990), pp. 62–66.

Schepens, P. "Euthanasia: Our Own Future?" *Issues in Law and Medicine* 3, no. 4 (Spring 1988), pp. 371–84.

Thomasma, David C. "The Range of Euthanasia." *Bulletin of the American College of Surgeons* 73, no. 8 (August 1988), pp. 4–13.

Abortion

Bolton, Martha Brandt. "Responsible Women and Abortion Decisions." In *Having Children: Philosopical and Legal Reflections on Personhood.* Ed. Onora O'Neill and William Ruddick. New York: Oxford University Press, 1979, pp. 40–51.

Brody, Baruch. "On the Humanity of the Foetus." In *Abortions: Pro and Con.* Ed. Robert L. Perkins. Cambridge, MA: Schenkman, 1974, pp. 69–90.

Butler, J. Douglas. *Abortion and Reproductive Rights: A Comprehensive Guide to Medicine, Ethics and the Law.* CD-Rom. Westminster, MD: http://www.qis.net/butler.1996.

Dworkin, Ronald. *A Matter of Principle.* Cambridge, MA: Harvard University Press, 1985.

———. *Life's Dominion: An Argument about Abortion, Euthanasia, and Individual Freedom.* New York: Knopf, 1993.

Englehardt, H. Tristram Jr. "The Ontology of Abortion." *Ethics* 84 (April 1974), pp. 217–34.

English, Jane. "Abortion and the Concept of a Person." *Canadian Journal of Philosophy* 5 (October 1975), pp. 233–43.

Feinburg, Joel, ed. "Postscript on Infanticide." *The Problem of Abortion*, 2d ed. Belmont, CA: Wadsworth, 1984.

Finnis, John M. "'Shameless Acts' in Colorado: Abuse of Scholarship in Constitutional Cases." *Academic Questions* 7 (Fall 1994), pp. 10–41.

King, Patricia. "Should Mom Be Constrained in the Best Interests of the Fetus?" *Nova Law Review* (Spring 1989), pp. 393–404.

MacKinnon, Catharine A. "Abortion, Precedent, and the Constitution: A Comment on Planned Parenthood of *Southeastern Pennsylvania v. Casey*" *Notre Dame Law Review* 68 (1992), pp. 11 ff.

Noonan, John, ed. *The Morality of Abortion: Legal and Historical Perspectives.* Cambridge, MA: Harvard University Press, 1970.

Pojman, Louis P., and Francis J. Beckwith. *The Abortion Controversy: A Reader.* Boston: Jones and Bartlett, 1994.

Tooley, Michael. *Abortion and Infanticide.* New York: Oxford University Press, 1983.

Warren, Mary Anne. "On the Moral and Legal Status of Abortion" in *Arguing About Abortion,* ed. Lewis M. Schwartz (Belmont, CA: Wadsworth, 1993): pp. 227–42.

Genetic Engineering

Anderson, W. French. "Human Gene Therapy." *Science* 256, no. 5058 (1992), pp. 808–13.

———. "Human Gene Therapy." *Nature* Supplement (April 30, 1998), pp. 25–30.

Areen, Judith. "The Greatest Rewards and the Heaviest Penalties." *Human Gene Therapy* 3, no. 3 (June 1992), pp. 277–78.

Cosset, F.L., and S.J. Russell. "Targeting Retrovirus Entry." *Human Gene Therapy* 3 (1996), pp. 946–56.

Epstein, Suzanne L. "Regulatory Concerns in Human Gene Therapy." *Human Gene Therapy* 2, no. 3 (Fall 1991), pp. 243–49.

Fisher, K.J. et al. "Recombinant Adeno-Associated Virus for Muscle Directed Gene Therapy." *Nature Med* 3 (1997), pp. 306–12.

Fletcher, John C., and W. French Anderson. "Germ-Line Gene Therapy: A New Stage of Debate." *Law, Medicine & Health Care* 20, no. 1/2 (Spring/Summer 1992), pp. 26–39.

Fletcher, John C., and G. Richter. "Human Fetal Gene Therapy: Moral and Ethical Questions." *Human Gene Therapy* 7 (1996), pp. 1605–14.

Juengst, Eric T., ed. "Human Germ-Line Engineering—Special Issue." *Journal of Medicine and Philosophy* 16, no. 6 (December 1991), pp. 587–694.

Ledley, Fred D. "Are Contemporary Methods for Somatic Gene Therapy Suitable for Clinical Applications?" *Clinical and Investigative Medicine* 16, no. 1 (February 1993), pp. 78–88.

Palmer, Julie Gage. "Liability Considerations Presented by Human Gene Therapy." *Human Gene Therapy* 2, no. 3 (Fall 1991), pp. 235–42.

Tauer, Carol A. "Does Human Gene Therapy Raise New Ethical Questions?" *Human Gene Therapy* 1, no. 4 (Winter 1990), pp. 411–18.

Von Tongeren, Paul J.M. "Ethical Manipulations: An Ethical Evaluation of the Debate Surrounding Genetic Engineering." *Human Gene Therapy* 2, no. 1 (1991), pp. 71–75.

Walters, LeRoy. "Ethical Issues in Human Gene Therapy." *Journal of Clinical Ethics* 2, no. 4 (Winter 1991), pp. 267–74.

Zohar, Noam J. "Prospects for 'Genetic Therapy'—Can a Person Benefit from Being Altered?" *Bioethics* 5, no. 4 (October 1991), pp. 275–78.

The Right to Health Care

Bayer, Ronald, Arthur L. Caplan, and Norman Daniels, eds. *In Search of Equity Health Needs and the Health Care System. The Hastings Center Series in Ethics.* New York: Plenum Press, 1983.

Beauchamp, Tom L., and Ruth R. Faden. "The Right to Health and the Right to Health Care." *Journal of Medicine and Philosophy* 4, no. 2 (1979), pp. 118–31.

Bole, Thomas J., and William B. Bondeson., eds. *Rights to Health Care.* Vol. 38, *Philosophy and Medicine Series.* Dordrecht, The Netherlands: Kluwer Academic, 1991.

Brody, Baruch. "The President's Commission: The Need to Be More Philosophical." *Journal of Medicine and Philosophy* 14, no. 4 (August 1989), pp. 369–83.

Callahan, Daniel. *What Kind of Life: The Limits of Medical Progress.* New York: Simon and Schuster, 1990.

Daniels, Norman. *Just Health Care. Studies in Philosophy and Health Policy.* Cambridge: Cambridge University Press, 1985.

Dula, Annette, and Sara Goering. *"It Just Ain't Fair": The Ethics of Health Care for African Americans.* Westport, CT: Praeger, 1994.

Engelhardt, H. Tristram, ed. "Rights to Health Care." *Journal of Medicine and Philosophy* 4, no. 2 (June 1979), pp. 113–215.

Fried, Charles. "Equality and Rights in Medical Care." *Hastings Center Report* 6, no. 1 (February 1976), pp. 29–34.

Jecker, Nancy S., and Alfred Berg. "Allocating Medical Resources in Rural America: Alternative Perceptions of Justice." *Social Science and Medicine* 34, no. 5 (March 1992), pp. 467–74.

Menzel, Paul T. *Strong Medicine: The Ethical Rationing of Health Care.* New York: Oxford University Press, 1990.

Pan American Health Organization. "A Human Right to Health Under International Law." *Bulletin of the Pan American Health Organization* 24, no. 4 (1990), pp. 624–28.

Porter, Susan. "Does Everyone Merit Health Care?" *Ohio Medical Journal* 83, no. 1 (January 1987), pp. 16–18.

Roemer, Ruth. "The Right to Health Care—Gains and Gaps." *American Journal of Public Health* 78, no. 3 (March 1988), pp. 241–47.

Sterba, James P. "Justice." In *Encyclopedia of Bioethics,* rev. ed. Ed. Warren T. Reich. New York: Simon & Schuster/Macmillan, 1995, pp. 1308–15.

Allocation of Organs for Transplant

Aaron, H.J. and W.B. Schwartz. *The Painful Prescription: Rationing Hospital Care.* Washington, DC: Brookings Institution, 1984.

Benjamin, M., et al. "What Transplantation Can Teach Us about Health Care Reform." *New England Journal of Medicine* 330 (1994), pp. 858–60.

Caplan, Arthur L. "If I Were a Rich Man Could I Buy a Pancreas? Problems in the Policies and Criteria Used to Allocate Organs for Transplantation in the United States." In *If I Were a Rich Man Could I Buy a Pancreas? And Other Essays on the Ethics of Health Care.* Bloomington, IN: Indiana University Press, 1992.

Childress, James F. "Policies for Allocating Organs for Transplantation: Some Reflections." *Biolaw* 11, no. 3/4 (March–April 1995), pp. 29–39.

Daniels, Norman. *Am I My Parent's Keeper? An Essay on Justice between the Young and Old.* Oxford: Oxford University Press, 1988.

Evans, Roger W. "Organ Transplantation and the Inevitable Debate as to What Constitutes a Basic Health Care Benefit." In *Clinical Transplants.* Ed. Paul Teresaki and J. M. Cecka. Los Angeles, CA: UCLA Typing Laboratory, 1993.

Fabry, Thomas L., and Franklin M. Klion. *Guide to Liver Transplantation.* New York: Igaku-Shoin, 1992.

Jarvis, Rupert. "Join the Club: A Modest Proposal to Increase Availability of Donor Organs." *Journal of Medical Ethics* 21, no. 4 (August 1995), pp. 199–204.

Kilner, J. F. *Who Lives? Who Dies? Ethical Criteria in Patient Selection.* New Haven, CT: Yale University Press, 1990.

Kubo, Spencer, Sofia M. Ormaza, Gary S. Francis, et al. "Trends in Patient Selection for Heart Transplantation." *Journal of the American College of Cardiology* 21, no. 4 (March 15, 1993), pp. 975–81.

Margolis, Robin Elizabeth. "Are Transplanted Organs Being Allocated Unfairly and Illegally?" *HealthSpan* 10, no. 6 (June 1993), pp. 14–17.

Moskowitz, Ellen. "In the Courts: Livers." *Hastings Center Report* 25, no. 4 (July–August 1995), p. 48.

O'Connell, Dolores A. "Ethical Implications of Organ Transplantation. *Critical Care Nursing Quarterly* 13, no. 4 (February 1991), pp. 1–7.

Rescher, N. "The Allocation of Exotic Medical Lifesaving Therapy." *Ethics* 79 (1969), pp. 173–86.

Schmidt, Volker H. "Selection of Recipients for Donor Organs in Transplant Medicine." *Journal of Medicine and Philosophy* 23, no. 1 (1998), pp. 50–74.

Swazey, Judith P., and Renée Fox. "Allocating Scarce Gifts of Life." *Trends in Health Care, Law & Ethics* 8, no. 4 (Fall 1993), pp. 29–34.

Acknowledgments

Chapter Three

"Precautionary Reason as a Link to Moral Action," by permission of the authors: Deryck Beylevel, professor of Jurisprudence and director of SIBLE at the University of Sheffield, UK; and Shaun Pattinson, University of Sheffield.

Chapter Four

Paternalism and Autonomy

Hilary Jones, "Autonomy and Paternalism: Partners or Rivals?" *British Journal of Nursing* 5.6 (April 10, 1996): 378–381. Reprinted with permission.

Savulescu, Julian, "Rational Non-Interventional Paternalism: Why Doctors Ought to Make Judgments of What Is Best for Their Patients." *Journal of Medical Ethics* 1995, 21:327–331. Reprinted with permission of the BMJ Publishing Group.

N.S. Jecker, "Is Refusal of Treatment Unjustified Paternalism?: *The Journal of Clinical Ethics*, 6, no. 2 (Summer 1995): 133–137. © 1995 *The Journal of Clinical Ethics*, all rights reserved. Used with permission of *The Journal of Clinical Ethics*.

Robert D. Orr, M.D. "Confessions of a Closet Paternalist." *The Western Journal of Medicine*, 162.3 (1995): 279–280. Replies to Dr. Orr: 162.6 (1995): 556–557. Reprinted with permission of *The Western Journal of Medicine*.

Privacy and Confidentiality

Paul Cain, "The Limits of Confidentiality." *Nursing Ethics* 5 (1998): 158–165. Reprinted with permission of Edward Arnold Publishers.

Katharine V. Smith and Jan Russell, "Ethical Issues Experienced by HIV-Infected African-American Women." *Nursing Ethics* 4 (1997): 394–402. Reprinted with permission of Edward Arnold Publishers.

Carol A. Ford et al., "Influence of Physician Confidentiality Assurances on Adolescents' Willingness to Disclose Information and Seek Further Health Care." *Journal of the American Medical Association* 278 (1997): 1029–1034. Reprinted with permission of the American Medical Association.

Grant Kelly, "Patient Data, Confidentiality, and Electronics." *British Medical Journal,* 316 (1998): 718–719. This article was first published in the BMJ and is reprinted with permission of the BMJ.

Informed Consent

Julian Savulescu and Richard W. Momeyer, "Should Informed Consent Be Based on Rational Beliefs?" *Journal of Medical Ethics,* 23 (1997): 282–288. Reprinted with permission of the BMJ Publishing Group.

Discussion of Informed Consent and Medical Research. *British Medical Journal,* 316 (1998): 1001–1005. This material was first published in the BMJ and is reprinted with permission of the BMJ.

Ellen Agard, D. Finkelstein, and E. Wallach, "Cultural Diversity and Informed Consent." *The Journal of Clinical Ethics,* 9, no. 2 (Summer 1998): 173–176. © 1998 *The Journal of Clinical Ethics,* all rights reserved. Used with permission of *The Journal of Clinical Ethics.*

Ronald Bayer, "Discrimination, Informed Consent and the HIV-Infected Clinician." *British Medical Journal,* 314 (1997): 915–916. This article was first published in the BMJ and is reprinted by permission of the BMJ.

Gender Issues

Mary B. Mahowald, "On Treatment of Myopia: Feminist Standpoint Theory & Bioethics," from *Feminism and Bioethics: Beyond Reproduction,* edited by Susan M. Wolf. Copyright © 1996 by The Hastings Center. Used by permission of Oxford University Press, Inc.

Marcia Angell, "Caring for Women's Health—What Is the Problem?" *The New England Journal of Medicine,* 329 (1993): 271–272. Copyright© 1993 Massachusetts Medical Society. All rights reserved.

Debra Leners and Nancy Q. Beardslee, "Suffering and Ethical Caring: Incompatible Entities." *Nursing Ethics,* 4 (1997): 361–369. Reprinted with permission of Edward Arnold Publishers.

Chapter Five

Euthanasia

Daniel Callahan, "Killing and Allowing to Die." *Hastings Center Report,* 19 Special Supp. (1989): 5–6. Reprinted by permission. © The Hastings Center.

Pieter V. Admiraal, "Justifiable Euthanasia." Reprinted by permission of the Publisher *Issues in Law & Medicine,* Vol. 3, No. 4 (Spring 1988). Copyright © 1988 by the National Legal Center for the Medically Dependent & Disabled, Inc.

Leon Kass, "Why Doctors Must Not Kill." *Commonweal,* 14 Supplement (August 9, 1991): 472–475. © 1991 Commonweal Foundation, reprinted with permission. For subscriptions, call 1-999-495-6755.

John M. Dolan, "Death by Deliberate Dehydration and Starvation." Reprinted by permission of the Publisher *Issues in Law & Medicine,* Vol. 7, No. 2 (Fall 1991). Copyright © 1991 by the National Legal Center for Medically Dependent & Disabled, Inc.

John Jefferson Davis, "Concerning the Case of 'Mr. Stevens.' " Reprinted by permission of the Publisher *Issues in Law & Medicine,* Vol. 3, No. 4 (Spring 1988). Copyright © 1991 by the National Legal Center for Medically Dependent & Disabled, Inc.

Caplan, Arthur and Cynthia Cohen, "Hastings Center Newborn Project." Excerpt 7–9, 30–32. Reprinted by permission. © The Hastings Center.

Winifred J. Pinch and Margaret L. Spielman, "The Parents' Perspective: Ethical Decision-making in Neonatal Intensive Care." *Journal of Advanced Nursing,* 15.6: 712–719. Reprinted with permission of Blackwell Science.

Abortion

John Noonan, ed., *The Morality of Abortion: Legal and Historical Perspectives.* Cambridge, MA: Harvard University Press. Copyright © 1970 by the President and Fellows of Harvard College. Reprinted by permission of the publisher.

Judith Jarvis Thompson, "A Defense of Abortion." Copyright © 1971 by Princeton University Press. Reprinted by permission of Princeton University Press.

Chapter Six

Nils Holtug, "Altering Humans: The Case For and Against Human Gene Therapy." *Cambridge Quarterly of Healthcare Ethics,* Vol. 6, No. 2 (Spring 1997): 157–174. Copyright © 1997 Cambridge University Press. Reprinted with the permission of Cambridge University Press.

Edward M. Berger and Bernard M. Gert, "Genetic Disorders and the Ethical Status of Germ-Line Gene Therapy." *Journal of Medicine and Philosophy* (1991): 667–683. © Swets & Zeitlinger. Used with permission.

Kathleen Nolan, "How Do We Think about the Ethics of Human Germ-Line Genetic Therapy?" *Journal of Medicine and Philosophy* (1191): 613–619. © Swets & Zeitlinger. Used with permission.

Dorothy Nelkin and M. Susan Lindee, "Cloning in the Popular Imagination." *Cambridge Quarterly of Healthcare Ethics,* Vol. 7, No. 2 (Spring 1998): 145–149. Copyright © 1998 Cambridge University Press. Reprinted with the permission of Cambridge University Press.

Søren Holm, "A Life in Shadow: One Reason Why We Should Not Clone Humans." *Cambridge Quarterly of Healthcare Ethics,* Vol. 7, No. 2 (Spring 1998): 160–162. Copyright © 1998 Cambridge University Press. Reprinted with the permission of Cambridge University Press.

John Harris, "Cloning and Human Dignity," *Cambridge Quarterly of Healthcare Ethics,* Vol. 7, No. 2 (Spring 1998): 163–167. Copyright © 1998 Cambridge University Press. Reprinted with the permission of Cambridge University Press.

Chapter Seven

The "Right" to Health Care

Charles Fried, "Equality and Rights in Medical Care." *Hastings Center Report,* 6.1 (1976): 29–34. Reprinted by permission. © The Hastings Center.

The Allocation Problem

Rosamond Rhodes, "A Review of Ethical Issues in Transplantation." *The Mount Sinai Journal of Medicine,* Vol. 61, No. 1 (1994): 77–82. Reprinted with permission of the publisher.

Brain Smart, "Fault and the Allocation of Spare Organs." *Journal of Medical Ethics,* 20 (1994): 26–30. Reprinted with permission of the BMJ Publishing Group.